HUDDERSFIELD

A MOST HANDSOME TOWN

Letters Patent dated 1 November 1671 whereby
Charles II granted to John Ramsden (1648-1690) the right to hold
a weekly market in Huddersfield. (WYAS, K)

HUDDERSFIELD

A MOST HANDSOME TOWN

Aspects of the history and culture of

a West Yorkshire Town

Edited by

E. A. Hilary Haigh

KIRKLEES CULTURAL SERVICES

Published by
Kirklees Cultural Services
Red Doles Lane
Huddersfield
HD2 1YF
ISBN 0 900746 51 3 (hardback)
      0 900746 52 1 (softback)
© E. A. Hilary Haigh 1992

Typeset in Janson Dutch Old Style
Cover photograph and project co-ordination by Arrunden Associates, Huddersfield.
Cover design by Jill Briggs of Applied Design Management, Huddersfield.
Book design, typesetting and artwork by Armitage Typo/Graphics, Huddersfield.
Printed by Amadeus Press, Huddersfield.

Cover Illustration: Harold Blackburn (1899-1980) Ceramic
Mural, 1967 Ramsden House, Ramsden Street, Huddersfield.
Front end paper: Map: Ramsden Estate, Huddersfield, 1716
Back end paper: Map: Ramsden Estate, Huddersfield, 1778

Contents

Introduction

Since 1859 several histories of Huddersfield have been produced, by C. P. Hobkirk (1859 and 1868), G. W. Tomlinson (1885), D. F. E. Sykes (1898), Taylor Dyson (1932 and 1951) and Roy Brook (1968). All these authors wrote in the style of their times, in a chronological narrative, and all their books have an honoured place in Huddersfield's historiography. None of them is still in print, however, and the time has been judged right to publish a modern history in a modern style.

Huddersfield has a fascinating history and many of the topics only touched on by previous writers have attracted detailed research by specialist historians, using documentary sources not always available to past generations. The present volume is a collection of work by twenty-six such specialists, each an expert in his or her chosen field, arranged in a thematic, rather than chronological, style.

The book comprises twenty-six chapters on different aspects of the history and development of Huddersfield. Readers will find sections on a wide range of topics, and all the chapters are self-contained units, complete in themselves. However, certain topics are relevant to several chapters, for instance the Cloth Hall is described as an architectural feature, as part of the Ramsden family's contribution to the town's development and as a trading centre and market. Similarly, references to the Ramsdens pervade the whole volume, as befits a family which owned the manor of Huddersfield from 1599 to 1920 and which oversaw the profound changes made to the town during that period.

The index is a vital tool in bringing together all references to any topic and readers are urged to make full use of it. The chapters have been grouped together as far as possible to form a logical progression of subject matter.

This book cannot claim to be comprehensive, however. A work such as this is inevitably selective, since it depends for its contents on the research which has been done and the willingness of scholars to make a contribution. Much research remains necessary; there is yet more to discover about Huddersfield. I hope that many readers will be encouraged to take up the challenge.

The Contributors have made the book, and I owe them my grateful thanks for agreeing to participate in the project and for all their research, checking, proof-reading and patience. All have approached their task with enthusiasm and professionalism. Many of the authors are from Huddersfield, several live and work in the town and others have developed research interests because of Huddersfield's unique history.

Most of the illustrations have been provided by Kirklees Cultural Services (KCS) (Huddersfield Local History Library, Kirklees Technical and Commercial Unit and Tolson Memorial Museum) and thanks for them are due to Jane Helliwell, Katrina Ward and John Rumsby. Thanks are also due to Janet Burhouse of West Yorkshire Archive Service, Kirklees (WYAS,K), Robert Frost and Alan Betteridge (WYAS,W) and (WYAS,C) and to Warwick Price and the staff at the University of Huddersfield Library. They have also assisted the Contributors with their research and I am also grateful to the following people for allowing the inclusion of illustrations: Mrs Gordon-Duff-Pennington, Roy Brook (RBC), Richard Crowther, agent for the Thornhill Estate (TEP), Richard Dennis (RD), D. Rawlinson, R. B. Schofield and Katrina Ward (KW) and the Royal Commission on the Historical Monuments of England (RCHME).

I am grateful for all the assistance in checking and proof-reading provided by Joanne Gascoigne and Isobel Schofield of the Technical and Commercial Unit of Kirklees Cultural Services and to Liz Hayes of the Kirklees Graphics Department for reproducing many of the illustrations. The suggestion of publishing a new history of Huddersfield came from the Huddersfield Library Anniversary Working Group and I must thank them for the idea and Peter Gill-Martin, Stuart Davies and Judith Hodge for entrusting it to me and allowing me to pursue my own plan to compile and edit a collection of scholars' work. It has been an unforgettable experience!

The book itself has been designed, typeset and printed in Huddersfield. My thanks go to Richard Armitage, Karen Matthews and Jules Vickerman for all their hard work in preparing the text and illustrations, to Richard Cook for the printing and to Arrunden Associates for co-ordinating the production of the book. The volume was truly made in Huddersfield.

Finally, but most importantly, I must thank John and Sarah, my mother, Joan Turner and all the family for their encouragement, support and enthusiasm for the project over the three years they have had to live with *Huddersfield: a most handsome town.*

E. A. Hilary Haigh

Figures, Illustrations & Maps

CHAPTER I

'A Castle Well Guarded': the Archaeology and History of Castle Hill, Almondbury

JOHN H. RUMSBY

Prehistoric hill-fort

The summit of Castle Hill, Almondbury is by far the most conspicuous landmark in the Huddersfield district. It is not particularly high, 900 feet (273 metres), but its isolation and distinctive shape, and the tall tower on the top, make it easily recognisable from the surrounding moors or from the streets of Huddersfield itself. The hill has for hundreds of years been a place of recreation for the people of Huddersfield, and the easily discernible remains of past occupation have made it a subject for legend, speculation and, more recently, scientific study.

The hill owes its shape to an outlying cap of hard Grenoside sandstone, which has protected the softer stone beneath from erosion. The first people to set eyes on Castle Hill were probably hunters and gatherers of the middle Stone Age (Mesolithic), camping amongst the forests which at that time covered the land. In the later Stone Age (Neolithic) and Bronze Age, there appears to have been widespread travel or trade along the river valleys connecting the Yorkshire Wolds, the Peak District and the Mersey and Ribble estuaries. This is shown by finds of various characteristic types of stone and bronze tools in a place far from their points of origin.

Any study of the history of Castle Hill should start with the little book published by Philip Ahier in 1946.[1] This is an invaluable collection of early descriptions and other information about the hill. Its main drawback is its account of the prehistoric period, since Ahier, like earlier writers, had to rely on identification of the hill from vague classical descriptions. Post-war archaeological excavations transformed our understanding of the prehistory of Castle Hill. Dr. W. J. Varley carried out excavations in 1939, from 1946 to

Fig. 1:1 View from the Victoria Tower, with the Castle Hill Hotel in the centre, 1912. (KCS)

1947 and between 1969 and 1973. It is interesting to compare successive accounts by Dr Varley of his interpretation of the hill-fort, as he moved from the traditional view of the hill as a fortress of the Brigantes, destroyed by the Romans, to a realisation that the hill-fort was constructed and then abandoned centuries before the Roman occupation of the area.[2]

The earliest written description of the hill and its antiquities seems to be that of the antiquary William Camden, whose pioneering work *Magna Britannia* was published in 1586. His description is still recognisable:

Six miles from Halifax, and not far from the river Calder, near unto Almondbury, a little town standing upon a high and steep hill, which has an easy passage or even ground unto it but on one side, are seen the manifest tokens of a rampart, some ruin of walls and a castle, which was guarded with a triple strength of forts and bulwarks.[3]

Camden, like other scholars trained in the classics, was eager to identify visible remains with sites mentioned by the ancient authors. He claimed that Castle Hill was in fact the Roman site of Cambodunum, mentioned by the geographer Ptolemy. He went on to describe it as the seat of an Anglo-Saxon king and the site of a cathedral founded by St. Paulinus and dedicated to St. Alban (hence the name Almondbury, a corruption of 'Albanbury'). According to Camden, the fortress met its end in the wars between the native Britons and the early Saxons. However, none of the archaeological excavations have uncovered any evidence for this Roman and Saxon occupation described by Camden and other writers following him.

The excavations in fact tell their own long and dramatic story about the hill, although much remains to be discovered. The archaeologists concentrated mainly on elucidating the various phases of construction of the defences. There remains great potential for excavation within the defences, to discover the nature of the occupation, the type of people who lived there, and more about their social and economic life.

The earliest occupation is indicated by finds of the late Neolithic period, which have been dated by radiocarbon tests on associated material to around 2100 BC. These finds consist of simple flint tools, such as knives and scrapers, and part of a polished stone axe, a useful tool for felling trees in the surrounding forests. Flint is a stone not found locally, and was imported, therefore, probably from east Yorkshire. Little is known of the nature of this settlement, and it was not defended by fortifications. After the abandonment of the site, it remained uninhabited long enough for a new soil surface to form over the remains.

The next occupiers of the hill lived in a different age, an age in which iron was used instead of stone tools, and where people were subject to pressures which forced them to defend their settlement against attacks by other tribes. These people built a single bank, without a ditch, around the south-western and highest part of the summit (roughly the area surrounding the later Victoria Tower). There was a single entrance, through the part of the bank that crossed the summit. The bank turned inwards at the entrance, and a hearth was found at this point, indicating a guardroom to shelter those on duty at the gate. The bank was well constructed, being delineated by a double row of flagstones set in slit trenches, with the sides built up from drystone walling, infilled with rubble and clay. The top of the bank was

3

probably crowned by a palisade, or an entanglement of thorny branches. Unfortunately, no remains of habitation were found within these defences, dated to the late seventh century BC.

This first defence in turn fell into ruin, and the next inhabitants of the hill obviously did not feel threatened, since they built no walls of their own, and constructed their huts against and over the earlier ramparts. These huts were circular, built of stone with clay floors and central hearths, the smoke presumably escaping through conical thatched roofs.

Later occupation of the hill was not so peaceful, and tells a story of increasingly complex and sophisticated stone, earth and timber defences, which must reflect a time of threat and disturbance, perhaps due to pressure of population, and powerful tribal groups striving for the best territories. Such defences would require a large and concentrated work-force, organised by a united authority. The first phase of these defences was a new fort, roughly following the line of its predecessor to enclose the highest part of the summit. The single bank was revetted with drystone walls, but had internal bracing as well, forming a series of cells filled with clay, stiffened with occasional timbers. The top of the rampart was pierced by stone-lined post-holes, probably to take the supports of a stout wooden stockade. The defences were completed by an external V-shaped ditch. The fort was dated by the excavators to the early sixth century BC.

The settlement must have prospered and grown, since a decade or two later the ramparts were enlarged to enclose the whole of the summit (roughly the area enclosed by the innermost bank). The ends of the old ditch across the summit were blocked off by boulders, and a new rampart and ditch of the same construction as the old were built to enclose the new area. The floors of huts and shelters attached to the rear of the ramparts have been discovered, showing that the hill-fort was actually occupied, and not just used as a refuge in time of war.

In the mid-fifth century BC the inner rampart was raised and widened, and a new ditch cut. Furthermore, a new rampart was built outside the existing one, on a natural shelf of rock, and the defences at the vulnerable north-east end of the hill were strengthened where the shallower slope made attack easier. An interesting "annexe" was also built at this end, alongside the approach to the fort entrance. This was a rectangular enclosure defended by a bank and ditch and containing a small two-roomed hut. It may have been

Fig. 1:2 Archaeological excavations at Castle Hill in 1941, showing a trench dug through the defences. (KCS)

intended to shelter livestock against raids by neighbouring tribes. Slighter defences were also added further down the hill.

This proud and powerful stronghold seems to have come to an abrupt end, its ramparts destroyed by fire at the end of the fifth century BC. The excavators discovered evidence for large areas of burnt and collapsed ramparts, with subsequent decay, indicating abandonment. The burning was intense and irregular, and affected the interior of the ramparts, where it could not have been caused, for example, by an enemy piling up wood and setting fire to it to bring down the walls. These extensive areas of burnt stone, now not visible, were remarked on and speculated upon by many early writers, among them William Camden:

> The fire that burnt it down seems to have been exceeding vehement, from the cinders which are strangely solder'd together. One lump was found, of above two foot every way, the earth being melted rather than burnt.[4]

5

A date of 431±180 BC was obtained from this burnt material, proving conclusively that the prehistoric defences were much earlier that the Roman occupation of the first century AD. Dr Varley, after experimentation, and discussion with Coal Board officials, came to the conclusion that the fire was caused not by the hand of man, but by spontaneous combustion of the timbers inside the ramparts due to pressure, a process similar to that which occasionally causes fires on coal waste-tips. As far as can be told from the archaeological record, the hill top remained unoccupied from the fifth century BC until the Middle Ages. It is interesting to note that the ancient British name for the hill may have survived in the name 'Catterstones', used for a small group of cottages on the slope of the hill. The first element appears to be the British 'cater' or 'catter', meaning a hill or even a hill-fort.[5]

Medieval castle and town

The banks and ditches which remain are not those left by the Iron Age peoples. They are much more the result of the recutting and other alterations carried out during the Middle Ages, modified by centuries of erosion. After the Norman conquest, Almondbury became part of the territory known as the Honour of Pontefract, which was held by the de Laci family. It was they who established the castle on the hill, no doubt as a post to keep order in this outlying part of their domain. The castle is mentioned in a charter of King Stephen to Henry de Laci of about 1142 to 1154, and excavation has provided a wooden stake, radiocarbon dated to the late 1140s, and a coin of about 1160. It can be assumed, therefore, that the castle was complete and occupied by the 1140s.

The construction work was considerable. The Iron Age defences were disguised under extensive remodelling and additions, which surrounded the whole summit with a bank and deep ditch to produce Camden's 'castle well guarded'. The summit was divided into three sections, or baileys, by cutting two transverse ramparts with ditches, one on the site of the prehistoric transverse ditch, and another further to the north-east, beyond the site of the later public house, where the modern road enters the car park. The ramparts were constructed from large blocks of local shale, faced at the front and back with unmortared stone blocks, and guarded by V-shaped ditches. No doubt the ramparts were topped by wooden palisades.

The three baileys would have been used for different purposes. The inner or south-western bailey (where the Victoria Tower stands) provided the lord's accommodation and was also the last and strongest line of defence. The centre bailey was probably occupied by the garrison and their workshops, and the lower, or outer, bailey would have given temporary shelter to local people and their livestock in times of trouble. However, little or nothing has been found of internal buildings except in the inner bailey, where a staircase was found when the public house was being built in 1810. In the inner bailey there was a strong tower, built at first of timber, but later replaced in stone. It was served by two wells, one of which remains; the other was discovered when the foundations for the Victoria Tower were built.

The archaeological record makes it clear that towards the end of the thirteenth century there was a change in function at the castle. The outer bailey seems to have been turned over to agriculture. The buildings in the inner bailey became a hunting lodge, presumably being visited by the de Lacis on occasional hunting trips for much of the rest of the century. The remaining well, that can still be seen on the hill, provided vivid evidence of the change of use. The well was 82 feet (25 metres) deep, and from the bottom came two stave-built wooden buckets, the wood preserved by the damp conditions. The disuse of the well is signalled by layers of clean silt, interspersed with layers of occupation debris, when the well was used as a rubbish pit. These layers were full of broken pottery, and the remains of the hunters' animals and their quarry. These included the skulls of fifteen dogs, five of which were breeds capable of attacking wild boar and stags. The hunted animals were represented by bones of red, roe and fallow deer, wild boar, badger, partridge, woodcock, wood pigeon, dove and greylag goose. Falconry was attested by a bone of a goshawk, and a falconer's bell.

Fig. 1:3 Wooden buckets excavated from the well on Castle Hill. The wooden parts were preserved by the damp conditions, and date to c. AD 1200. The metal hoops and rope handles are modern reconstructions. (KCS)

The upper part of the well was used as a dump for building materials, indicating demolition on the site. This probably coincided with the execution of the Earl of Lancaster in 1322; the Earl had married a de Laci and thus gained control of the Honour of Pontefract. After his execution for treason the Honour passed to the Crown.

In the early fourteenth century there was an attempt to found a town on the hill.[6] A successful town could be a useful source of income to a lord, generating rents, market dues and other payments. The town was laid out in the lower bailey (and possibly elsewhere on the hill), and aerial photography under certain conditions reveals a central roadway flanked by regularly laid-out plots. The inhabitants of this town or borough would have held agricultural land in the surrounding area, and it has been suggested that the local name Bumroyd is a derivation of 'Borough-man's clearing'.[7] This town was probably abandoned by the 1340s, although memory of it may have lingered, since the map of Almondbury drawn up in 1634 marks the hill as the site of a town.

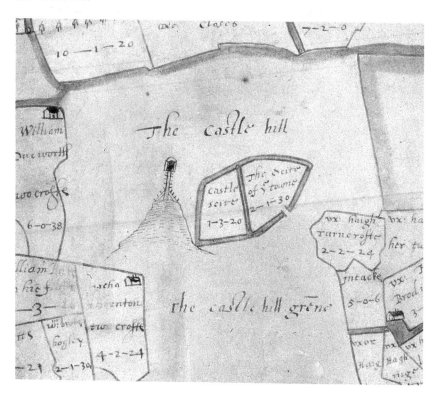

Fig. 1:4 Castle Hill as depicted by Senior on his 1634 map of the township of Almondbury. Note the illustration of a warning beacon and the 'scite of the towne'. (WYAS, K)

Fig. 1:5 Castle Hill from the air. (Private collection)

A place of resort and recreation

After the end of the Middle Ages, Castle Hill remained uninhabited until the early nineteenth century. Its prominant position made it an ideal site for a warning beacon. This consisted of an iron basket set on a long post and filled with combustible materials such as wood and tar. There was a network of such beacons on prominent hills all over the country, spreading out in lines from the coast. On the approach of an invasion fleet, the coastal beacons would be lit, followed by the others in turn. The first of these beacons seems to have been placed on Castle Hill around the time of the Spanish Armada in 1588. The beacon was replaced during the War of the Spanish Succession (1702-14), and again during the Napoleonic Wars, when Napoleon assembled an invasion force at Boulogne in 1804-05. On this occasion mischief-makers lit the beacon, and it is said that the local volunteers were called out and had marched as far as Marsden before it became known that it was a false alarm![8] In 1988, a replica beacon on Castle Hill once more became part of a chain of beacons, lit all over the country to celebrate the quater-centenary of the Spanish Armada.

Castle Hill's flat top was a useful venue for large political, religious and other meetings. An unofficial beacon on the hill in 1820 was lit to signal an abortive march on Huddersfield by four columns of insurgents. Chartist rallies were held on the hill at least four times, in 1843 and 1848. During the great weavers' strike of 1883 a rally of between two and three thousand people, accompanied by brass bands, braved bitter weather to listen to speeches by union leaders. Sunday school and other church and chapel 'outings' have regularly visited the hill-top and, in contrast, 5,000 people gathered in 1861 to attend the annual meeting of the Secularist Society of Huddersfield, when they were addressed by Charles Bradlaugh.

Less serious pursuits have also been popular on Castle Hill. A tavern to cater for pleasure-seekers was first built on the hill in about 1810-11. The existing Castle Hill Hotel (shown on page 2) was built in 1852, its architect being William Wallen, who also designed the George Hotel in St George's Square. Early photographs show other buildings surrounding two sides of the later car park. These were probably stable buildings, although they may have incorporated the early tavern; Ahier says that the 'first public house then became a Temperance Hotel in the days when the Hill was a popular Saturday afternoon resort'.[9]

Fig. 1:6 Castle Hill from the Catterstones area.

CASTLE HILL HUDDERSFIELD   (H.55.)

A bowling-green was formerly situated near the Hotel. However, the hill was also known for less gentle sports, such as the bareknuckle prize-fight that took place in 1865, between George Hulme of Huddersfield and Squire Sutcliffe of Deighton, which was stopped by the arrival of the police. Dogfights and cockfights also took place, no doubt encouraged by the landlords of the Hotel, who always benefited by crowd-pulling events on the hill.

By 1897 Queen Victoria had reigned over the British Empire for sixty years, longer than any other monarch. The whole Empire rejoiced. In Huddersfield there were processions, feasts, concerts and shows. Almondbury staged its own festivities, with decorations in the streets, and a procession and tea for 1,700 local Sunday School pupils. A beacon, once again, was lit on Castle Hill, and from the summit over twenty other beacons could be seen.[10] A more permanent memorial to the Jubilee was called for by the people of Huddersfield and, apparently at the suggestion of Isaac Hordern, cashier to the Ramsden Estate, it was decided to build a tower on Castle Hill.

The first scheme for a tower on the hill had been put forward as early as 1851. It was to have included a restaurant, museum and observation room.[11] Given the prevailing climate on the summit, it is unlikely that this would have been a popular establishment, and the plan was never proceeded with. The 1897 plan met with more success. A public appeal was launched, and the corner stone was laid on 25 June 1898.[12] Despite some difficulty in raising all the money required, the tower was opened by the Earl of Scarborough on 24 June 1899. Although often referred to as the Jubilee Tower, the correct name is the Victoria Tower. Permission to call it by this name was granted by the Queen herself in 1898.[13]

The Victoria Tower was designed by Isaac Jones of London, and built by the firm of Ben Graham and Sons of Folly Hall, using stone from Crosland Hill. It cost £3,398, and was 106 feet (32.3 metres) high, which, added to the height of the hill itself, made the top 1,000 feet (305m.) above sea level. The walls, 4 feet thick at the base, taper to 2 feet thick at the top. Visitors climb 165 steps to reach the main platform. In 1960, the top few feet of the Tower were removed for safety reasons. However, the height was restored in 1977 by the addition of a lantern, paid for by public subscription organised by the Huddersfield Civic Society, to commemorate the Silver Jubilee of Queen Elizabeth II.

During the Second World War it was suggested that the Tower should be pulled down, to prevent it from being used as a navigation aid by German bombers. In fact a few bombs were dropped near the Tower in 1940 and 1941, but these were probably just random jettisonings. There was an anti-aircraft battery near the south-west end of the hill, the remains of which may be seen, and pieces of shrapnel are occasionally picked up in the adjacent fields.

Mystery and legend[14]

Castle Hill, dominating the surrounding countryside and marked by a history that stretches back thousands of years, has always attracted speculation about its past, as well as less likely myths and legends. For some of these legends archaeology and documents may be used to guess at an origin. Others may be pure invention to frighten children, or to impress fellow-drinkers at the tavern. Still others hint at beliefs held by people living in an age so remote that no explanation can be offered.

Like many other conspicuous natural features, Castle Hill is associated with the activities of the Devil. He is said to have made a great leap from Scar Top at Netherton to Castle Hill, a distance of about eight miles. Having accomplished this Olympic-standard feat, he appears to have spent a while wandering in the maze of tunnels that supposedly lie beneath the hill. Such tales may have been made up simply to scare children into good behaviour, or they may be a veiled reference to cruelties thought to have been practised in the castle dungeons during the Middle Ages. Unfortunately for this theory, during the archaeological excavations on the hill, no traces were found of dungeons, or of any tunnel for that matter.

Medieval documents mention a piece of land near or on the hill, called 'Wormcliffe'. This name probably derives from the Anglo-Saxon 'wyrm', meaning a dragon.[15] Such dragons were associated with death; Saxon burial urns containing the cremated bones of the dead were sometimes decorated with wyrm symbols. These dragons often guarded treasure hoards and old ruins, as well as the dead, as the Saxon poet describes in *Beowulf*

> The primeval enemy that haunts the dusk; the scaly, malicious worm that seeks out funeral mounds, and flies burning through the night, wrapped about with flame, to the terror of the country folk. Its habit is to seek out treasure hidden in the earth, and mount guard over the pagan gold.

At sunset it is not too difficult to imagine that fire-breathing dragon guarding his lair, or even the Devil leaping through the air for an inspection tour of his tunnels!

Legend is very vague about the treasure the dragon might have guarded. Up until quite recent times, children in Almondbury were rocked to sleep with a tale of a mysterious Golden Cradle. This was said to be buried in one of the ditches of Castle Hill. No one seems to know who it was made for, nor why it was hidden.

One legend which may be discounted is that of the 'Almondbury Hoard'. This was a group of Celtic and Roman coins, thought to have been discovered on the hill in 1829. In 1961 it was proved that this belief was due to muddled nineteenth century accounts of the find. In fact the 'Almondbury' coins were part of a hoard from Lightcliffe, near Halifax.[16]

There is a tradition in Almondbury that the ditches of the hill were once filled with water. This water was miraculously supplied by an underground passage (some versions say an overhead pipeline!) from Lud Hill, near Farnley Tyas. One version of the tale even said that during a siege the defenders had to surrender when this water supply was cut off. Miraculous indeed: the low ground between Farnley Tyas and Castle Hill, and the difference in levels in the ditches themselves, would mean that the water would have to flow uphill. There certainly are springs in the slopes of the hill, and occasionally pools of water lie on some parts of the ditch, and these may have been the origin of the tales.

At least five tunnels are said to lead to the hill, from Deadmanstone at Berry Brow, from King Street under the River Colne, from St. Helen's Gate at Almondbury, from Longley Old Hall, and from Farnley Tyas. Most of these stories probably originate in the discovery of bricked-up cellars or old drains. Others may be memories of the two medieval wells found on the summit of the hill.

There is no record that the castle on the hill was ever besieged. As we have seen, the burnt remains of the Iron Age ramparts are thought to be the result of accidental spontaneous combustion, although the sudden bursting into flames of their defences would have been quite enough cause for the inhabitants to spread stories of attacks by devils or dragons. A battle did take place, however, in 1471 at the hamlet of Hall Bower, just below the hill. It seems to have been a small affair, the local families of Beaumont and Kaye settling old scores in a continuing feud. However, several people were killed, including Nicholas Beaumont of Newsome. The local volunteers held a sham fight on the hill one night in 1893, to test the efficacy of a new electric searchlight, but this time victory was won without bloodshed.

There is a long-standing tradition that from Castle Hill it was at one time possible to see, with the naked eye, the towers of York Minster, forty miles away. This wonderful sight, it was said, was eventually obscured by the smoking mills of Dewsbury and Batley. This story may have its origin in the use of the hill for a warning beacon. In 1588, at the time of the Spanish Armada, the Castle Hill beacon was described thus:

> Castle Hill giveth light to Halifax beacon and receiveth light from the beacon at Hoyland-super-montem, within Staincross, and at the said beacon one may see York Minster.

In other words, at night when the beacons were lit, one could see the beacon light at York from Castle Hill, although even this is scarcely credible.

In 1983 a local newspaper printed a 'history' of Castle Hill, suggesting that the hill-fort was the site of Camelot, the stronghold of King Arthur and capital of the Celtic kingdom of Brigantia, at the time of the Roman invasion.[17] None of this, of course, has any support from archaeology or history. Castle Hill had been deserted for hundreds of years when the Romans invaded, and Arthur, if he existed at all, lived at the time the Roman occupation ended, in the early fifth century AD; its defenders fought not against the Romans, but against the Anglo-Saxon invaders.

It is not surprising, perhaps, that Castle Hill has had the power to inspire fantasy. Its commanding bulk, looming over the streets of Huddersfield, and its history, imperfectly known, stretching back many thousands of years, have been a source of wonder and recreation to many generations of Huddersfield people.

John H. Rumsby

Biographical Note

After working in a regimental museum in Durham, and as Keeper of Archaeology with Hull Museums, John Rumsby joined Kirklees Museums Service in 1981 as Curator of the Tolson Memorial Museum, Huddersfield. Here he has been mainly concerned with the shaping of the collections and the modernisation of the displays and other services so that the Museum will serve as a centre for the study of the district's natural and human history through its material remains. His personal interests include military history, numismatics, architecture and ceramics.

NOTES

1. Philip Ahier, *The Story of Castle Hill, Huddersfield throughout the centuries, BC 200-AD 1945* (Huddersfield, 1946).

2. See the successive editions of W.J.Varley, *Castle Hill, Almondbury: A Brief Guide to the Excavations* (Huddersfield). The most recent edition, 1973, provides the best general summary. The most detailed interpretation of the prehistory of the hill is provided by W.J. Varley 'A Summary of the excavations at Castle Hill, Almondbury 1939-1972' in *Hillforts* edited by D. W. Harding (1976). Post-excavation work was halted by Dr Varley's untimely death in 1976, and the excavations have never been fully published. The finds and excavation records are held at the Tolson Memorial Museum, Huddersfield.

3. Quoted in Ahier, *The Story of Castle Hill*, p.1.

4. William Camden, *Britannia* revised by Edmund Gibson, 2nd edn (1722) Vol. II, p.855.

5. George Redmonds, *Almondbury Places and Place-names* (Huddersfield, 1983), pp.15-16.

6. *West Yorkshire: an archaeological survey to AD 1500*, edited by M.L. Faull and S.A. Moorhouse, (Wakefield, 1981), 3, pp.737-738.

7. Redmonds, *Almondbury Places*, pp.17-19.

8. Ahier, *The Story of Castle Hill*, pp.38-45.

9. Ahier, *The Story of Castle Hill*, p.77.

10. *Huddersfield Daily Chronicle*, 26 June 1897.

11. A copy of the proposal is in the W(est) Y(orkshire) A(rchive) S(ervice), Kirklees DD/RE/318, 23 June 1899. Letter re proposal for tower - 1851 from Isaac Hordern.

12. The photograph of this ceremony is found in Roy Brook, *The Story of Huddersfield* (1968), opposite p.138.

13. WYAS, Kirklees (uncatalogued): copy of a letter of 23 June 1898 from the Under-Secretary of State to Robert Welsh. A note on the copy states that the original was stolen from the Tower in 1906!

14. What follows is a revised text of a leaflet by John H. Rumsby: *Castle Hill - Mystery and Legend* (Huddersfield, 1984), published by Kirklees Museums Service and reproduced by their kind permission. See also Ahier, *The Story of Castle Hill*, pp.73-76.

15. Redmonds, *Almondbury Places*, pp.16-17.

16. Graham Teasdale, *Coin Finds of the Huddersfield District* (Huddersfield, 1961), pp.5-6.

17. *Huddersfield Examiner*, 28 January 1983.

CHAPTER 2

Settlement in Huddersfield before 1800

GEORGE REDMONDS

In 1801 the population of Huddersfield was 7,268 and this is often quoted, as a low figure, by historians anxious to emphasise how small the town then was and how rapidly it expanded in the nineteenth century. It should be remembered though that this was not a figure for the town alone, but for the whole township, and that the families represented, a total of 1,456, were scattered over a very wide area. In reality the nucleus of the town itself was very much smaller in 1801 than even the figure of 7,268 might indicate.

The exact status of the outlying districts of Huddersfield before c.1690 is not certain but, from that date at least, the township was divided administratively into five parts, or hamlets: Town, Bradley, Deighton, Marsh and Fartown.[1] However, these very different divisions reflected changes which had taken place in the sixteenth and seventeenth centuries; within each of the hamlets were smaller communities of varying size and importance, each with its own history. The development of the town centre before 1800 has already been the subject of a detailed study,[2] but the story of the hamlets has never been told. It is, therefore, the aim of this chapter to trace their origins and development, building up as accurately as possible the story of settlement in the whole township, from the Middle Ages up to the early stages of the Industrial Revolution.

Bradley hamlet

Bradley formed a logical hamlet division for it had recognised boundaries and had been an estate in its own right at the time of Domesday. It is true that it was then described as 'waste' but in this respect it was no different from its neighbours. It was independent of Huddersfield then and continued to be so for some considerable time. Important charters testify to significant expansion in Bradley in the twelfth century, providing firm evidence of clearance, cultivation and settlement.[3] By inference as many as ten to twelve families were living there in c.1190 and there are detailed references to houses, gardens, orchards and newly cleared land. Nevertheless, despite such signs of early growth, Bradley had certainly lost its independence by 1379 and had been incorporated into the township of Huddersfield. Afterwards the township was occasionally given the title Huddersfield cum Bradley.

The decline in status is likely to have resulted from depopulation and although it is tempting to attribute this to the Black Death of 1348-49 the reality may be that it resulted from Bradley's development as a grange estate of Fountains Abbey after c.1175. The abbey's records reveal how the Bradley lands passed into their possession from that time and also how they were immediately exploited for the production of iron and the pasturing of sheep. In fact, the period of expansion was relatively short and it is clear from a variety of sources that by the early 1300s the abbey was finding it difficult to operate the grange at a good profit.[4] The decision must then have been taken to relinquish direct control and to lease the property to a secular landlord; the earliest such landlord known to us is listed in the poll tax for Huddersfield in 1379 as 'John de Grenewode, Farmour de Graunge'.

The most important landlords were the Pilkingtons,[5] who held Bradley from 1478 until 1829, and under whose control it was eventually developed as a woodland estate, supplying bark, charcoal and timber for local industries. A tithe dispute of 1547, touching on Bradley's history before and after the Dissolution of the Monasteries, reflects the confusion which existed about its precise status, for it is referred to in the articles for the prosecution as 'the hamlet or township of Bradley' and in the articles for the defendants as 'the manor or grange'.[6] Similar descriptions occur in other documents both before and after this time. Significantly only half a dozen tenants figure in the dispute and this low number is probably a reasonably accurate indication of the hamlet's population.

The likelihood is that even this small population was scattered, and there is no evidence of a 'village' or nucleus of houses in Bradley in the sixteenth century. However, Bradley Hall (1547), which may have been the grange site, and Colne Bridge (1533), where there was probably a corn mill,[7] were important focal points for the community. There were also four named settlements in the years up to c.1600, all of which seem likely to have been occupied at the time of the tithe dispute. Possibly the most interesting of these are Shepherd Thorne (1557) and Lamb Cote (1565), for the names may date back to the years when large flocks of sheep grazed on the grange lands. Fell Greave (1554) and Lodge (1592) complete the total, tenanted respectively by the Brooks and Hirsts. These families, together with the Gibsons, were the only ones named in 1547 and all three appear under the heading for Huddersfield in the subsidy roll of 1545.

There appears to have been only limited expansion in Bradley between 1600 and 1800. A farm at Oak is referred to in the seventeenth century and there is some evidence for one or two new settlements along Bradley Lane in the eighteenth century. The name of one of these, Bradley Grange farm, was later to confuse the issue of where the original grange buildings might have been situated. Otherwise the major event in the hamlet's history was the building of the iron forge at Colne Bridge (c.1612), which survived into the 1790s, by which time there may have been a few cottages nearby for workmen.[8] The junction of highways just to the north of the forge, linking Bradley to the Calder valley via both Elland and Cooper Bridge, was emerging by then as the main focal point within the hamlet.

Deighton hamlet

Deighton also is a settlement site of considerable antiquity. This is implicit in the place-name which means 'farmstead by the dike'. This is first recorded in the twelfth century and may be much older. It can be compared in both meaning and form with several other Yorkshire places called Deighton, all of them Anglian in origin, so this may imply that the Huddersfield locality was named in the same period. It was also the surname of a Huddersfield family referred to as early as c.1200 and taxed in the township in 1297.

It has been suggested that Deighton may have had a degree of administrative independence in the Middle Ages,[9] and early references to 'Deighton brook' and 'Deighton field' appear to confirm that it was indeed an identifiable territory. Nevertheless, most of the evidence suggests that it remained a single dwelling into the early 1500s and that a family called Brook lived there as tenants. They were certainly there in 1425 and may even have been in occupation from c.1362 when the 'de' Deightons are judged to have moved into Kirkheaton parish.[10] By 1600 it was usual to describe the Brooks as 'of Deighton Hall' and, if this was on the site of the Deighton Hall shown on nineteenth century maps, it was probably the original settlement site.

Although the population of Deighton increased from c.1530 to c.1630, no new place-names are recorded, which may suggest that a small nucleus of dwellings grew up around Deighton Hall. Other family names occurring there alongside Brook in that period were Hirst (1533), Stead (1558) and Jagger (1560), the last two of these suggesting some movement into Huddersfield from other parts of the West Riding. From 1716 Deighton was occasionally referred to in the Quarter Sessions records as the vill of Deighton, or even the village of Deighton, further evidence perhaps that it was developing as a nucleated community.

Deighton seems to have been detached from the rest of Huddersfield manor at a very early date, possibly in 1362, and it was held by a succession of families, including the Mirfields and the Thornhills. During this period it was itself given the title of manor, although it is doubtful if it ever operated as such, but its boundaries were well established and it would logically fall into place as a hamlet in the seventeenth century. In 1854 it finally passed to the Ramsdens and so was reunited with Huddersfield manorially.

Marsh hamlet

The place-name Marsh can probably be taken at face value for it originally described the extensive area of waste and common which lay to the west and north-west of the town. It was not a settlement site and is first mentioned in 1436.[11] Eventually, after partial enclosure of the common in the late sixteenth century, there was some settlement there, particularly in Paddock, and at some time in the seventeenth century the population was sufficiently large for Marsh to be given hamlet status. The new territory incorporated the much older settlements of Gledholt and Edgerton.

The exact locations of the earliest settlements on Marsh common are not known, but two men, Edward Smith and Edmond Mallinson, made enclosures there c.1580 and were subsequently said to be 'of Marsh' in the parish registers. Other family names found there before 1600 were Batley, Brook and Gledhill, with Hirst and France recorded soon afterwards. No doubt some of these dwellings were cottages of the type described in the new statute,[12] and they were dispersed over the common. It was not long before the description 'of Marsh' was no longer an adequate identification and many of the settlements had to be named. By c.1650, for example, the Horsfalls were at 'Lathe', the Brooks at 'Coit', the Batleys at 'Lane end' and the Hirsts at 'the Cross'. These place-names all seem to have disappeared as the once isolated cottages were absorbed in later housing developments, but at least two families recorded in the late 1500s, the Heatons and the Blackers, are remembered in the place-names Heaton Fold and Blacker Road.

One of the first signs that the tenants at Marsh were being thought of as a community occurs in a manorial bye-law of 1657. In it the responsibility for repairing the highway between Marsh and Huddersfield was shared between the two places, with 'the inhabitants of Marsh' required to maintain the section 'leading from the house of John Hirst of the greene (Greenhead) to the Marsh yate'.

Fig. 2:1 Marsh in 1716, from Oldfield's map of the manor of Huddersfield. (WYAS, K)

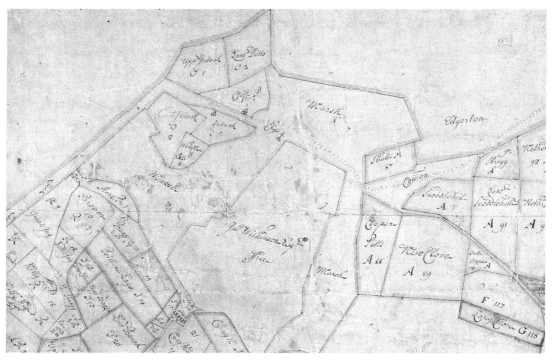

Paddock

The southern part of Marsh common was called Paddock and the place-name suggests that initially it may have referred to a small enclosure there. It is first mentioned by name in 1568 when Edmond Hirst was living at 'parockfote', but soon afterwards John Batley enclosed an acre 'on the head of the parock', so from the beginning it seems to have had a 'top' and a 'bottom'. Actually the first settlement there may have been a fulling-mill, referred to in 1501.[13] Its exact location is not clear but it was possibly on the site of the Paddock Foot mill operated by the Thorntons later in the century. Other families living in Paddock in Elizabeth's reign were the Hirsts, Sykeses and Dysons, all with Colne valley origins.

There were certainly more cottages built in the seventeenth century, although the number is uncertain. For example, the court roll of 1631 refers specifically to one occupied by Anthony Shaw and to four which had been recently erected, tenanted by Batley, Wilkinson, Blackburn and Sykes. It is, however, the estate survey of 1716 [14] which offers the first really detailed

Fig. 2:2 Paddock in 1716, from Oldfield's map of the manor of Huddersfield. (WYAS, K)

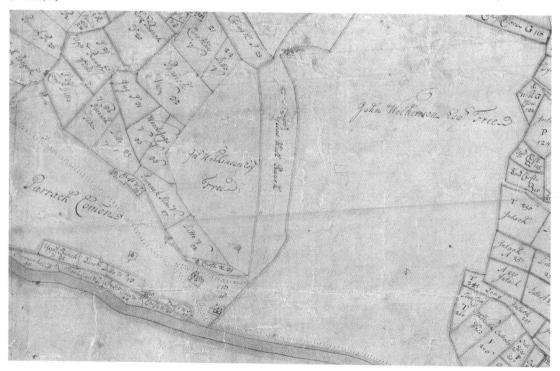

picture, listing something like twenty dwellings. These were scattered over the common, as both the text and the map make clear. Some were said to be located at 'the East end' or 'the Upper end', others at 'the North sid' and there were also cottages at 'the top oth Parrack' and 'Parrack Head'. Entries emphasise how the different sites were identified:

> Mr John Hodgson, a Cott. at the Nabend of the Parrack, in which Widow Illingworth inhabiteth in her Farme.

> Widow Heartley, a Cott. and a little Garth on the Parrack End

Even so, both in this survey and those later in the century, it is obvious that most of the dwellings were concentrated in two communities. The smaller of these, in 1771, was Paddock Head with perhaps ten families;[15] Paddock Foot had probably twice that number. It is noticeable that many of the buildings were in a poor condition, at least seven being described as 'bad' or 'in bad repair', compared with only one described as 'good'. On the other hand, it is clear that building had not stopped for there were at least half a dozen 'new' cottages and many tenants were paying rent on intakes. A cottage 'newly built' in 1797 was in the tenancy of John Moore, many of whose descendants bore the same name and who is remembered in the place-name Johnny Moore Hill.[16]

Edgerton and Gledholt

It has been suggested that both these localities once had hamlet status, but, whether or not that is the case, both later became part of Marsh. Edgerton is first referred to in 1311, but its meaning, Ecgheard's farmstead, suggests that it was a much older settlement site, probably of Anglian origin. It has a complicated manorial history and, as late as 1584, it was possible for the surveyors of Almondbury manor to say, 'Almondbury doth extend itself into . . . the lordship of Huddersfield, for that Edward Cowper . . . doth hold freely by socage a messuage and certain lands . . . called Edgerton'.[17]

It continued to be a single dwelling house for centuries, although some enclosure from the common did take place; for example the Marsh lease of 1436, referred to earlier, permitted William Cowper 'to dyke with qwykwode . . . from the hedge at the marche (Marsh) on the west side to the hedge on the hill'. Even so, Edgerton remained a small and identifiable territory into the nineteenth century. The Cowpers were the family most closely associated with it, for they are known to have lived there in 1425, and may have inherited the property from the 'de' Edgertons over fifty years earlier. In the poll tax of 1379, for example, Adam de Hegerton lived in Quarmby and the Huddersfield list contained a William Couper.

Gledholt means 'kite wood' and is not in itself indicative of settlement. Nevertheless it must be one of the oldest sites in the township and it had given rise to a family name as early as 1274. The 'de' Gledholts, who were quite prominent in the fourteenth century, were living in Huddersfield in 1379, but cannot be traced locally after that. In the early 1400s the Nettletons and the Shaws lived at Gledholt but then, in 1453, when the rent fell into arrears, the estate reverted to its owners, the Mirfields, and they granted the lease to William Hirst of Quarmby. [18] This family was still at Gledholt in the final years of the seventeenth century and it was Alice Hirst of Gledholt who, in 1692, sent a petition to the Quarter Sessions, declaring that her rates ought not to be assessed under Huddersfield, for she was an 'Inhabitant in a nother hamblit called Marsh'.

Fartown hamlet

The place-name Fartown is recorded from 1538 and may be much older, but it is likely in any case that it was first used as a convenient description of settlements in the eastern part of the township beyond the town brook. The history of the surname Brook, in Huddersfield, suggests that some families were living in the Fartown area as early as the thirteenth century and there was certainly a settlement at Woodhouse in the 1300s. However, it was in Tudor times when the most significant expansion took place in the 'far town' and, when the district was finally given hamlet status, it embraced the commons of Sheepridge and Cowcliffe and the territory of Birkby. However, it was always distinct from Bradley and Deighton.

Sheepridge and Cowcliffe

These are the names of two prominent hills which together formed an extensive common between Huddersfield and Bradley. As names of common grazing areas both appear to be self-explanatory, and Sheepridge can probably be taken at face value. However, Cowcliffe was originally 'Cawkecliffe' (*c.*1580) and has nothing to do with cows, except perhaps later through association with Sheepridge. The place-name, in this case, seems to contain the Old English element 'calc' (chalk, limestone) and yet neither of these is found naturally in the vicinity. Perhaps the very light coloured sandstone, quarried there from an early date, was confused with limestone.

As many as twenty named settlements are recorded in this area before 1608, and the part played in this expansion by the Brook family was very significant. The surname ramified strongly from *c.*1500 and was, numerically at least, the most important in the whole township. Its concentration in Fartown was remarkable and, of fourteen settlements first recorded before 1545, no fewer than eleven had a Brook as tenant. Equally interesting is the fact that eleven of the place-names employed the suffix 'house', and it is tempting to see all this deriving from the Brooks of Woodhouse. Expansion continued in Elizabeth's reign but, although Brook continued to figure prominently, the family's role was not as dominant as in earlier years and 'house' also ceased to be an important naming element.

Fig. 2:3 Bay Hall. A tanner named John Brook occupied Bay Hall in the 1560s. (KCS)

Table 1 Settlements in the hamlet of Fartown

Settlement	Earliest reference	Earliest tenants
Woodhouse	1383	Brook
Fieldhouse	1489	Brook
Greenhouse	1504	Blackburn/Brook
Newhouse	1521	Brook
Barkhouse	1524	Brook
Blackhouse	1524	Brook
Yatehouse	1524	Brook
Cloughhouse	1528	Blackburn/Boothroyd
Brockhole	1532	Brook
Hillhouse	1532	Brook
Bradley Gate	1533	Brook
Flashhouse	1542	Brook
Sykehouse	1542	Horsfall
Cuckold Clough	1543	Mellor
Copley Stones	1561	Horsfall
Stone Delves	1563	Brook/Batley
Longwood House	1563	Longwood
Bay Hall	1565	Brook
Intake	1585	Brook
Woodside	1608	Cowper

This list of place-names in Table 1 could be misleading about the exact number of settlements and families. For example Barkhouse, where John Brook was a tenant in 1524, is a name referred to once only and it is even possible that it was an earlier name for Bay Hall where a tanner, also called John Brook, was living in the 1560s. Also, Brockhole (bank) and Intake may just have referred to the same settlement (1817 Brook Hole Bank otherwise Intake).[19] On the other hand there were certainly two dwellings at Stone Delves in the sixteenth century and at Cloughhouse there was a corn mill attached to the 'nether house' in the early 1600s.[20] The following more detailed histories of two Fartown settlements illustrate what can lie behind such place names.

Newhouse Hall

This house owes its name to the fact that Thomas Brooke of Deighton was granted land on Sheepridge common in 1521 and built a new house there shortly afterwards.[21] In his will of 1554 he referred both to the land 'latelie taken of the west (waste) called Shipridge' and to the 'new house . . . lately builded'.[22] The exact date of its erection is not known but it must have been before 1533 when Thomas Brooke was said to be 'of Newhouse' in a list of local clothiers.

The deeds relating to Newhouse Hall contain interesting confirmation of the site of the house and of the continuing process of enclosure through the sixteenth century. The original grant of 1521 describes the land as 'lying to the west of a gate called Bradley Yatte, to the south of Bradley Wood, to the north and east of the said common' (Sheepridge), whilst a lease of 1611 took into account 'the expenses of Thomas Brooke . . . in taking in, enclosing, fencing and reducing into husbandry one piece of barren ground of the waste . . . called Sheepridge'.[23]

Between 1590 and 1630 there are references to the 'nethernewhouse' and the 'overnewhouse' which may seem to suggest that a second dwelling had been built on the site. However, the named occupants were Thomas and Edward Brook and there are good grounds for believing that Newhouse may simply have been partitioned in *c.*1590 and the old timber building incorporated into a larger stone structure. In such a case 'over' and 'nether' would simply refer to the two ends of the building.

Fig. 2:4 Newhouse Hall (KCS)

By 1630 Thomas Brook had acquired the status of 'gentleman' and possessed an estate which included property as far afield as Bingley to the north and Worsborough to the south, and it is almost certain that it was in this period that he built the surviving west wing.[24] Despite his improved status and circumstances there is no evidence yet that 'hall' had been added to the place-name and it seems more likely that this happened in the 1860s when Sir John William Ramsden, the new owner, had the east wing rebuilt.[25]

Cuckold Clough and Ash Brow

In the case of Newhouse Hall the building survives, although much altered and this, together with the documentary evidence, makes it possible for the history of the house and its occupants to be reconstructed with some accuracy. In contrast, the history of Cuckold Clough, also on Sheepridge common, illustrates how much more difficult it can be to identify a settlement site and estimate its antiquity when both the house and the place-name have been lost.

There are some facts: in 1543 James Mellor was granted a lease on a 'messuage and land called Cokewald Cloughe',[26] and the parish registers show that the family still lived there in the 1580s. As the house was already in existence in 1543 it seems unlikely that they were the first to live there and if the site had been named after Robert Cokewold, a Huddersfield tenant of the late thirteenth century, it was clearly of great antiquity. The Mellors increased their holding at Cuckold Clough, just as the Brooks did at Newhouse, and Alice Mellor's lease of 1565 mentioned 'land latlye enclosed of the waste . . . in one place called Cokwaldcloughe'.[27]

Other families were subsequently said to be 'of Cuckold Clough', for example William Whitworth (1636) and Thomas Hawkyard (1658), but eventually the place-name was used of the valley only, and the precise settlement site is not known. The decline of Cuckold Clough as a place-name is, however, compensated for by the emergence of Ash Brow on the same part of the common. In a deed of 1633 the Cuckold Clough land was described as 'lying upon a place called Sheepridge, of which ten acres doth abut upon Meller Eshe',[28] that is, Mellor's ash tree, and this tree seems to be the one later referred to in place-names such as Ash Hill and Ash Brow. The Huddersfield enclosure act refers to both names in 1789: 'one public bridle,

pack and driving road . . . leading across a valley called Cuckolds Clough
. . . which we call Ashbrow Road'. Ash Brow became the name of an inn just
to the west of the road to Bradford, looking out over the former Cuckold
Clough and probably not very far from the Mellors' house of 1543. The
change in the status of the two names may even have resulted from the new
highways built across the common at that point, particularly those of 1789
and the later Bradford turnpike.

There was further settlement on Sheepridge and Cowcliffe commons in
the seventeenth and eighteenth centuries and the estate rentals and surveys
list cottages in both localities. A few of these were given what appear to be
ironic names: Widow Sykes, for example, had 'cottages called Follyhall' and
Joshua Stannige a cottage entered in the rental as 'Brakenhall' (1716). Perhaps
Molewarp Hall was named in much the same spirit. Unfortunately, very few
of the new dwellings had such distinctive names and descriptions such as 'on
Browside' or 'at top of Sheepridge next Deighton' were considered to be
adequate. The rental of 1771 lists at least a dozen in the area, including James
Brook's 'good cott. and 1 acre intake' and James Tifney's 'bad Cottage and
small garden at Ash Hill'.

Some of the sites were new ones, as the surveys make clear, but others
had a long, if obscure, history and the following may be typical. In 1671
Anthony Allison, a poor man with a large family, petitioned the Justices
of the Peace saying that he had 'sustained diverse losses and was likely
to be put out of his house'.[29] He sought and secured permission to 'build
a cottage upon the Common . . . called Naithroyd Hill', (Netheroyd
Hill) and, although the exact location is not known, it must surely have
been close to the modern Allison Drive. Similarly Netherwood Drive recalls
Miles Netherwood who arrived in Huddersfield c.1680. This family
also settled near Naithroyd Hill and it was this that caused the confusion
between the surname and the place-name, finally converting the latter to
Netheroyd Hill.[30]

Birkby

The place-name evidence in this case poses a problem. The suffix 'by'
would suggest that Birkby was a pre-Conquest settlement site of
Scandinavian origin, possibly a single farmstead. Unfortunately, there is no

Fig. 2:5 Sheepridge and
Cowcliffe in 1716, from
Oldfield's map of the
manor of Huddersfield.
Note the description
Birkwith for Birkby.
(WYAS, K)

farmstead. Unfortunately, there is no record of the name until the sixteenth century and the earliest spellings are confusing. The name also appeared to have two values: on the one hand it was 'all that messuage and tenement called Birkbye' (1624), tenanted by the Midwoods from c.1580, and on the other hand it was used as a territorial name. Initially this territory may have consisted of the lands traditionally belonging to the messuage, but if that was so it subsequently embraced other settlements and areas of common. Even in the 1500s it had come to describe three quite separate dwellings.

Although these dwellings did not have distinctive names, something of their history can be traced. The first was probably 'all that messuage called Clayes' which had passed to the Midwoods by 1624. Robert Clay, taxed in Huddersfield in 1545, was said to be 'of Birkby' when he died in 1555, as was Percival Clay in the 1590s. A second property, with a similar type of name, was 'the messuage called Botheroides late in the occupation of Edmond Brooke and Elizabeth Botheroid' (1624). It may have been a partitioned house and indeed both the Brooks (1569-1631) and Boothroyds (1578-1620) were elsewhere said to be 'of Birkby'. Likewise 'of Birkby' were the Hasslegreaves who held a lease on a third unidentified property from at least 1561. This was probably 'the messuage called Thurdlebrough late in the occupation of John Hasslegreat' (sic) in 1624, but this place-name is not otherwise recorded and may have been miswritten on that occasion.

30

Neither Midwood nor Hasslegreave had obvious local connections. The former surname is particularly difficult to identify for there is no recorded earlier reference to it. One possibility is that it represents an abbreviated form of Middlewood, which originated in Darfield, but was essentially a Drax name in the period from c.1450 to 1650. Hasslegreave on the other hand seems likely to have arrived from Saddleworth where it was established between 1297 and 1545.

Lea Head and Storth

To the south of Birkby was a wide strip of common known as Stony Lee and enclosures were made here c.1580 by Edward Brook's widow. This family was said to be of Stony Lee from at least 1566, but the place-name then ceased to be used, except to describe the common, and it seems reasonable to assume that the site of the house came to be known as Lea Head. There were certainly Brooks at Lea Head (the head of Stony Lee) from 1589 and through most of the seventeenth century.

Further to the west lay Storth, probably deriving its name from a twelfth or thirteenth-century assart, but the site of a settlement by 1562 when Roger Shaw lived there. Soon afterwards the property appears to have been sub-divided and from c.1580 Storth was occupied by two families, although it remains uncertain whether this was in two dwellings or in the partitioned halves of the original messuage. One half was held by yet another family of Brooks into the 1700s, whilst the other in the same period is associated with several names, notably Shaw, Hirst and Gamble. The lease of Storth, in 1749, describes it as a 'messuage formerly two, now in the possession of William Hague'.[31]

The Poll Tax of 1379 was compiled a generation after the Black Death and the Huddersfield section contains the names of thirty-five married couples and fourteen individuals. It cannot be taken as a wholly accurate list of the residents, and we do not know exactly how to treat the information it provides; nevertheless it does suggest that the population could not have been much in excess of 200 to 250. The evidence already brought forward on early settlement shows that even this modest total was dispersed in at least six different sites.

By c.1550 a significant amount of expansion had taken place and most of this appears to have been in the area which came to be known as Fartown, and the adjoining parts of Bradley. It must have involved the clearance of substantial areas of woodland, and the evidence shows that this began in the 1400s and accelerated significantly in the reign of Henry VIII. There is no doubt also that the more systematic enclosures of Elizabeth's reign helped other parts of the town and township to develop and by the end of the century Paddock and Marsh were also emerging as important localities. Of these areas of expansion, Marsh, Cowcliffe and Sheepridge were part of the wastes and commons, and the older settlements of Edgerton and Gledholt did not become significant centres of population. Only Deighton was beginning to emerge as a community, probably as a second nucleus. By c.1600 there must have been close to fifty different settlement sites in the township, many of them distinctively named, and the role of the Brooks in this had been crucial, particularly in the earlier stages.

However, other names became important by the middle 1500s, notably Hirst and Horsfall, both from outside the township, and there was further evidence of immigration as the century progressed. Predictably, perhaps, much of this was from the Colne valley and Elland chapelry, but in cases such as Blacker, Midwood, Hasslegreave and Stead the families were from much further afield.

A pattern of settlement had been established which appears to have influenced the distribution of population throughout the township right up to the end of the eighteenth century. The fact that so few permanent settlement names were coined in the later period probably emphasises that point. It meant that as the Industrial Revolution got under way Huddersfield was still really a small village, its market and church ensuring that it served as a focal point for its own widely scattered population as well as for the district as a whole. It also meant that Marsh and Fartown were both given administrative status and emerged as communities at the expense of older settlements, whilst Bradley and Deighton, partly because of their distance from the town, and partly perhaps because of their different manorial histories, still remained on the fringe of things.

George Redmonds

Biographical Note

George Redmonds is a well known local historian. He has been a member of the Council for Name Studies (Great Britain and Ireland) from 1975 to 1992, a speaker at international conferences in England, West Germany, Australia and the USA since 1975, and between 1988 and 1992 has undertaken overseas lecture tours in Australia, New Zealand and the USA. He has been the joint editor of *Old West Riding* since 1981 and has published numerous articles on genealogy and surname development in journals in England, New Zealand and America.

His monographs include: *Yorkshire, West Riding,* English Surnames Series I (1973): *Old Huddersfield, 1500-1800* (1981); *The Heirs of Woodsome* (1982); *Almondbury: Places and Place Names* (1983); *Changing Huddersfield* (1985); *Huddersfield and district under the Stuarts* (1985); *Slaithwaite: Places and Place Names* (1988) *Yorkshire Surnames I: Bradford and district* (1990).

BIBLIOGRAPHY

The documents which identify families with particular named houses or localities are numerous and varied and the most important of these, as well as some of the more obscure sources, are referred to specifically in the footnotes. Other major sources used in this chapter are listed below:

'Lay Subsidy, 25 Edward I', edited by W. Brown, *Y(orkshire) A(rchaeological) S(ociety) R(ecord) S(eries)*, 16 (1894)

'Returns of the Poll Tax for the West Riding' 1379, *YAS RS*, (1882)

P(ublic) R(ecord) O(ffice), Duchy of Lancaster, Miscellaneous Books, DL 42, Vol.106, Folios 91-95, A Rental of Almondbury Manor, 1425.

'Index of Wills in the York Registry, 1389-1688', *YAS RS* 4, 6, 11, 14, 19, 22, 24, 26, 28, 32, 35, 49, 60, 68, 89, (1889-1934).

W.B. Crump and G. Ghorbal, *History of the Huddersfield Woollen Industry* (Huddersfield, 1935). Includes a list of Huddersfield clothiers for 1533 from the Exchequer Accounts, PRO.

'Dodsworth's notes for the Wapentake of Agbrigg', edited by G.Y. Armytage, *YAS Journal* 6, 7, 8. (1875-95).

'Subsidy Roll for the Wapentake of Agbrigg, 1524,' *YAS Journal*, 2 (1873).

W.B. Crump and G. Ghorbal, *History of the Huddersfield Woollen Industry* (Huddersfield, 1935). Includes a list of Huddersfield clothiers for 1533 from the Exchequer Accounts, PRO.

'Dodsworth's notes for the Wapentake of Agbrigg', edited by G.Y. Armytage, *YAS Journal* 6, 7, 8. (1875-95).

Subsidy Roll for the Wapentake of Agbrigg, 1524,' *YAS Journal*, 2 (1873).

'Lay Subsidy of the Wapentake of Agbrigg, 1545', *Thoresby Society Miscellanea*, 9, 11. (1899, 1904).

Huddersfield Parish Registers, 1562-1812.

P. Ahier, *Studies in Local Topography*, Part I (Huddersfield, 1934). Includes subsidy rolls for Huddersfield of 1570, 1588, 1603, 1620.

WYAS, Kirklees, Whitley Beaumont Papers, The Enclosure of Huddersfield Commons *c.*1580, WBE/II/I.

WYAS, Kirklees, Ramsden Papers, Account Books, DD/RA/f/4a and 4b.

D.F.E. Sykes, *The History of Huddersfield and the Valleys of Colne, Holme and Dearne* (Huddersfield, n.d.) includes a transcript of the Hearth Tax, 1666.

WYAS, Kirklees, Ramsden, Maps and surveys of Huddersfield, 1716, 1778, 1780, 1797, DD/RE and DD/RE/s.

WYAS, Kirklees, Ramsden, Rentals of Huddersfield, 1768-69, 1771-72, 1798-99, DD/RE/r.

NOTES

1. WYAS, Kirklees, Ramsden, DD/R/m. The court rolls of Almondbury, 1627-91.

2. G. Redmonds, *Old Huddersfield, 1500-1800* (Huddersfield, 1981).

3. *Chartulary of Fountains Abbey*, edited by W. T. Lancaster (Leeds, 1915).

4. C.T. Clay, 'Bradley, a Grange of Fountains', *YAS Journal* 29, 286-321.

5. William Ramsden of Longley married Rosamund, daughter of Thomas Pilkington of Bradley in 1589, thus connecting two wealthy local families.

6. 'Select XVI Century Causes in Tithe', edited by J. S. Purvis, *YAS RS*, 114, 20-23.

7. G. Redmonds, *The Heirs of Woodsome* (Huddersfield, 1982), p.38.

8. The estate was sold in 1829 and the Colne Bridge property included 'twenty-five Cottages for Workmen'. The sale particulars and map are in H(uddersfield) L(ocal) H(istory) L(ibrary). Folio Pamphlets.

9. *West Yorkshire: an Archaeological Survey to A.D. 1500*, edited by M. L. Faull and S. A. Moorhouse, (Wakefield, 1981), p.410.

10. HLHL, P. Ahier, *Huddersfield and its Manors*, Cuttings Book.

11. WYAS, Kirklees, Whitley Beaumont DD/WBD/VIII/10.

12. An Act against the erecting and maintaining of Cottages, 31 Eliz.,c.7.

13. WYAS, Kirklees Ramsden DD/R/dd/IV, no.1.

14. WYAS, Kirklees Ramsden DD/RE/s.

15. WYAS, Kirklees Ramsden DD/RE/r, (Rental 1771-72).

16. WYAS, Kirklees Ramsden DD/RE/s.

17. Several copies of this survey are held in Huddersfield Library, in WYAS, Kirklees and in the Local History Library: WYAS, Kirklees Ramsden DD/RE/s.

18. WYAS, Kirklees Ramsden DD/R/dd/I/3.

19. WYAS, Kirklees Ramsden DD/R/dd/VII/140.

20. The document which establishes this fact is a tripartite indenture of 1624, and it is frequently referred to in this section. It forms part of the Ramsden Estate Papers held at WYAS, Leeds RA/S/I.

21. WYAS, Kirklees Whitley Beaumont DD/WBD/VIII/24.

22. Borthwick Institute of Historical Research, York, Wills. Vol.14, Fol.115.

23. WYAS, Kirklees Whitley Beaumont DD/WBD/VIII/56.

24. WYAS, Bradford Miscellaneous Mss, Box 26, 47/D/75/5/10.

25. For more information about this house see the following. C. P. Hobkirk, *Huddersfield, its History and Natural History*, 2nd edition (Huddersfield, 1868); P. Ahier, *Studies in Local Topography*, Part I (Huddersfield, 1934); C. Giles, *Rural Houses of West Yorkshire, 1400-1830* (1986).

26.   WYAS, Bradford Spencer Stanhope Papers 4/11/70/2.

27.   WYAS, Kirklees Ramsden DD/R/dd/IV/2.

28.   WYAS, Kirklees Ramsden DD/R/dd/IV/12.

29.   WYAS, Wakefield Quarter Sessions Rolls, QS/I.

30.   e.g. 1841 Census Returns, George Neatheroyd of Neatheroyd Hill.

31.   WYAS, Yorkshire Archaeological Society, MD 43.

CHAPTER 3

The Ramsdens of Longley 1530-1690

DENNIS WHOMSLEY
and E. A. HILARY HAIGH

The story of the Ramsden family is central to any historical understanding of Huddersfield. The purpose of this chapter is to explain something of the Ramsdens' early history and their connection with Huddersfield over the centuries, especially during the period in which the family was resident at Longley. Their interest in the acquisition of land and in connecting themselves by marriage with other families with wealth and influence are major themes in the Ramsden story.

The Ramsdens established themselves in the Huddersfield area in the sixteenth century, when the township consisted of 'several houses grouped in an area to the east of the church and the parsonage'.[1] The family appears to have originated in Elland; and they were engaged in the wool trade, not uneventfully, however, as Ramsdens from there were named in 1533 as clothiers guilty of using flock in their cloth.[2] One of them was Robert Ramsden, who in 1528 bought from Henry Savile some scraps of land from the wastes of the manor of Elland to expand his own land holding;[3] he had already acquired Crawstone Hall in Greetland from his uncles, Gilbert of Sykehouse and Geoffrey of Stainland.[4]

William Ramsden (1513-1580)

It was probably at Crawstone that Robert Ramsden's eldest son, William, was born, in 1513 or 1514 (in a document dated 21 October 1546 he was stated to be aged 33). The name of Robert's wife is not known, except that she was a

Beaumont of Newsome in the parish of Almondbury; she bore him at least three more children, John, Robert and Elizabeth. Little is known about William's childhood, but the family seems to have been well educated. He and his brother John could express themselves in Latin, and in later life William bought copies of the Psalms and the Acts of the Apostles, as well as the songs and sonnets of Heywood, Wyatt and Surrey.[6]

In 1531 William married Joan (Joanne) Wood, one of the three daughters of John Wood of Longley, in the parish of Almondbury. The Wood family had been in the Huddersfield area for many generations and John was probably the wealthiest man in the local community. John's wife Elizabeth was the daughter of landowner Richard Beaumont of Whitley Hall; his eldest daughter Elizabeth married Thomas Savile of Exley and his youngest daughter married Thomas Kay, both from landowning families. By allying himself with the Wood family, William Ramsden was acquiring connections with local landed families of substance, who were also profitably involved in the flourishing wool trade of the district.[7]

Through his marriage, William Ramsden (and the Ramsden family) gained a foothold in the Huddersfield district. John Wood settled on his daughter and son-in-law 'lands, shops and workshops' in Huddersfield to the value of 200 shillings.[8] William increased his holding of land fairly quickly, and at the expense of his wife's family. He acquired a house and shops in Huddersfield from George, John Wood's illegitimate son: from his brother-in-law Thomas Savile, in addition to lands in Almondbury worth between £10 and £16 a year, he purchased Longley Hall,[9] which had come to Thomas by right of his wife, Elizabeth, John Wood's eldest daughter. By 1542 William had acquired much of the land in Huddersfield and Almondbury which John Wood had owned before dividing it among his daughters. He had also bought 'a mansion called the Parsonage in Huddersfield, and lands and cottages there which formerly belonged to St. Oswald's monastery'.[10]* This he had purchased from Richard Andrews and Leonard Chamberlain, agents who bought and sold monastic property, recently made available by the Dissolution.

Within a year of buying these monastic lands from Andrews and Chamberlain, Ramsden himself was buying monastic lands directly from the

*St. Oswald's Monastery, Nostell Priory, was suppressed in 1540. EDITOR.

Crown in association with Richard Andrews and, during the three years from 1543 to 1546, with other associates. On one occasion he obtained on his own account five large grants of land from the Crown for a total of £6,715 14s. 4½d. yet within a year he had disposed of nearly all the lands. The only parcels of land which he retained were in Halifax, Huddersfield, Hartshead, Leeds and Pudsey including a 'parcel of Huddersfield rectory' and the advowson of Huddersfield vicarage. Rather than buying monastic property to build up his own estates, Ramsden seems to have been acting as an agent and buying land for others. It may be, however, that those for whom he purchased land did not pay for it very quickly. At least, it is certain that in 1544 he owed the Crown £800 and that he had several spells in the Fleet Prison for debt.[11]

William's activities in the land market had brought him into contact with people organising the sale of monastic properties, and, in 1545, he was appointed 'Woodward of all the woods in Yorkshire within the Survey of Augmentations'[12]* and later he was appointed bailiff and collector of the manor or lordship of Tadcaster.[13]

William's later years, however, were overshadowed by debt and personal unhappiness. By 1559 he had separated from his wife, and his brother John was living at Longley Hall. It has been suggested that the marriage of Joan and William had been one only of convenience, but his work as a clothier and monastic agent had taken him from home regularly and his imprisonment may have been the decisive factor in the breakdown of a marriage which had produced no children. On 7 November 1580 he died in London and was buried there in St. Sepulchre's Church-without-Newgate. His lands passed to his brother John Ramsden.

John Ramsden (?-1591)

Everything that is known about John Ramsden suggests that he learnt as well as benefited materially from the activities of his elder brother, William. William's contribution to the fortunes and status of the family are clear, but it was John, who lived a quieter life, who consolidated the territorial and

---

*The Court of Augmentations was responsible for the revenue generated by the sale of monastic property at the Dissolution. EDITOR.

financial gains which he and his brother had made. It was John who built the symbol of the family's success, the New Hall at Longley and he was granted the family coat of arms. Before the end of his life his status was officially recorded as one of the gentlemen in the wapentake of Agbrigg.

John Ramsden's wife is thought to have been Margaret Appleyard;[14] their children were Elizabeth, Anne, William, John, Robert and Richard.[15] In 1546 John Ramsden had been appointed by the Court of Augmentations King's Woodward in Rayncliffe and Thurstanby and bailiff and collector of the lands of Monkbretton monastery,[16] possibly as a result of the influence of his brother William, who was Woodward General for the county from 1544 to 1545.

Sometime before 1561 John Ramsden leased from Queen Elizabeth the fulling mill and corn mill in the manor of Almondbury (but called Huddersfield Mills), thus becoming entitled to receive suit and soke from the tenants and inhabitants of Almondbury and Huddersfield, (although some of them had to be reminded to pay by being taken to court).[17] His main sources of income, however, were from the rearing and sale of sheep and cattle and the sale of wool, which, with the rents from the lands which he owned and the interest from money-lending, probably kept him and his family in relative comfort. Most of the records of the time show him exchanging or acquiring copyhold and buying freehold land.[18] An insight into his character is given by this entry in his accounts:

25 day off november 1588

William Loftehus, Crystofer Lofthouse servents and tenents to Mister Henrie Tempest and his son Stevyn dyd bryng unto me to bye [two cowes] the price fowre pounds sex shyllyngs eyght pence and yff they do not lyke of the pryce I shall keyp theym a weyke and dellywer theyme seyffe agayne.[19]

John was undoubtedly a man of substance; his brother William had acquired extensive lands in Leeds, Meltham and Dodworth as well as in Huddersfield and Almondbury. These lands had devolved on John when William died in 1580, yet when John died in 1591 they were valued at only £8 6s. 8d. per annum.[20] It is thought that they were worth possibly twice that amount, because a valuation was not given for all the lands, and Longley Hall, which John rented from William for a number of years, was valued at 'more than 40s' annually in 1591, yet John had been paying double that for it in 1559.[21] It is also difficult to assess John's income from money-lending, another of his interests.

Whatever the sources of his income, by 1575, with the grant of arms to the family by William Flower, Norroy King of Arms, it was clear that John Ramsden had enough money to sustain a way of life enjoyed by none of his ancestors and few of his contemporaries in the area; he had become a country gentleman. In 1576 he was appointed Royal collector of the fifteenth and tenths, a tax on movable objects, for the wapentakes of Agbrigg and Morley, Barkston, Skyrack and the liberty of Halifax.[22] Perhaps to keep up to his new status, but probably because he had the means to do so, John decided to build a house of his own, the New Hall at Longley.[23]

Work on the new house began on the Thursday in Easter week, 26 April 1576. Building was suspended for the winter on 18 August and began again about 18 March 1577. Most of the work was done by William Horsfall and Richard Longley, each with an assistant, but they were also helped occasionally by Edward Grieve and Denis Smith.

Vicesimo sexto die Aprilis anno domini 1576 be the Thursday in Ester week

I begone of my house	
Item the fyrst weyke	4s.
Richard Longley and his man	
William Horsfaull and his man	
Item the 5 of May	5s.8d.
Item the 12 May	9s.[24]

The building was completed on 3 August 1577, the total cost of labour being £17 0s. 5d. The house, described as the New Hall in the survey of Almondbury of 1584,[25] was situated to the north-east of the original Longley Hall. It has been lost in successive rebuildings and alterations.

At the time of the 1584 survey, John Ramsden was the owner of the largest area of freehold land in the district; including, since the death of his brother William in 1580, two halls, Longley Hall and New Hall. In Almondbury, John's lands were already considerable before he received his brother's, whereas in Huddersfield, although William had acquired some property,

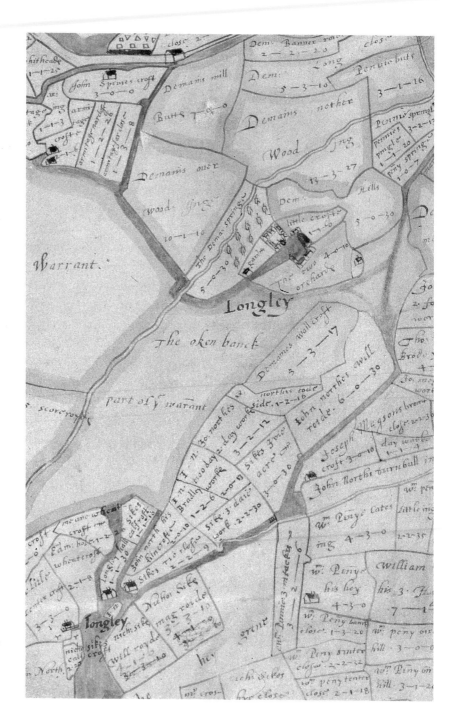

Fig. 3:1 Extract from Senior's 1634 map of Almondbury Manor, showing Longley Old Hall at the bottom left and Longley New Hall to the top right. (WYAS, K)

John appears to have held none until after the enclosure of the commons in c.1565.[26] Although neither John nor William received land directly as a result of the enclosure, John bought land from a major beneficiary, Sir John Byron, in 1571.[27] By the time of his death, in 1591, John Ramsden's lands in Huddersfield were worth slightly more than those in Almondbury, which were valued at about a quarter of the whole.[28]

During his lifetime, John Ramsden had improved and extended his estates. The steady accumulation of lands, rents and mills ensured his increase in wealth. The grant of arms to the family in 1575 and the building of New Hall proved his enhanced status. He had position and responsibility; in 1588 his contribution to the fund to defeat the Spanish Armada was the largest in Yorkshire. When he died on 3 July 1591 he left a family with wealth and good connections. His son William had married the daughter of Thomas Pilkington of Bradley, one of the richest people in the area; his daughter Anne married a merchant, Samual Saltonstall of Huntwick, and another daughter, Elizabeth, married Edward Beaumont of Whitley, a member of the well known local, rich and influential family, and in due course John Ramsden's grandson, Richard Beaumont, was to become a baronet.

Fig. 3:2 Part of John Ramsden's Longley New Hall may be seen to the right of this photograph. It was built in 1576-77. (KCS)

William Ramsden (1558-1623)

John Ramsden's son William succeeded to the estates on his father's death in 1591. Born on 27 August 1558, William had grown up at Longley. On 29 April 1589, he married Rosamund Pilkington and she bore him five children. She died young, however, and was buried at Almondbury on 4 May 1597.[29] William Ramsden inherited from his father extensive lands in Almondbury and Huddersfield, Leeds, Dodworth, Elland and Holmfirth, being granted livery of the lands on 7 February 1592.[30] William was evidently eager to acquire land, for, also in 1592 he was accused with others of intruding into lands in Marsden. A more prestigious acquisition was soon to come his way, however, when on 30 August 1599 he bought the manor of Huddersfield.

For over 250 years, from 1318 when Richard of Cloghes sold the land to Sir Richard Byron, the manor of Huddersfield had been in the hands of the Byrons of Clayton in Lancashire.[31] In the sixteenth century this family had also become involved in the purchase of monastic land. In 1540 Sir John

Fig. 3:3 Letters Patent of 30 August 1599 confirming William Ramsden's purchase of the Manor of Huddersfield for £965 0s. 9d. (WYAS, K)

Byron procured the grant of Newstead Priory in Nottinghamshire, later to become the chief seat of the family. On 2 March 1573 John Byron of Newstead mortgaged the manor of Huddersfield, for £700, to Gilbert Gerard, the Queen's Attorney General.[32] The mortgage appears to have been unredeemed and ownership passed to Gerard, who, on 12 June 1574, leased the manor, with other lands, for twenty-one years to Thomas Norris.[33] On 1 September 1578 Thomas Norris granted his interest in the property to Gilbert Gerard again[34] and on 10 May 1594, Sir Thomas Gerard, son of Gilbert, who had died the previous year, assigned the manor to William Ramsden for what was, in effect, one year.[35] On 30 August 1599 William Ramsden bought the manor from Queen Elizabeth for £965 0s. 9d.[36]

Huddersfield at that time was 'nothing more than a moor-edge village'.[37] For William Ramsden, however, it was an extension of his holdings and the acquisition of a manor was a status symbol. With arms already granted to the family, a new house built and the ownership of the manor of Huddersfield, the Ramsdens could justly substantiate their claim to be gentlemen.

William's personal life at this time, however, cannot have been happy. His wife, Rosamund, had died in 1597 and in his commonplace book survives a poem entitled 'This Lament':

All comfortles I may complayne   Alas far woo now may I saye
my hart is full of woo   gone ys that I loved best
right aspyros now ys my payne   more swete than the flowers that
My joy is gone me froe   grow in May
                                 fare well my joye ys and rest

To whome shall I now sew for grace
seyinge that she ys gone
And hath bene from me alonge space
the greatter ys my mone.[38]

With four children to look after, the eldest not yet six years old, it was important that William should marry again. The fact that it was almost two and a half years before he did so may be a further indication of his grief.

From William's commonplace book it is possible to surmise the organisation of his household at this time. A nurse, Mrs Turnbull, was hired for William's youngest son, also William, who had been baptised at Almondbury on 3 April 1597, a month before his mother died. Other

45

servants, hired between 1596 and 1601, were Arthur Firth, Susan Wilkinson, Isabel Cale, Edmund Hirst, John Shaw, William Wood, John Aneley, Agnes Towlson, John More, William Dale and Thomas Turner.[39]

When, in 1600, William Ramsden married for the second time, his bride was Mary, the widow of Henry Batte of Oakwell Hall, Birstall. They lived for twenty-three years together and both died in 1623.[40]

During his time as lord of the manor, William Ramsden occupied and personally ran his estates from Longley. His accounts record the collecting of rents, the lending (and borrowing) of money and details of farming transactions. The emphasis seems to have been on cattle and oxen rather than on sheep. In Halifax on 25 October 1606, for instance, William sold the following items:

one oxe to Ed. Hopkinson for	£6 6s. 8d.
one branded to a Lancashier man	£3 1s. 4d.
one little blacke to a Lancashier man	£3 13s. 4d.
one brown black to Giles Kaye	£4 10s. 0d.
one stoupeheaded black to one Priestley	£4 16s. 4d.[41]

In this period enclosure of the common land was a regular occurrence, often much to the distress of some people. On 20 April 1616 William Ramsden was informed by three of his tenants that his miller, Wrigley Moralew, to whom he had given permission to enclose 'some more common or waste' land, had far exceeded 'that compass which was appointed for him for he doth enclose and stop our waies and will not be staied from hedging . . .'. The petitioners asked either to be given 'our ancient waies' or for William to 'let us have the said common'.[42] In the following month another petitioner, Janet Taylor of Saddleworth, asked her 'dear and well beloved master' to tell her how many 'capons and hens I ought to pay your worship yearly' and to get these from her husband and children 'that I might live in some reasonable quietness'. She also requested that 'our house may be well repaired and upholden'.[43]

From this evidence, William Ramsden appears as working farmer and lord of the manor, one who could be approached by tenants with their grievances. However, William had problems of his own, caused by his son-in-law, Ambrose Pudsey. William Ramsden and Rosamund, his first wife, had a family of three sons, John, William and Richard, and two daughters,

Catherine and Rosamund. On 23 January 1616 Rosamund married Ambrose Pudsey of Bolton in Craven[44] and they went to live at Longley Green, in the parish of Almondbury. From this time payments to Ambrose, amounting in all to £290 16s. 5d., appear in William's commonplace book, starting with £100 for the wedding and continuing:

> £20 for him at his race at Gaterley
> Item to Ambrose Pudsey at his going to Barford 40s.
> Item when I went to Saddleworth in July to him 10s.[45]

In July 1618, Maria, the infant daughter of Rosamund and Ambrose died[46] and two months later, Rosamund herself died and was buried at Almondbury on 13 September 1619.[47] Relations between William and Ambrose were strained and by January 1620 they were not speaking. A draft letter from William to Mr Pudsey senior, written on 16 January 1620, illustrates the state of affairs:

> Brother Pudsey, I shall be very willing to meet you and your son at York in the Assize week, if health permit, for at this time for the most part I keep my bed being sore troubled with my old disease . . . . Although your son hath heretofore given me just cause of distaste, yet by his letters and some of his friends he hath shown himself so penitent, that he hath given me some part of satisfaction. For mine own part I desire that performance may be according to true meaning and shall be glad that love and amity may continue . . . .
> Your loving brother in law. W.R.[48]

William Ramsden was a sick man, old and suspicious, wanting more than words to convince him of his son-in-law's change of heart.

Between 1620 and 1624 there was a castatrophic depression in most parts of the country, with bankruptcies and riots. Between 1621 and 1623 there were three bad harvests.[49] In Suffolk it was reported in 1622 that two thirds of the textile employees had not been apprenticed and in Yorkshire and Lancashire the figure was probably higher.[50] The situation may have been similar in Huddersfield since in the parish 700 people, including 417 children, were described as poor, while in Huddersfield township 463 poor people, comprising 103 families and including 277 children, were enumerated on a list compiled on 22 December 1622.[51]

William Ramsden's Huddersfield was going through hard times and he was reaching the end of his life. He had brought increased status to the Ramsdens by the purchase of the manor of Huddersfield and seems to have run the estate himself, along with his other land holdings in Almondbury, Leeds, Dodworth, Elland and Holmfirth, keeping careful accounts of profit and loss, purchases and sales, money lent and money owing. He may have been difficult to deal with,[52] but he did grant in 1611 to the governors of the new free Grammar School at Almondbury an annuity of 20s. to increase the wages of the school master.[53]

William Ramsden died on 7 June 1623 at the age of sixty-four and his estates passed to his son, John Ramsden.

Sir John Ramsden (1594-1646)

John Ramsden was born on 10 October 1594 and baptised three days later at Almondbury, his sponsors being Robert Kaye, Thomas Pilkington Esq. and Lady Agnes Gargrayve.[54] Like his father and grandfather, he considerably increased the family estates, with the acquisition of the manors of Almondbury, Saddleworth and Byram, near Pontefract. A cousin of Sir Richard Beaumont of Whitley and a close friend of the influential Sir William Savile of Thornhill, his interests were broader than those of his father. He became a Justice of the Peace, High Sheriff of York and served in the Civil War as an ardent Royalist.

At the age of twenty-four John Ramsden had been knighted by the King; this ceremony took place at Nottingham on 12 August 1619. His father was still alive but a sick man and it is probable that for the last few years of his father's life Sir John played an increasing part in the management of the family estates. In 1623, for instance, a note entered in the family accounts stated that Sir John was owed £13 17s. 6d. for 15 hides by John Brooke of Storth 'to be paid on midsommer even next'.[55]

The year after his father died, in 1624, Sir John married Margaret, the sixteen-year-old daughter of Sir Peter Frecheville of Staveley in Derbyshire. She bore him two sons, William and John, but died, possibly in childbirth, and was buried at Almondbury on 18 September 1626, two days before her son John was baptised.[56] (Sir John later married Anne, daughter of Lawrence Overton of London).

In 1627 Sir John Ramsden acquired the manor of Almondbury with other lands.[57] He also became more involved in public affairs. In 1628, he was commissioned to act on a committee for compounding with recusants; the forfeitures were to be employed in maintaining six men-of-war to guard the coasts from the north-east to the mouth of the Thames.[58]

In the following year he was appointed to serve with the Lord President of the Council of the North and some other West Riding gentry, including Sir Richard Beaumont of Whitley, to consider the petition of poor clothiers of Leeds not to be forced into a company by the aldermen and chief burgesses. The petitioners had asked the King 'to refer the consideration of the inconvenience thereof to such of the Lords, Knights and Gentlemen of the county of York who best understood the nature of clothing'.[59]

In 1632 Ramsden and John Kay(e) of Denby Grange, two of his Majesty's Justices of the Peace in the West Riding were directed to enquire within the wapentake of Agbrigg which towns or places were the most convenient for the sale of tobacco. They themselves wrote to the chief officers of Wakefield, Almondbury and Huddersfield 'which towns we think fittest for that purpose'. The reply they received from Issac Wormall, deputy bailiff and John Kay constable of Almondbury, was that there were three people in Almondbury who had usually sold and were fit to sell tobacco there; two were mercers, Renne Trippier and John Kay; and one was an 'aledrawer' Francis Horne. However, in Huddersfield, according to John Hirst and the constable, Edward Cowper, only one man, John Stacy, mercer, 'is fittest for that purpose, and sufficient for our whole township because there [is] so little tobacco used in our town'.[60]

Some time before 1633 Sir John Ramsden had acquired the manor of Byram in Brotherton near Pontefract. Byram was to become the principal seat of the family in the eighteenth century but, at least until 1670, Longley Hall seems to have remained the centre of family activities. It is significant that Byram was not only a more splendid house than Longley but was much nearer York, the administrative capital of the north. Sir John had become a Justice of the Peace in 1631 and was increasingly involved in administrative and judicial matters.

49

Sir John was a loyal and conscientious as well as a rich knight of the shire. In 1636 his activities were rewarded with his appointment as High Sheriff of the County of York. The Sheriff was a very important official, only the Lord Lieutenant taking precedence over him. It was a great honour to hold the post, but it also involved its holder in a good deal of expense and financial risk. It was Sir John's doubtful privilege as Sheriff to collect £12,000 in ship money from the county to help Charles I in his attempt to avoid calling a Parliament to approve taxes. The first £9,000 to £10,000 appears to have been collected from the Justices of the Peace without too much delay, but the remainder was slow coming in and consequently Sir John was unable to take the money to London on the day he had promised. This was the occasion of a gentle but firm rebuke, on 3 January 1637 from Sir Edward Osborne, the half brother of his first wife, Vice-President of the Council of the North, who informed his 'affectionate loving brother' that the delay would detract much from his 'zeal and forwardness to his Majesty's service . . .'.[61] Sir John wasted little more time. On 7 February 1637 he paid £11,362 to the Treasurer of the Navy and obtained his receipt,[62] although it was not until December that final payment of £138 was made.[63]

Domestic affairs also demanded attention. In 1636 Sir John's uncle, John Ramsden of Lascelles Hall, died, and in the following year his cousin, William, also died, leaving a son, John, aged one year old. In 1639 Sir John was granted the wardship of the boy and obtained the lease of two-thirds of Lascelles Hall during the boy's minority.[64] Meanwhile, on 1 February 1639, Issac Wormall, yeoman, was confirmed as Sir John's bailiff of the manors and townships of Almondbury, Huddersfield, Slaithwaite, South Crosland, Meltham, Honley, Saddleworth and Quick, with an allowance of four shillings in every one pound of royalties that he collected from them.[65]

It was perhaps the seriousness of the national situation which had prompted Sir John to try to get his domestic affairs in order. A Parliament was summoned in April 1640 to grant money to the King, and the King's ministers arranged that many of the gentry in favour of his policy were returned. Among them was Sir John Ramsden, Member for Pontefract, who sat on the Committee of Privileges (16 April) and the Committee for Trade (30 April).[66] In face of the protests from the Commons and Lords, Charles I dissolved Parliament on 5 May 1640.[67]

The gentry of Yorkshire, most of them still loyal to the King, were becoming increasingly irritated by the continual demand for money, to which was now added the trouble and expense of making the largest levy of troops within living memory, for a war on the Scots. Some of their grievances were expressed in a petition, signed by forty-seven gentry, including Sir John Ramsden, and sent to the King on 30 July 1640. Having recalled how in the previous year 'in the execution of your commands about the military affairs, this county expended £100,000 to our great impoverishment and far above the proportion of other counties' they expressed their resentment at the billeting of unruly soldiers among them 'to whose violence we are so daily subject that we cannot say we possess our wives, children, and estates in safety'.[68]

Two years later, however, when Charles I came to York he was received 'with great expressions of joy and duty' and all persons of quality of that great county, and of the counties adjacent, went to see him.[69] Sir John Ramsden was among them, his personal contribution being £300 towards the sadly depleted royal treasury.[70] The Queen had already taken the Crown Jewels with her to the Netherlands, where they were pawned to raise money for the provision of arms and ammunition. Parliament also began to raise troops. In the summer of 1642 armed clashes occurred between the supporters of the two parties and the Royalists had laid seige to both Hull and Manchester fully a month before the King raised his standard at Nottingham on 22 August 1642.

In Yorkshire 'by much the greatest part of the persons of honour, quality and interest' were for the King; but 'Leeds, Halifax, and Bradford, three very populous and rich towns (which, depending wholly upon clothiers, naturally maligned the gentry)' were Parliamentarian.[71] There seems no reason not to link Huddersfield with Leeds, Halifax and Bradford except that the place was neither so populous nor so rich.

Certainly the local gentry were Royalist. Sir John Kaye of Woodsome was Colonel of a regiment of horse in the war, receiving a baronetcy for his services. Thomas Beaumont of Whitley was a major in the Royalist army and deputy governor of Sheffield Castle, and Sir William Savile of Thornhill was commander of the Royalist forces in the West Riding and Governor in turn of Sheffield and York. Sir John Ramsden was no exception; he too was a colonel in the Royalist army.

*Fig. 3:4 Sir John
Ramsden, Kt.
(1594-1646) by Richard
Walker (Private collection:
photograph Courtauld
Institute
of Art).*

It is more difficult, however, to determine the support for the Parliamentary cause in the area. Clothiers, in the nature of things, have not left as many documents as knights. The inhabitants of Holmfirth, it is well known from their own evidence, 'did make and set forth a hundred musqueteers for the Parliament service' and they suffered for it by having 'above thirty houses burnt down by the army against the Parliament'.[72] In Huddersfield one important member of the local community, Thomas Hirst of Greenhead, supported the King[73] and it seems highly likely that another, Edward Hill, the vicar, supported Parliament. (Hill was known to have Nonconformist leanings and his burial on 29 January 1669 was attended by seven Nonconformist ministers, including Oliver Heywood).*

In July 1644 the Parliamentary army defeated the Royalist army at Marston Moor. Sir John Ramsden's regiment fought in the battle, but he himself was a prisoner in the Tower of London, having been captured at Selby, nine miles from Byram, on 11 April that year. He and his commanding officer, John Bellasis, had been tried for high treason. Sir John Ramsden was released in August 1644 as part of an exchange of prisoners and returned to Yorkshire.[74] By this time, the northern counties were firmly in the hands of the Parliamentary forces, with the exception of a few well-garrisoned towns and castles. Sir John Ramsden went to Pontefract Castle as one of four commanders of the gentlemen volunteers, where he had forty-one men under his command. The Castle was besieged by Parliamentary forces under the command of Lord Fairfax. The first siege lasted from 25 December 1644 to 1 March 1645 and the second siege started on 22 March 1645. On 13 June 1645 General Poynz took command of the besiegers and much heavier artillery was used. A month later, on 18 July 1645 a committee of five, including Sir John Ramsden, was appointed to negotiate with the enemy. On 20 July 1645 an honourable withdrawal was agreed and, on the following day, the beseiged garrison marched out to Newark.[75]

The Royalist cause was virtually lost. At Naseby, on 14 June 1645, they had been defeated beyond hope of recovery. Many Royalists had compounded for their estates and, by leave of Parliament, gone abroad, Sir John's brother-in-law, Sir John Frecheville, among them. Ramsden himself was in his fifty-first year and, as he was not enjoying the best of health, this

---

*more information on Hill may be found in Chapter Five. EDITOR.

might have been a good time to retire from the fray. His two sons, as minors, were safe, William being twenty, and John nineteen years old. His second wife, Anne, and his sons were probably living at Longley Hall, comparatively secure in its remoteness. However, a Royalist commander at Newark, Lord Bellasis, as Sir John Bellasis, had been his fellow prisoner in the Tower. Perhaps it was affection for his old friend which determined Ramsden, whatever his private hopes and fears, to join the garrison at Newark, where Bellasis was appointed Governor in November 1645, an appointment which caused Prince Rupert to withdraw his troops to Belvoir.

Provisions at Newark began to fail by March 1646 and the Royalist soldiers had to eat horseflesh, because 'the want of provisions and plague within and the enemy without did expose us to enevitable dangers'.[76] It was all too much for Sir John Ramsden, he died about a month before the castle submitted to the Parliamentarian army. He was buried in the parish church of Newark on 27 March 1646. Three months later, with the capitulation of Oxford, the first Civil War came to an end.

It is difficult to evaluate the life of Sir John Ramsden as lord of the manors of Huddersfield and Almondbury and there is no contemporary opinion of him. That he was loyal to the King and served him well was obvious. In the process it would have been possible to neglect his family and risk losing his estates, but he was aware of this and determined that the family estates, including land near London,[77] would not be sequestrated by conveying all his lands in Yorkshire to two friends, Francis Nevile of Chevet and John Farrer of Ewood, who on 12 February 1643 returned all Sir John's possessions to the son, William Ramsden, then twenty-two years of age.[78] This action of Sir John's probably saved the estates and made possible their subsequent recovery at the cost of a heavy fine by way of composition with the Commonwealth government. It can therefore be said of Sir John Ramsden that, although he gave his life in the service of the King, he at least ensured that his estates remained where he knew they belonged – with the Ramsden family.

William Ramsden (1625-1679)

The post-civil war period was difficult for landed families, especially when they were known to be Royalist. William stayed at Longley; his father's house at Byram had been occupied by Oliver Cromwell and his troops possibly left it in no fit state to be lived in by the family. Times were hard and in 1654 William sold the manor of Saddleworth.

William Ramsden's wife was Elizabeth Palmes from Naburn, North Yorkshire, the daughter of George Palmes. They had three sons, John, Frecheville and Peter, and five daughters. The family was the last of the Ramsdens to reside at Longley. However William left little record of his days there; his son John (1648-1690) was created the first Baronet in 1689 and it was he who obtained in 1671 the letters patent granting the right to hold a market in his manor of Huddersfield.

Sir John Ramsden (1648-1690)

It seems likely that Sir John was born at Longley; he was baptised in Almondbury church in May 1648. Little is known about his early life but at the age of twenty-five John married Sarah, then aged twenty-two, daughter and heir of Charles Butler, esquire, of Coates in Lincolnshire: the marriage took place at Armthorpe in Yorkshire on 7 March 1670. In the following year he was granted a licence to hold a market for cattle and merchandise every Tuesday at Huddersfield and to receive the tolls and profits.[79] Almondbury had held a market on Mondays since the thirteenth century; Huddersfield now became a rival as a market not just for cattle, but for the sale of the much more important narrow kerseys, which were being made in ever increasing quantities in the surrounding countryside. Huddersfield soon proved a more convenient centre than Almondbury, and an open-air market in cloth grew up around its churchyard.[80] Huddersfield was a small village of perhaps 650 people,[81] and a market would increase the value of the estate, would bring in people to trade on Tuesdays and the tolls and profits would go to Sir John Ramsden. However he was probably much more interested in becoming Sheriff of Yorkshire, the post to which he was appointed in 1672.[82]

It seems likely that John moved to Byram on his marriage to Sarah Butler; his eldest son William was born there and baptised at Brotherton on 22 October 1672. Although the fact that the manor house at Byram was available when John married Sarah is sufficient reason for his going there, he probably also regarded Byram, as his grandfather Sir John Ramsden had done when he bought it, as a much more convenient place, nearer the administrative and social heart of the county than Longley. His parents,

Fig. 3:5 Sir John
Ramsden, 1st Baronet
(1648-1690) by
Sir Godfrey Kneller
(Private collection:
photograph Courtaulds
Institute of Art).

William and Elizabeth, stayed at Longley until they died, and both were buried at Almondbury, William on 26 April 1679 and Elizabeth, who outlived her eldest son, on 27 July 1691. Elizabeth was the last of the Ramsdens to be buried at Almondbury: 'Mr Leake preached from Numbers xxiii, 10. There was a very great congregation; and she was buried in great pomp. All her honours are now laid in the dust'.[83]

Meanwhile Sir John had become involved in national politics, at first in opposition to James II, but primarily in support of William of Orange. The reasons for this are not clear; probably he was most strongly alienated, as were so many of the gentry, by James' attack on the established political power of the aristocracy and major gentry between 1686 and 1687.[84] Himself a Catholic, James wanted to promote Catholicism in England and was convinced that 'by assiduous management it would be possible to ensure the election of a Parliament which would favour his designs'.[85] In October 1687 letters were sent to the lords lieutenant requiring them to obtain answers from their deputies, the sheriffs and the justices within their area, to three questions:

1. Will you, if returned to Parliament, vote for the repeal of the penal laws and the Test?

2. Will you support candidates who are in favour of such a measure?

3. Will you live neighbourly and friendly with those of a contrary religion?

The replies generally were evasive. Sir John Ramsden's name was among the many Yorkshire gentry who replied to the first question, that if elected to Parliament they would be guided by the reasons emerging from the debates in the House; to the second that until such penal laws and Tests are made to appear repugnant to the Protestant interest they could not 'contribute to any such election'; to the third that they would live peaceably with everyone else.[86]

This was not rebellion but it was resistance. Sir John Ramsden 'appears to have been closely associated with Sir Thomas Osborne, afterwards Earl Danby, Duke of Leeds, in supporting William and Mary in Yorkshire and the North'.[87] Sir Thomas Osborne had been appointed Lord Lieutenant of the West Riding in February 1674. That Sir John Ramsden was active in local politics from this time is suggested by his attendance as a Justice of the Peace at local Quarter Sessions. From 1674-1689 he attended fifteen meetings of the

General Quarter Sessions, mostly when they were held at Pontefract, Wakefield, Doncaster and Rotherham.[88] These meetings combined the maintenance of law and order with social and political activities; after the Sessions at Rotherham in July 1682 Sir John Ramsden was invited with the other seven Justices to dinner with the Duke of Norfolk.[89] There is, however, no clear and particular evidence linking him with the opposition to James II. It is certain, however, that Sir John Ramsden actively supported William III once he was in England: 'Our dear John Ramsden maintained 30 footmen in our army in our kingdom of Ireland for three whole years for the defence of that realm and the security of the plantation of the province of Ulster'.[90] For service he was 'created and made . . . in the state and grade of a baronet' on 30 November 1689.

Sir John did not live long to enjoy his new position. Just over six months later (on 11 June 1690) he died at the early age of forty-two and was buried at Brotherton; his wife Sarah had already died, in 1683, at the age of thirty-four. In the thirteen years of their married life they had seven sons, five of whom were living when Sir John died.

With the death of Sir John Ramsden in 1690, the direct link with Longley as the Ramsden family home was broken. Succeeding generations of Ramsdens lived at Byram, although of course, they continued to own the manors of Huddersfield and Almondbury. During the period from 1531, when William Ramsden married Joan Wood of Longley, until 1690, when Sir John Ramsden Bt. died, the history of Huddersfield was inextricably linked with the Ramsden family. In them, the two manors of Huddersfield and Almondbury were united, thus enabling them to be developed under one management. The granting of powers to hold a market in Huddersfield, to replace the declining market at Almondbury, ensured that Huddersfield became a thriving centre for trade, which led to its development as a commercial centre.

The story of the town's subsequent expansion owed much to the encouragement of the Ramsden landlords, whose later involvement in the development of Huddersfield is set out in other chapters of this volume.

The Ramsdens of Longley and Byram

```
Gilbert                    Thomas of          = Alice                    Geoffrey
of Syke House           Crawstones, Greetland                           of Stainland
                           (1461?–c.1525)

                                        Robert = daughter of Beaumont of Newsome

William     =   Joanne          John    = Margaret           Robert          Elizabeth
(1513–1580)     Wode           (d.1591)   Appleyard
                of Longley                 (d.1590)
                (d.1565)
                                      ②
                               Mary    =    William    =   Rosamund
                               Batte       (1558–1623)  ①  Pilkington
                               (d.1623)                     (d.1597)

                                          ①            ②
                            Margaret   =    John     =   Anne
                            Frecheville   (1594–1646)    Poole
                            (d.1626)       Knight

                               William   =  Elizabeth
                               (1625–1679)  Palmes
                                            (d.1691)

                            Sarah   =   John
                            Butler     (1648–1690)
                            (d.1683)   1st Baronet

                               William   =  Elizabeth
                               (1672–1736)  Lowther
                               2nd Baronet  (d.1764)

                                  John    =  Margaret
                                  (1698–1769) Bright
                                  3rd Baronet (d.1775)

                               Louisa  =   John
                               Ingram    (1755–1839)
                               (d.1857)  4th Baronet

                            Isabella   =  John Charles
                            Dundas       (1788–1836)
                            (1790–1887)

                  Helen Guendolen  =  John William
                     Seymour          (1831–1914)
                  (1846–1910)         5th Baronet

                     Joan     =  John Frecheville
                    Buxton       (1877–1958)
                    (b.1881)      6th Baronet

        Veronica = Geoffrey William Pennington-Ramsden
         Morley          (1904–1986)
         4 daughters      7th Baronet

    Caryl Oliver Imbert Ramsden   =   Anne
        Great Grandson                Wickham
     of the 4th Baronet
        (1915–1987)
        8th Baronet

           John Charles Josslyn  =  Jane
               (b.1950)             Bevan
               9th Baronet
```

A much more detailed version of this genealogy
may be seen in Huddersfield Local History Library.

Dennis Whomsley

Biographical Note

Dennis Whomsley was educated at the University of Wales, where he also took an archive qualification. After national service with the RAF, he was appointed as Huddersfield's first Archivist in 1958, a post he held until 1961, when he left to become a lecturer at Manchester Regional College of Art, later Manchester Polytechnic, from which he retired as Principal Lecturer in 1988. Dennis Whomsley has undertaken research on the Ramsden family for many years and has published several papers on Huddersfield history.

E. A. Hilary Haigh

Biographical Note

E. A. Hilary Haigh was born and brought up in the Huddersfield area and educated at Holme Valley Grammar School before taking a degree in History and English Literature at the University of Leeds. She was successively Archivist and Local Studies Officer for Huddersfield and then Kirklees from 1968 to 1982. A founder member and Honorary Secretary of Huddersfield Local History Society, Hilary Haigh is a freelance local historian and adult education tutor. She has also been employed as Archivist for the Polytechnic, now University of Huddersfield. She is the author of several books and articles on the history of Huddersfield and the Holme Valley.

NOTES

The research for this chapter was undertaken by Dennis Whomsley and edited for this volume by Hilary Haigh.

1. G. Redmonds, *Old Huddersfield 1500-1800* (Huddersfield, 1981), pp.3-4.

2. W. B. Crump and G. Ghorbal, *History of the Huddersfield Woollen Industry* (Huddersfield, 1935), p.44.

3. W(est) Y(orkshire) A(rchive) S(ervice), Kirklees Ramsden papers DD/RA/f/25 p.24.

4. WYAS, Kirklees Ramsden DD/RA/f/25 p.23.

5. J.S. Purvis, 'Select XVI Century causes in tithe from the York diocesan registry' *Y(orkshire) A(rchaeological) S(ociety) Record Series*, CXIV (1947), 23.

6. D. Whomsley, 'William Ramsden of Longley, Gentleman, 1514-1580, Agent in Monastic Property' *YAS Journal* XLII (1967) pt CLXIV 144.

7. Crump and Ghorbal, *Woollen Industry*, p.29-30.

8. WYAS, Kirklees Ramsden DD/R/dd/II/4.

9. For a fuller account *see* Whomsley, 'William Ramsden . . .'.

10. *S(tate) P(apers)* Henry VIII v17, 443 (39), p.261 and Henry v17, 443 (60) June 1542; WYAS, Kirklees Ramsden DD/R/dd/II/6.

11. For a more detailed account of this *see* Whomsley, 'William Ramsden . . '.

12. *S.P. Foreign and Domestic* Henry VIII v 20 pt.1, 1336, p.673 and WYAS, Kirklees Ramsden DD/RA/f/4a ff.23.

13. *S.P. Foreign and Domestic* Henry VIII v20 pt 1, 1336, p.676.

14. WYAS, Kirklees Ramsden DD/RA/f/25/26.

15. WYAS, Kirklees Ramsden DD/RA/dd/V/30 f1.

16. *S.P. Domestic* Henry VIII, vol.21, pt.1 (20 March 1546, and 28 November 1546), pp.770, 775.

17. Duchy of Lancaster, Calendar of Inquisitions Post Mortem, Edw I - Car I vol.2, pp.256, 270.

18. WYAS, Kirklees Ramsden DD/R/dd/V/30 ff.25^v, 26, 28^v.

19. WYAS, Kirklees Ramsden DD/R/dd/V/30 f.2^v.

20. P(ublic) R(ecord) O(ffice), C142/275/224.

21. WYAS, Kirklees Ramsden DD/RA/f/4a f.35.

23. WYAS, Kirklees Ramsden DD/R/dd/V/30 ff.13,13^v.

24. WYAS, Kirklees Ramsden DD/R/dd/V/30 ff 13,13^v.

25. WYAS, Kirklees Ramsden DD/R/dd/V/28.

26. WYAS, Kirklees Ramsden DD/WBE/II/1.

27. WYAS, Kirklees Ramsden DD/R/dd/V/7.

28. PRO C142/275/224.

29. Almondbury Parish Register.

30. S.P. Domestic Elizabeth (1591-1594) p.179.

31. *YAS Journal*, 7, 276-7.

32. D.F.E. Sykes, *History of Huddersfield and its vicinity* (Huddersfield, 1898), pp.211-214.

33. WYAS, Kirklees Ramsden DD/R/dd/IV/5.

34. WYAS, Kirklees Ramsden DD/R/dd/IV/6.

35. WYAS, Kirklees Ramsden DD/R/dd/III/1.

36. *S.P. Domestic*, Elizabeth (1598-1601), p.315.

37. *YAS Journal*, 7, 281.

38. WYAS, Kirklees Ramsden DD/RA/f/4a f.212.

39. WYAS, Kirklees Ramsden DD/RA/f/4a f.56.

40. Ramsden family tree by E. Rothwell in R Brook, *The Story of Huddersfield* (1968).

41. WYAS, Kirklees Ramsden DD/RA/f/46 f.62.

42. WYAS, Kirklees Ramsden DD/RA/f/19 p.38.

43. WYAS, Kirklees Ramsden DD/RA/f/19/40 letter dated 7 May 1616.

44. Almondbury Parish Register.

45. WYAS, Kirklees Ramsden DD/RA/f/19 p.54.

46. Almondbury Parish Register.

47. Almondbury Parish Register.

48. WYAS, Kirklees Ramsden DD/RA/f/19 p.54.

49. C. Hill. *The Century of Revolution* (1961) p.321.

50. Hill, *Century of Revolution* p.26.

51. WYAS, Kirklees KC337.

52. WYAS, Kirklees Whitley Beaumont papers DD/WBC/31 letter dated 24 March 1609 from George Clay of Middleton to Sir Richard Beaumont mentioning that he would have liked to have asked Mr. Ramsden to lend him a hen, 'dare I have been so bold with him and not have been censured too audacious'.

53. WYAS, Kirklees Ramsden DD/R/dd/II/22, 10 November 1611.

54. Almondbury Parish Register 13 October 1594.

55. WYAS, Kirklees Ramsden DD/RA/f/4a f.110.

56. Almondbury Parish Register.

57. WYAS, Kirklees Ramsden DD/R/dd/II/27, 28.

58. *S.P. Domestic*, Charles I (1628-1629), p.205.

59. WYAS, Kirklees Ramsden DD/RA/f/29/2 and *S.P. Domestic* Vol. 139 No. 24 21 March 1629.

60. WYAS, Kirklees Ramsden DD/RA/f/29/5.

61. WYAS, Kirklees Ramsden DD/RA/f/29/1.

62. *S.P. Domestic* Charles I (1637-1638), p.428.

63. *S.P. Domestic* Charles I (1637-1638), p.19.

64. WYAS, Kirklees Ramsden DD/R/dd/II/31, 32.

65. WYAS, Kirklees Ramsden DD/RA/f/19 p.56.

66. *Commons Journal* Vol.2, pp.4, 17.

67. Sir Charles Firth, *Oliver Cromwell* (1961, edition), p.44.

68. *S.P. Domestic* Charles I (1640), pp.523-524.

69. G. Huehns, *Selections from Clarendon* (1955), p.194.

70. WYAS, Kirklees Ramsden DD/RA/f/29 loose paper no.8.

71. C. Hill, *Puritanism and Revolution* (1958), p.202.

72. D.F.E. Sykes, *The History of Huddersfield and the valleys of the Colne, the Holme and the Dearne (Huddersfield, n.d.)*, p.175.

73. Sykes, *Huddersfield and the Valleys*. p.171.

74. *Commons Journal III*, pp.589, 716.

75. Nathan Drake, *A Journal of the First and Second sieges of Pontefract Castle* 1644-1645 Surtees Society 37 (1860), 80-81.

76. Historical Manuscript Commission *Ormonde Mss.*, New Series II, pp.391, 394.

77. *Commons Journal* III, p.279.

78. WYAS, Kirklees Ramsden DD/R/dd/II/33.

79. *S.P. Domestic*, Charles II (1671), p.533.

80. Crump and Ghorbal, *Woollen Industry*, p.102.

81. This figure is based on a number of people paying the hearth tax of 1664-139; assuming the average size of a household to be 4.47, the population in 1664 would be 621. See E.A. Wrigley *An Introduction to English Historical Demography* (1966), p.87.

82. WYAS, Kirklees Ramsden DD/RA/f/17.

83. From the contemporary diary of Revd Robert Meeke, quoted in C.A. Hulbert, *Annals of the Church and parish of Almondbury* (1882), p.30.

84. J.H. Plumb, *The Growth of Political Stability in England*, (1967), pp.58-61.

85. D. Ogg, *England in the Reigns of James II and William III* (1964), pp.187.

86. Sykes, *Huddersfield and its Vicinity*, p.241.

87. WYAS, Kirklees Ramsden DD/RA/f/29.

88. WYAS, Kirklees Handlist of attendance of Justices at Quarter Sessions, according to the Indictment Books, 1637-1699.

89. *Memoirs of Sir John Reresby*, edited by A. Browning (1948), pp.271, 348-9.

90. WYAS, Kirklees Ramsden DD/RA/f/20. *S.P. Domestic* William and Mary (1689-90), p.323.

CHAPTER 4

Markets, Fairs and Tolls in Huddersfield

EDWARD J. LAW

Fairs are known to have existed by 1584, the time of a survey of the manor of Almondbury,[1] conducted for the owner, Queen Elizabeth. This survey included reference to three 'little fairs', commonly called tyde days, held within the town of Almondbury, and that the Queen, or the farmer of the Manor, received a certain rent for the tolls arising therefrom, together with the toll of two other 'little fairs' held in the town of Huddersfield on St. Ellen Day and on St. Peter the Apostle Day. It was also reported that there were no stalls, standings, shops, booths or suchlike belonging to the said fairs or tydes. The right to hold a market in his manor of Almondbury had been granted in 1294, to Henry de Laci, Earl of Lincoln (who in the same year also had similar grants in respect of Campsall, Pontefract and Slaidburn[2]). Almondbury market must have fallen into disuse by 1584, for the terms of the survey included an enquiry into both fairs and markets, yet the latter are not mentioned. Indeed, report of the fairs at Huddersfield appeared to be almost an afterthought.

The next hundred years saw the reversal of the relative importance of the towns of Almondbury and Huddersfield, and the Ramsden family, who had purchased the manor of Huddersfield in 1599 and the manor of Almondbury in 1627, rather than reviving the market at Almondbury, applied in 1671 to the Crown for the grant of market rights in Huddersfield. The Crown had to be assured that any grant would not prejudice existing rights, and ordered a local enquiry. A translation of Charles II's order in the matter and of the findings

Fig. 4:1 Huddersfield Market Place.

65

are given by Taylor Dyson.[3] The writ ordering the enquiry was issued on 23 June 1671, and the inquisition itself took place on 12 September following, when twelve 'good and honest men' attested that the grant of market rights would not be to the detriment of the King or any others. Satisfied by the findings of the enquiry the King, by letters patent dated 1 November 1671, granted John Ramsden the right to a weekly market in Huddersfield.[4] Apart from the immediate objective of assuring to himself a further source of income from his estate, John Ramsden may have been looking to the long-term development of the town as a trading centre, with a consequent increase in property rentals for himself and his heirs.

An indication of the nature of the market in its early days is found in a lease of 1718, letting, among other things, 'all the tolls and profits belonging to the market place and fairs of the town of Huddersfield. Also the three old fairs of Huddersfield and Almondbury, with the tolls of all sorts of corn and grain'.[5] The lessees were to be responsible for the repair of all the stalls and trestles in and belonging to the Market Place, and were to keep 'a measure and standard and all other things belonging to a clerk of the markets'. We may imagine from this that the nature and format of the open market has changed very little down the centuries, comprising movable stalls, probably with their own canopies or covers. In the inventory of the effects of Jennet Williamson, taken in 1696, are 'Certaine Boards and Broaken Wood £1, Certaine Loose Stalls and other wood ith Market place £5'.[6] Jennet was the widow of Richard Williamson, probably the first farmer of the Huddersfield market, and had inherited the lease of the Market Place from her husband. Also in the inventory were 'the Brass Stroake, the yardwand and the Cryer Bell £1-10-0'. Clearly Jennet had continued to administer the market. The brass stroke was the measure, and the wand the standard, which the previously-mentioned lease required the clerk of the market to keep.

The market must have been a feature of weekly life for miles around; a case at Almondbury Manorial Court in 1689 records John Hurst of Busker, in the Parish of High Hoyland, as attending in the customary market place in Huddersfield. From its inception the market probably had a good variety of stalls. John Brook, a bookseller and binder, commenced business on a stall in the mid-eighteenth century. The following century a local nailmaker was a stallholder for between thirty and forty years; vendors of cutlery, market gardeners, fruiterers and fishmongers are among those known to have been market traders. Probably the one class of tradesmen who were not represented were the butchers, who operated from their specialist market, the Shambles. However, before the first shambles were erected, *c.*1771, it is possible that butchers too were to be found on the market.

Demand for stalls in the nineteenth century was very keen, one stallholder securing a site in the Market Place only after having a stall at the top of King Street for some twenty years. In the early part of the day, some of the stalls were occupied by wholesalers of fruit and vegetables who, when they had disposed of their stocks, sublet the stalls to retailers. Whilst the official, principally observed, market day was Tuesday, there were always one or two stalls on the market during the week, a fruit stall and sometimes a fishmonger's and Saturday night was very busy. Indeed, in the enquiries of 1852 it was stated that a Saturday market had been held for upwards of forty years. In 1821 a petition had been presented to Sir John Ramsden to alter the Huddersfield market day to Thursday, because Tuesday clashed with Leeds. Those mainly affected by such a clash would have been the clothiers and merchants. Tuesday was retained as the market day, however. This description of the market was published in 1795:

> The markets of Huddersfield are very well supplied with beef, mutton, veal and pork, which are exposed for sale in shambles built by the lord of the manor. The market-day is Tuesday, but mutton and veal may be had on other days at the butcher's (*sic*) shops. It is also tolerably supplied for a considerable part of the year with sea-fish from the Yorkshire coast. The fat cattle and sheep are brought out of Lincolnshire and the neighbouring counties, and generally bought at the fortnight fairs of Wakefield, which supply much of the western part of Yorkshire and the adjacent parts of Lancashire. Butter, eggs and fowls, are not usually sold at the market cross, but may sometimes be bought in the neighbourhood. A moderate quantity of corn is brought to the market by the farmers round, and a larger quantity is brought by water from the more southern counties, much of which is carried forwards into Lancashire. There are small quarterly fairs, at which some horses and lean cattle are exposed to sale; but the principal fair for this purpose is on May 4.[7]

It is interesting to note that there were not at that time regular sales of butter and eggs, traditionally a sideline of the wives and daughters of farmers. This trade seems to have developed years later for in November 1851 Sir John

William's mother, the Hon. Isabella Ramsden wrote to her son's agent: 'A covered market for the women who bring their poultry, butter and eggs from the country to Huddersfield is as I believe much wanted'.[8] The matter was taken up immediately, and a local architect, William Wallen, prepared plans for a glass cover for the Market Place. It is not known why the project was not pursued; it could well have been on account of the tolls controversy which erupted the following May.

The market of 1671 was probably first set up in the area of the present Market Place, but it may then have lain behind buildings on Kirkgate. The accompanying enlargement from the map of 1716 shows that the Market Place was not fully open to the principal street of the town, the present Kirkgate. A substantial house is shown on the north side, with access to the square being via entries on either side of the building. Across the street from that building was what was to become, and may even then have been, the George Inn. Whilst the Market Place would undoubtedly have been the focal point on market days, other areas were also utilised. The more important aspects of the trade may be gathered from the following headings into which the income was analysed in 1741: pieces, bystands, rents, corn, wool, cattle and bell.

Woollen pieces must have been a very important commodity; they were brought into the town from a very wide area, notably from Saddleworth. As trade developed, the Market Place would not be sufficiently large to meet the needs of the clothiers, leading to the practice of displaying their wares on the walls of the churchyard, and on the tombstones themselves. This facet of trade was eventually provided with its own market, the Cloth Hall, which Sir John Ramsden started to have built in March 1765 and which opened in November 1766. A suggestion made in 1863 when Cloth Hall charges were being considered, that they revert to the old plan, a toll of two pence for each piece, may refer to the days before the erection of the Cloth Hall.

Bystands and rents were probably synonymous, the only distinction being of physical location; the rents relating to those stalls on the actual Market Place, the bystands being the remainder, whether on the streets, in yards or in the adjoining fields.

A toll was taken on all corn which was offered for sale in the town. It was taken in kind, the collector carrying a one-pint brass measure, which amount was taken from each sack displayed. It is no surprise to learn that the farmers

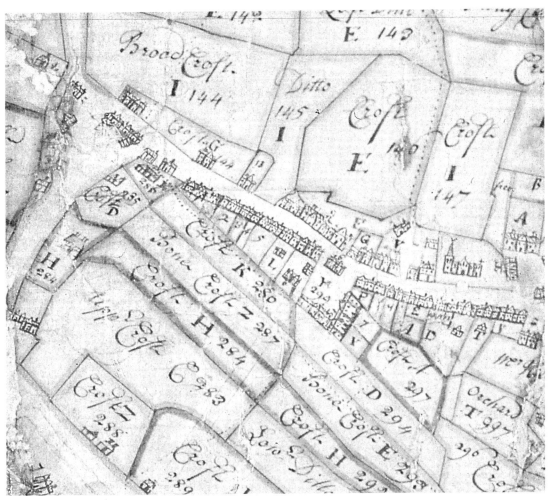

Fig. 4:2 Market Place in 1716, from Oldfield's map of the manor of Huddersfield.

tried to evade the toll, and the Almondbury court rolls of May 1735 record that corn was being sold in public houses and other places, a practice still being followed a hundred years later, when the collector reported that it was being displayed in the yards of inns. The toll on corn was allowed to lapse in the 1840s, when the amounts coming into the town were so small that its collection was no longer worthwhile. It is probable that the toll also extended to malt and other grain, which we know from a note in the day-books of John Turner were being sold in the market in 1757.[9]

At one time a toll was levied on every pack of wool displayed for sale, but it is said that the woolstaplers brought and won a court case to discontinue the toll,[10] and certainly it had ceased to be collected by 1810. Probably wool ceased to be sold on the streets in the last quarter of the eighteenth century, as the Cloth Hall became the focal point of the textile trade and the inns of the town incorporated shops and chambers for merchants, woolstaplers and others. In 1795 the income of the White Hart, a new inn in Cloth Hall Street, included £156 15s. od. per annum in respect of rents of thirty-six shops and other buildings in its yard. The tenants came not only from the surrounding villages, but as far afield as Manchester, Penistone, Saddleworth and Leeds.[11] Such premises were described by a visitor to the town in 1862, '3 or 4 yards or courts are fitted up with stairs and galleries on the outside of the buildings. Separate rooms which are marked with the names of the occupiers are to be seen with their doors open about 7 or 8 o'clock in the morning of the Tuesday'.[12] Perhaps the last of these in something resembling its original condition, with external steps and stone galleries, is the enclosed yard behind Cloth Hall Chambers.[13]

Cattle sold in the town on market and fair days were also subject to toll, although the amount is not known. There appears never to have been a definitive list of tolls. Even during the nineteenth century, when the whole question of fairs and tolls was being aired, no lists of tolls or charges were known. In the lease of the market tolls in 1718 the tenants were instructed not to charge above the usual rate that had already been received and paid, but without specifying such rates.

Clearly the restricted area of the Market Place was not suited for the display and sale of cattle on a busy market day and it is probable that from the very inception of the Tuesday market they were dealt with in the area which took the name Beast or Cow Market, between Kirkgate and Northgate. That toll also was allowed to lapse, in about 1810, on account of the very small numbers being presented for sale. The Ramsdens may have been partly to blame for the decline of the cattle market; indeed there may have been a conscious decision to discourage weekly cattle sales in order to promote an image of the town as a business and commercial centre. In later years a small area was cleared on the north side of Beast Market, but by that time sales of cattle took place only at fair times. It is recorded in 1837 that several houses at the head of Westgate had been removed to widen the approach and to make room for a cattle market.[14] How long it operated in that area is not known; it is probable that the commercial development which came with the railway in the next decade increased pressures to remove cattle sales to the periphery of the town. Huddersfield's principal cattle fair was held in October, with others in March and May. Cattle or beast fairs were also held at Slaithwaite and Marsden.[15]

The term cattle market probably included all agricultural livestock and references are found at various times to horses and pigs. As with cattle, the horse sales declined from a weekly event to periodic fairs, and in a plan of the town of *c.*1780 an area to the south of Kirkgate is designated 'Horse Fair'.[16] There is evidence to suggest that the area was utilised for horse fairs for something less than ten years, and possibly for a much shorter period. The Market Place on a Tuesday would have been thronged with stalls and people. No doubt because of this it was the natural centre for selling of all kinds, however inappropriate, sometimes with fatal consequences. The *Leeds Mercury* of 12 September 1786 carried the following report: 'Tuesday se'nnight as a horse dealer was showing a horse in the Market Place, Huddersfield, he rode against a woman who was knocked down and died'. A pig market is noted in the Ramsden rental of 1836 as part of the holding of Joseph Kaye; it seems probable that he administered that market in addition to many other business interests, for in 1833 he is on record as supplying pigs to the Huddersfield Infirmary.[17] The pig market was to the south of the shambles, the area being known as Swine Market in the 1840s, and later as Victoria Street.

All knowledge of bell tolls appeared to have been lost with the passage of time; it had already passed into obscurity in 1852. However, it is evident that it was a levy paid to the town crier or bellman to announce sale times and such like[18]. The town crier in 1766 was Edmund Sykes, who was also landlord of the Cross Keys. He and a partner held the tolls under Sir John Ramsden, and Sykes is stated to have encouraged persons to bring pieces of cloth to him, under pretence that they were lost, in return for a pint of ale, as he received a perquisite of 4d. for crying things lost, 'and frequently more'. The day-books of John Turner contain several references to the town crier; on 25 June 1755 he noted 'Paid William Sykes for crying notice to prosecute persons that trod down grass etc. in Priestroyds, 2d'.

There were certain markets which did not fall under the control of the Ramsden family. The principal one was the Huddersfield Statutes, the local hiring fair which was in reality a labour market. The Statutes was held annually one Wednesday in October. Domestic servants, agricultural labourers and the like attended in the town and held themselves out for hire for the next year. Clearly, from entries in John Turner's day-books, it was a functioning market down to the middle of the eighteenth century.[19] In 1749 Turner hired a young boy for £3 15s. od. per annum and in 1760 his wife was able to hire a maid for £2 10s. od. The Statute Fair is mentioned in Arthur Jessop's diary,[20] and the editor of the published edition states that it was followed some few days after by the Mop Fair, to 'mop up' those who had not been hired at the Statutes. However, in 1768, when John Turner was unable to hire a maid at the Huddersfield Statutes, he went to that of Barnsley on the following Saturday. It is not known when the last Huddersfield Statutes was held, but it is interesting to find one still being held in Leeds in 1823.

Another independent market is recorded in the recollections of John Hanson.[21] The Fud Market appears to have been a specialised wool sale, which in the early 1800s was held in a room over the Plough Inn, which stood at the corner of Half Moon Street and Market Street. Fud was a form of woollen waste, the strippings from carding engines, but the term may also have been applied to the products of such waste, for Hanson tells of the sale of hanks of yarn.

As well as being Lords of the Manor of Huddersfield, the Ramsdens were virtually the sole owners of the soil, and as such they considered themselves entitled to conduct the markets and fairs wherever they wished. Sir John Ramsden erected new shambles in the town around 1771, where as many as forty butchers were housed. They stood where King Street joins New Street and may be seen (Slaughter H.) on the plan of the town of 1778.[22] They were removed in c.1807, possibly to release valuable New Street frontage, and were replaced by new shambles behind the original site. The area between the shambles and King Street was utilised for stalls and came to be known as the New Market.

The corn market was held at the doorstones of the White Horse Inn,[23] giving the area at the top of Beast Market, known as Amen Corner, the alternative name of Corn Market, found on the 1778 map and in the directory of the town of 1814.[24] The corn market had been the centre of a riot in 1799. Corn prices had risen beyond the means of the poorer classes and the women of

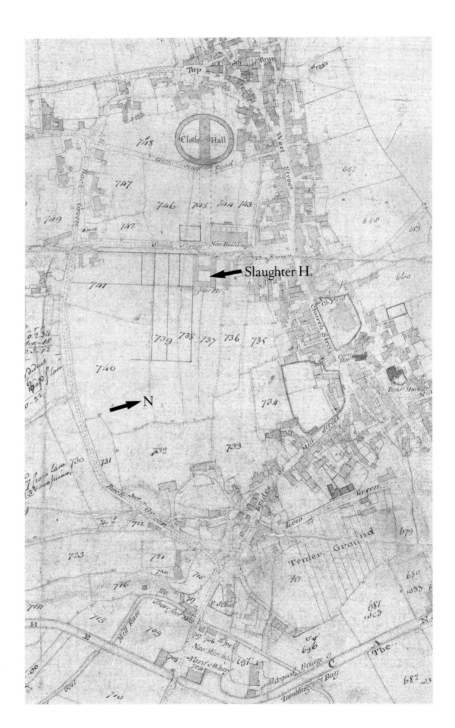

Fig. 4:3 Huddersfield in 1778. The Shambles is labelled Slaughter H. The Corn Market is below the Church. (WYAS,K)

the area determined to do something about it. On 19 November numbers of people, principally women, assembled in villages around Huddersfield and marched on the town, where an immense mob seized all the corn which had been brought to the market. Joseph Radcliffe of Milnsbridge, the local magistrate, who was later to pursue the Luddites with such determination, read the Riot Act, and, with the aid of two officers of the local volunteer force, arrested three people. Martha Bray, who appears to have been one of the ringleaders, had sold much of the wheat at six shillings a bushel, stating that that was quite enough. She was committed to York prison for a year. Abraham Broadbent, who had kicked Radcliffe's horse, and the third person each received three months in the House of Correction.

The market cross was probably set up shortly after the granting of market rights in 1671, a view supported by the heraldic evidence upon the cross itself. It is said that at a time of disturbances there were fears that the cross would be damaged, and it was removed to Longley Hall for safe keeping. The date of its removal is not known. The mention in Aikin's survey would indicate that it was in the Market Place in 1795, and the definition of the scope of the Act for Lighting . . . the Town of Huddersfield, as '1200 yards each way from the spot where the old cross stood in the centre of the Market Place' shows that it had been removed by 1820. Whether by design or neglect it was to remain at Longley Hall for the next thirty years. In 1851 Joseph Kaye was asked to consider the best method of replacing it in the Market Place, and Isaac Hordern notes that it was re-erected there on 2 June 1852.[25] One must wonder if the timing was a deliberate act on the part of the Ramsdens to assert their private ownership of the Market Place, for it was at the May fair, only a fortnight earlier, that opposition to the tolls first emerged. Whilst the Market Place was private property, and was assessed for taxes as such, it had come to be the centre of the public life of the town. Mass meetings were held there, crowds assembled there to listen to orations from the upper windows of the George, and at the County elections the polling booths were sited there. At one time it was the location of the town stocks, and on Sundays it became the pulpit of itinerant preachers. One may therefore excuse the townspeople if they had no knowledge of the private nature of the area, and for their feelings of resentment when the Ramsdens asserted their legal rights.

It is not known how the Huddersfield market was administered at its inception. It is known that by 1677[26] it was farmed out and it is probable that this was the manner of operation instituted by John Ramsden on being granted the market rights. This was a common practice; in the previous century, in September 1548, King Edward VI had farmed the tolls, markets and fairs in the Lordship of Almondbury for nine shillings per annum.[27]

It is probable that the first farmer of the Huddersfield tolls was Richard Williamson, a Huddersfield coalminer, upon whom the benefit of the Market Place was assessed in 1677. Although Williamson called himself a coalminer, it is clear from his will of 1686 that in fact he was a prosperous businessman. He left his wife the benefit of the unexpired term of the lease of the Market Place and sufficient money to pay any outstanding rent of the same. His two sons were each left a house in the town, and one of them, Richard, also inherited coalpits at Huddersfield, held from Madam Ramsden, with all the tools and implements for working them.[28] In 1677 an assessment was laid on the Constablery of Huddersfield for the rebuilding of thirty ships of war.[29] The second-largest levy, following William Ramsden, was upon Richard Williamson. He paid two shillings and fivepence for

Fig. 4:4 Market Place; the George Inn may be seen at the far end of the square. (KCS)

'Water Royds farm and for Coale pit', and the one shilling and sixpence which he paid for the 'benefit of markett place' was more than was paid by all but one other townsman. It is interesting to find the tolls and collieries already associated, an association which persisted for much of the period down to the 1850s. The Ramsdens also chose to farm out their mineral rights, and not until 1862 did they become involved in winning their own coal, at Springwood colliery.[30]

Richard Williamson's widow, Jennet, died in 1698, and whilst she did not mention the tolls in her will, items in the inventory of her estate, which have already been mentioned, indicate that she continued to hold the market rights. As previously noted, the lease entered into in November 1718 was for a period of twenty-one years, and it seems likely that the previous lease would have been for a similar period, which would accord with a new lease being made following Jennet Williamson's death; she died early in 1698, and the lease of November 1718 may well have been completed some months before it was to commence.

The families of Richard and Jennet Williamson were rather complex. He had had an earlier marriage to Alice Read, and Jennet, who was the sister of Robert Read of Backside Of Town, Huddersfield, and may also have been sister to Alice, had had two previous husbands, Francis Nicholl and Gervase Kaye. Nothing is known of Richard's two sons, despite the fact that they inherited property in the town. Jennet had several children by Francis Nicholl, and it seems likely that following her death Daniel Cooper, the husband of Margaret, her eldest daughter, took the lease of the tolls. The survey of the town in 1716 and the map which accompanied it both indicate that the site of the Market Place was part of the holding of Widow Cooper. Daniel Cooper had been an innkeeper in the town and in 1711 kept a new house at the south-east corner of the Market Place.[31] Sarah Nicholl, another of Jennet's daughters, married Thomas Dransfield, and the names of both Dransfield and Cooper were later associated with the Market Place and with the tolls.

In 1718 the tolls, in association with all quarries of stone on the common, were leased for twenty-one years to James and William Murgatroyd and James Whittaker, all of Huddersfield.[32] The Murgatroyds were described as yeomen, but James was the landlord of the town's premier hostelry, the George.[33] Whittaker was a butcher. It is significant that a later note to the

1716 survey of the Ramsden estates shows Whittaker to have been the successor to Widow Cooper, the tenant of the Market Place, for he was probably her son by a previous marriage. Another note to the survey records that the Murgatroyds and Whittaker were to surrender their lease, taking a new one for twenty-one years at an annual rental of £34 and paying a fine of £500; these were the terms on which the 1718 lease was taken. A provision of that lease was that the tenants were forbidden to assign their rights to anyone other than their children without the permission of Sir William Ramsden. A draft endorsed on the lease indicates that an assignment was considered, with the Murgatroyds' two-thirds interest going to Henry Wentworth, and the other third passing to John Nicholl of Brighouse. The latter was another of Jennet Williamson's children, and a series of deeds memorialised at the Registry of Deeds indicate that the assignment was a form of mortgage. In his will of January 1736 John Nicholl left his son John 'all my interest, right, tythes, property, claims and demand whatsoever of, in and to all the tolls and other profits yearly arising, growing and increasing within the town of Huddersfield'.[34]

It is not known what became of the tolls for the next thirty years. On 14 June 1739 William Elmsall, agent for the Ramsden family, noted 'to Huddersfield about the tolls,'[35] and it may well be that they were offered to the highest bidder. That method had been used in 1734 in renting out the tithes when Elmsall recorded 'Tythe folks bid, Richard Booth got it'. Whatever the method by which they were leased it seems probable that they remained with the descendants of Jennet Williamson, for there was at one time a book in the possession of the Ramsden family which recorded the tolls collected in 1761-62 by Thomas Dransfield, and it may be that he was the contractor for the tolls at that time. The next known lessees of the tolls were George Crowther and Edmund Sykes, the latter being the landlord of the Cross Keys Inn in the town.

Papers relating to a dispute of 1766, which have already been referred to,[36] record that Sir John Ramsden had let the tolls of Huddersfield Market to Edmund Sykes and George Crowther for a considerable yearly rent and accused them of using several arts to enhance their profits. The Ramsden rental of 1768 shows that the rent was in fact £50 per annum. George Crowther was at the same time in partnership with John Bradley as joint lessees of a colliery from the Ramsdens, and it seems probable that it was the same John Bradley, a Huddersfield innkeeper, who in 1784 bequeathed his half of the tolls of the market, and of collieries in Huddersfield and Almondbury, to his son Joseph.[37] Joseph in turn left them to his brother William, by whom they continued to be held to the end of the century, at which time the tolls, at a rent of £30 per annum, were very subsidiary to the collieries, for which the annual rental was £400.

In 1814 the tolls and collieries were again leased together, to Messrs Ogden & Co., who are said to have held them even before that date. When the lease was renewed in 1821 it was to Messrs Ogden, Horsfall & Co., a partnership which included Nathan Whitley of Stile Common. The Whitleys were to be associated with both tolls and collieries for the next thirty years, and Nathan had already been involved many years, having collected the tolls for Messrs Ogden & Co. as early as 1813. The partnership was dissolved in 1828 when Nathan Whitley took the lease of the tolls and the collieries for himself. Shortly before his death in 1837 he had assigned all his tolls of corn and cattle in Almondbury and Huddersfield and all the market tolls in Huddersfield to his son James,[38] who was in possession in 1852 when the market question came to a head.

The mention in Nathan Whitley's assignment of Almondbury may have been a matter of form, in that the manors of Almondbury and Huddersfield were one for administrative purposes. It should not be assumed, however, that because there is little evidence of fairs and markets at Almondbury, they did not exist. It is possible that the Almondbury tyde days mentioned in the survey of 1584 continued to be observed in some form over the centuries. There is in fact evidence of the survival of one, that which in 1584 was held at St. Martin the Bishop in winter (11 November), for John Turner recorded in his day-book at 22 November 1756 'attended Almondbury fair and purchased a pig'. (With the alteration of the calendar in 1752, 11 November would convert to 22 November). Market rights in respect of Almondbury had been granted in 1294; it is unlikely that those rights were ever extinguished, and no doubt there continued to be some agricultural trading in the village down the centuries, though probably on not much more than a local level. *Bailey's Northern Directory* of 1784 recorded that the market day at Almondbury was Friday, although the original grant of 1294 had been for a Monday.

As with Almondbury, the day-books of John Turner provide evidence of the continuation into the eighteenth century of one of Huddersfield's ancient fairs, that of 29 June. Turner recorded Huddersfield Fair on that date in 1732, and, on the same day in 1747, Peter's Fair. The 29 June was the feast day of St. Peter and St. Paul, it seems likely that it was one of the town's ancient fairs. The principal Huddersfield fair day, 14 May (4 May before the change of the calendar in 1752) was St. Ellen's or St. Helen's Day, by which name it is recorded in the diary of John Murgatroyd on 14 May 1781.[39] The origins of these fairs are no longer known. It was usual for a festival day to be held annually on the feast day of the saint to whom the Parish Church was dedicated, so that 29 June may have been Huddersfield Feast.

At a time when the lives of the great mass of people demanded six days of toil, any form of diversion would be heartily welcomed, and almost every township had festive days of one sort or another. Rushbearing was an annual religious ceremony, originally a community duty when parishioners would allocate a day to the cutting and collection of rushes with which to carpet the bare earth of their church floor. Rushbearing continued as a festive occasion at Kirkburton, Almondbury, Longwood, Slaithwaite, Meltham, Marsden and Deanhead. The rushbearing was still serving its utilitarian purpose in 1690, for Meeke records that Slaithwaite 'had a second rushbearing because the water had been in the chapel'.[40] It is surprising that there is no evidence of a rushbearing at Huddersfield; could it be that the church had, from its foundation, a flagged floor?

Another religious festival was the feast day which was observed with rejoicing and feasting, as opposed to the fast days. Each church had its own feast day, and evidence has been seen for Kirkburton, Emley, Honley, Deanhead, Slaithwaite, Marsden, Longwood and Holmfirth. In the 1830s, at a time when locally the domestic textile industry was giving way to the factory system, the millowners made provision for holidays at the local feast, albeit unpaid, of up to three days.[41]

At the Huddersfield May Fair all manner of stalls and sideshows were erected on the streets to cater for a festive public who flocked to the town from surrounding villages. The following account appeared in the *Leeds Intelligencer* of 17 May 1851: 'On Wednesday and Thursday, the annual Spring pleasure fair was held, and the weather being fine, was very numerously attended. The King street and the bottom end of Ramsden Street, were literally crammed with stalls, booths, caravans and the usual attendants at a fair ground. In the cricket field in the New North Road a "Grand Gala" was given the only attraction being the harmonious strains of Mr Moore's excellent band'.[42] The log-book of Lower Slaithwaite National School in 1870 records that 'being Huddersfield Fair Week the attendance today is considerably affected'.[43]

The concentration of large numbers of people in relatively small areas which came with the fair and market days inevitably attracted a criminal element. The *Leeds Mercury* of 22 May 1787 carried the following report: 'at Huddersfield fair yesterday se'nnight a boy of about ten picked a gentleman's pocket of his pocket book. Committed to Wakefield House of Correction. Same day a person had his pockets picked of seven and a half guineas'. Possibly the juvenile thief was John Sanders, whose sentence to a private whipping for pocket-picking was noted in the *Leeds Mercury* of the following 31 July. When the Quarter Sessions ordered a public whipping (and it was probably only Sanders's youth which saved him from that ignominy) it was usual to stipulate that it be carried out on a market day, no doubt to set an example to the greatest number of people. Probably it was for that same reason that the stocks had originally been sited close by the Market Cross.

Schofield, in his reminiscences, notes that at one time the May fair was held on land to the south of the present High Street, and that it had then removed to the Back Green and finally to fields on the east of Chapel Hill.[44] It was the latter site which in 1852 the Ramsdens allocated for the fair in order to relieve the congestion being created in the town streets by side-shows and stalls. There would appear to have been some discussion on the market rights in 1849 when the stalls were removed from the street to within the kerbstones of the Market Place, but the matter must have been forgotten, for the dispute in 1852 came as a complete surprise to the Ramsdens' local agent.

The Watch Committee of the Improvement Commissioners, who had not been consulted about the removal of the fair-ground, issued posters objecting, not to the new arrangements, but to the tolls being taken for stalls erected on public streets. One may imagine that little encouragement was required for stall-holders to withhold tolls, and the notice had a predictable effect in ensuring that the streets were full of stalls whilst the fair-ground was empty. Whitley approached all the stall-holders for the toll and was duly refused, and he distrained on the goods of several of them. Whilst the dispute arose from the annual May fair, popular feeling imposed the same objections to the actual Market Place, and whilst the Ramsdens had undoubted rights to market tolls, there were various matters which clouded the issue; principal among them was whether the payments by the stall-holders were tolls (a levy on goods) or rent. The Ramsden estate managers appear to have taken an early decision to extricate themselves from the whole matter as diplomatically as possible. In 1853 they advised the Improvement Commissioners that arrangements would be made to transfer the tolls and the management of the market and fairs to them. The matter dragged on, until in 1864 the Commissioners were granted a fourteen-year lease at £30 per annum for three years, and £50 per annum thereafter. However, the lease was not to run its full course, for in 1876 all market rights were transferred to the Corporation for a figure of £39,802; the deal included 41,930 square yards of land for the sites of the covered and cattle markets.

The agitation of 1852 served the purpose of abolishing the tolls for the remainder of the period that the rights remained with the Ramsden estate, but it was a temporary respite only, for an extensive list of tolls was incorporated in the town's bye-laws when the Corporation acquired the rights.

There is one subsequent development relating to the town's markets which it is thought has not previously been noted. In 1869 the Ramsden estate management considered the idea of creating a covered market. In the previous year they had commenced a major project, the erection of Estate Buildings. The eminent Huddersfield-born architect whom they commissioned for that project, W. H. Crossland, was asked to prepare a proposal for a market at the bottom end of the town on a site bounded by Kirkgate, Cross Church Street, King Street and Old Kirkgate. His proposals were made in May 1869 when the probable cost was estimated at over £33,000.[45] However, the project was not pursued, possibly because the estate managers decided to concentrate their resources on the more commercial developments of Byram Building, Byram Arcade and the Post Office. As it was, the town had to wait for a permanent covered market until 1880, when the Market Hall in King Street was completed.

Edward J. Law

Biographical note

A native of Lindley, Edward Law was educated at Huddersfield College before training to be a Chartered Accountant. He now works as a professional genealogist and historian. He is the author of several works on the history of Huddersfield and district.

ACKNOWLEDGEMENT

The preliminary results of my research on this topic were published by Huddersfield Local History Society in Newsletter No. 3, (1985).

SOURCES

General

Rentals and surveys of the Ramsden estates and deposit DD/RE/198, which are held by W(est) Y(orkshire) A(rchive) S(ervice), Kirklees. The *Huddersfield Chronicle* and *Huddersfield Examiner* for 1852 and 1853, copies of which are held by H(uddersfield) L(ocal) H(istory) L(ibrary).

NOTES

1. WYAS, Kirklees DD/R/dd/V/29.

2. K. L. McKutcheon, 'Yorkshire Fairs & Markets' *Thoresby Society* XXXIX (1939).

3. Taylor Dyson, *History of Huddersfield and District* (Huddersfield, 1932), pp.116-119.

4. Taylor Dyson, *History of Huddersfield and District*. Dyson dates all the documents to 1672; they are in fact 1671. There are also some misrenderings of the names of those who were examined at the inquisition. They were: William Batte esq., Richard Langley gent., John Greene gent., James Taylor gent., John Taylor gent., Daniel Thorpe gent., Abraham Lockwood, John Crosley, George Dawson, John Ledgeard, John Marsden, Abraham Woodhead and John Walker.

5. WYAS, Kirklees DD/R/dd/IV/23.

6. B(orthwick) I(nstitute) of H(istorical) R(esearch), York, Pontefract Wills March 1697.

7. J. Aikin, *A Description of the Country from Thirty to Forty Miles Round Manchester* (1795).

8. WYAS, Kirklees DD/RE/c/90, 2 November 1851.

9. Edward J. Law, *18th Century Huddersfield: the Day-Books of John Turner 1732-1773* (Huddersfield, 1985), p.26.

10. *Huddersfield and Holmfirth Examiner*, 13 May 1853.

11. WYAS, Calderdale RP/1435/2.

12. William Dawbarn, *Essays, Tales etc., etc.* (1872), p. 81.

13. L. Browning & R. K. Senior, *The Old Yards of Huddersfield* (Huddersfield, 1986), p.14.

14. William White, *History*, & *Gazetteer Directory of the West Riding of Yorkshire* (Sheffield, 1837).

15. WYAS, Kirklees KC242/1 10 May 1781 & KC242/7 25 April 1804.

16. Collection of John Goodchild, Wakefield. A Map of the Estate Belonging to Hirst & Kennet. A copy is held by HLHL.

17. HLHL, Minutes of Huddersfield & Upper Agbrigg Infirmary, 7 January 1833 & 20 June 1833.

18. WYAS, Kirklees KC165/73.

19. Edward J. Law, *18th Century Huddersfield*, p.9.

20. 'Two Yorkshire Diaries, the Diary of Arthur Jessop & Ralph Ward's Journal' edited by C. E. Whiting *Yorkshire Archaeological Society Record Series* CXVII (1951).

21. *Huddersfield Examiner, 25 May 1878*.

22. *Huddersfield Maps From 1634* [edited by E. A. H. Turner] (Huddersfield, 1971) and *Almondbury & Huddersfield: A Map Collection 1634-1860.*

23. *Huddersfield Chronicle*, 7 May 1853.

24. Pigot's *Directory* 1814-15.

25. WYAS, Yorkshire Archaeological Society, MS491.

26. WYAS, Kirklees DD/WBM/78.

27. WYAS, Kirklees DD/R/dd/II/7.

28. BIHR Vacancy Register July 1686.

29. WYAS, Kirklees DD/WBM/78.

30. W.P. Hartley, 'Springwood Colliery Huddersfield: a Portrait of a Yorkshire Estate Coal Mine 1862-1877' *Yorkshire Archaeological Society Journal* 53 (1981), 93-96.

31. HLHL.

32. WYAS, Kirklees DD/R/dd/IV/23.

33. Edward J. Law, 'History of the George Hotel, Huddersfield to 1900', *Essays in Local History*, No. 11. (Huddersfield 1988), p.85.

34. BIHR Pontefract Wills March 1731.

35. Sheffield City Libraries Archives Division A65.

36. WYAS, Kirklees KC165/73.

37. BIHR Pontefract Wills 1784 (John Bradley) & 1787 (Joseph Bradley).

38. BIHR Prerogative Wills July 1837.

39. WYAS, Kirklees KC242/1, 14 May 1781.

40. Henry James Moorhouse, *Extracts from the Diary of the Revd Robert Meeke* (1874)

41. Factories Inquiry Commission, *Employment of Children in Factories, Supplemental Report*, part 2, section C (1834).

42. The author is indebted to Mrs J. Stead for this reference.

43. WYAS, Wakefield D120/24.

44. *Huddersfield Examiner* Supplement 15 September 1883.

45. WYAS, Kirklees DD/RA/c/26/1, 6 May 1869.

CHAPTER 5

The Church in Huddersfield
600-1743

JOHN ADDY

The Pre-Conquest Church

It is impossible to determine with any accuracy the precise date when Christianity arrived in Huddersfield. No doubt it must have been in the reign of King Oswald who, after his defeat of the pagan King Cadwallon of Wales at the battle of Heavenfield in 664, set about the task of bringing Christianity to his subjects. This important task Oswald entrusted to Bishop Aidan, whom he brought from Iona. Thus the pattern of Christianity which became established in the north was the Columban pattern, which was based upon the monastery. The Venerable Bede states that there was an abbey of Thirdwulf, 'in the forest of Elmet'. There was also a strong tradition that connected an earlier evangelist, St. Paulinus, with Dewsbury.[1] At some date during the latter half of the seventh century, Dewsbury became the chief Christian centre for this region, due to its connection with one of the great Anglian abbeys. Prior to the Norman Conquest the parish of Dewsbury came to include within its boundaries Thornhill, Mirfield, Kirkburton, Kirkheaton, Almondbury, Huddersfield and Bradford, which suggests that a chapel of ease or a mission church existed in Huddersfield before the period of the great Norman church building. This is attested by the numerous archaeological remains that survive in these churches.

Medieval Huddersfield

The peoples of the north resented the arrival of the Normans and the imposition of their rule. Naturally, plots were made with the Danes to restore the old kingdom of Jorvik. In an attempt to bring this to fruition the

Norman garrison at York was massacred in 1068, with the inevitable consequence that William ordered the ravaging of the north in 1069. So extensive was the destruction that the north was a desert; it took some 150 years to recover. In fact, the region became one that was suitable for the re-settlement later undertaken by the monks of the Cistercian Order.

Norman landowners tended to build a church to serve the tenants on their estates. These proprietary churches, as they were called, were owned by the founders and their descendants, who endowed them with land for the support of the rector of the parish, glebe land, and demanded the levy of a tenth of all the produce of the parish, tithes.

The founders retained the advowson, or right to present an incumbent to the living; it was his duty to serve the church and parish. The Norman family of de Laci was granted by William I the great Honour of Pontefract, which included Huddersfield within its boundaries. An honour consisted of a very large number of manors under the control of a single lord. The first church in Huddersfield was a small intimate Norman building designed to serve the needs of a very tiny community.

As the country became settled under the strong Norman government, so the church organisation with which we are familiar began to emerge. Huddersfield formed part of the enormous diocese of York which, for administrative purposes was divided into the four archdeaconries of York, East Riding, Richmond and Nottingham. To assist the archdeacon in his administrative work, each archdeaconry was divided into rural deaneries. Huddersfield formed part of the large rural deanery of Pontefract, which extended westwards from Goole to Holmfirth, Marsden, Huddersfield and Halifax.[2] The acts of the Archbishops of York concerning Huddersfield are to be found in their registers and visitation court books. No archdeacons' visitation court books survive for the Middle Ages.[3]

Alongside the building of churches went the endowment and founding of monasteries and nunneries. The principal method of endowing a monastery was by gifts of land, the rents from which gave the monastery a regular income. The de Laci family followed this custom and founded the Cluniac priory of St. John the Evangelist at Pontefract with an offshoot at Monk Bretton. Following the lead given by the de Lacis, a small colony of hermits at Nostell became a community of Augustinian Canons.[4] Nostell Priory, situated close to the Great North Road, became one of the leading monasteries in Northern England. This priory acquired several parishes in the West Riding, including that of Huddersfield, in order to provide it with sufficient income to enable it to offer hospitality to important travellers between England and Scotland.

Parish churches given to a monastery were said to be alienated, that is changed from their original purpose. This custom of granting a parish church to a monastery illustrates the belief that medieval men and women were concerned for the ultimate salvation of their souls. It was believed that the prayers of members of religious orders were far more efficacious than those of the parish priest. Furthermore, medieval people were convinced that it was of great importance to ensure that their souls together with those of their ancestors, parents, heirs or assigns should arrive safely in heaven as quickly and as painlessly as possible.

The prior and convent of St. Oswald, Nostell Priory, had acquired the advowson of St. Peter, Huddersfield from Hugh de Laval in about 1130. This grant was later confirmed by Henry I to Archbishop Thurstan of York:

> For the souls of my father and mother and of my brother William, King of England, and for my soul and my wives' *(sic)* and sons, all those lands which were given to God and St. Oswald and the monks serving God there in pure and perpetual alms vizt: (amongst others) the Church of South Kirkby and the Church at Batley and the Church at Huddersfield with the lands appertaining there to as Hugh de Laval gave them to them ....[5]

Once a parish church was alienated to a religious order, be it an abbey or priory, the status of the parish priest changed; the rectory became a vicarage and the parish priest a vicar (meaning a substitute). So Nostell Priory became the rector of Huddersfield with the responsibility to provide a priest to serve the church and meet the spiritual requirements of the people. In order to make provision for a vicar, a vicarage had to be ordained, setting out in detail what rights should be attached to it. In 1216 Archbishop Walter de Gray, on the occasion of the institution of Michael de Wakefield to the living of Huddersfield ordained that the vicar was to receive all the 'oblations and emoluments from the offerings at the altar, reserving to the Prior and Convent all the tithes of corn, hay, pease and beans in the lands and farms belonging to the said Church...'. Also a suitable parsonage house was to be built by the prior and convent of Nostell for a residence for the vicar for the time being, 'bearing all the costs, customary charges and oblations of the said church'.[6]

At some date before 1243 the prior of Nostell found it necessary to raise more money. To achieve his object, Prior Robert of Nostell leased the living of Huddersfield to one Master Robert Talbot, clerk, to hold for the term of his natural life, on the following terms,

> . . .yielding and paying to us eight marks and four shillings within the Quinzane of Pentecost and four shillings at the feast of St. Martin in Winter and he shall sustain all the honours of the said Church . . . .[7]

A lease of a parish had to be approved by the Archbishop of York. So in 1243 Archbishop Gray issued his mandate to the rural dean of Pontefract instructing him that, as the Church of Huddersfield was now alienated to the prior and convent of St. Oswald, he should take care to see that the rights of the prior and convent of St. Oswald were not injured by the lease to Robert Talbot but were protected in every way.[8]

The fabric of the church appears to have been poorly maintained; each archbishop's register contains a reference to this matter. For instance, Archbishop Greenfield in 1313 issued his mandate to the prior and convent of Nostell not to exact one quarter part of the value of the Church of Huddersfield, now appropriated to St. Oswald, because there were defects in the fabric to the value of fourteen marks.[9]

The Black Death of 1348-49, which created havoc amongst both the clergy and the laity, forms a watershed in church life. Attitudes and beliefs began to change; this was marked in one way by the decline not only in the endowment but also the founding of monasteries and churches. The peasantry were restless, demanding that labour services were replaced by the right to hold land at an annual rent of fourpence an acre. The wealthy, afraid of a possible outbreak of revolt, saw the church as the only bulwark against such an event and gave it more support by endowing chantries in parish churches. Often a school was attached to a chantry to find the priest additional employment.

A chantry was a chapel within a parish church, endowed with revenue to support a priest to sing mass for the repose of the soul of the founder, his ancestors and his descendants. There were two chantries in St. Peter's church, Huddersfield: one dedicated to the Holy Trinity and the second to

Our Lady. The former was founded by Thomas Stapleton of Quarmby, but that of Our Lady appears to have had no specific founders.[10]

The economic prosperity of the fifteenth century saw either a partial or even a complete rebuilding of many parish churches, of which Halifax and Wakefield are good examples. St. Peter's Huddersfield was demolished and rebuilt, and in 1503 was consecrated by the Bishop of Negropont, acting for the Archbishop of York. This new church was built with inferior materials and was reported to be in serious decay in 1575.[11]

Fig. 5:1 The old Parish Church, built in 1503. (KCS)

From Reformation to Civil War

When Henry VIII decided to suppress the monasteries in 1536, the majority of the northern abbeys and priories managed to survive this threat until 1539, when all were dissolved. The property held by Nostell Priory, including the vicarage of Huddersfield, was sold by the Court of Augmentations to Richard Andrews of Hale, Gloucester and Leonard Chamberlain of Woodstock, Oxford. These two merchants bought '. . . all that mansion and messuage called the Parsonage of Huddersfield with its appurtenances, late property of the recently dissolved monastery of St. Oswald'.[12]

This property included a toft next to the parsonage house in the tenure of Roger Brook, a cottage called Sykehouse in the tenure of Richard Horsfall and all the court yard, lands, pastures, hereditaments whatsoever belonging in Huddersfield. Later this property was sold to William Ramsden of Longley.*

The vicarage house and garden were valued separately in 1534. One Peter Longfellow was the incumbent of Huddersfield and his parsonage house and garden were valued at three shillings and fourpence annual rental. The tithes totalled £20 13s. 2½d. from which £2 3s. 4d. was paid to the vicar of Dewsbury as altarage. (This payment dated from the time when Huddersfield was part of the parish of Dewsbury). Three shillings was paid to the Archbishop of York for synodals, being the contribution towards the cost of holding a synod, and seven shillings and sixpence to the Archdeacon of York for his visitation fees, so the actual money to support the vicar was £17 9s. 10½d. plus fees.[13]

In 1548 the Council of Edward VI decided to dissolve the chantries on the grounds that they encouraged superstition. In reality the government was bankrupt and required another source of revenue to plunder for funds. A survey of the chantries was undertaken. Holy Trinity chantry had as its priest Richard Blackburn. His duty was to pray for the soul of the founder, Thomas Stapleton, and celebrate mass in the church on all feast days. In order to provide the priest with a stipend, in 1525 the founder had given certain lands in Nottingham to the use of the incumbent. The material goods were valued at twelve shillings, being chiefly rents, and the communion plate at forty-eight shillings.[14]

The Chantry of Our Lady was endowed with lands in Slaithwaite, Stainland, Rastrick and Huddersfield. The rents from these funded the chantry priest who, in 1548, was Richard Brooke. His duties were to pray for the well-being of the parishioners and their souls, to assist the vicar to administer the sacraments in the parish church, whose congregation was said to number about nine hundred. The total value of the chantry was £2 10s. 4½d.[15] A former vicar, Thomas Rogers, had founded an obit, that is the right to have a requiem mass said annually on the date of his death, which he intended should 'continue for ever'. An annual sum of seven shillings was

*More details of William Ramsden's dealings in monastic property are found in Chapter Three.
EDITOR.

provided for maintaining the obit. George Kay had willed that a lamp should burn in the church for twenty years, 'whereof twelve be expired'; an endowment of property yielded an annual rent of eight shillings for its support.[16] In 1552 the government of Edward VI terminated all such lights and obits on the same grounds as those used to dissolve the chantries. At the same time priests were allowed to marry and many took advantage of this, among them Gabriel Raynes who held the livings of Huddersfield and Almondbury in plurality, and was in sympathy with the ideas of the Protestant reformers.

There was a reaction under Queen Mary; she had all the church legislation of Edward VI repealed, including the freedom of priests to marry, so all married clergy had to divorce their wives or face deprivation. Raynes was one who refused to obey and confessed to the charges brought against him at York on 21 April 1554; on 23 May he was deprived of his benefice and replaced the same October by Edmund Baynes, on the presentation of William Ramsden:[17] Baynes conformed to the Church of England in 1561.

The Reformation did not spread in the north as rapidly as it did in the south and east, for in 1559 many of the pre-Reformation church furnishings remained in churches, among them rood lofts, which divided the nave from the chancel; the crucifix flanked by images of Our Lady and St. John stood on this loft. Queen Elizabeth had ordered that all rood lofts be removed as these encouraged superstition. When it came to removing the one in the parish church in 1571 there were objections, however:

> contra Humphrey Blackburn, Richard Greenhowe and John Thewles for calling such thieves as pulled down the rood loft.[18]

For this objection they were presented before Archbishop Grindal for correction and were given a public penance.

Although the church had been rebuilt in 1503, it appears to have had little attention given to the fabric in the way of repairs. In 1571 the following report was made to Archbishop Grindal about the state of the chancel:

> The chauncell is oute of reparations and the rayne raineth into the churche, and it fell down vii yeres sence and slewe the parishe clerk, and thoughe it have bene verie often presented yet the sworne men saie they can never gett any amend any waie.[19]

The churchwardens tried to put the blame on Queen Elizabeth and the patron of the living, John Ramsden, but to no avail. In those parishes which had a rector it was his responsibility to repair the chancel, but in the case of a vicarage then those who held the advowson, the Ramsdens in Huddersfield, were responsible. By 1590 the sermon had replaced the sacrament, so the use of the chancel was restricted to the occasional Communion service and, therefore, repairs were neglected.

Similarly, the churchwardens began to neglect repairs to the nave, for which they were responsible; this was due to the increasing difficulty they experienced in collecting church rates. This problem was reflected in Huddersfield when in 1574 the churchwardens, Hugh Gledhill, Roger Brook and John Brokesburn, were presented at the Visitation on the grounds that, '. . . the church is in great decay. Ordered to repair and certify before Michaelmas next coming'.[20] Despite this order to repair, little appears to have been done, for the same complaint was made in 1582 and again in 1595.

During the second half of the sixteenth century there was a steady growth of Puritanism in Huddersfield parish. This growth is well illustrated by the case of Crosland v Crosse, heard before the Consistory Court at York in 1617. John Crosse was a grocer's apprentice in London, who in 1612 left his situation intending to study divinity and 'was made a full minister on 25th March 1616', being ordained deacon and priest the same day. He then came to Huddersfield as the assistant curate to Joshua Smith, who sent Crosse to serve Scammonden chapel. Although he had no licence to preach, he expounded the Scriptures in Huddersfield parish church and, by invitation, in other neighbouring chapels. His style of preaching drew crowds to Scammonden, attracting a great deal of attention, which the lesser Puritan enthusiasts usually escaped. He was eventually cited to appear before the Consistory Court at York in 1617, where he was charged with the following errors:

> Item: that the said John Crosse hath publiquely and privately taught and defended or maintained all or the most of the erroneus opinions following vizt; that all unpreaching ministers are dumb doggs and damned persons and whosoever goeth to hear them cannot be saved.

> Item: that noe preacher sanctifieth the Sabboath or is a sanctified person or lawfully called to the ministry unless he preache twice every Sabboath day.

> Item: that the signe of the Cross in baptisme and weareing of the surplesse in time of divine service and other laudable rites and ceremonies of the Church of England are damnable and anti-Christian.

Item: that it is not lawfull to use the Lord's praier nor any other form prescribed in the booke (of Common Prayer) affiraminge that noe praier is available but that whereunto the Spirit at that time moveth and all other is damnable.

The charges are further developed in the following statement:

. . . that the said John Crosse by his phantasticall and irregular proceedings hath gathered after him many followers persons of little or noe understanding, discontented in mind and not well affected to our present church government, sundry of whom being taught by the said John Crosse have openly affirmed that the Sign of the Crosse in baptism is the mark of the beast in Revelation, others by his strange doctrine have been distracted and driven into madness and forsake their ordinary trades to follow him.[21]

Each witness cited to appear in the cause affirmed that persons who were disaffected from the Church of England flocked to hear him at Scammonden. Crosse read the General Confession, which he mixed with his own comments and expressions, then read a psalm and expounded it, followed it by a psalm which he sang, prayed then preached and prayed again, but never wore a surplice. All the symptoms of religious enthusiasm were there, large congregations, violent denunciations of party shibboleths and emotional disturbances. One witness stated that his wife had been distracted for a month after hearing one of Crosse's sermons.

It is clear from the evidence that Crosse had been given unlimited scope by Joshua Smith to exercise his ministry in Huddersfield parish. It so happened that Crosse foolishly accepted an invitation to preach in Slaithwaite church, which at that time was under the oversight of Revd George Crosland, vicar of Almondbury. As a consequence, Crosland took an action against him in the York Consistory Court. Judgement was deferred from October 1617 to March 1618 to give Crosse time to settle out of court. Sentence was eventually passed against Crosse, who never appeared in court to hear it, but was fined in costs the sum of eight pounds, which at that time was a curate's annual stipend. Later in the year Crosse's costs were paid anonymously, revealing that Crosse had some substantial backing in the parish. No record survives of the parish to which he moved in 1617, but Joshua Smith also resigned the living of Huddersfield and was succeeded as Vicar of Huddersfield by Edmund Hill.

The Civil War and Commonwealth

The mid-seventeenth century was a traumatic period for Huddersfield. In 1642 the Civil War began and Huddersfield, being a Parliamentarian stronghold, supported the opposition to Charles I. In 1644, Parliament decided to abolish the Church of England so the 'Root and Branch' Bill, was brought into Parliament. Under this Bill the Church of England was declared to be 'utterly abrogated and put down for ever'.[22] The defeat of the Royalist forces meant the creation of a Commonwealth and the imposition of Presbyterian form of worship, even the use of the *Book of Common Prayer* was forbidden.

The period also saw the extreme Protestant sects coming to the fore, and alongside the Presbyterians, the Independents and the Baptists, infiltrated into the chapelries of Huddersfield parish. This latter body acquired a strong foothold in several parts of the parish but their strongest centre of influence was in Lindley.

The Restoration to 1743

Edmund Hill had been removed from his post as vicar of Huddersfield in 1652 as a suspected Royalist and replaced by a Commonwealth man, Henry Hyrst. The Restoration of the King in 1660 meant also the restoration of the Church of England. The new Archbishop of York, Accepted Frewen by name, held his primary Visitation in Huddersfield in 1662-63. The only defects that he noticed were that the Communion table needed a new carpet or covering, the alms boxes needed replacing and the church gates required repair. The churchwardens, Richard Massie and John Brooke, were ordered to send copies of their parish register and the glebe terrier, or catalogue of church plate and church property, to the registrar at York.[23]

Edmund Hill, the deprived vicar, continued to live in the parish unmolested and untroubled by authority until his death in 1668. He was a most respected man and friend of the Nonconformists, especially Oliver Heywood, who described his funeral like this:

> 1668 Jan.29 This day we have been interring the corpse of old Mr Hill and his wife, he was aged 80, within a few weeks, she near as old and they had lived many years together. He died on Wednesday between eleven and twelve o'clock and she died at three o'clock the same day. Seven Nonconformist ministers laid him in the grave. Lord sanctify it.[24]

Some Restoration clergy were intent on revenge for the conditions endured by many of them under the Commonwealth. Oliver Heywood had a poor opinion of one of these, Thomas Clarke (1675-1696):

> Mr Clarke vicar of Huddersfield hath behaved himself with strange insolency since he came there in many things, particularly concerning a house and land worth £10 a year, given to the poor decayed house keepers of Huddersfield, but he would needs have it in his hands that he might give it to the common poor of the parish, whereby he lost the favour of the townsmen, with many other strange acts. He hath made a law that if any weddings come to church after the clock had struck twelve they must pay five shillings or not be married.[25]

The Visitations that followed after 1663 until the first of the new style in 1743 recorded little if anything about the fabric of the parish church. After 1662, both clergy and churchwardens appear to be more concerned about the growth of dissent and breaches of the moral code than about the church fabric.

Until 1850, the church was responsible for controlling the morals of the parishioners, with clergy and churchwardens responsible for presenting offenders to the archbishop or the archdeacon for correction. Punishable offences were numerous and included working on Sundays and saints' days, non-attendance at church, not bringing children to be baptised and burying the dead in gardens and orchards. Above all, offenders, such as those who were common swearers, drunkards, fornicators, those living together in adultery and having illegitimate children, were to be punished. The church could not punish offenders by imprisonment but only by excommunication, if the offending parties refused to perform a penance. In one such case, the offending couples were to be present in Huddersfield parish church 'on Sunday next bare headed and bare footed in a white sheet and there penitentlie perform and declare their penance as is enjoyned'.[26]

The primary Visitation of Archbishop Neil in 1633 revealed a clutch of offenders, among them James Haigh and his wife, George Sykes and his wife Marian, all for ante-nuptial fornication. In the case of George Sykes and his wife, they escaped punishment by moving into Almondbury parish, out of the reach of Huddersfield churchwardens. In some cases the man responsible would disappear, as happened when John Savile left Sara Midgley to face the charge alone.[27]

One feature of Puritanism was to take quite literally St. Paul's words 'fervent in business, serving the Lord'. Clothiers and other artisans began to ignore the Act of Uniformity, which required all adults to attend divine service on Sunday, under the penalty of one shilling fine for every absence. Churchwardens found it impossible to levy and collect the fines. Absence from church on Sundays to follow secular employment tended to increase with the passage of time. In 1633 Godfrey Hinchliffe and Walter Butler were presented to the archbishop for working on Sundays.[28] Presentments for non-attendance at church tended to increase after 1662 because of the growing influence of dissent. The Quakers fell foul of the Act of Uniformity and in 1680 'John Brook, Abraham Key, Edward Horsfall and his wife Sarah being Quakers'[29] were presented to the archdeacon. In 1689 the Toleration Act removed these offences from the Statute Book.

Church rates were the only or virtually the only means of raising the necessary funds to finance church repairs. The growth of dissent gave many Nonconformists a valid reason for refusing to pay their church rates. As time passed there was an ever increasing number of those who steadfastly refused to support a Church whose teachings they found to be unacceptable. In 1705 William Preston was excommunicated for refusing to pay his church rate of one shilling, while James Sparold and John Hirst received the same sentence for refusing to pay church rates at one shilling and three shillings respectively. Maria Priestley was another penanced for refusing to pay her rates towards the repair of the parish church.[30]

Parishioners were encouraged to make provision for the relief of the poor in their wills but there were few examples before the eighteenth century. In 1647 Thomas Armitage left £83 1s. 6d. to buy wool for poor people on Christmas Eve, to which was added £5 by the Revd Thomas Clarke.[31] In 1662 a legacy of £100 left for the poor of the parish by Edmund Taylor of London was withheld; a tragic note is appended to the report that, 'he is in the Fleet Prison for debt'.[32]

The practice of passing General Acts of Pardon relieved those sentenced by the church courts from the humiliating task of performing a public penance. Not only were the church courts in decline but churchwardens too were becoming unreliable in the manner in which they made their returns to the archdeacon, merely contenting themselves with an, 'omnia bene', or 'all is well', reply.

In 1743, Archbishop Herring made the incumbent responsible for compiling the Visitation returns, so bypassing the churchwardens. These returns show that Nonconformist numbers had increased to more than one hundred souls. The largest group, the Anabaptists, had their own meeting house, while the numbers of Methodists and others only warranted meeting in private homes. There were very few benefactions for the poor and nothing at all towards the repair of the parish church.[33]

The Visitation returns of 1743 reveal that the population growth since 1548 had increased by less than one thousand as the Industrial Revolution had not then made an impact on the town. However, the second half of the eighteenth century was to see religious life in Huddersfield completely transformed.

Fig. 5:2 The old Parish Church. (KCS)

John Addy

Biographical Note

Dr John Addy is a Senior Research Fellow at the University College of Ripon and York St. John. He was Head of History at Darton Boys Secondary School (1957-1962) and, after a year as Fellow of Balliol College, Oxford, at Darton High School (1963-1970) before being appointed Senior Lecturer at St. John's College, York in 1970, a post he held until 1978, when he became the College Archivist. Dr Addy's publications include: *The Agrarian Revolution* (1964); *A Coal and Iron Community in the Industrial Revolution* (1973); *The Textile Revolution* (1976); *The Agrarian Revolution*, Seminar Studies (1978); *Sin and Society in the Seventeenth Century* (1989); *Death, Money and the Vultures; a study of contested* wills (1992).

NOTES

1. W.G. Collingwood, *Angles, Danes and Norse in the district of Huddersfield* (Huddersfield, 1929), p.10-11.

2. J. Addy, *The Archdeacon and Ecclesiastical Discipline in Yorkshire 1559-1714* (York, 1965), p.4-9.

3. Archdeacon's Visitation Court Books, Y/V 1664-1740 B(orthwick) I(nstitute) of H(istorical) R(esearch).

4. D.F.E. Sykes, *Huddersfield and its Vicinity* (Huddersfield, 1898), p.135.

5. Sykes, *Huddersfield*, p.135.

6. Sykes, *Huddersfield*, p.136.

7. Sykes, *Huddersfield*, p.137.

8. Sykes, *Huddersfield*, pp.137-138.

9. *Register of Archbishop Greenfield*, edited by W. Brown, Surtees Society 149, no. 815.

10. *Register of Archbishop Greenfield*, p.57.

11. *Chantry Certificates*, edited by W. Page, Surtees Society 92, 282-283.

12. G. Lawton, *Collectio Rerum Ecclesiasticarum* (1842), p.127.

13. Sykes, *Huddersfield*, p.141.

14. *Yorkshire Chantry Surveys*, Surtees Society 92, p.282.

15. *Yorkshire Chantry Surveys*, p.283.

16. *Yorkshire Chantry Surveys*, p.418.

17. BIHR, *Sede Vacante Register*, f. 662 v.

18. J.S. Purvis, *Tudor Parish Documents* (1948), p.181.

19. BIHR, Visitation Court Book V1571, f. 163.

20. BIHR, Visitation Court Book V1578, f. 163.

21. BIHR, Cause Papers CP/H1300.

22. J.P. Kenyon, *The Stuart Constitution* (1969), p.171.

23. BIHR, Archbishop's Court Book V 1662-3, f.109.

24. Sykes, *Huddersfield p.*147.

25. Sykes, *Huddersfield, p.*148.

26. BIHR, Archbishop's Court Book V1575, f. 72.

27. BIHR, Archbishop's Court Book V1632-3, f. 152.

28. BIHR, Archbishop's Court Book V1632-3, f. 155.

29. BIHR, Archdeacon of York's Court Book Y/V 1664.

30. BIHR, Archdeacon of York's Court Book Y/V 1705 f. 34.

31. BIHR, Archbishop's Court Book V1662-3 f. 155.

32. BIHR, Archbishop's Court Book V1662-3 f. 157.

33. *Archbishop Herring's Visitation Returns 1743* edited by S.L. Ollard and P.C. Walker, Yorkshire Archaeological Society Record Series LXX (1928).

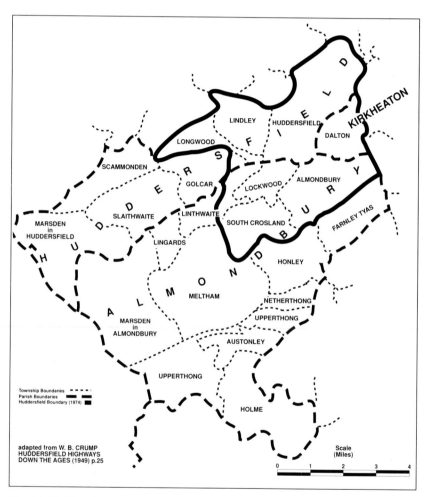

Fig. 6:1 The Townships, Parish and Borough of Huddersfield and adjacent areas.

CHAPTER 6

Religion in Huddersfield since the mid-Eighteenth Century

EDWARD ROYLE

The borough of Huddersfield, defined by its pre-1974 boundaries, included several townships from three ancient parishes: Almondbury, Lockwood, South Crosland and parts of Linthwaite in Almondbury parish; Dalton in Kirkheaton parish; and Huddersfield, Lindley, Longwood and parts of Golcar in Huddersfield parish, which also extended westwards to include Slaithwaite, Scammonden and parts of Marsden. The River Colne for the most part formed the south-eastern boundary of Huddersfield parish, cutting through some of the major settlements: Milnsbridge was situated in Golcar, Longwood and Linthwaite townships; Slaithwaite extended into Linthwaite and Lingards; and Marsden was divided, with the village chapel-of-ease in the Almondbury half.[1] (See Map)

Getting to the furthermost corners of these far-flung parishes in the eighteenth century was not easy. Until 1759, one of the main routes up the Colne valley ran north westwards by way of Lindley to Outlane, beyond which it joined the packhorse track from Halifax over Pole Moor and through Merrydale to Marsden and thence to Manchester. A second track ran up the Almondbury side of the valley over Crosland Moor and through Lingards to Marsden. This latter was turnpiked in 1759 but the valley-bottom turnpike was not constructed until the early 1820s.[2]

The position of the church in these upland areas was relieved by chapels-of-ease. For Almondbury there were chapels in Honley, Meltham and

Marsden; Huddersfield was served by chapels in Scammonden and Slaithwaite. These chapels were not permitted to detract from the revenues of the mother parish church and so no baptisms or marriages were conducted in them. Inconveniently long distances over difficult terrain to the parish church were to prove a considerable handicap to the Established Church as population and settlements grew from the mid-eighteenth century onwards.

The Evangelical Revival

The two most influential families in the area were the Ramsdens, lords of the manor of Huddersfield and patrons to the living, and the Dartmouths of Woodsome Hall, with extensive landholdings in Almondbury and Slaithwaite. William, the second Earl of Dartmouth, was one of the foremost national supporters of the evangelical revival and through his influence Sir John Ramsden appointed Henry Venn Vicar of Huddersfield in 1759. Within twelve years Venn had indelibly changed the face of Huddersfield religion. When he arrived, the Church of England had a virtual monopoly of religious expression: of 1,500 families in that part of the parish served by the parish church, there were only 100 families of Dissenters – Independents, Quakers and Moravians – and there was only one Meeting House, belonging to the Independent Baptists at Salendine Nook. The latter had been built in 1739 by Henry Clayton, evangelist and pastor, who saw his congregation diminish while Venn occupied the pulpit at the parish church. In Slaithwaite there were 300 families, only one Dissenting; and in Scammonden all seventy-one families were counted true to the Church.[3]

These figures, however, did not include the Methodists who were still an active evangelising element within the Church of England, often meeting in private homes but with no chapels of their own in the area until Netherthong was opened in 1769 and none in Huddersfield itself until the 'Old Bank' chapel was built at the edge of the town, on the hill down to Lockwood, in 1776. Methodists were welcomed by Venn in parishes where the spirit of revival within the Established Church was weak or non-existent, but he saw no need for such a movement of irregular auxiliaries in his own parish, and for a time John Wesley agreed to restrict the visits made by his preachers to the little Methodist society which had been formed before Venn's arrival. His departure in ill-health in 1771, and the Ramsden Trustees' failure to appoint

Fig. 6:2 The first Highfield Chapel, 1772. (KCS)

another Evangelical as his successor, brought home the extent to which the new forces of religious revival had taken hold in the parish. If the Established Church would not provide for them, then others would. In 1769 the Quakers had leased from the Ramsden estate a small parcel of land in Paddock, on which a Meeting House was licensed in February 1771; Highfield chapel, built on the northern edge of the town beyond the Ramsden monopoly of land, was opened at the beginning of 1772 as the first home of Independency (later known as Congregationalism) in Huddersfield; and with the Wesleyan Methodists acquiring the Old Bank site for their first chapel in 1775, and other Dissenters swelling the numbers at Salendine Nook, the monopoly of the Church of England was broken.[4]

The expansion of the Church of England

The capacity of the Church of England to respond to this challenge was severely limited by institutional and legal constraints. The Church could seek subscriptions for privately-funded chapels, such as the one built at Longwood in 1749 under the auspices of the Radcliffe family, which became a public chapel-of-ease in 1798, but a later generation of local subscribers seems to have been more willing to put its money instead into a Nonconformist chapel. At Slaithwaite some discontented parishioners, led by a local innkeeper, started a Baptist meeting in 1787 and then built a chapel in 1790 on Pole Moor, beyond the reach of Dartmouth on the old Marsden pack-horse track.[5]

Evangelical leadership was restored to the parish church in 1791 when John Coates (curate since 1785) was appointed to the living by Sir John Ramsden.[6] By the time of Coates's death in 1823 the face and fortunes of Huddersfield had been transformed, with a township population of 13,284 (24,220 in the whole parish) and a central built-up area which now extended from Westgate and Kirkgate to Upperhead Row, High Street, Ramsden Street and Queen Street. New churches were needed. The first to be built, Holy Trinity, founded by Benjamin Haigh Allen of Greenhead, was a private proprietary chapel, erected across the way from Greenhead and not far from Highfield Independent Chapel. A special Act of Parliament had been obtained in 1816 and the building, completed at a cost of £16,000, was consecrated in October 1819. Allen provided an endowment of £100 a year and was patron to the living. The income of the parish church was safeguarded by an arrangement whereby double baptismal and burial fees were charged and then divided between the perpetual curate and the vicar. Such were the complicated devices which the Church of England had to adopt in order to respond to the flexible chapel-building programmes of the Dissenters.[7]

This initiative was copied in 1824 by Allen's brother-in-law and fellow evangelical, John Whitacre of Woodhouse, whose Christ Church, Woodhouse Hill, was built to serve Fartown, Deighton and Bradley. Then, as Parliament began to deploy the Austrian war indemnity to fund new churches after 1818, public money was at last made available to support the extension of the Established Church through the building of what were sometimes called 'Waterloo', 'Million' or 'Parliamentary' churches. St. Paul's was one of these, built at the end of Queen Street, on land given by Sir John Ramsden, at a cost of nearly £6,000 and opened in 1831. Beyond the town centre other townships to receive 'Waterloo' churches between 1828 and 1831 were South Crosland, Golcar, Lockwood, Paddock, Linthwaite and Lindley. All remained legally subject to the mother church in either Almondbury or Huddersfield. Not until an Act of 1843 could ecclesiastical districts readily be carved out of existing parishes and only after 1856 could new parishes be created.

Even though by the 1840s the government was no longer willing to put state finance into church building programmes as it had in the 1820s, the Church was not without wealthy local patrons to continue the work, not only Dartmouth and the Ramsdens but also wealthy new manufacturers. St. Paul's, Armitage Bridge, (1848) was paid for by the brothers John and Thomas Brooke, while St. Thomas's, Longroyd Bridge, was erected by the widow of Thomas Starkey of Springwood and his brothers John and Joseph and completed in memory of all three in 1859.[8] The problem was that such churches were associated with authority – landlord, employer or local gentry. This is not to imply that many Dissenting places of worship were not similarly dominated – the great Independent and Wesleyan chapels were made possible only by the industrial and commercial wealth of their trustees and principal seat-holders – but there was a difference. The Church of England continued to exercise authority as of right; the Dissenters expected to earn it. The chapel may seldom have been the home of democracy, but it did see itself as home to the meritocracy – proud and fiercely independent self-made men.

The rise of Methodism

Protestant Dissent was the result of this independent temperament among the weavers and clothiers of the rural areas, who supported chapels in their scattered communities, and among the independent tradesmen, manufacturers and commercial men of the larger centres. Their independence did not stop at one branch of Nonconformity, but led to repeated splinter groups, as each settled into that religious, social and political configuration which best suited its temperament and inclinations.

The Wesleyan chapel at Old Bank (Chapel Hill) remained the only Methodist chapel in the central area until 1797, when national divisions over lay representation in the Conference (the governing body of Methodism after Wesley's death) led to the creation of the New Connexion. Feelings ran high in Huddersfield. The original Huddersfield Circuit, which had been formed in 1780 with 795 members, had grown to 1,700 members on the eve of the split in 1797. A year later it was down to 1,200 and reached a low of 520 in 1802. Some of the smaller chapels were entirely lost to the New Connexion. In Huddersfield the reformers took possession of the chapel and retained it until 1814. The original Huddersfield society lost a third of its members in two

*Fig. 6:3 Queen Street Chapel.
(KCS)*

years, and in 1798 the Wesleyan Conference voted special assistance for Huddersfield which helped finance the building of a new chapel in Queen Street in 1800. Thereafter numbers quickly recovered.[9] Meanwhile the New Connexion had grown to a membership of 588, with churches in Huddersfield, Lindley, Shelley and Deighton by 1814. After vacating the Old Bank Chapel premises in January 1814, the New Connexion continued to worship in a warehouse until, in May 1815, a new chapel was opened in High Street.[10]

Further national splits in Wesleyan Methodism in the 1820s and 1830s had little impact in Huddersfield. The revivalist Primitive Methodists made some progress, with a chapel in the town centre (begun in Springwood and moved to Northumberland Street when displaced by the railway in 1847) and a circuit was created in 1824 with 228 members, but they never became a major

Fig. 6:4 Queen Street Chapel interior. (KCS)

force in the area.[11] After 1814 the Original Connexion Wesleyans continued to use the new Queen Street chapel as their principal place of worship and their recovered Old Bank Chapel as a Sunday School. Their numbers so prospered that in 1819 Queen Street had to be rebuilt on a monumental scale – sufficient to hold over 1,800 people – and still, in 1837, the Old Bank chapel (now re-named Buxton Road) needed rebuilding to hold a congregation of 1,300. By 1844, when two Wesleyan Circuits were created, their combined membership was 2,820.[12]

Then catastrophe came. The 1849 Wesleyan Conference expelled three ministers for refusing to deny they were the authors of anonymous pamphlets attacking the leaders of the Connexion. Nationally Wesleyan Reformers rallied to the cause of greater openness and lay participation in the government of Wesleyanism; and, as in 1797, Huddersfield was one of the hardest hit places. At Buxton Road, with a circuit of 1,350 members in 1850, the loss of 433 members was reported at the end of the first quarter in 1851 – numbers which were not recovered until the end of the decade. At Queen Street the agony was more prolonged as the Reformers determined to seize control of the circuit. Membership, which had slumped from 1,435 in 1850 to 1,060 in 1853, crashed to only 539 a year later; at Queen Street itself, 640 members in June 1850 became 160 in June 1855 and the number of classes fell from thirty-seven to thirteen. Yet not until April 1857 did the Reformers finally secede, taking with them many of the most substantial seat-holders and leaders as well as the entire Sunday School, bar one class. With a membership of 346, the Reformers met for worship in the Philosophical Hall in Ramsden Street until their new chapel in Brunswick Street was ready in 1859.[13]

The development of Baptist and Congregational Independency

The Baptists and Congregationalists, with their independent church polity, were spared such constitutional wrangles: where they differed was over doctrine. Whereas all branches of Wesleyan Methodism were agreed on an Arminian theology, that is a belief that the saving grace of Christ was available to all who repented and believed, the old Dissenters shared with most evangelicals in the Church of England the Calvinist view that a special elect had been chosen by God to benefit from the saving grace of Christ. The problem was, how rigorously should this view be taken? Most Church of England evangelicals were moderates; the Baptists and Congregationalists were uncertain and so vulnerable to division, especially as theological liberalism developed later in the nineteenth century.

The Baptists initially held the high ground in the Huddersfield area, extending from Salendine Nook (1743) and Pole Moor (1787) down to the valley floor at Lockwood (1790), Slaithwaite (1816), Golcar (1835) and Milnsbridge (1843) as population and industry migrated from the scattered hillside communities to the more compact industrial villages near the river Colne. Early pastors were close to the weaving and farming communities to which they ministered. The cause at Salendine Nook grew steadily after the departure of Venn from the parish church in 1771: a larger chapel was opened in 1803 and another new chapel in 1843.[14] Meanwhile other members had been dismissed to form daughter churches: in 1790, Benjamin Ingham, a prosperous cloth-merchant and convert of Venn, opened a room for a Baptist meeting more convenient for the people of Lockwood. He provided a chapel at a cost of £800 in 1792 and a church was formed in 1795. However, a doctrinal dispute arose with a new pastor, John Poynder, in 1831 which led the latter and fifty-five members to secede and form a new church in 1832 along more strictly Calvinist lines. This was Rehoboth Chapel in Yews Lane, opened later that year by the Revd William Gadsby of Manchester, the acknowledged leader of the strict Calvinists.[15] A similar dispute had divided Pole Moor after 1804, leading to a 'Gadsbyite' secession to form Providence Chapel, Slaithwaite, in 1816.[16] Not until 1846 did the Baptists put down roots in the town centre, when a church of twenty members was formed in a schoolroom in Spring Street.[17] The following year a larger school room was taken in King Street, but in 1850 a dispute led to the temporary formation of a second meeting in Princess Street.

Fig. 6:5 Ramsden Street Chapel, built in 1825. (KCS)

If the Baptists began in the hills, the Congregationalists belonged to the valleys. Highfield remained the principal chapel for many years under its first pastor, William Moorhouse (1772-1823). The only other churches in the area were in Marsden (1790) and Honley (1795). Population increase in the town centre and a shortage of seats for the more prosperous members, however, led some of the latter to project a new chapel soon after Moorhouse's death. They acquired a site in Back Green, shortly to be dignified as Ramsden Street, where a chapel to hold 1,400 was built in 1825 at a cost of over £6,500; it was the first place of worship in Huddersfield to be lit by gas. The erection of a new and fashionable chapel in the town centre at first weakened the cause at Highfield but some parity between the two churches was restored in 1844 when a new Highfield chapel was opened for a similar outlay.[18]

Other Churches

Though Methodist, Congregational and Baptist chapels, along with the Church of England, dominated religious provision in early-nineteenth century Huddersfield, they were not the only providers. In Paddock, the Society of Friends (Quakers) had built a new Meeting House in 1810 and by 1850 had ninety-two members, divided equally between men and women;[19] in Dalton, members of the New Church, the followers of Emanuel Swedenborg, opened a chapel in Grove Place in 1825;[20] and early in 1846 a small group of Unitarians began meeting in rooms in New North Road. The following year they took a lease on a chapel in Bath Buildings, erected in 1839 by the followers of Robert Owen as the Hall of Science.[21] A few years earlier, in 1828, the Huddersfield Roman Catholic Mission had been founded to minister to the needs of the increasing numbers of Irish, mainly labourers and hawkers, who were settling in the town. Mass was initially said in a room in the Wool Pack Yard until, in 1832, St. Patrick's chapel, built with financial support from a number of prominent Protestant mill-owners, was opened in New North Road.[22] The extent of this religious diversity becomes apparent in the findings of the unique Census of Religious Worship, conducted on 30 March 1851.

Fig. 6:6 St. Patrick's Church. (KCS)

The 1851 Religious Census

On mid-Lent Sunday (Mothering Sunday) 1851, census forms had to be completed in every church and chapel, showing the extent of accommodation available and the number of adults and children actually attending each service on that day. The findings of this census were flawed: some places of worship failed to return the form; some returns alleged that the previous Sunday some chapels had announced the census and urged a good turn-out; others complained about the inclement weather which had kept people at home. Nevertheless, the returns can be used to give a broad picture of religious worship on one Sunday in the mid-nineteenth century. (Table 1).

Table 1 Census of Religious Worship, 1851

Date	Place of Worship	seats		adult attendance			total
		free	total	morning	aft.	even.	
Church of England:							
pre-Ref.	Huddersfield St. Peter	460	1,460	800	250	1,200	
1590	Slaithwaite St. James	407	1,500	200	727		
1846	Upper Slaithwaite School	260	260		(100)	35	
1615	Scammonden St. Bartholomew	50	350	45	86		
1749	Longwood St. Mark	60	460	93	195		
1819	Huddersfield Holy Trinity	500	1,500	900	(300)	900	
1841	Hillhouse schoolroom	50	50		20		
1824	Woodhouse Christ Church	105	530	200	291		
1829	Golcar St. John	100	400	(100)	(150)		
1830	Lindley St. Stephen	460	850	60	80	100	
1830	Paddock All Saints	450	850	140	100		
1831	Huddersfield St. Paul	250	1,200	700	550		
	Aspley room	200	200			200	
pre-Ref.	Almondbury All Hallows	454	950	120	134		
1841	Lowerhouses schoolroom			26	57		
pre-Ref.	Marsden St. Bartholomew		600	350	400		
1829	South Crosland Holy Trinity	219	607	140	220		
1830	Lockwood Emmanuel	400	900	180	163		
	Rashcliffe factory room					(50)	
1845	Milnsbridge St. Luke	337	602	125	147		
1848	Armitage Bridge St. Paul	320	320	137	146		
		5,082	13,589	4,316	4,166	2,435	
							10,917

Date	Place of Worship	seats		adult attendance			total
		free	total	morning	aft.	even.	
Wesleyan Methodist							
1776	Buxton Road	300	1,340	480		450	
1795	Lindley	30	257	147	183		
1800	Queen Street	298	1,862	777	77	672	
1816	Almondbury	148	300	84	85	118	
1822	Outlane		210	45	62	88	
1822	Sheepridge	300	48	40	56	35	
1824	Deadmanstone (Berry Brow)	118	286	93	111	121	
1824	Marsden	18	148	41	25	61	
1835	Moldgreen	300	526	90		142	
1835	Netherton preaching room	40	100	46	60	66	
1836	Cowcliffe		72	26	40		
1839	Slaithwaite Centenary	250	536	71	140	118	
1845	Crosland Moor	20	128	98	94	110	
1850	Paddock				70	100	
–	Dalton shared room	40	40			32	
–	Lockwood (Reformers)	26	182	130		207	
		1,888	**6,035**	**2,168**	**1,003**	**2,320**	
							5,491
Methodist New Connexion							
1805	Deighton	66	276	60	100		
1812	Lindley Zion	100	536	305	287	268	
1815	High Street	120	812	340		402	
1825	Berry Brow Salem	38	278	115	140	120	
1825	Paddock (Sunday School)						
1842	Wellhouse		319	60	140		
		324	**2,221**	**880**	**667**	**790**	
							2,337
Primitive Methodist							
1847	Northumberland Street	200	432	348	240	600	
							1,188
Total Methodist		**2,412**	**8,688**	**3,396**	**1,910**	**3,710**	
							9,016

Date	Place of Worship	seats		adult attendance			total
		free	total	morning	aft.	even.	
Baptist							
1743	Salendine Nook		300	1,050	333	437	
1790	Pole Moor			470	200	350	
1792	Lockwood First	200	800	259	265	255	
1816	Slaithwaite Providence		376	70	127		
1832	Lockwood Rehoboth		417	74	95		
1834	Golcar		630	300	500	150	
1843	Milnsbridge Aenon		750	220	245	51	
–	King Street Meeting Room	40	120	44		48	
–	Princess Street		200	61	80	170	
		240	3,593	2,538	2,045	1,461	
							5,584
Congregational							
1772	Highfield	50	990	430	261	352	
1807	Marsden Buckley Hill	48	366	110	180	30	
1825	Ramsden Street	60	1,570	635		556	
1843	Netherton schoolroom	40	100	46	60	66	
		198	3,026	1,221	501	1,004	
							2,726
Catholic							
1832	St Patrick		400	400		300	
							700
Others							
1771	Paddock Friends		310	73	41		
1825	Dalton New Church		452	170	175		
1846	Unitarian	100	220	70		90	
1848	Christ's Disciples	100	100	40	70		
1851	Latter Day Saints	250	250	40	30	80	
							879
Totals		8,382	31,098	2,004	9,088	8,730	
							29,822

Note: Numbers in parentheses are estimates or averages.
(*source:* Public Record Office, Home Office Papers 129/497, Census of Religious Worship, Returns)

What these figures show is the extent to which ten new district churches (and five small mission rooms) had enabled the Church of England, despite its many difficulties, to meet the accommodation needs of the Huddersfield area and to be the main supplier of free seats for the poor. Indeed, most of these churches had been built considerably larger than their ability to attract a congregation actually warranted. Despite the leading position of the Established Church, almost two out of every three attendances at church or chapel on census Sunday were made at non-Anglican places of worship. (Table 2)

Table 2 Percentage Shares, 1851

Denomination	seats		adult attendance			total
	free	total	morning	aft.	even.	
	%	%	%	%	%	%
Church of England	61	44	36	46	28	37
Wesleyan Methodist	23	19	18	11	27	18
New Connexion	4	7	7	7	9	8
Primitive Methodist	2	1	3	3	7	4
(Total Methodist)	*29*	*28*	*28*	*21*	*43*	*30*
Baptist	3	13	19	24	13	19
Congregational	2	10	10	6	12	9
Roman Catholic	–	1	3	–	3	2
Other	5	4	3	3	2	3

The figures show the extent to which Methodism had advanced to a position not far short of that held by the Established Church, though the Baptists, with fewer small chapels and less coverage than the Wesleyans, were actually attracting a slightly higher number of attendances; and, excepting the Catholics whose one church was reported full on the Sunday morning, the Baptists were the only denomination to report their chapels on average more than half full. The Congregationalists were considerably less numerous and largely a town centre denomination dependent upon the fortunes of Highfield and Ramsden Street.

Church growth in the later nineteenth century

i. The Church of England

In the first half of the nineteenth century the diverse denominational nature of religion in Huddersfield had been firmly established, with over thirty new churches and chapels to accommodate the expanding population of both the town and its surrounding communities. In the second half of the century this process continued at an accelerating rate in response to the growth of suburbs and the need for mission. In 1851, Lockwood and Paddock were still detached from the main urban centre, Highfield Chapel and Holy Trinity Church were still beyond the built-up area, Hillhouse and Fartown were still to be developed, and Moldgreen was no more than a cluster of houses at the foot of the hill to Almondbury.

Expansion to the north began with the building of St. John's, Bayhall, by Sir John William Ramsden, in 1853 to serve the Birkby-Hillhouse-Fartown area; further out, St. Thomas's, Bradley, was built in 1863; to the south, the Starkey family built St. Thomas's, Longroyd Bridge, in 1857; while to the east, Christ Church, Moldgreen was opened in 1863. With Paddock and Lindley already provided for, the needs of the area north of the Colne had, with one exception, largely been met until the church of St. Philip the Apostle, Birchencliffe, was opened in 1877. The exception lay in the rapidly expanding streets of working-class housing near the river and canal, from Aspley to Leeds Road. St. Andrew's church was opened here in 1870 at a cost of £5,000 towards which Sir John William Ramsden gave £1,000; closer to the town centre, St. Mark's was built in Lowerhead Row in 1887. Finally, there was a major area of residential growth to the south, from Lowerhouses (St. Mary's, 1888) across to Primrose Hill (St. Matthew's, 1904) and Newsome (St. John's, 1872) through Lockwood to Rashcliffe (St. Stephen's, 1864) and Crosland Moor (St. Barnabas's, 1902). Such expansion continued to depend upon the munificence of local landowners and employers. The site for Newsome Church was given by Sir John William Ramsden and the main subscriber was John Arthur Brooke of Armitage Bridge. The Brooke family again, along with Bentley Shaw and Robert John Bentley, had earlier constituted the committee which had built St. Stephen's, Rashcliffe. Elsewhere such men put money into rebuilding, extending or beautifying older buildings.[23]

*Fig. 6:7 St. Peter's Parish
Church designed by
J.P. Pritchett, built
1834-36. (KCS)*

It was during the second half of the nineteenth century that worship in
these churches assumed something like a recognisably modern form.
Previously, churches, like Nonconformist chapels, had been principally
preaching houses. The aim was to seat as many people as possible within
viewing and hearing distance of the pulpit. New churches could even look
like chapels, in some cases without chancels or towers. All this had changed
by 1900, in response not only to the High Church revival in the Established
Church, but also as a more general reflection of changing taste, so that by
1900 chapels were looking like churches instead of vice versa. When
St. Peter's parish church was rebuilt in 1834-36 by J. P. Pritchett, a leading
Nonconformist chapel builder, the internal layout was that of an eighteenth-
century preaching house. It was only in 1873 that the old box pews and three-

*Fig. 6:8 St. Peter's Parish
Church interior; note the
box pews and three-decker
pulpit. (KCS)*

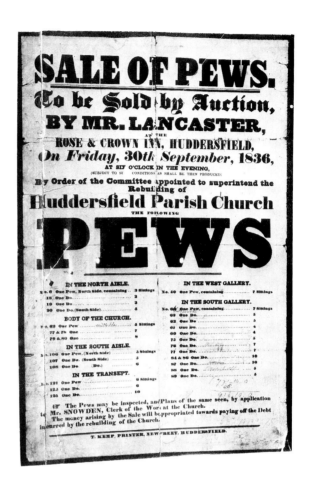

Fig. 6:9 Poster advertising the sale of "sittings" in the Parish Church.

decker pulpit were removed, the latter being replaced by a modern side pulpit, thus opening up the chancel as the central feature of the church.[24]

The first 'high' church in Huddersfield was St. Thomas's, Longroyd Bridge, designed by Giles Gilbert Scott in full Gothic splendour and with stained glass windows; at the opening the choir wore surplices, the first to assume this mode of dress in Huddersfield. Change was similarly apparent in the pioneering evangelical church of Holy Trinity; although the organ remained in its traditional position in the west gallery until 1880, the choir moved into the chancel in 1858. When the organ was placed in the north-east vestry in 1880, the chancel was raised two steps, the pulpit was changed and the choir was surpliced.[25]

ii. Nonconformity – The Baptists

Chapels followed the same lines of expansion, often beginning as school-missions and then being replaced by larger, purpose-built chapels if the cause prospered. But first the Baptists had to extend their influence from the outer communities to the town centre. In 1853 they purchased the former Unitarian chapel in Bath Buildings and in April 1855 reopened it as a Baptist Chapel with forty members. The Revd John Hanson, formerly pastor at Milnsbridge, was called to serve the new church; when he left, twenty years

Fig. 6:10 New North Road Baptist Chapel. (KCS)

later, the membership had quadrupled and plans were afoot for building a new chapel, which was opened in New North Road in April 1878 at a total cost of almost £15,000. Its outward appearance was that of a church, in decorated gothic with a bell tower topped by a small spire. In the new building membership rapidly increased and by the end of the 1880s had doubled to over 300.[26]

New North Road church had one mission station, in Birkby, begun in a barn in Hillhouse in the 1850s by the Salendine Nook Baptists. By the time New North Road took over the mission in 1879 there were just eighteen members, but with the growth of housing in the area in the next few years, the mission rapidly expanded until a separate church, with over 200 members, was formed in 1907. Its chapel, in Wheathouse Road, was opened in 1910. Salendine Nook was also active in the Lindley area, where a separate church was formed in 1864 and a chapel built at Oakes in 1869. A third development on the edges of the town came from Lockwood, which began to evangelise Primrose Hill in 1872: a schoolroom was opened in 1874 and a chapel in 1881. (Table 3)

Table 3 Baptist Churches and their Memberships, 1851-1901

Church and Date of Formation	1851	1861	1871	1881	1891	1901
Salendine Nook (1743)	229	281	304	302	356	380
Pole Moor (1787)	142	178	177	256	209	289
Lockwood First (1790)	144	202	270	343	257	254
Slaithwaite Providence (1816)	na	na	46	43	67	na
Lockwood Rehoboth (1832)	na	na	72	72	na	64
Golcar (1835)	122	146	233	214	317	337
Milnsbridge (1843)	90	77	119	162	273	326
Huddersfield (1846)	(40)	(86)	151	244	303	327
Hillhouse/Birkby (1853, 1879)		na	14	24	116	164
Lindley Oakes (1864)			63	88	169	153
Scapegoat Hill (1871)			28	116	171	235
Slaithwaite Zion (1886)					37	78
Primrose Hill (1889)					112	108
Sunny Bank (1890)					44	63
Totals	767	930	1,477	1,864	2,431	2,778

(*source: Baptist Handbook*; na = not available; numbers in parentheses are estimates)

The main area of Baptist growth was in the Colne valley, where Salendine Nook and Pole Moor had long been centres of strength. The isolated position of these chapels prompted a dispersion of Sunday school work for which Salendine Nook opened rooms in Longwood in 1838, Scapegoat Hill in 1850 and Jagger Green in about 1859. A church was formed at Scapegoat Hill in 1871. Pole Moor opened schools at Clough Head in 1876, Outlane in 1882 and Slaithwaite in 1885. The latter became a church ('Zion') the following year, with a school-chapel opened in Crimble in 1891. A further church was created out of an amicable division at Pole Moor, when thirty members objected to the use of fermented wine in the communion service. They left and opened a chapel at Sunny Bank on Bolster Moor in 1889.[27]

iii. Nonconformity – The Methodists

No less influential were the Methodists, although their divisions, exacerbated in the early 1850s, weakened their overall thrust and led to much competitive chapel building. The First Wesleyan Circuit (Queen Street) included, by 1851, chapels in Lindley (1795), Almondbury (1816) and Cowcliffe (1837), to which were added Sheepridge (1859), Leeds Road (1866), Moldgreen (1869) and Fartown (1880). The main growth point here was Fartown which, with 186 members in 1902, was second only to Queen Street itself (and, indeed, became head of the circuit when Queen Street became a separate mission in 1906). The rest of the circuit extended into the Kirkheaton and Kirkburton areas, beyond the scope of this study. No other society in the circuit had more than a hundred members; Almondbury was in decline and Moldgreen growing only slowly, though both were to become important centres with further housing development in the twentieth century.[28]

Buxton Road circuit (created in 1844) extended into the Holme and Colne valleys and included societies in Outlane (1822), Deadmanstone (1824; replaced by Birch Road, Berry Brow, 1893), Marsden (1824), Netherton (1835), Slaithwaite (1839), and Longwood (1837). By 1888, when a third circuit was created, chapels had also been opened in Crosland Moor (1864), Lockwood (1872) and Paddock (1873). With a new church opened in Mount Pleasant, Lockwood, in 1881, the latter cause rapidly expanded to over 200 members by 1884. Longwood similarly prospered, with 224 members in 1888 leading to a new, Gothic, chapel in 1904. Small societies were also established in the expanding Lockwood area at Crosland Hill (1889), Rashcliffe and Brierley Wood (1893) and Thornton Lodge (1897).[29]

The decision to divide the circuits further in 1888, bringing all the Colne valley chapels together, was linked with the building of two new chapels, one at Gledholt to head the circuit and to serve the villas of Edgerton, the other in the less rural surroundings of Milnsbridge. Both were initially very successful, attracting over a hundred members each during their first decade. But whereas Gledholt then went from strength to strength in the twentieth century, Milnsbridge faltered and suffered financial difficulties. Two smaller mission chapels were added to the circuit before the First World War: the Mount (1913) and Kew Hill, purchased from the Elland Primitive Methodists in 1890.[30]

The New Connexion operated on a much smaller scale, its main centres being the chapel in High Street (1815) and Lindley Zion (1812) – both of which had developed directly out of the 1797 split. There were smaller societies in Deighton (1808), Berry Brow (1824), Paddock (1825), Outlane (1832) and Wellhouse (1842). With the exception of Deighton, all the New Connexion chapels in the area lay in the Holme and Colne valleys to the south and west of Huddersfield. Many of these societies acquired new chapels during the second half of the nineteenth century, notably High Street itself which built a magnificent decorated gothic structure in 1867 at a cost of £12,000. Smaller

Fig. 6:11 High Street Chapel, built in 1867. (KCS)

chapels were also opened in Marsh (1863), Primrose Hill (1867) and Newsome (1891). The New Connexion continued in an undivided circuit until 1876, when the Colne Valley societies were formed into a separate Lindley circuit, and Wellhouse was immediately asked to start a Sunday service in Golcar. Providence chapel was opened there in 1883.[31]

The Reformers of the 1850s inclined towards independency with small circuits. When the reform storm broke in 1851, almost the entire memberships in Moldgreen and Crosland Moor, together with substantial numbers elsewhere, were expelled or left and eventually constituted a new circuit with societies at Almondbury (Zion), Lindley (Thornhill Street), Lockwood (Bentley Street), Longwood (Parkwood), Sheepridge (Providence), and Slaithwaite (Carr Lane). The breach was slow, painful but not always acrimonious. At Slaithwaite, the Reformers were permitted the use of a room in the Wesleyan Sunday School for preaching on alternate Sunday evenings – the second service in the chapel was usually in the afternoons. Alternative temporary premises were not acquired until June 1853; a permanent chapel followed in 1871. At Netherton, the Reformers seceded and for a time held services in the Oddfellows Hall, but resolved their financial difficulties in 1860 by reuniting with the parent body.[32]

The Queen Street Reformers followed a rather different path, running their Brunswick Street chapel from 1859 on independent lines. Only in 1866 did they accept a United Methodist Free Churches Minister, the Revd Marmaduke Miller (1866-72). He took them into the Connexion, raised their membership from 320 to 427 and attempted a Mission in Hillhouse where the New Connexion had previously failed. A chapel was opened in 1874 and became head of its own circuit ten years later. Miller also began a Mission in Rashcliffe in 1871.[33]

Lastly, the Primitive Methodists extended their influence through small and often short-lived societies throughout the whole area. Membership in the Huddersfield vicinity was only about three hundred, of whom half were in the central Northumberland Street society. Among the more successful causes elsewhere were those at Taylor Hill (1857) and South Street (1865). The latter was begun in Albion Street in 1857 to serve the western end of the town centre; it moved to Senior's Schoolroom in East Parade in 1862 before settling in a small chapel in South Street, amid the terraces of the Springwood area, in 1865.[34] (Table 4)

Fig. 6:12 Brunswick Street Methodist Chapel. (KCS)

Table 4 Methodist Circuits and Membership 1851-1901

Circuit	1851	1861	1871	1881	1891	1901
Wesleyan Methodist						
First/Queen Street	1,273	866	865	806	897	927
Buxton Road	872	1,134	1,241	1,372	967	1,014
Gledholt					1,205	1,192
Total	2,145	2,000	2,106	2,178	3,069	3,133
New Connexion						
High Street	672	858	1016	446	558	797
Lindley				680	702	721
Total	672	858	1,016	1,126	1,260	1,518
United Methodist Free Churches/Free Methodist						
First/Moldgreen		208	563	523	561	733
Brunswick Street		†310	399	435	368	322
Hillhouse					101	112
		518	962	958	1,030	1,167
Primitive Methodist						
Northumberland St.	664	625	629	*365	390	303
All Methodists	3,481	4,001	4,713	4,627	5,749	6,121

*The sudden loss of members which occurred in 1872 and again in 1878 is accounted for by a rearrangement of circuit boundaries and the consequent loss of outlying societies in the Dewsbury area.

(*source:* Minutes of the Conferences and Circuit Schedules;
†number from B. W. Rose, *Brunswick Street*, p. 85)

iv. Nonconformity – The Congregationalists

Congregationalism in Huddersfield kept to the low land much as the Baptists kept to the high and the two denominations tended not to overlap.[35] Highfield was led from 1854 until 1904 by Robert Bruce, an Aberdeen-born and educated pastor, who became one of the foremost citizens in his adopted town, for services to which he was made a freeman in 1906. His opposite number at Ramsden Street from 1847 until 1878 was Richard Skinner. The two were both excellent pastors and good friends.[36] Together they gave Congregationalism a position of religious and civic leadership in what was basically a Nonconformist and Liberal town.

The Congregationalists' missionary efforts from Highfield and Ramsden Street were aimed principally at the town centre and immediate suburbs. A mission in Paddock (1861) became a separate church in 1870 and acquired its own chapel the following year. There was also a chapel in South Street from 1856, served by the Ramsden Street missioner, William Hotchkiss, appointed in 1854. An independent chapel in George Street, affiliated to the Evangelical Union, also built in 1856, was bought by the Congregationalists in 1870 to replace South Street and was home to a church from 1874 until 1887. Thirdly, Highfield started a Sunday school in the Beaumont Street Board School in 1878, which led to the building of the Great Northern Street school-chapel in 1888 and the formation of a church in 1897.[37]

Meanwhile, Hotchkiss had begun missionary work in Hillhouse and Moldgreen, and a proposal was made that the bicentenary of the ejection of Nonconformist ministers in 1662 should be commemorated with a new church in Hillhouse. The result was a splendidly gothic structure with spire, costing £3,650, opened in February 1865. In Moldgreen, after an anonymous donor had promised to finance Hotchkiss's work for five years and provide £1,300 towards the building of a school and chapel, a church was formed in 1865 and a chapel opened the following year.[38] On receiving an illuminated address to celebrate twenty-five years at Ramsden Street in 1870, Richard Skinner could remark with justifiable pride:

> They had to thank God that the two churches of twenty-five years ago had multiplied into five. That had been done without any material weakening of the Churches from which the others had sprung. It had not been the result of division, or split, but had taken place with the most entire agreement and co-operation of the older Churches, from pure motives, with a sincere and earnest desire to extend God's kingdom, and to benefit their fellow men.[39]

Robert Bruce made the same point when addressing the Congregational Union meeting in Huddersfield in 1874. Including Paddock, there were now six chapels with 6,000 seats and a combined church membership of 1,150.[40]

The boast of unity was to be short-lived. In 1875 the aging Skinner took J. T. Stannard to be his assistant pastor. However, Stannard was a liberal Calvinist and so when Skinner retired in 1878 some of the congregation opposed his appointment as sole pastor. Of the twenty-one trustees, eleven, led by Charles Henry Jones, held that Stannard's teaching was contrary to

*Fig. 6:13 Milton Church,
Queen Street South.
(KCS)*

the Trust Deed. Jones was a political heavyweight, a member since his arrival in the town in 1841, deacon, trustee and treasurer, first Mayor of the Borough of Huddersfield in 1868 and 'a sturdy Nonconformist of the old-fashioned type'.[41] He took the case to the Court of Chancery and won. Stannard left Ramsden Street, taking with him all but 111 members and many of its leading figures. In February 1881 they constituted themselves an independent church with 168 members, meeting first in the Victoria Temperance Hall and then, calling themselves the Milton Church, in premises of that name in Queen Street South opened in June 1884.[42] Ramsden Street never fully recovered. (Table 5)

Table 5 Congregational Membership in 1903

Church	membership
Highfield (1772)	331
Marsden (1790)	104
Ramsden Street (1825)	255
Netherton (1843)	22
Hillhouse (1865)	221
Moldgreen (1865)	158
Paddock (1871)	165
Milton (1881)	457
Great Northern Street (1897)	86
Netheroyd Hill (1899)	38
Crimble (1903)	(34)
Total	1,871

(source: *Congregational Year Book*, 1904; Crimble membership is for 1904 from *Congregational Year Book*, 1905)

v. *Other Denominations*

The Roman Catholic Irish community was initially concentrated near the town centre and the Catholics, therefore, followed the economical policy of multiplying services rather than buildings. Increasing numbers following further Irish immigration in the 1840s warranted the appointment of a second priest at St. Patrick's in 1858. By the 1880s it was becoming necessary to open a second centre for Mass near the bottom end of town in Kirkgate and a third priest was appointed. Finally, in 1895, St. Joseph's, Commercial Street, became a separate parish.[43]

The Paddock Friends (Quakers) also maintained their position, with numbers fluctuating between eighty and a hundred until 1875. Thereafter they went into a steady decline, but in the 1890s the number of non-members attending their meetings (especially of females for some unaccountable reason) began to increase and this was followed by a doubling of female members (mainly by convincement) after 1906. By 1911 they had seventy-two members (forty-seven of whom were female) and a further forty-eight adherents. Their principal missionary work came through their Adult School, started in 1856.[44]

Among the new arrivals in Huddersfield in the later nineteenth century was the Salvation Army. Corps No. 400 was opened in March 1883, meeting at the Armoury in Ramsden Street and at a hall in Outcote Bank. As frequently happened when the Salvationists first appeared, there were demonstrations against them by what was usually termed 'the rougher element', but their brass band and a visit from General Booth on Whit Monday, 1884, served to establish their position in the town.[45]

Lastly, in 1902, the Presbyterians formed their first church and bought Waverley House on Portland Street for meetings. The cause prospered and by 1906, with over two hundred communicants, they decided to build a chapel, St. James's, opened in 1911 at a cost of £3,570.[46]

Sunday Schools

The majority of the Victorian middle classes were regular church and chapel goers. However, the total numbers recorded at public worship can only be explained by the presence also of many working men and women, although contemporaries were agreed that the majority of the working classes – especially the lower working classes – were not regular church and chapel goers. They had to be wooed through special missions like the interdenomination 'Rock' Mission in the Turnbridge area (1877-1945).[47] But for most people their sole point of contact with organised religion was likely to be as children in the almost universal Sunday Schools.

The earliest Sunday Schools were interdenominational and had paid teachers, but by 1811 the denominational school with voluntary teachers was becoming the norm.[48] The original purpose of the schools was to teach on a Sunday those basic skills of literacy which middle-class children could expect to learn at weekday school. Indeed the Highfield Sunday School (begun in 1811) turned away any children who attended day school 'as it is contrary to the original design of Sunday Schools, and also to common equity and reason'.[49] The first Wesleyan school was started by the Queen Street society in 1812, and was housed in the Old Bank chapel after its recovery from the New Connexion in 1814. In that year the Highfield and the Wesleyan Schools met together to celebrate the end of the Napoleonic wars; from 1817 this meeting became an annual event and the origin of the first Huddersfield Sunday School Union. By 1822 there were twenty schools in the Union, with 3,666 children and 959 teachers. This was impressive, but by the time that the second Sunday School Union (founded 1859) celebrated the centenary of the Sunday School movement in 1880, the growth had been extraordinary, all the more so when one recognises that some schools managed to produce more children for the procession than they had on their books! (Table 6)

Table 6 Sunday Schools in Huddersfield, 1879-1880

Sunday School (with date of formation)	numbers on books	av. att. 1879 morn.	aft.	scholars in the 1880 procession
Wesleyan				
Almondbury (1808)	421	125	236	421
Buxton Road (1812)	948	218	555	750
Queen Street (1812)	806	123	396	700
Lindley (1815)	205	75	123	–
Sheepridge (1823)	165	64	93	130
Deadmanstone (1824)	157	94	102	169
Cowcliffe (1836)	118	53	78	90
Paddock (1853)	139	68	93	148
Crosland Moor (1865)	236	115	158	196
Leeds Road (1866)	141	57	89	120
Moldgreen (1869)	121	39	59	80
Lockwood (1872)	130	75	96	150
Total	3,587	1,106	2,078	2,954
New Connexion				
Lindley (1803)	649	250	362	–
High Street (1814)	255	126	176	308
Deighton (1816)	158	62	93	160
Paddock (1825)	459	172	258	480
Berry Brow (1828)	388	178	230	384
Marsh (1860)	110	54	83	100
Primrose Hill (1864)	219	94	130	200
Total	2,238	936	1,332	1,632
Primitive Methodist				
Northumberland Street (1837)	216	84	129	170
South Street (1856)	131	57	89	130
Taylor Hill (1869)	110	68	86	90
Paddock (1873)	58	38	49	53
Lowerhouses (1878)	87	43	70	102
Total	602	290	423	545
United Methodist Free Churches/Free Methodist				
Moldgreen (1835)	575	110	258	490
Crosland Moor (1845)	235	122	161	349
Lockwood (1848)	229	96	168	256
Almondbury (1853)	45	25	38	45
Brunswick Street (1857)	430	122	258	400
Sheepridge (1858)	192	130	148	164

Table 6 Sunday Schools in Huddersfield, 1879-1880 (cont.)

Sunday School (with date of formation)	numbers on books	av. att. 1879 morn.	aft.	scholars in the 1880 procession
Rashcliffe (1870)	207	69	107	150
Hillhouse (1872)	289	93	176	300
Northgate (1872)	170	63	77	130
Crosland Hill (1877)	84	67	75	with Crosland Moor
Newsome (1878)	68	36	40	72
Total	2,524	933	1,506	2,356
Total Methodist	8,951	3,265	5,339	7,487
Baptist				
Salendine Nook (c.1800)	195	109	116	–
Longwood (1838)	163	101	83	–
Lockwood (1821)	615	229	363	540
Lockwood Rehoboth (1832)	175	106	124	194
Milnsbridge (1844)	556	200	300	510
New North Road (1849)	276	58	147	300
Oakes (1866)	285	106	181	300
Primrose Hill (1874)	315	146	162	200
Total	2,580	1,055	1,476	2,044
Congregational				
Highfield (1811)	420	127	236	475
Ramsden Street (1826)	731	272	477	750
Paddock (1844)	412	161	281	450
George Street (1862)	266	70	122	210
Hillhouse (1865)	472	142	315	472
Moldgreen (1865)	351	136	256	330
Beaumont Street (1878)	465	162	236	405
Total	3,117	1,070	1,923	3,092
Other				
Hall Bower Independent (1814)	250	136	179	260
Netheroyd Hill Independent (1814)	156	116	123	140
Paddock Friends (1856)	199	49	62	280
Bradford Road Christian Church (1861)	97	41	41	109
New Church Dalton (1830)	191	93	132	230
Total	893	435	537	1,019
Total	15,541	5,825	9,275	13,642

(*source*: R. Bruce, *Huddersfield Sunday School Centenary Memorial* (1880), pp. 36-43).

These figures are a useful guide but they underestimate the true position. Requests for information were sent only to schools within the then borough boundaries, so the great Colne Valley Baptist schools at Pole Moor (492), Golcar (380) and Scapegoat Hill (251) are omitted. Also, only three Anglican replies were received, although every church had its Sunday School just as every chapel had.[50] The size of these Anglican schools at the Visitation of 1858 (when they would have been much smaller than at the later date) gives some indication of their magnitude. (Table 7)

Table 7 Church of England Sunday School Numbers in 1858

Church	Sunday School
Almondbury All Hallows	202
Lowerhouses schoolroom	70
Armitage Bridge St. Paul	210
Golcar St. John	280
Huddersfield St. Peter	640
Huddersfield St. John	204
Huddersfield St. Paul	213
Huddersfield Holy Trinity	250
Woodhouse Christ Church	260
Lindley St. Stephen	95
Lockwood Emmanuel	459
Longwood St. Mark	135
Marsden St. Bartholomew	228
Milnsbridge St. Luke	246
Paddock All Saints	150
Scammonden St. Batholomew	210
Slaithwaite St. James	226
Lingards schoolroom	106
Upper Slaithwaite	171
South Crosland Holy Trinity	225
Total	4,580

(*source:* WYAS, Leeds, Visitation Returns of the Clergy, 1858)

These figures indicate how energetic action by the Church of England had, by mid-century, resulted in a Sunday School movement within the Established Church comparable to that undertaken by the

Nonconformists.[51] These huge church and chapel Sunday schools dominated religious life in the Huddersfield area for a hundred years. The peak of membership at Salendine Nook, for example, was 623 (with 125 teachers) in 1908 and the number did not fall below 300 until 1946. Great Northern Street Congregational school peaked at 501 (with 34 teachers) in 1905 and fell below 300 only after 1916. The Free Methodist schools at Brunswick Street and Rashcliffe totalled 730 children in 1883 (with 78 teachers) and did not consistently fall below 300 until after 1919.

The Twentieth Century

From the time of the evangelical revival in the mid-eighteenth century until the end of the nineteenth, religious organisations and observance were in the ascendant, a trend accentuated by the rapid increase in population. In the twentieth century an initial period of consolidation gave way after the Second World War to one of decline and massive cultural change.

i. Suburban growth and inner-city decline

Already by the later nineteenth century, acute observers were becoming aware of the problem of inner-city decline. Improved communications, and particularly the electric tramway from 1901, facilitated the spread of population – especially that part of the population which was most active in church and chapel going – from the centre to the suburbs. In response, Queen Street chapel was reorganised as a Mission Chapel in 1906 and Ramsden Street followed in 1909. Queen Street, High Street and Buxton Road were all identified as 'down town' chapels in the United Methodist Church handbook of 1923, which drew attention to the impact of the tramways on church life. Of course, not all was loss. Suburban churches continued to thrive and even to grow whilst others declined. With the development of the 'up town' area towards Edgerton, Holy Trinity Church and Highfield Chapel, which had been peripheral when founded, were now extremely well-placed and were joined by new chapels in quest of congregations – Gledholt Wesleyan (1890) and St. James's Presbyterian (1911); and, far from being remote, Salendine Nook chapel now had tramcars passing its door and was able to move its second Sunday service from the afternoon to the evening.[52]*

*Details of the tramcar service are to be found in Chapter Sixteen. EDITOR.

Fig. 6:14 Places of Worship in Huddersfield Borough and Parish, c.1914.

ii. Changing patterns of leisure

Before the mid-nineteenth century, religious activities outside formal worship were strictly confined to such matters as religious education and philanthropy. Mutual Improvement Societies were common and, from the 1870s, the Band of Hope became an essential adjunct of any well-regulated church or chapel. But by the end of the century new features were creeping in of a less obviously religious nature.

The strength of churches and chapels lay in their integration with the needs of their communities and they had few rivals save the public house. Towards the end of the century, new forms of competition were emerging to occupy the time and interests of young adults and others whom the churches might hitherto have hoped to monopolise, and they had to respond in kind. When St. James's began in 1902, it had a Sunday School, a Bible Class – and a Bowling Club, to which a Sewing Meeting and a Mothers' Meeting were soon added. By the 1920s there were Women's and Girls' Guilds, Scouts, and Tennis, Literary, Bowling and Rambling Clubs. Lindley Zion Sunday School Young Men's Class started a highly successful Cricket Club in 1893; the Dalton New Church had a gymnasium before the First World War and formed a Tennis Club in 1924. The story was the same in every church and chapel, although none was quite so blatant as Ramsden Street in its quest for congregations in the early years of the century, when immensely popular lantern slide displays were given at the end of the evening service.[53]

The impact of the 1914-18 war was disruptive of church life, but not decisively so. Ancillary premises were sometimes requisitioned, as at Milton Church where the Sunday School work was continued in the Technical College next door. Young men went off to war but, though most came back, they did not always resume the ties established in Sunday School. Churches between the wars began to complain of a lack of workers. They were less able to face the second period of disruption between 1939 and 1945.[54]

iii. Consolidation and rationalisation

Though regular congregations appear to have been falling in the inter-war years, membership at most of the larger chapels remained stable, though ageing, until the 1950s. After this, Methodist numbers were kept up in those chapels which remained open, by amalgamation with those which closed; but the Congregational and Baptist chapels saw their numbers dwindle.

Highfield experienced a steady decline, from 331 in 1904 to 247 in 1939; Milton fell more dramatically from 457 in 1903 to 149 in 1939, while Ramsden Steet went into terminal decline in the 1920s. Discussions about an amalgamation of Ramsden Street with Milton failed in 1927 when each wished the other's chapel to be the redundant one. Then, in 1933, financial pressures brought about the closure of Ramsden Street and the dispersal of the membership. The Corporation bought the site for its new Public Library and Art Gallery.[55]

In 1907 the New Connexion and the United Methodist Free Churches (along with the Bible Christians) amalgamated nationally to form the United Methodist Church, which joined with the Wesleyans and Primitive Methodists in 1932 to become the Methodist Church. This gradually brought about a reorganisation of the nine Methodist circuits and a rationalisation of premises: High Street chapel joined Brunswick in 1944 which joined Gledholt in 1949, Buxton Road was closed in 1950 and Northumberland Street was sold to the Y.M.C.A. in 1957. Out in the suburbs and villages, former rivals and neighbours learned to live together and then were united: three chapels in Slaithwaite; three in Lindley; two in Almondbury, Berry Brow, Crosland Moor, Lockwood, Longwood, Moldgreen, Outlane and Paddock. Amalgamation was not always easy and was sometimes painful; members were lost.

Although no such formal arrangements were made between other denominations until the Presbyterians and Congregationalists became the United Reformed Church in 1972, leading to the closure of Highfield in 1979 and transfer of members to St. James's, some informal local arrangements were agreed between Methodists and Congregationalists. Joint churches with a shared ministry were created in Paddock and Marsden (1968) and Sheepridge (1985). With the spread of the ecumenical movement, the Church of England was also brought into these local arrangements, the Newsome Ecumenical Project, for example, bringing together the work of St. Paul's Armitage Bridge, St. John's Newsome, Primrose Hill Baptists and Newsome South Methodists.

Decayed buildings, slum clearance and road widening also took their toll. St. Mark's, Lowerhead Row, was closed in 1939 and its benefice reunited with the parish church when slum clearance made it redundant. Negotiations for Lockwood Rehoboth to rejoin Lockwood First Baptist Church were accelerated by the dangerous state of Rehoboth in 1970.[56] Sometimes, as with New North Road Baptist Church and Moldgreen United Reformed Church, road widening led to the erection of new and more economical buildings.

The new diversity

If some buildings were lost during the course of the twentieth century, new ones were gained, with slum populations being rehoused and suburbs spreading ever further from the town centre. New Baptist churches were started in Lowerhouses Lane, Longley (1938) and Dalton (1955), a new Congregational church was formed at Brackenhall (1940) and the Church of England opened several new churches and missions, including St. Cuthbert's, Birkby (1932), St. James's, Rawthorpe (1955), St. Hilda's, Cowcliffe (1953) and St. Francis's, Fixby (1954). But the greatest growth was achieved by the Roman Catholics. They began the century with just two places of worship: St. Patrick's, and St. Joseph's which was moved from Commercial Street to Somerset Road in 1954. Two further churches were built in the Colne valley: the Church of the Holy Family, Slaithwaite (1915) and St. Brigid's, Longwood (1919). Then the great corporation rehousing schemes dispersed the old Irish communities and necessitated new chapels-of-ease, parishes and churches in the suburbs: Our Lady of Lourdes, Sheepridge (1938); St. Bernadette, Bradley (1953); St. James the Great, New Hey Road (1960); English Martyrs, Dalton (1970). Chapels-of-ease were also established in the former Plaza cinema, Thornton Lodge (1956) and St. Andrew's Church, Leeds Road (1976).[57]

The Catholic Church in Huddersfield had always had the character of an immigrant church. St. Patrick's supplied the needs of the Irish community and of successive waves of further immigrants for over a hundred and fifty years, and most of the priests during this time were themselves Irish. But the Second World War brought not only new Irish settlers but also Poles and Ukrainians of the Catholic faith. These were provided with their own priest at St. Patrick's in 1949, but in 1962 they acquired the former Unitarian chapel in Fitzwilliam Street which was re-dedicated to Our Lady of Czestochowa, Queen of Poland.[58]

As the origins of new immigrants became more diverse, in the latter half of the twentieth century, so too did their forms of religious expression. To the New Jerusalem, Christian Apostolic, Christadelphian, Plymouth Brethren and Spiritualist Churches of the nineteenth century were added twentieth-century sects of American origin such as Christian Science and Elim Four Square Gospel Pentecostalism. The Latter Day Saints (Mormons) were present in Huddersfield in the nineteenth century, but never more visibly so than when they opened their Tabernacle in Birchencliffe in the 1960s. The charismatic movement and an increase in population of Carribean origin brought a further crop of small revivalist and prophetic churches in the 1970s and 1980s.

Even more diversity accompanied the formation of substantial immigrant communities from India, Pakistan and Bangladesh, settling in inner suburbs such as Fartown and Thornton Lodge, where the better-off sort of working man and his family first lived and worshipped a hundred years earlier. To the churches and chapels of that era the 1970s and 1980s added the mosques and temples of Islam, Sikhism and Hinduism, sometimes occupying former chapels and schools no longer needed by their original occupants. Just as Christian diversity became the norm in the nineteenth century, so in the later twentieth century multi-cultural and multi-faith diversity came to characterise the ever-changing face of Huddersfield religion.[59]

Edward Royle

Biographical Note

Edward Royle was educated at King James's Grammar School, Almondbury, and Christ's College, Cambridge, where he read History. His postgraduate research was on Secularism in nineteenth-century Britain, directed by Dr G. Kitson Clark. After four years as a Fellow of Selwyn College, Cambridge, he returned to Yorkshire to take up a lectureship at the University of York in 1972. Among his publications are *Radical Politics, 1790-1900* (1971), *Victorian Infidels* (1974), *The Infidel Tradition* (1976), *Chartism* (1980), *Radicals, Freethinkers and Republicans* (1980), *English Radicals and Reformers, 1760-1848* (1982), two Borthwick Papers on *The Victorian Church in York* (1983), and *Nonconformity in Nineteenth Century York* (1985), and most recently, *Modern Britain, A Social History 1750-1985* (1987).

A NOTE ON SOURCES

Huddersfield was in the diocese of York until 1836 (records in the Borthwick Institute of Historical Research, York); then in Ripon until 1888 (records in W(est) Y(orkshire) A(rchives) S(ervice), Leeds, and Brotherton Library, University of Leeds); then in Wakefield (records in WYAS, Wakefield). Most Methodist circuit and chapel records are in the WYAS, Kirklees Methodist Church Records, unless otherwise stated. Some Methodist records are in WYAS, Wakefield; Baptist, Congregational and Unitarian chapel records are in WYAS, Kirklees Nonconformist Records. Society of Friends records are in the Brotherton Library, University of Leeds.

Statistics of Methodist circuit membership are taken from the Wesleyan Methodist (1780-1932), Methodist New Connexion (1801-1907), Primitive Methodist (1824-1932), United Methodist Free Churches (1859-1907), United Methodist Church (1908-1932) and Methodist Church (1933-1969) annual Minutes of Conference or equivalents, full sets of which are available in the John Rylands University Library, Manchester. Baptist church memberships are taken from the annual *Baptist Handbook* given from 1847; and Congregational church memberships are from the *Congregational Year Book* given from 1904, full sets of which are in Dr. Williams's Library, London.

Early secondary accounts used generally in this chapter include J. G. Miall, *Congregationalism in Yorkshire* (1868); R. Bruce, 'Congregationalism in Huddersfield', *Congregational Year Book* (1875), pp.120-24; D. F. E. Sykes, *The History of Huddersfield and its Vicinity* (Huddersfield, 1898), pp.337-61; J. Mallinson, *History of Methodism in Huddersfield, Holmfirth and Denby Dale* (1898); *The Baptists of Yorkshire* (Bradford and London, 1912); and local Directories, especially Tindall's (1866), White's (1894) and Kelly's (1917).

The individual church and chapel histories referred to in these notes, usually without place or date of publication, are principally drawn from the extensive collection of such works in the Kirklees Cultural Services H(uddersfield) L(ocal) H(istory) L(ibrary).

NOTES

1. Churches and chapels which were in neither the ancient parish of Huddersfield nor the former County Borough – those in Linthwaite (except for Centenary and Providence chapels), Honley, Dogley Lane, and Blackley – have generally been excluded from this study. Methodist circuit totals, however, do include some small societies from the wider region. The only area north west of the river not to be in Huddersfield parish was Turnbridge (in Kirkheaton).

2. W. B. Crump, *Huddersfield Highways down the Ages* (Huddersfield, 1949; reprinted, 1988), pp.69-70, 85-86, 100-101.

3. B(orthwick) I(nstitute) of H(istorical) R(esearch), Bp.V 1764 Ret., Archbishop Drummond's Visitation Returns for Huddersfield, Scammonden and Slaithwaite (1764); J. Stock, *History of the Baptised, Independent and Congregational Church meeting in Salendine Nook Chapel, Huddersfield* (London and Huddersfield, 1874), pp.10-28; P. Stock, *Foundations* (Halifax, 1933), pp.66-77.

4.   Mallinson, *Methodism*, pp.12-15, 23-24; Brotherton Quaker PA/61, 'Copy of Deeds belonging to Friends' Meeting House and Grounds at Paddock'; *Memoirs of the Rev. Joseph Cockin . . . written partly by himself, and continued by his son, John Cockin* (Holmfirth, 1828; second edition, London 1841), pp.80-86; *The Life and a selection of the letters of the late Rev. Henry Venn . . .*, ed. by Henry Venn (1834; 4th edition 1836), pp.44-49; Stock, *Foundations*, p.77; J. W. Dicks, *Highfield Congregational Church. The Inheritance of Faith* (Huddersfield, 1972), pp.1-4.

5.   C. A. Hulbert, *Annals of the Church in Slaithwaite . . . from 1593 to 1864* (London and Huddersfield, 1864), p.107; Stock, *Foundations*, pp.390-94; A. Crawshaw and M. Wilkinson, *Tabernacle on the Hill. A History of Pole Moor Baptist Chapel, Scammonden, 1787-1987* (1987), pp.6-9.

6.   For Coates, *see* H. J. Maddock, *The Loss of Ministers Improved, being the substance of A Sermon occasioned by the death of the Rev. John Coates, M.A., late Vicar of Huddersfield and preached at The Holy Trinity Church, in that town, on Sunday Evening, July 13th, 1823* (Huddersfield, 1823), p.32.

7.   A. S. Weatherhead, *Holy Trinity, Huddersfield. Three Lectures on the History of the Church and Parish, 1919-1904* (1913), pp.5-35. Population figures from White's *Directory* (1837).

8.   C. A. Hulbert, *Annals of the Parish of Almondbury* (Huddersfield, 1880-81), pp.275-78; *The Church at Longroyd Bridge, 1859-1899* (Huddersfield, 1899), pp.10-11, 17-18.

9.   Mallinson, *Methodism*, pp.46-53; J. Firth, *Buxton Road Wesleyan Sunday School, Huddersfield, AD 1812-1912. Historic Sketch and Centenary Celebrations* (Huddersfield, 1913), pp.2-3.

10. HLHL, Press Cutting, 13 May 1944.

11. H. B. Kendall, *The Origin and History of the Primitive Methodist Church*, 2 vols. (n.d.), vol. 1., pp.492-94; HLHL, Press Cutting, 8 May 1937.

12. Sykes, *Huddersfield*, pp.357-8; Firth, *Buxton Road*, pp.19-20.

13. WYAS, Kirklees NMW/HSC/II/1, Buxton Road Quarterly Meeting Minute Book; N/QS/HC/2, Queen Street Circuit Quarter-day Minute Book; B. W. Rose, *Brunswick Street Free Wesleyan Church and School. Origin and History, 1857-1907* (Huddersfield, 1907).

14. Stock, *Salendine Nook*, pp.27, 38; J. W. Shaw, *Salendine Nook Baptist Church and Sunday Schools*, (Manchester, 1905), p.9.

15. Stock, *Foundations*, pp.396-98; *Lockwood Baptist Church, 1790-1953. Souvenir Handbook and History* (1953); WYAS, Kirklees N/B/R/4, Rehoboth Chapel Minute Book.

16. Hulbert, *Annals of Slaithwaite*, p.108; Crawshaw and Wilkinson, *Pole Moor*, p.18. Providence Chapel, in Kitchen Fold, is technically in Linthwaite.

17. *New North Road Baptist Church, Huddersfield. Souvenir of the Jubilee* (1928), p.8.

18. Dicks, *Highfield*, pp.4-7; A.W. Sykes, *Ramsden Street Independent Church, Huddersfield. Notes and Records of A Hundred Years, 1825-1925* (Huddersfield, 1925), pp.4-20.

19. 'The Friends' Meeting House at Paddock', *Huddersfield Chronicle*, 28 December 1882; Brotherton Quaker PA/36, Statement of Members in the Brighouse Monthly Meeting, 30 June 1849, 30 June 1850.

20. H. Barnes, *A History of the Dalton Society of the New Church to the Centenary Year, 1925* (1925).

21. *New North Road*, pp.8-9. For the Hall of Science, *see Huddersfield Examiner*, 4 November 1939, 20, 21 March 1946.

22. F. X. Singleton, *A Historical Record of St. Patrick's Church* (Huddersfield, 1932), pp.15-17.

23. There is a useful summary of church building in Kelly's *West Riding of Yorkshire Directory* (1917), pp.446-52; see also Hulbert, *Annals of Almondbury*, pp.269-86, 386-423. The population of Huddersfield increased rapidly between 1871 (70,253) and 1891 (95,417) – see White's *Directory* (1881, 1894).

24. For the rebuilding of the parish church, see P. Ahier, *The Story of the Three Parish Churches of St. Peter the Apostle, Huddersfield. Part 3* (Huddersfield, 1950). Pritchett had earlier been the architect of Ramsden St. Chapel. An apse was added to St Paul's, Queen Street, in 1883 and a tower to St. Mark's, Longwood, in 1914. On the other hand, Lindley Wesleyan acquired a chancel in 1896 and Dalton New Church was remodelled internally in 1891 – see photographs in Barnes, *Dalton New Church*, pp.23, 25 and in A. R. Bielby, *Churches and Chapels of Kirklees* (Huddersfield, 1978), pp.41-48, 92-95.

25. *The Church at Longroyd Bridge*, pp.12-16; Weatherhead, *Holy Trinity*, pp.35-38, 71, 79-82, 84. Although St Thomas's is usually regarded as the first 'high church', John Coates, junior, son of John Coates, Vicar of Huddersfield, had preached in a surplice when curate of Longwood (1822-47) and may be regarded as the first 'high churchman' in the town – see G. Hinchliffe, *A History of King James's Grammar School in Almondbury* (Huddersfield, 1963), p.103.

26. *New North Road*, pp.9-12. The Unitarians had built a new chapel in Fitzwilliam Street.

27. Stock, *Salendine Nook*, pp.47-49; Shaw, *Salendine Nook*, pp.17-30; Crawshaw and Wilkinson, *Pole Moor*, pp.32, 36-38; N. Haigh, *A Short History of the Baptist Church, Scapegoat Hill*, (Huddersfield, 1921), pp.31-39. There was also a small Mission in Leymoor.

28. WYAS, Kirklees KC 34/5, Huddersfield First Circuit Quarterly Schedules, 1845-58; WYAS, Wakefield C 311/15-21, Wesleyan Huddersfield First Circuit/Queen Street/North East Circuit Quarterly Schedules, 1858-1953.

29. WYAS, Kirklees NM/MSC11/9-13, Buxton Road Circuit Quarterly Schedules, 1884-1950.

30. WYAS, Kirklees NM/HSC/12-13, Gledholt Circuit Quarterly Schedules, 1889-1909; [A. Hill], *The Story of Gledholt Circuit, Huddersfield, 1888-1948* (1948). Milnsbridge was attached to the Queen Street Mission between 1918 and 1927.

31. J. W. Walls, 'High Street Circuit', in *United Methodist Church Conference Handbook, 1923* (1923), pp.67-69; WYAS, Kirklees NM/MNC/1-4, Methodist New Connexion Quarterly Meeting Minute Books, 1846-1919; WYAS, Kirklees NM/HSC/VI 2-5,

Lindley Circuit Quarterly Meeting Minute Books, 1876-1915. Golcar Providence transferred to High Street Circuit in 1885 after a dispute with the Lindley Circuit.

32. WYAS, Kirklees KC 34/5, Huddersfield First Circuit Quarterly Schedules, 1853-57; F. Taylor, *The History of Carr Lane Methodist Church, Slaithwaite, 1853-1953. Centenary Brochure* (1953), pp.5-8; J. Feather, *Netherton Methodist Church Centenary, 1867-1967* (1967), pp.7-8.

33. Rose, *Brunswick Street*, pp.31-3, 79-83. The Rashcliffe Mission was conducted in an iron school-chapel from 1878 until a chapel was built in 1904. Brunswick and Hillhouse continued to use the name 'Free Wesleyan' and Lindley 'Wesleyan Reform'.

34. WYAS, Kirklees C311/36, Primitive Methodist Account Book, 1851-1870.

35. There were village Congregational churches in Marsden (1790) and Netherton (1843), but only Crimble had both Baptist (1886) and Congregational (1904) churches.

36. Robert Bruce (1829-1908) – obituary in *Congregational Year Book*, 1909, pp.162-4; Richard Skinner (1806-1885) – obituary in *Congregational Year Book*, 1886, pp.211-13.

37. Sykes, *Ramsden Street*, pp.36-39; WYAS, Kirklees N1/GN/11, Great Northern Street Congregational Chapel, Records Book and WYAS, Kirklees N1/GN/3, Minute Book.

38. Sykes, *Ramsden Street*, pp.37-38; *Hillhouse Congregational Church, Clara Street, Huddersfield. Jubilee Celebration* (1915), pp.3-8; *Congregational Year Book*, 1865, 1867.

39. quoted in Sykes, *Ramsden Street*, pp.46-47.

40. *Congregational Year Book*, 1875, pp.120-4.

41. Sykes, *Ramsden Street*, pp.54-58; Jones is described on pp.99-100.

42. WYAS, Kirklees Ni/M/7, Milton Congregational Church, Minute Book; *The New Independent Church Year Book*, (1881).

43. Singleton, *St. Patrick's*, pp.21, 24, 26, 32.

44. Brotherton Quaker PA 1-3, List of Members and Tabular Statements; Brotherton Quaker EE 3, Minute Book, 13 April 1856.

45. *The Salvation Army. Huddersfield Citadel Centenary, 1883-1983*. Other corps were later opened in Milnsbridge and Lockwood.

46. *The Semi-Jubilee of St. James's, Huddersfield, 1902-27*; *The Official Handbook of the Presbyterian Church of England*, Huddersfield St. James's.

47. WYAS, Kirklees RMT/1, 'History of the Mission known as the Rock now situated at Turnbridge'. The Mission began in Thomas Street, moving to Rosemary Lane in 1879, and the 'Rock' in Lord Street in 1886, before building its own wooden mission chapel in Turnbridge in 1889. It was later attached to the Queen Street Mission.

48. The best-known surviving non-denominational Sunday School is that at Hall Bower – see S. W. Roebuck, *Chapel Folk. The Story of the First 175 years. Hall Bower Sunday School* (1989).

49. R. Bruce, *Huddersfield Sunday School Centenary Memorial* (1880), p.20.

50. Bruce, *Sunday School Centenary*, p.32. The three Church of England Returns in 1880 were:

Sunday School (with date of formation)	numbers on books	av. att. morn.	1879 aft.
Almondbury (1807)	299	192	217
Lindley (1828)	431	na	na
Lockwood (1830)	529	291	388

51. *See*, for example, the efforts made in Slaithwaite with the help of Lord Dartmouth, leading to the building of the Upper Slaithwaite (Shred) (1846) and Lingards (1852) school-chapels – Hulbert, *Annals of Slaithwaite*, pp.177-79, 188-90.

52. Shaw, *Salendine Nook*, p.41. The second service being in the afternoon remains the norm in remoter parts such as Pole Moor and Upper Slaithwaite. The advantages of the afternoon service were that worshippers needed make only one journey if they brought their dinners with them and they could return home before dark; the disadvantage was that Sunday School teachers missed both adult services.

53. *Handbook of the Presbyterian Church*, passim; *The Story of Lindley Zion Methodist Church* edited by J. R. Firth (1947), pp.27, 30-32, 35, 41; Barnes, *Dalton New Church*, pp.30, 35; Sykes, *Ramsden Street*, p.70.

54. *Milton Congregational Church. Programme of Jubilee Celebrations* (1931), p.46; Barnes, *Dalton Society of the New Church*, pp.32-34; Crawshaw and Wilkinson, *Pole Moor*, pp.51, 54.

55. HLHL, Ramsden Street Press Cuttings Book. At its close, membership at Ramsden Street had fallen to 117.

56. WYAS, Kirklees N/B/R/4, Rehoboth Minute Book, 18 March 1970.

57. *Leeds Diocesan Directory* (1980).

58. The Unitarians had moved out to premises in New North Road.

59. Directories give details of places of worship until the 1950s; thereafter one can follow the references in the excellent newspaper index in the HLHL.

CHAPTER 7

'Attentive Soldiers and Good Citizens': Militia, Volunteers and Military Service in the Huddersfield District 1757-1957

JOHN H. RUMSBY

The study of military history is often regarded as 'difficult' field, with its overtones of militarism, and its esoteric jargon of 'militia', 'battalions', 'rifle corps' and so on. Yet reference to military service often occurs in studies of local and family history. The Militia Ballot, for instance, was a significant factor in many lives during the Napoleonic Wars, while some volunteer regiments were raised to combat not foreign invaders, but the 'enemy within', in the tumultuous days of the early nineteenth century. All explorers of family trees will have come across soldier or sailor ancestors, and ex-servicemen have formed a significant part of the local population, veterans of Britain's colonial wars.

The earliest military unit to carry the county name was the West Yorkshire Militia.[1] This force, like other county militias, had a long history, stretching back to Saxon times, but was first established on a proper footing by an Act of Parliament in 1662. It was completely reorganised in 1757, when three militia regiments were established for West Yorkshire. Men from the Huddersfield district seem to have been posted to serve in the 3rd Regiment, under the command of Colonel Earl Fitzwilliam.

The Militia was a professional army, serving full-time during times of war, when it was 'embodied', but was restricted to home defence in Great Britain and Ireland. The officers were career soldiers, drawn from the gentry of the country. The other ranks, unlike those of the regular army (who were volunteers), were recruited by a form of conscription known as the Ballot.

Lists of eligible men were drawn up for each township, and the names, to the number required, were picked by ballot. A man so chosen could arrange for someone to take his place, and in fact the majority of the other ranks in the Militia were substitutes, who were paid a bounty by those whose places they took.

Local archives contain among their civil parish records many 'call-up papers' for men chosen by ballot to serve in the Militia. John Hobson, for example, received a form notifying him that

> you are balloted to serve in the Militia of the United Kingdom, raised within the West Riding of the County of York, and that you are personally to appear at the George Inn, in Huddersfield, at Ten o'clock in the forenoon of Wednesday the Sixth Day of March 1822 . . . to be examined and take the Oath appointed . . . and be enrolled. . . .

The form did, however, point out that he could

> provide a proper person of the same Riding, or of some adjoining Parish or Place, able and fit for service, under 45 Years of Age, and at least 5 Feet and 4 Inches in Height, and who has not more than One Child born in wedlock . . . to serve as your Substitute. . . .[2]

Although both officers and men were drawn from the county, with the Lord Lieutenant acting as Colonel and responsible for recruiting, militia regiments rarely served in their home counties. This was partly due to the need to garrison ports and other strategic towns.[3] It also minimised possible conflicts of loyalty during times of civil disturbance. During the Luddite troubles of 1812-13, for example, the main militia force in the Huddersfield area was the Cumberland Militia. Claims of support for the Luddites from 'local militia' are therefore misleading; any such suppport would be based on common social class rather than local feeling.

In time of peace, the Militia was 'stood down'. The officers and men (except for a small permanent staff) returned to civilian life, except for occasional musters for training. In 1853, however, the Militia was completely reorganised, the ballot being replaced by an entirely voluntary system of recruiting. Three new regiments were added to the existing three West Riding regiments. Of these the 6th West Yorkshire Militia was recruited in the Huddersfield and Halifax districts.[4] In 1881, militia regiments became battalions of their county infantry regiments. Thus the 6th West Yorkshire

Militia (which had expanded into two battalions in 1879) became the 3rd and 4th Battalions the Duke of Wellington's (West Riding) Regiment. In 1890 these were amalgamated as the 3rd Battalion.

Although intended as a home service force, some militia battalions did serve overseas during the crisis of the South African War (1899-1902). The 3rd Duke of Wellington's served in South Africa from March 1900 to May 1902. They were mostly engaged in the safe but unglamorous task of guarding Boer prisoners, but nevertheless lost ten men from disease. During the First World War the Battalion was designated a 'Special Reserve', training and supplying recruits to the active service battalions of the Regiment. At the end of the war, all the old militia battalions were placed in 'suspended animation'. Despite a brief revival of the term for certain forces during the Second World War, the old militia saw no further service, and was finally disbanded in 1953.

The forerunners of the Home Guard of the Second World War were the volunteer regiments of the Napoleonic Wars. These were raised as spontaneous gestures of patriotism against the excesses of the French Revolution and the despotism of Napoleon that followed. The duties they were prepared to undertake varied. The officers of the Upper Agbrigg Local Militia (formed from volunteers, despite its title) volunteered the services of corps 'to do Garrison Duty in any of the Garrison Towns in the County or elsewhere', in order to relieve Regular troops for service overseas.[5] The Huddersfield Armed Association, by contrast, was founded in 1798 specifically 'in order to assist the civil power in case of emergency within the Parish of Kirkburton, but not to be subject to Military Law, nor to act outside the said Parish except on our own accord'.[6]

Like all volunteers, the Huddersfield corps were largely self-financed; they provided their own uniforms, although subscriptions and other fund-raising helped the less wealthy members, and the government provided arms and accoutrements to efficient regiments. The officers of volunteer regiments were generally drawn from the lesser gentry and prominent businessmen and mill-owners. Other ranks were made up of small businessmen and the farming and 'respectable artisan' classes. Volunteer cavalry units (sometimes called Yeomanry) had a higher social standing, since the provision of a horse and more expensive uniform was only possible for wealthier citizens. It can be seen that such men had a vested interest in supporting the established order, and upholding the law against such working-class uprisings as Luddism and Chartism.

The earliest volunteer unit in the Huddersfield district was the Huddersfield Fusilier Volunteers, raised in 1794, with Sir George Armytage of Kirklees Hall as its commanding officer.[7] Like most volunteer corps, they chose their own uniform of red with blue facings, which did, however, correspond in style to the government regiments.[8] Amongst the officers were William Horsfall, shot dead by the Luddites in 1812, and Thomas Atkinson, also a potential target for the Luddites, whose mill at Colne Bridge became notorious when it burned down in 1818, killing seventeen girls and women trapped inside.[9] Within two years of its formation the Fusiliers numbered 300 men, organised in four companies, and in 1796 they volunteered to serve anywhere in the United Kingdom. In 1802, however, when the Peace of Amiens brought a temporary lull in the war with France, the regiment was disbanded.

Other volunteers of this early phase of the war included the Huddersfield Armed Association, formed in 1798 for 'internal security' duties, as we have seen and an off-shoot, the Huddersfield Volunteer Cavalry, commanded by Captain Law Atkinson. This corps had a reputation for poor discipline, caused no doubt by a lengthy dispute over command between Atkinson and another anti-Luddite figure, Joseph Radcliffe of Milnsbridge House, Major Commandant of the Armed Association.[10]

When war with France was renewed in 1803, the volunteer movement was also revived. A Huddersfield Corps of Volunteer Cavalry was formed in 1803, under the command of John Lister Kaye of the well-known landowning family. It consisted of only eighty-eight men, and was disbanded in 1810. More long-lived was the successor to the old Huddersfield Fusiliers, now called the Upper Agbrigg Volunteer Infantry. The uniform was slightly different (red with buff facings), but the commander was again Sir George Armytage.[11] The regiment was exceptionally large, averaging nearly 1,300 men for much of its existence. Although never called upon to fight (although there were occasional false alarms of French invasion), it attended many musters and training camps, and its men earned a high reputation as 'attentive soldiers and good citizens'.[12]

The same could not be said of many of the 240,000 volunteers in the country in 1807. Many corps were below strength, or badly trained and equipped. In 1808 and 1809 therefore, the government created a new force, the Local Militia. Volunteers were encouraged to transfer to this new force,

Fig. 7:1 Sword-belt plate of an officer of the Upper Agbrigg Volunteer Infantry, 1803. (KCS).

and support for the old corps was withdrawn. Any short-fall in recruiting was to be made up by use of the ballot, as in the Militia. Many local historians tend to confuse the (regular) Militia and the Local Militia, but the two forces were distinct, and the use of terms such as 'local Militia' serve only to confuse still further.[13]

In most cases the Local Militia were the direct successors to the volunteers, and this was certainly the case in Huddersfield. The Upper Agbrigg Volunteer Infantry were officially replaced by the 3rd West Riding Local Militia, but the regiment's colours (flags) bore the title 'Upper Agbrigg Local Militia'. A marksmanship medal won by Joseph Jenkinson in 1812 (in the Tolson Memorial Museum) refers to the regiment as the 'Huddersfield Volunteers'. This view of the Local Militia as a continuation of the volunteers is entirely born out by a return of 24 November 1809, which lists 1,182 NCOs and men as enrolled voluntarily, none enrolled by ballot, and forty-one still needed to complete the establishment.[14]

Although only part-time soldiers (with 24 training days each year), Local Militiamen served under full military discipline when assembled. Private John Cock found this out to his cost at York in 1813, when he was found guilty of stealing money from a comrade. He was sentenced to '50 lashes on his bare back at the Head of the Regiment'. Luckily for him, this was commuted to three months in York Castle jail.[15] Another soldier, Lot Lockwood, neglected to attend a training session, and was allowed to join the regular army rather than go to prison.[16] It should be noted that there was no attempt to use the Local Militia against the Luddites in 1812-13. The regiment was disbanded in 1814, when Napoleon's first abdication appeared to dissipate the French menace for ever.

Internal threats to the established order continued, and led in 1817 to the raising of the Huddersfield Yeomanry, with the expressed aim of suppressing 'riot and tumult'. It had its first chance on 8 June 1817 when a patrol of six yeomen under their Commanding Officer, Captain John Armytage (son of Sir George) discovered a mob of about 300 men gathered near Folly Hall Bridge, on the outskirts of Huddersfield. Both sides were probably equally surprised. In what became known as the 'Folly Hall Fight', shots were exchanged, a yeoman's horse was killed, and the patrol retired for reinforcements (or fled, depending on where the narrator's sympathies lay). The mob dispersed, and six alleged leaders were later tried and found not guilty at York Assizes. This appears to be the only occasion before the Boer War when Huddersfield's 'part-time soldiers' actually faced enemy fire.[17]

In 1820 the Yeomanry, now under the command of Captain Thomas Atkinson, was again called out, patrolling the roads around Huddersfield to defeat alleged plots to seize magistrates and march on the town. Atkinson was proud enough of his service to have his portrait painted in uniform by the fashionable artist John Frederick Herring senior.[18] The uniform was modelled on that of the 13th Light Dragoons, with a blue coatee with white facings and gold lace. When the regiment was disbanded in 1828 the ladies of Huddersfield presented Atkinson with a fine sword, which is in the Tolson Memorial Museum.

Fig. 7:2 Volunteer swords 1. Worn by Capt. Lewis Fenton of the Upper Agbrigg Volunteer Infantry, 1803-08

2. Presented to Capt. Thomas Atkinson of the Huddersfield Yeomanry in 1828. (KCS)

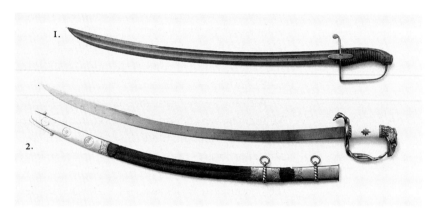

In 1820 an infantry corps was also formed, reviving the old name Huddersfield Armed Association.[19] Its aims were to act in aid of the civil power and for the protection of the town and neighbourhood, although it was unkindly suggested that some members joined to gain exemption from the Militia ballot. Its commanding officer was another former officer of Napoleonic War volunteers, Lewis Fenton. The members of the corps were dressed as riflemen (dark green uniforms with black facings), and seem to have been disbanded by about 1825.

The volunteer corps discussed so far were formed to meet specific threats, and lasted only as long as those threats were apparent. Later volunteer corps grew and changed over a long period of time, reflecting the political and social changes of the Victorian period, and the cataclysmic demands of two world wars in the twentieth century.

The formation of the Morley and Agbrigg Yeomanry Cavalry in 1843, however, must have seemed a routine response to internal threats to law and order. During the 'Hungry Forties' a large proportion of Huddersfield's population were on poor relief, and the Plug riots of 1842 were fresh in mill-owners' memories. The Yeomanry's officers were once again local landowners and gentry, and the other ranks were merchants and professional men. Two troops were raised in Halifax, one in Huddersfield, and from 1844 another in Bradford, giving a total of about 250 men. In June 1844 the title of the corps was changed to the 2nd West York Yeomanry Cavalry (often abbreviated to 2nd WYYC).

The regiment was called out during the Chartist disturbances of 1848, but during the second half of the nineteenth century the civil threat receded. The regiment, like other yeomanry, became as much socially as strategically important, although remaining a smart and efficient corps.[20] Much of this efficiency was probably owed to the presence in it of men who had been on active service with the regular army. The adjutancy, with its duties of internal discipline and administration, was held from 1869 to 1881 by Major Thomas George Johnson. He had worked his way up through the ranks of the 13th Hussars from Private to Captain, and was a veteran of the Charge of the Light Brigade at Balaclava in 1854.[21] Lieutenant Colonel Charles S. Greenwood, who commanded the 2nd WYYC from 1891 to 1894, had served as an officer of the 10th Hussars in the Second Afghan War (1878-80) and in the Egyptian campaigns of the 1880s. He received a medal from the Royal Humane Society for saving one of his men from the Kabul River in 1879, and lived until 1941.[22]

With no Luddites to hunt, and no danger of another Peterloo Massacre, service in the Yeomanry came to be seen as a gesture of patriotism, as well as providing healthy pursuits such as riding, target-shooting and camping. Annual camps, parades, attendance at local events and marksmanship competitions were all congenial elements of the life of a yeoman. More generous allowances from the government also meant that a broader social cross-section of citizenry could now serve.

However, the government decreed in 1893 that there were too many yeomanry regiments in the West Riding, and that the 2nd West York Yeomanry Cavalry was therefore to be disbanded; this took place in 1894. To help compensate for this, the Yorkshire Dragoons, based at Doncaster, raised an extra squadron ('D' Squadron) consisting of men from Huddersfield, Halifax and Bradford who had served in the 2nd WYYC. Thus the Yorkshire

Fig. 7:3 Daniel Albert Royston of the 2nd West York Yeomanry Cavalry, photographed in the yard of the family firm of Kenworthy Royston, Dale Street, in the 1880s. (KCS)

Dragoons came to be regarded as Huddersfield's own cavalry regiment, and many men from the town served with the regiment in the First and Second World Wars. After various amalgamations the Yorkshire Dragoons was reduced to a 'cadre' in 1967.[23] In 1983 a plaque commemorating the services of the Yorkshire Dragoons was placed in Huddersfield Town Hall.

The infantry equivalents of the yeomanry were the Rifle Volunteers. The rifle volunteer movement had its origins in the 1850s, when the demands on the regular army made by the Crimean War (1854-56) and the Indian Mutiny (1857-58) almost denuded the country of defenders. Fears that French expansionism threatened an invasion of Britain led to a popular clamour for the formation of a voluntary army that could support the regular forces in the field or in fortresses in the event of invasion. Reluctant government approval was finally given in 1859, and by May of that year 134,000 volunteers had responded. The numbers continued to grow until by 1861 the volunteers actually outnumbered the regular army.

Most of the volunteers were drilled as 'riflemen': that is, they were trained to fight in skirmishing order and guerilla warfare, taking advantage of any cover and exploiting good marksmanship. Uniforms were usually 'rifle green' (actually black) or various shades of grey, to camouflage the wearer when harassing the enemy. Some districts also raised artillery, engineers, 'light horse' and ambulance corps, so that, with the yeomanry, a complete force of all arms was formed.

As with their Napoleonic forebears, the rifle volunteers at first had to pay for their own uniforms and equipment, and for 75 per cent of the cost of their rifles. Public subscriptions and fund-raising events supplemented the volunteers' own funds, and later government allowances were more generous. It is probably due to this financial assistance that a larger proportion of these later volunteers were working class (up to 75 per cent in the larger cities).[24]

The first interest shown in Huddersfield towards the new movement seems to have been a proposal by various gentlemen in the early summer of 1859 to form a 'Rifle Club or Corps'. Nothing came of this, but on 9 June 1859 a public meeting took place in the Gymnasium in Ramsden Street, to consider the formation of a volunteer rifle corps. This was by no means a gentlemanly meeting of like minds. The chairman set the tone in his opening speech by remarking that 'to expect anything like unanimity in Huddersfield would be a hopeless affair'. Feelings ran high, with the proposition being strongly opposed by Joseph Woodhead, the Liberal politician and editor of the *Huddersfield Examiner*. Several shows of hands were indecisive, scuffles broke out and furniture was damaged, and the meeting broke up in disorder. The chairman remarked prophetically that the scheme 'will be carried, whether it is carried here or not'.[25] Another 'meeting of gentlemen' followed on 22 June, and here it was resolved to form a 'Huddersfield Rifle Club'. The term 'club' was quickly changed to 'corps', and it was from this date that the Huddersfield Rifle Volunteers can claim their formation.

At first the corps was designated the 10th West York Rifle Volunteers, but in July 1860 it was renumbered as the 6th. The first roll contains seventy names.[26] The officers were Captain Henry Frederick Beaumont of Whitley Beaumont Hall, Lieutenant Joseph Batley junior, a solicitor, Ensign Joseph Acheson Harrison, a merchant, and Honorary Surgeon Thomas A. Bottomley. The first drill instructor, paid for by the corps, was Sergeant

*Fig. 7:4 Riding School, or
Armoury, Ramsden Street.*

Fig. 7:5 Cross-belt plate of an officer of the 6th (Huddersfield) West Yorkshire Rifle Volunteer Corps, 1859-1874.

Horatio France, a former non-commissioned officer in the 34th Regiment of Foot. Annual subscriptions by members and honorary members, together with public subscriptions, helped to pay for uniforms, equipment and other necessities. An early requirement was a drill hall. After some difficulties, and various changes of venue, the 'Riding School' in Ramsden Street was obtained in 1863. This building remained the regiment's home until the St. Paul's Drill Hall was erected in 1901. The St. Paul's Hall continued to be used by the Territorial Army, descendants of the rifle volunteers.

A meeting was held at the George Hotel on 5 September 1859 to decide the essential matter of a uniform. Considerable interest was aroused by Mr J.C. Laycock, a former member of the Huddersfield Armed Association of 1820, who had brought with him part of his old uniform. This was modelled by Mr John Freeman, but the smart appearance of the bottle-green jacket, green epaulettes, crimson sash and tall black cap was somewhat marred by the contrast with Mr Freeman's own black and white check trousers. Despite this display of sartorial elegance, the uniform adopted was a smart and workmanlike black tunic trimmed with black braid, black cap and trousers, and patent leather accoutrements.[27] Although rifle regiments traditionally did not carry colours (flags which acted as rallying points in battle), since they could not be properly protected whilst skirmishing, it is interesting to note that in 1868 a committee representing the ladies of Huddersfield presented a pair of colours to the corps.

Initially each rifle volunteer company was entirely independent, with its own uniform, equipment and training. As companies were raised, they were numbered consecutively in the county. Thus the third company raised in Huddersfield was actually designated the 27th West Yorkshire, and the company raised in Holmfirth was the 32nd West Yorkshire. This could cause confusion, then as now, and did not help military effectiveness. Therefore in 1862 the volunteer companies were grouped into 'administrative battalions', with an overall command structure. The 5th Administrative Battalion, WYRV was formed from the 6th (Huddersfield) Corps (consisting of four companies), and the 32nd (Holmfirth) Corps. In 1864 the 41st (Mirfield) Corps was raised, and immediately joined the 5th Battalion. The 44th (Meltham) Corps, raised in 1868, also joined the Battalion, but was disbanded in 1876. In 1877 the 34th (Saddleworth) Corps, which from its formation in 1860 had stubbornly maintained its independence, finally joined the Battalion.

Fig. 7:6 Marksmanship medal, awarded to Josiah Thomas of the 6th (Huddersfield) West Yorkshire Rifle Volunteer Corps. 1861. (KCS)

Fig. 7:7 Glengarny cap badge worn by other ranks of the 2nd Volunteer Battalion, Duke of Wellington's (West Riding) Regiment, 1883-1895. (KCS)

The 6th Huddersfield Corps had meanwhile been expanding. The original company of 1859 had been joined by three more in 1860, and another in 1864. In 1867 two more companies were raised, the sixth from Outlane and district, and the seventh from Lindley (mainly from employees of Joseph Sykes and Sons, Joseph Walker and Sons, and Liddell, Bennett and Martin). Finally, in 1868 an eighth company was raised in Lockwood. At this time the strength of the Huddersfield Rifles stood at 732, all ranks. However, the first flush of enthusiasm had worn off, and a decline set in. In 1873, with the muster roll down to 313, the number of companies was reduced to four.

The story of the volunteers during the late nineteenth and early twentieth centuries is one of consolidation, and closer integration with the strategic structure of the regular forces. In 1880 the companies of the 5th Administrative Battalion were consolidated as the 6th West Yorkshire Rifle Volunteer Corps. In 1883 closer links were forged with the regular regiments when volunteer corps became volunteer battalions of their county regiments. The 6th WYRVC therefore became the 2nd Volunteer Battalion, Duke of Wellington's (West Riding) Regiment.[28]

In 1908 came a new, much more far-reaching reorganisation, with the formation of the 'Territorial Force' (from 1922 the 'Territorial Army'). This was designed to be a strategic reserve in the event of a major war.[29] New conditions of service were offered, some units were disbanded and others raised, and volunteer regiments were grouped into brigades and divisions, with their own general command, infantry, cavalry, artillery and support arms. The old 2nd Volunteer Battalion was transformed into the 5th (T.F.) Battalion, Duke of Wellington's, and was joined by a new formation, the 7th Battalion, raised amongst men of the Colne valley, with its headquarters in Milnsbridge.

Until the turn of the century, it had been a peaceful life for the volunteers. Drill, summer camp, concerts, rifle competitions had been the routine in the regiment. Volunteers were undoubtedly respected in the community, and this could have advantages when applying for jobs. The South African War (1899-1902) provided the first opportunity for the 'Saturday Night Soldiers' to prove their patriotism the hard way, by going out to foreign parts to fight the Queen's enemies.

The shortage of regular troops, especially cavalry, during the later stages of the Boer War led the government to authorise the formation of 'service companies', made up from fully-trained members of volunteer regiments. No yeomanry or volunteer corps fought as a complete regiment. Men from the Yorkshire Dragoons formed several independent companies of Imperial Yeomanry, and men from the 2nd Volunteer Battalion fought alongside their regular counterparts in the Duke of Wellington's Regiment.[30] The service of the citizen soldiers was marked by the erection of public monuments in Greenhead Park and in the Drill Hall (later the Civic Hall) in Holmfirth. It is interesting to note that the Greenhead Park memorial also records regular soldiers from Huddersfield who died in the war. This would have been most unusual before the Boer War, and marks a new identification between soldiers and the communities from which they came, an identification for which the participation of the volunteers may have been at least partly responsible.

A much sterner test awaited the Territorials during the First World War (1914-18). The space available here does not permit more than a dry enunciation of battalions raised and the theatres of war in which they served.[31] The dogged courage, lit by flashes of heroism, of the men in the trenches should not distract from a realisation of the awfulness and futility of that conflict. Something of the feeling of the loss to the Huddersfield communities can be experienced by reading the rows of names on war memorials, crosses and plaques in villages up and down the valleys.

The two Huddersfield Territorial battalions, the 5th and 7th Dukes, went to war as part of the 49th (West Riding) Division, although the 5th later transferred to the 62nd Division. Both spent the entire war on the Western Front. In common with most Territorial battalions, the 5th and 7th doubled and then tripled their numbers as the relentless demand for larger armies made itself felt. This expansion was indicated by the designation system 1/5th, 3/5th. The 2/5th and 2/7th joined their comrades on the Western Front, serving in the 62nd Division. The 3/5th and 3/7th remained at home as training establishments, supplying reinforcements to the other battalions.

Early in the war Lord Kitchener realised that the regular and territorial armies combined were not large enough to sustain an extended war against other European powers. He therefore called for the formation of new volunteer forces, the so-called 'Kitchener's Army'. Extra Service Battalions

Fig. 7:8 Badge of Huddersfield District Volunteer Corps, 1914-1918. (KCS)

were raised by each regiment. The Duke of Wellington's raised the 8th, 9th, 10th and 11th Service Battalions, a 12th (Labour) Battalion and a 13th (Garrison) Battalion, and Huddersfield men probably served in all of these. Over-age, under-age and unfit men, and those awaiting enlistment (conscription was introduced in 1916) often served in the little-known Volunteer Training Force, guarding local strategic points and providing military transport using their own vehicles.

The First World War was the first conflict to affect the civilian population directly, and not just through the vast numbers of men and women who served overseas. The shortage of men led to the employment of many women who would not otherwise have left the home, although often they were forced out of their jobs when the war was over. The misery of food, clothing and petrol rationing affected all, although not so equally as was officially claimed at the time. The numerous wounded were cared for by taking over general hospitals and large private houses as War Hospitals, run partly by

Fig. 7:9 Stretcher-bearers of the 2/5th Battalion, Duke of Wellington's (West Riding) Regiment, 1914-1915. (KCS)

army medical teams, but mainly staffed by volunteer female nursing staff. Royds Hall (later a school) was opened in October 1915 as a War Hospital, and by July 1916 had nine auxiliary hospitals attached to it, at Huddersfield Royal Infirmary, Kirkburton Volunteer Aid Detachment (V.A.D.) Hospital, Holmfirth, Shepley, Honley, Meltham, Lightridge House, Boothroyd Hospital and Spring Hall, Halifax.[32]

In 1919 the war-raised battalions were disbanded, and the 5th and 7th Dukes went back to peace-time soldiering. In the 1930s the Territorial Army had to face up to new methods of warfare, with more specialisation to take account of advances in armoured and aerial combat. The 5th Battalion found itself transformed in 1936 into an anti-aircraft (A.A.) searchlight battalion of the Royal Engineers (R.E.), with the long-winded title of 43rd (5th DWR), A.A. Battalion, R.E. (Searchlight). In 1940 they became the 600th Garrison Regiment, Royal Artillery, still in an anti-aircraft role, and despite their designation they served in France in 1944.

Duke of Wellington's West Riding Reg.t

On the approach of the Second World War the 7th Dukes was once again split into the 1/7th and 2/7th. The 1/7th served in Iceland in 1940, and in the hard-fought battles in north-west Europe in 1944-45. The 2/7th, understrength and ill-equipped, played a courageous part in the 'Dunkirk' campaign in France in 1940. After that it changed its role to that of an armoured regiment, in 1942 becoming the 115th Regiment, Royal Armoured Corps.[33] In recognition of the Regiment's services during the war, in 1952 the County Borough of Huddersfield granted it the right to march through the town 'on all ceremonial occasions with bayonets fixed, Colours flying and bands playing', a privilege the Regiment has occasionally exercised.

A postwar reduction of the army in 1957 led to the reversion of the 5th Dukes to its infantry role, and its amalgamation with the 7th Battalion. Since then, further reductions and alterations in role have taken place, but Huddersfield still has its contingent of volunteer soldiers, who can trace their lineage back directly to the rifle volunteers of 1859, and in spirit to the town's defenders against Napoleon.

Life on the 'Home Front' during the Second World War was much more organised than during the Great War. The Local Defence Volunteers with their makeshift weapons quickly developed into the Home Guard, two battalions of which (the 25th and 26th) were raised in the Huddersfield area.[34] Although the target of affectionate ridicule, members of the Home Guard were soon well-trained and equipped, and relieved full-time soldiers for overseas service by guarding potential targets from sabbotage. Occasional incidents worthy of 'Dad's Army' could occur however:

> We were ordered to stop all traffic on a lonely moorland road to look for escaped enemy prisoners. A car was being checked when a weird and very suspicious-looking equipage approached. It was an ancient saloon car with two rough-looking customers inside, full of old junk and with several sacks roped on the roof. The car was signalled to stop and appeared to be doing so when suddenly the driver accelerated and tried to get away. . . . One of my men jumped forward and, running alongside, crashed the butt of his rifle into the side window. This caused a hullabaloo. The driver stopped and threatened us and could only be quietened by the sound of live ammunition entering the chamber of the corporal's rifle. . . . It turned out that these gentlemen were only open-air market men who travel from town to town.[35]

The A.R.P., Fire and other emergency services also played a full part, with many men and women serving in them after doing a very full day's work in mill or factory. Huddersfield's textile, chemical and engineering industries were of vital importance to the country's war effort, and it is fortunate that the town had to sustain comparatively little bombing. For example, David Brown's made gears for Spitfires and tanks, Thomas Broadbent's made midget submarines, and W.C. Holmes and Co. made munitions, prefabricated decks for frigates and parts for Churchill tanks.[36]

Finally, a word should be said about the many servicemen and women who went from the Huddersfield district to serve all over the world, in the many wars, just and unjust, fought by Britain and its empire over the last two hundred years. Such veterans have formed a significant proportion of the population since the end of the Napoleonic Wars and include people who served in Queen Victoria's 'small wars' of empire-building days, as well as the 'civilian' servicemen and women of two world wars. The immigrant communities of Asian and Afro-Caribbean origin include veterans who fought for Britain against fascism and Japanese imperialism, as do the Polish and other central European groups, whose members ironically could not return to their own countries after the overthrow of fascism, due to the takeover by other totalitarian regimes.

The conventional picture of the attitude towards soldiers in nineteenth century Britain is that they were despised as the 'scum of the earth'; their victories were rejoiced over, but the veteran was consigned to the gutter. There is, however, much evidence from the Huddersfield area that veterans were regarded with interest and affection, and occasionally were afforded some local fame.[37] In the middle of the century it was thought noteworthy to record the services of veterans who died in the parish of Kirkheaton. Thus we know of John Fitton, a weaver, 'late a private in H.M. 51st Regiment, Rowley, Lepton, aged 66 years'. Other sources tell us that in 1848 Fitton was awarded a medal for services in the Peninsular War, including his participation in seven pitched battles. Stephen Cliff, also a weaver, who lived at Hole Bottom, Kirkheaton, and died in 1856 aged sixty, had fought with the 1st Life Guards at the Battles of Toulouse and Waterloo, at the latter of which he was wounded and twice had his horse shot from under him.[38]

When Benjamin Smith, a weaver of Kirkburton, died in 1845, an elaborate gravestone was erected in the parish churchyard; it was carved with a representation of the medal he had been awarded for serving at Waterloo with the Royal Artillery in 1815. Smith was born in 1793, the year the Great War with France started, enlisted in 1812, and was discharged in 1819. No doubt he was a respected 'character' in the village, wearing his medal on special occasions.[39]

News from 'our lads' overseas was eagerly sought, and letters sent home were proudly submitted by families to local newspapers. The *Huddersfield Examiner*, for example, printed a series of letters in 1854-56 from soldiers serving in the Crimea.

When the celebrations were being planned for Queen Victoria's Diamond Jubilee in 1897, a local solicitor and volunteer officer, Robert Welsh, had the idea of including in the parade local veterans of the Crimean War and Indian Mutiny. Nearly forty such veterans took part in the parade, and there survives a photograph of them, wearing their medals and sashes, taken at the Cloth Hall.[40]

Welsh was shocked by the poor circumstances of many of these men. Most were still working, although none was under sixty and the oldest was seventy-five. Many were broken down in health after up to twenty-one years' service in unhealthy climates. Welsh and several other businessmen of the town set out to form a society 'to recognise and keep from being forgotten all veteran soldiers who have been in active service for their country'. The archives of this society, the Huddersfield and District Army Veterans' Association (HDAVA) contain fascinating details about the Association's activities, and about the men it served.[41] Members were helped with advice about obtaining increased pensions, work was obtained through acquaintances of the committee, and fuel, clothing and other items (such as spectacles, donated by a local oculist) were distributed. A team of doctors gave their services free. Social life was not forgotten, with a round of socials, parades, concerts and outings.

A study of the HDAVA archives gives a glimpse of the lot of the veteran at the turn of the century. In the 1900s an average of ten out of the forty members were workhouse residents. This was not necessarily too terrible, if the obituary of one inmate (probably written by Welsh) can be believed: Zachariah Schofield, a veteran of campaigns in Afghanistan and Burma, had been in the Crosland Moor Workhouse for five years 'where he was perfectly happy, and was held in esteem by the officials'.

Many veterans in Huddersfield, as elsewhere, joined the police, where the uniform, comradeship and authority would appeal to them after their army service, and where soldierly qualities would be an advantage. Thomas Galvin, once a private soldier in the 83rd Regiment during the Indian Mutiny, rose to be a 'highly esteemed' inspector in the Borough Police. The struggle for survival which some older veterans had to face is illustrated by John Cunningham, a Crimean War Sapper, who, after a period of unemployment, obtained a place as watchman with the Corporation Tramways. Deteriorating eyesight probably forced him to give up this post in 1901, and the Association purchased a pedlar's licence for him (at the age of sixty-four). However, he died only a year later.

John Ford, a Mutiny veteran, had an even greater struggle. He came to Huddersfield in 1871 (his birthplace was in Sussex), and for twenty years was Armoury attendant to the Volunteers, for which he received one pound per week. Since he had a wife and seven children, this did not go far, even with his army pension of one shilling and fourpence per day. He also did evening work at the Theatre Royal, and his wife took in lodgers. The HDAVA committee was asked to consider his case as, at the age of *seventy-nine*, he was likely to have to give up his evening work! He was described as a 'proud old fellow who never was behind with his rent . . . and never received parish relief'. He died in 1911 and was buried in Edgerton Cemetery.

Such examples could be multiplied many times. These veterans were part of the fabric of local society, and often became well-remembered characters. The present author has spoken to people who still remember Thomas Settle, a Crimean veteran nursed by Florence Nightingale, who ended his days in Holmfirth.

Britain has never been regarded, despite its imperial past, as a militaristic nation on the Prussian model. Nevertheless, locally-raised regiments of militia and volunteers, and the presence in the community of considerable numbers of veteran servicemen and women, call for a study of military institutions if a full historical picture of local society is to be produced.

Table 1: Summary of Militia and Volunteer Corps drawing recruits from the Huddersfield District

Title	Raised	Disbanded	Other Titles	Uniform	Remarks
MILITIA INFANTRY					
1st, 2nd, 3rd West York Militia	1757	Stood down 1814		Scarlet jackets	Recruiting by ballot (conscription)
6th West York Militia	1853	'suspended animation' 1919; disbanded 1953	1879 became two battalions; 1881 3rd & 4th battalions D. of W. (W.R.) Regt.; 1890 amalgamated as 3rd Battalion D. of W. (W.R.) Regt.; 1908-1919 Special Reserve	Scarlet, sky-blue facings	Recruiting by voluntary enlistment
VOLUNTEER CAVALRY					
Huddersfield Volunteer Cavalry	1798	1802		Scarlet hussar jacket, silver lace, white breeches, light dragoon helmet	Operated as a cavalry troop of the Huddersfield Armed Association (q.v.)
Huddersfield Corps of Volunteer Cavalry ('Major Kaye's Regiment')	1803	1810	West Yorkshire Volunteer Cavalry; West Yorkshire Yeomanry Cavalry	not known	
Huddersfield Yeomanry	1817	1828		Blue jacket, white/buff facings, gold lace	
2nd West York Yeomanry Cavalry	1843	1894	1843-44: Morley and Agbrigg Yeomanry	Dark blue jacket, white facings, light dragoon shako, replaced by helmet 1853	On disbandment, some men transferred to Yorkshire Dragoons, as D Squadron
VOLUNTEER INFANTRY					
Huddersfield Fusilier Volunteers	1794	1802	1798: Huddersfield Volunteer Corps, or Royal Huddersfield Fusilier Volunteer Corps	Red jacket, blue facings, white breeches, cocked hat	
Huddersfield Armed Association	1798	1802		Blue jacket, scarlet facings, white pantaloons, round hat	Two companies of infantry, with a troop of cavalry (q.v.)
Upper Agbrigg Volunteer Infantry	1803	1808		Red jacket, yellow/buff facings, white breeches, stove-pipe cap	Re-mustered as Upper Agbrigg Local Militia (q.v.)
Upper Agbrigg Local Militia (3rd West Riding Local Militia)	1808	1814	Huddersfield Volunteers	Similar to Upper Agbrigg Volunteer Infantry	
Huddersfield Armed Association	1820	c.1825	Huddersfield Independent Association; Huddersfield Infantry; Huddersfield Riflemen (1825)	Bottle green jacket, black facings, green epaulettes, stove-pipe cap	
10th West York Rifle Volunteer Corps; 27th WYRVC	1859 1859		1860: 6th WYRVC 1862: 5th Administrative Bn. WYRV 1880: 6th West Yorks. RVC 1883: 2nd Vol. Bn. D. of W. (W.R.) Regt. 1908: 5th (TF) Bn. D. of W. (W.R.) Regt. 1936: 43rd (5th DWR) AA Bn. RE (Searchlight) 1940: 600th Garrison Regt. RA 1947: 578th (5/DWR) Heavy AA Regt. RA (TA) 1957: Amalgamated with 7th Bn. as 5th/7th Bn. DWR (TA)	1859: rifle green (black), black facings, forage cap; 1863: dark green, scarlet facings, shako 1874: scarlet jacket; from c.1880 uniform corresponded to regular army with variations in insignia	2/5th and 3/5th Bns. raised during first World War Reverted to infantry role
7th (Territorial Force) Battalion, Duke of Wellington's (West Riding) Regiment	1908		1957: amalgamated with 5th Bn. as 5th/7th Bn. DWR (TA)		Raised in Colne Valley. 2/7th 3/7th Bns. raised during first World War 2/7th raised during Second World War; became 115 Regt. RAC 1942
25th and 26th Bn. (Huddersfield) Home Guard	1940	1944			Home Guard re-raised with differing organisation, 1950-53

Glossary of Military Terms

Battalion   The usual Infantry tactical/administrative unit. A *regiment* might consist of one or more battalions. A battalion was usually between 500 and 1,000 men strong.

Cavalry   Soldiers who travel and fight on horseback.

Colours   The flags of a corps. Their original function was to act as a rallying point on the battlefield. They embodied the honour of the corps. British regiments usually carried two: the Royal (King's or Queen's) Colour had a design based on the Union flag, and the Regimental Colour, bearing regimental titles, badges and battle honours.

Company   A sub-division of a battalion, or occasionally an independent corps (as in the early days of the rifle volunteers). Usually about fifty to 100 men.

Corps   A vague term for an independent unit of soldiers.

Facing   Collars, cuffs and other trimmings of a contrasting colour or texture to the body of the coat

Yeomanry   Volunteer cavalry.

John H. Rumsby

Biographical Note

> After working in a regimental museum in Durham, and as Keeper of
> Archaeology with Hull Museums, John Rumsby joined Kirklees Museums
> Service in 1981 as Curator of the Tolson Memorial Museum, Huddersfield.
> Here he has been mainly concerned with the shaping of the collections and
> the modernisation of the displays and other services so that the Museum will
> serve as a centre for the study of the district's natural and human history
> through its material remains. His personal interests include military history,
> numismatics, architecture and ceramics.

NOTES

1. For a general account *see:* G.J. Hay, *An Epitomized History of the Militia (The
   'Constitutional Force')* (1908; reprint, Newport, Gwent, 1987)

2. W(est) Y(orkshire) A(rchive) S(ervice), Kirklees KC312/8/9. J.R. Western, *The English
   Militia in the Eighteenth Century: the Story of a Political Issue 1600-1802* (1965), pp.245-264
   gives an account of how the ballot worked.

3. See, for example the travels of Private David Greenwood of the 3rd West Yorkshire
   Militia: I. Dewhirst, 'The northward march of a West York Militiaman during the
   Napoleonic Wars' *Old West Riding* 1(2) (1981) 19, 29.

4. N. Moore, *Records of the 3rd Battalion The Duke of Wellington's (West Riding) Regiment,
   formerly 6th West York Militia . . . 1760-1910;* K.D. Pickup, 'Some badges of the Sixth
   West York Militia 1853-1881' *Bulletin of the Military Historical Society* XXV (97) (1974)
   23-25.

5. WYAS, Calderdale KMA 1552/1. Letter of 26 November 1813.

6. WYAS, Kirklees KC 271/55.

7. For this and other volunteer infantry corps see R.P. Berry, *A History of the Formation and
   Development of the Volunteer Infantry . . . illustrated by the local records of Huddersfield and its
   vicinity from 1794 to 1874* (Huddersfield, 1903), a detailed history quoting many original
   documents, and giving biographical details of officers of the various corps.
   (D.F.E. Sykes did much of the research for this book. Editor).

8. See Berry, *Volunteer Infantry* plates opposite p.70 for the uniform, and p.311 for the
   Colours. These colours were sold off with the other contents of Kirklees Hall in 1987.

9. There is a monument to the victims of the fire in Kirkheaton churchyard.

10. For this and other volunteer cavalry corps see R.P. Berry and B.F.M. Freeman, *History of
    the old Second West York Yeomanry Cavalry 1843-1894 . . .* (Huddersfield, 1905).

11. Muster rolls for the regiment 1803-1808 are held at the P(ublic) R(ecord) O(ffice), Kew, WO.13.4605 The collections of the Tolson Memorial Museum, Huddersfield, include a belt plate of the regiment and the sword of Lewis Fenton, commissioned captain in 1803, and elected in 1832 as Huddersfield's first Member of Parliament.

12. Berry, *Volunteer Infantry* p.354.

13. A useful summary of the formation of the Local Militia is given in R. Glover, *Britain at Bay: Defence against Bonaparte 1803-14* (1973), pp.143-146.

14. WYAS, Calderdale KMA 1551. KMA 1551 and 1552 include a large collection of documents relating to the Upper Agbrigg Local Militia.

15. WYAS, Calderdale KMA 1552/2 (31 May 1813).

16. WYAS, Calderdale KMA 1552/2 (22 June 1813).

17. Berry & Freeman, *History of the Old Second W.Y. Yeomanry Cavalry.*

18. Reproduced in colour in R.G. Harris, 'An Officer of the Huddersfield Troop of Yeomanry Cavalry 1822' J(ournal of the) S(ociety for) A(rmy) H(istorical) R(esearch) LX (241) (1982) 1-3.

19. Berry, *Volunteer Infantry*, pp.375-381.

20. *See* the painting of 1849 reproduced in W.Y. Carman, '2nd West Yorkshire *(sic)* Yeomanry Cavalry, 1849' *JSAHR* LXIII (256) (1985) 191-193, and also W.Y. Carman, *Some English Yeomanry Sabretaches* (MHS Special Number 1988). The collection at the Tolson Memorial Museum includes a drum banner, helmet and other relics of the regiment.

21. WYAS, Calderdale HAS/B:10/4; W.M. Lummis and H.G. Wynn, *Honour the Light Brigade* (1973), p.177.

22. J.M.A. Tamplin, 'M.B.E. - late in life' J(ournal of the) O(rders and) M(edals) R(esearch) S(ociety) 28 (204) (1989), 177.

23. Col. Hanwell, *A Short Record of the Queen's Own Yorkshire Dragoons 1794-1954* (Doncaster, 1954); L. Barlow and R.J. Smith, *The Uniforms of the British Yeomanry Force 1794-1914: No. 7 The Yorkshire Dragoons* (1984); T.G. Manby, *The Doncaster Yeomanry* (Doncaster, 1972). There are photographs, medals and other relics of the Regiment in the Tolson Memorial Museum, including the uniform of George Cowley, who served both on horseback and later in mechanised transport during the Second World War.

24. For a general account of the rifle volunteers see E. Cousins, *The Defenders* (1968). Huddersfield and district volunteers are dealt with in Berry, *Volunteer Infantry*. Berry drew on the copious correspondence and other documents in the Ramsden archives now held in WYAS, Kirklees. Local units are listed, with an emphasis on uniform and badges, in D. Pickup *West Yorkshire Rifle Volunteers 1859-1887* (Leicester, 1977).

25. A full description of this entertaining meeting is given in Berry, *Volunteer Infantry*, pp.384-389.

26. Printed in Berry, *Volunteer Infantry*, p.392.

27. Berry, *Volunteer Infantry*, plate opposite p.403. It should be noted, however, that there is in the Tolson Museum collection a hand-coloured photograph of Pte. Benjamin Hutchinson of the 1st Company, taken in 1860, which shows him wearing a *grey* uniform. The uniform was changed in 1863: see plate opposite p.454. The Tolson Memorial Museum collections include many badges and other items relating to the Huddersfield companies, as well as the 32nd (Holmfirth) and 34th (Saddleworth) corps.

28. The string of abbreviations 'E.COMPY. 2nd V.B.DWW.R.REGT.' on the old Drill Hall at Holmfirth (now part of the Civic Hall) thus becomes comprehensible as 'E Company, 2nd Volunteer Battalion, Duke of Wellington's West Riding Regiment.'

29. A.V. Sellwood, *The Saturday Night Soldiers* (1974)

30. A photograph of South African War volunteers from Holmfirth is printed in the *Huddersfield Examiner*, 12 August 1976, p.4.

31. For the services of the Territorial and Service battalions during the First World War, *see* J.J. Fisher, *History of the Duke of Wellington's West Riding Regiment during the First Three Years of the Great War from August 1914 to December 1917* (Halifax, 1917); L. Magnus, *The West Riding Territorials in the Great War* (1920); E. Wyrall, *The History of the 62nd (West Riding) Division 1914-1919* (2 vols. 1924).

32. John H. Rumsby, 'The Huddersfield War Hospital in the First World War' *JOMRS* 27 (201) (1988) 241-243.

33. C.N. Barclay, *The History of the Duke of Wellington's Regiment 1919-1952* (1953).

34. The story of the West Yorkshire Home Guard is the subject of research by Paul Laycock of Huddersfield.

35. C. Graves, *The Home Guard of Britain* (1943), p.360-361 (26th Battalion).

36. The experience of war for some Kirklees people is chronicled in *Words on War* by Helga Hughes, (Huddersfield, 1991) based on memories recorded by the Kirklees Museums Sound Archive.

37. See, for example, the chapter devoted to James Grime in L.B. Whitehead, *Bygone Marsden* (Manchester, 1942), pp.131-133.

38. I am indebted to Mrs Carol Ronayne of, appropriately, Waterloo, Huddersfield, for drawing to my attention these entries in the Burial Registers of Kirkheaton. Between 1850 and 1866 thirteen veterans are recorded, including Edmund Berry, who died of wounds received in the Crimea, aged twenty-one.

39. The gravestone is illustrated in the *Huddersfield Examiner*, 18 June 1936. Smith's service records are in the PRO, Kew, WO.97.1262. The Kirklees Museums collections contain several medals of local veterans, such as Absolem Bradley, who fought at the Battle of Gwalior (India) in 1843, and Sidney Herbert Drake, who served in South Africa in 1851-53.

40. John H. Rumsby, 'Crimea and Indian Mutiny Veterans in Huddersfield' *JOMRS* 23 (183) (1984) 118-122, where the photograph is reproduced and the men's names and services are listed.

41. I am most grateful to the officers of the HDAVA for granting extended access to their archives. See also John H. Rumsby and R. Wade, 'Veterans Remembered' *Huddersfield Examiner,* 17 September 1987. The HDAVA was by no means unique. There was a veterans' association in Rochdale in the 1850s, the Balaclava Commemorative Society was formed in London in 1877, and there were others in Sheffield (before 1897), King's Lynn and Manchester by 1906, and Nottingham in 1911. After the Boer War a Huddersfield South African Veterans' Association was formed. National societies such as the Royal British Legion came later.

CHAPTER 8

The Origins of the Co-operative Movement in Huddersfield: the Life and Times of the 1st Huddersfield Co-operative Trading Association

ROBIN THORNES

"They helped everyone his neighbour; and everyone said to his brother, be of good courage." (Isaiah XLI, v.6)

The origins of the co-operative movement are traceable to the publications of Robert Owen in the second decade of the nineteenth century. Owen argued that the pursuit of wealth by individuals in the competitive society would not result in 'the greatest happiness of the greatest number', but in conflict and misery. He thought it an indictment of the present state of society that 'in the midst of the most ample means to create wealth, all are in poverty, or in imminent danger from the effect of poverty upon others'.[1] The abolition of competition could be brought about, he became convinced, by the establishment of communities, or, as he termed them, villages of 'unity and mutual Co-operation'.[2] In these the inhabitants would receive, by direct exchange, the full value of their labour. Owen first advocated his Villages of Co-operation as a way of dealing with unemployment and pauperism, but gradually came to see them as the key to the creation of more rational and equitable society. As interest in Owen's ideas grew apace it became increasingly obvious that the financial backing would not, as he had hoped, be forthcoming from either the state or wealthy philanthropists.

From 1824 to 1829 Owen was to spend much of his time outside the country, devoting himself to a communitarian experiment at New Harmony, Indiana. In his absence groups of Co-operators, drawn largely from working class, began to work towards creating communities in England. These Co-operators, however, found it difficult to raise the money necessary to found communities. By the spring of 1827 the movement seemed to have reached an impasse. At this point William Bryan, a Brighton Co-operator, wrote to the *Co-operative Magazine* suggesting that they should do all their own retailing, the profits of which would be accumulated, and used to finance communities.[3] Co-operative retailing did, indeed, appear to offer a way ahead. Stores were soon established in London and Brighton. By the end of the following year the number of societies known to the Brighton based journal, *The Co-operator* had risen to nine. It was in 1829, however, that the movement began to attract a larger degree of support, no less than one hundred and thirty societies having been established by the end of that year.

The first Huddersfield Co-operators

Between 1827 and 1832 some thirty-eight co-operative societies are known to have been established in West Yorkshire, making the area one of the movement's principal strongholds. The most important and influential of these societies was, without question, the 1st Huddersfield Co-operative Trading Association, founded in April 1829. The society's first President was Amos Cowgill, a local labour leader who had come to prominence as President of the Fancy Weavers' Union (founded at Kirkheaton in September 1824). From the outset, the society worked to encourage the spread of Co-operation, employing a full time lecturer at a wage of 18s. weekly.[4] Eighteen months after its establishment, the *Birmingham Co-operative Herald* reported of the Huddersfield society: 'it has been in existence little more than twelve months, and although it commenced trading at the outset with the insignificant sum of nineteen shillings, its trading capital now amounts to SEVEN HUNDRED POUNDS!!!'[5]

By 1830 the society was weaving woollen cloth for sale in its shop, in Westgate. The Co-operators of Huddersfield found, though, that it was one thing to make goods and another to be able to sell them. The Halifax Co-operators, faced with the same problem, suggested that the societies should agree to take each others goods.

> I am happy to inform the various societies that if they will take and wear our merinoes, for gowns and frocks for their wives and children; and our

lastings . . . we will engage to wear their linens . . . calicoes, for various uses, woollen cloths for coats, waistcoats and trousers.[6]

The Huddersfield society decided to seek customers for its wares by employing one of its members, David Green, who was supplied with a pattern book which he was to take to those parts of the country 'where he may think likely to get sales'.[7] The society also established a clothing club, which it was felt might 'be of great use in disposing of co-operative produce and thereby finding employment for our brother co-operators'.[8]

The Huddersfield Co-operators, in common with others in the industrial areas of the north of England, were more concerned to press for an expansion of the co-operative manufacturing of goods, than to work for the establishment of a community. At the London Congress in 1832, the Co-operators of Rochdale urged

the utility of bringing the following subjects before the Congress — first the establishment of a Co-operative woollen manufactory. As the Huddersfield cloth, Halifax and Bradford stuffs, Leicester and Loughborough stockings, Rochdale flannels etc. etc. require in several respects similar machinery and processes of manufactures, might not these societies be brought to work together, on Co-operative principles, and procure mutual advantages not attainable by separate establishments.[9]

The fact that the Huddersfield society wrote to Congress on the subject suggests that there may well have been a degree of collusion with the Rochdale Co-operators. This letter recommended that

some one manufactory upon a large scale should as soon as possible be got into operation, that each society might have the produce thereof at prime cost, and in order that this may be carried into immediate execution, it would only require a certain sum of money from each society according to its members.[10]

Thomas Hirst, representing Huddersfield at the Congress, underlined the importance of co-operative manufacturing by displaying a selection of manufactured goods. These included cutlery, Britannia metal teapots and, most importantly, textiles:

> I have on my back . . ., a Co-operative shirt, and here's a Co-operative coat, and here's a Co-operative waistcoat (loud laughter). All my friends have Co-operative clothes; and for my own part, I would sooner go without clothes at all, than be clothed in any other way, so strong an advocate am I for Co-operation.[11]

Hirst's attitude to the idea of establishing an Owenite community was, in contrast, somewhat lukewarm. He voiced the fears and reservations of many Co-operators when he 'earnestly beseeched them, not to allow themselves to be carried away by wrong calculations', and went on to stress that 'they should not attempt a community without a certainty of success'.[12] That is not to say that Hirst and his fellow Huddersfield Co-operators were opposed to the idea of community *per se,* quite the contrary. Hirst himself in one lecture exhorted his audience 'to keep your eyes fixed upon the ground plan of Community as a second Canaan'.[13] Where he and his fellow Yorkshire Co-operators differed from Owen was in their definition of community. For Owen, and his closest followers, Co-operation meant self-supporting colonies planted in rural environments, at some distance from the nearest centre of population. In these communities the Co-operators would live in specially designed buildings. The communities would be, in essence, a microcosm of a new society, and would need, therefore, to remain distant from the world they sought to change by their example. This Owenite view of community seems to have been regarded by the northern Co-operators as neither practical nor desirable. The vision of these men and women was one in which their existing communities were transformed into Co-operative ones. For many it was in the opportunities offered for collective self-employment, and the gaining of the full value of their labour, that the principal attraction of Co-operation lay. These ends, they believed, could be achieved without creating model communities of the type advocated by Owen. The Cumberworth society, for instance, hoped to see 'a manufacturing community rise up amongst us, as we should have no doubts of its success'.[14]

They did not, on the other hand, 'have such good hopes of an agricultural community succeeding amongst the manufacturing population'.[15] Neither did they see the necessity of Co-operators engaging in agriculture when they would always be able to 'command the produce of the land in any market by their manufactured goods'.[16]

That is not to say that these Co-operators, or at least a proportion of them, were not interested in a fundamental tranformation of society. Thomas Hirst reported to the *Lancashire and Yorkshire Co-operator* that one society in the Huddersfield area had gone so far as to drop many of the old formalities, in favour of a more homely and familiar approach. At a tea party held by this society he noted that

> the company consisted of men and women, and almost every woman had a bairn (child) on her lap. There was none of the old custom of "Mr President", but all appeared to be brothers of one family.[17]

Spreading the word

The wish to encourage the spread of Co-operation, while at the same time attempting to ensure that new societies worked with a common sense of purpose, resulted in the movement resolving to establish an organised network of Co-operative lecturers. Thomas Hirst, speaking at the Birmingham Congress in October 1831, described the qualities he felt these lecturers should possess. They should, he believed, be men

> who had already, as it were, like good soldiers, fought to their knees in blood against the objections and opposition, arising from the prejudices and ignorance of the members of their own societies. Men were wanted who could tell the different societies how to overcome their difficulties, who could give a practical lecture as well as a theoretical one.[18]

The London Congress, in 1832, agreed to divide the country up into districts for, among other purposes, the supplying and funding of lecturers, or "Co-operative Missionaries" as they came to be known. The Co-operative stronghold of Pennine West Yorkshire was included in the North West District, centred on Manchester. Within this district were defined a number of sub-districts, one of which comprised the towns of Bradford, Halifax and Huddersfield.

Of all the Co-operative Missionaries active in the district, Thomas Hirst was, without doubt, the most tireless. Hirst devoted himself to spreading the gospel of Co-operation with a single-mindedness that would, within two years, cost him his life. He travelled throughout Yorkshire and the surrounding counties, often on foot, lecturing and advising on Co-operation.

At the Birmingham congress he described how he, and other members of his society 'went nine or ten miles to lecture in the evenings and walked back again afterwards, sometimes not reaching home till morning'.[19] His style of oratory was characterised as 'peculiar yet animating', and the forcefulness with which he argued was described as being capable of creating an 'extraordinary sensation' among his audiences.[20] Hirst rapidly established himself as one of best known and respected figures in the movement. Among his friends he counted Lady Noel Byron, with whom he corresponded until his death.

Another prominent Yorkshire lecturer on Co-operation, and Hirst's co-delegate from the Huddersfield district to the London Congress, was the Revd C.B. Dunn, curate of Cumberworth. It was unusual to find a curate of the Church of England actively working for a movement which was so closely identified with the "infidel" Robert Owen. Owen's attacks on established religion had, from the early days, caused anger and embarrassment among Co-operators. As early as 1830, Dr William King – founder and editor of *The Co-operator* – denounced Owen, though not by name, for having 'pretended to doubt of the real truth of the Gospel', and for trying to make 'a new Gospel out of Co-operation'.[21] When Owen's views on religion became a topic of discussion at the London Congress of 1832, Hirst 'thought the less co-operation was associated with peculiar abstract doctrines the better', and felt assured that 'many were driven from co-operation by supposing it to be a system of infidelity'.[22]

Mr Dunn does not appear to have had any qualms about taking an active part in a movement that was so closely associated with Robert Owen. Indeed, he claimed that 'he considered the philanthropic sceptic far better than the orthodox believer. His religion said that those prayed best who loved all men'.[23] As an Anglican clergyman, it was not his interest in social reform that is unusual, but, rather, the body with which he chose to associate himself. From 1831 onwards an increasing number of churchmen involved themselves with the movement for factory reform. There was, however, a fundamental difference between the beliefs of Dunn, and those of factory reformers such as Richard Oastler and Revd G.S. Bull. The reforming zeal of the latter men was based on a world view that was, backward looking – to a pre-industrial society where the throne and the cottage, not factory chimneys, were the pillars of the nation. Those ministers of the Church of England who were attracted to the Factory Movement were often Tory in their politics. The philanthropy that brought them into the movement was reinforced by their hostility towards the increasingly powerful and influential manufacturing interest; an interest that tended to be Whig in politics and Nonconformist in matters of religious belief. Dunn, on the other hand, was very much a product of the Enlightenment, with strong Liberal principles that did not stop short at free trade and a limited extension of voting rights. He believed, on the contrary, that competitive industrial capitalism was a stage in social development that might soon be transcended and replaced with a society organised on more equitable, efficient and Christian principles. He made his views on the present system very clear in a lecture he delivered to his own parishioners:

> To my plain understanding all this appears more like the work of the devil for certain I am that the genius of Christianity condemns the principle upon which the social fabric has hitherto been erected, and evidently inclines towards a system of mutual co-operation, which promotes the greatest happiness of the greatest number, in preference to the competitive system which requires an army of mercenary attornies and military butchers to preserve its monstrous and unnatural existence.[24]

Co-operators, Trade Unionists and Radicals

The growth of the co-operative movement in the early 1830s coincided with the expansion of the trade union movement, and the mass agitation which culminated in the Reform Act of 1832. The Co-operators were not wholly opposed to either of the other two movements, but felt that neither would make lasting improvements to the conditon of the working classes. They argued that the trade unions would do better to use their funds to establish co-operative manufacturing ventures. Thomas Hirst summed up this view when he told a Halifax audience that he disapproved of strikes 'except the men turned out for good, in order to work for themselves'.[25] Similarly, when speaking of the political agitation for reform, Dunn declared that 'God helps them, remember, who help themselves. If you expect any considerable benefits from the great measure of National Reform now pending in Parliament, I am afraid that you will find yourselves egregiously mistaken'.[26] Hirst was alarmed by the violent language employed by some

Radicals, and beseeched them 'to cease from exciting the lower orders against the higher'.[27]

This criticism of Radicalism did not, however, prevent many Co-operators and Radicals from working together. In Huddersfield, the co-operative society held meetings in the Radicals' rooms in Swan Yard and in 1832 the local Co-operators donated £3 towards the election expenses of the Radical candidate, Captain Wood of Sandal.[28] Speaking at the Birmingham Congress, Hirst proposed to the Radical papers 'that they should bring out a plan, such as was adopted at Huddersfield, to amalgamate the political unions and co-operative societies, so they might pull together'.[29] This involvement with the town's Political Union resulted in the arguments of the Co-operators influencing the thinking of local Radical leaders. In his address to the electors of Huddersfield, Captain Wood acknowledged the influence of the Co-operators:

> Had we even as my intelligent friend Mr Thomas Hirst observed, a railway to the moon to carry off our manufactured produce; the poor workman would not ultimately be benefited: for machinery can be increased to such an infinite extent as would supply the greatest possible demand. And where would he then be? Precisely where he is now – at the point of starvation.[30]

The movement in decline

By the autumn of 1832 the first flush of enthusiasm for Co-operation had already faded, the failure of an increasing number of societies bringing to a halt the movement's forward march. The failure rate was, however, greater in the south than the north. The Huddersfield society, though, continued to thrive, and was actively engaged in furthering the cause of community – still declared by Hirst to be 'the principle object of their pursuit'.[31] To that end the society had entered into 'a treaty with a gentleman for some land in the neighbourhood of Huddersfield, upon a loan forever, with the power to purchase at a stipulated price'.[32] The relative good health of the societies in the Huddersfield was noted in a report to the *Lancashire and Yorkshire Co-operator*: 'the societies in the neighbourhoods of Huddersfield and Halifax, were getting on in a comfortable manner so far as the competition they have to contend with, and the ignorance of the people will allow them'.[33]

It was the strength of the West Yorkshire societies that was to be the deciding factor in determining where the movement's spring conference would be held in 1833. Owen, among others, wanted it held in London; but the northern Co-operators opposed the idea – Wilson of the Halifax society moving that 'the next congress be held in Huddersfield'.[34] William Carson, of Wigan, spoke in favour of a Yorkshire venue, pointing out that:

> a good majority of the societies were in the north, and a great number had sprung up around Huddersfield and Halifax within the last six months, and he had no doubt but that the holding of a Congress in that district would tend very much to the advancement of the cause generally.[35]

The Huddersfield Congress of April 1833 should have been a great triumph for the Co-operators of West Yorkshire, but in the event it was overshadowed by the fact that Thomas Hirst lay on his death bed. His illness had been brought on, it was reported, by over-exertion on behalf of the cause. At a special meeting of Congress, on the evening of 8 April, it was resolved

> that the thanks of Congress be given to our dear brother in Co-operation, Thos. Hirst, for his unwearied zeal and distinterestedness, both as a Co-operator and Missionary, in the latter of which he sacrificed his health, and greatly endangered his most valuable life.[36]

Lady Noel Byron's concern for Hirst's health had led her to ask Dr. William King, the Brighton Co-operator, to visit him 'both as a friend and physician'.[37] King was, unfortunately, unable to leave Brighton at that time. In a letter to Hirst's wife, written in the same month, Lady Byron wrote:

> It is with great sorrow that I receive your account of your husband's situation. Tell him not to doubt that God will raise up friends to the "widow and fatherless", and I pledge myself to be one of them. Tell him, too, that as his life has been the means of doing good, his memory shall be likewise. . . . I write this letter with tears, and will only add – God bless you and yours – A.I. Noel Byron[38]

Lady Byron was as good as her word, sending £50 to Hirst's widow and paying for the education of his sons at the school kept by E.T. Craig – a fellow Co-operator – at Ealing Grove, Middlesex. The size of Hirst's funeral procession was a reflection of the esteem in which this popular Huddersfield

Co-operator was held, it being attended by some thousands of people, including Trade Unions, and several other societies, and headed by Mr. William Stocks, jun. (the Radical Chief Constable of Huddersfield) and Captain Wood of Sandal. Everything was conducted in the most respectable manner, and the sight of so many men attending to his last rest this popular orator, proves the esteem entertained by his own class for him.[39]

In April 1835 the last Co-operative Congress of the first series was held. On this occasion it was hosted by the Co-operators of Halifax. The congress was a small and very local affair, the eleven societies represented all being West Yorkshire ones, the Huddersfield society among them. Although weakened by the failure of numerous societies, and lacking the cohesion that had been provided by the congresses, the movement was far from dead. A number of societies survived, and continued to cling to the Co-operative *idea*. In 1836 the Huddersfield society decided to purchase a horse and cart, and to employ a member as a permanent manufacturer to the society at the generous wage of £1 5s. weekly.[40] The Huddersfield Co-operators also agreed that 'young men from Halifax who desire to join the society should be admitted'.[41] The implications of this resolution would appear to be that, either the Halifax society was not admitting new members, or that it had failed. Given that nothing is known of the society after 1835, it seems likely that the society had, indeed, ceased to exist.

The Huddersfield area, always one of the principal strongholds of the co-operative movement, was now its last major bastion in West Yorkshire. Not only did a number of the societies founded in the 1820s and early 1830s still survive, but new ones continued to be founded. In 1836 a society was established at the village of Hopton and in the following year one at Carr Green.

Within the law

On July 30th 1834 an Act of Parliament was passed amending the law relating to friendly societies. Existing legislation – introduced originally to afford a measure of legal recognition to those societies that had as their purpose the relief of their memberships in sickness, old age and death – now extended its scope to all societies established for 'any purpose that is not illegal', provided that their rules were certified by the Registrar of Friendly

Societies as being in conformity with the terms of the act.[42] The wording of the act meant that it was possible for co-operative societies to enrol under it and gain, for the first time, legal recognition and a degree of financial security.

The first West Yorkshire co-operative society to take advantage of the change in the law was the 1st Huddersfield Co-operative Trading Association, which enrolled on 4 July 1838, under its new name – The Huddersfield Co-operative Trading Friendly Society. Other societies copied the example of the Huddersfield Co-operators. In October 1838 the Skelmanthorpe Co-operative Trading Association enrolled, to be followed, in 1839, by societies at Paddock and Clayton West. The enrolled rules of the Huddersfield society make it clear that its objective continued to be to employ its members, and hopefully, to establish a community based on co-operative principles:

> The object of this society shall be to raise from time to time by subscriptions amongst the members thereof, or by voluntary contributions, or donations, or loans or trading, and to find employment, educate and instruct all its members, or the purchase or rental of lands whereon to erect suitable dwellings or other buildings wherein the members shall by united labour support each other, under very vicissitude, including the establishment of schools for children, or any other purpose not lawful, by these and every other means consistent with honesty and impartial justice, to arrange the powers of production, distribution, consumption and education in order to produce among the members feelings of pure charity, and social affection for each other, and practically plant the standard of peace and good will on earth to all men.[43]

It is interesting to note that this continued commitment to the creation of co-operative manufacturing communities, with mutually supportive populations, was not restricted to societies that had been founded in the late 1820s or early 1830s. The rules of three societies established in the Huddersfield area – Skelmanthorpe (1834), Hopton (1836) and Clayton West (1838) – subscribed to the same objectives as the Huddersfield society. However, the majority of the rule books that have survived from this period made no mention of either co-operative manufacturing or community. The rules of the Paddock Society (founded 1832) employ a phraseology similar to that found in those of the Huddersfield society – also wishing 'to plant the standard of peace and good will on earth towards all men' – but differed in restricting its objectives 'to such purposes, as will conduce to the happiness and general improvement of the society'.[44] Similarly, the two neighbouring societies at Kirkheaton and Colne Bridge (founded 1835 and 1842 respectively) shared identical rules, which show their objectives to have been limited to the raising of a capital 'sufficient for the purchase of food and raiment at the wholesale market and retail them out to the members and other customers at the lowest possible price in order to give to industry as large a share of its products as the present exigencies of the Country will admit'.[45]

A small number of societies in the Huddersfield area (Carr Green, Chapel Hill, Meltham Mills and Paddock) are known to have paid dividends according to the amount of goods purchased by individual members. Credit for devising the system, known as dividend on purchase, has tended to be given to the Rochdale Pioneers (established 1844), although by the end of the century historians of the movement were noting that other Co-operators had employed it prior to the founding of the Rochdale society. The four Huddersfield societies mentioned above all pre-date the Pioneers' – the oldest, Meltham Mills, being founded in 1827. The rules of the Paddock society (founded 1832 and registered in 1839) are the oldest surviving West Yorkshire ones to incorporate dividend on purchase. The rules of the society anticipated the Rochdale Pioneers' in making interest (at a rate of 5 per cent) on all loans, subscriptions and donations, the first call on profits; the remainder of the profits, if any, 'to be divided among the members according to the amount of monies paid for the purchase of goods, by each individual member'.[46]

The Chartist years

On Whit Tuesday 1837 a mass meeting was held on Peep Green, near Mirfield, its purpose to petition Parliament for the repeal of the New Poor Law. The culmination of months of preparation, it was a spectacular success. On the platform the factory reformer Richard Oastler stood alongside the Radical leaders Feargus O'Connor, Bronterre O'Brien and Henry Hetherington. Even Robert Owen lent his support to the occasion. The meeting was one of a chain of events which would, within a year, revive the fortunes of popular Radicalism, and lead to the establishment of the Chartist movement.

In the same month as the Peep Green meeting, Oastler contested the parliamentary election for the Borough of Huddersfield. At the poll he received the vote of the Huddersfield Co-operative Trading Friendly Society, cast on behalf of the membership by William Hodgson.[47] The Huddersfield society's support for Oastler was but one manifestation of its continued deep commitment to the cause of economic, social and political reform. The wide scope of its commitments is illustrated by the range of toasts offered at the society's annual festival, on New Year's Eve, 1837:

> "The Huddersfield Co-operative Society, and may it flourish and increase and answer the end intended." "The People, The Producing People, the Source of all Wealth." "The Principles of Co-operation," "Robert Owen, Esq., the Friend of Co-operation." "Richard Oastler, Esq., the Perservering Friend of the Factory Child, and the Advocate of the Ten Hours Bill." "May Temperance and Sobriety increase till all the people become intelligent." "John Fielden, Esq., the Patriotic Member for Oldham." "Feargus O'Connor, Esq., and may the principles of Radicalism advance." "G.S. Buckingham, Esq., the Perservering Advocate of Temperance and Civil and Religious Liberty." "The Liberty of the Press" "The Friends of Co-operation all over the World."[48]

The Huddersfield Co-operators were sympathetic towards the new agitation for political reform, working individually and collectively to further the cause of Radicalism. George Barker, a prominent member of the co-operative society, was also a founder member of the Huddersfield Northern Union, the town's first Chartist body. In October 1838 – a month after the founding of the branch – Barker spoke at a Chartist meeting, at Peep Green, denouncing the Reform Act of 1832 as 'a measure evidently intended to unite the middle with the higher classes, in order to oppress the working classes (cheers)'.[49] The Peep Green meeting was a great success, but it was also expensive to organise. At a meeting of the Huddersfield Northern Union held shortly afterwards, the local Chartists acknowledged their debt to the town's co-operative society for its financial help, thanking the Co-operators

> for the handsome manner in which they have come forward in granting their subscription towards defraying the general expenses of the Great West Riding Meeting. If all other public societies would come forward in like manner to assist the labouring classes to obtain their rights, oppression would no longer reign.[50]

With the rejection of the Chartists' National Petition, in July 1839, the movement was left without a clear strategy. Responses to the failure of the petition included calls for a run on the banks, a general strike and armed insurrection. Another, and less extreme alternative, was a decision to boycott all shopkeepers who did not sympathise with the Chartist cause. This tactic, known as 'exclusive dealing', was taken up by a number of Chartist branches. At an illegal Chartist meeting in Huddersfield, on 10 August 1839, George Barker spoke in favour of the boycott. He declared that under capitalism the national wealth went to, among others, 'the wholesale and retail dealers, to those who live by buying cheap and selling dear'.[51] The following speaker, James Mathewman, also a Co-operator, chided the working classes for being 'more willing to trade with other people than among themselves'. 'There was only one society in that town', he asserted (referring to the co-operative society), 'that had carried out the recommendations of the (Chartist) Convention. If the working people of that town had acted upon the principle of that society they might have been successful'.[52]

The Co-operators continued, however, to believe in the superiority of their approach to that adopted by the Radical reformers.[53] Speaking at the society's festival, on New Year's Eve 1840, Joseph Bray, himself an active Chartist, claimed that Co-operation had the potential to 'emancipate the labouring classes physically, and went on to assert that if all the working classess had done as they had done 'the Charter would be the law of the land before this'.[54] George Barker, chairman of the festivities, saw the financial success of the society as proof of the practicability of their strategy:

> They tell us that our system is impracticable, but when we commenced we had but one store, now we have three, and have been manufacturing woollen cloth for six years, and can now supply our brethren with as good an article for the same price as any manufacturer in the kingdom.[55]

Further proof that the co-operative *idea* was resilient is provided by the fact that in 1841 there were no less than thirty-one West Yorkshire co-operative societies on the books of the Registrar of Friendly Societies, John Tidd Pratt. Yet even this would appear to be a conservative estimate, for evidence derived from trade directories suggests that there may have been at least sixty societies in West Yorkshire by 1842, thirty-two of them in the Huddersfield area.[56]

Social and economic historians have, in the past, tended to divide the development of the co-operative movement into two distinct phases: the first 'rising to a peak of influence in the years 1828-34 . . . the second, heralded by the foundation of the Rochdale Pioneers' Society in 1844'.[57] It is a view that, while acknowledging similarities between the phases, believes that there were fundamental differences which set them apart; making them 'so divergent in object and inspiration as to constitute, in fact, two separate lines of development'.[58] There is, however, a growing awareness that the development of the co-operative movement should be seen as a continuous process, in terms of the evolution of both its theory and practice. The Co-operators of Huddersfield, whose faith in the destiny of their movement did not falter, provided the continuity between the first societies and those of the present. The first Huddersfield Society continued in business until the 1850s, White's *Directory* for 1853 describing it as the 'Co-operative Stores, Smith and Fitton 11, Westgate and Moldgreen'.[59] Around this time the society appears to have gone out of existence, the shop becoming an ordinary grocery store. However, by then the future of the movement was already beginning to look reasonably secure. In 1851 a report from the Newsome Trading Society to the *Christian Socialist* reported the existence of '3 or 4 societies in Huddersfield, 1 at Berry Brow, 3 at Henley (Honley), 2 at Netherthong, and one at Crosland'.[60] The next stage in the development of the co-operative movement in Huddersfield began within a few years of the demise of the town's first trading society. In 1860 the Huddersfield Industrial Society was founded. This society, later a part of Co-operative Retail Services, survived for over a hundred years – forming the link between the Co-operators of the 1820s and the modern movement.[61]

Robin Thornes

Biographical Note

Robin Thornes was born in Dewsbury in 1954. He attended Queen Elizabeth's Grammar School, Wakefield, after which he went on to study history at the University of Sussex, where he was awarded the degrees of Bachelor of Arts and Doctor of Philosophy. On leaving University in 1979 he spent two years working for the Archaeology Unit of the former West Yorkshire Metropolitan County Council. In 1981 he moved to the Royal Commission on the Historical Monuments of England. At present, he is Head of Architectural Survey at the Royal Commission.

NOTES:

1. Robert Owen, *Report to the County of New Lanark* (Glasgow, 1821), p.68.

2. Robert Owen, *A New View of Society* (1817, reprinted 1949), p.222.

3. Sidney Pollard, 'Co-operation: from Community Building to Shopkeeping', in *Essays in Labour History* edited by A. Briggs and J. Saville (1967), p.80

4. Owen Balmforth, *The Huddersfield Industrial Society Limited: a History of Fifty Years Progress, 1860-1910* (Manchester, 1910), p.34.

5. *Birmingham Co-operative Herald,* 1 Oct. 1831.

6. *Lancashire and Yorkshire Co-operator,* No. 1 (new series).

7. Balmforth, *The Huddersfield Industrial Society,* p.24.

8. *Lancashire and Yorkshire Co-operator,* 29 Oct. 1831.

9. *Proceedings of the Third Co-operative Congress held in London . . .* (London, 1832), p.121.

10. *Proceedings* (London), p.122.

11. *Proceedings* (London), p.38.

12. *Proceedings* (London), p.92.

13. *Lancashire and Yorkshire Co-operator,* No. 1 (new series).

14. *Proceedings* (London), p.49.

15. *Proceedings* (London), p.49.

16. *Proceedings* (London), p.49.

17. *Lancashire and Yorkshire Co-operator,* No. 1 (new series).

18. *Proceedings of the Second Co-operative Congress held in Birmingham* (Birmingham 1831), p.5.

19. *Proceedings* (Birmingham), p.6.

20. *Lancashire and Yorkshire Co-operator,* No. 1 (new series).

21. *The Co-operator,* 1 July 1830.

22. *Proceedings* (London), p.118.

23. *Proceedings* (London), p.100.

24. *Lancashire and Yorkshire Co-operator,* No. 6 (new series).

25. *Halifax and Huddersfield Express,* 24 March 1832.

26. *Lancashire and Yorkshire Co-operator,* No. 6 (new series).

27. *Proceedings* (London), pp.91-92.

28. Balmforth, *The Huddersfield Industrial Society,* p.24.

29. *Proceedings* (Birmingham), p.16.

30. Captain John Wood, *The Rights of Labour to Legislative Protection . . .* (1832), p.13.

31. *Proceedings of the Fourth Co-operative Congress held in Liverpool . . .* (Manchester, 1832), p.23.

32. *Proceedings* (Liverpool), p.23.

33. *Lancashire and Yorkshire Co-operator*, No. 7 (new series).

34. *Lancashire and Yorkshire Co-operator*, No. 10 (new series).

35. *Lancashire and Yorkshire Co-operator*, No. 10 (new series).

36. *Crisis*, 9 April 1833.

37. Balmforth, *The Huddersfield Industrial Society*, p.25.

38. Balmforth, *The Huddersfield Industrial Society*, p.23.

39. Balmforth, *The Huddersfield Industrial Society*, p.25.

40. Balmforth, *The Huddersfield Industrial Society*, p.24.

41. Balmforth, *The Huddersfield Industrial Society*, p.24.

42. Friendly Societies Act, 1834 (5 Wm. 4. c.40).

43. *Rules of the Huddersfield Co-operative Trading Friendly Society* (Huddersfield, 1838), p.6.

44. PRO FS 1/811/210, Rules of the Paddock in Huddersfield Co-operative Trading Friendly Society.

45. PRO FS 1/818/349, Rules of the Colne Bridge Friendly Co-operative Society; PRO, FS 1/819b/423, Rules of the Kirkheaton Trading Friendly Society.

46. PRO, FS 1/811/210.

47. *A Copy of the Poll . . . in the Borough of Huddersfield . . . 6th May 1837* (Leeds, 1837).

48. *Northern Star*, 1 Jan. 1838.

49. *Northern Star*, 13 Oct. 1838.

50. *Northern Star*, 5 Jan 1839.

51. PRO HO 40/5/463.

52. PRO HO 40/5/471.

53. For a fuller account of the relationship between Co-operation and Radicalism from the 1830s to the 1850s see Robin Thornes 'Change and Continuity in the Development of the Co-operation, 1827-1844' in *New Views of Co-operation* edited by Stephen Yeo (1988), pp.27-51.

54. *Northern Star*, 16 Jan 1841.

54. *Northern Star*, 16 Jan 1841.

56. William White, *Directory and Topography of the Borough of Leeds, and the whole of the Clothing District of the West Riding of Yorkshire*, 1842 (Sheffield, 1842). Many co-operatives societies traded, for business purposes, under the names of the agents or trustees. The Huddersfield society, for example, traded under the name of 'Christopher Wood &c.', while the Kirkheaton society traded under that of 'David Dawson &c.'. There is a close correlation between localities known to have had co-operative societies, and those in which trade directories list grocers styled '&c.'. Given that joint-stock formations, other

than co-operative societies, had not by this time entered the field of retailing, it is reasonable to assume that the majority of these shops were co-operative ventures of one sort or another.

57.   Sidney Pollard, 'Co-operation: from Community Building to Shopkeeping', p.74.

58.   Sidney Pollard, 'Co-operation: from Community Building to Shopkeeping', p.110.

59.   William White *Directory and Gazeteer of Leeds, Bradford, Halifax, Huddersfield, Wakefield and the whole of the Clothing Districts of Yorkshire* (Sheffield, 1853).

60.   *Christian Socialist*, 25 Oct 1853.

61.   For a fuller account of the early history of the co-operative movement in West Yorkshire see: Robin Thornes 'The Early Development of the Co-operative Movement in West Yorkshire, 1827-1863' (unpub. D.Phil thesis, University of Sussex, 1984).

CHAPTER 9

'A Metropolis of Discontent': Popular Protest in Huddersfield c.1780–c.1850

JOHN A. HARGREAVES

'A wilder people I never saw in England', John Wesley recorded in his Journal after his first visit to Huddersfield in 1757, when dirt had been thrown at him in the Market Place and the crowds had 'appeared just ready to devour us'.[1] Eighteenth century Huddersfield, as Methodist preachers learned to their cost on more than one occasion, was not quite so tranquil as some historians have supposed.[2] However, during the last two decades of the eighteenth century and the first half of the nineteenth century, Huddersfield was to experience a frequency, intensity and scale of popular protest unprecedented in the town's history, earning Huddersfield notoriety by 1813 as 'a hotbed of disaffection' and 'a metropolis of discontent'.[3]

Food rioting erupted in the town on three separate occasions during the 1780s and 1790s, decades which also saw the emergence in the town of new forms of political radicalism inspired by transatlantic and continental revolutions and rebellion in Ireland. In 1812, following a decade of industrial protest by croppers engaged in the hand finishing of woollen cloth, Huddersfield was the epicentre of the Yorkshire Luddite disturbances and one of only a handful of provincial centres where disturbances recurred in 1817, at the time of the Pentrich rising in Derbyshire, and in 1820, in the months following the Cato Street conspiracy in London. A population explosion in the town during the 1820s and the onset of a chronic depression amongst domestic handloom weavers, particularly those engaged in the fancy trade in the villages on the southern perimeter of Huddersfield, heightened the tension within the town during the struggle for parliamentary reform between 1829 and 1832; the electoral contests in the new borough constituency after 1832 and the popular protest movements of the 1830s. With the notable exception of the Plug Plot riots of 1842, the last major disturbances in the town before 1850, Huddersfield remained relatively quiescent during the Chartist decade (1838-48) and in 1848, the year of the last great Chartist demonstration in London and a plethora of revolutions across Europe, Huddersfield was conspicuously more peaceful than either Bradford or Halifax.[4] However, during the 1850s, when other towns were generally settling down to a period of greater tranquillity, Huddersfield witnessed a further decade of protest, firmly in the tradition of the protest movements of the preceding two decades, in the form of the Tenant-Right dispute, masterminded by the veteran factory reformer, champion of press freedom, Owenite and Chartist, Joshua Hobson (1810-1876).[5]

Food riots

The most persistent and widespread riots of the eighteenth century were those aimed at securing fair distribution and pricing of food in times of dearth and distress.[6] In June 1783, with the price of wheat at its highest for nine years, 'riotous mobs' at Bradford, Halifax and Huddersfield 'demanded an immediate reduction in the price of corn and on the market days compelled the dealers to sell at such prices as they chose to fix'.[7] In 1795, another year of soaring wheat prices, when 'for some time the manufacturing districts were the frequent scenes of riots and clamorous cries for bread', Almondbury apprentices vented their anger at the extortionate prices charged by local corn-dealers by attacking both them and their premises.[8] The last and most serious Huddersfield food riot erupted in November 1799. Following another poor harvest, an immense crowd consisting mainly of women 'assembled in the villages in the neighbourhood and proceeded to Huddersfield with determination to seize all the corn brought that day to market'. Sacks of wheat belonging to a Golcar shopkeeper were seized and then sold off to the rioters by Martha Bray, the wife of a Deighton waterman, who had taken a prominent part in the disturbances. When Joseph Radcliffe (1743-1819), the local magistrate, appeared on the scene to read the Riot Act, his horse was kicked 'with the greatest violence' by a Netherthong clothier, who was promptly arrested, together with Martha Bray and a Deighton cropper's wife, who had bought some of the corn. There were bitter recriminations when seven members were expelled from the local militia 'in a public and ignominious manner' for their refusal to answer the call to arms and their denunciation of those of their comrades who had rallied to the call of duty as 'the scum of the Country'.[9]

Radicalism and the Parliamentary Reform Movement

The American War of Independence (1776-83) reawakened in Britain a movement for parliamentary reform which was sustained during the 1780s by Major John Cartwright's radical constitutional societies; the Reverend Christopher Wyvill's more moderately inclined Yorkshire Association of gentry and merchants and Protestant Dissenters in their unsuccessful campaigns for civil and religious liberty. It was not until the 1790s, however, that an organised popular radical movement developed in the West Riding, stimulated by the outbreak of the French Revolution in 1789; the publication of Tom Paine's avowedly republican *Rights of Man* in 1791-92; the foundation of the Society for Constitutional Information in Sheffield in December 1791 and the London Corresponding Society in January 1792.[10] By 1793, a Jacobin corresponding society in Huddersfield was appealing to the metropolitan society: 'for God's sake send us the word of enlightenment and philanthropy. Huddersfield abounds in true patriots, but we are beset by masses of ignorant aristocracy'.[11]

Mass meetings were held in the open air at Sheffield and Halifax in the early months of 1794, attended by 'friends' from Huddersfield, at which plans were approved for a general delegate meeting at Bristol and a National Convention.[12] The correspondence of George Dyson, a book-keeper and warehouseman at Whitacre's Mill, Huddersfield, who attended the reform meetings at Sheffield on 28 February and 7 April, provides insight into the escalating radical activity, which led to the suspension of Habeas Corpus on 18 May. 'In our parts', Dyson confided early in March to Thomas Stutterd, the firm's commercial traveller and a fellow Baptist, 'I believe things are growing very serious'. He referred to a recent communication from Edinburgh, where a French-style British Convention had been held in November; described a membership ticket for a radical society, portraying a woman holding the cap of liberty aloft and trampling under her feet the chains of slavery, which he had been shown, and recounted an incident where 'a person in our neighbourhood' had declined to execute an order for fifty stands of arms. 'There is something of secrecy in the societies going forward', he concluded, 'which very few even of the Members know of, save the principal or leading men'. A later letter, written to Stutterd in June, after a local magistrate had ordered the arrest of the agent of the *Sheffield News* and alerted Dyson's employer of his purchase in Sheffield of 'seditious papers', revealed that 'about sixteen or seventeen' of Dyson's friends were subscribers to the *English Chronicle* and concluded ruefully: 'we are now at a horrible pass in this country, people must not talk nor read nor write . . . perhaps I shall date my (next) letter from the Bastille'.[13]

In 1795 Pitt's government introduced two acts extending the law of treason and prohibiting mass meetings unless approved by the magistracy, but there were relatively few prosecutions under these acts, whose effect was to drive the radical movement underground, necessitating further legislation outlawing secret oaths in 1797; imposing a stricter control over newspapers in 1798 and belatedly proscribing named radical societies in 1799. During Pitt's so-called 'Reign of Terror', much was left to the discretion of local magistrates, who were reluctant to involve themselves in the expense of prosecutions. The Crown was prepared to prosecute in only one of the three cases of seditious speech brought before Joseph Radcliffe during the period between 1798 and 1803, much to the annoyance of Radcliffe. His impatience with the Home Office during this period earned him the rebuke of the Home Secretary, the Duke of Portland, who informed Earl Fitzwilliam (1748-1833), Lord Lieutenant of the West Riding, in 1803 that Radcliffe 'has somehow or other not formed a correct idea . . . of his own situation and authority as a justice of the peace'. The Crown had agreed to prosecute only David Norcliffe, who had toasted success to 'Bonaparte and . . . his undertaking' in January 1798, because the seditious words had 'been spoken in the presence of soldiers'. They declined to prosecute a second offender, John Taylor, for a seditious speech delivered in February 1798, and a third offender, James Jubson, who had boldly marched into the Huddersfield guardhouse in April 1803 declaring that he had been 'on board ship with the Glorious Parker', the leader of the naval mutiny at the Nore and that 'if soldiers were not fools to themselves they might have plenty of friends in this Town'. 'I feel within my own breast', he concluded impassionately, 'that your Master the King is not fit to rule over me' and that 'I wish the King and all his ministers were in Hell'. The Home Office advised that he might be discharged if he were suitably contrite before a magistrate.[14]

Revolutionary republican organisations, formed in imitation of the United Irishmen, sprang up in the late 1790s in London and the provinces. Whilst there is certainly evidence of individuals affiliated to such organisations in the Huddersfield area, it is difficult, from the fragmentary evidence available, to determine whether these associations symbolized widespread popular hostility to the social and political order or formed part of a coordinated national network of secret revolutionary organisations linked with Colonel Despard's ill-fated military conspiracy in London in 1802.

In July 1800, James Gledhill of Battyeford wrote to Edmund Norcliffe of Mirfield, enclosing a song, which he had composed for Bastille Day, extolling republican France as 'the bright star of freedom', which he hoped Norcliffe would read 'to our Friends at Almondbury'. In March 1801 the West Riding magistracy was hastily convened to examine reports 'that an Insurrection was in contemplation among the lower orders and oaths administered to such multitudes purporting an engagement to overthrow the Government'.[15] In April 1801, Earl Fitzwilliam informed the Home Office that 'the lower Orders of the People . . . talked of revolution as the remedy for Famine', however, in the absence of solid evidence of insurrectionary conspiracy, Fitzwilliam did not attach 'much importance to any supposed Conspiracies or Combination' and felt no 'alarm on account of the Temper of the People'.[16]

Two months later, a spy in the employment of a Bolton magistrate reported that 'the better sort of people' in Huddersfield and other places were deserting the radical movement as more extreme elements came to the fore. In March 1802, other spies from Bolton obtained the names of a joint Wakefield and Almondbury committee of the United Englishmen, which was seeking affiliation with the national committee. On 20 July 1802 Radcliffe was informed that betting had been taking place in Huddersfield Market, with only short odds being offered against 'a general Insurrection in less than a month' and a few days later he forwarded to Earl Fitzwilliam a copy of both an address and a membership card, numbered ninety-nine and bearing the United Briton's oath, which had been obtained for him by a government spy in Almondbury, and which Fitzwilliam, although usually suspicious of the activities of spies, promptly despatched to the Home Office as evidence that 'the true Jacobinical sort of conspiracy . . . does exist'.[17]

On 24 August, Radcliffe gained a fuller picture of the underground movement in Almondbury when he received a visit from Edward Harling, an Almondbury merchant, who had been suspicious for some time about the activities of some of his neighbours, and Mark Haigh, an Almondbury yeoman farmer, who had actually been drawn into those activities. They came to Milnsbridge House to volunteer information, probably at the suggestion of another magistrate, George Armytage, with whom Harling was acquainted. Haigh told Radcliffe 'that he had strong grounds to suspect that seditious meetings are held frequently at the houses of David Midgley and Samuel Buckley . . . that five or six Sundays past, eight or ten people who are strangers in Almondbury have come to the Houses . . . and stayed there during the whole of the afternoon Service' and that he had been informed 'that the Books or Accounts of a Seditious Society are kept at the house of Midgley', an Almondbury cordwainer. Haigh also revealed that Robert Lodge, an Almondbury clothier and part-time barber, was implicated. On 28 August, Radcliffe had Lodge arrested 'on suspicion of being a member of a seditious society'. Lodge denied the charge, but acknowledged that around June 1801 he had been persuaded by Buckley to subscribe a penny for 'a Paper', in return for which he was given a small numbered card bearing the initials 'D.M.', which Radcliffe's information suggested were those of David Midgley, the treasurer of the Almondbury section of the United Britons. Some time later Thomas Sykes, an Almondbury clothier, had demanded a further twopence from him, but he had handed over only three halfpence, giving him a shave instead of the other halfpenny. Radcliffe wrote immediately to the Home Secretary for advice on how to proceed, but then decided to raid the house on 29 August before waiting for a reply. By the time a military detachment arrived at the house, however, the occupants had had time to remove or conceal any incriminating evidence and Radcliffe regarded his seizures, two songs of liberty, including the song written by Citizen Gledhill for Bastille Day in 1800, and a manuscript on democratic organisation, as 'of little if any consequence'. After the raid, Radcliffe received the reply to his letter from the Home Office, which advised that there appeared to be insufficient evidence for a raid. In the circumstances, Radcliffe chose not to notify the Home Office of his actions, but remained determined to investigate further the provenance of the documents that had fallen into his hands. However, his attention was diverted to other matters when industrial unrest arose among the croppers in 1802 following similar disturbances in the West Country.[18]

Alongside the popular radical movement of the 1790s there developed an upsurge of popular patriotic sentiment behind the war effort, which was actively encouraged by the authorities, especially during the invasion scare of 1797. At Huddersfield, in May 1794, according to George Dyson, eighty-eight men enrolled themselves as volunteers for infantry and those coming forward to testify against David Norcliffe in 1798, for expressing support for Bonaparte, were described by Radcliffe as being 'too poor to bear the expense of the prosecution'. British naval victories at Camperdown in 1797, the Nile in 1798 and Copenhagen in 1801 were received with great popular rejoicing and the renewal of the war with Napoleon in 1803, after the short-lived Peace of Amiens, was accompanied by a resurgence of chauvinism, displayed publicly when the Huddersfield Volunteers paraded on Crosland Moor to receive their Colours in 1804.[19] The detrimental effects of economic warfare during 1807-08, however, fuelled a growing peace movement, culminating in what one newspaper decribed as perhaps 'the most numerous public meeting ever held in the West Riding', at Huddersfield on 1 March 1808.[20] The failure of the ensuing mass petitioning campaign and continuing economic hardship – by May 1808 one clothier's piece had lain in the Huddersfield Cloth Hall so long that a bird had nested in it – stimulated a 'numerous and respectable' reform meeting in Huddersfield on 30 May 1809 to call for 'a radical reform in the representation of the Commons'.[21]

Luddism

The repeal of protective legislation for woollen workers in 1809, following two unsympathetic parliamentary enquiries and a petitioning campaign which had drawn together workers from the West Country and the West Riding in a common cause, together with the growing pressure on

*Fig. 9:1 Factory children,
1812, (Walker's 'Costume
of Yorkshire').*

*Fig. 9:2 Perpetual
shearing frame. Machines
similar to this were
manufactured locally at the
foundry of Enoch and
James Taylor of Marsden .
(KCS)*

manufacturers to cut costs on account of the wartime dislocation of trade, paved the way for the introduction of labour-saving gig mills and shearing frames into the finishing processes of woollen cloth manufacture. This jeopardised the status of the croppers, hitherto a well-paid, highly-skilled labour élite, whose fiercely protected craft had been to raise the nap on the surface of the woollen cloth by hand with teazles after it had been woven and fulled and then to trim it deftly by the careful manipulation of heavy iron shears.[22]

In 1812, with Napoleon's power in Europe and food prices in Britain at their peak, Luddism, which had previously been confined to the East Midlands, erupted in Yorkshire.[23] Following an initial arson attack in January on a factory near Leeds employing gig mills and the ambush and destruction of a consignment of shearing frames destined for William Cartwright's Rawfolds Mill early in February, no fewer than thirteen

Fig. 9:3 A print published c.1860 claiming to show the interior of John Wood's cropping shop, Longroyd Bridge. Several pairs of cropping shears are illustrated and at the rear of the building a cropper is shown raising the nap with a teazle brush on a piece of cloth stretched across a frame or nelly. (KCS)

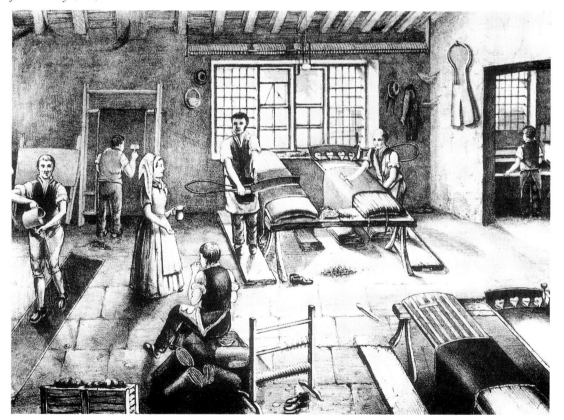

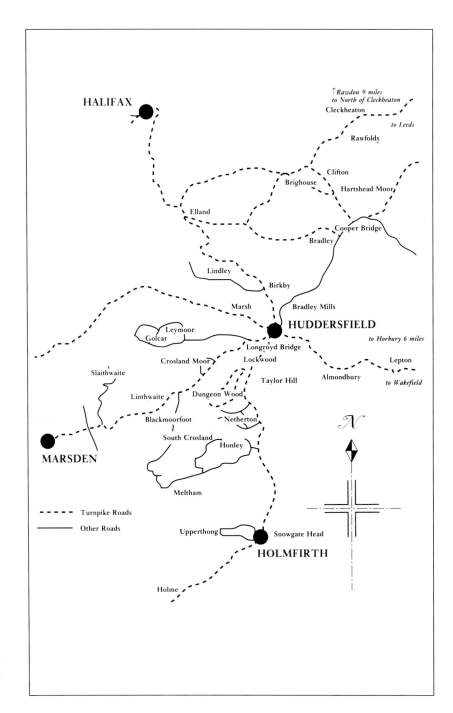

Fig. 9:4 Locations of machine breaking in West Yorkshire 1812. (KCS)

machine-breaking incidents occurred in the vicinity of Huddersfield within the space of three months, resulting in the destruction of forty shearing frames, three gig mills and 129 pairs of handshears and a bill for damage amounting to nearly £700. Groups of between thirty and fifty men, organised in companies and equipped with muskets, pistols, pikes, hammers and hatchets, were involved in a spate of daring late-night raids on small workshops across a swathe of moorland around Huddersfield, extending south-westwards from Marsh into the Colne valley as far as Slaithwaite and into the Holme valley as far as Snowgate Head, near Holmfirth. By far the most vituperative local attack was on the premises of the Wesleyan manufacturer Francis Vickerman, at Taylor Hill, on the evening of Sunday 15 March, when men with blackened faces smashed windows, a clock and twenty to thirty pairs of shears in the name of 'Ned Ludd of Nottingham'.[24]

Early in April, the Huddersfield Luddites, supported by contingents from other parts of West Yorkshire, launched two large scale attacks on targets further afield, at Horbury, eleven miles east of Huddersfield and Rawfolds, seven miles north of Huddersfield. An estimated 300 men were involved in the first attack, on Joseph Foster's mill at Horbury on 9 April, when the millowner's three sons, unceremoniously bundled out of the house at gunpoint in their nightshirts, were forced to witness the destruction of machinery and cloth to the value of nearly £300 by Luddites wielding the heavy sledgehammer 'Enoch', which had become the trademark of the Luddite attacks in the Huddersfield area. These hammers were given the name of the ironfounder who had made them, Enoch Taylor of Marsden, whose foundry, ironically, also held the patent for the local manufacture of the shearing frames for which they became the instruments of destruction, hence the Luddite warcry: 'Enoch hath made them, Enoch shall break them'.

There was a second attack on William Cartwright's Rawfolds Mill at Liversedge on 11 April, this time by a contingent of between 100 and 150 men mainly from the Huddersfield area, who had hoped for support from reinforcements from Halifax and Leeds which, in the event arrived too late to be of assistance. Here the Luddites met with their first serious resistance from Cartwright and a detachment of soldiers stationed at the mill. In the furious twenty-minute assault on the heavily defended premises, John Booth (1793-1812), a curate's son from Leymoor, apprenticed to a saddler in Huddersfield, was one of two Luddites left mortally wounded in the mill

Fig. 9:5 Rawfolds Mill, Liversedge, owned by William Cartwright, was attacked by Luddites during the night of 11 April 1812. (KCS)

yard, whilst other men were dragged away into the darkness by their comrades. Booth's body was hastily interred at Huddersfield Parish Church at dawn a few days later, in order to forestall an expected Luddite demonstration at the funeral, originally planned for noon.

With the failure of the Rawfolds attack, machine breaking in Yorkshire virtually came to an end and Luddism entered a more violent phase, in which armed robberies and threats of vengeance came to the fore, culminating in the assassination, on 28 April 1812, of William Horsfall (1771-1812), a local manufacturer who had once proclaimed his intention to ride up to his saddle girths in Luddite blood rather than capitulate to their demands. He suffered mortal gunshot wounds to the abdomen and thighs on Radcliffe's plantation at Crosland Moor, returning to Ottiwells Mill, Marsden, from the Huddersfield Cloth Hall. Despite sustained activity on the part of the authorities and a heavy military presence in the town, no arrests were made for the murder until October. In January 1813 at York, three croppers from Longroyd Bridge, George Mellor (b.1791), William Thorpe (b.1790) and

Fig. 9:6 Joseph Radcliffe (1743-1819) of Milnsbridge House, the local magistrate who played a leading role in the maintenance of public order in the late eighteenth and nineteenth centuries. This portrait was presented to him in June 1813, together with the congratulatory address seen on the table at which Radcliffe is seated. (KCS)

Thomas Smith (b.1791) were convicted of the murder of William Horsfall, largely on the evidence of an accomplice, Benjamin Walker (b.1788), also a cropper at Longroyd Bridge, who had turned King's evidence. Fourteen others, including five Huddersfield men, Thomas Brook (b.1781), Jonathan Dean (b.1785), James Haigh (b.1785), John Ogden (b.1785) and John Walker (b.1782), were hanged eight days later for their part in the attack on Rawfolds Mill.

Interpretations of Yorkshire Luddism have diverged sharply. The main controversy has centred upon the aims of the Luddites. Was Luddism primarily a form of industrial protest or was it essentially a politically motivated movement, linked with an underground revolutionary conspiracy? The evidence is fragmentary and problematic. The list of Luddite prisoners at York in January 1813 reveals that, whilst other occupational groups were

REWARDS.

WHEREAS, two Villains did, on the Night of Wednesday the 22nd. Day of July Instant, feloniously SHOOT at and WOUND *John Hinchliffe*, of *Upper-Thong*, in the West Riding of the County of York, Clothier, with intent to MURDER him, of which Wound he lies in a dangerous state.

A Reward of 200 Guineas

will be given to any Person who will give such Information, as may lead to the Apprehension and Conviction of either of the said Villains.

AND WHEREAS, John Scholefield Junior, of Nether-Thong, in the said Riding, is strongly suspected of being concerned in the said Murderous attempt, AND HAS ABSCONDED.

A Reward of Twenty Guineas

is hereby offered to any Person, who will apprehend the said John Scholefield, and lodge him in any of his Majesty's Prisons, and give Information thereof, or give such Private Information as may lead to his apprehension; *and Inviolable Secrecy will be Observed.*

The said John Scholefield is by Trade a Cloth-Dresser, about 21 Years of Age, 5 Feet 10 Inches High, Brown Hair, Dark Complexion, rather stout made: commonly wears a Dark coloured Coat, made rather short, and Lead coloured Jean Pantaloons.

The above Rewards will be paid upon such Information, Apprehension, and Conviction as above mentioned by

Mr. John Peace, of Huddersfield,

in the said County of York, Treasurer to the Huddersfield Association.

Huddersfield 27th. July, 1812.

LANCASHIRE, PRINTER HUDDERSFIELD

Fig. 9:7 Reward poster, 1812. (WYAS,K)

represented amongst the sixty-four accused, all the twenty-four men from Huddersfield and its adjoining townships of Dalton and Lockwood were croppers, with an average age of twenty-seven.[25] Few of the Huddersfield croppers would, therefore, have been old enough to have been actively involved in the underground movement from 1796 to 1802. Although the provenance of a bundle of United Britons' papers found on the road to Horbury after the attack on Foster's Mill remains a mystery, it does suggest, perhaps, that there might have been some vestiges of a Jacobin underground tradition amongst the large crowd involved in the attack. The threatening letter received by a Huddersfield manufacturer, however, warning that there were '2,782 Sworn Heroes . . . in the Army of Huddersfield alone' seems to have represented more the rhetoric of revolution than evidence of actual revolutionary conspiracy.[26] Moreover, the croppers' petitioning campaigns of the early nineteenth century had been characterised more by their retrospective appeal to traditional rights than by their identification with insurrectionary Jacobin ideology. It is possible that the repeal of the Tudor protective legislation for woollen workers in 1809 and the deployment of the military to counteract Luddite machine breaking at Rawfolds resulted in an increasing politicisation of the movement, which was reflected in the insurrectionary tone of some Luddite propaganda in 1812. Whilst some alarmist West Riding magistrates imputed revolutionary aims to the Luddites, the Lord Lieutenant, Earl Fitzwilliam, did not concur with this view, and no evidence emerged at the trials implicating any of the Huddersfield Luddites in insurrectionary conspiracy.[27] Moreover, the decline of machine breaking and the upsurge in arms thefts and intimidation does not necessarily imply that Luddism entered an insurrectionary phase after Rawfolds.[28] Earlier Luddite successes had virtually eliminated the use of cropping machinery outside the larger well-defended enterprises and the resort to violence in April 1812 may have arisen out of a growing sense of frustration and outrage after encountering armed resistance at Rawfolds. It may also have reflected a determination to maintain a conspiracy of silence in the face of increasing pressure from the authorities, given that since February, when the disturbances around Huddersfield had begun, machine breaking had been a capital offence. Intimidation might have appeared the most effective means of weakening both the resolve and the capacity of the authorities to bring to justice the large numbers implicated in the disturbances and discourage those with knowledge of Luddite activities from making potentially damaging disclosures to the authorities. Certainly, after the collapse of Yorkshire Luddism, nineteen of the twenty-four Huddersfield Luddites held at York signified their support for a petition for parliamentary reform, but this was part of a widespread revival of the radical movement cultivated by Major John Cartwright (1740-1842) and should not be interpreted as evidence of Luddite motivation during the disturbances in the first half of 1812, when radical leaders generally disapproved of Luddite machine breaking.[29]

Another question which has been posed in the continuing debate about Yorkshire Luddism is whether the men hanged for the murder of William Horsfall were guilty of the crime which sent them to the gallows.[30] The main problem with the argument that there was a serious miscarriage of justice at York in January 1813 is that it discounts both the King's evidence of an accomplice and others closely associated with the accused and the weight of an oral tradition presumed to be derived from Luddite sources and preserved in the writings of Frank Peel and D.F.E. Sykes, neither of whom challenged the verdicts of the trial.[31] Moreover, it perhaps also attaches too much credence to alibi evidence which was collected at least six months after the murder and has too little regard for the inherent weakness of the defence position which was tacitly acknowledged by contemporary opinion, including that of the celebrated Luddite defence lawyer, Henry Brougham, whose brilliant performance at the Lancaster Assizes in May 1812 had secured the acquittal of thirty-eight Lancashire Luddites.[32] Even if it is conceded that some aspects of the legal process left much to be desired, for example the lack of courtroom procedures to establish a proper identification of the accused, the fact remains that those who have questioned the validity of the verdicts of the court on Mellor, Thorpe, Smith and Walker have failed to identify another group of men with both a strong motive for the murder, namely their sense of outrage against a leading Luddite antagonist following the Luddite losses at Rawfolds, and a perfect opportunity for the murder, given their precise knowledge of Horsfall's regular route to the Huddersfield Cloth Hall, which took him close to the cropping shops at Longroyd Bridge, where the accused men worked and where they were conveniently placed to observe his movements.

Fig. 9:8 Exterior view of John Wood's cropping shop, Longroyd Bridge. (KCS)

Parliamentary Reform

Arriving in Huddersfield a week after the Luddite executions at York, at the invitation of Samuel Clay, a respectable linen draper, Major Cartwright and a number of his local supporters, mainly 'working mechanics', were arrested and only the Major's demonstrable knowledge of constitutional law prevented further harassment from the authorities.[33] A radical club, named after John Hampden, the seventeenth-century champion of parliamentary rights, was formed and by January 1817 the Huddersfield Political Union Society was well-established. Alarmed at the extent of post-war unrest, the government temporarily suspended Habeas Corpus, banned meetings which did not have the approval of magistrates and made extensive use of spies and agents provocateurs, including W. J. Richards, alias William Oliver, a discharged debtor, in an attempt to infiltrate plans for a general rising in the spring of 1817 in the industrial districts. When Oliver visited Huddersfield in early May, he found local preparations for a planned general rising on 26 May already in progress and Joseph Mitchell, a Lancashire weaver, who had links with extremist radical Spencean groups in London was arrested near Huddersfield on 5 May. Although Oliver had complained at one point of the apathy of the Huddersfield conspirators, Huddersfield was one of only two places to experience an actual rising at a later date in June. On 6 June ten West Riding conspirators, who had been brought together by Oliver, were arrested at a secret meeting at Thornhill Lees, near Dewsbury. Despite this obvious setback, after a weekend of frenetic activity, late on the Sunday evening of 8 June, George Taylor of Honley, who was rumoured to have been a veteran of the Rawfolds attack, led a crowd of croppers, weavers, artisans and labourers from the Holme valley towards Huddersfield, exhorting them as they marched: 'now lads, all England is in arms – our liberties are secure – the rich will be poor and the poor will be rich!' The aim was to place a guard on the bridge at Folly Hall and then march into Huddersfield disarming the soldiers. When the insurgents reached Folly Hall they were challenged by Captain John Armytage, commander of the recently formed Huddersfield Yeomanry, George Whitehead, the deputy constable, and six privates. After a brief exchange of shots, during which the horse of one of the soldiers was wounded in the head, the soldiers galloped back to Huddersfield for reinforcements. Meanwhile, the seventy or eighty strong crowd, only about a tenth of whom carried firearms, quietly melted away into the night.[34] That evening a more serious insurrection unfolded in the villages around Pentrich in Derbyshire, where a march on Nottingham was planned. In the aftermath of the disturbances numerous arrests were made, but the timely exposure in the *Leeds Mercury* of the role of Oliver in the Huddersfield disturbances led to wholesale acquittals at the York summer assizes of those implicated in the Huddersfield incident, whereas three of the Derbyshire insurgents, including their leader, Jeremiah Brandreth, who had unintentionally killed a man when firing through an open window, were hanged and a further fourteen were sentenced to transportation.[35]

In 1819 there was a revival of the movement for parliamentary reform in Huddersfield, which rose to a crescendo after the horrific Peterloo Massacre in Manchester in August, when eleven people died and 462 were injured as the yeomanry charged into the crowd to arrest the radical orator, Henry Hunt.[36] After Peterloo, women, such as those forming the Paddock Female Reform Society, and banners, such as the celebrated Skelmanthorpe flag, became more prominent in the local protest meetings and prosecution witnesses travelling through Huddersfield for the trial of Hunt at York were 'assailed with hisses, groans and imprecations'.[37] In February 1820, a conspiracy to assassinate the cabinet at dinner in Cato Street was uncovered in the capital and during March it became clear to the authorities that insurrectionary conspiracy was again rife in parts of the north and Scotland. On 31 March magistrates, fearing an attempt by insurgents to seize Huddersfield, sat all night in the George Hotel surrounded by detachments of infantry and cavalry, but, when the signal to attack the town came from Castle Hill, the expected support failed to materialise. On 11 April a more serious march of about 300 men from Barnsley to Grange Moor, where the men had expected to meet with reinforcements, quickly retreated on the approach of the dragoons from Huddersfield.[38]

When the unpopular King George IV attempted to divorce his estranged wife, Caroline of Brunswick, after his accession in January 1820, Huddersfield radicals expressed their sympathy for the Queen in an address containing over 4,300 signatures and the Queen's acquittal was celebrated in November by an illumination of the town and sheep-roasts for the poor.[39] During the early 1820s there was considerable support for Richard Carlile's republican atheism in Almondbury, Huddersfield and the Colne valley and by the end of the decade there were plans to build an Infidel Hall in

Fig. 9:9 The
Skelmanthorpe Flag
carried in procession at
radical protest meetings
after 1819 and now in
Tolson Memorial
Museum. (KCS)

SKELMANTHORP
Will not rest Satisfied
with the Suffrage being
any thing but Universal

Truth and Justice
Powring Balm into
the Wounds of the
Manchester sufferers.

May never a Cock
in England Crow,
Nor never a Pipe
in Scotland Blow,
Nor never a Harp
in Ireland Play,
Till Liberty regains
Her Sway.

Am I not a Man & Brother?

Fig. 9:10 Poster
advertising a public
demonstration in support
of Queen Caroline, the
estranged wife of King
George IV, in Huddersfield
in November 1820.
(WYAS, K)

THE
Friends of the Queen.

THE Gentlemen who are Promoters of the intended
ILLUMINATION on Thursday Evening next, in honor of
Queen Caroline's TRIUMPH!
Earnestly request that all LADIES who join with them
in thinking her Conduct deserving of Imitation, and are
desirous of being thought like her, will make a point of
Appearing at their Windows,
During the Illumination, in order that Gentlemen may
know their Female Friends.

Huddersfield, November 15h, 1820.

Huddersfield.[40] There had also been a revival of trade unionism following the repeal of the Combination Acts in 1824. The most significant development at the end of the decade, however, was the revival of the struggle for parliamentary reform following the enactment of Roman Catholic Emancipation in 1829 and the collapse of the Duke of Wellington's Tory administration in the following year.

Mass meetings held on Almondbury Bank in November 1829, on a scale which had not been witnessed for a decade, were attended by thousands of distressed fancy weavers. In July 1830 Huddersfield radicals welcomed news of the revolution in France and also, no doubt, Henry Brougham's well-reported speech in the Yorkshire election campaign, declaring: 'we don't now live in the days of Barons . . . we live in the days of Leeds, of Bradford, of Halifax and Huddersfield. We live in the days when men are industrious and desire to be free'. On 1 November 1830 the Huddersfield Political Union was formed, but there were problems to be resolved before Huddersfield's inclusion in the list of new parliamentary boroughs was assured.[41]

Sir John Ramsden (1759-1839) had accepted that the boundaries of the new constituency ought to extend beyond the central township, but had confided to Earl Fitzwilliam in October 1831 that: 'it would never do to take in more of Almondbury than Lockwood for in the whole of the West Riding I am sorry to say there is not to be found so notorious and radical a Population as that Parish contains'.[42] In the event, however, only the parish of Huddersfield was included within the boundaries of the new constituency,* but this did not prevent non-electors from the town's radical hinterland from making their presence felt in the five electoral contests in as many years after 1832, which produced some of the most turbulent scenes in the town's electoral history.

After the first contest for the new borough seat in the general election of 1832, rioters smashed every window in the house of the victorious Whig candidate, Captain Fenton, who, writing to General Bouverie of the Northern command at the end of the year, claimed that, had the military not intervened, the combination of the fury of the mob and gale force winds might have produced worse scenes than at Bristol, parts of which were razed to the ground in 1831. He concluded:

> Huddersfield is surrounded on all sides by a dense population, composed
> principally of the operative classes, with a very small number of the leading

*A map of the constituency appears in Chapter Nineteen. EDITOR.

classes in proportion. A vast number of the working classes have joined those dangerous societies which under the designation of trades, political and other unions, some of which are bound together by oaths of a most execrable nature, are constantly aiming at the subversion of all social order.[43]

The Factory and Anti-Poor Law Movements:

The main challenge to the Ramsden Whig interest in Huddersfield during this period came from a remarkable Tory-Radical alliance forged by local radical leaders with Richard Oastler (1789-1861), the Tory land agent of the absentee Thomas Thornhill (1780-1844) of Fixby Hall, in the cause of factory reform. A tragic fire at a Huddersfield cotton mill in 1818, in which seventeen young girl nightshift workers had perished, had strengthened the Lancashire campaign for factory reform, but Sir Robert Peel's Act of 1819 lacked effective provision for the enforcement of its restrictions on child labour and applied only to the cotton industry.[44] On 29 September 1830, Richard Oastler, encouraged by his friend John Wood (1793-1871), a prominent Tory evangelical worsted manufacturer of Bradford, wrote his celebrated letter to the *Leeds Mercury*. In the letter, which was published in October, he exposed the plight of thousands of children who worked a thirteen-hour day 'in those magazines of infantile slavery – the worsted mills in the town and neighbourhood of Bradford'. This dramatic intervention appealed to members of the newly-formed Huddersfield Short-Time Committee and, on a Sunday morning in June 1831, the general dealer John Leech (1803-71) and the furniture dealer James Brook (1797-1870) led four delegates: the woollen merchant Samuel Glendinning (1802-83); the fancy weaver John Hanson (1789-1877); the apprentice cabinet-maker and former handloom weaver Joshua Hobson (1810-76) and the merchant Lawrence Pitkethly (d.1858) to Fixby Hall, to invite Oastler to assume the leadership of the revived Factory Movement in the famous Fixby Hall Compact. His oratorical and journalistic skills and charismatic leadership qualities soon earned him popular acclamation as the 'Factory King', and he became central co-ordinator of the movement until 1838. An effective propaganda machine was established at Fixby Hall and central committees, delegate conferences and impressive mass demonstrations were organised at York in 1832 and Wibsey Low Moor in 1833 in support of the Ten Hour Bill.

Fig. 9:11 Richard Oastler
(1789-1861), land steward
at Fixby Hall, who played
a leading role in the
Factory Movement
following the publication of
his letter on 'Yorkshire
Slavery' in the **Leeds
Mercury** in 1830. (KCS)

*Fig. 9:11 Richard Oastler
(1789-1861), land steward
at Fixby Hall, who played
a leading role in the
Factory Movement
following the publication of
his letter on 'Yorkshire
Slavery' in the* **Leeds
Mercury** *in 1830. (KCS)*

Oastler's unwearied personal commitment to the cause was illustrated when he returned to Fixby and removed his boots after the marathon trek to York and the skin from his feet pealed off with his socks. Three successive factory bills were debated during the period from 1831 to 1833. The bill which finally reached the statute book, although not the Ten Hour Bill the movement had wanted, did go further than any of its predecessors in limiting the hours of work of children and young people and in its provision for education and inspection.[45]

Fig. 9:12 Fixby Hall, the Yorkshire home of the Thornhill family, where Richard Oastler met a delegation from the Huddersfield Short-Time Committee in June 1831, forming the 'Fixby Hall Compact', an agreement to work together for the regulation of factory labour. (KCS)

Fig. 9:13 Oastler's triumphal return to Huddersfield, 12 July 1832; his procession along Cross Church Street was led by Lindley Band. Oastler went on to address the Friends of the Ten Hour Bill in Back Green Field. (KCS)

The Factory Movement had received strong support in the columns of the unstamped press and in particular from Joshua Hobson's *Voice of the West Riding*, an unstamped penny paper, published in Huddersfield between June 1833 and June 1834. Hobson developed links with a national network of Owenite booksellers and newsagents and printed his paper on a home-made wooden hand-press. The *Voice* reflected the increasingly class conscious tone of radical politics in the early 1830s and enjoyed a wide circulation throughout the West Riding and Lancashire. In August, Hobson was sentenced to six months imprisonment after refusing to pay a fine for publishing an unstamped paper and after his release moved to Leeds, where he later published the *Northern Star* for Feargus O'Connor. Huddersfield remained a stronghold of Owenism into the mid-1840s and the movement had considerable impact on the character of the radicalism in the town in the 'hungry forties'. In 1835 the first Yorkshire branch of Robert Owen's Association of All Classes of All Nations was established in Huddersfield and in 1837 the first Owenite Social Institution in the county. By November 1839 Huddersfield had its own purpose-built Hall of Science, though the maintenance of the new building proved to be a serious drain on the movement's finances in the next decade.[46]

Fig. 9:14 Joshua Hobson, publisher of the Voice of the West Riding *and the* Northern Star. *(KCS)*

THE
COTTAGER AND HIS WIFE,
AND THE
NEW POOR LAW:

BY AN OPERATIVE.

I WELL did know both John and Sarah Loy;
I recollect, though I was but a boy.
When they were married and appeared so gay,
With joy and mirth they crown'd their wedding-day.
John Loy was honest and to Sarah true,
And she was modest as there are but few;
Love to each other heightened all thair joys,
And they were blest with pretty girls and boys.
John early rose his business to pursue,
And laboured hard to pay each one their due;
And Sarah too, she drew her useful thread,
Swept clean the hearth, prepared their household
  bread;
To make their cottage clean was her delight,
And all things neat, when John came home at night:
The children ran to share their father's smiles,
Their frugal meal and chat the time beguiles;
When from their daily labour they did cease,
They spent their nights in sweet content and peace;
When time for rest the village clock did sound,
They slept together in sweet sleep profound;
This happy pair they lived for many years,
Till age and poverty brought on sad tears.

When John no longer could maintain the board,
And not one child to help them could afford,
They for relief must to the parish go;
With heavy sighs and hearts o'erwhelmed with woe.
No kindness there, but harshest words were said,
While John and Sarah stood as if afraid.
The affecting separation now takes place,
While paleness next to death was in each face;
John to the left, and Sarah to the right,
They looked, they sighed, shook hands, and bid
  good night.
No more for them the cottage fire-side glows—
No more they in each others arms repose;
Those happy days and nights will ne'er return,
They for each other on their pillows mourn.
Tho' nature's fountain may be nearly dry,
Yet pure affections in their bosoms lie.
You, that are called the *Guardians* of the poor!
Oh! think on this if you ne'er thought before;
Pay due respect to God's most holy laws,
Protect the poor, and lessen human woes.
Such ways I ne'er approved in all my life
To separate the husband and the wife!

C. Tinker, Printer, Huddersfield.

Fig. 9:15 Broadsheet published in Huddersfield by Christopher Tinker, the radical bookseller, attacking the New Poor Law of 1834. (WYAS, K)

After 1837 the indignation and energy of the leaders of the Factory Movement, including Oastler and Pitkethly, was channelled into resisting the implementation of the 1834 Poor Law Amendment Act, which aimed to replace the Tudor system of parish relief by a system of indoor relief in workhouses, administered by newly elected Boards of Guardians. When assistant commissioner Alfred Power arrived in Huddersfield, which was to be the administrative base for the second largest poor law union in the country, in January 1837, his meeting with local officials was stormed by an angry crowd, which had been urged by Christopher Tinker, the radical bookseller, to mark their names on a piece of lead and 'send it through anyone who came to enforce the accursed law'. In June, the old workhouse was sacked by a crowd composed largely of women and effigies of the Act's supporters were burned. Later in the summer, after another riotous election campaign, Richard Oastler, who had run the Whig candidate close in a by-election in April, came within an ace of winning the Huddersfield seat and, for the next eighteen months persistent obstruction prevented the Board of Guardians from implementing the new system, which was never fully operated in the West Riding and Lancashire.[47]

Chartism

By 1839, the Tory-Radical alliance, which had never involved a total identification of interests between the two parties, was beginning to come apart with the departure of Oastler from Fixby in 1838, sacked by his employer, ostensibly for alleged financial irregularities, and the rapid growth of the campaign for universal suffrage, which Oastler had consistently opposed. During his northern tour in December 1835, Feargus O'Connor had founded a Radical Association in Huddersfield and, on 26 September 1838, only four months after the publication of the People's Charter, a branch of O'Connor's Great Northern Union was established in the town. A public meeting, called to adopt the Charter and the First National Petition, was attended by nearly a thousand people, a quarter of whom were immediately enrolled as members. Three of those serving on the committee, Lawrence Pitkethly, John Leech and John Hanson, had made the Fixby Hall Compact with Richard Oastler in 1831.[48]

Pitkethly, who had been Oastler's right-hand man, became the most prominent local Chartist, speaking at the massive West Riding rallies at Peep

Green on Hartshead Moor alongside Feargus O'Connor and other radical leaders and attending the Chartist National Conventions of 1839 and 1842. In 1841 he was nominated as Chartist candidate for the West Riding election, along with the militant G.J. Harney, but did not proceed to the poll. He was equally at home in the Owenite and Chartist movements and, after 1842, returned to his Owenite roots, preaching moral regeneration. The Chartist historian R.G. Gammage described him as 'a man of a benevolent turn of mind, somewhat of the Cobbett school of politics; a speaker whose earnestness, rather than his oratory, made him popular'.[49]

A Huddersfield Anti-Corn Law League Association was founded early in 1839 and an Operative Anti-Corn Law Association in 1840. There were frequent bitter clashes between Chartists and Leaguers until the Corn Laws were repealed in 1846. Some 19,432 signatures were collected in Huddersfield alone for the first Chartist National Petition, which was rejected by Parliament on 12 July. Huddersfield Chartism enjoyed only limited trade union support, as was evident in the muted local response to the abortive Sacred Month or general strike for the Charter in August 1839, following which local Chartism fell into sharp decline and the *Leeds Mercury* gloated that Huddersfield, formerly 'a seat of turbulence' had now become an example of 'peace and good citizenship'.[50]

The founding of the National Charter Association in July 1840 revitalised Chartism and, within a few weeks, a branch had been established in Huddersfield, with Edward Clayton, a local bookseller, as chairman. The movement underwent sustained growth during the winter of 1841-42 and, during 1842, 630 membership cards were taken out. However, it suffered severe disillusionment after the rejection of the Second National Petition in May and serious divisions during the Plug Plot disturbances in August, which occurred during one of the most severe depressions of the nineteenth century.[51]

On the 12 and 13 August, thousands of rioters from Saddleworth swept down the Colne valley drawing the plugs from the boilers and opening the dam sluices. At Longroyd Bridge, Joseph Starkey attempted to halt the progress of the rioters, but was quickly overwhelmed, and they continued unimpeded into Huddersfield where at an impromptu meeting at Back Green, some local workers declared: 'we'll join you for the Charter', whereupon the meeting adopted the Charter by show of hands, amidst cheering. The disturbances continued for another five days. More Lancashire strikers arrived in Huddersfield via the Holme valley, but twenty-seven local rioters were also arrested during the disturbances. The local Chartist leadership promptly dissociated itself from the disturbances, announcing that 'the Chartists of Huddersfield ... cannot countenance any riot or any disturbance, or any proceedings likely to lead to a breach of the peace'. The disturbances underlined the tactical and philosophical divisions within the movement and represented a watershed in the development of working class radical politics.[52]

During the winter of 1842-43 Chartist meetings in Huddersfield were poorly attended and the movement lost one of its stalwarts with the death of the veteran radical Tom Vevers (1776-1843), who had been associated with virtually every radical cause since the turn of the century. Another mainstay of the movement was lost when Edward Clayton was expelled for embezzlement a year later. By 1844, as the economic climate improved, the Chartists were struggling for survival and were obliged to share accommodation with the Owenites. During these years the energies of local Chartists were diversified. Lawrence Pitkethly was preoccupied with securing the release of Oastler from imprisonment for debt and, when this was accomplished in February 1844, a revived Ten Hour movement finally succeeded in getting an act on the statute book in 1847. Joshua Hobson, fresh from his experience of municipal Chartism in Leeds, conducted a successful campaign for sanitary improvement in Huddersfield in the period between 1844 and 1848. There was also considerable local Owenite and Chartist interest in emigration and land schemes during this period. By 1847 the Huddersfield District Co-operative Land Society had 264 members, more than half of whom were textile workers.[53]

Harvest failures, commercial crises and revolutions abroad stimulated a Chartist revival, culminating in the presentation of a Third National Petition on 10 April 1848. But the revival in Huddersfield was transitory and the town remained tranquil during May and June whilst disturbances were erupting elsewhere. The *Leeds Intelligencer* commented: 'the Chartists in Bradford and other places appear quite indignant at the peaceful behaviour of their Huddersfield brethren and accuse them of cowardice and want of pluck'.[54] Huddersfield Chartism, with its Owenite and Oastlerite associations, had never fully recovered after 1842. However, the tranquillity of 1848 did not mean that the propensity for popular protest from within the town was extinguished altogether. Joshua Hobson carried the politics of social protest into the 1850s and 1860s in the Tenant-Right dispute thereby denying Huddersfield the social harmony which many other towns experienced after 1850.[55]

John A. Hargreaves

Biographical Note

John A. Hargreaves was educated at Burnley Grammar School and Southampton University, where he obtained an honours degree in History. He has taught History locally since 1971 at King James's School, Almondbury and Howden Clough High School, Batley, where he is currently Head of History. He obtained an M.A. with distinction in 1985 and was awarded a Ph.D. in 1992, both following part-time study at Huddersfield Polytechnic. He has lectured and written extensively on aspects of local history and was awarded the Yorkshire History Prize in 1989 for an essay on the relationship between Methodism and Yorkshire Luddism. He has recently written *Halifax in Old Picture Postcards* and is currently writing a new history of Halifax.

NOTES:

1. J. Mallinson, *History of Methodism in Huddersfield, Holmfirth and Denby Dale* (1898), pp.11-12.

2. R. Brook, *The Story of Huddersfield* (1968), p.79; Mallinson, *Methodism in Huddersfield*, pp 19-20.

3. *Report of the Proceedings under Commissions of Oyer and Terminer and Gaol Delivery for the County of York, 1813* (1813), pp.x, viii.

4. The best general surveys relating to the theme of this chapter are E. Royle and J. Walvin, *English Radicals and Reformers, 1760-1848* (1982) and D.G. Wright, *Popular Radicalism: the Working-Class Experience, 1780-1880* (1988). I am grateful to Dr Royle and Dr Wright for commenting on a preliminary draft of this chapter.

5. D Whomsley, 'Radical politics in the 1850s and 1860s: Joshua Hobson and the Tenant Right Dispute in Huddersfield', *J(ournal) of R(egional) and L(ocal) S(tudies)*, 17 (1987), 14-33.

6. J. Stevenson, 'Food Riots in England, 1792-1818' in *Popular Protest and Public Order* edited by R. Quinault and J. Stevenson (1974), p.33.

7. J. Mayhall, *Annals of Yorkshire* (Leeds, 1861), pp.154, 164; *Leeds Intelligencer*, 5 August 1783; J.A. Hargreaves, *Factory Kings and Slaves: South Pennine Social Movements, 1780-1840* (Hebden Bridge, 1982), p.6.

8. Mayhall, *Annals*, p.184; R.A.E. Wells, *Dearth and Distress in Yorkshire, 1793-1802* (York, 1977), p.25.

9. *Leeds Mercury*, 1 February 1800; W(est) Y(orkshire) A(rchive) S(ervice), Leeds, Radcliffe MSS, 1,578 handbills and depositions, November 1799.

10. Wells, *Dearth and Distress*, p.35; J. Stevenson, *Artisans and Democrats: Sheffield and the French Revolution, 1789-97* (Sheffield, 1989), pp.v-vi, 1-6.

11. Letter from Huddersfield to the London Corresponding Society, 1793, cited in G.A. Williams, 'True-Born Britons' in *The Long March of Everyman*, edited by T. Barker (1975), p.62.

12. E.P. Thompson, *The Making of the English Working Class* (1963; 1968 edition), pp.143-44; G.A. Williams, *Artisans and Sans-Culottes* (1968), p.78.

13. P. Stocks, *Foundations* (Halifax, 1933), pp.488-92.

14. C. Emsley, 'An Aspect of Pitt's "Terror": prosecutions for sedition during the 1790s', *Social History*, 6 (1981), 155-84; S(heffield) C(ity) A(rchives), W(entworth) W(oodhouse) M(uniments), F45/119 copy of deposition. I am grateful to Olive, Countess Fitzwilliam, the Wentworth Settlement Trustees and the Director of Sheffield City Libraries for access to this collection.

15. R.A.E. Wells, *Insurrection: the British Experience, 1795-1803* (Gloucester, 1983), pp.172, 209.

16. Wright, *Popular Radicalism*, p.35.

17. Wells, *Insurrection*, pp.209, 221, 228-29; A.J. Brooke, 'The Social and Political Response to Industrialisation in the Huddersfield area, c.1790-1850' (unexamined Ph.D. thesis, Manch. Univ. 1988), pp.152-53. I am grateful to the author for permission to consult and cite material from a copy of this thesis deposited in the Huddersfield Local History Library.

18. Wells, *Insurrection*, pp.209, 227-37.

19. Stocks, *Foundations*, p.490; Emsley, *Social History*, 6, p.161; Mayhall, *Annals*, pp.189, 193; Wells, *Dearth and Distress*, p.44; *Leeds Mercury*, 17 March 1804.

20. C. Emsley, *British Society and the French Wars, 1793-1815* (1979), pp.137-39; *Leeds Mercury*, 5 March 1808.

21. Brooke, thesis pp.161-63; *Leeds Mercury*, 5 June 1809.

22. J.G. Rule, *The Labouring Classes in early Industrial England, 1750-1850* (1986), pp.363-67.

23. This account of Yorkshire Luddism is a synthesis from the extensive range of literature now available on the subject. The most reliable narrative of the movement is now R. Reid, *Land of Lost Content*, (1986), though F. Peel, *The Risings of the Luddites, Chartists and Plug-drawers* (Heckmondwike, 1888), which draws on the surviving oral tradition of the movement, is also worth consulting. The best survey of the historiographical debate is contained in Rule, *Labouring Classes*, pp.369-75, updated in J.G. Rule, 'Popular Protest in Britain, c.1811-1850', *The Historian*, 25 (1990), 9-10. Two indispensable detailed assessments of the movement from different perspectives are E.P. Thompson, *The Making* and M.I. Thomis, *The Luddites*. A collection of source material is available in E.P. Greenleaf and J.A. Hargreaves, *The Luddites of West Yorkshire* (Huddersfield, 1986 edition). The relationship between Methodism and Luddism in Yorkshire is explored in J.A. Hargreaves, 'Methodism and Luddism in Yorkshire, 1812-13', *Northern History XXVI* (1990).

24. *Leeds Mercury*, 21 March 1812.

25. *Report of Proceedings under Commissions of Oyer and Terminer*, pp.xiv-xix.

26. P(ublic) R(ecord) O(ffice), H(ome) O(ffice) Papers, 40/41 copy of undated letter to a Huddersfield master; reprinted in G.D.H. Cole and A.W. Filson, *British Working Class Movements. Select Documents 1789-1875* (1965), pp.114-15.

27. J. Stevenson, *Popular Disturbances in England, 1700-1870* (1979), pp.160-61.

28. Stevenson, *Popular Disturbances*, pp.157-58.

29. J.R. Dinwiddy, *From Luddism to the Reform Bill* (1986), pp.23-24; M.I. Thomis and P. Holt, *Threats of Revolution in Britain, 1789-1848* (1977), p.36; Thomis, *Luddites*, p.24.

30. L. Kipling and N. Hall, *On the Trail of the Luddites* (Hebden Bridge, 1982).

31. Peel, *The Risings*, p.220; D.F.E. Sykes, *The History of the Colne Valley* (Slaithwaite, 1906), p.319.

32. Reid, *Land of Lost Content*, pp.201, 233-34, 246, 258.

33. *The Life and Correspondence of Major Cartwright*, edited by F.D. Cartwright, vol. II (1826), pp.47-52.

34. A.J. Brooke, 'The Folly Hall Uprising, 1817', *Old West Riding*, 4, I (1984). A.J. Brooke's estimate of the numbers involved is considerably lower than that of Mayhall, *Annals*, p.263 and Thompson, *The Making*, p.725, who, following the *Leeds Mercury*, suggest that several hundred were involved. *See also* Chapter Seven.

35. J. Stevens, *England's Last Revolution: Pentrich 1817* (Buxton, 1977).

36. Mayhall, *Annals*, p.280.

37. Brooke, thesis pp.213-17. The Skelmanthorpe flag is a part of the permanent collection at the Tolson Museum, Ravensknowle Park, Huddersfield

38. Brooke, thesis, pp.218-30; Royle and Walvin, *Radicals and Reformers*, pp.105, 123; Thompson, *The Making*, pp.776-77.

39. WYAS, Kirklees, DD/HF/z/II poster in support of Queen Caroline, 1820; *Leeds Mercury*, 25 November 1820.

40. Brooke thesis, pp.230-36.

41. Brooke thesis, pp.239-66; *Leeds Intelligencer*, 29 July 1830.

42. SCA, WWM, Rockingham Correspondence, G83/143b Sir J. Ramsden to Earl Fitzwilliam, 23 October 1831. I am grateful to Miss S. Richardson of the University of Warwick for this reference and for discussing with me her research on Huddersfield politics in the 1830s. For another account of this episode *see* Chapter Nineteen.

43. PRO, HO 40/31 (3) Captain Fenton to General Bouverie, 29 December 1832, cited Brooke, thesis, p.294.

44. Hargreaves, *Factory Kings*, pp.9-11.

45. C. Driver, *Tory Radical. The Life of Richard Oastler* (New York, 1946); J.T. Ward, *The Factory Movement, 1830-55* (1962); J.T. Ward, 'Richard Oastler on Politics and Factory Reform', *Northern History*, XXIV (1988), 124-45; F. Driver, 'Tory Radicalism? Ideology, Strategy and Locality in Popular Politics during the Eighteen-Thirties', *Northern History*, xxvii (1990), 120-38.

46. Royle and Walvin, *Radicals and Reformers*, p.150; J.F.C. Harrison, *Robert Owen and the Owenites in Britain and America* (1969); S. Chadwick, *A Bold and Faithful Journalist. Joshua Hobson, 1810-76* (Huddersfield, 1976); S.C.E. Cordery, 'Voice of the West Riding. Joshua Hobson in Huddersfield and Leeds' (unpub. M.A. thesis, York Univ., 1984). Cordery is highly critical of Chadwick's treatment of aspects of Hobson's radicalism.

47. M.E. Rose, 'The Anti-Poor Law Movement in the North of England', *Northern History*, I (1966), 70-91; *N.C. Edsall, the Anti-Poor Law Movement, 1834-44* (Manchester, 1971); J. Knott, *Popular Opposition to the New Poor Law* (1986), pp.149-58, 177-97.

48. Wright, *Popular Radicalism*, p.117; E. Royle, *Chartism* (1980), pp.17-23; J. Rhodes, 'Chartism in Huddersfield, 1838-48' (unpub. B.A. dissertation, York Univ. 1986). I am grateful to Mr Rhodes for allowing me to use this dissertation.

49. J.T. Ward, 'Lawrence Pitkeithley', *Huddersfield Daily Examiner*, 2 June 1958; R.G. Gammage, *History of the Chartist Movement* (1894), p.64.

50. Rhodes, thesis, pp.15, 26; Brooke, thesis pp.365, 396, 421; D. Thompson, *The Chartists* (1984), p.352.

51. Rhodes, dissertation, pp.20-36; Thompson, *Chartists*, p.352.

52. Brooke, thesis, pp.404-418.

53. Thompson, *Chartists*, p.217; Rhodes, dissertation pp.36-47; Brooke, thesis, pp.419-51.

54. Wright, *Popular Radicalism*, pp.136-39; *Leeds Intelligencer*, 3 June 1848.

55. Whomsley, *JRLS*, 17, 14-33.

CHAPTER 10

Labour Disputes and Trade Unions in the Industrial Revolution

ALAN J. BROOKE

The transition from artisans' craft societies to workers' trade unions was shaped by the struggle against industrialisation. The clothdressers, or croppers, were in the forefront of resistance to the introduction of machinery and the factory system into the wool textile trade. In 1787 'journeyman clothdressers of Leeds and district' brought a legal action against Richard Atkinson of Bradley Mill for contravening a law of Edward VI by finishing cloth with a gig mill.[1] By the following decade a 'Huddersfield Cloth Dressers' Society' was in existence, until outlawed by the Combination Laws. A notice appeared in the *Leeds Mercury* on 7 September 1799 requesting over 500 members to bring their membership tickets to the White Swan Inn so that the funds could be disbursed by the 'steward' and to 'bring change and none need apply without their Tickets or Numbers which are attended (*sic*) to be destroyed'.[2]

The croppers' organisation did not disband but assumed the dual role of a legal sick brief Institution, operating as a friendly society and an illegal Institution, seeking regulation over trade questions such as machinery and unapprenticed labour.[3] Institution committees in Leeds, Huddersfield, Halifax and Wakefield sent delegates to central meetings at Birstall and also had links with croppers in the West Country where, in 1802, premises using gig mills were being attacked.[4]

In August the Huddersfield committee attempted to stop the use of gig mills by Fisher & Mallinson and Law Atkinson. Threats to twenty-eight strikebreakers that 'they would gig them as they gigged at Bradley Mill' resulted in seven croppers being sentenced to two months hard labour at

Wakefield House of Correction for intimidation. Cloth on Atkinson's tenters was also slashed and in December 1804 Bradley Mill was damaged by a 'mysterious' fire. Although Atkinson did not think it was arson, an anonymous letter sent from Huddersfield to the Royal Exchange Insurance offices in London in 1805 warned against insuring machinery, 'N.B. Only remember Bradley Mill in this county, which did not do one sixth of what was wished for; and expect more about December'.[5]

As well as the illegal direct action, the croppers carried out an overt campaign to petition Parliament to maintain the Tudor laws curtailing machinery. Subscriptions were collected in each cropping shop, sometimes of 1s. to 2s. 6d. per member a week. (Wages, paid according to the length and quality of cloth dressed, varied from 18s. to 30s. per week). A few pence was also levied for the sick brief fund. As the Institution was not supposed to exist and could not legally possess any finances for trade union purposes, any funds had to be classed as the expenses of the parliamentary campaign, required for such things as paying lawyers and sending witnesses to London. Two representatives from Huddersfield attended the 1803 select committee inquiry and in 1806 five Institution members were supported by two fine drawers who claimed not to belong to any society. The "clerk" of the Huddersfield Institution, Abraham Nutter, was called upon to present his books and the 1806 Inquiry showed as much interest in the functioning of the Institutions as in the effects of machinery. One witness, John Ardron, a former cropper at Bradley Mill, later had to refute allegations that he had lied about gig mills damaging the cloth.[6]

The croppers' campaign was supported by the Clothiers' Institution, which embraced both journeymen weavers who worked for others and clothiers who sold their own cloth. Clothiers from the Huddersfield area met at the George Inn, Honley, on 28 May 1806 and adopted a resolution, passed at Saddleworth a few weeks previously, calling for compliance with a law of Philip and Mary limiting the number of looms under one roof to five and jennies to a total of 160 spindles 'in order to preserve and secure the domestic system of manufacture of woollen cloth'. Like the croppers, the clothiers also supported the Elizabethan law making seven-year apprenticeships statutory.[7]

Following a wave of disputes amongst various trades in Leeds in 1805, the employers began an offensive against 'unlawful combinations', which was joined by woollen manufacturers in Halifax and Huddersfield. In September they issued a declaration that they would not employ anyone belonging to the Institution or any illegal combination supporting strikes to advance wages or enforce regulations against machinery.[8]

The 1806 Inquiry concluded that machinery posed no threat to manufacture and that the Institutions were 'still more alarming in a political than in a commercial view', equating them with the subversive organisations behind the French Revolution. Its parliamentary campaign proving futile and the economy reeling from the war with Napoleon, the croppers' Institution declined. When a Bill to repeal most of the laws regulating woollen manufacture was introduced in 1808, a meeting of Huddersfield croppers passed a conciliatory resolution regretting 'those unhappy differences which have so long existed in the clothing districts betwixt the Employer and the Employed' and called for 'Love and Unanimity to prevail amongst all Classes of his Majesty's subjects'.[9]

Their appeals went unheeded. The following year the Bill became law and the number of gig mills and shear frames increased. When the croppers again turned to direct action with the outbreak of Luddism in 1812, an anonymous cropper voiced what must have been a common lament. Thousands of pounds had been expended on petitioning to no avail, 'We petition no more, that won't do, fighting must'.[10]

The West Riding Fancy Union

Although Huddersfield was notable for its political radicalism between 1812 and 1820, there is no evidence of trade disputes such as that of the Barnsley linen weavers or even of organisation.[11] However, at least a year prior to the repeal of the Combination laws in 1824, a trade union apparently existed among the handloom fancy weavers.[12] Fancy weaving, which used a variety of woollen, worsted, cotton and silk yarns to produce patterned cloth, had developed rapidly since the 1790s. The fancy weavers worked at home and were not directly threatened by machinery, the powerloom was not widely introduced into their trade until the 1840s, but from around 1819 they were faced with constant attempts to drive down wages, both by direct cuts and by the manufacturers' practice of using a measure longer than a standard yard.

Following a meeting at Almondbury on 24 August 1824, the fancy weavers' union was 'newly organised' and the 'Articles and Regulations' of the West Riding Fancy Union (WRFU) agreed by delegates at Kirkburton on 6 September, included the declaration:

> As labour is the only inheritance of a poor man, to endeavour to obtain a fair remuneration for it by honourable and fair means is not only a right derived from nature but a duty. . . .

Over the previous two years the payment for weaving some goods had been reduced from 8d. to 3d. a yard and more than five yards in every fifty could be taken by the manufacturer using a long measure. The WRFU took action against Joshua Boothroyd, who made a halfpenny a yard reduction in winter when trade was slack, and Francis Farrand, who imposed reductions from 5½d. to 3d. a yard on pieces still in the loom. An attempt by Boothroyd to put out his work to Slaithwaite weavers was countered by a meeting called by the Union to explain the wage cuts and thirty new members were recruited as a result. Weavers brought in from Stockport to strikebreak by Eli Chadwick, a shawl manufacturer, were met off the coach by a Union official, John Swift of Newsome, and offered alternative work. Chadwick, asserting that he refused to be dictated to by the Union, offered an increase of 6d. per shawl more than the demand. In general the wage increases were met, but Swift found himself unable to find work, 'the shawl manufacturers have turned me quite adrift', he complained. Amos Cowgill, a WRFU president, was similarly victimised.[13]

The most bitter struggle was against Norton of Clayton West, who employed 300 weavers. He claimed that measurement was a matter of custom: 'there is no such thing as a yard; we have forty inches'. An attempt by him to commit all the manufacturers to sign a bond not to employ members of the WRFU failed. On 31 January 1825 a union deputation met several leading manufacturers at the Rose and Crown in Huddersfield, to discuss grievances. Swift dismissed the argument that wage reductions were necessary because of 'foreign competition' and, in a paraphrase of the biblical maxim, described the wealth of the manufacturers as coming 'through the eye of a shuttle'. The following week the *Mercury* reported '. . . a strong public feeling in favour of the workmen'.[14]

In March the woollen cord weavers, who were paid by the length of yarn they wove, not the finished piece, also presented a wage demand, in the form of a printed circular. This was followed by a deputation which secured an agreement with leading manufacturers, including Learoyd of Huddersfield and Armitage of Milnsbridge. Weavers' wages varied according to the type of goods and the regularity of employment. Cowgill stated that a 2s. 6d. to 3s. advance had been secured over the previous year and a toilinette weaver working about fourteen hours a day was now averaging 14s. per week, 2s. of which had to pay the bobbin winder. Swift said £1 could be earned shawl weaving, of which 3s. went to the winder and 5s. to the drawboy who operated the healds. Eli Chadwick claimed, however, that his shawl weavers could average 30s. per week.[15]

Whatever the actual figures, wages were relatively high in the area, according to Amos Cowgill, who announced to striking woolcombers on Bradford's Fairweather Green in July that Huddersfield workers had donated £300 to the strike fund. Two months later Swift promised that support so far was as 'drops before the shower' and, when John Tester, the woolcombers' union leader, visited Huddersfield, some workers gave as much as 10s. each. By the end of the dispute the defeated woolcombers had received £1,688 12s. 1d. from the area – only £150 less than from Leeds. Support for the woolcombers reveals a widespread network of solidarity, which included support from Kidderminster, Loughborough and London. Cowgill claimed the WRFU had contact with, 'many bodies of men at a distance with whom he held correspondence'.[16]

By May 1825 the WRFU had around 5,000 members and was still growing, but its success was short-lived. In December Dobson's Bank collapsed, followed within a month by Sikes', as Huddersfield was hit by the general financial panic. Merchants and manufacturers were left holding worthless notes, international trade slumped and bankruptcies proliferated. Thousands of weavers were turned away from the manufacturers' warehouses without new warps to weave. When the following year an Almondbury weaver complained to the magistrate, John Horsfall, that the parish overseer had refused him relief work on the roads, he was asked only if he was a 'Union man'. On answering in the affirmative the case was dismissed. The Union, explained the *Mercury*, was 'combined in the course of last year to obtain an advance of wages but which now has no existence'.[17]

The rise and fall of 'John Powlett'

Wage cuts were also imposed indirectly by the illegal practice of 'truck payments'. Weavers might receive up to three-quarters of their wages in oatmeal, meat, cloth or other goods, 'not of the best quality nor at so cheap a rate as they might be bought elsewhere'.[18] Although there were at least two strikes for wage increases (in Dalton and Clayton West, where John Heaton, formerly of the WRFU, was secretary to the 'Weavers' Committee' which conducted the strike against Norton), widespread unemployment meant that the weavers had little power. A series of open air meetings on Almondbury Bank led to the formation of an Operatives' Committee, which sought cooperation with 'fair manufacturers' to end the truck system. The Committee also carried out extensive surveys of Huddersfield and the out-townships, revealing the enormous extent of poverty and hardship.[19]

Factory and mill workers, although hit less than the handloom weavers, also suffered wage cuts. However, by 1830 trade union organisation was again making ground, as Huddersfield workers joined the Clothiers' Union, affiliated to the National Association for the Protection of Labour established by the Manchester cotton spinners. The Clothiers' Union, whose objective was to unite all West Riding workers, was usually referred to as 'the Leeds Trades' Union' or simply 'John Powlett', after its secretary. Following an improvement in trade, 200 weavers at Gott's factory in Leeds successfully struck in 1831 for a restoration of wages to pre-1826 levels. At Huddersfield the weavers of Henry Brook and Sons of Wells Mills, whose wages had been reduced in line with Gott's, struck for a 20 per cent increase in 1832, followed by the croppers employed by Thomas Pedley at Paddock. Major firms, such as Brookes of Armitage Bridge, agreed to pay their weavers, 'according to Messrs Gotts' statement' and other firms followed suit.[20] Only at Holmfirth did the manufacturers bitterly resist any wage increase. Events here were recollected a generation later as 'the "Powlett" strike, the suffering resulting from which was so terrible it is not forgotten today'.[21]

The fancy weavers also reorganised and disturbances were 'daily becoming more serious and alarming' as 'blacksheep' strikebreakers in Almondbury and Clayton West were threatened by unionists. According to a sympathetic cotton warp dealer, the unions had achieved a 20 to 25 per cent wage increase for weavers of woollen and higher quality fancy cloths. In an attempt to curb such successes, twenty-three leading woollen manufacturers agreed not to employ any worker unable to provide a character reference from his former employer.[22]

Other trades were also organising. In 1834 masons struck for a wage increase and young millworkers at Norris & Sykes amused themselves at mealtime by 'bah-ing' at the blacksheep carrying out building at the mill. Cardmakers at Lindley struck against an attempt to lower wages to 11s. per week and shoemakers were prosecuted for ducking a non-unionist's head in a puncheon of water. There was even a lodge of 'Operative Agriculturalists' at Farnley Tyas.[23]

A glimpse of the inner-workings of the unions is given by the ledger of the Journeyman Steam Engine and Machine Makers and Mechanics, founded in 1831. The mechanics bought sixty sets of rules from Manchester and a 'pistil' (pistol) and Bible for the initiation ceremony.[24] Details of this were later revealed by George Beaumont, an Almondbury fancy weaver and former member of the Operatives' Committee, who claimed credit for founding thirty-six union lodges. In addition to the ritual elements known from other sources, such as blindfolds, mock thunder, skeletal apparitions and oaths, Beaumont said that lately the imagery had been improved by the depiction of a 'Large Factory' and a carriage containing, 'two wealthy and portly men, riding over the skeleton of the labourer'.[25]

Both government and employers were apprehensive about the secretive and potentially subversive nature of these organisations. Although the Leeds Trades' Union publicly declared in 1832 'that any interference in politics is positively prohibited', its Huddersfield members were openly involved. During the town's first Parliamentary election the trades' unions joined in the great welcome for the Radical factory reformer, Captain Wood, while his opponent, J.C. Ramsden, accused them of intimidating the shopkeepers who made up the electorate.[26] Both Wood's campaign committee and the Trades' Union committee were based at the White Hart and after the election it was a 'principal member' of the Trades' Union who led a deputation to the magistrates to protest against accusations that the workers' organisations had fomented riots on polling day.[27] Leading Radicals such as Lawrence Pitkethly and Joshua Hobson lent their support to the trades unions and Hobson's illegal paper, the *Voice of the West Riding* provided a platform for trade union news.

A few months later the town was again thrown into a ferment by an election campaign in which trade unionism became a central issue. The Whig candidate, Blackburne, described trade union members as 'bulls, tigers and serpents' and exhorted the workers instead of putting two shillings a week into a union 'bag' to 'keep a bag of your own at home'.[28] A poster was published challenging him to explain why, if unions were the danger he claimed, there were no disturbances in the 'entirely "UNIONIZED" ' Huddersfield area, while in the agricultural districts, where there were no unions, property was being destroyed and blood shed.[29]

This time electioneering produced disagreements within the Trades Union, reflecting the division amongst the Radicals about whether to again support Wood, or Richard Oastler's friend, the Tory factory reformer Michael Sadler. A vote of censure passed by the Trades' Union against members canvassing for Sadler was published as a poster by Wood's committee. Three Sadler supporters countered by stating that although they had not been authorised by the 'permanent committee' of the Trades' Union it was nothing to do with Wood's committee. Another Union member published his own poster supporting the three and threatening to leave the Union. This public bickering was seized upon by the Whig *Leeds Mercury* to expose the Union's claim that, 'the sole object of that body was to ensure the operative a fair remuneration for his labour'.[30]

Further ammunition was provided by two Union defectors. On 2 January 1834 George Beaumont, who had recently come into conflict with the Union over his handling of a strike involving his own employer, went before the magistrate, Joseph Armitage, and swore a detailed affidavit claiming that he had been approached by members of Wood's committee to organise 'exclusive dealing', a boycott of shopkeepers who opposed the Radicals. He said that a woollen weaver, Joseph Threppleton, had been given £5 by Wood's treasurer and offered 3s. per day expenses to assist the campaign.[31] On 28 January Threppleton was summoned to a meeting at the White Hart to answer 'some very serious charges of swindling', namely, that in the previous March he had continued to collect subscriptions from shopkeepers without authorisation and appropriated the funds. Pitkethly was present at the inquiry, as was John Swift, formerly of the WRFU, whose son was one of the shopkeepers who had given donations to Threppleton.[32]

Beaumont's warning that Union members were arming and prepared to march into town on polling day did not materialise, but the authorities remained alert. A spy sent to the town in March by the army's Northern Commander, General Bouverie, concluded, 'the Trades Unions are very strong and there is a strong radical feeling'.[33] A demonstration of Union strength was staged on 30 March when a procession four abreast and almost a mile long escorted a member's funeral to Lindley Methodist Chapel.[34] On 4 April a large demonstration was held in the Market Place in support of a deputation led by Hobson and Pitkethly which presented to the new MP, Blackburne, a petition protesting against the sentences on the Tolpuddle labourers.[35]

Beaumont, now under suspicion as an informer, warned that a 'general simultaneous strike' was being planned and provided eleven names, including oath administrators.[36] Letters appeared in the *Mercury*, ostensibly from Threppleton, accusing the Union committee in the White Hart of spending all their time drinking ale and playing billiards and, more seriously, of diverting the Union towards the establishment of the 'Commercial Order'.[37] This scheme, to establish producers' co-operatives and build a Guild Hall for all the trades, had indeed been discussed in March.[38]

Threppleton and Beaumont were the least of the Union's worries. As well as the Tolpuddle arrests there were major lock-outs in Derby and Leeds. Police raided a Union lodge in Oldham where there was serious rioting and one unionist was shot dead. Five thousand met on Huddersfield's Back Green on 19 April to hear demands from Oldham unionists for a general strike until the Tolpuddle unionists were returned home and the eight hour day introduced. The meeting cautiously agreed to await the results of a West Riding meeting on Wibsey Moor on 28 April.[39] With the economy again depressed this came to nothing. Bouverie reported:

> in Leeds, Huddersfield and other towns in the clothing districts it is believed that the unions are falling very much to pieces, the great poverty of the working classes at this moment tells very much.[40]

In June the *Mercury* claimed that the Leeds Trades' Union had been dissolved and the following month that, 'The Trades Unions are selling up all over the country'.[41] A correspondent from Huddersfield gleefully reported:

> The box with its contents belonging to Lodge No.4 of No.1 District of the Fancy Weavers Union held at the New Inn, Linthwaite, was sold on

Wednesday night last for £1 10s. when the company joyfully partook of a bowl of punch on the occasion, with the exception of one individual who went home weeping at the death of the invincible and renowned John Powlett.[42]

Trade Unions and Chartism

A decade passed before efforts were made again to create a union embracing all trades.[43] In this period the rights of trade unions were seen as part of the wider struggle for the political rights of the working classes embodied in the People's Charter. The Chartist leader Feargus O'Connor was present at a meeting in the town in 1838 to hear delegates from the Glasgow cotton spinners, whose executive committee had been arrested on serious conspiracy charges.[44] The link with trade unionism was also evident at a great West Riding demonstration in support of the Charter at Peep Green in October, when Pitkethly read an open letter bearing the signature of 'John Powlett' on behalf of 'the prisoners' of those Huddersfield millowners who had threatened with dismissal workers attending the meeting.[45]

Among the workers and trades subscribing 'National Rent' to the Chartists was a Fancy Trades' Union at Kirkheaton, workers at Kaye's Folly Hall factory and Dewhirst's textile block-printers at Aspley. When O'Connor was arrested, Dewhirst's workers expressed sympathy by signing a temperance pledge until his release.[46] Forty cordwainers also attended a Chartist meeting in Huddersfield and joined as a body.[47] However, the local Chartists were well aware of the limitations of their support. One of the 'ulterior measures', proposed to secure the Charter if petitioning failed, was a 'sacred month', or general strike, from 12 August 1839. At a meeting the week before Huddersfield Chartists passed a resolution describing the venture as 'unwise . . . seeing the improbability of getting the factory hands in this district to make a general stand'. Although the Almondbury fancy weavers responded with a three day 'holiday', the strike in the area and nationally was a failure.[48]

The Chartists' agitation coincided with a growing trade depression and deeper poverty for the handloom weavers. In September 1840 the Lepton fancy weavers initiated the formation of a union for 'protection and relief'.

Meetings were held throughout the area over the following month and a demand for 'an equalisation of the price of labour' was put to the main manufacturers by a deputation.[49] A trial of strength between the union and one of the leading firms broke out in March 1842 when Wood & Norton of Fenay Bridge Mill imposed a wage reduction, provoking a strike of most of their 400 weavers. Attempts to send work to Bolton and to employ about fifty local 'blacksheep' aroused fierce hostility. The 'Central Committee' of the union condemned acts of intimidation for which fourteen strikers were arrested, but the dispute was overtaken by greater events.[50]

On the afternoon of Saturday 13 August thousands of men, women and children entered Huddersfield after marching down the Colne valley, stopping at every workplace on their route. Many were 'turnouts' from Saddleworth, Lancashire and Cheshire but they had gathered local forces; even the hostile *Mercury* acknowledged that 'very generally amongst the working class they met with much sympathy'.[51] On Monday reinforcements of strikers from the Holme valley and over the Pennines were met by a cavalry charge, but the strike continued to spread. The following day several hundred people marched on Fenay Bridge Mill, draining the dam and extinguishing the boiler. Others ranged as far as Clayton West before the movement petered out.[52]

As well as weavers, those arrested included delvers, labourers, shoemakers, coalminers and millworkers. Not only mills and factories but mines, quarries, foundries and other works were shut down. The nature of the strike mystified contemporary commentators and even took the Chartists by surprise. Although at the mass meeting at Back Green, greeting the arrival of the strikers, some local workers shouted 'We'll join you for the Charter', the strike certainly had no clear political objective.[53] Nor is the economic demand of 'a fair day's work for a fair day's pay' made by the Lancashire strikers an adequate explanation of the scale of the strike. Rather it must be seen as a combination of factors in which agitation for the Charter, economic distress and a deep rooted hostility to industrialism all played a part.[54]

Arrests and internal divisions forced Chartists to explore new strategies. O'Connor was one who saw Trade Unions as an increasingly important factor in protecting the working class. In late 1843 trade was again improving and workers sought to recover wage levels. The most militant campaign was by the Miners' Association, which began recruiting in the area in December with a tour by the Lancashire Chartist William Holdgate. By the following March subscriptions from Lockwood, Birchencliffe, Meltham and Lepton were recorded at the delegate meeting in Barnsley. At a meeting at the White Hart on 7 May, to which the Huddersfield coalowners had been unsuccessfully invited, pit delegates discussed the miners' demands and reported that there was no sympathy from the employers for a wage increase. Strikes were called at selected collieries and, supported by subscriptions from other miners, factory workers and trades people such as the tailors, increases were won at local pits, including Waterhouse & Co. of Birchencliffe. Strikes continued in other areas and in August the *Northern Star* reported of Huddersfield 'the trades of this town are rousing to the assistance of the miners of the north'.[55]

Following the introduction of a Masters and Servants Bill, limiting the rights of workers to leave work without notice, the ironmoulders and mechanics held a protest meeting in April 1844, chaired by the Chartist moulder John Chapman. The following year he was again elected to the chair of a meeting at the White Hart to discuss the formation of the National Union of Allied Trades (NAUT) to organise united opposition to such legislation. A bootmaker, William Spurr, was chosen to represent the town's trades at the founding conference. The Huddersfield United Tailors Protection Society and the Skelmanthorpe fancy weavers joined the NAUT in 1847.[56]

Disputes occurred in a number of trades in the mid 1840s. Dewhirst's block printers struck in a wage dispute, journeymen slop tailors denounced their masters as 'tyrants and oppressors of the poor' and masons stopped work on Quay Street mill in protest at their 'tyrant foreman'. Work on the railway tunnel and viaduct was also halted by masons demanding a wage increase. Plasterers struck for a 6d. per day increase to bring wages up to 24s. per week and cabinet makers at John Hanson's struck against joiners working mahogany.[57]

The factory workers

By 1848 the economy was again in deep crisis. However, the violent trade fluctuations had stimulated rather than held back the process of industrialisation. The size and number of factories grew in the 1840s, as spinning and weaving became increasingly mechanised. Factory workers rather than domestic weavers and artisans were to become the main trade union force in the second half of the century, as they struggled to overcome workplace sectionalism and other divisions. Cotton, with its long history of mechanisation had a strong tradition of factory trade unionism. More spindles were spinning cotton than wool in Huddersfield by 1860 when a strike, or lockout, occurred as a result of workers joining the Oldham based Operative Cotton Spinners' Association. Despite a mass picket placed on the station to prevent the bringing in of non-union labour, the return to work was conditional on the men abandoning the Union.[58]

A large proportion of the workers in mills and factories were women and children, considered cheaper and more acquiescent by the employers. However, in 1835, soon after the introduction of the powerloom into Starkeys' Longroyd Bridge factory, fifty women and girls struck against a reduction of wages from 7s.6d. to 6s. per week. In 1857, 400 female weavers at Milner & Hales', Learoyd's and John Day's at Leeds Road and Moldgreen demanded the restoration of a wage cut. They claimed that they could not average 7s. per week, of which 2s. might have to be paid to a child minder. Milner & Hale claimed that a 'good and attentive' weaver could average a weekly wage of 8s. and a girl winder 5s. A Weavers' Committee based at Moldgreen collected donations out of which 2s. per week strike pay was distributed. The women won a partial victory and it was first intended to use the £5 the Weavers' Committee had left to begin a 'Labour Protection Fund' but a few months later it was donated to the Huddersfield Infirmary.[59]

In 1865 Huddersfield Cloth Dressers' Association was founded and within a year had 978 members. Links were established with London trade unions. George Potter, editor of *The Beehive* addressed a meeting in 1866 and £12 was donated to striking tailors in the city. As factory workers, clothdressers were now earning 18s. to 20s. for a sixty-hour week, a decline in real wages as well as status from the early 1800s. In 1871 a demand for 24s. a week was conceded.[60]

A circular in 1869 called for a union for both hand and powerloom weavers, but in 1872 a separate Handloom Weavers Protection Society was set up and met regularly at the Hope and Anchor public house at Shorehead. Unjust measurement was still one of the main grievances. In 1874 the Society registered under the 1871 Trade Union Act which gave some legal protection to union funds.[61]

The foundations of a Powerloom Weavers' Association were laid in 1866, although disputes at various mills continued to be run by Weavers' Committees, which existed just for the duration of the strike and had no permanent finances, as in the case of Cliff End Mill at Longwood in 1871-72, when money remaining after the strike was subscribed to the Infirmary enlargement fund. In 1875 the Huddersfield & District Power Loom Weavers' Association appears on the list of donations to the heavy woollen weavers' dispute, but the majority of subscribers were from individual workplaces. It was only after the bitter strike against Taylors of Newsome in 1881 that a Weavers' Association was formed to unite most of the district's weavers, culminating in the great strike of 1883.[62]

Enthusiasm for a Trades Council resulted in an inaugural meeting in 1875 addressed by Joseph Arch, the agricultural labourers' leader, but conditions were inopportune for union growth. 'Foreign competition' was blamed for the onset of a serious trade depression in 1878. The following year almost 200 weavers of Martin & Co. at Lindley struck against a 10 per cent reduction. When 300 local masons working on the construction of the Market Hall struck over a 2s. per week wage cut, outside labour was brought in to impose it; cotton spinners and twiners were subjected to both lower wages and longer hours. The machine makers' week was increased from fifty-four to fifty-seven and a half hours, resulting in the lock-out of sixty engineers at John Haigh's of Firth Street and other firms; this action nearly broke the descendant of the 'Old Mechanics'' Union of 1831.[63]

By the 1880s, the foundations of modern industrial Huddersfield had been laid by workers who created the economic basis of the town's prosperity and literally built the factory system. Out of their struggles against the exploitation and poverty involved in this process of industrialisation the modern labour movement emerged as a vital part of Huddersfield's culture and political tradition.

Alan J. Brooke

Biographical Note

A socialist since school days at Honley High School, Alan Brooke worked from 1971 to 1975 as a miner at Emley Moor Colliery and was an NUM branch delegate to Huddersfield Trades Council.

In 1978 he graduated from Manchester University with a BA in Ancient History and Archaelogy.

From 1980 to 1983 he carried out research into the Industrial Revolution in the Huddersfield area. He has worked on archaeological excavations and surveys of sites of various periods in Fair Isle, Orkney, Italy and the Jordan Valley. He has travelled in Nicaragua, Ireland, Eustadi (Basque Country) and Palestine, researching into anti-imperialist movements. He is currently compiling a history of the textile mills of the Huddersfield area before the First World War.

NOTES AND REFERENCES

This Chapter is adapted from A.J. Brooke, 'The Social and Political Response to Industrialisation in the Huddersfield Area *c.*1790-1850' (unpub.1988). (Copy in Huddersfield Local History Library.) I would like to thank the staff at the various libraries and archives used during the research, but particularly those of Huddersfield Local History Library and West Yorkshire Archive Service, Kirklees.

1. (W)est (Y)orkshire (A)rchive (S)ervice, Kirklees, Crossland & Fenton, solicitors' papers KC 165/36 25 July 1787. John Robinson versus Richard Atkinson at York assizes.

2. *Leeds Mercury*, 7 September 1799.

3. Most inside information on the Institution comes from the evidence of John Tate, a Halifax cropper, in (P)arliamentary (P)apers 1806 (268) III *Report of Select Committee Inquiry into the State of Woollen Manufacture*, pp.352-358.

4. For a full account of the West Country connection see A.J. Randall, 'The Shearmen's Campaign' (Unpub. M.A. thesis, Sheffield Univ. 1972). (P)ublic (R)ecord (O)ffice. (H)ome (O)ffice. 42/66 William May at Leeds to Mary Tucker. A. Aspinall, *The Early English Trade Unions* (1949), pp.40-69. E.P. Thompson, *The Making of the English Working Class* (1976), pp.570-578.

5. *S.C. on Woollen Manufacture*. 1806 James Fletcher's evidence, pp.263-273; p.312.

6. *S.C. on Woollen Manufacture*. 1806 John Tate's evidence, pp.352-358; *Leeds Mercury*, 16 Aug. 1806.

7. *S.C. on Woollen Manufacture*. 1806 Document presented 7 June.

8. *Leeds Mercury*, 7 Sep. 1805.

9. *Leeds Mercury*, 4 June 1808.

10. Letter from 'Clerk (to) General Ludd' to 'Mr Smith of Hillend shearing frame holder', from Benjamin Gott's papers reprinted in W.B. Crump, *The Leeds Woollen Industry 1780-1820* (Leeds, 1931), pp.229-230.

11. *Leeds Mercury*, 10 Oct. 1818; 7 Nov. 1818; 21 Nov. 1818; Dewsbury weavers had a union by 1819 for example.

12. (P)arliamentary (P)apers 1825 IV *Proceedings of the Enquiry into the Repeal of the Combination Laws* John Swift's evidence, pp.129-141.

13. P.P. 1825 IV *Proceedings* . . . John Swift's evidence.

14. P.P. 1825 IV *Proceedings* . . . John Swift's evidence; *Leeds Mercury*, 12 Feb.; 19 Feb. 1825.

15. *Leeds Mercury*, 9 Apr. 1825. A copy of circular dated 3 Mar. 1825 is in Tolson Museum. Toilinette (or toilinet) was a coloured, patterned cloth made from wool, cotton and silk yarns usually used for waistcoats.

16. *Leeds Mercury*, 16 Jul. 1825, Cowgill's speech; 17 Sep. 1825 Swift's speech; *Bradford and Huddersfield Courier*, 1 Sep. 1825 for Tester's visit to Huddersfield; *Leeds Mercury*, 17 Jun. 1826, for Bradford Union of Woolcombers and Stuff Weavers strike accounts.

17. *Leeds Mercury*, 16 Sep. 1826.

18. *Bradford and Huddersfield Chronicle*, 20 April 1826; *Leeds Mercury*, 8 Jul. 1826; 13 Jan. 1827; 3 Oct. 1829; 14 Nov. 1829; One cropper complained of receiving his wages in herrings. WYAS, Kirklees, solicitors' papers, KC 165/329 John Armitage against John Williamson, Paddock at Pontefract Assizes, 23 Apr. 1827.

19. *Bradford and Huddersfield Chronicle*, 4 May 1827; *Leeds Mercury* 3 Feb. 1827; 16 Jun. 1827; 23 Jun. 1827;
For surveys see *Leeds Mercury*, 12 Aug. 1826; 3 Aug. 1829; 19 Sept. 1828; 12 Dec. 1829.

20. *Leeds Mercury*, 19 Feb. 1831; 8 Oct. 1831; 21 Apr. 1832; 5 May 1832; 20 May 1832; 9 Jun. 1832; *Halifax and Huddersfield Express*, 5 May 1832; 16 Jun. 1832.

21. *Leeds Mercury* and *Huddersfield and Halifax Express*, 4 Aug. 1832 to 27 Sep. 1832; *Huddersfield Examiner*, 12 Feb. 1870 John Hinchcliffe's obituary.

22. *Leeds Mercury*, 1 Jun. 1833; *Halifax Guardian*, 19 Apr. 1834 (Fancy weavers); PP VI 1833 (690) *Select Committee on Present State of Manufacture, Commerce and Shipping*, pp.597-637 William Stocks' evidence. Stocks had extensive local knowledge, not only due to his occupation, which made him familiar with the woollen industry and his position as Parish Constable, but also through his radical sympathies and involvement in the operatives' surveys of working class conditions. However the *Leeds Mercury*, 26 Oct. 1833 attributed the wage increases solely to the improvements in trade. For wages and the workforce in local mills and factories at this time see PP 1834 (167) XIX,XX *Report from Commissioners Relative to the Employment of Children in Factories, Supplementary Report. Voice of the West Riding*, 27 Jul. 1833 (manufacturers opposing Trades Unions – in August, Huddersfield manufacturers also joined those of Leeds in signing a memorial attacking Trade Unions for, 'impeding trade', *Leeds Mercury*, 17 Aug. 1833.

23. *Halifax Guardian*, 27 Apr. 1833; *Voice of the West Riding*, 6 Jul. 1833 (Masons); *Leeds Mercury*, 5 Oct. 1833 (shoemakers); *Pioneer*, 5 Oct. 1833 (Operative agriculturalists).

24. The Ledger was found in the box of No.1 AEU Branch during the 1922 engineers' strike by Fred Shaw and reported in *The Worker*, 15 Jul. 1922; Also in J.B. Jeffries, *The Story of the Engineers* (1945), pp.20-21.

25. PRO.HO 52/25. 189. Huddersfield Magistrates, Walkers and Battye to the Home Office 15 Feb. 1834. Deposition by Beaumont and Threppleton. Although Beaumont was a fancy weaver he claims the ceremony described, obviously from first hand knowledge, was that of the cordwainers. The similarity of the Tolpuddle oath to that administered by Unions in the West Riding was noted by the *Leeds Mercury*, 29 Mar. 1834. John Tester (the former woolcombers' leader) who defected from the Union in July revealed that the initiation rites in Leeds and Huddersfield were the same as the Rochdale Flannel weavers who had adopted 'the death scene' from a division of Oddfellows.

26. J. Hobson, *The Whig, Tomfoolery Election*. . . . (Huddersfield, 1833); Sheffield City Record Office, Wentworth Woodhouse Muniments. G9. 2. Ramsden to Fitzwilliam, 4 Aug. 1832.

27. *Leeds Mercury*, 2 Feb. 1833.

28. *Leeds Mercury*, 11 Jan. 1834.

29. WYAS, Kirklees. Tomlinson Collection. KC/174.

30. *Leeds Mercury*, 28 Dec. 1833.

31. PRO.HO 52/25 (171), (172). G. Beaumont's deposition 2 Jan. 1834.

32. *Voice of the West Riding*, 1 Feb. 1834; *Leeds Mercury*, 29 Mar. 1834, 5 Apr. 1834.

33. PRO.HO. 40/32 General Bouverie to Home Office, 19 Mar. 1834.

34. *Voice of the West Riding*, 5 Apr. 1834.

35. *Voice of the West Riding*, 29 Mar 1834; *Leeds Mercury* 5Apr. 1834.

36. PRO.HO 52/25 (100) Beaumont to Melbourne 21 Apr. 1834; J. Kaye 27 Apr. 1834, enclosure of affidavit signed by Beaumont.

37. PRO.HO 52/25 copy of letter from editor of *Leeds Mercury* to Huddersfield magistrate J. Walker 11 Apr.1834 referring to the publication of letter by Threppleton; *Leeds Mercury*, 24 May 1834.

38. *Voice of the West Riding*, 5 Mar 1834.

39. *Voice of the West Riding*, 26 Apr. 1834; *Leeds Mercury*, 26 Apr. 1834.

40. PRO.HO 40/32 (67) Bouverie to Home Office. 17 Apr. 1834.

41. *Leeds Mercury*, 14 Jun. 1834.

42. *Leeds Mercury*, 5 Jul. 1834.

43. Apart from a short lived effort in late 1834 to establish Robert Owen's Grand National Consolidated Trade Union and its successor the British and Foreign Consolidated Association for Industry, Humanity and Knowledge. *Leeds Times* 27 Sep. 1834, 25 Oct. 1834, 1 Nov. 1834.

44. *Northern Star*, 17 March 1838.

45. *Leeds Mercury*, 20 Oct. 1838.

46. *Northern Star*, 9 Mar; 30 Mar; 20 Jul. 1839; *Northern Star*, 13 Jun. 1840. It was reported that the pledge was broken by one of Dewhirst's pattern designers who, after a binge, ran amok in a butcher's shop with a cleaver! *Leeds Times*, 31 Jun. 1840.

47. *Northern Star*, 3 Aug. 1839.

48. *Northern Star*, 3 Aug. 1839.

49. *Northern Star*, 5 Sep. 1840, 17 Oct. 1840, 7 Nov. 1840.

50. *Leeds Times*, 20 Mar, 1842, 9 Apr. 1842, 16 Apr. 1842, 23 Apr. 1842; *Halifax Guardian*, 2 Apr. 1842, 28 May 1842, 4 Jun. 1842, 25 Jun. 1842; *Northern Star*, 9 Apr. 1842, 21 May 1842, 25 Jun. 1842.

51. *Leeds Mercury*, 20 Aug. 1842. Although as, tradition emphasised, some workers at the mills of the magistrates Joseph Starkey at Longroyd Bridge and Willam Brook of Wells Mills may have offered to defend their masters' property, thousands more enthusiastically joined the movement.

52. *Northern Star*, 3 Sep. 1842.

53. *Northern Star*, 20 Aug. 1842.

54. See also Halifax Guardian, 20 Aug. 1842, 27 Aug. 1842; *Leeds Times*, 20 Aug. 1842, 27 Aug. 1842; *Leeds Mercury* 3 Sep. 1842.

55. *Northern Star*, 6 Jan. 1844 meetings at Honley, Meltham and Lockwood.; *Northern Star*, 9 Mar. 1844, Barnsley delegate meeting Binchencliffe appears as 'Cliff Birchin'; *Leeds Times*, 18 May 1844, White Hart meeting; *Northern Star*, 18 May 1844, 25 May 1844 Lepton strike.; *Northern Star*, 29 June 1844, 27 July 1844, 17 Aug 1844 lists of donations; *Northern Star*, 20 Jul. 1844 list of collieries where increase won; *Northern Star*, 17 Aug. 1844 support of trades; *Northern Star* 5 Oct. 1844, 'very successful' meetings at Lockwood, Birchencliffe with D. Swallow.

56. *Leeds Times*, 27 Apr. 1844, moulders' meeting; *Northern Star*, 17 Apr. 1847; tailors; *Northern Star*, 31 Jul. 1846, fancy weavers.

57. *Northern Star*, 9 Oct. 1844, blockprinters; *Leeds Times*, 29 Mar. 1845. slop tailors (makers of low quality 'off the peg' type clothes); *Leeds Times*, 23 Aug. 1845, *Leeds Mercury*, 24 Apr. 1847, masons; *Leeds Mercury*, 4 Jul. 1846, plasterers; *Leeds Times*, 21 Feb. 1846, cabinet makers.

58. *Huddersfield Chronicle*, 27 Oct. 1860, 3 Nov. 1860; *Huddersfield Examiner*, 3 Nov. 1860, according to the manufacturer John Ogden the men returned after a meeting with the masters at the Zetland Hotel and renounced the Union.

59. *Leeds Mercury*, 9 May 1835, refers to women as 'power loom tenters'; *Leeds Times*, 9 May 1835, points out how power looms were undercutting the handloom weavers' wages; *Huddersfield Examiner*, 24 Feb. 1855, Edward Learoyd summonsed 12 women and girls, striking against a reduction, for leaving work. *Huddersfield Examiner*, 24 Oct. 1857, 31 Oct. 1857; *Huddersfield Chronicle*, 3 Oct. 1857.

60. *Huddersfield Chronicle*, 13Oct. 1865; *Huddersfield Weekly Examiner*, 2 Sep. 1870 9 Sep. 1870.

61. WYAS, Kirklees, KC 381 leaflet, *An Address to the Hand* & *Power-loom Weavers of the Huddersfield District*. Huddersfield 10 July 1869 ; *Huddersfield Weekly Examiner*, 4 Jan. 1873, 8 Mar. 1873, 5 May 1873, 5 Sep. 1874, 29 Sep. 1874.

62. *Huddersfield Examiner*, 31 Mar. 1866, 14 Apr, 1866. *Huddersfield Weekly Examiner*, 10 Feb. 1872 ; WYAS, Kirklees, Ben Turner papers DD/BT, Leaflet, *Heavy Woollen Weavers' Strike and Lockout . . . Report of Income and Expenditure*. Dewsbury Apr. 5 1875 ; Ben Turner *Short History of the General Union of Textile Workers* (Heckmondwike, 1920), Chapter V.

63. *Huddersfield Weekly Examiner*, 30 Jan. 1875., 8 Feb. 1879, Martin & Co strike, 3 May 1879, masons 14 Feb. 1880, spinners, 18 Jan. 1879, 25 Jan. 1879, 1 Feb. 1879 ; J.B. Jeffries *The Engineers . . .*, pp.97-99.

CHAPTER 11

Textiles and Other Industries, 1851-1914

DAVID T. JENKINS

"As a merchant, knowing the makes both of the Continent and the West of England, I assert most strongly, that as far as ability is concerned, the Huddersfield makers are quite at the top of the tree". (J.C. Broadbent, 1905).[1]

The pioneering study of the Huddersfield Woollen industry by W.B. Crump and Gertrude Ghorbal took the history of textiles up to 1851, the year of the Great Exhibition at the Crystal Palace in Hyde Park, London; an exhibition at which the manufacturers of the Huddersfield district were well represented and received due recognition.[2] Huddersfield in 1851, like neighbouring towns, was heavily dependent upon its textile trades, which were overwhelmingly at this period the spinning of woollen yarn and the weaving of woollen cloth. Of the town's male workforce of just over 10,000, one third was directly employed in textile manufacture. Of its female labour force, 27 per cent were recorded in textile manufacture. Textiles were by far the major local occupation. No other manufacturing trade was of particular significance at this time but, like its neighbours, Huddersfield's population of 30,880 engaged in a wide range of industrial and commercial activities.[3]

The second half of the century was one of contrasting fortunes in the textile trades. The cotton industry, no sooner recovered from the difficulties of the cotton famine in the 1860s, began to encounter fierce competition in world markets both from competing industries and from the rising home production of some of its traditional markets. The British worsted industry

Fig. 11:1 Huddersfield Cloth Hall. (KCS)

experienced fashion gradually moving against its staple product, cotton-warped cloth, in favour of the French all-wool worsted. In the British woollen trade fortunes likewise varied. The West of England continued down its long path of decline, loathe to change its products, methods and attitudes. The Scottish trade showed more dynamism, but its products were particularly susceptible to the vagaries of the market and the protectionist barriers of foreign countries. Within Yorkshire the woollen trade was much more progressive. The heavy or low woollen trade of Dewsbury, Batley and Morley gained great advantage from its adoption of recovered wool as its main raw material. It clothed the military forces of the world and the rising army of working men. The Leeds woollen industry was less progressive. The Leeds economy diversified into other industries early and the remnants of its woollen industry showed only little innovation in design and product in the second half of the nineteenth century.

The Huddersfield textile trade stands out, however, as being particularly innovative and active. It both successfully continued to excel in most of those products it had displayed in 1851, adapting them to changes in fashion and to the possibilities created by the availability of new raw materials and techniques, and it diversified its textile activity into other successful specialisms, particularly low and medium quality tweeds, worsted coatings and cotton spinning and doubling.

In 1862 another major exhibition was staged, on this occasion in Paris. The reports of that exhibition described the Huddersfield trade in glowing terms. Some fifty local firms exhibited. The United States Commission on the exhibition wrote of Huddersfield:

> There is no place which produces so large a variety of fabrics of every quality, from the lowest to the highest. It is celebrated for plain cloths and doeskins, fancy trouserings and waistcoatings of the best designs and execution, beavers and paletot cloths of every description, ladies' cloakings of elegant design and richest quality, mohairs, sealskins, Hudson's Bay rugs, cotton warp, and mixed cotton and woollen doeskins and angolas, Bedford and worsted cords, kersey, linsey, quiltings, challies, and articles for children's dresses, and an endless variety of other fabrics . . . .[4]

The report goes on to describe the excellence of quality and neatness of style of trouserings, particularly the silk mixtures. Waistcoatings were mentioned for their variety 'calculated to meet the wants and suit the taste of every market'. This Huddersfield speciality was described as being without rival. The report stressed the richness of quality, variety of design and fabric, and cheapness of manufacture. And specific mention was made of union fabrics for trousers, coats and suits at 8d. (3.3p) per yard upwards, said to be unrivalled for cheapness and produced in large quantities.[5]

In fact the range of type and quality of woollen cloth in Huddersfield and district was wider than in any other area of the Yorkshire woollen trade or the British wool textile industry. The majority of production was for the home market, but the local specialisms were finding markets abroad in Europe, North America and the colonies. A notable development was the tweed trade, geared to supplying 'cheap and useful articles of clothing which come within the reach of the humbler classes who otherwise would be imperfectly clothed'.[6]

The Tweed trade

The growth of the manufacture of low and medium quality tweeds, mainly in the Colne valley but also by mills within the Huddersfield municipal boundary, may be seen as a development out of the local fancy woollen industry. But its success was closely connected with the increasing use of recovered wool, shoddy and mungo, in the woollen trade. The history of the shoddy industry is well recorded and initially related more to the heavy woollen district of Dewsbury and Batley, than to the town of Huddersfield.[7] Developments in the processing of recovered wool for re-use in the woollen industry had taken place through the early decades of the century. Gradually shoddy and mungo was adopted by the industry as a cheaper substitute and supplementary raw material. Recent research has suggested that by the 1870s over one quarter of all clean wool used in the British wool textile industry was recovered wool. That proportion had risen to over one third by the first decade of the twentieth century. Bearing in mind that very little recovered wool, if any, was used in worsteds, and allowing for the relative size of the two main sectors of the industry, it has been calculated that, by 1879, 39 per cent of clean wool used by the British woollen industry was recovered wool. Thirty years later, the proportion was nearer 60 per cent. Allowing for Yorkshire's share of national woollen cloth weaving capacity and the comparatively small amount of recovered wool used in the other major woollen districts of Scotland and the West of England, it would seem that in the decade before the First World War recovered wool formed, remarkably, the majority of all clean wool woven into Yorkshire woollen cloth.[8]

The advantages to Yorkshire woollen manufacturers of using recovered wool were substantial. The most obvious was that although the price relativity between new and recovered wool varied over time, the latter was always significantly lower. Comparison would depend on the type of shoddy and type of new wool, after washing and scouring, but it is not unrealistic to argue, that for the late nineteenth century, the use of shoddy could reduce raw material input cost for that proportion of input shoddy accounted for by 50 per cent or more. Moreover, cheaper recovered wool was also used to advantage as a buffer against rises in new wool prices. It gave woollen manufacturers the ability to make rapid changes in the proportions of raw materials in blends in response to changes in relative price levels of fibres. In periods of rising new wool prices, careful alterations in blends of recovered and new wool allowed woollen firms to stabilize costs and thus prices, as long as the customer was prepared to sacrifice quality slightly to limit price increases.

Another price advantage of recovered wool may be described as the 'colour value'. Dyeing of wool, yarn or cloth was a costly process. The use of recovered wool could enable manufacturers to avoid having to dye their product. Rags were sorted into hundreds of different colours by dealers and manufacturers were often able to buy such rags and produce shoddy in the colour that they required for spinning. The use of recovered wool did increase the cost of blending, and of spinning because of the lower speeds necessary to spin the shorter fibre. Overall, however, it is clear that the use of shoddy gave the Yorkshire industry a competitive advantage over the West of England and Scotland and over manufacturers on the continent of Europe, particularly in France where little recovered wool was used. The British woollen industry performed better in overseas markets than its French counterpart in the fifty years before 1914.[9]

The term 'shoddy' has acquired a derogatory meaning in the English language, but it is not correct to assume that the use of recovered wool in yarn and cloth necessarily meant poor quality in relation to the service the final product had to provide. Moreover, recovered wool should not be seen just as an adulterant. Better types of it had qualities that gave advantages over some lower grades of new wool. Staple length of shoddy could be longer than some very short new wools. Moreover it was not just a substitute for virgin wool. Its use produced particular qualities in cloth, notably a fullness of surface finish. Thus manufacturers might use it as a supplementary or complementary raw material.

Although the main area of shoddy production and use was the low woollen district of Dewsbury and Batley, Huddersfield became a secondary centre for its production through such firms as the Mill Hill Wool and Rag Extracting Company, which displayed its products at a number of international exhibitions. Shoddy was of particular significance in the manufacture of low to medium quality tweeds. This tweed production grew very successfully in the second half of the nineteenth century. It benefited from the design skills of the fancy woollen manufacturers and quite deliberately copied the higher quality products of the south of Scotland, undercutting on price through the use of recovered wool. Initially Scottish manufactures scorned the potential competition of Colne Valley tweed. One Hawick tweedmaker boasted in 1855:

> in comparing Huddersfield cloth with our own, the sun shines on the gaudy Yorkshire suit, and the colour shines no more. A shower of rain pelts its wearer and diffuses the cheap dyes on his linen and person. The suit in a few weeks looks seedy and miserable. Our hero in Tweeds faces sun and rain without fear. Honesty and innate goodness triumph. The colour is permanent. . . .[10]

Before long, however, south of Scotland tweedmakers were rueing the rise of Huddersfield tweed. It was a trade that was assisted by the wool carbonizing innovations of John Nowell and George Jarmain,* which enabled vegetable matter and other detritus to be destroyed in wool, allowing lower and cheaper grades of wool to be processed, as well as more shoddy to be produced. There were many Huddersfield and district firms in the trade. Several were commended at the 1876 Philadelphia Exhibition, notably Jesse Clegg 'for economy in cost in the manufacture of cotton warp fancy cheviots

---

*Jarmain's career is discussed in Chapter Twenty-Two. EDITOR.

of considerable merit, and adaptation for general use', and Thomas Mallinson and Sons for a 'small assortment of fancy cheviots of superior manufacture, at low prices, and adapted for general consumption'.[11] A similar comment was made about the products of John Day and Sons. Clegg's cloth received very favourable mention again at the Paris Exhibition of 1878.[12]

This tweed trade found a healthy market amongst the home population at a time when real incomes for the majority were rising and the working man was gradually becoming more conscious about his dress. In 1877 a trade journal described 'well to do agriculturalists wearing more tweeds instead of fancy or black coats'.[13] Leisure and outdoor pursuits and increased travel were stimulating more regular fashion change and perhaps the market was becoming less concerned about the durability and wearing qualities of cloth. Huddersfield succeeded in bringing the tweed down market. Home business was also encouraged by the ready made clothing trade of Leeds and, on a smaller scale, of Huddersfield itself.[14] In foreign markets, notably the United States, the Huddersfield and district tweed trade undercut the renowned Scottish product, to the annoyance of Scottish manufacturers. It was reported that by careful rag sorting, local manufacturers were able to obtain tones remarkably near Scottish tweed.[15] A substantial foreign trade was developed but it was a business that was particularly susceptible to the tariff pressures of the 1890s. Some compensation was found by producing, on tweed looms, Khaki for the Japanese army during its conflict with Russia in 1905, a war which gave a great boost to the Yorkshire woollen industry generally. The *Economist* was able to report in 1905 that the means of production in the local tweed trade had doubled in the previous thirty years, primarily by the faster working of looms.[16]

Worsted coatings

A significant new departure for the Huddersfield textile industry, which was to have long term beneficial implications for the state of local trade, was the innovation of worsted coatings manufacture. In the last third of the nineteenth century the Yorkshire worsted trade generally faced substantial problems that it was slow to overcome. The root of these difficulties was in the 1840s, when the two main worsted manufacturing countries of Europe began to pursue quite different strategies in production and trade. Developments in dyeing methods in Yorkshire allowed long sought for improvements in the manufacture of mixed worsted cloth; cloth of cotton warp and worsted weft. The British worsted industry rapidly converted its production to the cheaper 'mixed' worsteds for a much wider market. One estimate suggests that by the late 1850s only a little of the output of the industry remained all-wool cloth.[17] France, on the other hand, continued to specialize mainly in the production of softer all-wool worsteds, woven from dry spun yarn produced on the mule; yarn which dyed better to both brilliant and delicate shades. The result of these different strategies was that from the 1840s to the 1860s the British worsted industry gained much of the world market expansion for low to medium quality worsted cloth. These cheaper worsteds provided some competition for cotton cloth and allowed a period of considerable prosperity for Bradford manufacturers. France retained clear command of the higher quality market for all-wool worsted cloth; a fact continually stressed in the reports of the major international exhibitions.[18]

From the 1860s new market influences began to occur. Fashion changes, perhaps partly the result of the American Civil War, the resultant cotton famine and consequent alterations in relative raw fibre prices, favoured the French, and growing German, worsted industry. Moreover tariff barriers in major markets, and notably the United States, were particularly effective against lower and medium quality goods to the disadvantage of Britain. As a result the British worsted industry began to lose trade. It was much criticized at the time for its seeming unwillingness to adapt to French competition and there has subsequently been debate about whether it was lethargic in changing its technology and product to the new market conditions. It is, however, realistic to argue that the scale of the problem the industry faced did not permit easy and rapid solutions. The raw materials, technology and labour skills required for all-wool worsted production were quite different and a rapid conversion to French methods of wool preparation and spinning was not quickly feasible. Instead the Bradford industry pursued a policy, initially rather slowly, of adapting its existing machinery and innovating new products. In the two decades before the First World War it did succeed in recouping some of its previous trade losses.[19]

Whereas the main worsted industry was solidly based on Bradford, the most important innovation in worsted cloth manufacture took place initially in the Huddersfield district and was only adopted by Bradford at a rather later stage. That innovation was worsted coatings, the one bright area of the worsted industry in the late nineteenth century. Various manufacturers claimed to have initiated the trade. Perhaps the strongest claimant was J.T. Clay of Rastrick. In a letter to the *Huddersfield Chronicle* he suggested that John Beaumont of Dalton brought out, about 1853, a vesting of a novel character, made of four-fold woollen yarn twisted with a thick thread of silk. It apparently looked well but was clumsy and wore badly owing to the paucity of threads, with only sixteen ends to the inch and sixteen picks. Clay seems to claim that this innovation encouraged him to experiment. He was advised by a Savile Row tailor to use cashmere to produce a much neater and more serviceable article. Further modifications apparently led him to make a 'coating cloth' for a coat for the Prince of Wales. He stated that 'the trade took time to find public favour but by degrees developed into an enormous trade'.[20] Thus it would appear that the original experimentation with worsted coatings was in the 1850s. None appear to have been exhibited at the international exhibitions of 1862 and 1867, but by the 1870s the trade was well underway in the Huddersfield district. The *Huddersfield Examiner* in 1870 reported that 'the better class coating trade goes on increasing year to year', and worsted coatings began to figure large in the state of trade reports of the Huddersfield district. In the late 1870s those reports record 'very large orders' and 'exceptional demand'.[21] In June 1877 the *Textile Manufacturer*, the leading trade journal, commented on 'the deservedly high reputations of Huddersfield black cloth coatings and of black doeskins' and the journal regularly wrote of good business in Huddersfield worsted coatings, amongst other bleak reports of failures and poor trade in the 1880s and 1890s. At the Philadelphia Exhibition of 1876, which encountered opposition from the Bradford trade, two Huddersfield firms displayed worsted coatings. Those of Ainley, Lord and Company were described as 'well made worsted coatings of good quality'; those of Liddle and Brearley 'a very creditable exhibit . . . in neat designs, well manufactured, and adapted for general use'.[22]

Worsted coatings only appear as a separate category in British trade statistics from 1882. But it is clear from those statistics (Table 1) that the decade of the 1880s saw the great extension of the trade overseas, at a time when many other types of cloth were experiencing severe problems in export markets.

Table 1 Export from Britain of Worsted Coatings

annual average	million yards	annual averages	million yards
1882-84	4.3	1900-04	17.6
1885-89	15.0	1905-08	20.0
1890-94	25.5	1909-13	23.6
1894-99	23.7		

By the 1880s Bradford firms were beginning to get involved in manufacture but the business was still primarily based in Huddersfield and district. A very good description of it was written in 1883:

> The extension and development of the worsted coating trade has formed, perhaps, the most important feature in the progress in the year now closed. This comparatively modern branch of local manufacture has rapidly advanced into the first place in importance, and the increased favour which, year by year, the public regard this class of goods is conclusive as to their appearance and durability. The plain twills have been most in favour, the fancy patterns now being reduced to the smallest and neatest designs. These goods, for which Huddersfield by common consent now stands unrivalled, are produced here in all qualities, though it is no doubt in the better class goods in which our manufacturers most excel. These cloths are being largely woven, not only for coatings, wherein they replace to a large extent black superfines, but also for overcoatings, and for ladies' jackets and mantles.[23]

The yarn used was either spun locally or imported from Belgium. Huddersfield worsted coatings appear to have successfully competed against Leeds woollen coatings and West of England coatings, to the extent that by the mid-1870s some West of England firms were attempting to experiment with worsted cloth production.[24]

The trade became quite dependent on the American market and was affected in the 1890s by the fluctuations in American tariffs. The McKinley tariff of 1890 disturbed trade but the Wilson tariff of 1895 reduced restrictions and created a boom in American demand. In 1895 57 per cent of exports of worsted coatings went to the United States. The revival was shortlived however. The Dingley tariff of 1898 curtailed business. But other markets were successfully developed in Empire countries and South America.

Key

A Main Entrance
B Office and Workpeople's Entrance
C Timekeepers' Lodge
D Office
E Hoistway
G Yarn Store
H Weaving Shed
I Office Entrance
J Counting House
L Store Rooms
M Shearing
N Milling
O Washing and Scouring
P Tentering and Pressing
Q Engine House
R Boiler House
S Economiser House
T Water Closets
U Designing and Pattern Weaving
V Cloth Inspection
W Examining and Mending

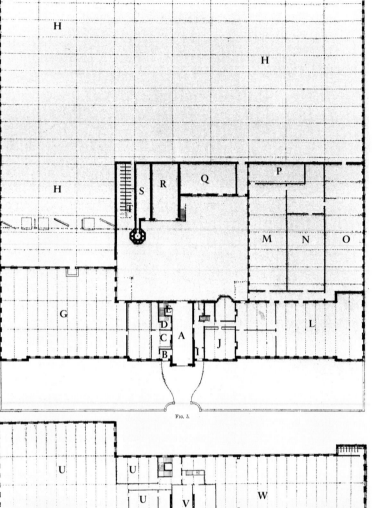

Fig. 3.

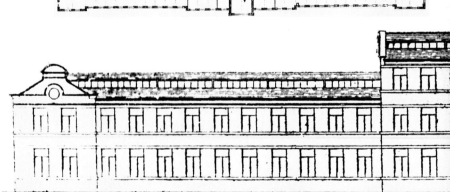

Fig. 11:2 Messrs Learoyd Bros. Fancy Worsted Mills, 1896. Designed by John Kirk & Sons, Huddersfield, 'The Textile Manufacturer', 15 December 1896. (Univ. of Leeds)

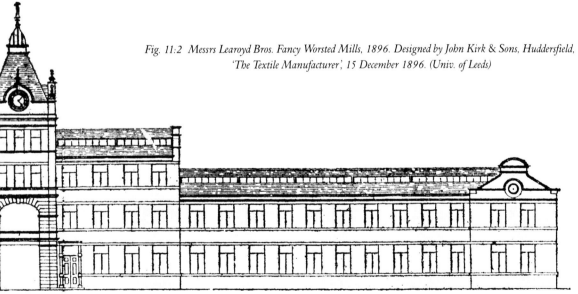

Worsted coating production in Huddersfield also paved the way for other innovations in worsted cloth manufacture in what had previously been entirely a woollen cloth district. From about 1900 the district began to establish its subsequently longstanding reputation for all-wool worsted suitings. This important trade gave rise to a number of famous firms and a host of small specialist weaving businesses that bought in yarn. In 1921 the town claimed that the high class worsted cloth of Huddersfield possessed 'distinctive features of texture, pattern, quality and finish that place them first in any country.'[25] Bradford may not have totally agreed but Huddersfield worsted cloth had attained a reputation that was to survive through the twentieth century.

The rise of local worsted manufacturing can be roughly traced from occupational data in the census. Enumeration and classification cannot be assumed to be entirely accurate. However, the 1861 census records only sixteen men and seventeen women engaged in worsted manufacture in Huddersfield registration district. By 1881 794 men and 926 women were employed in the trade.[26] Ten years later the numbers were 1,295 and 2,195 respectively, clearly reflecting the expansion of local worsted manufacture as reported in the trade press and indicating how worsted manufacture had become the great growth area of local textile production. In 1891 almost one quarter of Huddersfield's wool textile workers were engaged in the worsted branch of the industry.[27] One assessment in 1905 suggested that tweeds and worsteds were of roughly equal importance to the local economy in terms of the value of labour employed.[28]

Fancy woollens

The traditional local manufacture of fancy woollen cloth, often with very intricate designs and weaves, continued through the second half of the nineteenth century but was overshadowed by the growth of tweeds and worsted coatings. However, the fancy trade still showed great versatility and adaptability. Some of its traditional products gradually went out of favour, for example fancy waistcoats, which were reported as declining in demand in the 1870s.[29] But a very wide range of products continued to be manufactured. 'To enumerate the sub-varieties of these goods' wrote the *Textile Manufacturer*, 'would almost read like an auctioneer's catalogue'.[30]

Manufacturers quickly reacted to fashion and experimented to influence fashion. The 'novelty trade', as it became known, showed a great deal of ingenuity. Local manufacturers tested the market and tried to influence fashion with some quite outrageous designs and fabrics. They experimented with various fibres. Dog hair, feathers, rabbit fur and other furs and hairs were incorporated in cloth. The Huddersfield district was at the forefront of the craze for imitating animal skins when that was in vogue. At one stage it had a major business in black doeskins for trouserings. The fancy trade made much use of silk both in elaborate weaves and in embroidery.

The instability of fashion and the demand for novelties required new ideas and designs annually. 'Fashions now multiply *ad infinitum* . . . eclecticism is universally practiced' wrote a trade journal in 1881.[31] The risks that manufacturers had to take in responding to such changes were great. The rapid changes in, and variety of, demand meant that it was often only possible to produce short runs of cloth. This may have kept profit margins low but it did allow a place for the small firm. The difficulties caused were well described by a local witness to the Government Commission on Depression in Trade and Industry in 1884:

> I should say that business is now more difficult to do and to manage on account of the changes in fashion, which entail considerably more labour on the part of manufacturers; and we have to make a quicker response in the matter of taste and demand for style.[32]

Business was more hand to mouth, to use a contemporary term. Reading fashion trends wrongly could be disastrous, leaving manufacturers with useless stock. On the other hand, fashion changes presumably increased total expenditure on clothes. Surviving patterns suggest the district was capable of maintaining high design standards. Some firms employed their own designers, others bought in patterns, including some from Paris.[33] Manufacturers watched carefully the patterns of the Scottish designers. Piracy of designs in the United States was annoying local manufacturers early this century, but perhaps they could hardly complain as they had clearly previously benefited from the designs of Scotland and elsewhere.

Handloom weaving remained an essential part of local enterprise until at least the 1890s. The intricacy and elaborateness of some of the designs of the period required the handloom, especially where production runs were short.

Patterns were also often woven on the handloom. One estimate suggests that as late as 1866 one quarter of the looms in the Huddersfield fancy woollen trade were still operated by hand. In the 1880s at one stage attempts were being made to attract handloom weavers from Scotland to some of the villages south of Huddersfield. Handlooms were still being manufactured in the district in 1885.[34]

Other textile activity

In 1851 some 400 Huddersfield inhabitants were engaged in cotton manufacture. By the end of the century the number was nearer 2,500, employed by some fourteen firms and and working half a million spindles.[35] During a period when both the Yorkshire woollen and worsted industries made substantial use of cotton warps, Huddersfield developed as the main Yorkshire district to service their needs for the doubling of cotton.[36] No estimate has been made of the amount of cotton yarn the Yorkshire wool

Fig. 11:3 Advertisement for John Beever & Sons, Yorkshire Textile Directory 1911-12. (KCS)

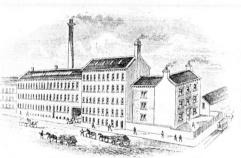

textile industry consumed. Nor can we be sure about what part of those needs Huddersfield supplied. Huddersfield also doubled yarn for Lancashire. In 1901, one in six local textile workers were engaged in the cotton trade.

Besides these main areas of Huddersfield textile activity, there were firms engaged in other areas of textile manufacture. There was an important local group of hearth rug manufacturers; some fifteen firms in 1900. There were flannel and shawl manufacturers at the same date and also a ramie, or china grass, manufacturer.[37]

Dyeing and finishing operations were in some instances carried on within the local woollen and worsted mills. Much work was also done by specialist firms on a commission basis. All classes of dyeing were said to be carried out in the district and each firm claimed particular expertise. There was much debate about the quality of Yorkshire dyeing the late nineteenth century. Some manufacturers believed that local dyers were incapable of emulating the best of Continental standards. Types of fibre used, manufacturing processes and machinery employed and the nature of cloth produced determined dyeing quality, not just the skill of the dyer. Within the Huddersfield district the problems of attaining a sufficiently high quality of dyeing seem to have been less than in Bradford. Huddersfield dyers claimed that it was the excellence of the dyeing and shades and finishing operation that helped to account for the high reputation of Huddersfield fabrics, as regards quality and appearance.[38] But there were complaints from time to time about Huddersfield dyers not matching continental standards.[39]

Relatively few textile factories were situated within the municipal boundary, compared with those in neighbouring townships; not surprisingly because of the constraints on available, suitable land and consequent land prices. But the town itself was a focal point for commercial and merchanting activity, for both the home and export trades. The Huddersfield Cloth Hall survived better than than the cloth halls of neighbouring Yorkshire towns. Built in 1766, it was enlarged in 1780 and in 1848, and extended again in 1864, perhaps reflecting the extent of survival of small clothiers south of Huddersfield. The last extension was ill-planned, however, because by 1870 demand for its services had much declined.[40]

Another aspect of commercial activity was the packing of cloth for export. For reasons which are not clear, but may relate to the existence of a local American consul, Huddersfield became a significant centre for the

*Fig. 11:4 Plan of the
Huddersfield Cloth Hall.
(KCS)*

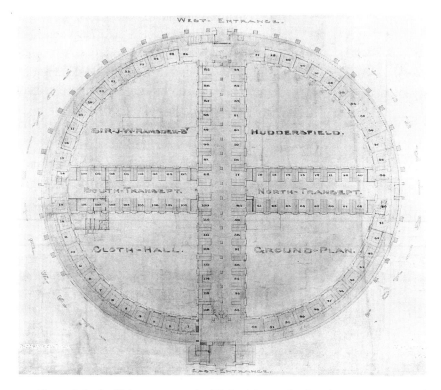

packing of cloth. Shipments to the United States had to have contents and value certified by a consul. Manufacturers from the West of England and Scotland, and many from elsewhere in Yorkshire, used the services of Huddersfield packing firms to send their goods abroad. Tariffs on packing cases to America, at one stage 55 per cent *ad valorem* hurt the business in the 1890s and a local packing case industry, reported to have employed twenty workers was almost put out of existence.[41]

Some local cloth, particularly tweed, was manufactured in the town into ready-made clothing. This industry was small compared with Leeds. Dressmaking and tailoring employed 1,303 men and 2,611 women in 1911, amounting to 3.7 per cent and 13 per cent of the male and female occupied labour respectively. Apart from domestic service, this was the second biggest category for women's employment, after textiles.

The Huddersfield Chamber of Commerce quite actively represented the commercial interests of the local textile trade. Constituted in 1853, it seems to have taken up some issues with alacrity. It paid close attention to treaties and changes in trading restrictions. Its main interests were primarily local; it was active in the promotion of other commercial facilities and was an alert watchdog over the provision and efficiency of postal and rail services for example.[42]

On the eve of the First World War the textile business of the Huddersfield district was greater in volume, and possibly in value, than at any previous time and a very wide variety of cloth continued to be manufactured. Some of the types of woollen cloth manufactured in 1851 had been ousted by fashion movements or superceded by new methods. Many local specialisms were still largely unrivalled by the products of other districts. Thus Huddersfield stands out as the most successful of the Yorkshire, and British textile districts in the half century before the First World War, an opinion held by contemporary commentators. The *Textile Manufacturer* described Huddersfield as 'the most thriving and prosperous manufacturing district of Yorkshire' in the 1880s.[43] Favourable contemporary comments about local textile manufacture abound and hindsight suggests that they were largely justified.

To what can this success be ascribed? Maybe Huddersfield was lucky not to have suffered major exogenous fashion movements against its products as Bradford did. Maybe it was lucky that the fickleness of fashion in the period was advantageous to it. Weight should be put not just on luck, but on judgement. The same trade journal wrote two years later:

> ...one of the strongest points in our progress has been the increased facility and promptitude with which our manufacturers and designers have adapted themselves to the ever changing requirements of public taste, equally in respect of fashion and pattern.[44]

The variety of Huddersfield's industry may have prevented entrenched attitudes, such as those suffered by the West of England woollen industry, and encouraged experimentation and emulation. There seems to be evidence that its commercial enterprise outshone its neighbours'. It showed greater interest in the international exhibitions; although perhaps some of its products were more suitable for the nature and purpose of those exhibitions. Local firms exhibited more regularly than was typical for West Yorkshire. For example, at the 1878 Paris Exhibition nineteen Huddersfield manufacturers exhibited, compared with only seven from Leeds, although, of course,

Huddersfield's trade was larger by this time. The local standard of display at the exhibitions was often, but not always, favourably commented on. At the Paris Exhibition the Huddersfield display was described as neat, chaste and compact and well presented and it won the Grand Diploma of Honour, and its Chamber of Commerce reports on exhibitions were often the most revealing and perceptive.[45] Local enterprise and innovation in the textile industries would seem to stand out more than that of any other district.

Chemicals and dyestuffs

The development of the Huddersfield chemical industry in the nineteenth century was closely related to the colour needs of textile manufacture, but the pioneering local firm, Read Holliday, the leading enterprise in local chemical manufacture, had interests far wider than the manufacture of dyestuffs. Moreover this, at times, very dynamic firm was instrumental in providing skills and ideas which gave birth to other local firms and related industrial activity. So important was this one firm to the creation and later prosperity of the Huddersfield chemical industry that it is relevant to trace its history in some detail.[46]

Read Holliday established himself in business in rented premises at Tanfield, off the Leeds Road, in 1830 at the age of twenty-one. His family had been variously engaged in tanning, flour milling, wool spinning and tin smithing in the Bradford and Otley areas. He gained experience with chemicals at a Wakefield works producing sal ammoniac, which was used in tin plating and as a flux for soldering.

The opportunity that Read Holliday initially saw at Huddersfield was the distillation of ammonia from the ammoniacal liquor wastes from the works of the Huddersfield Gas Light Company. The ammonia provided an alternative to stale human urine or 'sig' for cloth scouring and Read Holliday gradually built up a trade with local cloth manufacturers. Thus the birth of this new industry was directly related to the needs of wool textile manufacture.

Within a few years, local opposition to the pollution created by Read Holliday's works forced him to move to the site at Turnbridge on which the firm's huge chemical complex developed over later decades. His ammonia based products diversified into washing powder, soda ash and other domestic

Fig. 11:5 Read Holliday.
(KCS)

chemicals. He began to sell some natural dyes and appears to have traded in other chemical products, including ink, black lead, tapers and matches.[47]

A major step forward in the firm's activities from the 1840s was experimentation with the distillation of coal-tar. He began producing creosote, at a time when it was much in demand for preserving railway sleepers, and pitch, which he exported to the continent as a binding medium for coal dust for making coal briquettes. Further experimentation at the works produced a sufficiently high quality of naphtha for burning purposes and the firm also started manufacturing naphtha lamps, for which patents were taken out in 1848 and 1853.

The firm's expertise in coal-tar distillation and manufacture of by-products encouraged it to establish plants elsewhere in Yorkshire and at Bromley by Bow in East London. Through the 1850s, the still quite small enterprise was highly active in experimenting with coal tar and its derivatives. Read Holliday visited France to acquaint himself with developments there and made contacts with other chemists working in the field. He bought in technical expertise and developed an association with the chemist, Charles Blackford Mansfield, who had also invented a naphtha lamp and had an interest in colour chemistry. Read Holliday's products diversified through the 1850s at a time when the needs of the local economy were becoming much more extensive and varied. Production of benzene for degreasing and spot removal on textiles created another link with the local textile industries. That link was extended further when the firm entered the dye industry in the 1860s.

W.H. Perkin began to manufacture his artificial aniline dye mauvine in 1857. Demand developed rapidly for the magenta dye and Read Holliday, by then one of the country's largest coal-tar distillers, was well placed to get involved in the business. Paraffin lamps were affecting his naphtha business and local opposition to the pollution from his works was creating difficulties for some production processes. Thus the invention of synthetic dyes came at the right time for the firm. Read Holliday's sons, Thomas and Charles, both developed an interest in colour chemistry and entered the firm. Business activity swung rapidly towards the manufacture of aniline dyes and from the 1860s through to the 1880s the firm was remarkably innovative in the field of artificial dyestuffs, and dyeing methods and machinery. A subsidary company to manufacture magenta was set up in New York in 1864. Read

Holliday himself retired from the business in 1868 and control passed to his sons, who maintained and extended the firm's research activities, and during the 1870s developed a broader portfolio of aniline dyes, extending the colour range significantly. The firm experimented successfully with natural indigo dyeing, until overtaken by German synthetic indigo.[48]

The decade of the 1870s was a frustrating period for the business. Its dyestuff innovations allowed it to expand from a labour force at Turnbridge of forty-two in 1870 to, at one time, over 140. Relocation of distilling to Wakefield and fierce German competition had reduced the workforce to fifty by 1880.[49] In spite of continued successful technical experimentation, the firm, like the British dyestuffs industry in general, suffered from the ferocious competition and well protected methods of the German giants. It again looked for means to diversify. The brothers, Thomas and Charles, became engaged in woollen manufacture in Normandy. But the emphasis on dyestuffs manufacture continued and a new lease of life appears to have occurred in the 1890s. At the beginning of the decade the firm, Read Holliday and Sons, became incorporated as a private limited liability company and found the capital to expand. The site was extended, plant modernised and the company's product range increased. The policy was successful. An account of the firm in the mid-1890s describes it as employing 1,500 work people 'in some seventy departments and fifteen laboratories'. It was consuming 25,000 tons of coal a year, some of which came from local collieries owned by the firm, and it was processing some 21,000 tons of raw materials annually. By this time the circumference of its works at Turnbridge extended over two miles.[50]

The firm clearly tried to keep abreast of German dye developments, in spite of patent problems. It appears at times to have been a little devious in its production and marketing methods to cope with the force of competition. The business was restricted by the need to use imported intermediates. A new departure, but one perhaps influenced by the firm's earlier interest in lamps, was experimentation in the 1890s with acetylene generators and lamps. Thomas Holliday took out a patent for an acetylene generator in 1890 and subsidary companies were created to manufacture and trade in this area. But the death of Thomas, and then his brother Robert, brought this branch of the firm's activities to an end, although one important spin off for Huddersfield was that acetylene development had begun to lead the company towards the manufacture of electric dynamos, under the management of Ernest Brook, who went on to establish his own company in 1904.[51]

From the close of the century the firm began to encounter severe business and financial problems. The death of Thomas Holliday in 1898 deprived it of a sound business leader. The other brothers died within the space of a few years and for a while there was a vacuum in leadership. The United States branch was encountering problems. Production costs were rising in a period when competition was fiercer than ever. The firm responded to Government encouragement to enter the chemical explosives field and invested in plant to produce Lyddite (picric acid). It also started large scale production of 'synthetic' phenol. The picric acid plant, and much of the neighbouring factory, was wrecked by an explosion in 1900 and the firm's attentions had to be diverted to rebuilding.[52]

The result of these problems was a decision in 1901 to rationalize severely. The non-dye activities were curtailed; soap manufacture ceased; the common dyehouse was closed; the acetylene and electric dynamo projects were brought to an end. The labour force was reduced to 750 by 1914. Business was concentrated on artificial dyestuffs to meet German competition. Plant and methods were modernised and sales improved. The rationalization was subsequently to prove helpful when war curtailed supplies of German dyes. But war brought to an end to the firm of Read Holliday and Sons Ltd. The desperate need to divert the British chemical industry to the war effort led to Government action to create a national dyestuffs enterprise, British Dyes Ltd., which subsumed the Holliday business and led to a huge expansion of chemical manufacture on the eastern fringe of Huddersfield. In 1919 British Dyes Ltd. was amalgamated with Levinstein Ltd. to form the British Dyestuffs Corporation. Seven years later Imperial Chemical Industries (ICI) was formed to acquire this and other chemical manufacturers, in order to form an organisation with sufficient financial, commercial and technical resources to compete with the continental chemical giants.[53]

The Read Holliday enterprise formed the core of Huddersfield's important chemical manufacturing industry. That importance was far more

Fig. 11:6 A Read Holliday advertisement from c.1900, indicating the firm's range of products, 'Britain's Greatest Manufacturers'. (WYAS, C)

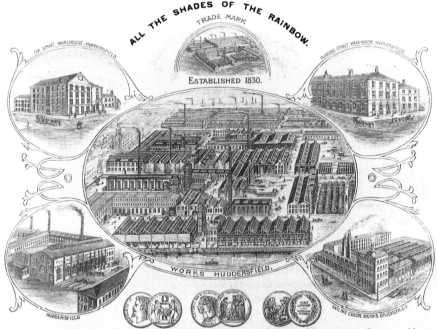

Fig. 11:7 Advertisement for James Robinson &Co. in 'Britain's Greatest Manufacturers'. (WYAS, C)

than local in terms of innovation and production, but its innovatory activity was an example to others locally and the labour skills that it imparted were instrumental in creating a local labour force from which other firms no doubt benefited. It is interesting to note, however, that other local chemical firms developed in the second half of the nineteenth century quite independently. The firm of Dan Dawson, which became the Colne Vale Chemical Company, was also a pioneer in the manufacture of artificial dyestuffs. It was involved in the 1860s in the development of magenta and other basic dyes. Part of the firm's premises at Milnsbridge were taken over in 1890 by John Walker Leitch, who rapidly developed an aniline dye manufacturing concern and then, from 1902, started producing trinitrotoluol (TNT), the first large scale production of it in Great Britain.[54] Other significant Huddersfield chemical firms included James Robinson & Co of Hillhouse Lane which maintained a large business in natural dyestuffs through the second half of the century in spite of competition from synthetics. But after 1900 its trade

Table 2 The Occupational Profile of Huddersfield in 1911

Occupation	Men		Women	
	Number employed	% of total occupied	Number employed	% of total occupied
National & local government	530	1.5	76	0.4
Professional	909	2.6	841	4.2
Commercial	2,101	5.9	239	1.2
Public utilities	522	1.5		
Domestic offices & services	615	1.7	3,271	16.4
Transport & storage	3,356	9.4	75	0.4
Agriculture	701	1.9	34	0.2
Mining & quarrying	510	1.4	1	
Building & construction	2,974	8.3		
Food, drink & lodging	2,295	6.5	1,266	6.3
Metal work, machine making and engineering	4,410	12.4	106	5.3
of which				
General engineering & machine making	*3,169*	*8.9*	*48*	*0.2*
Chemicals, oil, soap etc.	712	2.0	67	0.3
Skins, leather etc.	205	0.6	38	0.2
Textile manufacture & dealing	12,785	35.9	13,219	66.3
of which				
Cotton	*695*	*2.0*	*1,339*	*6.7*
Woollens & worsted	*8,641*	*24.3*	*8,085*	*40.5*
Carpets, rugs & felt	*92*	*0.3*	*478*	*2.4*
Bleaching, dyeing etc.	*928*	*2.6*	*67*	*0.3*
Dealing	*727*	*2.0*	*300*	*1.5*
Dressmaking	*1,517*	*4.3*	*2,725*	*13.7*
Other occupations	2,977	8.4	1,201	16.0
TOTAL OCCUPIED	35,622	100.0	19,956	100.0

(*source:* Census of Population, 1911.)

declined and it diversified into merchanting artificial dyestuffs and refining fats and spinning oils from wool wastes.[55] Twenty-two manufacturing chemists were reported as polluting local rivers by the Rivers Pollution Commission in 1867.[56]

The census of population categories, the variety of employment within the Huddersfield chemical industry and the geographical location of Read Holliday do not permit accurate measurement of total employment and the role of the industry in the local labour market. Table 2 records employment for the town of Huddersfield in 1911. Although the numbers employed are much below the figures for textile manufacture, the industry had a very significant role within the local economy and the base created in the second half of the nineteenth century has continued to serve the town's economy well in the twentieth century.

Other industries

Like other major manufacturing towns, Huddersfield experienced a progressive diversification of its industrial base during the nineteenth century. That diversification resulted from a variety of influences. With a substantial population within the town and with a considerable hinterland, for which it served as a market and distribution centre, Huddersfield had to provide for the day to day needs of its people. Many, perhaps most, of those needs were provided by local firms. Other industry resulted from local raw material supply, coal and stone, for example. However, the growth of other major industrial activity, rather than the development of individual firms, arose out of the increasingly complex and specialist needs of the textile and chemical trades. The town spawned a range of engineering and machine making businesses in particular. Other industry developed as a result of local construction needs. Some firms established themselves in Huddersfield without any obvious links to existing industry or particular local needs. Industrial diversification is primarily explicable through market influences, but skilled labour availability and wealth generated within existing industry contributed to the process.

By 1850 there was already a range of local industries to provide for local consumer needs and to service the day-to-day requirements of the local economy. White's *Directory* of 1853 lists 92 boot and shoe makers, 13 braziers

Wm. Whiteley & Sons Ltd

LOCKWOOD, HUDDERSFIELD.

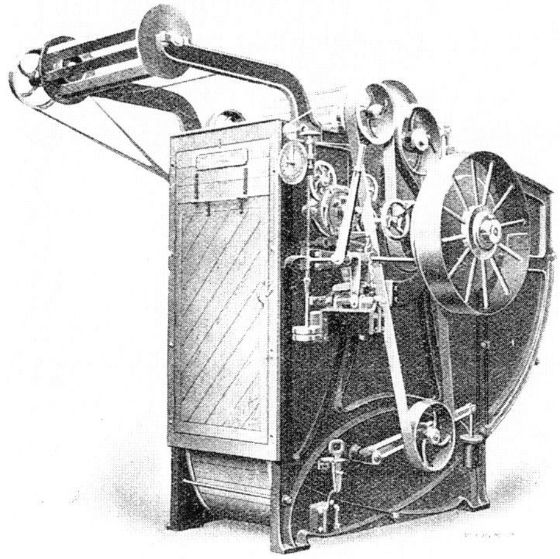

Milling Machine, Friction Drive.

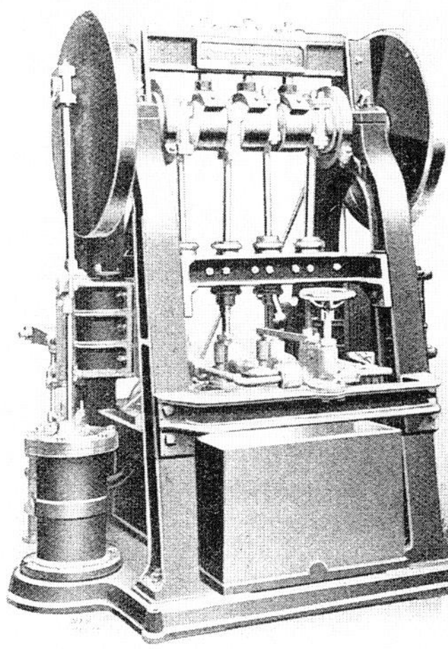

Hydraulic 4 Plunger Pump, Direct Driven.

CONTINUOUS ROTARY (HYDRAULIC) PRESSING MACHINE.

IMPROVED PATENT TWISTING AND FANCY DOUBLING MACHINE for Woollen, Worsted, Silk and Cotton Yarns.

TENTERING AND DRYING MACHINES of all descriptions, fitted with either Clip or Pin Chains.

MERCERISING MACHINERY for Cloth and Yarn.

Makers of IMPROVED SELF-ACTING MULES.

HYDRAULIC HOT PRESS, and all other kinds of Finishing Machinery.

PLANT FOR CARBONISING OR EXTRACTING WOOL.

PATENT WOOL AND COTTON DRYING MACHINES.

PATENT HANK DRYING MACHINE.

STEAM BLOWING MACHINE for Lustre.

Improved BOBBIN or PIRN WINDING MACHINES on Triple Cone System.

PATENT QUICK TRAVERSE CROSS DRUM AND SPLIT DRUM WINDING MACHINES.

IMPROVED WARPING MILLS, with Patent Sectional Dividers.

Makers of COMBINED WARP SIZING AND COOL AIR DRYING AND BEAMING MACHINES, also OTHER WOOLLEN MACHINERY.

SOLE MAKERS OF PRATT'S PATENT RETURN STEAM TRAPS, FOR RETURNING CONDENSED WATER FROM STEAM HEATING PIPES BACK INTO BOILERS.

CATALOGUES ON APPLICATION.

MALLEABLE IRON AND STEEL CASTINGS.

Fig. 11:8 Advertisement for Wm. Whiteley & Sons Ltd, 'Yorkshire Textile Directory' 1911-12. (KCS)

and tinners, 21 cabinet makers, 5 coach builders, 9 coopers, 68 joiners and builders, 16 straw hat makers, 14 wheelwrights, and many other trades besides. The *Directory* lists 27 coal owners and dealers and 39 quarry owners and stone masons.[57] That range had considerably extended by the end of the century as a result of rising real incomes, a larger local market, and the much more diverse needs of local society.

During the second half of the century the development of textile machine making and associated engineering trades, as well as the engineering requirements of the chemical industry, provided Huddersfield with another major focus of industrial activity. The history of this engineering industry is primarily one of individual firms creating successful specialisms initially for local needs, but then spreading their reputations, in some instances, further afield. Some firms remained as specialist businesses. Others considerably extended their engineering products beyond the needs of textiles and chemicals. By the 1880s Huddersfield considered machine making as one of its major trades. In its Chamber of Commerce submission to the Royal Commission on Depression in Trade and Industry in 1886, machine making was listed after textiles and chemicals as a significant local industry[58] and this is borne out by census of population employment data which show over 4,500 employed in metal work, machine making and engineering on the eve of the First World War (*see* Table 2).

Of particular note was the business of William Whiteley and Sons of Lockwood. Founded in 1854, its main specialism was finishing and cloth drying machinery. By the 1890s it was employing 400 people, had become a private limited liability company and was enjoying a national reputation.[59] The firm of Thomas Broadbent and Sons, founded in 1864, came to dominate the supply of centrifugal hydro-extractors, claiming in more recent times to have installed machinery in over 90 per cent of the textile mills of Britain. At various times the firm diversified into the manufacture of horizontal steam engines, overhead cranes, electrical capstans, bridge operating gear and, during the First World War, steel aerial bombs.[60] The business of Brook Motors, founded in 1904, initially specialized in electric drives for textile machinery.[61] And before becoming famous for tractors and machine tools, the firm of David Brown, founded in the 1860s and based in part of Thomas Broadbent's works, was a manufacturer of gearing.[62] Within the field of textile engineering other local firms specialised in packing

Fig. 11:9 Advertisement for J. Charlesworth, 'Yorkshire Textile Directory', 1910-11. (KCS)

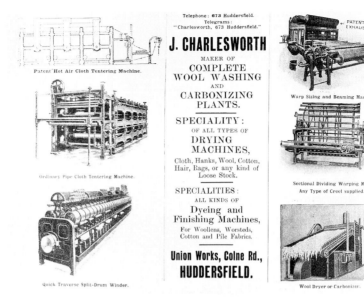

Fig. 11:10 Advertisement for William Whiteley & Sons Ltd, 'Britain's Greatest Manufacturers'. (WYAS, C).

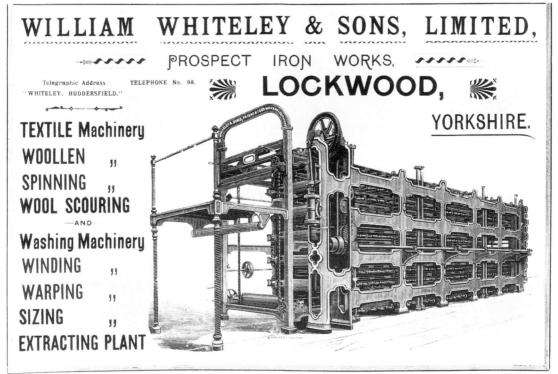

machinery, card clothing, conveyors, and shearing and cropping machines. As late as 1885 the firm of Samuel Crossley was still making handlooms.[63]

Boiler making and associated activity was another engineering trade which developed out of the needs of textiles and chemicals. By 1921, the firm of J. Hopkinson and Co., founded in 1843, was employing 1,500 workers in the manufacture of valves and boiler fittings.[64] The firm of William Arnold, which moved to Huddersfield from Barnsley in 1847, appears to have had an active trade in boiler manufacture and repair, and diversified into making gasometers, dyepans, brewpans, cisterns, condensors, and crane ladles. In 1866 it exported a set of boilers to St. Petersburg.[65]

Gas plant manufacture was linked to the activities of the local chemical industry. One firm, W. C. Holmes and Co., was described as gas apparatus manufacturers by 1853 and developed into a major supplier of gas plant and complete gas works.[66] By the First World War electrical engineering was becoming a significant local employer.

A profile of Huddersfield as an industrial centre, just after the end of the period with which we are concerned, is provided by the 1921 Official Handbook of Huddersfield Corporation. Besides stressing the variety of textile and chemical manufacture, the handbook lists a range of auxilliary trades including valves and boiler fittings, electrical machinery, motor vehicles, sheet metal goods, leather working, tool making, wood working and furniture, boots and shoes, bricks and cardboard boxes. Other local firms were engaged in metal casting, oil and tallow refining, fireworks, wire making and card clothing.[67] The earlier industrial base of textiles and chemicals would appear to have been significantly diversified into a far broader industrial structure, within which many firms gained strong reputations. It is realistic to argue that the flexibility and innovativeness of the local nineteenth century textile and chemical trades continued to be reflected in other industrial activity.

David Jenkins

Biographical Note

David Jenkins has published extensively on the history of the British and European textile industries, including two books on the British wool textile industry: *The West Riding Wool Textile Industry, 1770-1835* (1975) and (with K. G. Ponting) *The British Wool Textile Industry, 1770-1914* (1982, 1987).

His present research interests include a study of the process of diversification of West Yorkshire industry between 1840 and 1914, and an analysis of the international competitive performance of the British wool textile industry in the nineteenth century.

NOTES

1. *Report of the Tariff Commission. Vol 2. The Textile Trades* (1905), para. 1787.

2. W.B Crump and Gertrude Ghorbal, *History of the Huddersfield Woollen Industry*, (Huddersfield, 1935; reprinted Huddersfield 1988), pp.128-32; *Exposition Universelle de 1851, Travaux de la Commission Française sur l'Industrie des Nations* (Paris, 1854), Vol IV.

3. Census of Population, 1851.

4. *Report of the U.S. Commission to the Paris Exhibition* (Washington, 1862), Class XXI, p.12.

5. *Report of the U.S. Commission*, p.12.

6. *Report of the U.S. Commission*, p.12.

7. See particularly J.C. Malin, 'The West Riding Recovered Wool Industry, 1813-1939' (unpublished D.Phil. thesis, Univ. of York, 1979).

8. D.T. Jenkins and J.C. Malin, 'European competition in woollen cloth, 1870-1914: the role of shoddy', *Business History*, 32, 4, (1990).

9. Jenkins and Malin, 'European competition'.

10. C. Gulvin, *The Tweedmakers: a History of the Scottish Fancy Woollen Industry, 1600-1914* (Newton Abbot, 1973), p.132; quoting the *Hawick Advertiser*, 27 October 1855.

11. *Textile Manufacturer*, February 1877.

12. *Textile Manufacturer*, September 1878.

13. *Textile Manufacturer*, November 1877.

14. *Tariff Commission*, para. 1759.

15. *Tariff Commission*, para. 1358.

16. *The Economist Trade Review for 1905*, Supplement, January, 1906; Huddersfield Corporation, *Huddersfield as an Industrial Centre*, (Huddersfield, c.1921), p.8; *Tariff Commission*, para. 1358.

17. J. James, *A History of the Worsted Manufacture* (1857), p.579.

18. See D.T. Jenkins and K.G. Ponting, *The British Wool Textile Industry 1770-1914* (1982), p.150.

19. Jenkins and Ponting, *British Wool Textile Industry*, pp.261-66.

20. W(est) Y(orkshire) A(rchive) S(ervice), Calderdale. Clay Mss., 274(52).

21. WYAS, Calderdale. Clay Mss., 274(52); Jenkins and Ponting, *British Wool Textile Industry*, p.164; and see, for example, reports in the *Textile Manufacturer*, November 1877, January, June and July 1878, January 1883. See also *Reports of the Royal Commission on Depression of Trade and Industry*, Second report, pp.1886 (c.4715) XXII, paras., 3787, 3795, 3924. Evidence of H. Mitchell.

22. United States Centennial Exhibition, *International Exhibition, 1876, Reports and Awards*, Vol. 5.

23. *Textile Manufacturer*, January 1883.

24. E.M. Sigsworth, *Black Dyke Mills: a history. With introductory chapters on the development of the worsted industry in the nineteenth century* (Liverpool, 1958), pp.110-12 citing *Bradford Observer*, 31 December 1874; J. de L. Mann, *The Cloth Industry of the West of England*, (Oxford, 1971), p.214.

25. *Huddersfield as an Industrial Centre*, p.27.

26. The Huddersfield municipal boundary was extended in 1868 and 1890. Thus figures are not comparable over time. Owen Balmforth, *Jubilee History of the Corporation of Huddersfield* (Huddersfield, 1918)

27. Censuses of Population, 1861, 1881, 1891.

28. *Tariff Commission*, para. 1308.

29. *Textile Manufacturer*, September 1877.

30. *Textile Manufacturer*, June 1877.

31. *Textile Manufacturer*, October 1881.

32. *Reports of the Royal Commission on Depression of Trade and Industry*, Second report. 1886. Evidence of Henry Mitchell.

33. WYAS, Kirklees. John Taylor & Sons Ltd., Bought Ledger 3, 1852-62.

34. *Textile Manufacturer*, June 1884, June and October 1886, March 1887; T.R. Ashenhurst, *A Practical Treatise on Weaving and Designing of Textile Fabrics*, (3rd. edn. Huddersfield, 1885), advert for Samuel Crossley; J.H. Clapham, 'Decline of the Handloom Weaver', *Bradford Textile Journal*, June, 1905; J.H. Clapham, *The Woollen and Worsted Industries*, (1907), pp.128-29.

35. Owen Balmforth, *Huddersfield Past and Present; in its social, industrial and educational aspects* (Huddersfield, 1894).

36. *Textile Manufacturer*, March 1887.

37. Census of Population, 1901; *The Yorkshire Textile Directory and Engineer's and Machine Maker's Advertiser*, 16th. edn., 1900.

38. *Huddersfield as an Industrial Centre*, p.20.

39. There was much debate in the trade press in the 1880s and 1890s and conflicting opinions were expressed.

40. Crump and Ghorbal, *Huddersfield Woollen Industry*, pp.105-6.

41. *Tariff Commission*, paras., 1355, 1760, 1768.

42. WYAS, Kirklees. Huddersfield Chamber of Commerce, Minute Books.

43. *Textile Manufacturer*, March 1883. The previous month the same journal had reported: 'Huddersfield of late years has displayed a creditable amount of enterprise and has reaped a corresponding degree of prosperity as its reward'.

44. *Textile Manufacturer*, January 1885.

45. *Report of Henry Mitchell upon the Paris Exhibition together with the Report of the Artisans*, 1878; also published as part of *Papers Relative to Industry and Commerce*, pp.1878 (c.2085) LXXVI, No. 18. See also Huddersfield Chamber of Commerce, *Artisans Reports on Scribbling Machinery and Yarns, Dyeing, Designing Woollen Fabrics and Cloth finishing at the Paris Exhibition* (Huddersfield, 1878).

46. A very detailed analysis of the firm's development is provided in M.R. Fox, *Dye-makers of Great Britain, 1856-1976: a history of chemists, companies, products and changes* (Manchester, 1987). The discussion that follows is indebted to that source.

47. Fox, *Dyemakers*, pp.63, 68 note 3; *The Dyer and Calico Printer*, 20 January 1915.

48. Fox, *Dyemakers*, p.71; *The Dyer and Calico Printer*, 20 January 1915. L.F. Haber, *The Chemical Industry during the Nineteenth Century. A Study of the Economic Aspects of Applied Chemistry in Europe and North America* (Oxford, 1958), pp.86, 144, 164-5.

49. Fox, *Dyemakers*, Ch. VIII: Haber, *The Chemical Industry during the 19th. Century*, p.165.

50. Fox, *Dyemakers*, p.78.

51. W.J. Reader, *Imperial Chemical Industries. A History. Vol. 1. The forerunners 1870-1926*, p.264; Fox, *Dyemakers*, p.90 note 3; Brook Motors, *About Ourselves: the story of Brook Motors*, (Huddersfield, 1957).

52. L.F. Haber, *The Chemical Industry, 1900-30. International Growth and Technological Change* (Oxford, 1971), p.14; Fox, *Dyemakers*, p.85.

53. W.J. Reader, *I.C.I.*, Vol. 1, pp.263-68; Fox, *Dyemakers*, Ch. X; Haber, *Chemical Industry, 1900-30*, pp.148-49.

54. Fox, *Dyemakers*, pp.85, 140-41.

55. D.W.F. Hardie and J.D. Pratt, *A History of the Modern British Chemical Industry* (Oxford, 1966), p.316; Fox, *Dyemakers*, pp.139-40.

56. *Report of the Commissioners on River Pollution*, B.P.P., 1867 (3850) XXXIII, p.13.

57. William White, *Directory and Gazetteer of Leeds, Bradford, Halifax, Huddersfield, Wakefield and the whole of the clothing districts of Yorkshire* (Sheffield, 1853; reprinted Newton Abbot, 1969), pp.609-40.

58. *Commission on Depression in Trade and Industry*, first Report, 1886, p.89.

59. *Men of the Period: England* (1896), p.285; *Wool Year Book*, (Manchester, 1909).

60. T. Broadbent and Sons Ltd., *Broadbents complete 100 years, 1864-1964*, (Huddersfield, 1964) F.W. Derbyshire, *A History of Thomas Broadbent and Sons Ltd., 1864-1950* (1959), typescript in Huddersfield Local History Library. N.C. Gee, *Shoddy and Mungo Manufacture* (Manchester, 1950), adverts p.10.

61. Brook Motors, *About Ourselves, 1904-1939* (Huddersfield, 1939).

63. Advert in T.R. Ashenhurst, *A Practical Treatise on Weaving and Designing of Textile Fabrics* (3rd. edition, Huddersfield, 1885).

64. *Huddersfield as an Industrial Centre*, p.31.

65. H. Arnold, *Boiler Making a Hundred Years Ago: the early history of Wm. Arnold and Son (Hfd.) Ltd.* (privately printed, not dated).

66. W.C. Holmes & Co. Ltd., *The Story of the Hundred Years of Endeavour in the service of the Gas Industry* (Huddersfield, c.1950).

67. *Huddersfield as an Industrial Centre; Wool Year Book* (Manchester, 1909, 1913).

CHAPTER 12

The Huddersfield Woollen Industry and its Architecture

COLUM GILES

The town of Huddersfield and its hinterland – the Colne and Holme valleys, the Fenay Beck valley, and all the high land between – have enjoyed a diverse economy for centuries. Agriculture has always been important, engineering and chemicals have played a significant role since the middle of the nineteenth century, and, of course, textiles have long been a major employer. The textile industry is itself extremely diverse, and Huddersfield has at different times played host to woollen, worsted, cotton, silk and recovered wool production. Woollen cloth manufacturing, however, was until the late nineteenth century the dominant aspect of the local textile scene. It provided employment for a large part of the urban and rural population in the pre-factory era and continued to do so in the age of mills. Furthermore, it spawned other industries, like the dyeware and machine-making trades. In acknowledgement of its local importance, this chapter takes the woollen manufacturing sector for examination, but uses architectural evidence to illustrate developments which, in broad outline, have been well treated by previous published studies.[1] The changing methods of manufacturing are fully reflected in buildings, which tell a story starting in a cottage industry and ending in fully-mechanised factory production. The area chosen for study is centred on the town of Huddersfield, but because the town's functions in relation to the woollen industry were for so long complemented by those of the outlying settlements, these too will be included.

The architecture of the domestic system before 1770

The typical figure of the domestic system of woollen cloth production before 1770 was the small manufacturer, working both in Huddersfield itself and throughout the surrounding area. Crump and Ghorbal give a good picture of his way of life and show how, while many such manufacturers were engaged solely in the production of unfinished cloth, others also undertook the important dyeing and finishing processes.[2] The workplace was the home, and probate inventories show how looms were set up either in a 'shop' or workshop, invariably a ground-floor room usually used exclusively for manufacturing, or in a chamber alongside beds and other furniture. In 1689, for example, Joseph Armitage, of Dudmanstone in Almondbury parish, had a work chamber with looms, press and shears, and at a more modest level, Edward Perkin of Slaithwaite had, in 1693, looms and a stock of wool in the bedroom over the main living room. Some of the more substantial clothiers had further rooms or outbuildings with an industrial function. Joshua Broadhead of Upperthong had a 'dying house' in 1733, and in 1734 Jonathan Hobson of Wooldale had a woolchamber containing £120 worth of wool, a dressing chamber for weaving and finishing, and a dyehouse with a lead grate, a pump trough and a range for heating.[3] Inventories suggest that these clothiers' houses varied widely in size, some being large and elaborate, others perhaps no more than small cottages.

The home was the centre of manufacturing activity both because processes were still hand-powered and because industrial organisation was based on the family. One process, however, that of fulling, had been mechanised since the Middle Ages, and had for centuries been located in water-powered fulling mills. By 1780 there were at least thirty-five fulling mills in operation in the Huddersfield region, including mills on the major rivers, like Ramsden Mill, Golcar and Linthwaite, on the River Colne, and Dungeon Mill, South Crosland, on the River Holme, and others in the upper valleys, in Hepworth, Cartworth and other upland townships.[4] The fulling mill's function was to take in the clothiers' pieces and to process them to give a dense felted finish through the action of prolonged pounding in fulling stocks (Figure 12:1). The mills, therefore, offered a public service for a fee, and were run by a fulling miller who was often a tenant of the local landed gentry family. The Earl of Dartmouth, for example, had come to have a major interest in fulling mills by the early nineteenth century.[5] Because

*Fig. 12:1 The fulling
stocks at Dewsbury Mills
(KCS)*

these early fulling mills were usually in prime locations for harnessing water
power, they tended to continue in use in the post-1770 period of industrial
expansion. As a result, they have been almost entirely swept away by later,
larger buildings constructed to serve a new age. There is little evidence for
their size and nature. They were doubtless stone-built, and may have been
single-storeyed or two-storeyed, with a store room over the working floor.
Waterwheels were probably housed within the mill on some sites, outside on
others. The mills' capacity depended to some extent perhaps on local
demand for their services but probably more on the amount of water power
available. Small streams might power only one or two pairs of fulling stocks,
but mills on large rivers or on sites with a good fall of water could have a
greater capacity.

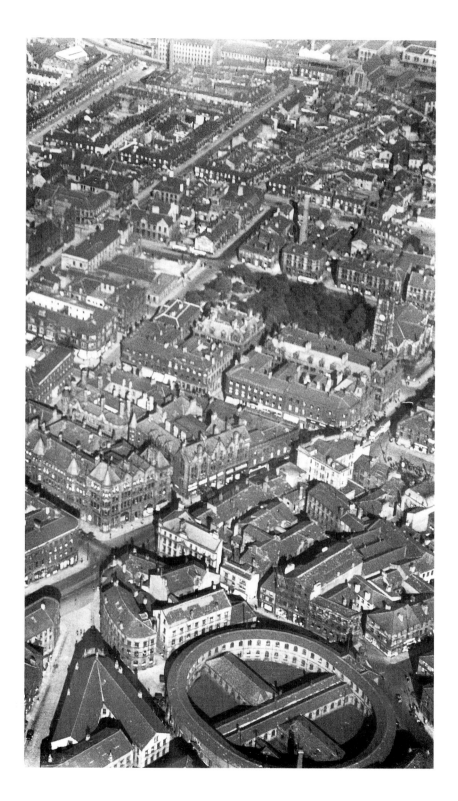

*Fig. 12:2 Huddersfield
Cloth Hall; the elliptical
plan is seen on this 1928
aerial photograph.
(Aerofilms)*

The finishing and market of cloth

Early production of cloth was, therefore, divided between the home and the fulling mill. The clothier usually sold unfinished cloth, and it was the merchant who commonly brought the cloth to its final state through the use of commission finishing establishments. These undertook the skilled operations of raising and shearing of the cloth nap, and usually worked from small premises, none of which survives in recognisable form. The marketing of cloth, however, created major monuments in the West Riding, for by the late eighteenth century all the principal towns had Cloth Halls, replacing the earlier outdoor markets for the sale of cloth. Both Almondbury and Huddersfield had open-air markets before the mid-eighteenth century, but in 1766 Sir John Ramsden built an elliptical Cloth Hall in the town.[6] Built in brick, an unusual material at that period, it presented blank walls to the exterior, thus giving a secure trading space internally. The importance of the building's function is revealed, however, in the treatment of the entrance area, which had round-headed openings, a pediment, and a clock tower with a belfry and cupola (Figures 12:2, 12:3). Built just before the advent of a new

Fig. 12:3 The entrance to the Cloth Hall; the blank perimeter wall gave a secure trading environment internally. (KCS)

industrial era, the Cloth Hall nevertheless played a significant role in the town's commercial life through to the mid-nineteenth century, when finally it became redundant.

Mixed domestic and mill production, 1770-1850

Between 1770 and 1850 the woollen industry was dramatically altered by technological and organisational innovation. Mechanised working, previously confined to fulling and, to a limited extent to raising, was applied successfully to scribbling and carding in the 1770s, to spinning in the 1820s, and to weaving in the 1830s. Some of the developments were only slowly adopted. Costs of textile machinery and of power generation, often in the form of a steam engine, proved too much for many manufacturers, and some early machines were too limited to threaten traditional methods of working. Nevertheless, the industry was, potentially at least, virtually fully mechanised by the mid-nineteenth century, only the weaving of fancy patterned cloths, a speciality of the Huddersfield area, remaining a hand-powered process.

This period, then, was one of slow but steady transition from a largely domestic system of hand-powered cloth production to one in which all or most processes were often conducted on a single site, largely by mechanised working. The mills of the period fall into different categories according to their role within the industry. Some represented only a modest change from the traditional public mill, simply offering a greater range of mechanised services to the domestic manufacturer. Others, however, were private mills, working only or mainly for the business of the millowner. Of these private mills, some worked in combination with a domestically-based waged-labour force employed by the millowner on a putting-out system, but others began as or became fully integrated factories. Still others were not owner-occupied but were designed to house a number of tenants who rented room and power. This organisational variety produced very different types of mill complex, for the grouping of buildings of different functions reflected the range of operations carried on within the mill.

The public scribbling and fulling mill

The most common type of woollen mill before 1825 was the public scribbling and fulling mill, housing the two principal powered processes in woollen manufacturing. Scribbling usually included carding, for the two processes were done in sequence at the preparatory stage of cloth production and involved the opening and straightening of the wool fibres before spinning could take place. Scribbling machines were in use in the 1770s and very quickly these machines and the similar carding engines replaced traditional hand-powered methods.[7] The new machines were commonly housed in mills, some of which were old fulling mills given a wider function and others being new constructions. Most of these new mills operated as fulling mills had done, providing mechanised services for the independent domestic clothier, and these 'public mills' were seen as an important complement to the domestic system, giving the small manufacturer access to the new technology without large capital outlay. Clothiers paid a fee for the services and thus the new mills altered only slightly the traditional organisation of woollen cloth production. The public mill continued in operation until after 1850, for as long, in fact, as the domestic-manufacturer survived. In 1833, Joshua Robinson of Smithy Place Mill, Honley, described the function of his public mill as 'scribbling, carding and fulling – it is no factory neither am I a manufacturer but work the mill for the country domestic manufacturers – there is no spinning or weaving carried on in the mill'.[8]

The public mill usually had a simple form. It was commonly a loose grouping of a number of buildings of different functions. The principal building was the mill itself, stone-built and perhaps three or four storeys high and five or seven bays long. Blackmoor Holm Mill, Slaithwaite, was sixty feet long and thirty-four feet wide and had an internal waterwheel, three floors and an attic.[9] A late eighteenth-century plan of Holmbridge Mill (Figure 12:4) shows how a mill of this type functioned.[10] That mill was three storeys high and had internal dimensions of seventy feet by twenty-four feet three inches. The ground floor had two waterwheels, five pairs of fulling stocks and a 'teasor', probably for opening the wool before scribbling. On the first floor were four 'ingens' for scribbling and carding, with space for two more, and a forty-spindle slubbing billy. At one end of this floor was a small heated 'dwelling house'. The top floor was used for wool storage. A reconstruction of the working arrangements of a public mill of this period is shown in

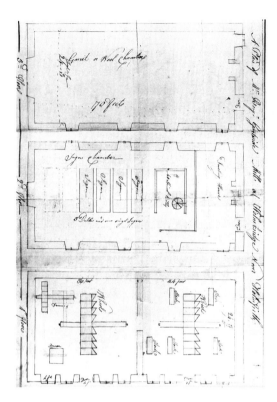

Fig. 12:5 This reconstruction of a scribbling and fulling mill of the early nineteenth century shows the use of water power and the arrangement of machinery, with fulling stocks on the ground floor and scribbling and carding engines and a slubbing billy on the upper floors. (RCHME)

Fig. 12:4 A late-eighteenth century plan of Holmbridge Mills. (RCHME, reproduced by kind permission of Mr G.C. Barber, Holmbridge).

Figure 12:5. The small scale of the typical mill building reflected both the small amount of power available on many sites and the scale of activity in the period. Despite its small size, however, the capital investment in buildings, power equipment and machinery was well beyond the means of the small domestic clothier.

Around the main mill building were grouped a number of ancillary structures. Warehouses stored wool awaiting scribbling and cloth ready for collection. Dyehouses, at this period invariably small single-storeyed buildings, formed a part of some public mills. Their main requirements were a system of heating the liquids in the dye vats and good ventilation. After fulling, cloth was tentered, which involved drying and stretching on tenterframes. Tenterfields were located beside many mills, and the mid-nineteenth century Ordnance Survey map of Huddersfield shows numerous tenterfields on all sides of the town. In the early nineteenth century, however,

Fig. 12:6 Aspley Mills, Huddersfield, in the early nineteenth century. (WYAS, K)

cloth dryhouses, sometimes called stoves or tenterhouses, were built to provide indoor drying, using warm air from a steam plant or gas installation. Cloth dryhouses were long narrow buildings, a form dictated by the need to extend the cloth to its full length.

Aspley Mills, Huddersfield, perfectly represents the typical public scribbling and fulling mill. Seen in a view of the 1830s (Figure 12:6), it has the main mill at the core of the complex, housing the powered processes.[11] Around this building are grouped smaller structures, probably a dyehouse, warehouse, and, in the foreground, a single-storeyed cloth dryhouse. Indoor drying was, at Aspley, combined with outdoor tentering, for the view shows cloth being hung on tenterframes. Only a very few mills survive in substantial form from this period. Aspley Mills itself no longer exists, illustrating how, like the earlier fulling mills, this generation of public scribbling and fulling mills was swept away when later developments demanded larger buildings with a greatly-increased stock of machines. Perhaps the best survival in the Huddersfield area is Lord's Mill, Honley, built in 1792 by the Earl of Dartmouth as a scribbling, carding and fulling mill (Figure 12:7). Its thirteen-bay length has at least three phases of construction, one of which involved the addition of steam power to the original water-powered building. Its mullioned windows and timber floors are typical of mills of the period.

Fig. 12:7 Lord's Mill, Honley; the early mill was water-powered, but a steam engine was added in the early nineteenth century. (RCHME)

Weavers' cottages and loomshops

Domestic production, modified by the new scribbling and fulling mills, continued to be the mainstay of the Huddersfield woollen industry. As late as the 1830s, nearly 800 clothiers used the Huddersfield cloth market.[12] The quickening pace of economic life found architectural expression after 1770 not only in the construction of new mills but also in the area of domestic manufacture. A well-established and expanding industry provided the incentive for manufacturers, speculators and landlords to erect special-purpose buildings combining both a dwelling area for a family and a workshop for textile production. These 'weavers' cottages' thus formalised an arrangement that had obtained for a century and more without being as clearly or permanently reflected in domestic architecture. Large numbers of weavers' cottages are found in the Huddersfield region, and the fact that most date from the period after 1780 reflects their connection with the heightened economic activity represented also in the new mills (Figure 12:8). Typically, the weaver's cottage was of three storeys, with the lower two levels for living

Fig. 12:8 The view over Jackson Bridge, near New Mill, shows how weavers' cottages form an important part of the rural landscape. (RCHME)

285

Fig. 12:9 The loomshop on the top floor of the Colne Valley Museum. (RCHME)

accommodation and a top-floor loomshop.[13] The Colne Valley Museum, Golcar, is a perfect example of the type. Built as late as the 1840s and thus revealing the importance of domestic production in the woollen industry even in the mid-nineteenth century, the house is built into the hillside to allow direct access to the loomshop from the rear. The loomshop is lit by a long window in the front wall and by a smaller window in the rear wall (Figure 12:9).

Weavers' cottages were occupied by small independent clothiers or by weavers taking in work from an employer. Within this period, there is evidence for a development from this building type to a similar type, one which, significantly, reveals an increased scale of production and a change from independent working to production under supervision. At Coffin Row, Linthwaite, built between 1820 and 1840, a terrace of four cottages was built with a large loomshop over with space for up to forty looms.[14] The loomshop in Ramsden Mill Lane, Golcar, is a four-storeyed building, giving storerooms on the ground floor, two single-room dwellings on the first floor, and large loomshops or workshops on the two upper floors (Figures 12:10, 12:11). The loomshops are well-lit by long windows and have taking-in doors in the gable walls. The inference to be drawn from the scale and design of such buildings is that manufacturers were providing workspace for a sizable waged-labour force to produce cloth under supervision. This change in the organisation of production is known in this period from other sources, but nowhere can it be seen more strikingly than in the architecture of these workshops.

Fig. 12:10 The loomshop in Ramsden Mill Lane, Golcar. (RCHME)

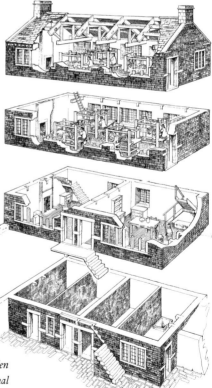

Fig. 12:11 A cut-away view of the Ramsden Mill Lane loomshop shows the probable internal arrangements. (RCHME)

The private mill

Alongside the public mill and the domestic manufacturer there developed private mills, working for the millowner alone. Built by manufacturers and merchants with greater resources, initiative or credit than the typical domestic clothier, these mills functioned in one of two ways. Some acted in precisely the same way as the public mill in concentrating entirely on powered processes. John Wrigley of Cocking Steps Mill, Honley, used his mill in 1833 for scribbling, carding, slubbing, fulling and finishing. The processes which were still hand-powered, spinning and weaving, were conducted off-site on a putting-out system, for Wrigley stated that he had 'all our spinning, weaving, burling, and wool picking worked at our servants' own houses, in the neighbourhood . . . from three hundred to four hundred of them are in our employ'.[15] Their mill, now partly ruinous, was of similar size and construction to the typical public mill.

A second and very different type of private woollen mill developed in the late eighteenth century. This type was characterised by the integration of all processes into the mill complex, marking a sharp break from the dispersed

Fig. 12:12 The warehouse at Armitage Bridge Mills, South Crosland; the original hand-spinning and handloom-weaving shops can be seen in the background. (RCHME)

method of production practiced even by substantial manufacturers like the Wrigleys. Most renowned of these early integrated woollen mills was Benjamin Gott's Bean Ing Mills in Leeds, built in the 1790s.[16] In the Huddersfield area the best example of the type is Armitage Bridge Mills, in South Crosland township. The Brooke family, large-scale manufacturers on the putting-out system and with mills in Honley for finishing their cloth, moved to Armitage Bridge in the second decade of the nineteenth century, building a mill complex on a new site and using the water power of the River Holme.[17] Their accumulated resources and standing in the industry allowed them to build on a large scale. Among the first buildings on the site were a substantial warehouse, on its own bigger than most public mills; a fireproof scribbling and fulling mill of five storeys and ten bays; and a wheelhouse with two powerful waterwheels (Figures 12:12, 12:13).

The significance of the site, however, is that the Brookes drew in to the complex the hand-powered processes habitually conducted in the houses of dispersed workers. Prominent among the early buildings is a long four-storeyed range providing hand-spinning and handloom-weaving shops, well-

Fig. 12:13 Mills 1 and 2 at Armitage Bridge. Mill 1 in the foreground is fireproof and was powered by waterwheels in the low building in front of it. The higher and wider Mill 2 of 1828-29 is in the background. (RCHME)

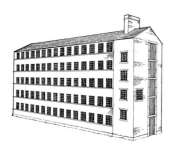

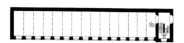

Fig. 12:14 The loomshop at Armitage Bridge Mills, built c.1830, could hold a large number of handlooms. (RCHME)

lit by large windows on one wall. Later, *c.1830*, a large five-storeyed loomshop was added with space for a substantial number of handlooms (Figure 12:14). Alongside these buildings were, in all probability, all the finishing buildings and dyehouses essential to give complete integration.

The advantages of integration were said to be the prevention of embezzlement of materials by domestic workers, convenience in terms of movement of goods, and ease of supervision during production.[18] The largest manufacturers, able to build integrated mills, had a strong advantage over the small producer, but it is interesting to note that the complete 'factory system', which in the woollen industry can be defined as integrated working, resulted not from purely technological advances – the mechanisation of production and the use of steam power – for in early integrated woollen mills only the first processes, scribbling and carding, and the last, fulling and perhaps some finishing stages, were mechanised. Instead, it was organisational logic which provided the impetus towards a radically new method of working. The buildings representing this significant departure are largely still evident at Armitage Bridge, giving the site a special importance in the Huddersfield industry.

Between the mid-1820s and the mid-1830s mechanically-powered spinning and weaving were introduced to the woollen sector after the successful adaption of machines in use in other textile branches.[19] The spinning mule rapidly replaced the hand-spinning jenny and spinning quickly became a mill-based operation using the new machines. The powerloom was only a limited success in woollen manufacture initially and well into the second half of the nineteenth century it was heavily outnumbered by handlooms. Both mules and powerlooms, however, had an effect on the architecture of mills. Mules were commonly housed in the main mill building, which, in addition, accommodated scribbling and carding engines and fulling stocks. Mills, therefore, tended to become larger after the mid-1820s, either because of the need to house more machinery or because economies of scale were sought by wealthy millowners able to build substantial mills. At Armitage Bridge Mills, the Brookes added a new mill in 1828-29 and used it at least in part for mule spinning, and it is significant that this mill is longer, taller and wider than the original scribbling and fulling mill (Figure 12:13).[20]

The initial reaction to the powerloom on the part of the Yorkshire woollen manufacturer was cautious. It is conspicuous that, in the

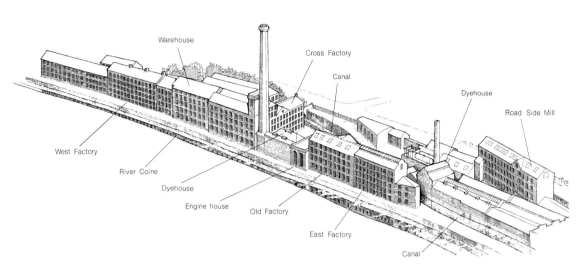

Fig. 12:15 This reconstruction of Starkey Brothers' Longroyd Bridge Mills shows how the site became fully developed by the mid-nineteenth century. (RCHME)

Huddersfield area as elsewhere, it was the largest manufacturers who first experimented with it, and then, its success for some products demonstrated, invested in buildings to house it. In 1835 Starkey Brothers of Longroyd Bridge [Springdale]Mills had seventy-two powerlooms and at Armitage Bridge in 1836 the Brookes bought a modest twelve powerlooms on a trial basis.[21] In the early years of powerloom weaving the machines were often housed in existing buildings, sometimes on the upper floors of mills. At Longroyd Bridge they were on the second, third and fourth floors of the five-storeyed 'West Factory'. The use of a storeyed building at Longroyd Bridge may be explained by the restricted nature of the site, on an island between the River Colne and the Huddersfield Canal (Figure 12·15), with no room for horizontal expansion. On other sites, however, the powerloom, once accepted, was commonly housed in single-storeyed sheds, first used for cotton manufacture in the 1820s. Armitage Bridge Mills, a pioneer in so many ways, was probably the first mill in the Huddersfield area to have a shed for powerloom weaving (Figure 12:16). The Brookes built a shed there in 1838 to house fifty new looms, and extended it after 1850.[22] Sheds had many advantages for weaving. They provided a good even top light from the north-facing glazed part of the saw-tooth roof, ventilation was easy to control, and single-storeyed buildings could withstand the vibrations set up by the powerlooms. The use of top lighting, moreover, allowed sheds to assume any shape or size, according to the requirements of the site and the number of looms to be housed.

Fig. 12:16 The weaving
shed at Armitage Bridge
Mills, first built in 1838
and later extended. (KCS)

Fig. 12:17 At Washpit
Mills, Wooldale, the 1840
spinning mill, with its
mill dam providing water
for its waterwheel, lies in
front of the steam-powered
weaving sheds, the first
phase of which was built in
c.1870. (RCHME)

The architecture of the woollen mill, 1850-1900

By the mid-nineteenth century, the woollen industry was fully mechanised in its principal processes, and the domestic system of production, while still important, entered a period of decline leading ultimately to extinction. Before 1850 perhaps the most important way of categorising mills revolved around whether they were public or private in their operation. Increasingly after 1850, most mills were private, reflecting the demise of the domestic clothier, and mills can be classified more easily according to whether they were integrated or concentrated instead upon a single major stage of production.

The rapid adoption of the powerloom after 1850 and the increasing significance of integration are closely linked. Less than 4,000 powerlooms were in operation in Yorkshire woollen mills in 1850, and only 20 per cent of those mills were integrated. By 1874, however, over 30,000 powerlooms were working and 56 per cent of Yorkshire woollen mills were involved in both spinning and weaving.[23] The trend towards integration in the Huddersfield area can be seen most clearly not so much in the construction of new mills but rather in the addition of powerloom-weaving capacity to existing mills concerned with scribbling, carding, spinning and finishing. At Washpit Mills, Wooldale, for example, the first phase of the weaving sheds was added c.1870 to one side of the 1840 mill building (Figure 12:17). The old mill was water-powered, but the new sheds were provided with a steam power plant, first with a beam engine but later, in 1909, with 'Agnes', a horizontal engine. Weaving sheds came to cover large expanses, and the great carpet of sheds in the valley floor at Milnsbridge developed to house powerlooms of integrated woollen firms. The form of the integrated woollen mill after 1850 was identical in general terms to that worked out at Armitage Bridge Mills before 1850, and showed a functional division between multi-storeyed mills for scribbling, carding, spinning and finishing (scouring and fulling) and sheds for weaving.

The development of industrial suburbs around Huddersfield after 1850 led to the construction of many entirely new mills. The function of these mills – whether integrated or not – is in some cases rather obscure, but many show similarities of form. Because they were developed on small plots, they were planned on an emphatically vertical plane (Figure 12:18), the main mill building frequently being of five or six storeys. Sheds, however, were either entirely lacking, as at Firth Street Mills when first built in 1865-66, or of small dimensions, like that at Albert Mills, Lockwood, added with a spinning mill extension in the mid-1860s (Figure 12:19). Fireproof construction, using cast-iron beams and brick-arched ceilings, was commonly employed in these mills (Figure 12:20), in sharp contrast to the structural forms used in most pre-1850 mills.

Some of these new suburban mills were probably built as specialist spinning works, obviating, therefore, the need for weaving sheds. Others, however, were certainly built by woollen manufacturers, by definition involved in both spinning and weaving. Firth Street Mills and Albert Mills were, for example, both built by manufacturers. It is possible that these firms used weaving capacity on other sites or employed outworkers even at this date. It is also possible, however, that powerlooms were housed within the main multi-storeyed mill building, just as had been the case at Starkey Brothers' Longroyd Bridge Mills during the 1830s, as previously described. Such a use of the upper floors is documented in the 1880s at Albert Mills, when the mill was occupied by a number of firms following the failure of the original builders. It is conceivable, therefore, that on sites too restricted to permit the normal division between storeyed mill and sheds, the main mill could, by itself, act as an integrated factory. The common use of fireproof construction in these mid-century suburban mills made the siting of powerlooms on the upper floors more practicable than was the case in timber-floored mills.[24]

After 1880 few entirely new woollen mills were built and most new building involved the addition of extra working capacity or the replacement of redundant structures by buildings suited to contemporary needs. There were few radical departures in the design and planning of the woollen mill, the functional division between storeyed mill and shed continuing to dominate the thinking of mill architects. One mill, Trafalgar Mill on Leeds Road, Huddersfield, was built by Learoyd Brothers in 1895-96 as a weaving and finishing mill on a single-storeyed layout (Figure 12:21), but otherwise new building tended to follow earlier forms. The woollen industry, however, was changing rapidly in this period, for in the last quarter of the century many firms which had developed as woollen manufacturing concerns diversified to include high-quality worsted production, giving Huddersfield its world-wide reputation for this type of cloth rather than for its traditional product.

Fig. 12:18 Firth Street Mills and, beyond, Larchfield Mills, tower above the canal and form part of the intensive development of the Colne Road/Firth Street area of Huddersfield in the 1860s. (RCHME)

Fig. 12:19 Albert Mills, Lockwood; this aerial view shows the layout of multi-storeyed mills, sheds, and on the street frontage the warehouse and the former dyehouse. (RCHME)

Fig. 12:20 An interior view of the multi-storeyed mill at Albert Mills shows the fireproof construction and spinning mules in operation. (RCHME)

Fig. 12:21 Trafalgar Mill, Leeds Road, Huddersfield; this view shows the single-storeyed layout of the complex. (RCHME)

Room and power mills

Most mills were either owner-occupied or run by a single tenant. A few, however, had a number of occupiers paying rent both for working space and for a share of the power to drive machinery. Some of these 'room and power' mills were simply adaptations of mills built for a single occupier. Albert Mills, Lockwood, for example, was built in the early 1850s and run by the firm of Berry and Turner through to the 1880s, when the company failed. The mill was then turned into a room and power factory and in 1884 it had eight, perhaps nine, independent companies renting space, taking a room or a floor according to their needs.

Other mills were built as room and power factories, often by a speculator seeking to profit from the demand for such facilities from small manufacturers. The best local example of a purpose-built room and power complex is Folly Hall Mills, Huddersfield, developed in and after 1825 by Joseph Kaye, the well-known local builder.[25] The mill was a speculative venture on Kaye's part, for he never intended to become personally involved as a textile manufacturer. An observer of Huddersfield in c.1830 noted that

Fig. 12:22 Folly Hall Mills, Huddersfield; the 1844 mill presents its best elevation to the town. (RCHME)

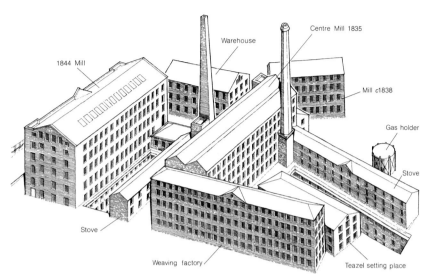

Fig. 12:23 Folly Hall Mills in the mid-nineteenth century, showing the grouping of buildings of different dates and functions. (RCHME)

several mills were in course of construction on the Manchester Road side of town and that 'the man that built the largest of them, I was told, built it for the purpose of letting to the manufacturers to make cloth, on hire'.[26] It is highly likely that the mill in question was Folly Hall Mills. The first of the multi-storeyed buildings, built in 1825, was six storeys high and seventeen bays long. It burned down in 1844 but was rebuilt on the same scale, this time as a fireproof building. Its handsome pedimented north front, carried out in ashlar masonry, makes the mill the most distinguished industrial building of its age in Huddersfield (Figure 12:22). Grouped around this mill are two others, one originally of six storeys and an attic, the other more modest in scale; stoves for the drying of cloth; a gas plant; and a 'weaving factory', a long, five-storeyed range lit by windows in front and back walls and clearly intended to house a large number of handlooms (Figure 12:23). The complex was occupied by a host of small businesses, many involved in the woollen industry but others with no direct connection. In 1844, the main mill housed a merchant, three manufacturers, two cloth finishers and two 'country jobbers', and in 1856 cotton warp spinners, woollen yarn spinners, cloth finishers and manufacturers were those most directly affected by a destructive fire in Centre Mill. The list of occupiers in 1861 numbered twenty-eight, and the complex operated as an industrial village (Table 1). The use of room and power facilities such as that provided by Kaye at Folly Hall was important in permitting many small manufacturers to participate in mill working without the prohibitive capital outlay which purchase of land and costs of construction necessitated.

Table 1 Folly Hall Mills, 1861; List of Occupiers

Woollen textiles Trades	Worsted trades	Cotton trades	Others
6 scribbling millers	1 worsted spinner	3 cotton spinners and doublers	1 machine maker
3 woollen manufacturers		1 cotton spinner	1 shuttle maker
3 cloth finishers		1 cotton warp manufacturer	1 steam saw mills
3 rag grinders			
1 fulling miller			
1 woollen spinner			
1 woollen spinner and scribbling miller			
1 woollen and cotton dyer			

(*source: Post Office Directory of Yorkshire*, 1861, p.357)

Later examples of purpose-built room and power mills in the Huddersfield area include two by the name of Britannia Mills. Britannia Mills, Lockwood, was built in 1861 by John Firth and Sons, who operated as woollen manufacturers from an adjacent earlier mill. The size of the new mill – a vast fireproof building of six storeys – indicates speculation on a large scale, and in 1872 nine companies occupied space in the building (Figure 12:24). The second Britannia Mills, this one on Colne Road in the canal area of Huddersfield, was built in and after 1860 by Joseph Hopkinson, a local engineer. As early as 1861 room and power were advertised to let, and the complex rapidly came to resemble Folly Hall Mills in the diversity, if not the numbers, of its tenants. In 1868 a cotton spinner, two yarn spinners, two woollen yarn spinners, two woollen manufacturers, a fancy woollen manufacturer, a cotton waste dealer, a wool cleaner and a woollen weaver all had space within the complex; in 1866 there had even been a silk waste dealer. The variety of trades represented within the complex reflects the broad base which Huddersfield's textile industry enjoyed by this date, for the town was very far from a one-industry settlement. Britannia Mills itself differs little in its design from owner-occupied mills, for its two large fireproof mills, its ranges of warehouses and sheds, and its power plant were typical features of mills of the period (Figure 12:25). Permanent divisions were not part of the design of the storeyed mills, for flexibility of use was the principal requirement. The basic unit available for rent was a floor in the mill, and the dimensions of 'three fireproof rooms' available for rent in 1866 (fifty by fifteen yards) corresponded exactly to the size of individual floors in the main buildings.[27]

Fig. 12:24 Britannia Mills. Built in 1861, it was one of the largest mills in the area and was occupied by a number of tenants. The earlier smaller woollen mill is seen in the foreground. (RCHME).

Fig. 12:25 Britannia Mills, Huddersfield. This room and power mill had main mills, sheds and warehouses grouped around a small yard. (RCHME)

The legacy of the textile industry

The woollen industry, like the other textile branches, has declined in the Huddersfield area since the early twentieth century. It is encouraging to record that many mills remain in their original use. The decline, nevertheless, is undeniable, and again buildings tell the story in a graphic way. In both urban and rural settings there are gaps in the landscape where mills once stood, there is darkness, dereliction and emptiness where formerly all had been vitality. It may be difficult now to imagine the overwhelming impression which Huddersfield's densely built-up mill suburbs of Lockwood, Rashcliffe, and the canal area around Colne Road and Firth Street made on the stranger to the town (Figure 12:26), for the impact of the towering mills on the landscape has been reduced by demolition. Huddersfield swept away part of its industrial past once before, in the 1930s when the Cloth Hall, the town's monument to the domestic system, was demolished and the site used for a cinema. The losses of recent decades combined with potential further demolition mean that Huddersfield's image as a mill town may become entirely a thing of the past.

Fig. 12:26 The Colne Road area of Huddersfield in the 1930s. Folly Hall Mills is in the foreground, Britannia Mills in the middle distance, with Firth Street and Larchfield Mills beyond. Many of the mills shown in the photograph have been demolished. (C.H. Wood).

Colum Giles

Biographical Note

Colum Giles is an investigator with the Royal Commission on the Historical monuments of England. After reading History at the University of London, Colum Giles studied for an M.A. in English Local History at the University of Leicester. He joined the Royal Commission in 1976, moving to West Yorkshire in 1978 to undertake a survey of vernacular houses (published in 1986 as *Rural Houses of West Yorkshire, 1400-1830*). He then went on to participate in a survey of textile mills in Yorkshire, published in 1992, as C. Giles and I. H. Goodall *Yorkshire Textile Mills 1770-1930*. Colum Giles lives in York, with his wife and daughter.

NOTES

1. Much of the general background for this article is taken from a number of published accounts of the history of the woollen industry both nationally and locally. The most important works are D.T. Jenkins and K.G. Ponting, *The British Wool Textile Industry 1770-1914* (1982); D.T. Jenkins, *The West Riding Wool Textile Industry 1770-1835* (Edington, 1975); and W.B. Crump and G. Ghorbal, *History of the Huddersfield Woollen Industry* (Huddersfield, 1935). Specific information relating to individual mills is drawn from the archive of the Royal Commission on the Historical Monuments of England. I would like to express thanks to the Royal Commission's Secretary, Mr Tom Hassall, for permission to use material in this archive. The findings of the Royal Commission's survey of Yorkshire's mills are published as C. Giles and I.H. Goodall, *Yorkshire Textile Mills 1770-1930* (1992). I would also like to acknowledge with thanks the work which Royal Commission colleagues have undertaken in the survey of Yorkshire mills; Dr Ian Goodall (investigation), Gillian Cookson (research), Anthony Berry (graphics), Terry Buchanan, Tony Perry, Bob Skingle and Peter Williams (photography), and Davina Turner (word processing). This article draws heavily upon their work. The archive resulting from the Mills Survey is held by the National Monuments Record, Fortress House, 23 Savile Row, London. A copy is held more locally, by the West Yorkshire Archaeology Service, 14 St John's North, Wakefield. The Archaeology Service was a partner in the survey.

2. Crump and Ghorbal, *Huddersfield Woollen Industry*, Chapters 4 and 6.

3. Borthwick Institute of Historical Research, Exchequer Probate Records, Deanery of Pontefract, May 1689, November 1693, May 1733, May 1734.

4. Jenkins, *West Riding Wool Textile Industry*, pp.6-8.

5. Jenkins, *West Riding Wool Textile Industry*, p.197.

6. Crump and Ghorbal, *Huddersfield Woollen Industry*, pp.102-7.

7. Jenkins, *West Riding Wool Textile Industry*, pp.19, 22. Dr Jenkins' evidence for the earliest use of scribbling machines in Yorkshire dates from 1779, when second-hand machines were advertised for sale in Huddersfield.

8. P(arliamentary) P(apers) (House of Commons) 1834 (167), *Employment of Children in Factories*, XX, C2, Mill No. III.

9. Jenkins, *West Riding Wool Textile Industry*, p.52.

10. Plan of Holmbridge Mill, private papers of Mr G.C. Barber, Holmbridge. The Publishers are grateful to Mr Barber for permission to reproduce this plan.

11. West Yorkshire Archive Service, Kirklees, KC 57.

12. W. Parson and W. White, *Directory of the Borough of Leeds and the Clothing District of Yorkshire* (1830), pp.319-25.

13. The weaver's cottage is discussed in L. Caffyn, *Workers' Housing in West Yorkshire 1750-1920* (1986), pp.9-18, 55-7, and in R.C.N. Thornes, *West Yorkshire; A Noble Scene of Industry, the development of the county 1500 to 1830* (Wakefield, 1981), pp.19-22.

14. H.A. Bodey, 'Coffin Row, Linthwaite', *Industrial Archaeology*, VIII (1971), 381-91.

15. PP 1834, Mill No. 136.

16. 'The Leeds Woollen Industry 1780-1820', edited by W.B. Crump, *Thoresby Society*, XXXII, (1931), 254-71.

17. Crump and Ghorbal, *Huddersfield Woollen Industry*, pp.93-95, 116-20.

18. P. Hudson, *The Genesis of Industrial Capital; a study of the West Riding Wool Textile Industry c.1750-1850* (Cambridge, 1986), p.71; Crump and Ghorbal, *Huddersfield Woollen Industry*, p.92; F.J. Glover, 'Dewsbury Mills; a history of Messrs Wormalds and Walker Ltd., Blanket Manufacturers of Dewsbury' (unpub. Ph.D thesis, Leeds University, 1959), p.378.

19. Jenkins, *West Riding Wool Textile Industry*, pp.121-7; Jenkins and Ponting, *British Wool Textile Industry*, pp.110-7.

20. Crump and Ghorbal, *Huddersfield Woollen Industry*, p.118.

21. Guildhall Library, Sun CR, MS 11937, Vol 214, Policy Number 1197383, 18 March 1835; Crump and Ghorbal, *Huddersfield Woollen Industry*, p.118.

22. Crump and Ghorbal, *Huddersfield Woollen Industry*, p.119.

23. Jenkins and Ponting, *British Wool Textile Industry*, pp.112, 179.

24. I am grateful to Mr A.J. Brooke for advice on the question of the direction taken by the Huddersfield textile industry after 1850.

25. E.A.H. Haigh, 'Joseph Kaye – Builder of Huddersfield', *Old West Riding*, IV, (Spring 1984), 30-32; E.J. Law, *Joseph Kaye, Builder, of Huddersfield, c.1779 to 1858*, (Huddersfield, 1989), pp.27-30.

26. PP 1833 (690), *Report on the present state of Manufactures, Commerce and Shipping*, vi, p.82.

27. Information kindly supplied by Mr A.J. Brooke.

CHAPTER 13

Architectural Design in Nineteenth Century Huddersfield

DAVID J. WYLES

It took a century of development to transform 'a miserable village'[1] into what Friedrich Engels called in 1845 'the handsomest by far of all the factory towns in Yorkshire and Lancashire by reason of its charming situation and modern architecture'.[2] By 1964 Huddersfield was recognised as 'a town of great character and Georgian and Victorian beauty'.[3] These changes were the result of a number of factors.

Sir John Ramsden had ensured the regional pre-eminence of Huddersfield with the building of the Cloth Hall (1766) and Sir John Ramsden Canal (1774-80). These stimulated further growth assisted by favourable market forces and technical innovations. Although this resulted in the first phase of planned development, the town remained generally cramped and poorly planned, with overcrowding resulting from a surge in population growth

In the early nineteenth century famine, war and general discontent exacerbated by an absentee landlord and incompetent agent resulted in the stagnation of commercial growth. Nevertheless, increased prosperity generated a group of craftsmen and architects whose work, stimulated by fashionable movements, introduced new levels of architectural sophistication which fulfilled the aspirations and doctrines of their clients. Elegant housing for the new middle class, public institutions and a frantic period of church and chapel building took place. The commercial revival was fully realised by the Trustees of the Ramsden Estate under the guidance of George Loch and local agent Alexander Hathorn. The construction of the Railway Station revolutionised the methods by which goods were transported, stimulating the development of the new town. The second half of the century saw the development of some of England's finest commercial buildings and domestic architecture and this growth was sustained until the beginning of the twentieth century. This chapter analyses the town's growth during the nineteenth century through its architectural developments. No attempt has been made to pass judgment on every building of note nor describe every architect; rather it attempts to set the period of Huddersfield's physical development against the influence of dynamic forces nationally.

The explosion of industry and population was, in the cities of the north, parallelled by an age of revivals when historicist styles emulated the glory of classical Greece and Rome, the power of the medieval church and the Renaissance of Italy and continental Europe. The great trading cities of Venice and Genoa became the source of inspiration for the new princes of industry. *The Builder* lamented, 'nothing is now left for it but to mime – with what ability it may the efforts of its palmier days … the universal refrain is, Copy, copy!'[4] And so they did, architects, craftsmen and clients, bringing great style, verve and character to Huddersfield. Huddersfield followed fashionable movements and occasionally anticipated them. The

Fig. 13:1 View of Huddersfield from Longley, 1837 by G.D. Tomlinson. (KCS)

energy of the town through the nineteenth century had its greatest manifestation in its buildings, crafted from the very sandstone on which it was built.

The builder, the architect and the client

It is the interrelationships of the architects, the builders whom they directed and the clients whose whims and resources they had to compliment, which underpin the stylistic development of the town. Many of the architects whose work is represented developed their knowledge from practical experience of the building trade. Both John Oates and William Henry Crossland, who produced some of Huddersfield's most notable buildings, were sons of quarry owners and stone merchants. Leeds architect Thomas Taylor (Holy Trinity Church, Trinity Street) had practised 'under Mr Andrews, a builder of eminence in London'[5] and the father of William Perkin (Highfield Chapel) was probably a master mason. Whilst some architects also trained under established names (W.H. Crossland under George Gilbert Scott, Taylor under James Wyatt), other local architects, such as John Kirk[6] and William Cocking,[7] whose fathers were both joiners, would have developed into architects as a natural extension of their practical building knowledge.

For most local architects formal training was limited and the development from the mechanical process of building to the technical preparation of drawing and supervision of the work was not clearly defined. Although the Architectural Society had been formed in 1831 and the Institute of British Architects in 1834 (the two united largely as a result of Sir William Tite's efforts in 1842), it is doubtful whether the newly established codes of practice would have been adopted by most local architects. 'A class in drawing and design was begun at the Huddersfield Mechanics' Institution in 1842,* to which were shortly added classes in mechanical drawing, architectural drawing and modelling.'[8]

In 1847, however, there were still only four architects listed in Huddersfield, including William Wallen and J.P. Pritchett of York. By 1853 the list[9] had increased to ten, including Joseph Kaye,[10] whose credentials as an architect were suspect and who would, with his other business interests,

* *The Young Men's Mental Improvement Society became the Mechanics' Institution in 1843.* EDITOR.

*Figure 13:2
Portrait of Joseph Kaye.
Folly Hall Mills may be
seen on the left and Kaye is
holding the plans for the
Huddersfield and Upper
Agbrigg Infirmary. (KCS)*

hardly have been able to satisfy the code of practice. As a result, although the autonomy of the master craftsmen, especially masons and joiners, was to diminish, local architects would maintain their close practical relationship with the building trade, blurring the definition between the two. This close understanding of practical skills helped to ensure that both the quality of stonework and the structural durability of a building were maintained. This relationship is clearly illustrated in *Joseph Kaye, Builder, of Huddersfield,*[11] which outlines the efforts made by John Oates in ensuring the terms of the contract for the building of the Infirmary were observed by Joseph Kaye.

Supervision by the architect or his Clerk of Works normally ensured a high standard of construction, as inferred in Alexander Hathorn's letter to George Loch concerning St. John's Church, Bay Hall, Birkby, where 'a sample of the proposed manner of walling is being set in dry courses for Mr Butterfield's inspection and approval'. The same letter, after assuring Loch of Joseph Kaye's good work, suggests '. . . it very often happens that the working masons in spite of very positive instructions from their employer, are careless and inattentive, from a desire to save themselves trouble and attention to secure the necessary quality and strength of work'.[12]

Joseph Kaye is a fine example of a master craftsmen, highly respected but, nevertheless, sometimes distrusted; a builder whose credentials as an architect have been questioned, but who created Huddersfield's finest buildings, often designed by 'architects' who in practice had little or no formal training. Kaye, however, remained the dominant figure for over fifty years of Huddersfield's building history. He was respected because he was one of a handful of masons who could deal with the scale of buildings proposed. A well organised workforce, the buying-in and transporting of materials and the handling of huge blocks of stone weighing up to ten tons, required a forceful, confident and skilled director.

No doubt masons such as Kaye would have to deal with the financial problems encountered by their employers, such as occurred during the construction of the Railway Station, but the masons themselves were prone to miscalculation. The Ramsdens' cashier, Isaac Hordern, for example, called Kaye 'a funny old man [who] has been known to say after taking a Contract for a Church, that he had forgotten the Estimate for the Tower'.[13] That the masons were a powerful body was illustrated during the building of the Union Bank and Chambers of Commerce in Westgate (demolished): 'its erection was greatly retarded by a local strike of masons, which occurred in the summer of 1865, and lasted eighteen weeks'.[14]

If the mason was the mechanic, it was the architect who held the responsibility for ensuring that the building was completed to specification and to the client's satisfaction. Edward Blore, the eminent London architect, furnished George Loch with a 'pretty sketch'[15] for the building of the Court House, Princess Street in 1844, prompting Isabella Ramsden to confirm 'that you [Loch] have been able to prevent the erection of a frightful building'.[16] His 'pretty sketch' resulted in a building of formal Georgian convention, perhaps confirming Colvin's assertion that 'a dull competence pervades all his work'.[17] In contrast, Blore's designs for St. John's, Bay Hall were rejected as being 'beautiful but too expensive'.[18]

The architect chosen for this commission was William Butterfield who, although producing a number of highly accomplished works, had little chance of expressing his considerable skills in the designs. He felt that the church should be sited amongst houses, while Hathorn preferred a position at the crest of the hill. Butterfield probably realised that little or no benefit derived from this, since financial constraints dictated an unspectacular solution. However Hathorn's report of November 1852 records, 'Mr Tite was quite delighted with the new church and expressed a high opinion of the masonry and general character and details of the whole building'.[19]

Tite himself was the perfect architectural representative for the Ramsdens. An eminent architect of the establishment, he was employed to ensure that high standards of design were maintained around St. George's Square. His tireless advocacy of the *Classical* style brought him into conflict with J.P. Pritchett, whose designs for Lion buildings on behalf of Samuel Oldfield he considered unsatisfactory. Isabella Ramsden had already insisted that Pritchett 'must not be employed in his profession on any work for which the Ramsden family are expected to pay',[20] although he retained his employment with the Earl Fitzwilliam at his Wentworth Woodhouse Estate. It was Fitzwilliam, as an influential Trustee of the Ramsden Estate and brother-in-law of Isabella Ramsden, who, in October 1846, laid the foundation stone of the new Railway Station, designed by Pritchett. During this period of great commercial activity when the town was being reshaped, Isabella Ramsden's strength and intuition, George Loch's astute direction and Alex Hathorn's (over-)fastidiousness provided a firm foundation of overall control.

By the 1870s Isaac Hordern, the most articulate but opinionated of the Ramsdens' employees, was interfering in design matters to a degree which must have proved infuriating to an architect of the stature of W.H. Crossland. In 1876 Hordern wrote, 'It will be a matter for consideration whether Sir John Ramsden would not prefer to have one important block made of the Byram Buildings and the Byram Arcade rather than cut up the elevation into three styles for one block'.[21] In February 1879 he advised Crossland, 'The square girders to carry the roof do not look very pleasing. Could you not have an iron arcading to take the place of the heavy looking girders. . .'.[22] His notes were accompanied by crudely executed sketches outlining his ideas.

Naturally the closed circle of builder, architect and client was occasionally breached by external forces. Joshua Hobson's personal criticism of original proposals for the new town and the concern voiced by the Improvement Commissioners, by whom he was employed, clearly influenced the Ramsden Estate into creating a public square which would 'leave nearly the whole of the elegant station front open to view from the very centre of town forming one of the finest architectural vistas in the

Fig. 13:3 Huddersfield in 1826. (WYAS, K)

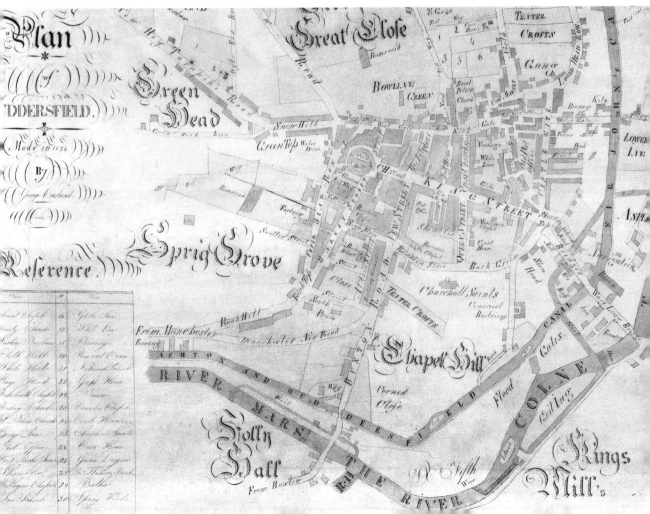

provinces'.[23] Whilst such control implied a level of public accountability it was the builder, the architect and the client who narrated the story of Huddersfield's development through most of the nineteenth century.

Commercial development

The importance of the Cloth Hall and the canal to the development of the town has been well documented. The *Universal British Directory* (1794) stated that 'the average return of the goods sold is supposed to be greater than that of any other market in the kingdom...'.[24] The wide main streets and planned development of the town initiated by Sir John Ramsden (1699-1769) was paralleled by the increase in finishing processes and warehousing associated with the textile industry, largely concentrated around the riverside and canal. By the early nineteenth century, however, the 'combination of an indifferent landlord and an incompetent agent brought commercial building in the town to a standstill'.[25] Famine, war and local discontent exacerbated the problems of mismanagement. Whomsley states, 'the more expensive commercial and industrial buildings, warehouses and mills were driven away by the policy on leases, and this policy, had it been allowed to continue, would have been ultimately disastrous for the town'.[26]

Fortunately the policy did not continue. In 1839 Sir John Ramsden died and during the next thirteen years the Estate was supervised by Trustees during the period before Sir John William Ramsden came of age. The control exerted by Sir John William's mother, Isabella Ramsden, and her influential brother-in-law, Earl Fitzwilliam, was to stimulate the period of Huddersfield's most rapid commercial growth. In 1844 the Trustees appointed George Loch as their agent. Loch, already a well established auditor, during the next nine years would provide the essential guidance under which the Estate flourished. The construction of the Railway Station (1846-50) created the perfect opportunity for growth and the story of these years has been well documented.[27]

In 1849 Loch, in consultation with local agent, Alex Hathorn, suggested that 'if the George were removed the main street might be carried forward'.[28] His recommendations were adopted. The old George Inn was removed to be re-erected in St. Peter's Street and a new hotel built adjacent to the station, creating an access to a large area on which the 'new town' would be developed.

Fig. 13:4 The George Hotel. (KCS)

Fig. 13:5 Tite's Building.
(KCS)

The Italianate façade of the George Hotel, designed by William Wallen, was to become the adopted architectural style for the new town over the next ten years. In 1851 the Trustees appointed the eminent London architect, Sir William Tite, as consultant to ensure high standards of design were maintained. Tite, a confirmed classicist, had established his reputation in the 1820s and in 1840 won the controversial competition for the new Royal Exchange in London, after which he was knighted, became President of the Royal Institute of British Architects and Liberal MP for Bath from 1855 to 1872. *The Buildings of Huddersfield* [29] examines his considerable influence on the appearance of the new town, including his indictment of work by other architects, in particular J.P. Pritchett's designs for Lion Buildings (1852-54). Following his request for alterations to the elevations he wrote: 'I don't think the changes made in the main front are improvements – but they are not very important and therefore I think they may pass ... I wonder that Pritchett and Oldfield are troublesome – I am sure without vanity, they are greatly indebted to me for putting a very crude design into shape and proportion'. [30]

The new buildings around the square provided warehousing and office space and grand façades disguised their utilitarian use. Offices were reached through entrances off the square, while the warehousing was served by intermediate courtyards. Certainly the palazzo architecture of Renaissance Italy fitted the purpose for which it was adapted. It was sophisticated and elegant, offering the merchants and buyers who arrived by train an immediate impression of well-being and quality. It offered a multi-storey building with a large capacity for storage. The formal arrangement provided a regular fenestration, providing a reasonable level of natural light. And sandstone was the perfect material, both resistant and easily worked, enabling the production of freestone dressings, sculpted elements and decoratively tooled features such as vermiculated quoins.

The limitations of Roman and Greek architecture with its giant pilasters, porticos and pediments, and Gothic architecture with its elaborate detailing resulted in the Renaissance palazzo becoming the characteristic norm for the northern industrial towns. And yet by 1870 a hybrid of French and Italian Gothic was being adopted for the building of offices in the new town. The influence of the Houses of Parliament (1840-60) and Ruskin's *Stones of Venice* (1851) have been outlined in *The Buildings of Huddersfield*.

Fig. 13:6 Estate Offices, Railway Street. (KCS)

Fig. 13:7 Design for the Estate Offices by W.H. Crossland. (KCS)

It was W.H. Crossland, not only Huddersfield's most notable architect by birth but a pupil of George Gilbert Scott, who brought the finest of Continental Gothic to Huddersfield. His designs for the Ramsden Estate Office (1871-72), Railway Street included the use of elaborate wrought iron, marble, tracery, heraldic shields and intricately carved birds, flowers and other beasts. Charles Eastlake said of Ruskin's converts, 'they made drawings in the Zoological Gardens and conventionalised the forms of birds, beasts and reptiles into examples of noble grotesque for decorative sculpture'.[31] Decorative elements are only one feature of Crossland's building, however. The form and bulk, reminiscent of the French châteaux of the early Renaissance, created a multi-storeyed building which maintained the advantages of earlier Italianate buildings. The picturesque groupings of parts, broken by projecting bays, pinnacled turrets and chimneys, subtle changes in the fenestration raise this above the ordinary.

A further result of the diversity of Gothic taste was its interpretation by local architects such as William Cocking. Cocking designed Britannia Buildings (1856-59), perhaps the finest of all those around St. George's Square, with the Italianate overlaid by sculpted elements such as the masks, festoons and Royal Arms over which Britannia rules.

Fig. 13:8 Britannia Buildings. (KCS)

Fig. 13:9 Detail of Kirkgate (Bulstrode) Buildings. (KCS)

Whether his work was tempered by Tite in his role as architectural overseer, or whether he plagiarised the Italianate buildings already completed is open to debate. Certainly the West Riding Union Bank (*c.*1860) in Market Place was even bolder with its use of marble columns, sculpted masks, foliate carving and Composite pilastrade. This eclecticism reached its peak in the main elevation to Eddison's, estate agents, on High Street where Cocking not only made use of the various elements incorporated into the bank but added favourites of High Victorian design such as the elaborate cast iron gates and polychromatic stonework in the voussoirs. It was this debased use of Gothic that led Ruskin to regret, with some bitterness, having created 'the accursed Frankenstein's monsters',[32] and by the late 1870s the use of Gothic for civil architecture was abandoned.

During this period the Queen Anne style became fashionable and again W.H. Crossland created the finest examples of it in the Waverley Hotel, Kirkgate, and Bulstrode Buildings, Byram Street (1880-1883). The style, noted by George Gilbert Scott as 'a vexatious disturber of the Gothic movement',[33] was appreciated by the Ramsdens' cashier Isaac Hordern who in 1876 wrote

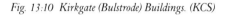

Fig. 13:10 Kirkgate (Bulstrode) Buildings. (KCS)

Fig. 13:11 Huddersfield Banking Company, Cloth Hall Street. (KCS)

'there would be a fair chance of introducing the Queen Anne style on the Kirkgate Block to good effect'.[34]

Further described as having 'a little genuine Queen Anne in it, a little Dutch, a little Flemish, a squeeze of Robert Adam, a generous dash of Wren and a touch of Francois I',[35] the form adopted for the Kirkgate block was primarily based on French and Flemish models. Gone is the Italian Gothic, to be replaced with the robust and vigorous Baroque with deeply tooled piers and above the eaves cornice the striking gabled dormers with their fanciful carving. Beneath these fashionable embellishments was the linear heir to the earlier Italianate around St George's Square and Crossland's earlier commissions in Huddersfield. Once again the architect's brief was to produce a building which would fulfil commercial requirements.

Edward Hughes' Huddersfield Banking Company premises (1881) (demolished) on the corner of Cloth Hall Street and New Street proved that local architects were no slave to contemporary fashion but made eccentric use of various revivals. From the predominantly Italianate ground floor, the style became more debased floor by floor, with the crowning onion shaped copper dome adding a hint of eastern promise. It would be wrong to be too critical about the work of such architects as Hughes, for, perhaps unknowingly, they added a little humour to the skyline of Huddersfield. It is such buildings as this which, once demolished, are affectionately remembered.

It took some time for Huddersfield to free itself from the Classical Revival. The availability of sandstone and craft skills resulted in a number of commissions which, although marked by individual characteristics, lacked the power and presence of earlier commercial buildings. One good example, built at the turn of the century, was Station Street Buildings by Abbey and Hanson.

Fig. 13:12 The Prudential Assurance Building on the corner of Ramsden Street and New Street. (KCS)

317

Two buildings broke the mould. The Wholesale Market (1887-89) on Lord Street, designed by the Borough Surveyor, R.S. Dugdale, made use of iron sections, pre-fabricated by the Whessoe Foundry Company in Darlington, and large expanses of glass, which introduced the maximum amount of light. Below this canopy was a highly functional flexible space.

It was the structural value of iron which determined the external rhythm and internal flexibility of the Prudential Assurance Company offices (1897-98), New Street, by Alfred Waterhouse. Although Waterhouse was one of the greatest Victorian architects, having designed the Town Hall and Assize Courts in Manchester and Natural History Museum in London, his link with Huddersfield was limited. This was because his designs for the Prudential followed a basic format which could be adapted throughout the country. Whilst the interior was carried on a steel frame the exterior walls were constructed of durable terracotta and red brick, which distinguished it from most other buildings in the town centre. Only decorative elements reveal its true Victorian pedigree. The Prudential building not only provided a suitable link with the standardisation and pre-fabrication of twentieth century Modernism but a symbolic break with a town created from stone and largely moulded by one family.

Fig. 13:13 Waterworks Building and Spring Street. (KCS)

Housing

George Searle Phillips' memory of a 'miserable village, the houses poor and scattered, the streets narrow crooked and dirty'[36] reflects a period during which the population grew at a rate faster rate than in any of West Yorkshire's principal towns. From 1801 to 1841 the population grew from 7,268 to 25,068.

The Royal Commission Report on the State of Large Towns and Populous Districts in 1844 observed that, 'here the poor are badly off for ventilation; they have scarce a sash or a pane that will open, and ventilation flues for cottages are almost unknown'.[37] Overcrowding was a particular problem, with domestic accommodation, often in squalid rooms and cellars, competing for space with workshops, stabling and warehousing. Especially notorious were the yards, particularly those centred around Kirkgate, Rosemary Lane and King Street. A number of yards, in particular Wormald's, Hammond's and Goldthorp's Yards off King Street provided some idea of these cramped conditions and vernacular construction. Buildings were constructed of coursed hammer dressed stone with stone slate roofs and both mullioned and sash windows with small panes sub-divided by glazing bars. Not all housing was as ramshackle, however; White's *Directory* of 1837 noted that, 'The Market Place is a large area lined with good houses and shops, mostly rebuilt during the last fifty years'.[38]

As the wealth of the town grew, so the growing number of tradesmen and merchants sought less cramped and more sanitary conditions. Their status dictated a style of town house which met the Georgian conventions of decorum, conformity and tradition. The symmetrical rigidity of the design was offset by classical detailing, as seen on the ashlar-faced town-houses along Queen Street (c.1830). Panelled doors with entablatures and Tuscan columns, bold eaves cornice with blocking course and sash windows originally with small panes and glazing bars completed a formula which, although criticised by Ruskin as 'utterly devoid of life, virtue, honourableness or power of doing good', combined elegance with characteristic economy of design. The same period saw the development of Huddersfield's first 'suburb', a speculative development of Georgian town houses occupying higher ground between Fitzwilliam Street West and Spring Street where the newly constructed Waterworks building formed a suitable focal point to the formal vista.

The beginning of Victoria's reign marked the beginning of the end for the purity of the Georgian aesthetic. Growing affluence and individual taste provided the spring board for the adoption of the Italian villa, with pictorial grouping of detached and semi-detached houses. The result was best seen along Trinity Street and New North Road where antique elements used decoratively created greater plasticity of design. The result was greater novelty and variety, inspired by the picturesque and the developing aspirations of an income group influenced by the extravagance of their social superiors. Even if the houses failed to match the romantic grandeur of the architecture of Vanburgh, Kent, Nash and Wyatt, the period saw the publication of a large number of manuals which offered the would-be architect a pattern book of ideas.

The Ramsden Estate itself lost no chance in recognising that the growing demand for villas provided a valuable means of income. Alex Hathorn asked surveyor Thomas Brook to prepare 'a plan of all the land from the Greenhead Estate (but not including it) to the New North Road, and hence to the boundary of the Bayhall Estate'. Hathorn considered that 'in order to serve the interests of the estate and to lead the people and to afford them the proper and reasonable facilities for building it is only necessary to show them some such plan and the style and character of the Building proposed to be erected'.[39] In July 1850 an application for a house on New North Road prompted Hathorn to write to George Loch, 'I expect shortly to be able to inform you that 3 or 4 additional applications will soon be made for Dwelling Houses in the Gothic Style fronting to New North Road'.[40]

Here is an illuminating insight not only into the control exerted by the Ramsdens' agents, but their determination to lead the people into a correct form of architecture. Ironically, this clear acceptance of Gothic was during the period when Italianate architecture was being rigorously applied to the new town around St. George's Square. By 1862 *The Builder* was to report:

> But the public demand for good taste is on the increase in England . . . I need only refer to the New North Road, in Huddersfield, for an example of pleasing Domestic architecture. In this street there is a great variety in point of style in the different houses; both Gothic and Classic examples are to be seen, frequently juxtaposed, and with an effect that is eminently satisfactory. One instance of a detached Classic villa is perhaps the most perfect specimen of Classic house architecture in England. But no two houses are alike where they are quite detached, and this is productive of a charm which as far as my own experience goes, is without example in England.[41]

Huddersfield's list of building plans and building registers[42] indicate the numerous applications in the area identified by Hathorn. A number of local architects were involved in designing houses, among them William Wallen, who probably designed the property on New North Road where he practised in 1853 and by the 1870s John Kirk was creating for wealthy clients new levels of eclectic finery, such as Ebor Mount (1873) on New North Road. During the last quarter of the nineteenth century housing extended northwards a far as the junctions of Birkby Road and Holly Bank Road with Halifax Road. As decisively as the mills and warehouses, these properties confirmed Huddersfield's standing as a manufacturing town of reknown. Cote Royd is one example, built in 1874 for Wright Mellor, the first Mayor of Huddersfield.

The wealth of carved stonework in the houses off Halifax Road, Thornhill Avenue, Bryan Road and Cleveland Road is matched by an equal variety of historic references, even glimpses of a vernacular tradition, with mullioned and transomed windows with hoodmoulds and the return of hammer-dressed stone for main elevations. The eclecticism of the period is illustrated by this description of Cleveland House, Cleveland Road:

> The two storey canted bays with sashes, Tuscan piers and entablatures at both floor levels and sculpted panels in between, 3-panelled door with semi-circular fanlight, moulded voussoirs and imposts, vermiculated keystone and sunk panels, in Doric porch with full entablature: metopes have sculpted Anglo-Saxon or Mediaeval style heads nearly in the round: ornamental cresting above blocking course. French casements above porch in marbled surround with moulded cornice on tall gadrooned consoles.[43]

And this is one of the less elaborate mansions of the Edgerton district! Nietzsche said 'Blessed are those who have taste, even although it be bad taste'. Here are some fine examples.

The presence of a skilled body of masons and joiners and the survival of a vernacular tradition produced a suitable platform for the growing Arts and Crafts movement, which prized individual craftsmanship in contrast to mass production and the sham nature of mass-produced items. The result was a number of exceptional interiors, such as the billiard room added to Stoneleigh, Bryan Road by the Manchester architect George Faulkner Armitage and illustrated in *The British Architect*, February 1891. However, it was another Manchester architect, Edgar Wood, whose commissions in

Huddersfield not only resulted in the most outstanding buildings of the late nineteenth century but whose work was nationally and internationally acclaimed. Briarcourt, Occupation Road, built for H.H. Sykes, included elements of West Riding vernacular, matched with a Jacobethan interior with stylised Art Nouveau motifs, best illustrated in the decorative plasterwork. Nevertheless, it is Banney Royd off Halifax Road, built for W.H. Armitage in 1900, which best illustrates the combination of craftsmanship, local vernacular and the anti-historicist freedom of Art Nouveau.

The house is built entirely of coursed hammer-dressed stone with ashlar dressings and a stone slate roof, windows with leaded lights have chamfered mullions and transoms. These features, combined with the rythmn and movement of the whole, create an illusion of traditional solidity and mass. But it is the detailing especially of the interior which make the house more than just a clever interpretation of the past, for the introduction of Art Nouveau decoration effects a complete break with tradition. Sinuous, flowing, and elongated forms are represented in the richly-decorated finger plates, plasterwork and tapering chimney breasts of old red sandstone with their sculpted elements and mottoes. Less obvious are the tapering pilasters dividing the panelled oak wainscotting, the slender panelling of internal doors, the stained glass and ornamental ironwork.[44]

Church and Chapel

Throughout the eighteenth century few Anglican churches were built. Those that were generally avoided clear references to Roman Catholicism, as expressed in the Gothic church architecture of the pre-Reformation, and adopted the simplicity and meeting-house style of the Nonconformist movements. The Gothic Revival in Church architecture occurred at a time of war, social upheaval and growing dissent, when the tenets of a no-frills approach contrasted with the decorative symbolism and extravagance of continental baroque.

Holy Trinity Church (1816-19), Trinity Street provides an interesting early example of this Revival, pre-empting the surge of Gothic churches brought about by the Million Act of 1818. It was designed by Thomas Taylor (1778-1826) of Leeds, who had practised in London in the office of James Wyatt. His commission to build Christ Church at Liversedge in 1812 had established his reputation for Gothic architecture and the Million Act provided him with extensive employment.

In the case of Holy Trinity the relationship between the architect and his client, Benjamin Haigh Allen is an important one. It was Allen's deep spirituality and his association with a growing circle of Evangelicals at the University of Cambridge which fuelled his desire to build a new church in a town with just one church serving a population of over 8,000. It was the Million Act which provided the greatest impetus to church building, establishing the names of architects and masons, such as John Oates and Joseph Kaye.

At a time of growing population and the increasing influence of Nonconformity, the Government sought to quell unrest and the seeds of discontent amongst the working classes. A growing middle class and the formation of the Church Building Society spurred the spending of £1 million towards the building of churches in populous districts.* Although a great deal more was spent during the next fifteen years, with 214 churches built as a result of the Act, the main consideration was one of economy in construction. The style chosen for most of the churches was Gothic, as in its most simple form it offered a less extravagant solution than the Classical style with its columns, pediments and grandiose proportions.

St. Paul's Church (1829) by John Oates exemplified several aspects of this period. It met the requirements of the Church Commissioners by adopting the Early English style, with plain untraceried lancets and the thrifty application of decorative features. Kenneth Clark asserted that no Commissioners' churches were effective and claimed that the buildings were shoddy and contemptible as architecture.[45] This is unfair. Given the constraints, Oates managed to avoid both meeting-house austerity and the frippery of baroque and its inference of popery. The result is a functional building of simple charm, honesty and adherence to the given brief.

A few years later the need arose to completely rebuild the Parish Church of St. Peter, which had fallen into decay. J.P. Pritchett was chosen as architect, and his designs using the perpendicular Gothic were perhaps a little excessive in view of the need for economy. The large mullioned and transomed windows enabled the introduction of elaborate tracery and

*See also Chapter Six 'Religion in Huddersfield since the mid-Eighteenth century' by Edward Royle.
EDITOR.

stained glass. The tower of six stages has designed buttresses, crocketed pinnacles and traceried crenellations. The galleried interior helped reduce the overall floor area, in common with many Million churches.

The problems created by the church's construction have been well documented. The lowest tender of £10,000, submitted by Mr W. Exley of York, was accepted, Exley not only used second-hand stone from the old church but laid it with its natural bed lying vertically, causing the face to laminate and disintegrate from the time of its completion in 1836.

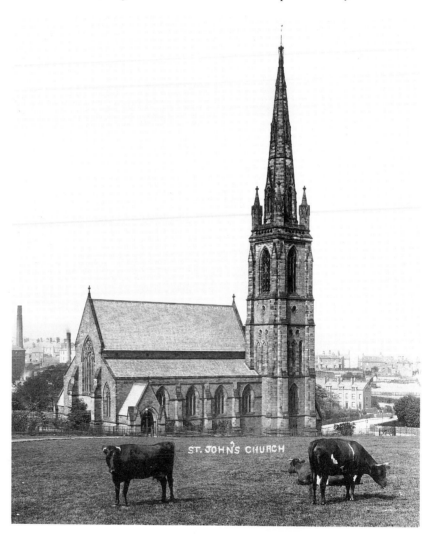

Fig. 13:14 St John's Church, Birkby. (KCS)

The second major phase of the Revival was greatly influenced by the fervour of a group of students and academics at both Oxford and Cambridge. In 1841 the first issue of the *Ecclesiologist*, the research magazine of the Cambridge Camden Society, set standards for both civil and secular architecture over the next thirty years. A passion for structural and historical honesty developed through deep spiritual faith, matched by a return to solemn ritual and symbolism. Growing nationalism, the publication of A.W. Pugin's enormously influential *The True Principles of Pointed or Christian Architecture*[46] and the influence of the university societies provided an inspirational source for the greatest architects of the age. Two such architects, George Gilbert Scott and William Butterfield were commissioned to design churches in Huddersfield. Both were stamped with the Revivalists' creed for honestly interpreting English Gothic, even though both departed from the true principles in their individual work.

William Butterfield was appointed by the Ramsden family to design St. John's, Bay Hall. The Ramsden papers indicate Butterfield's frustration over delays, local petitions for action and disagreement over siting. Joseph Kaye, however, having submitted an acceptable estimate for the building, of only £3,934 7s. 10d., had made good progress by August 1851 when Alex Hathorn wrote his long and fastidious letter to George Loch. For all the niggling attention to detail and Tite's satisfaction at the finished result, the building is restrained and orthodox in comparison with the High Church values and bold polychromy of Butterfield's finest work. This was value for money architecture but perhaps a waste of Butterfield's talents.

Scott's designs for St. Thomas's, Manchester Road provide a more rewarding example of Revival architecture. It was built in 1859 by the Starkey family, owners of the nearby Springdale Mill, at a cost of £9,000. Scott was asked to design the church through his childhood friendship with the Vicar of Huddersfield, Canon Bateman. The outstanding feature is the tower with its tall broach spire, the vertical thrust of which provides a symbolic link with the spirit of *Ecclesiology*.

The buildings of Huddersfield provide clues to the moral and social climate of their time and no more so than in the comparison of church and chapel. Queen Street Wesleyan Chapel, built by subscription in 1819 was, at the time of its completion, the largest of its kind, seating over 1,500 people. Classical influences are clearly reflected in the Tuscan columned porch, central overarched Venetian window and central pediment with oval oculus in the tympanum, creating an uneasy balance of Roman and Palladian elements. Here was a clear statement of confidence and influence, contrasting with the low profile and relative isolation of earlier Nonconformist chapels. Above all this fine building, costing £8,000 to construct, was completed at a time when the Million Act was stipulating economy of design.

Less grand but maintaining the impact of the 'town hall' style was Ramsden Street Independent Chapel (1825) (demolished), designed by Watson and Pritchett (J.P. Pritchett supervised the work). Its bold horizontal rustication, central bay with Ionic pilasters and pediment, stood as a further example of strong local support. Built as a result of the chapel at Highfield becoming too crowded, the townspeople raised the £6,514 to complete the building.

Highfield Chapel itself was, by the 1840s far too small for its growing congregation. Specifications were drawn up and an advertisement in the *Leeds Mercury* of 18 February 1843 invited architects to submit plans. The architects appointed were Messrs Perkin and Backhouse, a Leeds firm who had already undertaken a number of similar commissions.

The design, as with Queen Street Chapel, was a powerful if loose adaptation of Classical styles. The main elevation of five bays had the two end bays breaking forward and framed by giant Tuscan pilasters and Ionic Columns. Sash windows were linked by large round arched surrounds and the eaves cornice supported massive parapets.

St. Patrick's Church on New North Road emphasises a further strand in the social history of new buildings. The growing population of Roman Catholics, especially Irish immigrants, resulted in the building of Huddersfield's first Roman Catholic Church since the Reformation. The architect was John Child of Leeds who also designed St. Anne's, Park Row and St. Patrick's, York Road in Leeds. The builder was Joseph Kaye. It was built in 1832 with 'missionary zeal'[47] and although basically a functional box costing only £2,000, the main elevation in its scale and Gothic detailing has a certain charm.

The contrasting wealth of the chapel goers and the generally poor Irish immigrants, resulted in the raising of subscriptions from the local business community, who realised the importance of the church in maintaining the stability of an important source of labour.

The social and architectural development of church and chapel became generally less significant as the century progressed. Later additions such as the chancel to St. Paul's church in the 1880s reflected the changing nature of Anglican worship. The bold classicism of the earlier chapels was replaced by a less formal, through still dignified interpretation of the meeting house, the 720 seater Gledholt Methodist Chapel (1890) providing a good later example. The Gothic style was also adopted. Milton Congregational Church (1883-85), Queen Street South,* by Messrs Healey of Bradford with its 'fourteenth century' tracery, foliate decoration and tower, illustrated a move towards conformity and architectural assimilation.

As religious and doctrinal passions diminished, the symbolic associations as expressed through architectural design, also declined. Huddersfield may contain no individual gems, but taken as a whole its churches and chapels provide a lively insight into nineteenth century themes and values.[48]

Public buildings

In contrast to the Gothic Revival in church architecture the first of Huddersfield's major public buildings paid tribute to the classical architecture of Greece and Rome. The design of the Infirmary (1829), Lockwood Spa (1827) and the Railway Station (1846-50) gave full-blooded acknowledgement to classical elements, in contrast with the more refined architecture of the Chapel.

The Spa buildings and the Infirmary were designed by John Oates who, at a time when he was adapting church architecture to the financial constraints imposed by the Million Act, was creating public buildings of substance and grandeur. The Spa and the Infirmary provide some clue to the diversity of this Revival, for encapsulated in its interpretation were strands of both academic and romantic thought. The achievements of a civilised society, the concept of a temple to science, and the expression of the sublime and the picturesque were all present.

Both the fashion and symbolism of this Classical Revival found suitable expression in the growing demand for what would later be termed as health and leisure facilities. The *Universal British Directory* had noted in 1794, 'there

---

Later renamed Queensgate. EDITOR.

Fig. 13:15 J.P. Pritchett's design for the Railway Station. (KCS)

are several medicinal springs in the neighbourhood . . . which probably only want the attention of some person of abilities and influence to bring them into notice and more general use'.[49] The opportunity was obviously recognised, for in 1827 Oates designed a range of buildings, including shower baths and large swimming bath, with the spring water pumped into the building and heated. The group was fronted in the neo-classical manner with a tetrastyle Tuscan porch supporting a pediment and appropriately set 'in a deeply sequestered spot, sheltered by a lofty and well-wooded ridge on the east side of the river'.[50] Unfortunately the deeply sequestered spot became a hotchpotch of industry and housing leaving only the soot blackened façade and the Bath Hotel building on Lockwood Road.

Of grander proportions was the Infirmary; the dominant feature was an imposing entrance, a giant Greek Doric portico. John Oates won the commission, against competition from thirteen other architects, following an advertisement in the *Leeds Mercury*[51] inviting the submission of designs and specifications.

The Greek Revival did not eclipse the refined taste of Georgian architecture. The symmetry and proportion associated with human scale were satisfactorily applied to the Waterworks building, Water Street (1828), the Court House, Queen Street (1825) each with its ashlar façade, bays of sash windows with glazing bars and crowned by a pediment with an oval plaque in the tympanum bearing an inscription. The later County Court, Princess Street (1847) by Edward Blore was equally polite if a little dull.

The 1840s marked a crossroads with the Georgian, Neo-classical and Italianate styles all represented. In addition was the preference for late Gothic and Tudor architecture for educational establishments, welding the themes of scholarship and Christianity. J.P. Pritchett, for example, was commissioned to design Huddersfield College (1839-40) after an advertisement in the *Bradford Observer* had requested architects 'to furnish the design and superintend the erection of buildings'.[52] His design incorporated chamfered mullioned windows with hoodmoulds, within which diamond-paned glass was set within a pointed arch frame, and a castellated parapet.

The Neo-classical Revival was magnificently represented by J.P. Pritchett's Railway Station (1846-50), with its central pedimented portico of four Corinthian columns with parapet and balustrade. The terminal blocks have central porticoed bays with parapets bearing the names of the two railway companies at whose joint expense it was built. This 'stately home with trains in'[53] was in fact, a glorious façade, designed by a man who was obviously acquainted with Neoclassicism from his apprenticeship in London and commissions in Yorkshire. There was little of substance behind this façade, reflecting the view that the railways were 'as interested as insurance companies and banks in the representational dignity of Classical frontpieces'.[54] Only two stations, at Newcastle-upon-Tyne (1846-50) and Monkwearmouth by John Dobson, rival the monumental grandeur of Huddersfield.

Pritchett's design for a Town Hall on land later occupied by Britannia Buildings was blocked by the Improvement Commissioners. Had this been built it would have provided a fitting complement to the station with its central tetrastyle pedimented portico, flanking bays with round arched windows set between a giant pilastrade and a domed roof adding weight and balance to the overall design. The hall would have formed an impressive physical symbol of public government, contemporary with Leeds Town Hall and comparable to St. George's Hall, Bradford. It was never built and Huddersfield finally created a poor substitute in 1881 on Princess Street. Perhaps this was Huddersfield's greatest missed opportunity.

The mode for the Italianate palazzo was at this time asserting itself on the architectural vocabulary of the town. The first major buildings to adopt the style seem to have been the Riding School and Zetland Hotel, Ramsden Street (1848) by William Wallen. The Riding School was used chiefly for the local unit of the West Yorkshire Yeomanry Cavalry, but for several months of the year was also used as a theatre. Both buildings had rusticated basements and bold entablatures, the hotel with giant Tuscan pilasters and the Riding School a tall arched entrance flanked by panels bearing bas-reliefs with rampant horses.

The Mechanics Institution (1859), Northumberland Street, by Travis and Mangnell of Manchester was a heavy rendering of the Italianate style with Tuscan pilasters dividing windows, set within blind arches and capped by a prominent full entablature with 'Mechanics Institution' inscribed in the frieze. The growth of such institutions was parallelled by their architectural development, which provided for the expanding demand for further education facilities.

As with commercial buildings, the period from 1860 onwards was marked by a move away from the rigidity of the Classical Revival. Its place was taken by an ornate or debased form of historicism embracing elements of both Gothic and Renaissance architecture.

Edward Hughes' Market Hall (1878, demolished 1970), King Street was, like his bank on Cloth Hall Street, a building fondly remembered. It included a central clock tower with gabled spire, pointed two and three light windows separated by slender colonnettes, a central bay with a tall arched entrance with sculpted elements incorporated into the spandrels and frieze and flanked by octagonal tourelles. It was significant enough to feature in *The Builder* of 28 December 1878. His Technical College (1881-84) Queen Street South, makes use of similar elements. Windows are mullioned and

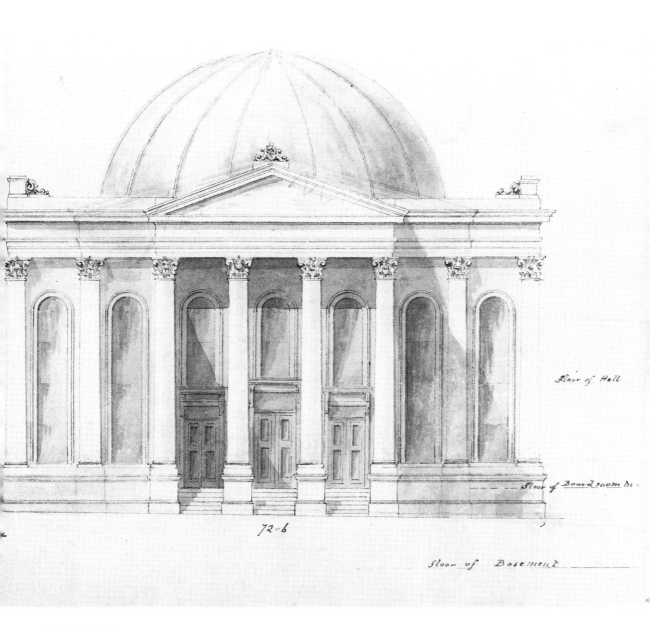

Floor of Hall

Floor of Board room &c.

72·6

Floor of Basement

*Fig. 13:16 The Town
Hall which was not built.
Pritchett's design for a
Town Hall in St. George's
Square. (WYAS, K)*

Fig. 13:17 Wholesale Market. (KCS)

transomed and upper lights have reticulated tracery. Octagonal tourelles support spires and the central bay includes a porch with balustrade and finials, the door flanked by colonnettes with trefoiled lancets in the fanlight.

The aim of creating a suitable headquarters for local government culminated in the building of the rather dull Municipal Offices (1875-76) on Ramsden Street designed by the Borough Surveyor, John Abbey. The main elevation, with its portico carried on four Doric columns with the arms of the borough and its bold horizontal rustication, contains a hint of civic pride.

The second phase of construction, incorporating a concert hall, was built between 1878-1881, with its main entrance on to Princess Street. Abbey was again the designer, but died before its completion. His building is Free Classic mixing the metaphors of Italianate, French Renaissance and Baroque architecture, with rusticated angle piers, giant order Corinthian columns, slender colonnettes, sculpted masks, a central bay with a round arched porch flanked by paired pilasters, and segmental pediments to the central and end bays of the side elevations. The concert hall interior has lavish stucco decoration and elaborate mouldings, with the magnificent Father Willis organ occupying centre stage.

The saga of the Town Hall exemplified a lack of conviction and commitment which, combined with characteristic caution and financial restraint, held back the dynamic forces which had shaped the town. Asa Briggs declared that 'the image of the city depended not only upon the facts but upon the imaginative power with which people arranged the facts . . .'.[55] Because it lacked the imaginative power, the borough failed to sustain a level of competitiveness with the other major West Riding towns, which would have produced public buildings of considerable note. This air of no-confidence has haunted Huddersfield since.

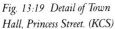
Fig. 13:19 Detail of Town Hall, Princess Street. (KCS)

Fig. 13:18 Municipal Offices, Ramsden Street. (KCS)

David J. Wyles

Biographical Note

David Wyles was born in Norfolk. He attended the School of Town Planning at Leeds Polytechnic from 1970-1974 and is a Member of the Royal Town Planning Institute. He joined Kirklees Metropolitan Council in 1974 becoming Senior Planner in the section dealing with Conservation and Listed Buildings in 1977. In 1983 he was invited to give a series of architectural walks around Huddersfield by the curator of Huddersfield Art Gallery. This was followed by *The Buildings of Huddersfield* published in 1984.

He has lectured on various aspects of art and architecture and was a member of the Banney Royd Group, preparing architectural background of the house for *Banney Royd – An Agreeable House* published in 1991.

He is currently Principal Tourism Officer for Kirklees Metropolitan Council and has contributed a range of articles for various publications associated with his work.

GLOSSARY

Art Nouveau

A movement prevailing at the turn of the twentieth century, characterised by the use of decorative elements, especially the use of curving lines and plant forms.

Baroque

Term originally applied to late Renaissance design using rich and bold ornamentation.

Bas-relief

Sculpture which stands out only slightly from surface.

Blocking Course

Course of solid masonry built on top of projecting cornice.

Buttress

A vertical mass of masonry built against a wall to resist outward thrust.

Canopy

An overhanging covering.

Classical
The architecture of ancient Greece and Rome, the rules and forms of which were revived during the Renaissance and later years.

Column
A cylindrical pillar usually serving as a support to same portion of a building.

Crocket
In Gothic architecture a projecting, carved ornament used to decorate spires and architecture

Ecclesiology
The science of church forms and traditions in relation to its rituals and architecture.

Entablature
In classical architecture the part which lays horizontally across supporting columns.

Fenestration
The arrangement of windows in the façade of a building.

Festoon
A carved garland of fruit and flowers usually supported from its ends.

Foliate
Ornamentally carved with leaf decoration.

Gothic
An architectural style prevailing in Europe from the thirteenth to the fifteenth century and widely revived in the nineteenth century. Its most distinctive feature is the pointed arch.

Historicist
Emphasis placed on historical truth and respect for past styles.

Hood-mould
Also known as a dripstone; a moulding projecting over and round the head of doors and windows in order to throw off rain water.

Jacobethan
Revival architecture using elements from the period of Queen Elizabeth I (1558-1603) and King James I (1603-1625).

Mask
A sculpted face used as an architectural ornament.

Mullion
A vertical member dividing window openings into various numbers of lights.

Orders of Architecture
Rules applied to the proportion and detail of columns in Greek, Roman and Revival architecture. The Greek types are the Doric, Ionic and Corinthian Orders. The Romans borrowed all three Orders and developed certain modifications, the Tuscan Order based on the Doric and the Composite Order, a combination of Ionic and Corinthian.

Palazzo
The palatial homes of the merchant princes of Renaissance Italy. Many of the buildings around St George's Square were modelled on High Renaissance (sixteenth century) examples.

Pediment
Term used in Classical and Renaissance architecture for the triangular section of wall above entablature or at roof end.

Pilaster
A rectangular pillar set against a wall and projecting slightly from it.

Pilastrade
A row of pilasters.

Pinnacle
In Gothic architecture a slender turret often ornamented.

Polychromy
Use of various colours achieving decorative effect on a building.

Portico
A roofed space, supported by columns. Open at least on one side.

Quoins
The large corner stone at the external angle of a building.

Rustication
Block of stone tooled to create boldly roughened surfaces and deeply recessed joints.

Terracotta
A hard burnt clay used for wall facings and architectural details.

Tracery
In Gothic architecture ornamental patternwork often geometrical or flowing, as in the upper parts of pointed windows.

Transom
A cross-piece dividing a window horizontally.

Turret
A small tower.

Vermiculation
Ornamental tooling of stone, creating worm like trails across surface.

Vernacular
Using local forms and traditional techniques.

Voussoir
One of the wedge-shaped stones forming part of arch.

GENERAL SOURCES

E.J. Law, *Architects of Huddersfield and District to 1860*, Paper no. 7, published by the author.

E.A.H. Haigh, 'Joseph Kaye – A Builder of Huddersfield' *Old West Riding* 4, 1 (1984) 30-32.

D. Whomsley, 'A Landed Estate and the Railway: Huddersfield 1844-94', *The Journal of Transport History*, New Series 2, 4 (1974) 189-213.

J.B. Eagles *John Benson Pritchett: first Medical Officer of Health for Huddersfield*, (Huddersfield, 1984).

NOTES

1. G.S. Phillips, *Walks Round Huddersfield* (Huddersfield, 1848).

2. F. Engels, *The Condition of the Working Class in England* (1845).

3. Sir John Betjeman, 'Huddersfield Discovered', *The Weekend Telegraph*, 2 October 1964.

4. *The Builder*, 18 July 1846.

5. H. Colvin, *A Biographical Dictionary of British Architects, 1600-1840* (reprinted 1978).

6. John Kirk's obituary, *Huddersfield Weekly Examiner*, 13 March 1886.

7. William Cocking's obituary, *Huddersfield Weekly Examiner*, 10 October 1874.

8. Quoted in D. Linstrum, *West Yorkshire Architects and Architecture* (1978), p.44.

9. W. White *Directory and Gazetteer of Leeds, Bradford, Halifax Huddersfield and Wakefield* 1847, 1853.

10. Joseph Kaye's obituary, *Huddersfield Chronicle*, 20 March 1858.

11. E.J. Law, *Joseph Kaye, Builder of Huddersfield* (Huddersfield, 1989).

12. W(est) Y(orkshire) A(rchive) S(ervice), K(irklees), Ramsden Papers DD/RE/c/74.

13. WYAS, Kirklees, Ramsden DD/RE/c/18.

14. *The Builder*, 22 May 1869.

15. WYAS, Kirklees, Ramsden DD/RE/c/5.

16. WYAS, Kirklees, Ramsden DD/RE/c/5.

17. H. Colvin, *A Biographical Dictionary of British Architects 1600-1840* (reprinted 1978).

18. WYAS, Kirklees, Ramsden DD/RE/c/74.

19. WYAS, Kirklees, Ramsden DD/RE/c/87.

20. WYAS, Kirklees, Ramsden DD/RE/c/3.

21. WYAS, Kirklees, Ramsden DD/RE/c/48.

22. WYAS, Kirklees, Ramsden DD/RE/c/87.

23. Joshua Hobson's three articles under the general title 'The Sanitary Movement' were published in the *Leeds Mercury* on the 1, 8 and 15 December 1849. For further criticism see also the *Huddersfield Chronicle*, 13 April 1850 and 3 August 1850.

24. *Universal British Directory*, Volume III, Exeter to Morton 1794.

25. D. Whomsley, 'Market Forces and Urban Growth: the influence of the Ramsden Family on the Growth of Huddersfield 1716-1853', *Journal of Regional and Local Studies*, 4, (1984), 27-56.

26. Whomsley, 'Market Forces and Urban Growth'.

27. Particularly, D. Whomsley, 'A Landed Estate and the Railway: Huddersfield 1844-1854' *Journal of Transport History* 2, 4 (1974), 189-213.

28. WYAS, Kirklees, Ramsden DD/RE/c/56.

29. D. J. Wyles *The Buildings of Huddersfield: Four Architectural Walks* (Huddersfield, 1984).

30. WYAS, Kirklees, Ramsden DD/RE/c/85.

31. C.L. Eastlake, *A History of the Gothic Revival* (1872).

32. In a letter to the *Pall Mall Gazette*, 16 March 1872.

33. G.G. Scott, *Personal and Professional Reflections* (1879).

34. WYAS, Kirklees, Ramsden DD/RE 48.

35. M. Girouard, *Sweetness and Light: The Queen Anne Movement 1860-1900* (Oxford, 1977), p.1.

36. Phillips, *Walks Round Huddersfield* (Huddersfield 1848).

37. Appendix to the *First Report of the Commissioners of Inquiry into the State of Large Towns and Populous Districts Royal Commission, 1844.*

38. W. White, *Directory and Gazetteer, 1837.*

39. WYAS, Kirklees, Ramsden DD/RE/c/74.

40. WYAS, Kirklees, Ramsden DD/RE/c/74.

41. 'House Architecture of the Provinces', *The Builder*, XX, 30 August 1862.

42. WYAS, Kirklees, Ramsden List of Plans for New Leases 1862-1868 DD/RA/c/7/3.

43. List of Buildings of Special Architectural or Historic Interest (Huddersfield): Unpublished list available for inspection at Kirklees Metropolitan Council (Planning Service).

44. Banney Royd Study Group, *Banney Royd: 'An Agreeable House'* (Huddersfield, 1991).

45. K. Clark, *The Gothic Revival* (third edition 1962), p.107.

46. A.W. Pugin, *The True Principles of Pointed or Christian Architecture* (1841).

47. Revd Francis X. Singleton, *A Historical Record of St. Patrick's Church* (1932).

48. For a discussion of religion in Huddersfield *see* Chapter Six.

49. *Universal British Directory*, volume III, Exeter to Morton 1794.

50. J. Mayall, *The Annals of Yorkshire* (Leeds, n.d.).

51. *Leeds Mercury*, 1829.

52. *Bradford Observer*, 4 April 1839.

53. Ian Nairn, 'The Towns Behind the Teams', *The Listener*, 28 August 1975.

54. H.R. Hitchcock *Architecture: Nineteenth and Twentieth Centuries*, The Pelican History of Art, edited by Nikolaus Pevsner, third edition (1968).

55. Asa Briggs, *Victorian Cities* (1963), p.87.

Fig. 14:1 Huddersfield Market Hall, King Street. (KCS)

CHAPTER 14

The Development of Huddersfield's Town Centre from 1870 onwards

IAN A. THOMPSON

The townscape of Huddersfield is unique. This is not to imply that Huddersfield's townscape is of especial value but merely to note that every settlement has an idiosyncratic character, reflecting the factors giving rise to its establishment and growth. This individual character was once, before the advent of mass-produced concrete and plate glass tower blocks, most strikingly apparent in the commercial hub of a town, its retailing centre and the surrounding core of offices, banks and other institutions.

The townscape of any urban centre does not develop in isolation from socio-economic or physical influences. Whitehand notes that 'the size and rate of change of the population of a hinterland of a town-centre and the nature and pattern of innovations are of considerable influence'.[1] Luffrum also establishes 'the existence of relationships between aspects of urban form and certain measures of economic activity in the town'.[2]

Huddersfield's embryonic evolution as a retailing centre may be traced back to the granting of a market charter in 1671. Physically the town was well situated to control local commerce as it was sited at the outfall of four upland drainage basins. By 1820 it had grown to such an extent that an Improvement Act was necessary.[3] The system of 'putting out' wool into the surrounding districts also aided the town's commercial expansion. The town took little part in the production process but was the centre at which buyers and sellers met.[4] The arrival of the railway in 1847 provided a further impetus to commercial development and also influenced the direction of new growth. By 1870, the date at which detailed planning records began to be kept,

Huddersfield had become established as a major commercial centre of the West Yorkshire conurbation.

By the mid-nineteenth century the consequences of the urbanisation accompanying the rapid commercial and industrial expansion experienced earlier in the century were becoming apparent. A large number of poorly designed dwellings had been constructed to house the denser population concentrations demanded by the factory system. In 1847 the Town Improvements Act was passed, enabling, rather than obliging, local authorities to regulate building.[5] Huddersfield began to implement these powers in 1869 and also obtained the Huddersfield Improvement and Town Government Act in 1870.[6] These powers effectively required any person wishing to construct a building to submit plans to a Building Committee set up by the local authority.

These building plans, and the documentary information contained therein, can be cross referenced with the records created by the Poor Law Act of 1869.[7] This Act required that records of all property owners and occupiers should be kept. Although each source has drawbacks, when used in conjunction one with another, and with supplementary information obtained from trades directories and Ordnance Survey 1:2500 plans, they provide a comprehensive source of information about townscape development from the mid-Victorian period onwards.

Between 1870 and 1939 a total of 979 building plans were approved by the Building Committee for work to be undertaken within the central area.[8] The number of applications fluctuated violently throughout the study period and successive years were often characterised by peaks and troughs (Figure 14:2). In general, each peak and trough attained a higher level than the previous one

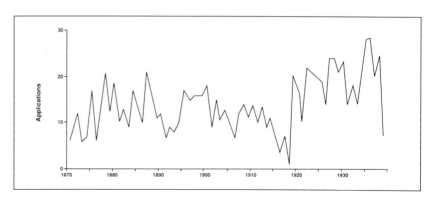

Fig. 14:2 Approved building applications, 1870-1939.

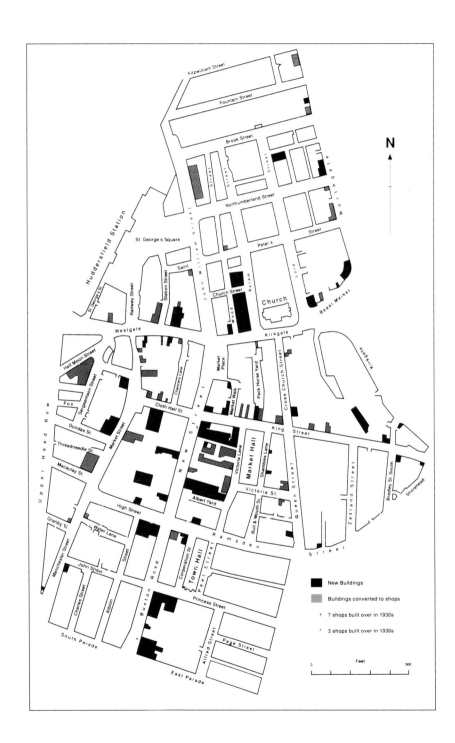

Fig. 14:3 Total retail provision, 1870-1939.

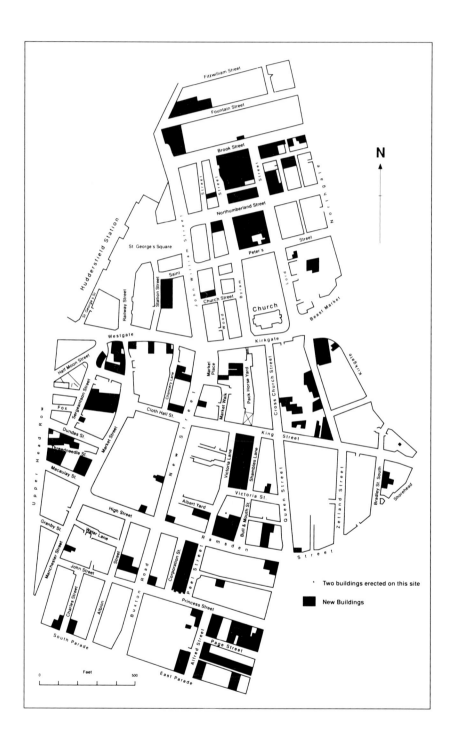

Fig. 14:4 Total non-retail provision, 1870-1939.

during the 1870s and 1880s but activity had declined by the Edwardian period. Activity revived during the inter-war years.

The inadequacy of simply recording the aggregate level of building applications in order to estimate the impact of change upon the central area building fabric will be self-evident. Simple structures such as wcs have been accorded the same importance as four-storey warehouses, for instance. The amount of floor space created by each new building is a much more valid measure. A detailed survey of floorspace provision shows that retailing provided only one-third of the new floorspace created within the central area, with institutions providing almost one-quarter (Figures 14:3, 14:4).

Table 1 New floorspace provision in Huddersfield central area 1870-1939.

Retailing	29.7%	Warehousing	15.8%
Institutions	24.9%	Non-commercial	8.8%
Commercial	20.8%		

These figures were obtained by placing $\frac{1}{10}$th inch tracing paper over the 1:2500 O.S plan and estimating the areal coverage of the ground floor. The total provision was estimated at 56,000 square feet.

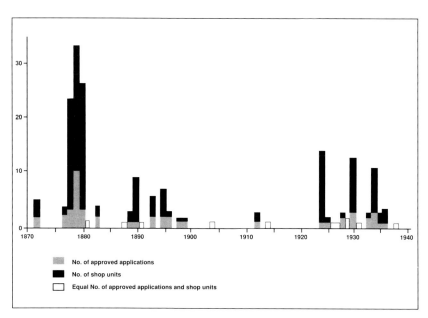

Fig. 14:5 The number of shops erected in Huddersfield, 1870-1939.

345

To a large extent the relatively low amount of new retailing space created can be attributed to Huddersfield's pre-1870 development. The town had expanded significantly in the Georgian and early-Victorian periods, consequently relatively few structures required replacement because of dereliction or dilapidation.

The pattern of new retailing provision is shown in Figure 14:5. The massive peak during the 1880s reflects the thirty-nine shops (at ground floor level) commissioned by Sir John William Ramsden in his Kirkgate and Westgate schemes. These speculative projects required a notable rearrangement of the street layout and marked the culmination of Ramsden's attempts to relocate the commercial centre of the town in the vicinity of the railway station.

These grandiose schemes were augmented by other speculative developments, erected on behalf of other property owners in Lord Street, King Street, Buxton Road and Victoria Lane in the same decade, which provided a further seventeen shops. Not unnaturally, the simultaneous provision of so many shops created a large amount of competition for tenants and the rent levels became depressed. The Ramsden Estate's agent, Major Graham, noted that, 'when trade revives the rental of each shop and office should be worth 15 or 20 per cent more'.[9] The Ramsden Estate was less affected than many speculative shop builders as the shop element in the Kirkgate Buildings was only intended to realise one-fifth of the anticipated income from the buildings. This was calculated as follows:[10]

	£	s.	d,
Shops	913	6	0
Offices	897	12	0
Warehouses	2,666	15	6

It may, however, be deduced from the rental rates per square yard that there was a ratio of 6:2:1 for the shop, first floor office and cellar respectively (Table 2). If this is accepted as the rental income of a typical speculative building it can be seen that two-thirds of the income was expected to be derived from the shop premises. In the Kirkgate and Westgate schemes the large proportion of warehousing and offices was intended to offset short term problems in letting the shops by spreading the risks across three markets.

Table 2 Examples of the rates charged for two shops fronting on to Westgate by the Ramsden Estate Office.

	Shop 1					Shop 2				
	Yards[3]	Rate	£	s	d	Yards[3]	Rate	£	s	d
Basement	60	5/-	15	0	0	60	5/-	15	0	0
Shop	50	30/-	75	0	0	53	35/-	94	10	0
Shop mezzanine floor[1]	50	12/6	31	5	0	30	12/6	18	15	0
Mezzanine	82	10/-	41	0	0	53	10/-	26	10	0
1st floor	78	10/-	39	0	0	53	10/-	26	10	0
2nd floor	78	5/-	19	10	0	45	5/-	11	5	0
Top floor[2]	78	2/-	7	16	0	45	2/-	4	10	0
			228	11	0			197	0	0

1. This would appear to be a gallery beneath the mezzanine floor.
2. This is an attic.
3. Presumably this means square yards.

(*source:* West Yorkshire Archive Service, Kirklees Ramsden Archives DD/RE/24).

With few exceptions this massive over-provision of shops in the town during the 1870s led to a hiatus in new retailing construction until the inter-war period, with the exception of the Huddersfield Industrial Society (Co-operative) premises in Buxton Road and the extension of shops into Northgate.

The inter-war revival in shop building also saw a change in emphasis as large scale department stores were constructed on behalf of Huddersfield Industrial Society, Marks & Spencer and F. W. Woolworth which, together, accounted for 28 per cent of the retailing floorspace provided during the seventy-year period. These stores relied upon a highly accessible location within the Central Business District, as their retailing policy was based upon selling a large quantity of goods at discounted prices and making their profit from economies of scale.   The highly efficient public transport systems that had evolved by the 1920s reached into the outlying areas and ensured that a sufficiently large clientele could be attracted to make them viable. The stores were orientated at right-angles to the street in order to acquire the cheap land available within the street blocks away from the street front, for example F. W. Woolworth, Figure 14:6.

Conversions from existing structures into shops accounted for almost one-third of the new retailing premises created during the study period. This method of expanding the retail area was particularly important during the Edwardian era, given the virtual cessation of new construction at this time. During the 1920s and 1930s conversions augmented rather than replaced new construction. In many instances the conversions occupied the ground floor of woollen warehouses at the periphery of the retailing area. This cheap method of expansion progressed along Cloth Hall Street and Market Street in the Edwardian era, culminating in the construction of twelve shops in Macaulay Street during the 1920s. In this manner the original woollen warehouse area became encompassed within the retailing core of Huddersfield.

Although the local authorities gained legislative control over building work from the 1870s, the physical alterations to the townscape were instigated by property owners and occupiers. The ownership and occupancy of property, therefore, had considerable implications for the manner in which the townscape evolved. The property ownership patterns of Huddersfield were, however, extremely complicated, in contrast to the land ownership pattern.[11] In all 1,118 persons were recorded as owning property in the central area.[12] Furthermore, on average, property underwent two or three ownership changes between 1870 and 1939. It might be expected that property ownership would have become concentrated in the hands of a relatively few owners during this period and that these might be expected to exert increasing influence upon the property market and, hence, townscape development. In actuality, however, ownership patterns tended to be cyclical in nature, with periods of consolidation fluctuating with the dispersal of property amongst a number of owners.

Whilst it would be naïve in the extreme to suggest that property transactions were the prelude to redevelopment in every instance, it is important to note that over half of the new buildings in Huddersfield town centre were erected at the behest of an owner who had recently acquired the property. One-third of the new buildings were, however, initiated by owners who had possessed the site for some considerable time prior to the commencement of construction. In the majority of cases the replacement building increased the intensity of land use by increasing the amount of floorspace. The Huddersfield Industrial Society's department store, built in Buxton Road in 1883, for instance, replaced a number of disparate structures

Fig. 14:6 Woolworth & Co. and fabric alterations in part of east New Street.

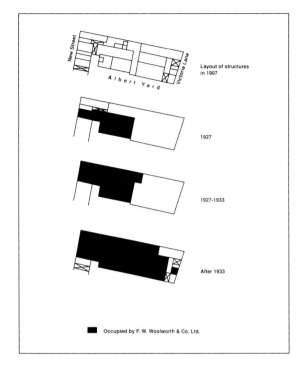

with a much larger bespoke building. Property acquisition was an obvious pre-requisite for building replacement. For indigenous companies, such as the Huddersfield Industrial Society, this posed less of a problem than for external companies seeking to construct large bespoke premises in the town as branch establishments of their national businesses.

The case of F. W. Woolworth provides a good study. They, of necessity, required a site in a major shopping thoroughfare. The fragmented nature of property ownership within the retail core rendered the acquisition of such a site impossible. In 1915 the company occupied two shops in New Street, owned by Rippon Brothers, and gradually expanded into the surrounding properties (Figure 14:6). In 1933, presumably after Woolworth had obtained ownership of the site, a large department store was erected.[13] This building retained occupation of the site although the store was extended to the building line in Victoria Lane, once again following the piecemeal acquisition of the relevant properties. The long gestation period prior to redevelopment may have been to Woolworth's advantage. The company could initially establish a branch outlet in the town for a small outlay and gradually build up trade until a level was reached at which a new building would be beneficial. If the turnover failed to fulfil initial expectations this expenditure would have been avoided. This gradual process of site acquisition could be circumvented if necessary. There remained a number of unoccupied sites within the central area, albeit at the periphery, despite the large scale development of the town during the early-Victorian period.

There were other structural alterations which had a significant impact upon the townscape. Shop façade replacement, although structurally a simple alteration to undertake, could radically alter the appearance of a building, particularly when it is considered that many people's perception of a town centre is heavily influenced by the ground floor aspects presented by the shops. Shop façade replacement grew in popularity during the inter-war years. The façade projected an image and its replacement was intended to favourably influence potential customers' attitudes to the shop and to increase trade.

Façade replacements were not related to property ownership. As the shop occupier, usually a tenant, stood to gain most from the alteration, they were normally installed at the expense of the occupier and reflected property occupancy patterns. These were extremely fluid. On average each shop underwent a change of occupant once every twenty years. This, however, is likely to be a conservative estimate.[14] The replacement rate of façades varied quite considerably. On average 51 per cent of the shops replaced their façades between 1900 and 1939. In the main shopping streets replacement rates were much higher, that in New Street being 70 per cent.

In the majority of cases where façades were altered the alteration was undertaken by the new occupier. In 78 per cent of these instances no modification was necessary. This may have been because the nature of the trade carried out at the premises remained unaltered and that only the firm conducting it changed. In other cases the reluctance to alter the façade may have been associated with the replacement of one business with another for which image projection was not an important enough consideration to merit the expense of altering the façade. It must be assumed that the only alteration undertaken was the replacement of the original sign by new nameboards.

In those cases where existing occupiers altered their façade, many were companies competing for a share of a fashion conscious market. These shops, such as shoe stores or ladies' millinery shops, tended to cluster in close

Fig. 14:7 Façade alterations undertaken by cobblers in New Street, 1900-1938.

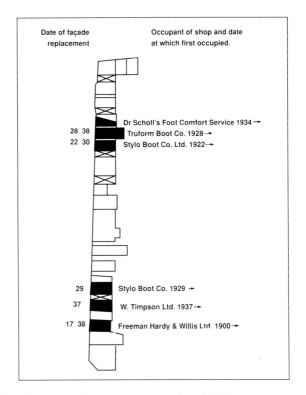

proximity to one another for economic reasons and replaced their façades at relatively frequent intervals.[15] The sequence of alterations exhibited by shoe shops in New Street provides a typical example (Figure 14:7). It will be observed that the acquisition of a shop by W. Timpson in 1937, and the replacement of its façade was followed by the Truform Boot Co. and Freeman Hardy and Willis altering their façades in 1938.

Each of these modifications to the building fabric required the preparation of a plan, not necessarily by a professional draughtsman but by someone connected with the building's construction. Three broad categories of designers may be recognised at Huddersfield. First there were the professional architects, albeit that many were also estate agents or surveyors.[16] Secondly there were specialist shopfitters. Thirdly there were the general contractors or builders. The plans were normally the work of one designer but on occasions a number of companies collaborated in the preparation of the plan, usually when a Huddersfield based company acted as an agent for a firm from outside the town.

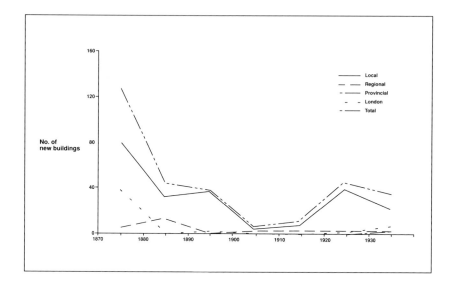

Fig. 14:8 The number of structures for which plans were prepared by designers from different locations during each decade.

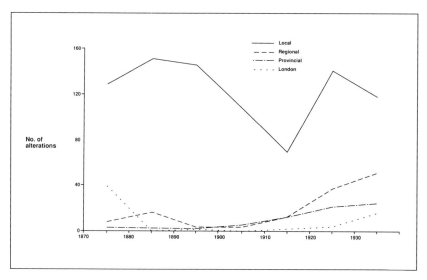

Fig. 14:9 The number of plans for new buildings prepared by each category of designer.

It will be apparent from Figure 14:8 that locally based designers, as might have been expected, predominated. This dominance was mirrored by their pre-eminence in the preparation of plans for new structures (Figure 14:9). Local designers sufficed for many new structures because they were simple in plan and utilitarian in appearance. Important buildings such as Sir J.W. Ramsden's Kirkgate Scheme were designed to impress and consequently employed externally based architects. The intense rivalry between the towns of West Yorkshire resulted in the construction of a number of imposing buildings. Ramsden's decision to employ W.H. Crossland, a Huddersfield born but London based architect, partially reflected Huddersfield's civic pride but also sought to gain credibility for his 'new town' close to the station. Large shopping schemes had been developed, or were being proposed in neighbouring towns at the time of Ramsden's development. Linstrum notes that, 'it was not until the 1870s that the vogue for arcades reached the major industrial towns' whereas 'there were early nineteenth century examples in London'.[17] In order to obtain the best quality product, therefore, it would have been desirable to commission a London designer. This lead was followed in the 1880s by two smaller schemes comprising altogether ten shops.

The trend towards the use of external designers continued into the Edwardian era, when plans were submitted for a bank, a warehouse, a theatre and a cinema. Rather surprisingly, given the catalytic effect of the First World War upon Edwardian social, economic and technological norms, outside influences remained rather limited during the inter-war period. The non-local designers achieved a much greater impact upon the townscape, however, than the more numerous local designers. This may be attributed to the employment of non-local designers upon large scale projects. This in part reflects the decision by a number of national and regional firms to erect new buildings in Huddersfield. Both Marks & Spencer (employing a Southport architect) and F.W. Woolworth (using their own Architect's Department) built department stores in New Street in 1933. A cinema was built upon the site of the Cloth Hall in 1935 and a theatre was built in Kirkgate in 1936.

Non-local designers were much more prominent numerically in the design of shop façades, gaining most impact during the inter-war period. Initially these external shopfitters were employed in the pre-1870 core area with comparatively few replacements taking place outside this zone before 1920. Regional designers from the surrounding towns provided the largest source of external shop façade designers and it is interesting to note that Huddersfield itself did not possess a prolific indigenous specialist shopfitter during the inter-war period. By the 1930s, 80 per cent of the façades installed in the town were to the designs of outsiders.

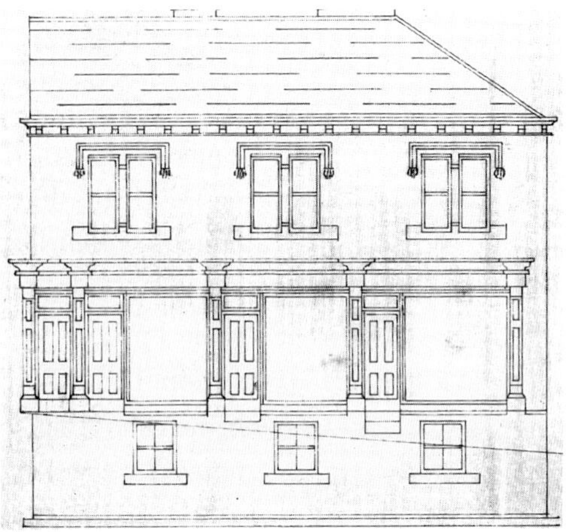

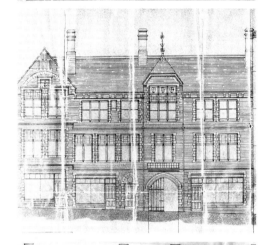

Fig. 14:10 3 shops,
Buxton Road. Stead
& Kaye
(707 Central 1879)
(WYAS, K)

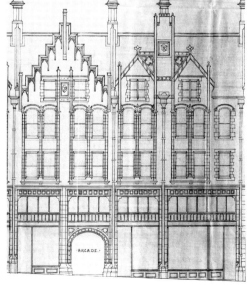

Fig. 14:11 3 shops and
offices Victoria Lane.
E. Hughes
(685 Central 1878)
(WYAS, K)

Fig. 14:12 Arcade (13
shops) Westgate
W.H. Crossland (London)
(700 Central 1878)
(WYAS, K)

354

*Fig. 14:13 Kirkgate
and Byram Street
W.H. Crossland (London)
(768 Central 1879)
(WYAS, K)*

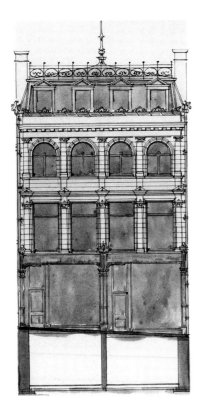

Fig. 14:14 2 shops, King Street.
W. Cooper (2480 Central 1897).
(WYAS, K)

Fig. 14:15 Prudential Assurance Offices, New Street and Ramsden
Street A. Waterhouse (London) (476 C.B. 1899). (WYAS, K)

Fig. 14:17 Shops and offices, Cloth Hall
Street and New Street, Prices (Tailors)
Staff Architect (Leeds) (23317 C.B.).
(WYAS, K)

Fig. 14:16 Shop, New Street, Jones & Rigby (Southport & Manchester
(21119 C.B. 1933). (WYAS, K)

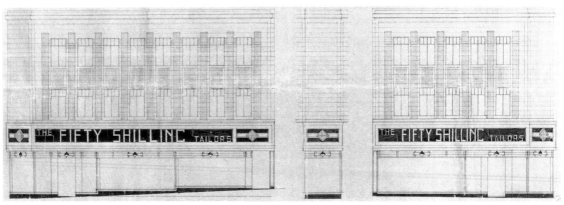

Fig. 14:18 Shop, New Street & King Street Healey & Baker (London) (25707 C.B. 1937). (WYAS, K)

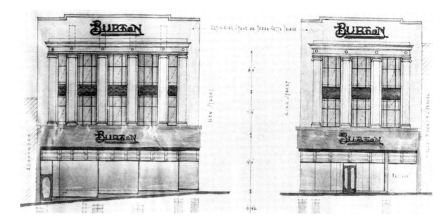

Fig. 14:19 2 shops, Greenwood's Yard, Victoria Lane. J. Berry & Sons (14448 C.B.). (WYAS, K)

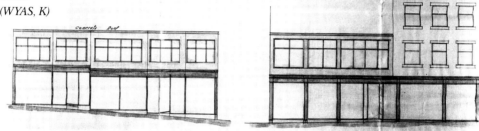

Fig. 14:20 9 shops, Venn Street J. Berry & Son (21381 C.B. 1933). (WYAS, K)

Except in the broadest terms, the physical impact of the structural alterations have not yet been considered. The sheer quantity of information available during the study period makes it necessary to be highly selective of the material examined. A number of buildings erected during the mid-Victorian period were simple unadorned structures erected at the periphery of the Central Business District. In the main these were designed by local workmen (Figure 14:10). The great upsurge of institutional building that characterised this period demanded more considered stylistic approaches.

The realisation amongst nineteenth century architects that the aesthetics of design were freed from constructional constraints led to a variety of revivalist approaches to building design. The Gothic Market Hall (14:1), decorated in the Classical style by Hughes, was reflected in the structures erected to the same architect's design in adjacent Victoria Lane (Figure 14:11).[18] The Kirkgate and Westgate Schemes of Ramsden almost simultaneously introduced the Gothic style to the designs of Crossland, a London based architect (Figures 14:12 and 14:13).

Other influences entered the town around the turn of the century. The structure by Cooper in King Street in 1897 incorporated elements of Art Nouveau whilst the Prudential Assurance Company office block in New Street in 1899, by Waterhouse of London, particularly broke with the aesthetic traditions of the town with its use of terra-cotta tiles (Figures 14:14 and 14:15). The movement away from the use of local materials and styles proceeded apace during the inter-war period. The bespoke developments of

Fig. 14:21 Shop façade New Street by J. Kirk & Sons (968 Central 1881). (WYAS, K)

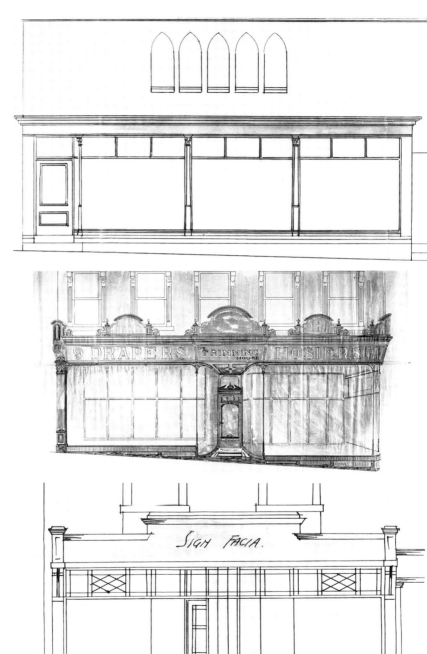

Fig. 14:22 Shop façade Brook Street by A. Lofthouse (2384 Central 1895). (WYAS, K)

Fig. 14:23 Shop façade for Kaye and Mornington, King Street and Market Walk by Parnall & Sons (Bristol) (1339 C.B. 1902). (WYAS, K)

Fig. 14:24 Converting 2 shops to 1 shop Westgate by J.T. Spratt (11010 C.B. 1915). (WYAS, K)

Marks & Spencer Ltd., F. W. Woolworth and Prices Tailors (*sic*) among others projected the corporate design of the relevant company (Figures 14:16-14:18). The modern construction methods, including girder frames and pre-stressed concrete used in these and other structures marked the decline of masonry construction techniques. As in the Victorian period, some of the simpler structures were basic shells devoid of decoration, whereas others made some rudimentary concessions to stylistic considerations (Figures 14:19 and 14:20).

Façade design was inextricably linked with image projection and consequently was subject to changes in the prevailing fashion. In the Victorian period the normal practice was to incorporate a large sash (window area) with the dado (the section between the window and the pavement) being virtually eliminated (Figures 14:21 and 14:22). The first externally designed façade was presented to the Building Committee in 1899 but, being designed in Halifax, was virtually identical with the indigenous designs. The façade erected in 1902 for Kaye and Mornington by Parnall of Bristol was more typical of the practices introduced to the town by outside shopfitters (Figure 14:23). It incorporated a number of innovative features, in the context of Huddersfield, which included plate-glass, an entrance lobby and a window specifically designed for display purposes. These features were eventually accepted into the repertoire of local designers, albeit with a considerable time-lag, the first locally designed façade incorporating such features being designed in 1915 (Figure 14:24).

Fig. 14:25 Shop façade Shambles Lane by W. Spratt (26040 C.B. 1937)

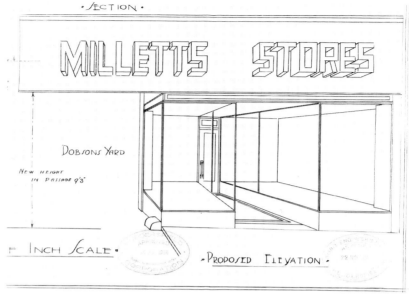

Fig. 14:26 Shop façade Cross Church Street by Fielding & Bottomley (Halifax) (2422 C.B. 1936)

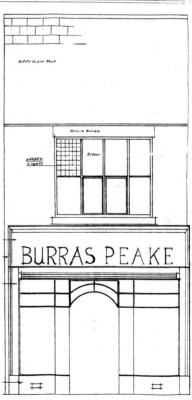

Fig. 14:27 Shop façade, Cross Church Street by L.S. Kempton (Leeds) (25833 C.B. 1937)

Façade design continued to be led by external designers throughout the inter-war period although the response time for assimilating innovations shortened to a time-lag of three or four years. The proliferation of non-local designers between the wars, especially of specialist shopfitters, created a great stylistic diversity by the late 1930s (Figures 14:25-14:27).

The cumulative effect of the changes in ownership and occupancy patterns, the ensuing alterations to the building fabric, the choice of designers and their stylistic preferences resulted in the evolution of Huddersfield's townscape. Three broad themes may, however, be discerned which have implications far beyond the boundaries of Huddersfield. First, building ownership changed frequently, giving developers ample opportunity to acquire property for redevelopment. Secondly, shop façades had a relatively short life span compared with the buildings into which they were inserted, therefore the ground floor character of shopping streets could change rapidly. Thirdly, the design of new structures and alterations became more specialised. The non-local designers, initially introduced into the main retailing streets of the town, disregarded the existing architectural norms of the town and introduced their own styles which were quickly imitated by local companies. This movement towards a cosmopolitan, standardised townscape culminated in the anonymous Central Business Districts which characterise so many British towns.

I. A. Thompson

Biographical Note

Ian Thompson was born in Batley in 1956 and educated at Batley Grammar School and the Universities of Birmingham and Hull. In 1979 he began the research for a Doctorate, upon which this article is based. He currently teaches geography in a Norfolk Comprehensive School.

NOTES

1. J.W.R. Whitehand, 'The study of variations in the building fabric of town centres: procedural problems and preliminary findings in southern Scotland', *Transactions of the Institute of British Geographers*, IV (New Series) (1979), 560.

2. J.M. Luffrum, 'The building fabric of the central areas of small towns in rural England: inter-urban variations and relationships', *Urban Geography*, II (1981), 176.

3. 1 Geo IV c. xliii (43).

4. F.S. Hudson, 'The Wool Textile Industry in the Huddersfield District', *International Dyer and Textile Printer*, (Dec, Jan 1965-1966), 951.

5. R. Johnston, 'Towards an analytical study of the townscape: the residential building fabric', *Geografiska Annaler*, Series B LI, (1969), 20-32.

6. 11 & 12 Vict. c.cxl. Other Acts were 34 & 35 Vict. c.cli, 39 & 40 Vict. c.c, 43 & 44 Vict. c.cxix, 45 & 46 Vict. c.ccxxxvi, 53 & 54 Vict. c. cciv, 60 & 61 Vict. c.xxvi.

7. 32 & 33 Vict. c.41

8. For the purposes of the study the central area was defined as the land within the inner-ring road, with the railway station forming the boundary to the north-west: Fitzwilliam Street was taken as the northern boundary. The time period was restricted by the availability of documentary evidence. The earliest date for which the requisite information was obtainable was 1869. The Huddersfield Rate Books cease to record owners after 1929. The post-1948 building plans had not been deposited with the West Yorkshire Archive Service, Kirklees at the time of this research.

9. W(est) Y(orkshire) A(rchive) S(ervice), Kirklees Ramsden Archives DD/RE/48.

10. WYAS, Kirklees Ramsden Archives DD/RA/c/20/4.

11. Where the land was unused for buildings it was common practice for the land owner to sell the freehold to a developer. In the centre of a town there was little unoccupied land therefore redevelopment was necessary rather than development. This required the purchase of existing properties, which in Huddersfield were held on a 999-year lease. The landowner therefore had relatively little influence in the central area.

12. This does not preclude the possibility of duplication owing to constraints in the way that the data were collected.

13. It is not possible to check this owing to the change in the way that information was recorded in the Rate Books.

14. Shop occupancy was surveyed at selected intervals. There is evidence to suggest that shops were occupied by businesses which were not recorded in the surveys.

15. P. Scott, *Geography and Retailing* (1970), Chapter 2.

16. Many architects added the description 'valuers, estate and insurance agents' or some permutation of the three. In one case the designer, Oakley of Ilford, Essex, described himself as 'shopfitter, coach builder and motor engineer'.

17. D. Linstrum, *West Yorkshire Architects and Architecture* (1978), p.322 *et seq*.

18. Linstrum, *West Yorkshire Architects and Architecture*, p.318.

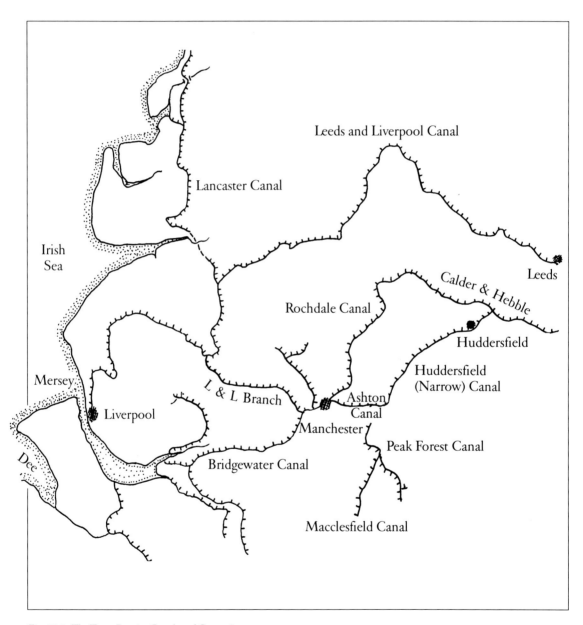

Fig. 15:1 The Trans-Pennine Canals and Connections

CHAPTER 15

The Construction of the Huddersfield Narrow Canal, 1794-1811

R.B. SCHOFIELD

The British system of navigable waterways was established between 1750 and 1840, although the peak period for legislation occurred in the canal mania years from 1791 to 1795[1] when Parliament authorised fifty-one new canals. About 4,000 miles of waterways were built to provide a transport system by means of which the industrial centres of the country developed and prospered. Some of the earliest canals were built to serve local interests and gradually an intricate network spread across the countryside. In retrospect, it seems fortuitous that national routes were eventually established in the same way as those projected in the railway era of a generation later.

In the north of England, however, three inter-regional canal routes were proposed to link Lancashire with the West Riding and the east-coast ports of Yorkshire. The Huddersfield Narrow Canal was the first of these to be built and the others, completed in later years, were the Leeds and Liverpool and the Rochdale Canals, both broad[2] navigations which followed more northerly, longer but easier routes. (Figure 15:1).

Proposals for a canal company were enthusiastically received in Huddersfield during May 1793, mainly as a result of the success and high premiums attached to the shares of the Manchester to Ashton-under-Lyne Canal Company which was then seeking an eastwards extension of trading links. The two companies had high expectancies of a cross-Pennine route, although it is unlikely that this would have been contemplated had the Rochdale Canal been completed beforehand.

None of these issues concerned the enthusiastic investors who flocked to a crowded meeting in Huddersfield on 22 October 1793 to listen to the civil engineer, Benjamin Outram, present his report[3] for a proposed navigable canal. There was very little dissension before subscriptions were invited for shares in the £200,000 required for the project, which comprised £182,748, estimated by Outram, for the construction of the canal, reservoirs and accommodation works, and a lesser sum for the promotion of the Act.

William Pontey, a local businessman, described the scene when bidding for the £100 shares commenced:

> Subscription papers were opened at 3 or 4 tables and happy was the wight who could get to write his name, deposit his cash or £1 upon each share subscribed for and then escape from the crowd. . . . Immediate dealing with shares soon put the premium up to £15 per cent although this soon came down. . . . The reason I could never ascertain probably others like myself were panic struck for very soon after prices began to decline and I sold 3 of the 6 shares I had hold of in the scramble at a premium of 5 guineas each and very soon after let the same person have the other 3 at par. . . .[4]

That hectic scene suggests that from the beginning the Company was in the hands of speculators. Although Outram's estimate was to prove too low, the Company was harassed from its inception by the failure of investors to pay calls promptly, as well as by those who evaded payment altogether.

The Company and its Managers

The Huddersfield Canal Company was formally established shortly after the Act of 1794[5] received the Royal Assent. The General Assembly of shareholders then elected a Management Committee of local businessmen, weavers, farmers and gentlemen, none apparently with any experience of managing a civil engineering project. From the beginning, however, they set about their tasks with confidence and gusto, first by appointing key personnel, including George Worthington of Altrincham, solicitor, as Clerk to the Company (a task he performed simultaneously for both the Ashton and the Peak Forest Canal Companies), bankers, treasurers and valuers and, most important, Benjamin Outram of Butterley Hall, Ripley, as Engineer.

Outram, then twenty-nine years of age, was one of Britain's promising young civil engineers who was already managing partner of an important ironworks in Derbyshire. His salary was fixed at three guineas per day whilst on the canal, plus ten guineas expenses for each journey. His half-yearly fees amounted to between £150 and £175,[6] which suggests that he would work four or five days on site each month and then attend the Committee. Remuneration was not large bearing in mind the many hours spent off the job planning and preparing designs and reports, in correspondence and when visiting companies to examine machinery and materials on behalf of his clients.

Outram's tasks were exacting but, as a young member of his profession, he does not seem to have acquired an entourage of well-tried resident engineers and contractors, who could be called on to execute works under his control. Instead he had to rely heavily on local appointees, notably the resident engineer Nicholas Brown, a youthful and inexperienced surveyor from Saddleworth, selected mainly through the patronage of friends among the proprietors.

Brown's annual salary was £315, from which he was expected to pay the wages of a book-keeper, besides personal expenses in supervising nearly twenty miles of canal construction across some difficult, mountainous country. The project was obviously under-staffed from the outset. It called for at least three assistant resident engineers and, although Brown was allotted some overlookers as work progressed, initially he had all the work to do himself. The conditions of his appointment discouraged him from spending too freely on assistants and on extensive travel about the line.

It is hardly surprising that Brown proved an ineffective manager and, although the company minutes are uncritical of him, the signs of inadequate supervision are all too plain. There were serious mistakes in setting out the works and some structures were even built in the wrong places! Moreover, there were frequent claims by riparian landowners for real, as well as imagined, damages and trespass, and substantial sums were paid out by the Committee on the flimsiest of evidence. A competent resident engineer would have stopped such practices by issuing clear instructions and by firm personal control of the works. The inexperienced Brown was unable to cope with such problems and this eventually led the Committee to appoint a group of proprietors to set out accommodation and other works. By such means, construction muddled along until, finally, the Committee lost patience with Brown after an unnecessary culvert was built. He was given notice to quit and was replaced by William Bailiffe of Marsden who, although fairly successful, resigned in 1801.[7] To some extent, Outram must be blamed for tolerating this state of affairs, but it did not help matters when he was forced through illness to absent himself for long periods during the critical years of 1795 and 1796.

After 1801, John Rooth of Manchester was appointed Superintendent.[8] A dominant personality, he remained with the Company with fair, but not outstanding, success until six years after the completion of the canal. By 1801 Outram had withdrawn as Engineer when work had all but ceased through lack of funds. The Company managed without specialist engineering advice until Thomas Telford, the famous Scottish engineer, visited late in 1806 to report on the state of the works and to prepare plans and estimates for the completion of the undertaking.[9]

Canal route, earthworks and tunnels

Documents prepared by Outram and Brown for the construction of the canal were restricted to the minimum then required by law.[10] These comprised a plan of the canal (Figure 15:2) with a book of reference as to land occupation, a rudimentary bill of quantities and an estimate of costs. The plan, an early example of Brown's work,[11] was an inaccurate plot, probably of a magnetic compass and chain survey.[12] It was of limited value for engineering purposes, but served as a useful illustration for the parliamentary procedures and for potential investors.

Outram recommended a route from Sir John Ramsden's Canal in Huddersfield to follow the Colne valley to Marsden, climbing 436 feet (438 feet 10 inches as built) to the summit level at 649 feet above sea level then, by tunnelling over three miles through Standedge, to emerge in Brunn Clough, from where the canal pursued the Tame valley on the Lancashire side, descending via Stalybridge to the Ashton Canal some 334 feet (338 feet 11 inches as built), with a tunnel of 200 yards at Scout Mill (220 yards as built).[13] The Engineer did not refer to another tunnel near Ashton which, though finished, was opened up in later years. He intended to leave the numbers and locations of locks to be decided at the construction stage and in fact, forty-two were built in Yorkshire and thirty-two on the Lancashire side,

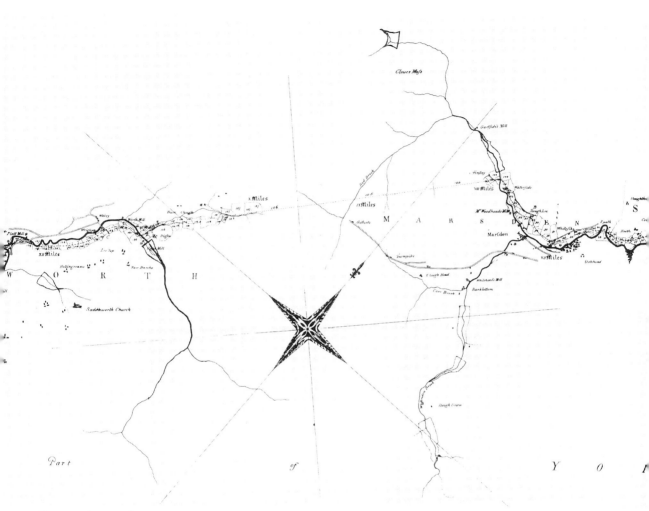

Fig. 15:2 A section of Brown's Survey of the route of the Huddersfield Narrow Canal, 1793. (Cheshire R.O.)

the average fall being 10 feet 6 inches per lock. The total length of canal was given as 19¾ miles (19⅞ miles finally).

Outram stressed that the route was the 'shortest communication yet between Manchester and the eastern navigations and it will pass through a country full of manufacturers . . . and by the vicinity of the proposed canal to the river the mills will receive their articles free from land carriage to the canal'. This was true; the numerous mills shown on the survey were located close to the canal because of the narrow valley floors. Moreover, the Engineer was aware of the mill-owners' fears for their water supplies, hence reservoirs to feed the canal were to be situated only in large and deep valleys where 'collected waters frequently produced torrents of floods'. He intended taking no water from the rivers, hence the canal's operation would not interfere with the thirty-six waterwheels on which the mills depended for their power.[14]

The Engineer did not see fit to mention the difficulties, foreseen by some of his critics at the time, of linking his narrow canal between broad navigations at Huddersfield and Manchester. That certainly was a defect in the design but, had the route been built with the generous dimensions of a broad navigation, it is certain that the costs would have been prohibitive and unlikely to attract investors. In any event, the estimate was pared down to less than a desirable minimum in spite of what must have been obvious at the start, that this was going to be a difficult project fraught with imponderables created by its remoteness, climate and uncertain ground conditions.

The major engineering task was the great tunnel at Standedge, for which Outram envisaged a five-year programme with costs of £55,187. He stated that the tunnel 'appears favourable, the strata consists of gritstone and strong shale and the low ground in the centre near Red Brook will afford the opportunity of opening works by steam engines so as to greatly facilitate completion'. The estimate included 5,380 yards of heading at £7 per yard, sinking eighteen shafts for £2,767 10s. (thirty-two were actually commenced on the main line) and lesser sums for steam engine operations. Unwisely, he did not include costs for lining and arching sections of the tunnel, assuming that even the shale strata required no support. He was to be proved incorrect in that assumption.

The aqueducts and bridges

None of the five remaining masonry aqueducts (at Paddock, Scarbottom, Diggle, Uppermill and Royal George) was built exactly to the original specification.[15] All are simple, functional bridges which carry few architectural embellishments and, with the exception of that at Diggle, all incorporate a skeen (or circular segmental) arch. This type allows for economies in earthworks and lockage besides giving reasonable clearance below soffit level. Too flat an arch can lead to settlement over the years, however, as had occurred at Uppermill and Scarbottom.

Floods in 1799 had a devastating effect on the entire canal, destroying embankments and reservoirs and washing away aqueducts at Marsden and Stalybridge.[16] The former, close by the tunnel entrance, could only be rebuilt in 1806 when funds allowed, but the latter had to be replaced immediately as that canal section was already in use for traffic. The headroom below the canal at the Tame crossing in Stalybridge was about five feet and because that gave insufficient height for a single arch, Outram originally designed a four-span arch bridge with three piers. Unfortunately, this bridge impeded river flow in the floods, causing the river to back up to such a depth that the pressure overturned the structure. Rather than replace with a bridge of the same design, Outram used a new structural type which readily lent itself to the site. This was the single-span cast-iron trough, built

Fig. 15:3 The cast-iron trough aqueduct crossing the River Tame at the Stakes, Stalybridge. (author's collection)

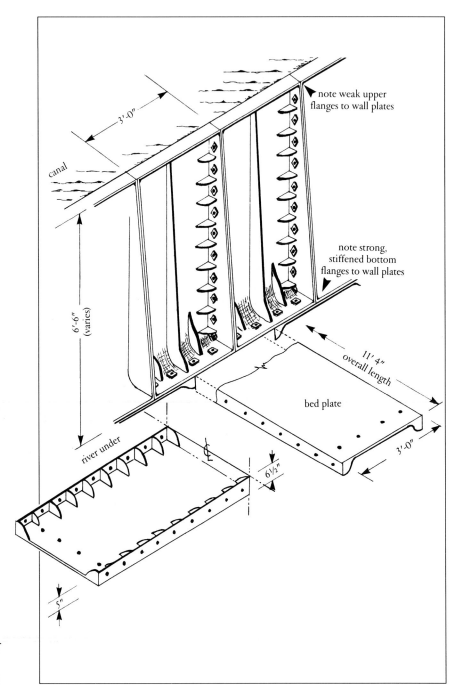

note weak upper
flanges to wall plates

3'-0"

canal

note strong,
stiffened bottom
flanges to wall plates

6'-6" (varies)

11' 4"
overall length

bed plate

3'-0"

river under

6½"

5"

Fig. 15:4 Half view of
underside of bed plate
(symmetrical about ℄)

from prefabricated iron plates. He had already constructed a similar aqueduct in 1795 to carry the Derby Canal across a narrow stream in Derby.[17] The location on the Tame was similar, which explains how 'one arch of cast-iron' was recommended for the 55 feet span. Components of this bridge were probably built at the Butterley ironworks, of which Outram was managing partner, and the high-quality finish of the manufactured units is indicative of the advances made at that foundry in the few years of its existence. The plates were assembled *in situ* and the aqueduct was probably commissioned by May 1800[18] (Figure 15:3).

The Derby aqueduct failed structurally by 1802 although its inherent defects were noted long before that date.[19] Failure seems to have been caused by severe buckling of the top flanges of the wall plates when the structure was fully loaded. In turn, this led to cracking and collapse of the floor plates. The Stalybridge aqueduct was an improved design, but Outram still did not appear to understand its action under load. He stiffened the floor of the aqueduct but instead of thickening the flanges at the top of the wall plates, he only strengthened those at the bottom (Figure 15:4). There was some movement in later years, probably as a result of this action, because a clumsy cross-bracing of wrought iron rods was bolted on to the structure in 1875 and the whole was supported by a vertical rod fixed to the centre of the adjacent arch. Farey visited the site in 1808 and his description then shows that little has changed over the years.[20] He also criticised the 'ridiculous stone arch' built immediately down-stream to act as a tow-path. Nevertheless, the iron aqueduct is handsome in spite of its defects and is probably the oldest surviving example of its type still in use.[21]

Outram's original estimate included for forty-nine accommodation and highway bridges, as well as thirty culverts.[22] In accordance with the practice of the day, there had been no formal negotiations with landowners at preliminary design stage and eventually, ten additional bridge crossings had to be agreed. Most of these were stone arches faced in squared rubble masonry, each costing from £64 to £100.

A standard bridge design was adopted which comprised a semi-elliptical opening, rounded at the shoulders to permit easy access along the towpath. Stone parapets were built upon a string course (or narrow projecting course of masonry) which defined the level of the crossing highway. The wing walls curved in plan to terminate in square-capped pilasters and the spandrel walls also curved in sectional elevation. These simple, inexpensive yet handsome bridges, built in local gritstone, were immensely strong and have withstood long periods of neglect (Figure 15:5).

Several timber footbridges were built before 1800 for reasons of economy but most deteriorated and were replaced by stone bridges, even before the canal was opened in 1811. Farey noted that several arches had unwisely been built without tow-paths[23] and Rooth claimed to have replaced nineteen of these in later years.[24]

The water supply

Heavily-locked canal routes are often vulnerable in times of drought and the Huddersfield Narrow Canal became notorious in this respect. Outram initially proposed feeder reservoirs 'to contain 14,900 locks-full of water to supply one hundred locks per day for four months altogether',[25] claiming this was more than enough for the largest trade that could be expected, and that with this 'capacious system' there was no need to tap the rivers in dry seasons and thus deprive the mills of vital water supplies. In spite of this claim the cautious weavers still insisted on increasing total capacity to 20,000 locks-full.

Brown's original survey showed a reservoir at Stayley Mill, another near Saddleworth church, three in the Wessenden valley above Marsden and others at March Haigh, Diggle and Slaithwaite. Only the last three were built by the company. The Wessenden chain was completed before 1800 by a consortium of mill-owners,[26] although the system was taken over eventually

Fig. 15:5 Masonry accommodation bridge built at the tail of Sparth lock. Note the slight skew, the semi-elliptical arch, the string course and the curving wing-wall. (author's collection)

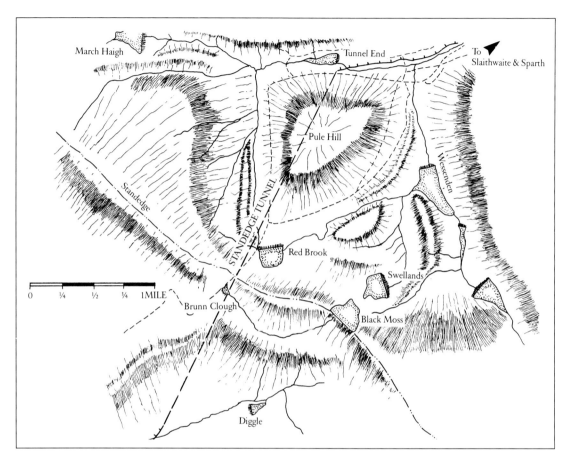

Fig. 15:6 Standedge summit level and reservoirs.

by Huddersfield Corporation and developed for potable water supply. A location on Swinshore Common was eventually preferred to that at Stayley Mill, although this was also abandoned after its partial destruction during the floods of 1799.[27]

Reservoirs were built as the canal sections were completed and opened to traffic. Thus Slaithwaite reservoir was being built in 1796 as the canal approached from Huddersfield, to be followed by a new reservoir at Tunnel End, above Marsden, in 1798. These were soon followed by March Haigh and Red Brook reservoirs which were used to augment the Tunnel End supply via the Red Brook and its tributaries. Similarly that at Diggle was under construction in late 1799 to provide for the section from Stalybridge to Woolroad (Figure 15:6).

All reservoirs were contained by earth dams with clay cores, although the design and construction methods are unknown. Most leaked for several years after completion and this can no doubt be attributed to ignorance of the engineering principles involved, lack of suitable plant for consolidation and, perhaps, also to the absence of skilled supervision. The state of the reservoirs on the summit level in 1800 was said by Rooth to be so bad that 'there was not one reservoir out of five that would retain any water' and 'there was a fairly well-grounded apprehension of great destruction to the property of the country below the Slaithwaite dam'.[28]

In 1807, Black Moss reservoir was under construction on the watershed of the Colne and Tame valleys such that flow could be directed into either valley as required. Thomas Telford also recommended that another reservoir should be constructed close by at Swellands, which he stated would be of 50 acres and 45 feet in depth.[29] A small capacity reservoir at Sparth in the Colne valley was constructed in 1807 to complete the original supply system for the canal.[30]

Work seemed to be drawing to a conclusion when a very serious accident occurred with the failure of Swellands dam on 29 November 1810. The reservoir was then only partially-filled with water to a depth of 7 feet but this proved sufficient to cause underseepage and collapse of the earthworks. Water rushed eastwards into the Colne valley at one o'clock in the morning, inundating the valley at Marsden and as far beyond as Paddock. The force of the water was such that a 15-ton boulder was washed two miles down from the summit and the mountainside was denuded of soil. Factories and homes were destroyed in what became known as the night of the Black Flood.[31]

Setting-out of the Works

Brown's inaccurate survey drawing, on which the canal line appears to have been sketched in freehand, could only have provided a rough guide for establishing a line on the ground by eye and personal judgment. Centre-line pegs, the tops of which were levelled to the proposed water surface, were driven in probably at two to three chain intervals, or closer where the canal was on an embankment or in a cutting.[32] For high banks, very long stakes were often used and in cuttings, holes were first dug before pegs were set in them at the correct level. Alignment between pegs was left to the overlookers to decide as work proceeded, a practice which in places led to short meanders, which are common enough on most waterways, although unnecessary and avoidable. It would have been a simple matter to calculate and then mark out toe positions of the earth banks and cuttings and then to set up wooden profiles to define the slopes. If that had been done before work commenced, the limits of the construction could have been fenced in and the land-take valued and agreed with land-owners. Outram, in common with other engineers of the period, preferred not to do this and left such matters until work was finished. Not surprisingly, this practice led to the disputes and claims for trespass and damages to property already mentioned.

A difficult matter was the control of line and level in the tunnel at Standedge. The principal surveying tasks comprised of the establishment of accurate surface alignment between the tunnel mouthings at Diggle and Marsden and the location of the shafts; the transfer of bench marks across the mountain and also to the top of each shaft to ensure a common basis for levelling; and the transfer of line and level down the shafts and into the workings.

Surviving records fail to describe how any of these problems was resolved, although survey methods and instruments used were of the simplest kinds. Surface alignment was probably obtained by an iterative process of traversing using a magnetic compass and chain, or even by means of a series of long poles, each of which was moved laterally by trial and error until a satisfactory alignment was observed. Accuracy was poor and the surface positions of existing shafts were only between 3 feet and 7 feet laterally of the correct positions. One of the two shafts at Red Brook (the pumping or downcast shaft) was offset from the centre line of the tunnel at the bottom by about 26 feet, but no doubt this was deliberate so as to ensure that the deep sump and pipe work at canal level would not impede movement along the tunnel (Figure 15:7). Transfer of surface alignment to the base of the shaft would be made by means of a pair of plummets hung at pit bottom on cords suspended from points a short distance apart on the survey line at the surface[33] (Figure 15:8). Thus a parallel line could be projected into the workings for the guidance of the miners. The correct level of the tunnel was generally obtained by calculating the depth of the shaft and measuring down from a bench mark by chain, as sinking proceeded.

Thomas Telford, after visiting the canal during the winter of 1806, wrote that 'the season was totally unfit for proving the general line of direction over

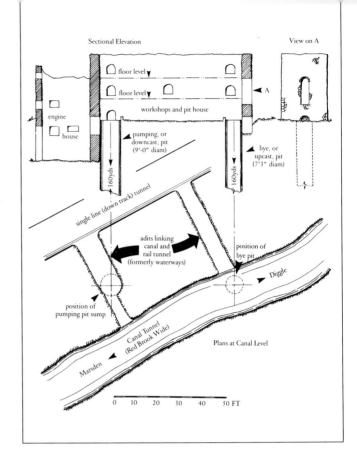

Fig. 15:7 Canal tunnel and engine house at Red Brook

Sectional Elevation

View on A

floor level

floor level

workshops and pit house

engine

house

pumping, or downcast, pit (9'-0" diam)

160yds

single line (down track) tunnel

adits linking canal and rail tunnel (formerly waterways)

position of bye pit

bye, or upcast, pit (7'3" diam)

160yds

Diggle

position of pumping pit sump

Canal Tunnel (Red Brook Wide)

Marsden

Plans at Canal Level

0   10   20   30   40   50 FT

Fig. 15:8 Method of transferring survey line into tunnel working

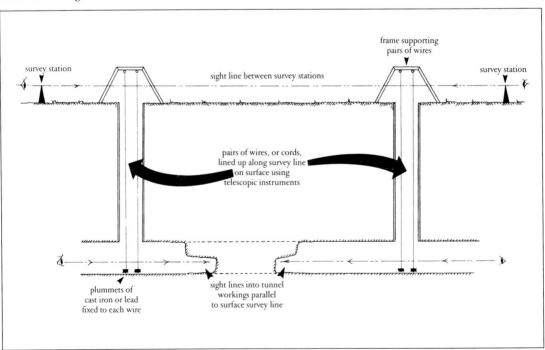

survey station

frame supporting pairs of wires

sight line between survey stations

survey station

pairs of wires, or cords, lined up along survey line on surface using telescopic instruments

plummets of cast iron or lead fixed to each wire

sight lines into tunnel workings parallel to surface survey line

the mountain and dialling and levelling below, but each end appears very direct in itself'. He was confident that all was satisfactory because he understood that 'they have been tried and found accurate by several properly qualified persons'. In fact, some serious surveying errors had been made prior to Telford's visit. David Whitehead, a surveyor associated with Outram on the Peak Forest Canal, checked the tunnel in 1802[34] and found several mistakes which were described by Rooth[35] in later years (Figure 15:9). At the Marsden end the tunnel invert (or lowest level) was found to be 2 feet deeper than the sill at the first lock. Moreover, the workings then dipped 3 feet deeper over a short distance to the rock face! Of greater concern however, was the difference between levels at the tunnel ends. The invert at Diggle was much higher than that at Marsden. Rooth did not record this difference in measurement, but on excavating at Diggle to equalise the levels, the foundations to the side walls were undermined and these, as well as the completed masonry arching, had to be dismantled and rebuilt. Beyond this length was a long, partially-finished section of tunnel which also had to be cut down to a correct level.

Fig. 15:9 Levelling errors in Standedge Tunnel (1802)

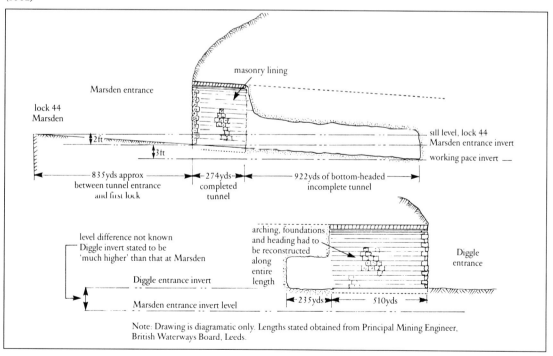

Note: Drawing is diagramatic only. Lengths stated obtained from Principal Mining Engineer, British Waterways Board, Leeds.

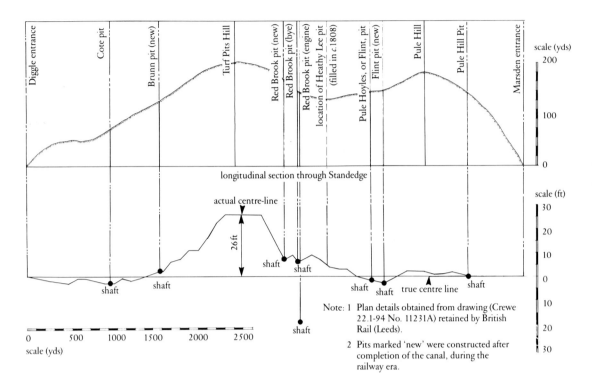

Labels on figure (left to right, top): Diggle entrance, Cote pit, Brunn pit (new), Turf Pits Hill, Red Brook pit (new), Red Brook pit (bye), Red Brook pit (engine), location of Heathy Lee pit (filled in c.1808), Pule Hoyles, or Flint, pit, Flint pit (new), Pule Hill, Pule Hill Pit, Marsden entrance

scale (yds)
200

100

0

longitudinal section through Standedge

scale (ft)
30
20
10

actual centre-line

26ft

shaft

shaft

shaft   shaft

shaft   shaft   true centre line   shaft

shaft   shaft

shaft

0   500   1000   1500   2000   2500
scale (yds)

Note: 1 Plan details obtained from drawing (Crewe 22.1-94 No. 11231A) retained by British Rail (Leeds).

2 Pits marked 'new' were constructed after completion of the canal, during the railway era.

10
20
30

Fig. 15:10 Plan of tunnel showing shaft positions on centre line.

Although these levels had been corrected before Telford's visit, a major error of alignment occurred in the months that followed. The final section of the tunnel from Red Brook to Brunn Clough was driven with a maximum deviation of 26 feet to the north-west of the true centre-line[36] (Figure 15:10). Not surprisingly, this was never mentioned in the company minutes, but that was not all: there were errors of 120 feet and 42 feet respectively in measuring between the longitudinal positions of three of the shafts. These were not discovered until the mountain was finally pierced in 1809 and direct measurement was possible.[37] The corrected length of Standedge Tunnel was then given as 5,477 yards.

Construction of the Great Tunnel

It is difficult to unravel the sequence of construction in the Standedge Tunnel during those sixteen years. Work should have been carefully planned, but instead it proceeded in haphazard fashion. Minds were changed, there were frequent stoppages, sections and machinery were abandoned for long periods and labour dismissed or switched between working faces. The basic reason for this was the shortage of funds, largely through the failure of shareholders to pay their calls. For example, by June 1796, when output should have been rising to a peak, some £92,000 had been called for of which £22,650 was in arrears and the company had only £889 in the bank.[38] In spite of this, the Management Committee persisted in maintaining several working faces with all the associated equipment and labour that entailed; all this was in a desperate effort to complete the link between the two ends of canal then nearing completion. Impatience only added to their troubles and costs and it was not surprising that £20,049 had been spent of the £55,187 estimated, for only one-seventh of the tunnelling work completed.

The proprietors' problems were compounded by their failure to find experienced and reliable contractors to take on their massive task. Two major contractors were financially ruined and had broken their agreements by 1798. They were never satisfactorily replaced and most of the remaining work was eventually executed by direct labour.

Something of the methods of working the tunnel can be gleaned from Outram's report of 1796[39] and also from a longitudinal section prepared by Brown about 1799.[40] A total of fourteen shafts were originally sunk at intervals of between 100 yards and 180 yards from each end, but pumping costs at all of these were high due to an unexpected ingress of water from the millstone grit strata; indeed at the sixth pit from Diggle (also known as the Cote Pit) costs were eleven guineas per week. A change of plan reduced the numbers of shafts to those at Cote (80 yards deep), Brunn Clough (140 yards deep), two at Red Brook (each 160 yards deep), Heathy Lee (146 yards deep), Pule Hoyles (160 yards deep) and Pule Hill (156 yards deep). That at Heathy Lee was later abandoned on Telford's instructions but the others remained (Figures 15:10 and 15:11).

An adit was driven into each of these shafts in a direction approximately at right angles to the main tunnel at depths between 28 and 49 yards below ground level, and as many as four shafts were sunk along the line of these adits in order to expedite construction (Figure 15:12). These apparently extravagant temporary works were completed in an effort to draw off ground water from the workings, but, more important, they also provided a drain for the 'water engines' used for hoisting spoil from the tunnel to the surface tips. These simple and effective machines were common in mining practice and operated by means of a water-filled kibble (or barrel) which moved down a shallow balance pit to the level of the adit. By this means and a gearing system, ratios of which were related to the depth of the shafts, spoil was lifted

Fig.15:11 The engine house and workshops at Red Brook. The engine, or pumping pit (which is also the downcast shaft) is inside the far end of the building; the bye pit (the upcast shaft) is at the near end. Both pits are approximately 480 feet deep.

Note:

A — the pits and adjacent engine house at Pule Hoyles.

B — the site of the abandoned Heathy Lee pits.

(author's collection)

Fig. 15:12 The 'Water Engine' used at several shafts on Standedge.

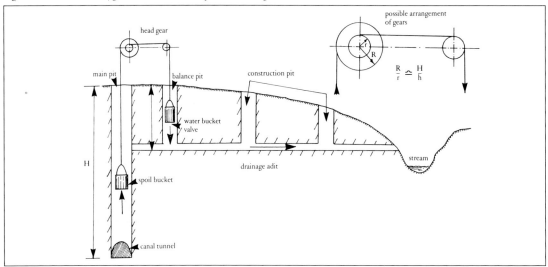

Fig. 15:13 Lined section of Standedge Tunnel under Pule Hoyles (New) pit. View towards south-west at distance marker 79, 3950 yards from the original Diggle end. Ground-water discharges through the joints of the shaft lining during wet weather. (Dr R.C. Witter).

out of the deeper pit from canal level up to the surface. Initially, some waterwheels were also used, notably at Pule Hoyles, where an elaborate water supply system was built, but generally these wheels provided insufficient power and were soon replaced by water engines. Steam engines of the Newcomen type, coupled to reciprocating pumps, were also utilised in the engine house at Red Brook and elsewhere for the drainage of the working levels (Figure 15:13). A small quantity of water was discharged into the top of the pumping shaft at Red Brook, falling as a fine spray and thereby inducing a strong draught of air down the shaft and into the workings far below. This ventilation system has continued in use.

The driving of the tunnels was achieved by hand-drilling and blasting with black powder. Shaft sinking proceeded in much the same way, although a description by Farey gives a graphic impression of the dangerous conditions of working.[41] A shallow hole would be drilled in the centre of the shaft floor, then thoroughly dried out with oakum before packing with gunpowder and a clay seal. On lighting a fuse, the miners clung, one above the other, on to a winding rope and at a signal were hauled some distance up the shaft, where they remained until the shots were fired. They were then lowered into the fumes to clear up the broken rock and to repeat the process. Farey noted that sometimes accidents occurred when the miners were not lifted sufficiently high above the danger zone!

A spirit of optimism was generated by the passing of a new Act in 1806 to finance completion of the waterway,[42] and also by the appointment of Thomas Telford to survey the canal, to plan for and estimate the costs of its completion. In his report Telford claimed

> . . . a thorough knowledge of the state of the works because I have examined everything twice and even checked the filling and emptying of every lock.[43]

His plans included for the completion of the tunnel, also an unfinished section of canal from Woolroad to Diggle and new reservoirs, as well as repairs to structures and earthworks. Estimates for these works were £45,000 for the tunnel and £37,498 for the remainder. Telford meticulously planned progress such as:

> 280yds commencing at the termination of the last length and ending the fourth pit at the rate of 8yds per week, which will occupy up the 1st November 1807.

The company assiduously followed these instructions during the ensuing years until their canal was finished in April 1811, just five months later than Telford's prediction. Regrettably, Rooth was to claim in later years that he alone had supervised completion of the works 'without the aid of any engineer', thus ignoring the substantial guidance and advice which had been provided by one of the leading civil engineers of that time.[44]

Throughout those troubled years it was the workforce of miners, tradesmen and labourers who suffered most from the frequent stoppages and shortages of funds. Their recompense for working in squalid, brutal conditions was small and too frequently the company was in their debt; indeed at one stage wages were paid only to those owed less than £30, greater sums being paid at five shillings in the pound.[45] Welfare of workers was of small account; only once was £1 1s. granted 'towards the expense of burying a workman who died today on the line of the canal'[46] and, although a sick fund was set up, the company subscribed only five shillings each week.

The workmen's origins are mainly unknown, although local parish records suggest that many were sojourners of northern stock such as the unfortunate 'John Kell who was killed in the tunnel, a native of Stanhope-in-Weardale 19.3.1810'.[47] It seems that upwards of fifty men lost their lives during the construction years, but added to this must be the wives and children who also suffered and died, having lived in the primitive shanty towns established near the works at Gilbert's Intack, on Puleside and elsewhere, in support of their menfolk who laboured on that great navigation.

Conclusions

The final costs of the canal project were quoted as £396,267 in June 1811,[48] but in view of the remedial work and modifications carried out in the following year it is more appropriate to include for this period also. Thus, total costs by June 1812 were £402,653.[49] This included £123,804 for the Standedge Tunnel, or £22.60 per yard compared with the original estimate of £10.25 per yard, taking into account costs of shafts and all ancillary works.

In retrospect it is easy to criticise the Canal Company's inept management organisation and its shaky financial arrangements, as well as the self-inflicted troubles and the shortcomings of many individuals involved. Such a view, however, ignores the pioneering nature of the task and the fact that the Huddersfield Narrow Canal was a major project even judging by exacting modern standards. Is it not surprising, therefore, that a group of citizens comprising weavers, farmers and others should establish a company, hire a few professionals and set about their immense task using only the crudest of equipment and methods? That they completed the task even in seventeen years is a tribute to their courage and faith in their country. Perhaps the canal never made fortunes for the proprietors and speculators but it greatly assisted in the development of the region which it served for generations to follow. Moreover, it did much for the common folk who populated those bleak moors and valleys, through improved communications and employment opportunities, and such factors cannot easily be expressed in monetary terms. For all its troubles and failings, the canal was successful; it was a splendid concept and its completion a wonderful achievement.

Later years saw the advent of the railway era and the construction of three tunnels through Standedge in 1849, 1870 and 1894. All utilised the canal tunnel for access and the removal of spoil and thus in a sense the waterway subscribed to its own demise and ultimate closure in 1944. The working life of the canal as a transport medium is long over but recently, moves have been made to secure its future for water supply and recreational pursuits, fitting enough purposes for this great navigational waterway after many years of industrial life.

R B Schofield

Biographical Note

Professor Schofield was educated at Bolton School and Corpus Christi College, University of Cambridge, where he graduated in Mechanical Sciences. After several years in the civil engineering industry as a chartered engineer, he returned to academic life in the University of Salford to specialise in fluid mechanics and hydraulics. His doctorate was awarded there for research into the phenomena associated with ships moving in restricted navigations. He left for Northern Ireland in 1975 and recently retired as Professor and Head of of the Department of Civil Engineering in the University of Ulster. He has published over sixty papers on fluids, engineering management and other topics and has a keen interest in engineering history.

NOTES

1. E.C.R. Hadfield, *British Canals, an Illustrated History* (1950).

2. Locks and structures of the Huddersfield Narrow Canal accommodate narrow boats of 70ft x 7ft x 3ft 6in draught. Broad canals vary in size; the Leeds and Liverpool Canal and Rochdale Canal take craft of 62ft x 14ft 3in x 3ft 9in and 72ft x 14ft 2in x 4ft draught respectively.

3. B. Outram, *Report on the Proposed Canal etc.*, 22 October 1793, in W. Pontey, *A Short Account of the Huddersfield Canal* (Cambridge, 1812), p.3-6.

4. Pontey, *A Short Account of the Huddersfield Canal*, p.6.

5. Huddersfield Canal Act: 34 Geo.III c. 53, 4 April 1794.

6. P(ublic) R(ecord) O(ffice), B(ritish) T(ransport) H(istorical) R(ecords), Minutes of the C(ommittee) of the H(uddersfield) C(anal) C(ompany), 11 July 1794.

7. PRO, BTHR, Minutes of the CHCC, 12 October 1798.

8. PRO, BTHR, Minutes of the CHCC, 23 April 1801.

9. W(est) Y(orkshire) A(rchive) S(ervice), K(irklees), B/HCC/z T. Telford, Abstract of the Report relating to the State of the Huddersfield Canal, 29 January 1807.

10. Standing Orders of the House of Commons, 14 March 1793.

11. Brown practised as a land surveyor in Wakefield in later years.

12. The chain formerly used by surveyors was the 22 yards long Gunter chain which consisted of 100 wrought-iron links, each measuring 7.92 inches.

13. B. Outram, *Report on the Proposed Canal etc.*, 22 October 1793, in Pontey, *A Short Account of the Huddersfield Canal*, p.3-6.

14. H(ouse) of L(ords) R(ecord) O(ffice), N. Brown, Survey of Proposed Canal between Huddersfield and Ashton under Lyne, 1793. The positions of waterwheels are marked on this drawing.

15. The original Diggle aqueduct can be found a short distance to the south-east of the present canal line. It has a semi-elliptical arch. The Marsden aqueduct was either buried or demolished during reconstruction of the Tunnel End reservoir outfall and related railway engineering works, at the end of the nineteenth century.

16. G. Worthington, Correspondence to Share-holders, 2 September 1799, in Pontey, *A Short Account of the Huddersfield Canal*, pp.22-23.

17. The Holmes aqueduct in Derby is reputed to be the first of its type to be built in Britain. It was demolished during town centre re-developments during the 1970s.

18. The adjacent tow-path arch was being built at that time. A date of 1801 has been given by J. Farey, *General View of the Agriculture of Derbyshire*, Vol. III, (1811), pp.373-374.

19. Derby Public Library. Minutes of the Committee of the Derby Canal Company, [February 1802].

20. Farey, *General View of the Agriculture of Derbyshire*, Vol. III, (1811), p.374.

21. Telford's Longdon-on-Tern aqueduct on the Shrewsbury Canal is the oldest extant cast-iron trough although the canal is disused.

22. HLRO, B. Outram, Estimate of the Expense of Making a Navigable Canal. Huddersfield Canal, 1794.

23. Farey, *General View of the Agriculture of Derbyshire*, Vol III, (1811), p.372.

24. WYAS, Kirklees KC 174, Tomlinson Mss., Correspondence of J. Rooth with R. Firth, 24 February 1817.

25. B. Outram, *Report on the Proposed Canal etc.*, 22 October 1793, in Pontey, *A Short Account of the Huddersfield Canal*, pp.3-6.

26. WYAS, Leeds Dartmouth Mss,D77/5/2. Minutes of a Meeting of Mill-owners situate on the River Colne, 4 April 1799.

27. In correspondence with the author, Mr A.I.B. Moffatt of Newcastle University wrote that the civil engineer, J.F. Bateman, reporting to the Manchester and Salford Waterworks Company in 1844, described the remains of Swinshore reservoir which he stated had failed through lack of an adequate overflow system.

28. WYAS, Kirklees KC 174 Tomlinson Mss., Correspondence of J. Rooth with R. Firth, 24 February 1817.

29. WYAS, Kirklees B/HCC/z T. Telford, Abstract of the Report relating to the State of the Works on the Huddersfield Canal, 29 January 1807.

30. PRO, BTHR, Minutes of the CHCC, 23 April 1807.

31. PRO, BTHR, HRP/6/8X/K979, Report to the General Assembly of the Huddersfield Canal Company, 27 June 1811.

32. *Art on Canals: Encyclopaedia or Universal Dictionary of Arts, Science and Literature*, edited by A. Rees (1819).

33. Sometimes known as Simm's Method, the technique is generally used today on shallow shaft construction for sewers and similar works.

34. PRO, BTHR, Minutes of the CHCC, 1 November 1802.

35. WYAS, Kirklees, KC 174 Tomlinson Mss, Correspondence of J. Rooth with R. Firth, 24 February 1817. Mr D.M. Stakes, British Waterways Board, confirmed that by the time of Whitehead's surveys, 489 yards of tunnel was finished at the Diggle end and a further 265 yards was incomplete. At the Marsden end, 1,051 yards was finished and another 176 yards was incomplete.

36. R.B. Schofield, 'The Construction of the Huddersfield Narrow Canal 1794-1811, with particular reference to the Standedge Tunnel', *Transactions of the Newcomen Society for the Study of the History of Science and Technology*, 53, (1981-82), 17-38.

37. J. Rooth, *Report on the Huddersfield Canal*, 29 June 1809, in Pontey, A *Short Account of the Huddersfield Canal*, pp.32, 33.

38. *Report on the State of the Finances and Works of the Huddersfield Canal to the General Assembly of Proprietors by the Committee and Engineer*, 30 June 1796, in Pontey, A *Short Account of the Huddersfield Canal*, p.12.

39. *Report on the State of the Finances and Works of the Huddersfield Canal*, 30 June 1796, in Pontey, pp.13-16.

40. PRO, BTHR, Rail 844/52/14143, Longitudinal and cross-sections of Standedge Tunnel, Huddersfield Canal.

41. J. Farey, *General View of the Agriculture of Derbyshire*, Vol.1, (1811), pp.325-326.

42. Huddersfield Canal Act: 45 Geo. III c.12, 31 March 1806.

43. WYAS, Kirklees B/HCC/z. Estimates given in Telford's printed report.

44. WYAS, Kirklees, KC 174 Tomlinson Mss., Correspondence of J. Rooth with R. Firth, 24 February 1817.

45. PRO, BTHR, Minutes of the CHCC, 18 December 1800.

46. PRO, BTHR, Minutes of the CHCC, 29 June 1797.

47. Parish Registers 1776-1812, St. Bartholemew's Parish Church, Marsden

48. PRO, BTHR, HRP/6/8X/K979, J. Rooth, Report to the G(eneral) A(ssembly) of the CHCC, 27 June 1811.

49. PRO, BTHR, HRP/6/8X/K979, J. Rooth, Report to the GAHCC, 25 June 1812.

CHAPTER 16

Passenger Transport in Huddersfield

ROY BROOK

Steam Tramways 1883 to 1902

On Thursday 11 January 1883 a Corporation steam tramcar made its way from Fartown to Lockwood. So began the first municipal transport service in Britain, soon to become the largest standard-gauge steam tramway in the country. In 1893 it became the first to carry postboxes and in 1904 the only municipal tramway to carry coal for private customers. After conversion to trolleybuses it became the third largest municipal system. And it began almost by accident . . . .

The construction of tramways in Huddersfield was first considered in connection with a Parliamentary Bill promoted by the London Tramways and General Works Company in 1877.[1] Powers were sought for lines from Huddersfield Market Place to Lindley Church via New North Road, Blacker Lane (Edgerton Grove Road) and Marsh; Fartown Bar via Bradford Road; Moldgreen (Broad Lane) via Kirkgate, Shorehead and Wakefield Road; Lockwood Bar via Folly Hall; and Paddock Foot (Shires Hill) via Manchester Road.

The Corporation decided to oppose the Bill on the grounds that the proposed lines were inadequate for the needs of the Borough and that they would prefer to retain control of the roads in their own hands. The Town Clerk sent circulars to seventeen boroughs asking for their views on the merits of tramways constructed by independent companies and all the replies received, in effect, condemned the principle.[2] Notwithstanding, the promoter proceeded with the Bill in full knowledge of the Corporation's disagreement, with the result that Parliament's Standing Orders Committee rejected it on 1 February 1878.[3]

Desiring to establish a system of tramways in the town, Huddersfield Corporation itself promoted a Bill in Parliament during the autumn of 1879, for powers to lay more than nineteen miles of track in the Borough, to the nominal gauge of 4 feet 8½ inches (in practice 4 feet 7¾ inches to allow railway wagons to run on the tramways). This was duly authorised by the Huddersfield Improvement Act, 1880 which received the Royal Assent on 2 August of that year. Table 1 shows the routes authorised to run from the town centre.

Table 1 Routes authorised to run from the town centre.

> Berry Brow (Golden Fleece) via Lockwood
> Borough Boundary, Meltham Road (for Beaumont Park)
> Crosland Moor (Park Road)
> Borough Boundary, Marsden Road, (Pinfold Well)
> Paddock Head via Longroyd Bridge
> Lindley, Circular route via Marsh and Edgerton
> Ashbrow (Listers Road) via Fartown
> Bradley (Woodman Inn) via Leeds Road
> Waterloo Inn via Moldgreen
> Almondbury via Somerset Road
> Newsome Church via Newsome Road

It was the normal practice at this time for tramways laid by a Corporation or other local authority to be operated on lease by a private concern. During the construction of the lines, which commenced in June 1881, every effort was made to effect such a lease, but this did not prove to be possible; would-be operators were possibly deterred by the steep gradients on almost every route. The only alternative was for the Corporation to work the tramways themselves, and power to do so was given by the Huddersfield Corporation Act, 1882. A seven-year licence was granted, renewable on expiry, on the proviso that if any Company offered to work the tramways for a period of not less than seven years (unless agreed otherwise by the Corporation) the operating powers would pass to that Company.

Steam traction was decided upon as being best suited to the hilly nature of the district and, on 19 September 1882,[4] the first tram engine was ordered from William Wilkinson & Co. Ltd of Wigan, and a single-ended double-deck four-wheeled tramcar, to seat thirty-eight passengers, from the Ashbury Railway Carriage and Iron Company of Manchester. Steam tramways in Britain were normally worked by a steam locomotive hauling a trailer car and, in exceptional cases, more than one car. Temporary accommodation for the engine and car took the form of a wooden shed erected in the middle of Lord Street, between Northumberland Street and St. Peter's Street, over track laid as part of a proposed route to Waterloo, later abandoned in favour of the King Street route. Both engine and car had arrived in Huddersfield by the end of October 1882 and were stored in the shed in Lord Street.

All was now ready for the Board of Trade inspection, a necessary preliminary to the opening for passenger traffic of lines governed by the Tramways Act, 1870, (or the later Light Railway Acts of 1896 and 1912). Major-General C.S. Hutchinson, R.E. inspected the routes on Thursday 16 November 1882.[5] He approved all the ten track miles then laid (apart from Longroyd Lane, which had not been paved, and Lidget Street, Lindley, which required widening in part). The certificate of fitness was received from the Board of Trade on 29 November 1882.[6]

The Corporation decided that the tram engine and its car should be used to open a service between Lockwood Bar and Fartown Bar,[7] and so on 11 January 1883 Huddersfield Corporation became the first municipality in the British Isles to operate its own tramways.[8] The driver and conductor employed were paid at the weekly rate of £1 12s. od. and £1 3s. od.[9] respectively and fares were fixed at 2d. inside and 1d. outside between town and each terminus.[10]

The tramcar fleet was in due course increased by five further Wilkinson engines[11] and five cars,[12] although these came from the Starbuck Car & Wagon Company, Birkenhead, and were double-ended vehicles with stairs to the upper deck at each end. They seated thirty-four passengers.

The need for improved depot accommodation was met by purchasing a wooden building in Northumberland Street, on the site of the present General Post Office building and formerly used by William Pinder as a circus, and expected to be vacant by the end of March 1883.[13] The temporary shed in Lord Street had suffered gale damage on 26 January 1883 and in any case was too small to accommodate the growing fleet.

About this time the Corporation entered into an agreement with the Hallidie Patent Cable Tramways Co. Ltd to lease two of the routes, to

Fig. 16:1 Steam tram engine (built by Thos. Green & Sons, Leeds) with Milnes-built trailer car in Railway Street on the Salendine Nook service, c.1892. The conductor (extreme right) is holding his Kaye's patent fare collection box in his right hand. (RBC)

Paddock and Moldgreen, for operation by cable trams, but difficulties with the curve from New Street into King Street and restrictions imposed by the Board of Trade caused the project to be abandoned, even though the Company had already excavated a site in Manchester Road (where the Grand Cinema was later built).[14]

In June 1885 Mr Joe Pogson, a Holmfirth-born engineer, was appointed Tramways Manager and remained in this post until October 1901, having successfully managed the department through its formative years and for most of the steam era.[15]

As the tramway system expanded, the Northumberland Street Depot in turn became too small, and in 1887 a new purpose-built stone-fronted Depot to the design of the Borough Surveyor, Mr R.S. Dugdale, was built in Great Northern Street. The building had a capacity for thirty engines and cars, and proved adequate for the steam fleet, which in the event never reached this figure. (This Depot, with subsequent alterations and extensions, was later used for housing the local bus fleet of Yorkshire Rider Limited).

The early tram engines were in due course replaced by more powerful types, built by the well-known Leeds builders Kitson & Co. Ltd and Thomas Green & Sons Ltd and the cars were superseded by larger models of the bogie type, fitted with top covers to the upper deck. These had seating for over sixty passengers and were mostly built at Birkenhead by George F. Milnes & Company.

For a three year period (1885 to 1888) the Moldgreen route was operated by horse trams as the route to and from the town centre was by way of the steep and narrow King Street.* This was a very busy shopping thoroughfare and it was not at first considered safe to operate steam trams. They did take over the service from 2 April 1888, however. Horse trams were also used at times on the Fartown route. After replacement by steam trams the four redundant horse trams were sold to the Stockport & Hazel Grove Tramways Co. Ltd in 1890-91.[16]

For turning steam trams with locomotive and trailer car, a turning circle was obviously the ideal layout, but only two were possible in Huddersfield, in St. George's Square (for cars from Lindley and Outlane) and at Bradley terminus. The other alternatives were a reversing triangle or a run-round loop. The triangle was preferred by the Board of Trade when a terminus was sited on a gradient. When a run-round loop was used the engine and car had to be uncoupled for the engine to run around the car and this was only acceptable on level ground. At Crosland Moor (Park Road) the Board of Trade ordered the use of a reversing triangle,[17] and a further ten were laid at Paddock Head, Moldgreen (Broad Lane), Lockwood Bar, Waterloo, Almondbury, Fartown Bar, Berry Brow, Salendine Nook, Stile Common Road, and Thornhill Road, Marsh.

In March 1893 Huddersfield became the first town in Britain to carry letter boxes on the trams. A suitable box was designed by Mr Pogson and painted in Post Office red.[18] This was attached to the rear end of each car and letters could be posted at all termini and other stopping places, although if a tram was specially stopped for the purpose one penny had to be inserted into the conductor's fare box. This service was maintained for forty-six years; post boxes in the trolleybus era were withdrawn only at the request of the Post Office, after the outbreak of war in 1939.

Horse trams were not the predecessors of steam trams in Huddersfield; the horse trams operated on the Moldgreen route for a temporary period and after the steam tramway service had been operative on other routes for two years. EDITOR.

The authority to operate the tramway system under licence granted to the Corporation in 1882 was revoked by the Huddersfield Corporation Act, 1897 and the operating powers were made absolute and permanent.

In October 1897 the Urban District Council of Linthwaite expressed interest in laying a single line tramway along the main Manchester Road through the Colne valley from the Huddersfield boundary at Pinfold Well to the Star Hotel, Slaithwaite, a distance of 3.01 miles. Application was made to Parliament for a Provisional Order[19] and agreement reached with Huddersfield Corporation for them to work the line on the Council's behalf as a through service from Huddersfield. By a similar Order Huddersfield was authorised to lay a connecting line from the Crosland Moor route at the Griffin Inn along what was then Marsden Road to Pinfold Well.[20] This connecting line was duly laid and inspected on 29 September 1899 and opened for passenger traffic on 2 October.

Construction of the Linthwaite UDC line began in September 1899 and was connected to the Corporation track at Pinfold Well in time for inspection and opening on 21 May 1900. Although Linthwaite was responsible for track laying in its area, the overhead equipment later to be erected and all things electrical, such as feeder cables and traction poles, were to be provided by Huddersfield Corporation.

Fig. 16:2 Huddersfield Corporation Steam Tramways 1900

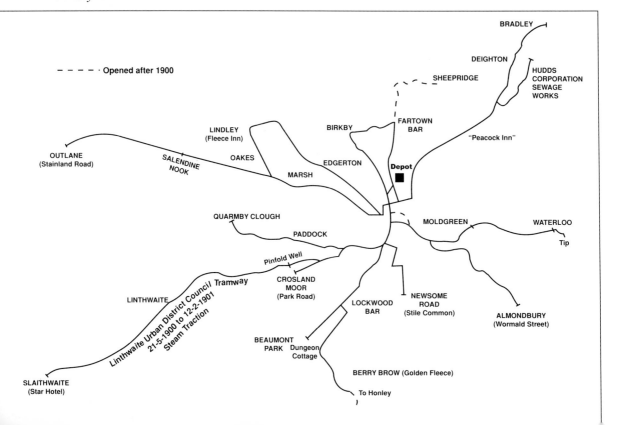

Table 2   Timetable of inauguration of steam tram routes.

Lindley (Bay Horse Inn)	9 June	1883
(extended to Fleece Inn)	June	1883
Edgerton (Bryan Road)	10 January	1884
Paddock Head	13 December	1884
Moldgreen (Junction Inn) Horse trams	9 May	1885
Steam trams	2 April	1888
Circular route to Lindley via Holly Bank Road	11 October	1886
Almondbury	15 February	1889
Crosland Moor (Park Road)	23 May	1890
Waterloo	26 September	1890
Peacock Inn (Leeds Road)	25 September	1891
Bradley	15 April	1892
Salendine Nook	15 April	1892
Berry Brow	2 June	1892
Birkby	1 December	1892
Newsome Road (Stile Common Road)	22 July	1896
Outlane	1 February	1899
Pinfold Well	2 October	1899
Slaithwaite	21 May	1900
Longwood (Quarmby Clough)	21 May	1900
Sheepridge	2 April	1901
Honley (temporary service of twelve days duration pending introduction of electric trams)	5 June	1902

The maximum route mileage of Huddersfield's steam tramway system was 29 miles 45 chains, the largest standard gauge system in the British Isles. The steam tram routes (after the initial opening of the Lockwood to Fartown route on 11 January 1883) were inaugurated on the dates shown in Table 2.

Service frequencies in steam tram days were usually every half-hour, with no trams on Sundays, although the Crosland Moor route worked by one engine and car had a forty-minute service. Waterloo had the most frequent service, with a car every fifteen minutes in the later days of the service. This line was always the busiest and in electric tram days (from 1924 to 1934) had a six-minute service all day.[21]

No tickets were issued in the steam era, fares being collected in the Kaye's Patent Fare Collecting Box by the conductor from every passenger after passing each successive fare stage. Bell Punch tickets of different colours according to value came during the early part of the twentieth century and remained in use until 1949, when machine-issued 'ULTIMATE' tickets were introduced, also printed in differing colours.

During the steam era two fatal accidents took place. The first, on 3 July 1883, was by far the worst, as seven passengers were killed and twenty-eight injured. The mishap occurred in Railway Street when the 2.30 p.m. car from Lindley, hauled by No. 2 engine, ran out of control in Trinity Street and failed to negotiate the left hand curve from Westgate into Railway Street, overturning and throwing passengers from the open upper deck with great violence.[22] The Tramways Committee later donated the sum of fifty guineas (£52.50) to the Huddersfield Infirmary funds for the magnificent help rendered to the sufferers.

The second fatal accident,[23] whilst not as serious as the first, nevertheless resulted in the death of a twenty-year-old Moldgreen man employed as a cleaner in Great Northern Street Depot. On 3 June 1891 Engine No. 9, working the 8.30 a.m. journey from Town to Crosland Moor, exploded whilst standing in the Longroyd Bridge passing loop. The cause of the accident was fire-box corrosion and arrangements were afterwards made to provide water from Longwood reservoirs, as these had less sulphuric acid content than other sources.

Electric Tramways 1901 to 1940

Electrification of the steam tramways was first considered in 1898, when additional rolling stock was needed, principally in connection with the proposed line to Slaithwaite. Reports were prepared by the Managers of the Tramways and Electricity Departments and the Borough Engineer, Mr K.F. Campbell.[24] On 25 April 1899 Mr Campbell's recommendation to electrify the entire system was adopted, and the stage was thus set for a modern electric tramway system for Huddersfield. The conversion was scheduled to be carried out in two stages, during 1900 and 1902.

A site alongside the River Colne at Longroyd Bridge, 4,474 square yards in extent, formerly occupied by the Corporation Refuse Destructor, was earmarked for a power station and car sheds to accommodate twenty-five tramcars, and the foundation stone for the new building was laid on 13 February 1900 by the Chairman of the Tramways Committee, Alderman Armitage Haigh.[25] The first routes chosen for conversion were those from St. George's Square to Crosland Moor (Park Road), Slaithwaite (Star Hotel), Longwood (Quarmby Clough), Outlane, and the Lindley Circular line via Marsh and Edgerton.

The main contract was awarded to Greenwood & Batley Ltd of Leeds, who sub-contracted various works, including the building and equipping of tramcars. Traction poles painted sage green, for the suspension of overhead wiring, were planted on all routes, whilst on John William Street, New Street and Buxton Road (that part of the main street from Ramsden Street to Chapel Hill) span wires were attached to rosettes bolted to the buildings flanking the road. Many routes had bracket arms adorned with wrought-iron scrollwork on one side of the road, but on wider roads it was necessary to use span wires attached to traction poles on each side. Each pole was topped with a ball and spike finial and had a decorative fluted cast-iron base. Such adornments were found to cause corrosion, however, and many were subsequently removed.[26]

Electric power for traction purposes was distributed to each route by means of underground feeder cables from Longroyd Bridge Power Station.

Early in 1901 the time was approaching for the opening of the new electric system. Twenty-five new trams, built by George F. Milnes & Co. Ltd of Hadley, Shropshire, painted in vermillion and cream, had been delivered and were in store at Great Northern Street Depot. They were luxurious vehicles when compared with the steam trams, with velvet-cushioned lower saloon seats for twenty-four passengers and curtains to the windows. Two electric heaters fitted under each of the longitudinal seats allowed warm air to pass into the car through perforated grids on the seat fronts. The upper deck was open and accommodated thirty-two passengers on rain-proof roof seats. The cars were mounted on bogies and had two 35 horse power motors.[26] On economic and operational grounds the bogies were later replaced by four-wheel trucks.

During January 1901 tests were carried out with the electrical sub-contractors, the British Thomson-Houston Company, the Borough Engineer, Tramways Manager, and Tramway Electrical Engineer, Mr H.N. Thomas (who succeeded Mr Pogson as Tramways Manager in October 1901). After their formal inspection on 30 January 1901 by Major E. Druitt, R.E. and Mr Alexander Trotter all electrified lines were certified fit, apart from minor adjustments to be made on Acre Street, Lindley and in St. George's Square.

The grand opening of the Power Station, attended by 150 invited guests, including the Managers from surrounding tramway systems, took place on 7 February 1901 and Table 3 gives the date on which public services of electric trams commenced.

Table 3 Timetable of commencement of public services by electric trams.

Outlane	14 February 1901
Lindley	14 February 1901
Slaithwaite	18 February 1901
Crosland Moor	18 February 1901
Longwood	25 February 1901

With the electric trams came more frequent services of ten, fifteen and twenty minute intervals.

Sunday running of trams in Huddersfield began on 9 June 1901, services commencing generally around 1.30 p.m.[27] Opposition to Sunday running had been experienced in the past from religious bodies, and any member of the tramway staff who had religious convictions about Sunday working was not compelled to do so.

The second stage of conversions followed with the Waterloo and Newsome Road sections being inspected on 14 May 1902, and new services were inaugurated the same day. The remaining routes opened as described in Table 4.

Table 4 Timetable of opening of electric tram services.

Sheepridge	20 May 1902
Fartown Bar via Birkby	10 June 1902
Almondbury	17 June 1902
Honley	17 June 1902
Bradley	13 July 1902

Huddersfield saw its last steam trams in passenger service on 21 June 1902 when three engines and cars were pressed into service to help clear heavy traffic in connection with the annual athletic sports meeting at Fartown rugby football ground.[28]

To operate these additional routes forty-four new tramcars and one second-hand car (No. 67) were acquired from the British Electric Car Co. Ltd of Trafford Park, Manchester, the fleet then totalling seventy cars. The seating capacities of the new cars were fifty-one or fifty-five and they were of the single truck (four wheel) type which was found more suitable than the bogie (eight wheel) type for the steeply graded routes in the town. All electric trams purchased before 1903 were open topped, but the first experiments in top covering were carried out in November 1902. Huddersfield was in the forefront with this development, and the General Manager of Glasgow Corporation Tramways visited the town to inspect the cars so fitted up. The new cars built in 1902 and 1903 were painted in a new livery of Indian red and cream and this colour scheme was in due course applied to all the tramcars.

Fig. 16:3 Tramcar No. 6 working on the St. George's Square – Crosland Moor (Park Road) service in the first decade of the twentieth century. The white band on the traction pole on the left denotes a stopping place. (RBC)

Unique to Huddersfield was the carriage of coal to three commercial buyers whose mill premises were near the Outlane tram route. The coal was collected from the railway coal chutes at Hillhouse Goods Yard by two specially-built coal trams, numbered 71 and 72 (later 1 and 2), mounted on tramcar trucks which took their current in tram-like fashion from the overhead wire. Special sidings were laid to Oakes Mill, Wellington Mills, and Gosport Mills by the Corporation on behalf of the mill-owners.[29] This service was developed by Mr H.N. Thomas, Tramways Manager. Deliveries to Gosport Mills ceased in 1926 and to Wellington Mills in July 1933 but the service to Oakes Mill continued until 31 May 1934 when conversion of the Outlane tram route to trolleybus operation was imminent.

Mr Thomas was appointed Tramways Manager for Durban, South Africa in 1904. The new General Manager who took over was Mr R.H. Wilkinson, the former Manager of Oldham Corporation Tramways. He was to manage the Huddersfield system for the next fourteen years, during which time the annual car miles operated rose from 1,632,000 to 2,774,328 and the passengers carried from 10,192,000 to 32,389,732. The tramcar fleet was increased by the addition of thirty-six top covered cars (all built at Dick, Kerr Works, Preston by the United Electric Car Co. Ltd) the last ten arriving in the autumn of 1914. The further route extensions are set out in Table 5.

Table 5 Route extensions

Quarmby Clough to Longwood (Rose & Crown)	6 July	1904
Crosland Moor, Park Road to Dryclough Road	27 September	1907
Stile Common Road to Newsome Church	19 July	1911
Holly Bank Road to Green Style Farm, Birchencliffe	29 August	1911
Birchencliffe to Elland Town Hall	14 January	1914
Elland Town Hall to West Vale	30 May	1914
Slaithwaite Star Hotel to Marsden (Peel Street)	3 October	1914

Commencing in 1905 through tram services were introduced, each route being linked with another on the opposite side of town, with the exception of the Newsome route which remained self-contained. The dates of linking are given in Table 6.

When the tram service via Holly Bank Road to Lindley ceased upon the extension of the line along Halifax Road to Birchencliffe, the Birchencliffe trams continued to run through to Almondbury, but a new through service was started between Lindley and Moldgreen (the Junction Inn) via Marsh, the date of commencement of which appears to have escaped record.

Table 6 Timetable of commencement of through services.

Honley – Town – Sheepridge	10 December 1905
Longwood – Town – Birkby	10 December 1905
Outlane – Town – Waterloo	7 July 1907
Lindley – Edgerton – Town – Almondbury	7 July 1907
Slaithwaite – Town – Bradley	14 July 1907
Crosland Moor – Town – Brighouse	18 December 1933

Another fatal tramway accident, in which three people were killed,[30] occurred at Aspley on 28 June 1902 when tramcar number 40 ran away out of control in Somerset Road and crashed into a grocer's shop in Wakefield Road. This was the last accident involving fatalities during the electric tramway era, despite the difficult terrain in which the trams operated. Several other tramcars ran away down gradients but, after trials with various types of brake, the Department later adopted a slipper brake specially designed for Huddersfield by Mr Charles Henry Spencer, younger son of the Halifax Tramways manager, Mr F. Spencer. This mechanical brake comprised a malleable iron shoe 3 feet 3 inches long, fitted between the wheels on each side of the tram, which could be quickly applied to the rails in descending such gradients as Newsome Road, Blackmoorfoot Road, The Ainleys, Birkby Hall Road and Norman Avenue, thereby keeping the tram under perfect control.

On 27 May 1910 Huddersfield Corporation agreed to purchase for £4,000 the track owned by Linthwaite UDC between Pinfold Well and Slaithwaite, although it was in urgent need of renewal. The Corporation undertook to renew the rails and double the track; work started on 1 August 1910 under the control of Mr K. F. Campbell, Borough Engineer. The task of laying over three miles of double track and its associated paving with granite setts was accomplished in two months and four days, no mean achievement.

In common with all other tramway operators, Huddersfield had to contend with great difficulties during the First World War. Tramway motormen (as the drivers were known), conductors and maintenance staff

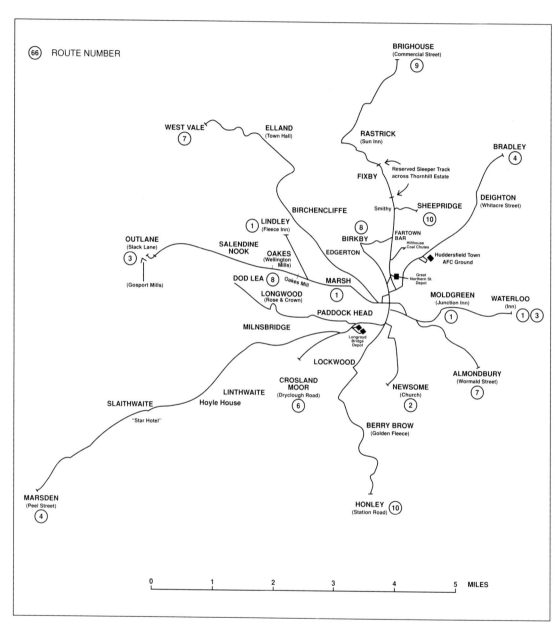

(66) ROUTE NUMBER

BRIGHOUSE
(Commercial Street)
(9)

WEST VALE
(7)

ELLAND
(Town Hall)

RASTRICK
(Sun Inn)

BRADLEY
(4)

FIXBY

Reserved Sleeper Track
across Thornhill Estate

DEIGHTON
(Whitacre Street)

BIRCHENCLIFFE

Smithy

SHEEPRIDGE
(10)

LINDLEY
(Fleece Inn)
(1)

OUTLANE
(Slack Lane)
(3)

SALENDINE
NOOK

OAKES
(Wellington
Mills)

BIRKBY
(8)

EDGERTON

FARTOWN
BAR
Hillhouse
Coal Chutes

Huddersfield Town
AFC Ground

(Gosport Mills)

DOD LEA (8)

Oakes Mill

MARSH
(1)

Great
Northern St.
Depot

MOLDGREEN
(Junction Inn)

WATERLOO
(Inn)
(1)(3)

LONGWOOD
(Rose & Crown)

PADDOCK HEAD

(1)

MILNSBRIDGE

Longroyd
Bridge
Depot

LOCKWOOD

ALMONDBURY
(Wormald Street)
(7)

CROSLAND
MOOR
(Dryclough Road)
(6)

NEWSOME
(Church)
(2)

SLAITHWAITE

LINTHWAITE
Hoyle House

"Star Hotel"

BERRY BROW
(Golden Fleece)

MARSDEN
(Peel Street)
(4)

HONLEY
(Station Road)
(10)

0   1   2   3   4   5   MILES

Fig. 16:4 Huddersfield Corporation tramways electric tram routes at maximum extent 1923.

Fig. 16:5 Tramcar No. 19 at Longwood terminus (c.1906). It is shown here after having been recently fitted with a top cover. (RBC)

were called up to serve in the forces. Women were recruited to act as conductors until 1919, but were never employed to drive trams in view of the arduous conditions found on most local routes. Maintenance of vehicles and track could not continue in the normal manner and arrears had to be made up when peacetime conditions returned.

Table 7 Route numbers and routes.

Route No.

1 Lindley – Moldgreen (later Waterloo)	7 West Vale – Almondbury
2 Newsome	8 Longwood (later Dod Lea) – Birkby
3 Outlane – Waterloo	9 Brighouse (from 12 March 1923)
4 Marsden – Bradley	10 Honley – Sheepridge
6 Crosland Moor	

*Fig. 16:6 Tramcar
No. 29 after being top
covered, in Imperial Road
loop around 1909. The
tram shelter on the right
still stands on the same site
which it has occupied since
the 1890s. (WYAS, K)*

In October 1918 Mr Wilkinson left Huddersfield to assume managership of the neighbouring Bradford undertaking and was succeeded by Dewsbury-born Albert A. Blackburn, former Tramways Chief Engineer in Belfast.

On 31 October 1918 the Tramways Committee relinquished control of Longroyd Bridge Power Station to the Corporation Electricity Department, who continued to generate traction current there until 1923, after which the Power Station in St. Andrew's Road supplied all the Tramways Department's needs.

In order to allow Great Northern Street Depot to be used exclusively as a works for the repair and building of tramcars, a new car shed was built in reinforced concrete in St. Thomas' Road, Longroyd Bridge, adjacent to the 1901 Depot and Power Station. It provided accommodation for 100 tramcars and was opened on 15 July 1921.[31]

As conditions improved, work started on two new route extensions, from the Rose & Crown, Longwood to Dod Lea (opened on 1 April 1920) and that from Smithy, on the Sheepridge route, to Brighouse. Although Huddersfield

Fig. 16:7 Wakefield
Road, Dalton, c.1927 after
road widening in 1924
and modernisation of the
Waterloo tram route with
new double track and
traction poles, which later
continued to support
trolleybus wires for
many years. (WYAS, K)

Fig. 16:8 The
Almondbury tram route
in Somerset Road at the
junction with Dog Kennel
Bank, showing tramcars
passing on a loop on a
single track and loop line.
The tramcar on the left
(No. 42) had been rebuilt
to all-enclosed form; it was
originally an open top car.
(WYAS, K)

407

Corporation was authorised under its Tramways Act of 1900 to build a route to Brighouse, which was to run via Birchencliffe, Fixby and Rastrick, the line was not built. However, under an agreement made in 1914 with Brighouse Corporation, a more direct route via Bradford Road and Rastrick was envisaged. The First World War delayed this development but in 1919 Huddersfield Corporation promoted a Bill in Parliament which resulted in the passing of the Huddersfield Corporation (General Powers) Act, 1920. The main lines authorised in this Act were the line to Brighouse (including the three-quarter mile stretch of double sleeper track across Thornhill Estate land at Fixby); the tracks leading to the new Longroyd Bridge Car Shed and a line via St. Thomas' Road to Folly Hall, which was never laid.

The Brighouse tram service opened on 12 March 1923 with great ceremony, involving officials of both Huddersfield and Brighouse Corporations; a special illuminated tramcar (No. 78) performed the opening and all fares collected were divided equally between Huddersfield Royal Infirmary and a charity chosen by the Mayor of Brighouse. Like the Marsden and West Vale tram routes, the ride to Brighouse proved to be very popular for the hundreds of people who enjoyed a trip by tramcar at weekends and Bank Holidays. On such occasions the service frequency was often increased to cater for the crowds of intending passengers.[32]

The post-war additions to the tramcar fleet from 1919 to 1932 consisted of thirty-eight cars built at Preston by the English Electric Company Ltd., eighteen of which were to an all-enclosed design. The final eight, designed by Mr Blackburn, were outstanding vehicles, painted in a new livery of Post Office red and cream, fully upholstered throughout and equipped with air-braking on both wheel and track, with two 50 h.p. motors each. They were used on the Bradley to Marsden through service usually and were the subject of much praise in the technical and local press of the day. One spokesman at the trial run of Car 138 on 20 August 1931 declared that the new Huddersfield cars were equal, if not superior, to the latest cars in Sheffield, Leeds or Birmingham![33]

Between 1920 and 1924 the tramway system recovered from the arrears in maintenance caused by the Great War and track doubling was undertaken from Hillhouse Lane to Fartown Bar, Moldgreen to Waterloo, and from Ashgrove Road to Bradley. Another improvement, opened on 25 August 1923, was the provision of a loop line for the parking of football special trams on

Fig. 16:9 Halifax Road, Birchencliffe c.1912-14 showing a tramcar en route for Elland. This extension was opened on 29 August 1911. The feeder cables supplying current to the overhead wires from the roadside section box can be seen. (WYAS, K)

the occasion of football matches at Huddersfield Town AFC ground in Leeds Road. This was the last extension made and the route mileage then totalled 38.16 miles.

Trolleybuses 1933-1968

During the latter part of the 1920s and up to 1933, track renewals were made on the Birkby route, in Leeds Road, Bradford Road, Lockwood Road, Manchester Road and Northumberland Street, but the cost of this work was becoming increasingly expensive. Early in 1932 the Tramways Committee considered the renewal of the single track and loop layout from the Lyceum

Cinema at Aspley to Almondbury, just over one mile in length. Here the margins of Somerset Road between the outer rails and pavements also needed total reconstruction and the cost involved was estimated at £13,000 for trackwork alone, in addition to the cost of the margins; the Committee decided in favour of tramcar abandonment and replacement by trolleybuses.[34]

A meeting was convened in London on 11 February 1932 between officals of the Corporation and the Ministry of Transport. The Corporation's parliamentary agents, Messrs Sharpe, Pritchard & Co., advised that the quickest way of obtaining powers would be under the Public Works Facilities Act, 1930 which had been enacted to allow local authorities to execute works which would contribute to the relief of unemployment. A suitable scheme was prepared and rushed through its stages to emerge with the Royal Assent on 22 December 1932. At the same time, work started on track removal at Almondbury, trams running to the railhead, until this had been moved back to Rookery Road. On 16 April 1933 the Almondbury trams were completely withdrawn. A motor bus service using vehicles hired from Huddersfield Joint Omnibus Committee ran from Byram Street to Almondbury via Almondbury Bank from 5 December 1932 until trolleybus wiring was erected and Somerset Road reconstructed.[35]

Mr A.A. Blackburn, the Tramways General Manager, retired in April 1933 and was succeeded by Mr H.C. Godsmark, formerly Deputy General Manager with Nottingham Corporation Transport Department. In transport circles Mr Godsmark was well-known as a trolleybus advocate and it is therefore not surprising that when the matter of track reconstruction in Trinity Street, Westbourne Road, and New Hey Road was discussed in June 1933, Mr Godsmark made his views known and the Tramways Committee decided on the cheaper alternative, to replace trams on the Outlane, Lindley and Waterloo routes with trolleybuses. Mr Godsmark's estimate of the cost of tramway modernisation, with new cars and the doubling of the existing single track from the Bay Horse to Salendine Nook and to Lindley, was £57,410, whereas trolleybus replacement would cost only £35,568.

Meanwhile, on 4 December 1933, Huddersfield's first trolleybus route between Byram Street and Almondbury was ceremonially opened, following Ministry of Transport inspection and approval. Six new double-deck three-axle trolleybuses entered service; they were painted predominantly in Post

Office red with cream bands edged in black, but with lower saloon panels in maroon. They provided a basic twelve-minute service with six minute frequency at peak periods.

Sunday morning tramcar and trolleybus services were introduced experimentally on Easter Sunday, 1 April, 1934. The frequency was half-hourly and they were an immediate success and in due course made permanent. Services were provided on all routes but the through services were different from those operated normally and no service was provided between Elland Town Hall and West Vale.

To put the Outlane, Lindley and Waterloo trolleybus conversions into effect a scheme similar to that used for Almondbury was drawn up and powers granted by Royal Assent on 28 March 1934. After the erection of trolleybus wiring, the last trams ran on Saturday 10 November 1934. Trolleybus services commenced the following day between Outlane and Waterloo and Lindley and Waterloo with additional Saturday and weekday peak hour buses between Marsh (the Bay Horse) and Moldgreen (Grosvenor

Fig. 16:10 Great Northern Street, 1940. Trolleybus No. 18, a Brush-bodied Karrier E6 built 1934 for the Outlane, Lindley and Waterloo routes. The buildings behind constitute Beaumont Street Schools. (RBC)

Road). Very frequent services were operated on these routes and the trolleybus became a popular vehicle from the passengers' viewpoint. Twenty-four Karrier E6 sixty-four seat trolleybuses were acquired to operate these routes, twelve having bodies by the Brush Electrical Engineering Co. Ltd. and twelve by Park Royal Coachworks Ltd. The trolleybus, having been thus established on three routes, was soon regarded as a satisfactory replacement for the tramcar and the Tramways Committee decided at its April 1935 meeting to convert all the tram routes, concentrating initially on short routes with a high proportion of single track. Newsome and Crosland Moor fell into this category and they were chosen for the first conversions.

Parliamentary procedures for abandonment were set in motion and on 14 July 1936 the Huddersfield Corporation (Trolley Vehicles) Act, 1936 received Royal Assent. Authority was given for total conversion to trolleybuses, with some routes being extended (Table 8).

Table 8 Route extensions, 1936.

Newsome tram terminus to junction of Newsome Road South and Caldercliffe Road. (Including a diversion via Colne Road.)

Crosland Moor tram terminus to Crosland Hill.

Fartown Bar via Fartown Green and Woodhouse Hill to Sheepridge.

Diversionary route for Brighouse trolleybuses via Bradford Road, Bradley Bar and Bradley Road (now Fixby Road) to avoid the Fixby tramcar sleeper track.

The erection of new overhead wiring, including replacement of traction poles necessary to support the added weight of trolleybus wires, was carried out by the Department's own Overhead Line Section, except on the Marsden route from the Griffin Inn and the Bradley route from the top of Northumberland Street, which were sub-contracted to Clough, Smith & Co. Ltd of Westminster.

Following the closure of the Marsden tram route on 9 April 1938, the eight newest tramcars were sold to Sunderland Corporation for £225 each. They served the Wearside town for another sixteen years.

The general conversion took three years from the closure of the Newsome route on 1 May 1937 to the running of Huddersfield's ceremonial last tram to Brighouse on 29 June 1940. Wartime conditions and the black-out during the summer of 1940 did not permit the end of the tramway era to be commemorated in the lavish manner accorded to trolleybuses twenty-eight years later.

A further 110 new trolleybuses, all with Karrier E6 chassis, ten with bodywork by Brush, eleven with Weymann bodywork, and eighty-nine with Park Royal bodywork, were acquired for the general conversion, and all, with the exception of No. 31, were of outwardly similar appearance.

All 110 were fitted with the braking systems prescribed by the Ministry of Transport for certain steep gradients, namely the coasting brake, which, when in use, limited the downhill speed to 15 mph, and the runback brake, which automatically prevented a bus running backwards at more than 2 mph unless, of course, deliberately reversing. Huddersfield with its steep gradients (up to 1 in 8.3) was Britain's largest fleet so equipped.

A large new depot to accommodate the new fleet of 140 trolleybuses was built during 1937-38, using the site of the original tramway depot of 1901, the former Power Station and the 1921 extension, which alone held 100 trams.

Tramway closure dates for the remaining routes are shown in Table 9.

Fig. 16:11 Longroyd Bridge trolleybus depot as new on 21 June 1938. The building occupies a site where formerly the old 1901 Tram Depot and Tramway Power Station stood. (WYAS, K)

Table 9 Tramway closure dates.

Crosland Moor	2 October	1937
Birkby	3 October	1937
Marsden	9 April	1938
Sheepridge	18 June	1938
Bradley (a)	20 April	1938
Deighton (Whitacre Street)	18 June	1938
Dod Lea	25 September	1938
Honley (b)	19 February	1939
West Vale	27 May	1939
Brighouse	29 June	1940

(a)   The last tram to Bradley ran on 20 April 1938. From 21 April 1938, to allow the road surface under the bridge carrying the Kirkburton Branch Railway Line over Leeds Road to be lowered to give adequate headroom for trolleybuses, the tramcar service along Leeds Road was terminated at Whitacre Street, where a crossover existed. Passengers had to change, and were conveyed to and from Bradley by single-deck motor buses hired from the Joint Omnibus Committee.

(b)   The Honley trams were only replaced by trolleybuses as far as Lockwood Church, as the limited clearance under the stone-arched railway bridge in Woodhead Road precluded the operation of double-deck trolleybuses. Honley was therefore served by existing Huddersfield Joint Omnibus Committee motor buses on Holme valley routes, the service being supplemented at peak periods.

The General Manager, Mr Godsmark left Huddersfield in March 1941 on being appointed to the managership of the Newcastle-upon-Tyne Transport undertaking; he was succeeded by Mr Harold Muscroft, a Yorkshireman, born at Thornhill, who had received his early training at Bradford, where his trolleybus experience eminently qualified him to fill the Huddersfield vacancy.

The trolleybus livery was modified during the summer of 1941 to become all-over Post Office red with cream bands, and in the following year the fleet was renumbered by adding 400 to each fleet number, trolleybus 1 became 401 and so on. The drab wartime liveries seen in some towns and cities were never applied to Huddersfield trolleybuses, and, considering the many restrictions imposed, the trolleybus fleet emerged from the Second World War intact, apart from the loss of the body of the original No. 28, which was burnt out in a fire in Trinity Street during thick fog on 6 January 1940 and consequently received a new Park Royal body.[36] The Karriers successfully weathered six years of war, including the winter of 1940 with 35 degrees of frost at Outlane, and snow on the roads which remained compacted for many weeks. The 1947 winter was not much better and these vehicles still had to persevere. Fleet replacement began during the summer of 1947 and between then and 1949 fifty-two new seventy-seater Sunbeam trolleybuses were purchased, thereby allowing pre-war vehicles to be withdrawn from service. Twelve of these, the Brush bodied Karriers of 1934, were sold to Reading Corporation, where six were placed in service after being reconditioned, the remainder being used as a source for spare parts.

On 27 March 1949 Huddersfield passengers faced their first all-round fare increase for almost thirty years when trolleybus fares were advanced by ½d. or 1d., according to distance travelled. The stable economy of the inter-war years allowed fares to remain static, but they have been subject to regular increases since. During the financial year ended 31 March 1949 Huddersfield trolleybuses carried 61,255,937 passengers, the highest number in their period of service.

Post-war trolleybus route extensions were made into the housing estates at Riddings and Brackenhall; services commenced on 6 March 1949 followed by the extension, on 2 April 1956 (Easter Monday), into the post-war estate adjacent to the Bradley route at Keldregate. Significantly, this was the first day on which Workmen's Return tickets were not available, the previous Saturday having been the last day of issue. The Keldregate extension proved to be the last one made in Huddersfield.

Between 1950 and 1957 thirty-eight further new trolleybuses entered service, fourteen of which were seventy-seater Sunbeams, and the rest seventy-two seaters of British United Traction manufacture. They were followed in 1959 by the last ten, which were seventy-two seater Sunbeams, and in fact the last three-axle trolleybuses built for service in the UK. A programme of re-bodying older vehicles began in 1949, giving the sixty-nine buses involved an added ten to twelve years of life.

As early as 1951 Mr Muscroft had recommended that the Brighouse service beyond the Fixby reverser should be abandoned,[37] providing that the Joint Omnibus Committee would supplement their existing motor bus service to Brighouse via Cowcliffe and Rastrick. This service was finally withdrawn after Saturday 9 July 1955,[38] despite much opposition from passengers in the Brighouse area, who in future would be faced with the higher scale of fares charged on the Joint Omnibus Committee services.

Mr Muscroft retired as General Manager in April 1958 and his replacement was Mr Edgar V. Dyson, former General Manager at Warrington. Born locally, Mr Dyson had commenced his transport career with Huddersfield Corporation Tramways in 1924.

During the early 1960s the trolleybus was found to be in the same situation as the tramcar had been thirty years earlier. The cost of renewal of overhead equipment and new vehicles had increased substantially, as had the price of electricity, together making trolleybus operation uneconomic. In April 1960 a proposal was made to replace trolleybuses on the West Vale, Marsden and Fixby routes; they ceased running to West Vale on Wednesday 8 November 1961 and were replaced by Huddersfield Corporation motor

Fig. 16:12 New Hey Road, Rastrick, near the Sun Inn on 9 July 1955, the last day of operation of trolleybuses on the portion of route between Lightridge Road, Fixby and Brighouse. The trolleybus is an East Lancs. re-bodied Sunbeam MS2. (RBC)

buses, the first such vehicles operated solely by the Corporation since 1930, when its motor buses were transferred to the newly formed Joint Omnibus Committee.

After a lengthy Council debate in October 1962, the decision was taken by a narrow margin of one vote to change over completely to motor bus operation.[39] Table 10 gives the dates on which trolleybus services were gradually withdrawn.

Table 10 Timetable of withdrawal of trolleybus services.

Marsden	30 January	1963
Birkby – Crosland Hill	5 February	1964
Almondbury – Fixby	14 July	1965
Riddings – Newsome South	13 July	1966
Brackenhall – Lockwood	13 July	1966
Bradley – Longwood	12 July	1967
Waterloo – Outlane	13 July	1968
Waterloo – Lindley	13 July	1968

Fig. 16:13 Thornhill Road, Longwood, 1966, conveying the village atmosphere of this hillside community. The old tram track formation can still be discerned from the sett pattern in the road. (RBC)

On 13 July 1968 the public of Huddersfield gathered in their hundreds to witness the end of an era, and for many, a lifetime's association with the trolleybus. The previous week, 7 to 13 July, had been labelled 'Last Trolleybus Week'; souvenir tickets had been issued, a brochure entitled *The Era of Electric Traction 1901 to 1968* was published by the Department, and a decorated and illuminated trolleybus (No. 623) ran in public service throughout the week. It was also used as the last civic trolleybus and conveyed municipal and departmental officials and their guests on the final return journey from Westgate to Waterloo and Outlane at 2.30 p.m. on Saturday 13 July 1968. The last trolleybus to carry members of the public (and the penultimate vehicle in the procession of five) was No. 629, which made the final journey to Longroyd Bridge Depot after returning from Outlane.[40]

In their hey-day in Huddersfield the trolleybuses were synonymous with frequent services, safe and silent travel, fume-free speedy journeys (especially uphill) and, above all, low fares. Their hill-climbing capabilities made them the ideal vehicle for Huddersfield's steep gradients. With the post-war route extensions between 1949 and 1956 in the Sheepridge and Bradley areas, the maximum street mileage of trolleybus routes totalled 4.36 miles of single and 38.08 miles of double track.

The Huddersfield trolleybus system* was recognised as one of the leading undertakings of its type in the British Isles and both in the tramcar and trolleybus eras Huddersfield was regarded by many as a first class training ground, and many Huddersfield men became successful candidates for managerial positions in other authorities.

---

*Discussion of the part played by the transport system in the expansion of Huddersfield may be found in Chapters Thirteen and Eighteen. EDITOR.

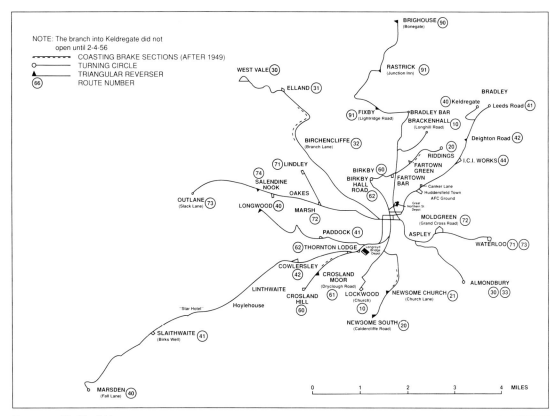

NOTE: The branch into Keldregate did not
open until 2-4-56

- - - - - - COASTING BRAKE SECTIONS (AFTER 1949)
○——— TURNING CIRCLE
▲ TRIANGULAR REVERSER
(66) ROUTE NUMBER

*Fig. 16:14 Huddersfield
Corporation trolley buses at
maximum extent 1955.*

Roy Brook

Biographical Note

Roy Brook was born and educated in Huddersfield. Upon leaving school he
obtained employment in the accountancy profession and studied commercial
subjects at Huddersfield Technical College. During the 1939/45 war he served
in the RASC and Royal Signal Regiment for a total of almost five years and upon
demobilisation returned to his pre-war occupation. It was at this time in the early
post-war years that he decided to carry out research into the history of passenger
transport in Huddersfield having had a very keen interest in tramways and
trolleybuses from boyhood. This was undoubtedly inherited from his father,
Herbert Brook, who spent his entire working life from 1905 to 1954 in the
Corporation Transport Department. This work has culminated in the
publication in recent years of detailed accounts of this aspect of the town's
history. Previous publications include *The Tramways of Huddersfield* (1959); *The
Trolleybuses of Huddersfield* (1976); *Huddersfield Corporation Tramways* (1983), *100
Years of Public Transport in Huddersfield* (1883-1983): *A Pictorial History* (Souvenir
Brochure published by West Yorkshire Passenger Transport Executive to
commemorate the 1983 Tramway Centenary).

ACKNOWLEDGEMENTS AND SOURCES

This account of the history of Huddersfield's steam and electric trams and trolleybuses has been abridged from the author's detailed histories *Huddersfield Corporation Tramways* (1983) and *The Trolleybuses of Huddersfield* (1976).

The author's interest in this subject dates back to 1930 and events since that date are from first-hand knowledge. Original research has been carried out since 1950 using Deposited Plans and Sections for each Tramways Bill, preserved copies of the *Huddersfield Chronicle, Huddersfield Examiner, Colne Valley Guardian,* Huddersfield Corporation Tramways Committee Minutes, departmental books and records held by West Yorkshire Archive Service at Leeds, Huddersfield and Wakefield, the MT 6 files of the Railway Inspectorate of the former Board of Trade at the Public Record Office, Kew, and bound volumes of *Tramway and Railway World* and *Light Railway and Tramway Journal* together with the annual issues of *Garcke's Manual of Electrical Undertakings.*

Thanks are also due to the Institutions of Civil, Electrical and Mechanical Engineers for their assistance.

NOTES

1. W(est) Y(orkshire) A(rchive) S(ervice), Wakefield, Tramways Bill 1877.

2. WYAS, Kirklees, Huddersfield B(orough) C(ouncil) General Purposes Committee Minutes, 18 December 1877.

3. WYAS, Kirklees, Huddersfield BC General Purposes Committee (Book 46) Minutes, 4 February 1878.

4. WYAS, Kirklees, Huddersfield BC General Purposes Committee Minutes, 19 September 1882 and Huddersfield BC Tramways Sub-Committee Minutes, 20 October 1882.

5. WYAS, Kirklees, Huddersfield BC Tramways Sub-Committee Minutes, 15 November 1882. *Huddersfield (Weekly) Examiner,* 18 November 1882.

6. *Huddersfield (Weekly) Examiner,* 2 December 1882.

7. WYAS, Kirklees, Huddersfield BC Tramways Sub-Committee Minutes, 3 January 1883.

8. *Huddersfield (Weekly) Examiner,* 13 January 1883.

9. WYAS, Kirklees, Huddersfield BC General Purposes Committee Book 'D' Minutes, 24 January 1883.

10. WYAS, Kirklees, Huddersfield BC Tramways Sub-Committee Minutes, 1 December 1882.

11. WYAS, Kirklees, Huddersfield BC Tramways Sub-Committee Minutes, 1 December 1882.

12. WYAS, Kirklees, Huddersfield BC Tramways Sub-Committee Minutes, 14 February 1883.

13. WYAS, Kirklees, Huddersfield BC Tramways Fund - Ledger 'A' Plant and Rolling Stock Account, 12 March 1883.

14. WYAS, Kirklees, Huddersfield BC Tramways Sub-Committee. Various entries January and February 1883. Abandonment by Hallidie Patent Cable Tramways Co. Ltd Book 'D' General Purposes Committee Book 'D' Minutes, 30 July 1884 and Tramways Sub-Committee Book 'E' Minutes, 20 October 1884.

15. WYAS, Kirklees, Huddersfield BC Tramways Sub-Committee Book 'E' Minutes, 22 June 1885.

16. H(uddersfield) L(ocal) H(istory) L(ibrary), Huddersfield C(ounty) B(orough) C(ouncil) printed Minutes Tramways Committee, 27 February 1891.

17. HLHL, Huddersfield CBC printed Minutes Tramways Committee, 25 April 1890.

18. HLHL, Huddersfield CBC printed Minutes Tramways Committee, 14 December 1892, 8 February 1893. *Huddersfield (Weekly) Examiner*, 25 March 1893.

19. Linthwaite Tramways Order 1898. Both orders confirmed by the Tramways Orders Confirmation (No. 2) Act 1898 61 and 62 Vict. c.ccii.

20. Huddersfield Corporation Tramways Order 1898.

21. Departmental Time Tables.

22. WYAS, Kirklees, Huddersfield CBC Tramways Sub-Committee Minutes, 4 and 25 July 1883. *Huddersfield (Weekly) Examiner*, 7 July 1883, Report of Accident; 14 July 1883, Inquest; 21 July 1883, Inquest; 28 July 1883, Inquest.

23. *Huddersfield (Weekly) Examiner*, 6 June 1891, Report of Accident. Board of Trade Official Report on Accident with pages 1159-1169, WYAS, Kirklees Huddersfield CBC Tramways Committee Minutes 1890-91.

24. Reports on Tramway Electrification by K. F. Campbell, Esq C.E. Borough Engineer and Surveyor, December 1898: J. Pogson, Esq M.I.M.E. Tramways Engineer and Manager, 1 July 1898: A. B. Mountain, Esq M.I.E.E. Borough Electrical Engineer, n.d.

25. *Huddersfield (Weekly) Examiner*, 17 February 1900. The foundation stone of the power station was removed on demolition and built into the wall of the new trolleybus depot at Longroyd Bridge, 1938.

26. *Tramway and Railway World*, 7 March 1901, *Huddersfield (Weekly) Examiner*, 9 and 16 February 1901.

27. *Huddersfield Examiner*, 15 June 1901.

28. *Huddersfield (Weekly) Examiner*, 28 June 1902.

29. *Tramway and Railway World*, 13 October 1904. *Huddersfield Weekly Chronicle*, 3 September 1904. *Huddersfield (Weekly) Examiner*, 3 September 1904.

30.   *Huddersfield (Weekly) Examiner*, Report on Accident 5 July 1902; Inquest 12 July 1902; Board of Trade inquiry 19 July 1902.

31.   *Huddersfield (Weekly) Examiner*, 16 July 1921. *Tramway and Railway World*, 18 August 1921. WYAS, Kirklees, Huddersfield CBC Borough Engineer's correspondence Ref No. 4170. HLHL, Huddersfield CBC Tramways Committee Minutes, 11 July 1921.

32.   *Huddersfield (Weekly) Examiner*, 17 March 1923.

33.   *Huddersfield (Weekly) Examiner*, 21 August 1931. *Tramway and Railway World*, 15 October 1931.

34.   HLHL, Huddersfield CBC Tramways Committee Minutes, 5 January 1932.

35.   Departmental Traffic Notice.

36.   *Huddersfield Daily Examiner*, 6 January 1940.

37.   HLHL, Huddersfield CBC Passenger Transport Committee Minutes, 19 February 1951.

38.   HLHL, Huddersfield CBC Passenger Transport Committee Minutes, 11 July 1955.

39.   *Huddersfield Daily Examiner*, 26 September 1962, 29 September 1962 and 4 October 1962.

40.   *Huddersfield Daily Examiner*, *Yorkshire Post*, 15 July 1968.

CHAPTER 17

The Social Geography
of Victorian Huddersfield

RICHARD DENNIS

When government commissioners examined proposals for the parliamentary borough of Huddersfield in 1832, they advised that its boundaries should be identical to those of the existing Huddersfield township: entirely to the north and west of the River Colne, and excluding the villages of 'Mould Green' and Lockwood.* They concluded that both these settlements, although connected to the town by continuous rows of houses, were still distinct and separate places. Moldgreen was also excluded because of the low value of its houses – perhaps they feared that if the parliamentary borough ever became a municipal borough the village would be a drain on the borough's resources, contributing little in terms of rate revenue, but requiring much in cleansing and the provision of basic services; whereas Lockwood was not only distinct from Huddersfield but was excluded because it had 'interests of its own', recognised by the inhabitants of both places.[1]

Thirty-five years later, on the eve of incorporation, a further report concluded that Lockwood was now 'a continuation of the Town. Land in the Township is rapidly being taken up for building purposes. The town delivery of letters extends into the district, which is supplied with gas and water from Huddersfield, and the pursuits and employments of the inhabitants are identical with those of the Town Population'. Likewise in Dalton, including Moldgreen, 'the occupations of the inhabitants are identical with those of the Town Population', while Lindley, which had not even merited

* A map showing the proposed boundaries may be found in Chapter Nineteen. EDITOR.

*Fig. 17:1 Trevelyan
Street, Moldgreen. (KCS)*

consideration in 1832, was now intimately connected to the town, and
its newly constructed villas were occupied by Huddersfield merchants
and traders.[2]

No doubt the change in perception was a matter of political strategy on
the part of those the boundary commissioners consulted as much as it was a
consequence of the town's physical expansion. But it also reflected a
profound change in social geography: the integration of a number of
disparate and relatively self-contained industrial villages into an emerging
town with distinctive social areas – such as the concentration of merchants
and traders in Lindley, contrasting with districts of a more solidly working-
class or lower middle-class status – linked together by a developing public
transport system, by the distribution of utilities such as gas and water, and by
central institutions such as the Mechanics' Institution and the Huddersfield
Industrial Society, with its growing number of branch co-operative stores.[3]

Of course, the process was not an overnight replacement of local 'communities' by the zones and sectors of uniform land use and social class that feature so prominently in the theories of modern urban geographers and planners. Nor was the change as negative as a transition from 'community' to 'segregation' has often been depicted – for example, by contemporary writers such as Disraeli, who lamented the absence of personal relations between employers and their employees in the new factory towns, and urged the development of planned industrial villages where employers could exercise a benign paternalism over their workforce.[4] Certainly, the self-contained, unplanned industrial village of the early nineteenth century was often insanitary and squalid in its built environment, and feudal and deferential in its social structure. Consider the observations of the radical educator, G.S. Phillips, in his *Walks round Huddersfield* (1848):

> Of all the sights one meets with in the manufacturing districts, the houses of the mechanics and factory workers are the most distressing. They seem to have been erected after no model; with no design after beauty; but piled together in savage haste, and contempt for the beings destined to dwell in them. This is literally true of the houses in Longley village. . . .[5]

Phillips went on to note how 'every factory master is a sort of feudal lord. He has *his* village struggling at the foot of his factory keep. . .'.[6]

But from the middle of the nineteenth century onwards, most new development took the form of one-class suburbs – Edgerton for the élite, Hillhouse for the lower middle class, Rashcliffe and Moldgreen for the working classes – with the poorest households confined to courts and yards sandwiched between main streets in the town centre. These new social areas could equally well function as 'communities': communities of choice and common interest, as in Hillhouse, where respectable clerks, tradesmen and master manufacturers shared similar political and religious attitudes; or communities of crisis, so-called 'mutualities of the oppressed',[7] as in Irish courts off Castlegate, where the poor were thrown back upon each other's resources during times of sickness, bereavement and unemployment.

Early nineteenth-century industrial villages were not all factory based. Many were collections of handloom weavers' cottages, where there was not even the deferential personal relationship between operative and master. Thus, S. Keyser on the handloom weavers of the West Riding:

> The moral condition of the weavers in general differs materially from that of other working classes; they are in a manner excluded from intercourse with society. Days and weeks pass over without a communication with any but their neighbouring fellow workman or the foreman of a warehouse. . . . neither the force of example, nor any other cause operating as a stimulus to improvement. . . .[8]

In these circumstances, the advent of factory employment offered both the potential for surveillance – 'the habits of a number of men working together at regular hours, under the eye of a master, must be improved' – and a stimulus to education and mutual improvement.[9]

The aim of this chapter is to illustrate the changing social geography of Huddersfield during the second half of the nineteenth century, and particularly the emergence of a new pattern of residential segregation, examining first some town-wide social indicators of wealth and poverty, then exploring in more detail the contrasts between two new social areas of the town, one respectably lower middle-class (the Thornhill estate in Hillhouse), the other substantially working-class (part of Moldgreen). Particular attention will be paid to the operation of the housing market in these two areas, and to the fluidity of population movement that lay beneath a seemingly stable and unchanging residential pattern.

The primary sources for reconstructing social patterns are the manuscript census enumerators' books, which record the name, address, age, marital status, occupation and birthplace of every resident of the town, at ten-year intervals from 1841 onwards.[10] The books are subject to a 100-year confidentiality rule so that when the research for this chapter was undertaken, the most recent census open to the public was that for 1881. Other more or less partial listings of the population are included in town directories, which recorded occupations but concentrated on middle-class or self-employed adult males, and ratebooks which listed the owner, occupier and rateable value of each property.[11] Indicators of lifestyle, behaviour and beliefs include marriage registers, from which we can reconstruct geographical and occupational patterns of marriage, pollbooks which, prior to the Secret Ballot Act of 1872, recorded how electors cast their votes, and the membership registers of churches and voluntary societies. By linking records through time, for example tracing names in successive directories or censuses, we can also see how individuals moved house or changed occupations as they progressed through the life cycle.[12]

One index of status was the distribution of households with resident domestic servants. Figure 17:2 shows the proportion of such households in each census enumeration district in 1851.[13] Within the five townships that became the borough in 1868, approximately 11 per cent of households employed at least one resident domestic servant. The map identifies districts in which the proportion exceeded this borough-wide average. Servant-keeping families were most common in and around New North Road and Trinity Street, in older middle-class streets around St. Paul's Church between the town centre and the canal, and around the Market Place, the latter no doubt reflecting the proliferation of inns and hotels. In one enumeration district including Edgerton and Belgrave Terrace, 62 per cent of households included at least one resident servant. By 1861 the overall proportion of households with servants had declined to about 9.5 per cent, indicative of the growth of a servantless, factory-employed working class, but in Edgerton the proportion of households with servants had increased to 72 per cent. Evidently, the pattern was becoming more polarised, especially as professional families abandoned their town-centre homes, or converted them into offices, moving their families to villas in Greenhead, Edgerton and Marsh.[14] Fewer town-centre tradesmen now lived over or behind their shops; rather it became their ambition to 'live away from business'[15] in new suburban streets, as on the

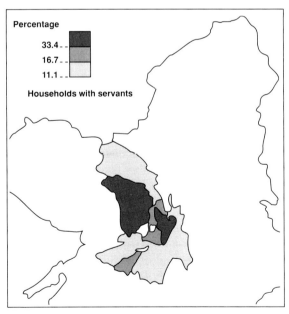

Fig. 17:2 The distribution of Huddersfield households with domestic servants, 1851 (plotted by census enumeration districts) (from R. Dennis, English Industrial Cities of the Nineteenth Century (Cambridge, 1984), p.216; by permission of Cambridge University Press).

Percentage

33.4 _ _

16.7 _ _

11.1 _ _

Households with servants

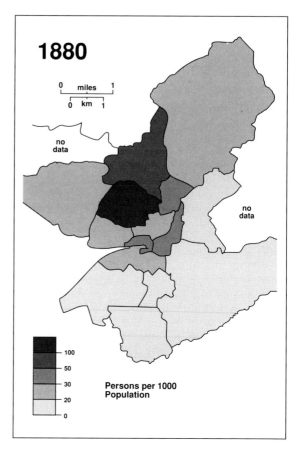

Fig. 17:3 The distribution of entries in the 'court' section of Kelly's Directory, 1881, shows the concentrations of Huddersfield's élite.

Thornhill Estate in Hillhouse. Even in 1880 there was a remnant of high-status families in the streets around St. Paul's Church but, as the distribution of persons whose names appeared in the 'court' section of Kelly's *Directory* reveals, the majority of Huddersfield's élite were now concentrated in Fartown and Woodhouse and along Halifax Old Road, in Highfield and Edgerton, Trinity Street and Greenhead, and in smaller outliers, for example on Primrose Hill (Figure 17:3).[16]

At the other extreme of social status were the majority of Irish migrants, who arrived in large numbers from the 1820s onwards and particularly in the wake of the great famine of the mid-1840s. In 1851 there were 1,688 persons born in Ireland enumerated in the five townships, almost all of whom lived in the central township where they comprised over 5 per cent of the total population. The most intense concentrations of Irish were in courts on either side of Castlegate, including Windsor Court, Post Office Yard and Boulder's Yard, and at the southern end of Upperhead Row, including Jowitt Square and Water Lane, just east of Manchester Street, and part of Swallow Street,

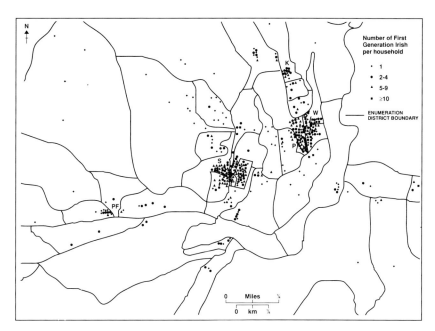

notably O'Connor's Yard, which was almost exclusively Irish (Figure 17:4).
New arrivals frequently found temporary shelter in Irish-run lodging houses,
as in Makin's Yard, off Water Gate, where a family of four, all Irish, ran a
lodging house in which sixteen lodgers, also all Irish-born, were enumerated

Fig. 17:5 Water Lane,
just east of Manchester
Street, housed intense
concentrations of Irish in
1851. (KCS)

on census night. In Windsor Court there were twenty-three households in 1851, sixteen with Irish-born household heads, and containing 107 persons who had been born in Ireland, thirty-five children born in England but to Irish parents, and only eight other non-Irish-born, some of whom may have been second-generation migrants. The seven non-Irish households in the court included a run of five successive households, presumably living next door to one another in the same part of the court, containing twenty-nine persons, none of whom was Irish-born, and only two, very small, households apparently resident in the midst of the Irish bloc – a seventy-year-old widow living on her own, and a fifty-five-year-old widower who shared his home with a thirty-seven-year-old female lodger.[17]

Irish males followed occupations that were ill-paid and unskilled, even by the standards of the Yorkshire-born population that shared the same areas of the town. For example, in one town-centre enumeration district, the nineteen Irish heads included fourteen labourers, a rag and bone collector and no more than four with skilled occupations, whereas the non-Irish population included textile workers, tradesmen and craftsmen, and only a handful of unskilled workers. The difference between the Irish and English poor was also reflected in the contrast between the population of the workhouse (in Bayhall), which accommodated hardly any Irish, and the forty-nine individuals enumerated under the heading of the Vagrant Office, Croft Head, of whom thirty-three had been born in Ireland.[18]

Visiting Huddersfield in his tour through the manufacturing districts in December 1849, Reach reported to the *Morning Chronicle* on 'the pot and rag trade, by which so many of the Huddersfield Irish live', collecting rags door-to-door in exchange for coarse earthenware pots and pans, supplied by rag merchants. Other Irish women peddled salt, tapes, laces and buttons.[19] Reach also noted the insanitary conditions in which many of the poorest inhabitants lived, including cellar dwellings, but he claimed that conditions were improving in the wake of sanitary legislation. As was common with 'improvements', problems were not eradicated but displaced. In this case the 'low Irish' were driven 'into the adjacent townships, where they cannot be hindered from pigging together on the floors of garrets and cellars by dozens and scores'.[20] One outlying slum district was Johnny Moore's Hill, in Paddock, still within Huddersfield Township, but beyond the jurisdiction of the Improvement Commissioners, where a mere nineteen houses accommodated twenty cases of cholera, seventeen fatal, during the epidemic of 1849.[21]

Several courts attracted the attention of an inquiry into the Huddersfield Improvement Bill in 1848. During 1847, 221 cases of fever were recorded in overcrowded lodging houses, mostly kept by Irish families. In Barker's Yard a cottage room roughly 5 yards square was found to accommodate twenty-one persons, eleven of them ill with the fever. No wonder typhus was referred to as 'Irish fever'. Windsor Court was notable for a 'terrible stench', inadequate and poorly constructed drains, and a lack of through ventilation.[22] Kirkmoor Place, off Northgate, was more mixed than Windsor Court – of thirty-one households in 1851, thirteen included a total of thirty-nine Irish-born members along with thirty-one English-born children, and only three adults born outside of Ireland. The place was noted for 'foul and offensive' drains, 'noxious matter' accumulating in front of most dwellings, a cesspool which was also 'foul and offensive' and two privies which had not been emptied for four years. Yet there were other courts where the houses were built back-to-back but which remained free of typhus, attributed to the cleaner state of the courtyards.[23]

In mid-century, therefore, the centre of the town still displayed a 'preindustrial' front street/back street pattern of segregation, substantial wealth within sniffing distance of extreme poverty. Even on New North Road, not every family could afford to employ a servant. And the majority of the town's residents, neither so poor to be restricted to courts and cellars off Castlegate, nor so rich as to afford a villa in Edgerton, still occupied districts that were socially and occupationally diverse. By the end of the century residential segregation had become much more obvious and larger in scale, involving the 'middle orders' of society as well as the extremes of wealth and poverty. Three examples are considered here: Primrose Hill, Hillhouse and Moldgreen.

Jane Springett has noted that Primrose Hill was first developed in a building boom in the 1850s.[24] Access to the town centre was via a footbridge across the river at the foot of Queen Street South, and the initial population was mainly lower middle- class. Of 103 household heads living there in 1861, only fifteen had been present ten years earlier; thirty-one had moved in from the adjacent out-townships, and twenty-two had been living in and around the town centre in 1851; thirty-five could not be traced anywhere in

Huddersfield in the 1851 census. Of the fifty-three who moved to Primrose Hill from other parts of the borough, only thirty had been married in 1851 but fifty-two were married in 1861, and forty-six were aged under fifty in 1861.[25] In other words, many of the families moving in were new households – the newly-married children of parents who lived in the town centre. Subsequently, the district attracted more working-class families, following the construction of a bridge across the Holme, giving access to mills in Rashcliffe and the Holme valley, and the building of poorer-quality back-to-earth houses on Whitehead Lane.[26] But these were towards the lower slopes of the hill. By the 1880s, the centre of Primrose Hill had acquired a range of lower middle-class institutions, including a Baptist Chapel and Sunday School, and a co-operative grocery store – opened in 1871 – incorporating a penny savings bank and, from 1878, a drapery store. In 1876 a board school for

Key	No. of Houses	Name of Owner		
		1871	1891	1896
A	15	Ralph Oddy	H. B. Lodge	H. B. Lodge
B	6	Joseph Crossland	Mary Wood	Mary Wood
C	6	John Wormald	Wormald Ex'rs	J. Wormald Ex'rs
D	5	Hillhouse Fdly. Soc.	Hillhouse Fdly. Soc.	Hillhouse Co-op. Soc.
E	5	James Brown	Walter Brown	Walter Brown
F	5	Michael Kaye	John Hy. Taylor	John Hy. Taylor
G	5	Thos. Winn. Ex'rs	Seth Senior & Sons	James Senior
H	4	Charles Dyson Ex'rs	Charles Dyson Ex'rs	William Hy. Dyson
J	3	Charles Smith	Joseph Wilkinson	Joseph Wilkinson
K	3	Joseph Battye	Joseph Battye	Joseph Battye
L	3	William Platts	William Platts	William Platts
M	3	Sophia Kaye	Sophia Kaye	Sophia Kaye
N	3	Robert Milnes	Rt. Milnes Ex'rs	Robert Milnes Ex'rs
P	3	John Womersley	Joseph Womersley	W. E. Wood
Q	2	George Rhodes	George Rhodes	Geo. Rhodes
R	2	Geo. Hy. Stead	Geo. Hy. Stead	Geo. Hy. Stead
S	2	Mallinson Ex'rs	Geo. Mallinson	Geo. Mallinson
T	2	Saville Crowther	Denton Brook	Geo. D. Widdows
U	2	Ben Proctor	Merab Tetley	Merab Tetley
W	2	Joseph Stoney	Joseph Stoney	Joseph Stoney
X	2	John Pitchforth	John Pitchforth	John Pitchforth
Y	2	John Platts	John Platts	Thomas Sykes
1	2	Thomas Tolson	Jason Hy. Best	J. H. Best
2	2	Joseph Mellor	J. Mellor Ex'rs	J. Mellor Ex'rs
3	2	Joseph Hoyle Ex'rs	Joseph Hoyle Ex'rs	Joseph Hoyle Ex'rs

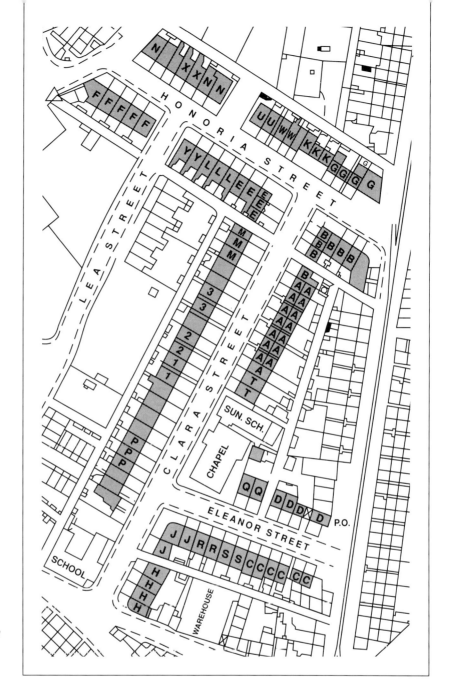

Fig. 17:6 Hillhouse in 1890, showing locations mentioned in the text (based on Ordnance Survey 25 inches: 1 mile plan, published 1893)

800 pupils was opened at nearby Stile Common, and in 1896, a steam tram service was introduced linking the town centre to Stile Common across King's Bridge.[27]

In Hillhouse (Figure 17:6), the Thornhill Estate granted 999-year leases under powers obtained in an estate act of 1852. Long leasehold was much more attractive to developers than the 60-year leases and tenancies at will still

433

current on the Ramsden Estate, but it allowed the Thornhill Estate to retain some control over the quality of development. On the three residential streets at the heart of the estate – Clara, Honoria and Eleanor Streets – restrictive covenants specified that houses 'should have a forecourt . . . kept entirely as a garden or lawn enclosed by a low wall not more than 3 feet in height or ashlar edge stone surmounted by iron railings or open work'. Ground rents of 2d. to 4d. per square yard were lower than those on Ramsden land closer to the town centre, but double the rents charged by the Thornhill Estate for leases on land fronting Bradford Road North. The naming of the three streets, after members of the Thornhill family, indicated the polite respectability of the development. There was also a site for a Congregational church and school on the corner of Clara and Eleanor Streets (opened in 1865), while the corner of Eleanor Street and Bradford Road North was occupied by the Hillhouse Co-operative Society (founded in 1860). On the entire estate (including Bradford and Whitestone Roads) forty-seven building leases were granted between 1853 and 1866, most for only two to four houses at a time. This pattern of development was still reflected in the structure of house ownership at the end of the century (see below).[28]

Hillhouse was more middle class than Huddersfield as a whole, and Clara, Eleanor and Honoria Streets were more middle class than the rest of Hillhouse (Table 1).[29] Nearly 26 per cent of all male householders, and more than 19 per cent of all adult males in Hillhouse in 1871 (including those who were not heads of household) had been eligible to vote in the by-election of 1868, which had been held on the pre-1867 register, in which the franchise was restricted to £10 householders. This compared with fewer than 13 per cent of adult males in the whole parliamentary borough. On Clara, Eleanor and Honoria Streets, more than half of all male household heads were eligible to vote. The 1868 election was won by Leatham (Liberal) by 1,111 votes to 789 for Sleigh (Conservative); but among Hillhouse electors the voting was much more even, ninety-seven for Sleigh to eighty-eight for Leatham. Hillhouse was one of a ring of new lower middle-class suburbs also including Fartown, Newtown and Trinity Street with a majority of Conservative voters, contrasting with the old commercial core of the town (e.g. Kirkgate, King Street) and the highest-status districts (Edgerton, Highfield, Birkby) where the merchant and manufacturing élite had their homes, which all returned clear Liberal majorities.[30]

Many of the respectable residents of Hillhouse commuted to work in the centre of Huddersfield. For example, the residents of Clara Street in 1871 included a hairdresser who ran a salon in Lion Arcade, John William Street, a partner in a firm of wholesale and retail drapers in Kirkgate, and a wholesale tea, coffee and spice merchant whose business was based in Victoria Buildings, New Street. Manufacturers resident on the same street included the co-proprietor of the Phoenix Iron Works in Leeds Road, and a dyer and a woollen manufacturer, both with works at Turnbridge.[31] Sampling the town's directories more widely for middle-class residents whose home and work addresses were both listed, Springett found a substantial lengthening of the journey to work during the 1870s. In 1864, 17 per cent of her sample either worked where they lived or travelled less than a quarter of a mile to work, while 28 per cent travelled more than a mile. By 1881, only 2 per cent went less than a quarter of a mile, and 42 per cent more than a mile.[32]

Table 1 Social structure in Hillhouse and Moldgreen in 1871

Occupation of household head	Hillhouse[1]	Moldgreen[2]
	% heads in each area	
Professional and business middle class	20	2
Clerks, salesmen, agents	26	–
Shopkeepers, dealers and other lower middle class	18	3
Master craftsmen[3]	6	3
Skilled manual workers[4]	23	70
Semi-skilled and unskilled	3	17
Not known	3	5
Total number of heads in area:	95	60

[1] Clara, Eleanor and Honoria Streets

[2] Eastwood and Victoria Streets, and Trevilian and Victoria Places

[3] listed in directory and assumed self-employed, or recorded in census as employing others

[4] no evidence from census or directory that they ran their own business

Note the female-headed households were classified according to the occupations of adult male members of household, where present.

(*sources:* census enumerators' books, 1871, RG-10-4370 (Hillhouse), RG-10-4363 (Moldgreen); William White's *Directory* 1870; George Harper & Co. *Directory* 1870).

Fig. 17:7 *'Victoria Terrace', on the east side of Clara Street, originally back-to-back dwellings; the entrances to the rear dwellings can be seen through the arches between pairs of front doors. The whole block was owned in 1871 by Ralph Oddy, a cabinetmaker and upholsterer, himself resident on Bradley Street South. Residents in 1871 included two joiners, a grocer, a stationer, a clerk, a draper and a warehouseman; two houses at the northern end of the row (to the left of the section in the photograph) comprised a small private dame school. (RD)*

Fig. 17:8 *The west side of Clara Street; the variegated roof-line and brickwork indicate the piecemeal pattern of building which was reflected in small-scale ownership. In 1871, 22 houses were divided among 15 owners, but only 5 houses were owner-occupied. Residents included an engineer with 15 employees, a cattle-food manufacturer with 5 employees, a stationmaster, an engine-driver and a variety of tradesmen. (RD)*

Fig. 17:9 *The north side of Honoria Street, owned in blocks of 2 or 3 houses, as reflected in the haphazard building line. Two houses were owner-occupied in 1871, only one in 1896. Most residents were engaged in the textile industry, including a spinner, cord cutter, merchant, agent and dyer. (RD)*

Figure 17:7

Figure 17:8

Figure 17:9

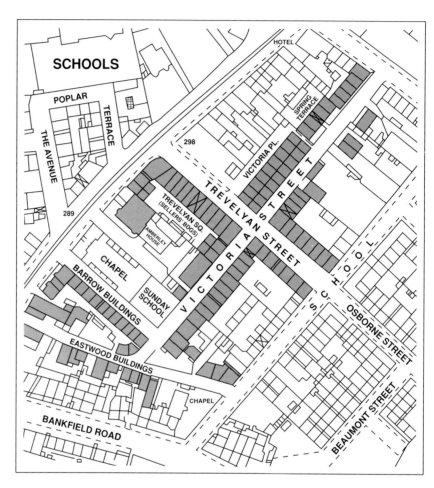

Fig. 17:10 Moldgreen in 1905, showing locations mentioned in the text (based on Ordnance Survey 25 inches: 1 mile plan, published 1907).

Comparing names and addresses in the poll book for 1868 with directories and censuses for 1870-71 and 1881, we can see where residents of Hillhouse had come from, and in some cases where they were to move subsequently. Several recorded 1868 addresses in older middle-class streets closer to the town centre, such as Stables Street, off Chapel Hill, and Fitzwilliam Street. By 1881 some had moved farther out again, along the Halifax Old Road into Birkby, or up Woodhouse Hill. On Clara Street, only about 20 per cent of households remained at the same address between 1871 and 1881 or between 1881 and 1891.

Rateable values on Clara, Eleanor and Honoria Streets ranged between £5 and £23 2s. in 1871, with a median of about £11. This implies a weekly rent of about five shillings. By 1891, values had increased by about 25 per cent, but generally by more at the bottom than at the top of the range (Table 2). Most houses were in short terraces of no more than five or six dwellings, although adjacent terraces constructed by different builders under separate leases might in practice form a continuous frontage, as on the west side of Clara Street. Surprisingly, on the east side of Clara Street a row of back-to-back dwellings was permitted, the front houses rated at £9 10s., the back houses at £7 10s. in 1891. The whole block of twelve back-to-backs plus a through house at each end of the terrace was owned as a single unit in both 1871 and 1891. In this respect, as well as in its built form, it resembled dwellings in Moldgreen; but in almost every other way, Moldgreen was a very different kind of suburb.[33]

While it proved relatively easy to match census, directory and ratebook entries in Hillhouse, it was almost impossible to do so in the sample area selected in Moldgreen (Figure 17:10). An attempt was made to match 1871 census entries for Eastwood Street, Victoria Street, Victoria Place and Trevilian Place with entries in the ratebook for the same year for Eastwood Street, Barrow Buildings, Trevelyan Street and Place, and Victoria Street and Place. Of sixty families recorded in the census, only twenty-five could be

Table 2   Rateable values of residential property in Hillhouse and Moldgreen

Rateable value	Hillhouse[1]			Moldgreen[2]		
	1871	1891	1896	1871	1891	1896
	% houses in each band of values					
Less than £3	–	–	–	21	12	2
£ 3-£ 4 19s. 11d.	1	–	–	44	28	16
£ 5-£ 7 19s. 11d.	26	15	16	27	48	71
£ 8-£11 19s. 11d.	30	21	24	2	10	10
£12-£19 19s. 11d.	43	52	50	5	3	1
£20 and over	1	13	11	1	–	–

[1] includes all ratebook entries for Clara, Eleanor, Honoria and Back Honoria Streets

[2] includes all ratebook entries for Barrow Buildings, Eastwood Street, Trevelyan Place and Street, Victoria Place and Street, and Beaumont Street (1896) only.

(*source*: Huddersfield Corporation Borough Ratebooks, 1871, 1891-92, 1896-97).

traced in the ratebook, and several of these were at addresses not originally included in the ratebook sample. For example, John Gardiner, M.D., surgeon and medical officer to the Kirkheaton district of the Huddersfield Union, along with his wife and four servants, was recorded in the census as living in Trevilian Place, somewhat improbable given that the rateable value of dwellings there was only £4 8s. In fact, the ratebook recorded Dr Gardiner as the owner-occupier of a house rated at £67 11s., with the address simply 'Moldgreen', but listed just prior to the entries for Trevilian Place. As subsequent directories reveal, this was Amberley House, a substantial villa on Wakefield Road, adjoining Trevelyan Place (Figure 17:10).[34]

Of the households listed in the census, most were skilled manual workers with jobs in the textile industry (including weavers, dyers, spinners, a slubber, a pattern maker and a cloth printer), or as masons, joiners or iron moulders. Apart from the doctor there were two self-employed craftsmen (who merited entries in the town directory) and one shopkeeper; but, overall, this was a much more modest and relatively homogeneous working-class population compared to the residents of the Thornhill Estate in Hillhouse (Table 1).

Yet in one respect at least, the two districts were quite alike. In neither did many people own their own homes: about 7 per cent of householders in Hillhouse, no more than 5 per cent in Moldgreen (Table 3). Moreover, many of those who were owner-occupiers also owned other property. Of seven owner-occupiers in Hillhouse in 1896, only two owned nothing but their own homes (and even they, of course, may have owned other property outside the sample area). Likewise in Moldgreen, of eight owner-occupiers in 1896, four also owned adjacent dwellings, while one owned a row of ten houses. Owners moved into and out of dwellings that they previously or subsequently rented to others. Evidently, the ownership of property was more important than whether one chose to occupy it; property provided

Table 3 Homeownership Hillhouse and Moldgreen

	% dwellings occupied by their owners		
	1871	1891	1896
Hillhouse	7.9	5.9	6.8
Moldgreen	3.5	4.9	5.2

For source and definitions, see Table 2.

status, income, wealth and political power.[35] But in the days before mortgage tax relief, before double-figure inflation, and before property taxation discriminated between landlords and owner-occupiers, homeownership yielded few benefits not equally applicable to landlordism. Security of tenure, for example, was rarely a critical issue. As long as tenants paid their rent on time, landlords were unlikely to evict them. In middle-class tenancies, rents were usually paid monthly or quarterly, and tenants were responsible for paying rates; working-class tenancies were normally on weekly terms, rent paid a week in advance and including rates which were then paid in a lump sum by landlords to the local authority. Tenants were as attracted by the possibility of leaving at a week's notice as landlords were by the possibility of evicting undesirable tenants equally quickly. In an age before state pensions, national insurance, and sickness and unemployment benefit, tenant-households could quickly adjust the level of rent they paid to the level of wages they received. Workers who changed jobs could easily move house near to their new place of work.[36]

So, in a town dominated by private landlordism, who were the landlords? In general, historical research has uncovered much more about the ground landlords – such as the Ramsdens and the Thornhills – than about the more modest, and less well documented, owners of houses erected on their land. Not many were full-time 'professional landlords' whose only source of income was from renting or dealing in property. In Moldgreen in 1871, Amelia Crossland, a sixty-five year old widow, returned her occupation as 'income from houses', corresponding to one stereotype of petty landlordism that will be familiar from numerous Victorian and Edwardian novels.[37] The ratebook recorded her as owner-occupier of a house in Spring Terrace, Victoria Street, rated at £9 4s., and as owner of another six houses in the same street, collectively rated at £29 8s.; but as two were occupied by other Crosslands we may doubt if even this much changed hands in rent, or that she really was solely dependent on her income from rents with her self-employed son living next door! Twenty years later, however, her executors had responsibility for not only the houses but also a heald shop, 'yarn place', warehouse and two engine houses, altogether valued at £88 10s.[38]

Increasingly, as owners died, property remained in the hands of executors, sometimes for decades. In the Moldgreen sample area, only two dwellings out of ninety-eight were recorded as owned by executors in 1871, but by 1896, seventy out of 170 were in executors' hands. Executors may have left the responsibility for day-to-day management to individual family members, but there must have been the possibility that management would become less personal, delegated to a paid agent, or that the final settlement of the estate would involve selling the property in order to realise a cash sum that was more easily divisible among beneficiaries. In this way the social relations associated with property began to change, and the dominance of private landlordism started to diminish, long before the introduction of rent control or legal security of tenure, traditionally assumed to have caused the collapse of the rental housing system.[39]

A few landlords were institutional – Hillhouse Co-operative Society owned houses adjacent to its store on the corner of Eleanor Street, the Harmonic Revised Independent Lodge of Oddfellows owned newly-constructed Beaumont Street in Moldgreen in 1896 – but most landlords were local tradesmen or industrialists. In Hillhouse most owned only a few houses – an average holding of 2.5 houses per owner – although some may also have owned property outside the sample area. In Moldgreen the average was about seven houses per owner, and several landlords owned more than twenty houses (Table 4), in the form of either a long terrace or a block facing an internal courtyard. So although most *owners* possessed only a few houses each, most *houses* in Moldgreen were owned by a small minority of landlords, who would have had some power locally, for example in blacklisting undesirable tenants or in showing favour when existing tenants requested accommodation for family or friends. This power would have been accentuated to the extent that prominent landlords shared similar views – for example, similar political or religious beliefs – or were also local employers, as appears to have been the case in Moldgreen (see below). By contrast, landlords in Hillhouse were not generally in the same position to discriminate between tenants. But in both suburbs, ownership patterns in the 1890s reflected the units of construction twenty to thirty years earlier. When property changed hands it did so in the blocks in which it had originally been built. Overall, there was not an active property market. Although it has been assumed that most housing was built speculatively, once they had purchased it landlords tended to retain ownership for long periods, drawing a regular income from rents. There were few quick capital gains to be made by dealing in property.

Table 4· Residential property ownership in Hillhouse and
        Moldgreen, 1896

	Hillhouse		Moldgreen	
No. of Houses	Owners (%)	Houses (%)	Owners (%)	Houses (%)
1	35	14	23	4
2-3	45	40	27	11
4-6	18	33	27	20
7-9	–	–	4	5
10-19	3	14	8	16
20+	–	–	12	44
Total no	40	103	26	170
Average no. of houses per owner	2.6		6.5	
% dwellings vacant	0.0		9.4	
% owner-occupied	6.8		5.2	

An example of how to interpret this table: In Hillhouse, 18% of owners owned 33% of houses,
each with 4-6 houses; in Moldgreen, 23% of owners, each owning one house, owned between
them only 4% of all houses.

For source and definitions, see Table 2.

Among the leading landlords in Moldgreen, Benjamin Graham was a
'builder, quarry owner, stone and ground lime merchant, manufacturer of
sanitary tubes and of bricks by steam power' with works at Bridge End, and a
house nearby at Park View, off Somerset Crescent. He owned all of Barrow
Buildings, and also twenty houses at Green Mount, a few streets farther east.
Charles William Frederick Taylor lived at Eldon House, Almondbury. He
was a partner in a firm manufacturing fancy woollen vestings, shawls and
mantle cloths, with an office in Cloth Hall Street and mills in Almondbury.
During the period under study, he gradually extended his ownership of
property in Trevelyan Street, Victoria Street and School Street. Smaller-scale
landlords included Jacob Schofield (ten houses in 1896), a stonemason, and
Richard Eastwood (eight houses on Eastwood and School Streets in 1871), a
joiner, both resident in their own blocks of property. Overall, it appears that
most landlords were local to Moldgreen or Almondbury, and many were
engaged in some aspect of the building industry.[40]

Hillhouse landlords were more often merchants or local tradesmen. The largest block of houses (the back-to-back terrace on Clara Street) was owned by Ralph Oddy, a town-centre cabinetmaker and upholsterer. By 1891, ownership had passed to Henry Bedford Lodge, a woollen commission agent (but probably a relative of Oddy's; the 1881 directory records a Sam Lodge Oddy who was an innkeeper). Other house-owners in Hillhouse included Joseph Crosland, grocer and postmaster of the post office in Bradford Road, who owned property on the corner of Honoria and Clara Streets; John Henry Taylor, a carpet merchant with premises in Westgate, who owned the most highly-rated terrace of houses on Honoria Street, occupying one himself; and John Wormald, whose more modest row on Eleanor Street complemented his saddlery in Wormald's Yard, King Street.[41]

Further research is needed, linking ratebooks to building permits or legal documents, such as building leases, to ascertain connections between the building process and subsequent ownership. It may transpire that building was less speculative than was once thought, if builders retained ownership of houses they erected. Even more fundamentally, we need to know more about the financing of house purchase, to counterbalance the attention that has been paid to well-documented but, in numerical terms, relatively unimportant building clubs and societies.[42] And just how profitable was landlordism to attract the investments of merchants and manufacturers? Why invest in bricks and mortar rather than in new industrial technology?

However infrequently property changed hands, its occupants were much more mobile. In the two sample areas, the proportion of householders who 'persisted'[43] for as little as five years (1891-96) was 45 per cent in Hillhouse and 36 per cent in Moldgreen. This includes cases where the original householder had been replaced by a widow or other relative with the same surname. It also includes several families who had moved house, but remained within the sample area. Indeed, short-distance residential mobility was very common, perhaps reflecting people's need to move to larger or smaller, more expensive or cheaper dwellings, as their family circumstances changed, but their desire to remain in the same neighbourhood as friends, on whom they could rely in times of crisis. A larger-scale survey of residential mobility, covering 1,449 male household heads enumerated in Lockwood and the Holme valley parts of Almondbury township in 1861, found that 37 per cent had been resident in the same enumeration district ten years earlier, while another 33 per cent could be traced to addresses elsewhere in Huddersfield. In general, the local-born were less likely to move than in-migrants, the young were more likely to move than the elderly, and the middle classes were less mobile than labourers. This might appear to contradict the argument above, that the poor needed to remain close to established friends and family; in fact, it demonstrates the extreme insecurity of the *very* poor, obliged to move from town to town in search of casual work, compared to the security of the local-born skilled working class.[44]

It has been argued in this chapter that Huddersfield was becoming a more differentiated place during the second half of the nineteenth century. From a residential segregation just of the extremes of wealth and poverty, the development process was creating a more subtle pattern of lower middle-class and skilled working-class suburbs. The pattern of development was sustained by continuing differences in ownership and management of housing, as exemplified in this chapter by the contrast between Hillhouse and Moldgreen. These are merely exemplars, chosen because they happened to lie on the route of the author's undergraduate fieldclass! Much the same contrasts could be made between other districts. But within an apparently stable pattern of segregation, individuals were constantly on the move, although many of their moves were over quite short distances, often within the same street, usually in the same sector of the borough. To return to the argument outlined at the beginning of this chapter, a sense of 'community' survived in areas like Moldgreen and Paddock, sustained by short working-class journeys to work, by membership of local churches, chapels and friendly societies, and positively enhanced by the identity of class interest among local populations of social equals. 'Community' flourished, not despite residential segregation, but because of it.[45]

Richard Dennis

Biographical Note

Richard Dennis has been on the staff of the Department of Geography, University College London, since 1974. He is the author of *A Social Geography of England and Wales* (co-authored with Hugh Clout) (Pergamon Press, 1980) and of *English Industrial Cities of the Nineteenth Century* (Cambridge University Press, 1984), which incorporated many of the findings of his PhD thesis on Huddersfield. More recently he has written widely about housing problems in nineteenth and twentieth-century London, and was a major contributor to *The Times London History Atlas* (Times Books, 1991). He is currently undertaking research on housing in turn-of-the-century Toronto.

NOTES

1. *Reports from Commissioners on Proposed Divisions of Counties and Boundaries of Boroughs vol. III, pt II* P(arliamentary) P(apers) 1831-32, XL, pp.187-88.

2. *Report of Boundary Commissioners for England and Wales* PP 1867-68, XX, pp.159-60.

3. F. Singleton, *Industrial Revolution in Yorkshire* (Clapham, Yorkshire, 1970), pp.127, 175; O. Balmforth, *Huddersfield Industrial Society Limited: Jubilee History* (Manchester, 1910).

4. B. Disraeli, *Sybil* (1845) esp. Book 3, chapter 8; B. Disraeli, *Coningsby* (1844) Book 4, chapter 3.

5. G.S. Phillips, *Walks round Huddersfield* (Huddersfield, 1848), p.22.

6. Phillips, *Walks round Huddersfield*, p.51.

7. R. Williams, *The Country and the City* (St. Albans, 1975), p.131; C. Bell and H. Newby, 'Community, communion, class and community action' in *Social Areas in Cities, Volume 2* edited by D. T. Herbert and R. J. Johnston (1976), pp.189-207.

8. *Reports from Assistant Hand-Loom Weavers' Commissioners* PP 1840, XXIII, pp.492-93.

9. PP 1840.

10. *The Census and Social Structure: An Interpretative Guide to 19th Century Censuses for England and Wales*, edited by R. Lawton (1978); D. Mills and C. Pearce, *People and Places in the Victorian Census* (Historical Geography Research Series, No. 23, 1989).

11. On directories, see G. Shaw, *British Directories as Sources in Historical Geography* (Historical Geography Research Series, No. 8, 1982); on ratebooks, see M.J. Daunton, 'House-ownership from rate books', *Urban History Yearbook* (1976), 21-27.

12. On the use of marriage registers and church records, see R. Dennis, *English Industrial Cities of the Nineteenth Century* (Cambridge, 1984) esp. chapter 9; see also R. Dennis and S. Daniels, 'Community and the social geography of Victorian cities', *Urban History Yearbook* (1981), 7-23.

13. Census enumeration districts each contained between about fifty and two hundred households, small enough to be covered by one enumerator; unfortunately there was no requirement for them to be socially homogeneous or geometrically compact, as the pattern of e.d. boundaries on Figures 17:2 and 17:4 clearly illustrates.

14. H. Marland, *Medicine and Society in Wakefield and Huddersfield 1780-1870* (Cambridge, 1987), pp.287-90 provides a good illustration of this process in the suburban migration of medical practitioners between 1822 and 1871.

15. The phrase is from Arnold Bennett's description of Darius Clayhanger's ambitions in *Clayhanger* (1910) Book 2, chapter 3.

16. *Kelly's Directory of Huddersfield and Neighbourhood* (1881); R. Dennis 'Community and interaction in a Victorian city: Huddersfield, 1850-1880' (unpub. Ph.D. thesis, Cambridge Univ. 1975), pp.140-44.

17. Census enumerators' books, Huddersfield 1851 (registration district 497-9a, e.d.s 3 and 4).

18. *Ibid.* Croft Head was in e.d. 18 (497-9c), Bayhall Workhouse in e.d. 26 (497-9d).

19. A.B. Reach, *The Yorkshire Textile Districts in 1849*, edited by C. Aspin, (Helmshore, 1974), p.5.

20. Reach, *Yorkshire Textile Districts*, p. 4.

21. Marland, *Medicine and Society*, p.45.

22. *Minutes of Proceedings on a Preliminary Enquiry of the Huddersfield Improvement Bill, held February 1848* (1851), W(est) Y(orkshire) A(rchive) S(ervice), Kirklees KHT9/1, para. 685-693, 837, 863-886.

23. WYAS, Kirklees KHT9/1 para. 408-13, 863-77; Census enumerators' books, Huddersfield 1851 (497-9a, e.d. 8).

24. J. Springett 'Landowners and urban development: the Ramsden estate and nineteenth-century Huddersfield' *J(ournal) of H(istorical) G(eography)*, 8 (1982), 129-44.

25. Dennis, *English Industrial Cities*, pp.266-67.

26. Springett, *JHG*, 8, 139.

27. *Handbook of the 27th Co-operative Congress* (Huddersfield, 1895), pp.68-102, 159: R. Brook, *The Story of Huddersfield* (1968), chapter XII.

28. J. Springett, 'Land development and house-building in Huddersfield, 1770-1911' in *Building the Industrial City* edited by M. Doughty (Leicester, 1986), pp.44-45. I am grateful to Jane Springett for additional details on covenants, ground rents and patterns of leasing on the Thornhill Estate in Hillhouse.

29. For further details, see R. Dennis, 'Class, behaviour and residence in nineteenth-century society: the lower middle class in Huddersfield in 1871' in *Class and Space: The Making of Urban Society* edited by N. Thrift and P. Williams (1987), pp.73-107.

30. I have explored the geography of voting behaviour in more detail in R. Dennis, 'Housing, class and voting behaviour in West Riding textile towns: a geographical analysis' in *Geography of Population and Mobility in Nineteenth-Century Britain* edited by C. Withers (Historical Geography Research Group, 1986), pp.46-70. For a map of voting behaviour in the 1868 by-election, see R. Dennis, 'Dismantling the barriers: past and present in urban Britain' in *Horizons in Human Geography* edited by D. Gregory and R. Walford, (1989), pp.204-08.

31. Census enumerators' books, Huddersfield 1871, RG-10-4370; William White's *Directory* (1870).

32. Springett (1986), p.42.

33. For both Hillhouse and Moldgreen, information on rateable values and patterns of ownership and occupancy was derived from Huddersfield Corporation Borough Rate Books for 1871, 1891-92, 1896-97, WYAS, Kirklees.

34. Census enumerators' books, Moldgreen 1871, RG-10-4363. Note that Trevelyan Place (spelt Trevilian by the census enumerator) was later known as Sellers' Buildings, after the name of its owner.

35.   For example, under the 1848 Improvement Act, candidates for the posts of commissioners had to be rated at £30 or more on the property they occupied, or to be in receipt of more than £50 per annum in rents from property, or to be worth more than £1000 in personal wealth; electors received more votes, the more property they owned; see D.F.E. Sykes, *The History of Huddersfield and its Vicinity* (Huddersfield, 1898), p.390; Marland, *Medicine and Society*, p.423.

36.   For comprehensive discussions of landlordism and homeownership in the nineteenth century, see M.J. Daunton, *House and Home in the Victorian City: Working Class Housing 1850-1914* (1983); P. Kemp, 'Some aspects of housing consumption in late nineteenth century England and Wales', *Housing Studies*, 2 (1987), 3-16.

37.   For example, Arnold Bennett *Hilda Lessways* (1911); Dennis, *English Industrial Cities*, pp.170, 173.

38.   Huddersfield Corporation Borough Rate Books 1871, 1891-92.

39.   On the decline of landlordism in Britain, see M.J. Daunton, *A Property-Owning Democracy? Housing in Britain* (1987), esp. chapter 2.

40.   Information on landlords was derived from directories for 1870 (Harper's), 1870 (White's), 1881 (Kelly's) and 1891 (Slater's).

41.   Directories, 1870, 1881, 1891.

42.   On housing finance and building societies, see Springett, 'Land development' and M.H. Yeadell, 'Building societies in the West Riding of Yorkshire and their contribution to housing provision in the nineteenth century', both in *Building the Industrial City* edited by M. Doughty (Leicester, 1986), pp.23-56 and 57-103.

43.   That is, persons who could be traced in the same sample area in successive records (in this case ratebooks for 1891-92 and 1896-97), irrespective of whether they had moved *within* that area. In many records, lacking house numbers, and, in early censuses for outlying villages, even street names, it is impossible to tell if households were still in the same dwellings.

44.   This paragraph is based on more detailed discussion in R. Dennis, 'Intercensal mobility in a Victorian City', *Transactions of the Institute of British Geographers* New Series, 2 (1977), 349-63, and in Dennis, *English Industrial Cities*, chapter 8.

45.   On working-class journey to work and church membership in Huddersfield, see Dennis and Daniels, *Urban History Yearbook* (1981), 7-23 and Dennis, *English Industrial Cities*, pp.132-40.

CHAPTER 18

Landowners and Housebuilders in the Nineteenth Century

JANE SPRINGETT

The nature of the house building process

The residential fabric of nineteenth century Huddersfield was the product of decisions of hundreds of individuals in response to local market forces. These were the building initiators (to distinguish from the profession itself) who brought together the land, labour, materials and capital necessary for house building. As entrepreneurs they were largely unskilled amateurs. For, while their perceptions of the needs of the market and consumer preference helped to determine the type of housing built, their judgment was often imperfect and based on personal considerations rather than profit maximisation. As in other Victorian towns, most of the home building was undertaken for rent and largely involved small scale savers seeking a low level of risk, a reliable repository of value and some promise for the future.[1] Consequently, the urban fabric was largely built in small units by jobbing builders, with few schemes during the first half of the century consisting of more than one or two houses. Even with changes in the structure of the building industry towards large scale enterprises in the latter part of the century, rarely did they exceed six and only exceptionally comprised of fifty houses.[2]

This large number of small scale capitalists was in part a product of the economic structure of Huddersfield, which saw the comparatively late emergence of factory organisation. This meant that the facility to accumulate capital was available to a large number of individuals creating a long tradition of small scale credit and only a partially developed industrial proletariat. The result was a rather haphazard approach to building involving the utilisation of

449

Fig. 18:1 Jowitt's Court: cited in government reports as having the worst sanitary conditions. (KCS)

infill space behind existing commercial buildings in the centre of town or tenter crofts, and creating densely packed and insanitary courtyard developments with a wide range of property types.[3] (Figure 18:1 and 18:2).

Remarkably, despite such a fragmented business structure, the building industry was surprisingly successful in terms of quantity if not quality in keeping pace with the demand for living space. However, while there was rarely a shortage of housing *per se* there were often times when there was insufficient *cheap* housing available. This particularly was the case towards the latter quarter of the century after the introduction of byelaws to control building standards in 1872.[4] Thus a correspondent to the *Huddersfield Chronicle* in 1877 wrote:

> houses of a superior class increase rapidly; the effect is that overcrowding is almost beyond control; the difficulty is serious because it is well known in Huddersfield that the outlay on a good dwelling house for the poor does not yield an adequate return for the owner.[5]

450

Fig. 18:2 Cooke's Buildings, Ramsden Street, pulled down 1876, illustrated the lack of competition for land during the early stages of urban growth and the proximity of the mill owner's residence to his factory. (KCS)

In 1899, the Medical Officer of Health claimed that the continued existence of some 355 cellar dwellings in Huddersfield was due to the lack of houses with two rooms for rent between 2s. and 2s. 6d per week.[6] Nor were such dwellings confined to inner Huddersfield, for in 1910, a report of the Inspector of Nuisances revealed the existence of seventy-four occupied cellar dwellings in Lockwood and Rashcliffe.[7]

Most new houses, therefore, in the second half of the nineteenth century were built for higher income groups, for the skilled artisan, the newly emerging white collar professions with a steady income untainted by cynical economic downturns, and for the élite of the town, the merchant manufacturers and their heirs whose wealth was based on a generation of investment in the cloth industry. With the development of class consciousness, social status began to accrue to location and so, over time, the aspirations of each group were met. First, there were the large villas in extensive grounds built in Upper Edgerton between 1855 and 1875 and smaller semi-detached villas with rather less land at Gledholt in the 1870s. Then after 1880 large scale developments of inferior terraced and back-to-back houses became the norm in areas such as Birkby, Fartown, Dalton, Moldgreen and Crosland Moor, serviced by the new tram routes and creating homogeneous suburbs in terms of physical infrastructure, if not social mix. It is these suburbs which remain today the main inheritance of the Victorian housebuilding process. With a few exceptions, the older crowded courts have disappeared, declared unfit for human habitation by the standards of the twentieth century.[8]

Landowners and the building process in Huddersfield

While the building undertaker took the initiative in determining the type, quantity and location of houses built, the residential fabric of Huddersfield cannot be understood without reference to the activities and decisions of local landowners. Builders operated against the background of an urban land market, the characteristics of which were the consequence of the spatial pattern of predevelopment landownership and eighteenth century values concerning land inheritance. The impact of these factors was stronger during the early stages of urban-industrial growth, for, as the spatial constraints on builders' choices were removed, landowners, under greater competition with each other, became from necessity less able to dictate the terms of the market and more responsive to short term economic considerations rather than longer term economic gains based on the maximisation of quality. It is on the management policies of these landowners and their implications for residential development that the rest of this chapter will concentrate.

The nature of the urban land market and land tenure policy

Huddersfield became notorious for the dominance of one landed estate in the town's development, the Ramsden Estate, although in reality this estate's monopoly was never absolute. The myth arose from the estate's involvement during the early stages of urban industrial development when it still enjoyed something akin to a patriarchal/feudal relationship with many of its tenants.[9] The structure of the urban land market, in fact, was more like an oligopoly – a few individuals offering differentiated products in a market

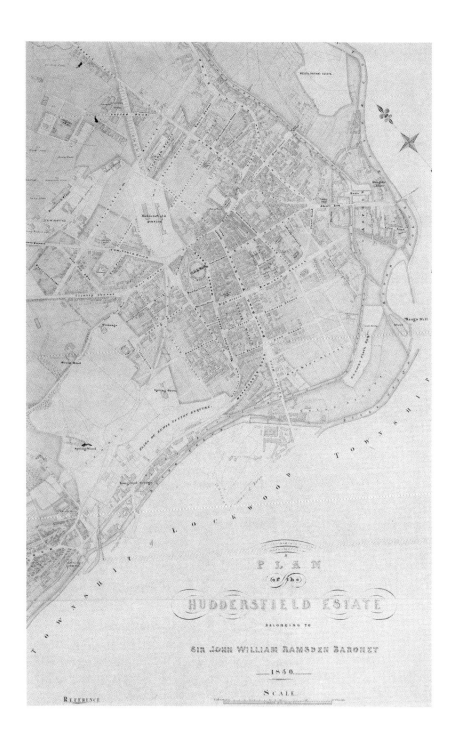

Fig. 18:3 Part of the 1850 Ramsden Estate plan, showing the town centre. (WYAS, K)

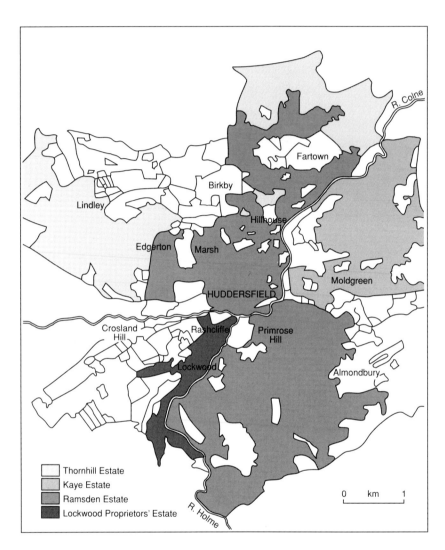

*Fig. 18:4 The spatial
pattern of landownership
in Huddersfield, 1850.*

where there was a high demand. This limited competition gave landowners
the opportunity to dictate the choice of tenure on which land would be made
available for building within their own inherited legal restrictions, financial
positions and family circumstances. However, since clauses in wills and
settlements could be nullified by Acts of Parliament, access to and power to
assimilate wealth was crucial, influencing their attitude to their land.

In 1850 the spatial pattern of landownership was such that the Ramsden
family owned most of the land in the immediate vicinity of the town centre

454

while the Lockwood proprietors, a business consortium, and the Thornhill family dominated Lockwood and Lindley respectively. In the villages of Fartown, Birkby, Crosland Moor and Marsh landholdings were fragmented Figure 18:4). Some of the smaller estates and most of the larger ones were subject to various restrictions in wills and settlements preventing sale, or, as in the case of the Thornhill Estate until 1852, the leasing of land.[10] There was generally a low level of market activity even amongst the remaining landowners and the overall structure of ownership remained unchanged for the greater part of the century. Some inroads were made into the dominance of the large estates, providing limited opportunities to purchase freehold land for building. In the 1820s a number of small estates on the fringes of the built-up area disposed of land to merchants and manufacturers for villas and factory development. The former were built at Newhouse some five minutes walk from the Cloth Hall; the latter were built along the canal.[11] The Kaye Estate, which was suffering financial problems, sold off land in Dalton in the 1820s which, although laid out as building plots, was purchased for the creation of small mansion house estates. The sale of some of the Thornhill Estate land in Lindley in 1854 gave landed property rights to many local millowners in the village of Lindley. In contrast to freehold land sales elsewhere in Huddersfield, demand was very strong and the prices obtained at the auction artificially high. This was to the considerable satisfaction of the managers of the Thornhill Estate, who attributed it to the employment of Frederick Robert Jones, considered to be 'the most eminent land agent in the West Riding of York'.[12] According to Christopher White, one of the estate's Trustees:

> I have every reason to believe that the judicious manner in which he lotted the property and met the claims of tenantry (a most difficult task) has secured for Miss Thornhill an addition of £20,000 over and above what would have been realised had the matter been placed as usual in the hands of a London firm of eminence.[13]

Pressure had been building up during the 1840s from tenants of the Thornhill estate for better tenure terms than the twenty-one years available. A number of potential industrialists, who had been tenants for many generations, had applied to the estate for sums of money exceeding £2,000 for the building of mills and it was these tenants who purchased most of its land. Any house-building that subsequently took place was on lease rather than freehold terms.

Indeed, throughout the Huddersfield area, although the 1850s estate agents advertised small estates as being 'freehold and not subject to ground rent or chief rent or the expense and trouble consequent upon the renewal of lease on a term of years',[14] most freehold land sold either ended in the hands of the Ramsden Estate or remained undeveloped. There seems to have been, as one contemporary observer put it:

> not the slightest inclination amongst lessees to purchase ground rents – all the capital they command they prefer to apply in business which will probably realise a much greater return.[15]

In the absence of strong demand for freehold land the Ramsden Estate was able to pursue a policy of purchasing estates which projected within its bounds, in an effort to protect itself 'from injurious competition'. Between 1844 and 1884 it purchased a total of 942 acres, much of it not advertised on the open market.[16] But the policy imposed an increasing financial burden on the estate and had to be abandoned when the estate found itself unable to compete in the market for small estates sold in the developing north-west of the town.

Towards the end of the century, competition between landowners in supplying building land became intense as demand fell during the recession of the 1890s and transport improvements* brought more land within the ambit of potential urban demand.

While the older established estates responded by lowering ground rents, the prospects of long-term holding of freehold land became increasingly unattractive to the smaller landowner. The depression in agriculture and calls for land nationalisation persuaded many of them to shed their landed property interest for other forms of investment. For the greater part of the century, however, the majority of landowners preferred to retain some continued interest in landed urban property and let their land for building on 999-year leasehold tenure. This enabled the builder to obtain a reasonable benefit from the capital employed, but at a respectable return to the landowner. The exception was the Ramsden Estate, who only pursued such a

*A discussion of the passenger transport system is found in Chapter Sixteen. EDITOR.

policy after 1867. Between 1859 and 1867 land was let on 99-year leasehold and previous to that on either 60-year renewable leases or tenancy at will. This partly reflected estate management practices and partly the financial and legal position of the Estate during the nineteenth century.

The estate in Huddersfield had originally been acquired in the sixteenth century by William Ramsden, a yeoman clothier and was subsequently augmented through judicious purchase and by marriage settlements.* Although the family owned some property in London and a country seat at Byram near Ferrybridge, the estates in Huddersfield were the chief source of the family's landed income in the nineteenth century. In the absence of adequate documentation little is known about the nature and extent of income from other sources. The few accounts available indicate that, whereas during the first half of the nineteenth century the estate was in a position of financial solvency, by 1873 the owner was complaining that he had to draw on his own independent income to reduce mortgages on the estate. A high proportion of rental income was siphoned off to pay interest on loans. In 1890 mortgages amounting to a total of £1,009,075 were charged on the estate, taking from a rental income of £58,910 interest charges of £35,317. Most aristocratic landowners were suffering from similar debts at this time and only those able to diversify their assets were able to survive into the twentieth century. In the case of the Ramsden Estate that survival only lasted until 1920, when the estate was sold to Huddersfield Corporation for £1,350,000.[17]

The importance of the estate to the family was reflected in the legal restrictions placed on it to preserve its continuity. In 1780 the estate was held in tail male. Under the terms of the original settlement any leases granted could not extend beyond the life of Sir John Ramsden, the tenant for life. Part of this land, most of it agricultural, was resettled on Sir John's son in 1814 and by his will in 1838 on his grandson, his son having predeceased him. This settlement could be broken in 1853 when his grandson came of age. The rest of the estate was devised to trustees during the lifetime of his grandson for use while he lived and to his male heirs successively. When Sir John died in 1839 his grandson, Sir John William, was a seven-year-old minor, thus the administration of the estate passed directly to these trustees, Earl Fitzwilliam, the Earl of Zetland and George Fox. The Earl of Zetland was Mrs Isabella Ramsden's brother and Earl Fitzwilliam was married to their sister. Sir John

*For more details see Chapter Three. EDITOR.

William assumed responsibility for running the estate in 1853 and retained control until 1909 when the estate was resettled on his son Mr John Frecheville Ramsden. For a greater part of that time, Sir John William took a direct interest in the running of the estate, visiting regularly and making policy decisions.[18]

Land-owner management policy during the early stages of urban growth

Different options were open to a landowner in developing an urban estate. He could take a passive role, merely supplying land when it was demanded either by sale or lease, the choice determined by the market, by the potential value of the land and by the financial circumstances of the owner. Alternatively, he could take an active entrepreneurial role through capital investment and by adopting a coherent development strategy.

Although there was some variation between landowners in the degree to which they effectively managed their estates, most chose to develop the land themselves. While economic considerations were paramount, perceptions on how best to maximise their assets changed as the century progressed, as each landowner adjusted to economic reality. The phasing of that adjustment varied from estate to estate, and it had consequences for the urban fabric, particularly when decisions did not accord with market conditions. During the first half of the century most adopted a passive role. In the case of the Thornhill Estate this passive role was almost cavalier, for the owner 'regularly milked the estate dry, timber had been cut to a fearful extent and buildings on the whole of the estate were in a frightful state of repair'.[19]

A more realistic approach was like that of the Lockwood Estate proprietors and Sir Joseph Radcliffe, who owned land in Crosland Moor Bottom. Both placed the management of their estates in the hands of the professional land agent, Frederick Robert Jones, who was of such assistance to Miss Thornhill. Jones remained responsible for maximising the assets, in this case letting land on straight forward 999-year leases.[20]

Up until 1844 the Ramsden Estate adopted a course somewhere between these two approaches. Although direct investment by the Ramsden family came early in Huddersfield's development with the building of the Cloth Hall and the canal before the development of the railway in the 1840s, entrepreneurial activity during the period of Huddersfield's most rapid growth was limited solely to the provision of wide main streets. Provided he received a continually increasing rental income the owner, Sir John Ramsden, was content to leave management entirely in the hands of his steward, John Bower. Bower visited Huddersfield twice a year, on rent days and to audit the accounts. He usually stayed two weeks, during which time he would examine applications for land, fix rents and, if requested, draw up leases, for which he charged a fee of fifteen guineas. For the rest of the year a local part-time agent, Joseph Brook, was responsible for recording any applications for land, staking out the plots and provisionally fixing rents. An investigation into the estate's affairs in 1840, following Sir John's death, revealed the consequences of this lax management.

Because Bower took all decisions concerning the estate, the increasing volume of work arising from the demand for building land generated a substantial backlog of work. This was aggravated by Bower's age and increasing infirmity. It also resulted in a considerable amount of corruption. Prospective tenants had to treat Brook to a drink in his public house before an application was favourably received, but people frequently erected a building without seeking any permission at all. The many who did so were not made liable to arrears and some were not entered in the rent book.[21]

It was a widely held local belief that Brook and Bower, as substantial property owners themselves, promoted the letting of land on tenancy at will. With this system, normally associated with agriculture, there was no written agreement or lease involved. An individual would build and then surrender his property to the landowner, thus becoming tenant at the will of the landowner from year to year. This was done in the full knowledge that he could be given notice to quit at any time. The management, however, inculcated a feeling amongst the tenants that they were unlikely to be disturbed and, in the event, few tenants were ever evicted. Thus the system came to be accepted as customary tenure and credit for house building was advanced simply on the strength of a tenant's name being in their rent book.

There was an alternative available – a 60-year renewable lease. Originally this was renewable on payment of a certain fine, but in 1816 a fine calculated on the basis of one year's improved value was introduced, with the result that the uptake of building leases declined from 138 between 1780 and 1816 to thirty-eight between 1816 and 1840. By then tenants viewed tenancy at will as a cut price perpetual lease for which no fine had to be paid. Even after the reintroduction of certain fines in 1844, only those building substantial middle-class houses and mills took leases.[22]

A two-tier system of ground rents existed, the rents fixed for land taken on tenancy at will being less than those charged for the equivalent land on leasehold. But, despite the relative cheapness of the land and the incentive inherent in the pricing system to acquire large plots, the intensity of development was high, most houses being built back-to-back, in close and confined courts. If the pricing system had no effect on the pattern of development, it influenced the process of building.

The size of a building project on the Ramsden Estate was substantially less than elsewhere, with most houses built in ones or twos, with additional houses being built some years later and few building projects consisted of more than six houses. On other estates where long-term leases could be obtained, some larger building projects were undertaken, comprising between ten and twenty-five houses.[23]

The ease with which small plots of land could be acquired encouraged the participation of a large number of workers in the building process, contributing to its small scale characteristics and the development of building clubs. The tendency was so unusual that it elicited this comment by a government visitor in 1847:

> There is a peculiarity observed in Huddersfield that workmen pride themselves in being able to build and have a house of their own. More cottages belong to workmen than in any other town.[24]

The same observer also remarked on the high proportion of building societies to the population. These were the small building clubs in which most individuals saved for about twenty years; the amounts were 4s. in the winter and 8s. in the summer, much less than normally quoted for building societies. Women as well as men were savers and not all savers built only for themselves. The quality of building was poor, for when such investors had accumulated perhaps fifty pounds, 'they will go and build a house that costs perhaps seventy or eighty pounds but are unable to complete it . . . the privies are the last things erected and they are generally badly done. They have no capital to go farther'.[25] This accounts for the generally poor sanitary condition of the town.

Such building clubs appear to have financed a large proportion of the working-class house-building in Huddersfield, particularly on the Ramsden Estate. In 1859, 1,794 members of forty-one such clubs subscribed £531,589, with £232,449 paid, for tenant at will property on the Ramsden Estate. Between 1859 and 1879, fifty-four clubs are mentioned as financing building on leasehold land from the estate. In the surrounding industrial villages, local merchant clothiers, doctors and solicitors more frequently supplied capital.[26]

Much political protest was levelled at the hardships a tenant at will would face in 1859 when the tenancies were finally abolished and converted to more expensive 99-year leases.[27] It was probably as much the informal nature of the acquisition of land as its cheapness, however, that encouraged this form of building process and successfully housed the working population during the early stages of modernisation.

Landowner management strategies after 1845

The first half of the century was followed by a period during which there was a more active attempt by the larger landowners, such as Thornhill and Ramsden, to control the character of development with varying success depending on market conditions. Amongst the smaller landowners, attitudes to land development by those who were resident differed from those who were absentees. Resident landowners were reluctant to open their estates to development no matter how great the pressure to do so. Thus, the Fisher Estate was only opened for development after the death of the owner Edward Fisher, and land adjacent to Henry Dewhirst's home in Fartown was not opened until after Dewhirst was certified insane and the estate passed into the hands of trustees. Landowners who were resident and did develop their estates also tended to show more concern for the character of development and often enforced extensive restrictive covenants.[28]

Such landowners were keen to benefit from middle-class demand and sought to satisfy that class's desire for preservation of the *status quo* in the hope of encouraging well-built and substantial properties. The existence of a general plan of an estate's development for the protection and guidance of all parties concerned also helped to induce stability in the market. A landowner who made no attempt to safeguard the interests of the middle classes did so at the risk of his future income. Frances Battye found it increasingly difficult to let land on her estate for superior villas after she had attempted to exploit the potential of land adjacent to Marsh for terraced houses. Tenants on her estate even petitioned the council about terraced houses being built behind their properties.[29]

The nature and content of covenants varied from estate to estate. The most wide-ranging restricted use to residential only and a defined level of maintenance. Some controlled house type by stipulating the value of the house to be built. Back-to-back houses were controlled by clauses specifying the location of windows. Sometimes specific types of houses were excluded. Thus leases granted on land belonging to G. W. Marsh specifically stipulated that no cottage with only one room on the ground floor should be built.[30]

The closest control of development on estates other than Ramsden was undertaken by the managers of the Thornhill Estate. Following the death of Thomas Thornhill in 1844, the Estate's management had passed to the hands of the Court in Chancery who oversaw its development on behalf of his heir, Clara, who did not come of age until 1857. Concerned with maximising income and improving the value of the Estate, the day to day management was placed under the aegis of a Dr Ramsbottom, a local agent, and eventually handed over to three trustees, including Dr Ramsbottom, under the Thornhill Estate Act in 1852. Under a deed of dedication appertaining to the Thornhill Estate Act of 1852, detailed covenants were laid down for the leases granted in each of three areas of development identified. This ensured that building followed the course stipulated by the Act. All plans and elevations were subject to close scrutiny by the agents of the Trustees and any change in use or ownership was with their consent.

For the Edgerton area, destined to be the most fashionable in Huddersfield, the covenant stipulated that no trade of any kind would be allowed and the only properties to be created would be villas (Figure 18:5). In the other two areas, at Lindley and Hillhouse (Figures 18:6 and 18:7), no offensive trade was to be allowed unless first sanctioned by the lessor and a penalty of £10 was to be exacted if such a trade was practised without consent. Villas in the Edgerton area were to be erected only when their exact location and architectural quality had been agreed by the agents of the estate. In Hillhouse the forecourt of each house was to be 'kept entirely as garden', while for houses in Lindley restrictions were placed on the construction of cellars. The range of covenants selected for each area was ideally suited for the market and largely the result of the expertise of F.R. Jones.[31]

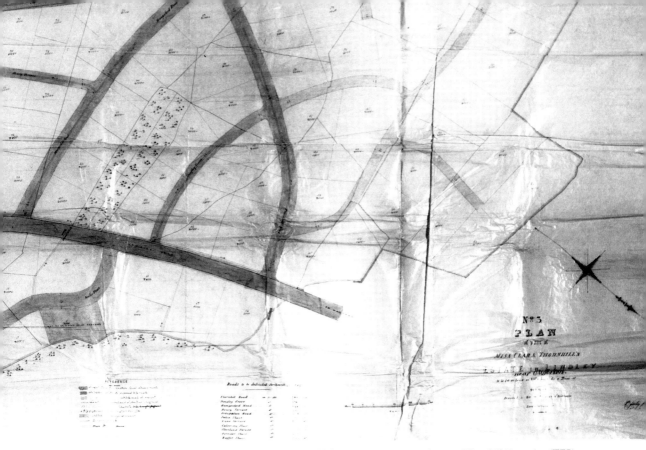

Fig. 18:5 *Plan of Clara Thornhill's estate of Edgerton from the deed of dedication appertaining to the 1852 Thornhill Estate Act. (TEP)*

Fig. 18:6 *Plan of Clara Thornhill's estate at Lindley from the deed of dedication appertaining to the 1852 Thornhill Estate Act. (TEP)*

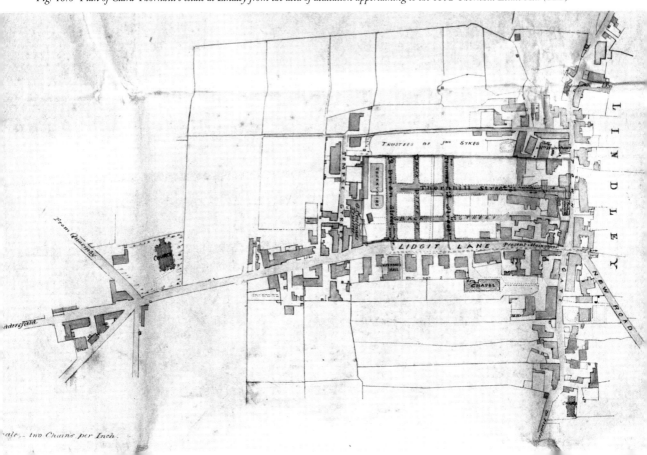

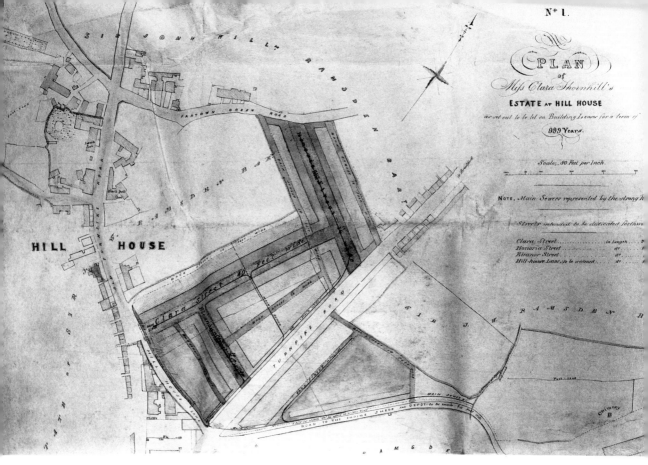

PLAN
of
Miss Clara Thornhill's
ESTATE AT HILL HOUSE
as set out to be let on Building Leases for a term of
999 Years.

Scale, 80 Feet per Inch.

NOTE. Main Sewers represented by the strong li...

Streets intended to be dedicated for thir...

Clara Street .... in Length ...
Honoria Street .... do ...
Eleanor Street .... do ...
Hill-house Lane (to be widened ... do ...

HILL HOUSE

Fig. 18:7 Plan of Hillhouse from the deed of dedication appertaining to the 1852 Thornhill Estate Act. (TEP)

The success of a covenant depended on its enforcement and continual surveillance of building was necessary. Only the Thornhill and Ramsden Estates maintained a high level of enforcement. Often landowners depended on professional surveyors rather than their own agents and in the final decade of the century found it difficult to impose covenants to ensure that only middle-class housing was built. The growing practice of offering either leasehold or freehold also reduced any effectiveness of a covenant.

The imposition of covenants reflected an attempt by landowners to take a more positive role in urban development through restrictions on builders' behaviour. In doing so they hoped to preserve or increase the value of their assets by attempting to exert some control over the output in the production process. The power of the landowner to dictate the terms of contract was dependent on the continuance of a monopoly in the supply of land, or at least an agreement amongst potential development landowners that they would act in a similar manner. The mobility of the middle class increased competition amongst landowners by providing the opportunity for choice in location. It also allowed choice between landowners concerning the terms of tenure offered. During the period 1859 to 1867, when the Ramsden Estate only offered leasehold on 99-years, builders sought land from other landowners who offered 999-year terms, despite a number of attempts by Sir John William Ramsden to stimulate development. This was most strikingly illustrated at Hillhouse where builders chose land solely from the Thornhill Estate during this period despite more accessible land made available by the Ramsden Estate.[32]

Some landowners also provided streets to encourage development. Although streetage charges were made, this provided a useful service to the building undertaker and facilitated development generally. The initial outlay could be considerable. Three roads in the Thornhill Estate, for example, cost a total of £1,498 12s. 3d. in 1863.[33] While builders were willing to tolerate restrictions that would increase their building costs in the 1850s, the rise in ground rents and the introduction of 99-year and then 999-year leases increased their sensitivity to such restrictions and charges and they gravitated towards landowners who did not impose them. Mention has already been made of the extent to which this was apparent to contemporaries and it was continually remarked upon by local agents in their correspondence with Sir John William Ramsden. In the depression of the 1890s all landowners stopped streetage charges. Indeed by the 1870s a new type of landowner/developer was emerging. Unconstrained by the mores of a previous age – the aristocratic notions of estate continuity, the role of the landowner and the reciprocal relationship between landowners and tenants – such entrepreneurs were concerned only with short term economic gain. They were, however, a fundamental necessity for a building industry that was dominated by petty capitalists.

Examples of such landowners/developers included Richard Brook, who purchased a block of lots from the Kaye Estate in 1857 and, having built a house himself, leased the remainder to building undertakers in small lots, financing their operations with the Moldgreen Permanent Benefit Building Society, of which he was secretary.[34] Nearly all of the new landowner/developers had some previous connection with the building industry or estate development. George Crowther, a local surveyor and agent for the Thornhill Estate, from 1880 onwards gradually acquired various shares in the Ashworth Estate at Row and in 1893 opened it for development.[35] Most active and dominant of all was J.A. Armitage, who initially gained experience in land development as a trustee of an estate at Crosland Hill in 1879. He entered into partnership with John Henry Hanson of the local firm of surveyors, Abbey and Hanson. In 1857 they purchased an estate at Thornton Lodge, laid out streets and drains, made the land available on 999-year leasehold at a bargain rent of 1d. per square yard and imposed no streetage charges. The extremely rapid uptake of plots, mostly for back-to-back houses, meant that within ten years all twenty acres were covered with buildings. In 1890 Armitage collaborated with one Sarah Martha Grove Grady in the purchase and development of an estate at Moldgreen. This time the option of either freehold or leasehold tenure was given. Finally, in 1897, again in partnership with Hanson, Armitage purchased forty-five acres at Clough House.[36] Here again leasehold and freehold terms were offered to the builder. Indeed, sale of land as freehold allowed the landowner to defray the expense incurred in laying out streets, for which no charge was made, and enabled land to be supplied with leasehold or freehold at the price the market would bear.*

The Ramsden Estate and the residential fabric of Huddersfield

Although the Ramsden Estate only belatedly attempted to capitalise on its monopoly power at a time when that power was already diminishing, decisions taken by that estate did have a substantial impact, if not always that which was intended, on the residential fabric of Huddersfield.

The death of Sir John Ramsden in 1839, and the takeover of the estate by trustees, heralded the introduction of a more formal system of management seeking to maximise long-term economic returns from the property. Responsibility for overall policy, including decisions on the location of new roads, on the quality of new buildings and on the level of rents, was separated from day-to-day management. The latter was left in the hands of a full-time local agent and a full-time surveyor. Estate surveys were commissioned, systems of registering leases and tenancies at will were formalised and new building was strictly monitored (Figure 18:8 to 18:15).

Initially the overall strategy was directed by George Loch, in consultation with Earl Fitzwilliam. Loch, who was appointed steward of the estate in place of John Bower, had been subagent to his father James Loch, agent to the Dukes of Bridgwater and Sutherland and Lord Carlisle. His appointment had

*For a discussion of land development, see Chapter Seventeen. EDITOR.

been urged by Mrs Isabella Ramsden, mother of Sir John William; she had had previously engaged Loch to oppose a bill for laying a railway across the Byram Estate. Loch's correspondence shows him to have been extremely efficient and it was on his advice that major changes were made in the administrative structure of the estate, for Loch maintained that 'in the management of all considerable affairs, it is useful to keep the arrangement of local details in separate hands from those to which general supervision should be entrusted'.[37]

Fig. 18:8 Church Street, Paddock. (KCS)

Fig. 18:9 Church Street, Paddock. (KCS)

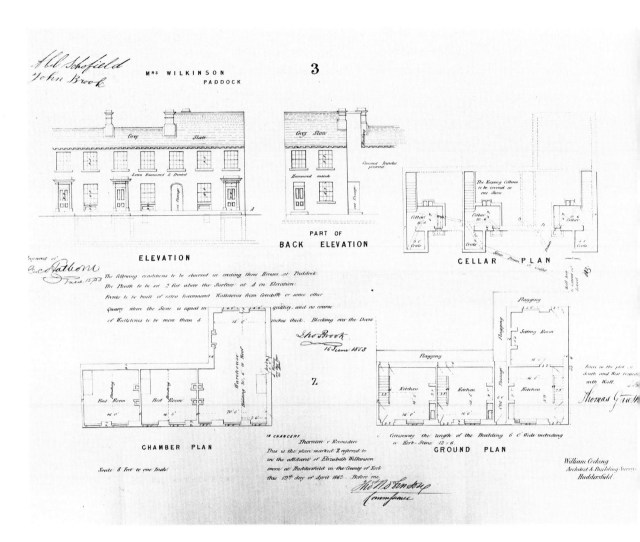

Fig. 18:10 Three houses at
Paddock, designed by
William Cocking. (KCS)

468

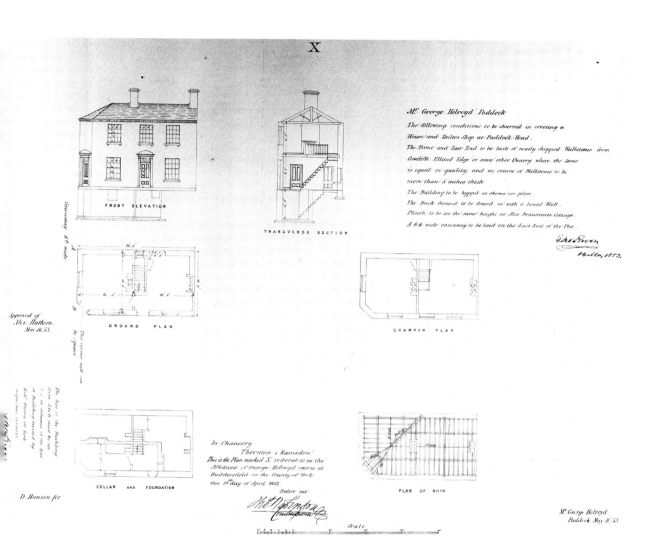

Fig. 18:11 House and
Tailor's shop at Paddock
Head. (KCS)

469

Fig. 18:12 House of
Hannah Holmes,
Highfield Road, 1863.
(KCS)

Fig. 18:13 Hebble
Terrace, Bradford Road.
(KCS)

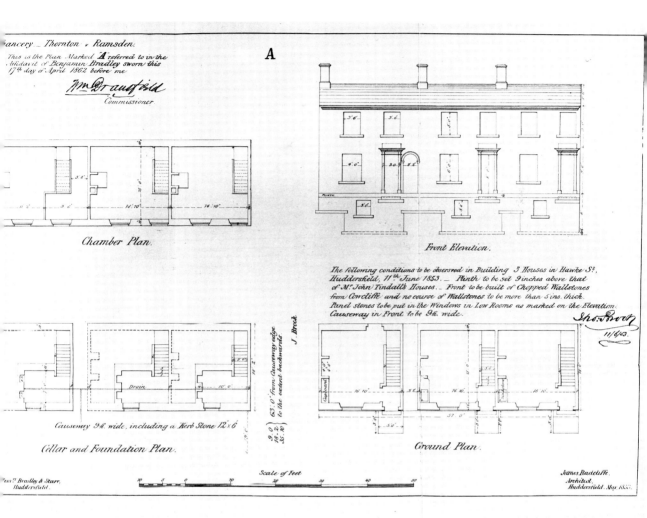

Fig. 18:14 Three houses
in Hawke Street,
Huddersfield, designed by
James Radcliffe. (KCS)

Fig. 18:15 Houses, New North Road. (KCS)

After 1853, when Sir John William Ramsden came of age, a London solicitor, Nelson, took over as steward and auditor. Then finally in 1859, Sir John William took direct control over decision-making, declaring his intention, 'to dispense as much as possible with the intervention of agents and cultivating a more direct personal intercourse on all business matters with the town of Huddersfield'.[38]

Each individual brought to bear his own view of the best way to maintain and improve the long-term value of the estate. Lord Fitzwilliam was reluctant to allow large-scale speculative developments, no doubt reflecting his experience in Sheffield where the activities of middlemen had led to 'jerry-building'. George Loch, an experienced estate manager, was very conscious of the need to maintain the tenants' confidence in the estate in order to promote its continued development, particularly in handling tenancies at will. Nelson, a solicitor, was more concerned with legality, and considered tenancies at will detrimental to the interest of the estate since they lowered the potential annual income. The way he achieved its abolition completely undermined the confidence upon which Loch had set great store; Nelson's substitution of London-style 99-year leases in 1859 illustrates his detachment from the reality demands of local builders in Huddersfield. Sir John William was more sensitive to local needs but his attitudes and decisions were coloured by aristocratic notions of long-term territorial growth, estate maintenance, private landed interest and his own personal prejudices against back-to-back houses and speculators. As a result he failed to be sufficiently responsive to changes in demand.[39]

On the Ramsden Estate all new building was strictly supervised, even when long-term leases were introduced. Each application was dealt with on its merits. Covenants in these leases gave considerable scope for discretion by the landowner, who had to approve all plans. It was necessary, however, to secure the erection of a good class of buildings short of imposing restrictions detrimental to the letting of land. Loch was more successful in maintaining this delicate balance than subsequent decision-makers. His task was in many ways much easier, because during the late 1840s and early 1850s the demand for building land on the estate reached a peak. Builders were so eager to obtain sites that they were willing to submit to restrictions and thereby incur higher costs. John Tindall wrote to Loch proposing that he should build a court of nine cottages, maintaining that if he were not allowed to include four cellar dwellings he would not build at all. When his application, following estate policy banning cellar dwellings, was refused, he omitted the cellar dwelling and built what Alexander Hathorn, the local agent, described as 'a respectable well-regulated pile of working men's cottages'. When William Brook sought permission to build a set of back-to-back cottages in Bradford Road and Hathorn convinced him of the disadvantages of such a plan, he built simple cottages instead.[40]

Whatever the economic reasoning behind such restrictions the effects on development were threefold. First, they accentuated a trend, apparent in most late Victorian cities, towards building for the lower middle classes, and thus contributed to pricing out the working class from the market for new houses. An early observer of this was Hathorn in 1853:

> When a builder takes a piece in that way he will erect a certain number of houses for the poorest classes. What they do is build the first two and than a back house . . . . However, in the last three years . . . I have refused in many cases back houses and made sure I only accept sites that provide through ventilation and a separate outlet. However, it has meant that rents rose to £12 rather than £6.[41]

A second effect was that builders sought sites from other landowners and continued to build such houses elsewhere. This trend was even more marked after the introduction of trams in 1883* made more distant estates potentially more accessible to the upper working class. A third effect was that intensity of development on Ramsden land was much lower than on similar land on adjacent estates.

Restrictions on back-to-back houses were not removed until 1900. The decision is recorded in Sir John's memorandum book, in which he recalls a visit to Fartown where the Dewhirst Estate abutted his own. On both estates new roads had been laid down and land was available on 999-year leases. The Dewhirst Estate, however, was being rapidly covered with back-to-back houses, while on the Ramsden Estate not one house had been built since 1885. He commented as follows:

> Wherever there is a bit of freehold, it is getting covered with houses, while hardly any building is in progress on my estate. The Corporation approves these houses and all the working class houses are now being built on this system. He (Colonel Beadon, the local agent) urges that I have stood against them long enough and now is the time to give way, that the public demand these cheap little houses and will have no others and that the only sound policy is to meet the public's wish. Sorely against my wish, I am constrained to admit he is right. What I have now seen of the buildings in progress proves my refusal is no good. It does not prevent these objectionable little houses being built, but only gives fictitious value to the small freeholds scattered about the town, over which I have no control.[42]

Although other estate policy had an indirect effect on new building, the estate also took some positive measures to steer particular developments to particular areas, more successfully in mid-century than later. As well as the position of streets, the estate encouraged industrial establishments, particularly chemical works, to locate at the extremity of the estate, away from residential areas. In 1863 a freehold estate was actually purchased with the sole object of preventing the erection of a chemical factory near the town.[43] Estate managers also considered it their responsibility to facilitate the provision of public amenities such as churches, schools and parks, through

*The tram service is described in Chapter Sixteen. EDITOR.

reductions in rent. Not only was this done to provide for growing needs, but also with a view to stimulating development. As early as 1850 Hathorn suggested that the recently acquired Gledholt Estate be set aside as a park to encourage the erection of villas. In fact the park was not made public until 1880, when the corporation acquired it with a contribution of £30,000 from Sir John William Ramsden. Almost certainly the location of St. John's Church on Clare Hill in 1853, was dictated primarily by the wish to encourage development in that area.

Such action could only be successful if the locations chosen were appropriate from the point of view of the market. By encouraging the segregation of land uses the estate was pandering to a trend already discernible amongst the middle classes. But the estate managers were insufficiently perspicacious to anticipate the demand for villa sites at a greater distance from the town in areas such as Edgerton. In the year when the Thornhill Estate was seeking powers to let land in Upper Edgerton for just such a purpose, Loch commented on Edgerton that 'land there can never be so eligible as New North Road'.[44]

The landowner undertook no development himself, but the lack of demand for land from the estate prompted an attempt at active land promotion in the early 1860s. The scheme was largely the idea of a London architect, Habenshon. Three areas adjacent to existing roads were selected and sites for villas, houses of the value £20 to £30 per annum and smaller houses, 'suitable for railway porters and superior mechanics', were laid out. Sketches of different house types were provided and the new parsonage of St. John's Church was built as a model villa in the gothic style to illustrate how such a dwelling might be erected at minimal cost. A letter containing these proposals was circulated to London builders inviting them to undertake building in Huddersfield, since it was anticipated that if such builders started projects, local builders would follow suit. Habenshon considered that the combination of full-scale architectural control and secure financial inducements would attract a greater response from the building profession. The finance came from Sir John William himself who agreed to advance 60 per cent of the cost after the builders had spent the first 40 per cent. The project was only of limited success. The response came from members of the local building profession building the cheapest houses.

Nevertheless, a further twenty acres adjacent to Greenhead Park was surveyed and laid out in villa sites 'making best use of slopes in harmony with the landscape and vistas'. This scheme failed since the demand for such sites was limited and by now Edgerton had already established itself as a dormitory for the élite, thus the entire project was abandoned.[45]

The nineteenth century saw the transformation of the housebuilding process. Early development took place in an *ad hoc* informal manner founded on personal relationships and set against the background of paternalistic property relations fostered by the Ramsden Estate. The end of the century saw the emergence of a more complex and professional building production process concentrating solely on the needs of the burgeoning middle classes. The changes seen in Huddersfield, from socially mixed and often insanitary housing clustered around industrial developments to increasingly monotonous rows of back-to-back and terraced houses interspersed with segregated middle class districts of large villas, were features characteristic of all nineteenth century towns. Its uniqueness, however, in terms of specific development patterns was the product of the interaction between the decisions of landowners and building initiators within the context of changing socio-economic and political conditions. Nevertheless, the nature of the housebuilding process had its roots in the spatial pattern of predevelopment landownership and the near monopoly power of the Ramsden Estate during the early stages of its development.

Jane Springett

Biographical Note

Dr Springett studied as an undergraduate and postgraduate at Leeds University between 1970-76. She became a lecturer in Human Geography at Wolverhampton Polytechnic. After working for a short time in the Health Service she took up a post at Liverpool Polytechnic as a lecturer in Human Geography. She was promoted to Principal Lecturer in 1988 and became Head of Centre for Health Studies in September 1990. She has a strong committment and involvement in the W/D Health, Cities Project. She has two publications in relation to the historical geography of Huddersfield.

NOTES

1. A. Offer, *Property and Politics, 1870-1914: Landownership, Law, Ideology and Urban Development in England* (1981). P.J. Aspinall, *The Size Structure of the House-building Industry in Victorian Sheffield* (1977). M.J. Daunton, *Coal Metropolis: Cardiff 1870-1914* (1977); *House and Home in the Victorian City: Working-class Housing 1850-1914* (1983).

   E.W. Cooney, 'The speculative builders and developers of Victorian London – a comment' *Victorian Studies*, VIII (1969), 355-8.

2. J. Springett, 'Landownership and Housebuilding in Huddersfield 1770-1911', in *Building the Industrial City* edited by M. Doughty, pp.23-56.

3. H(ouse of) L(ords) R(ecord) O(ffice), Report of the Commissioners of her Majesty's Woods, Forests, Land Revenue, Works and Public Building; Local Acts, Huddersfield Improvement Bill – unpublished minutes.

4. J. Springett, 'The mechanics of urban land development – Huddersfield 1770-1911'. (unpub. Ph.D. Thesis, Leeds University, 1979), p.263.

5. *Huddersfield Chronicle*, 28 April 1877.

6. Report of Medical Office of Health, Huddersfield Council Proceedings Minutes 1899.

7. L.W. Dair Moir, *Report on Back-to-Back Homes*, (1910).

8. Many of these inner courtyards were demolished in the 1930s.

9. Often referred to in Parliamentary Reports, for example: *Select Committee on Town Holdings* . . . 260 xiii (1887), 313 xii (1888), 251 xv (1889). Sir John Ramsden was Lord of the Manor and many of the traditions surrounding the manorial court continued into the nineteenth century, including biannual rent dinners. These ritual activities sustained this manorial tradition beyond its real life.

10. Thornhill Estate Papers, Thornhill Estate Act 1852.

11. WYAS, Wakefield W(est) R(iding) R(egistry) of D(eeds)
    ME/553/681 1820; HE 592/678 1820; HE 593/679 1820; HC700/749 1820; HC 702/750 1820; HF 453/501 1820; HG 48/51 1820; HN 214/218 1821; GY510/526 1821; 12 587/562 1827.

12. WYAS, Kirklees, Thornhill Estate Papers. Affadavit of Christopher White, 1855.

13. WYAS, Kirklees, Thornhill. Court in Chancery Proceedings, Affadavit of Christopher White, 1855.

14. *Huddersfield Chronicle*, 16 March 1861.

15. WYAS, Kirklees, Ramsden Estate Papers. Mr Beasley's Report, DD/RA, Box 24.

16. WYAS, Kirklees, Ramsden, DD/RE/c/32.

17. WYAS, Kirklees, Ramsden DD/RA Box 36 Abstracts of Receipts and Expenditure, 1845-1863 DD/RA36/4 Correspondence Sir John William Ramsden to Major Graham 1873 Ramsden. DD/RA Box 18, DD/RA/2. Miscellaneous Documents including notes on property mortgaged. The Dawson File.

18. WYAS, Kirklees, Ramsden. Case filed in Chancery, 9 June 1862 Joseph Thornton and Lee Dyson, plaintiffs and Sir John William Ramsden, 2 vols. Miscellaneous Documents DD/RA Box 24. Abstract of Title to Purchased Estates.

19. WYAS, Kirklees, Thornhill DD/T/351. Brief petition for the Transfer of Funds in Court and Other Purposes. Notes on the back. Anon 26 June 1857. DD/T/351.

20. WYAS, Halifax, Radcliffe Estate Papers. Register of Deeds c.1800, R.A.D. 115/5 L.C.A. WYAS, Kirklees, C/T/z/42, Lockwood, Radcliffe and Little Royd Conveyancing Deed 1854 Ingham Estate Act. House of Lords, WRRD, MH/311/801, 1836.

21. WYAS, Kirklees, Ramsden. DD/RA Box 24 Rough Draft of Report to the Ramsden Trustees by George Loch, 1 June 1844.

22. WYAS, Kirklees, Ramsden. DD/RA Box 12 Case filed in Chancery 6 June 1862 between Joseph Thornton and Lee Dyson and Sir John Ramsden, 2 vols. Miscellaneous Documents relating to the tenant-right case received from Mr Nelson, 1874.

23. WYAS, Wakefield, WRRD. WYAS, Kirklees, Huddersfield CBC Archives C/T/z/42. Applications for leases and tenancies at will 1845-53. Register of Leases 1859-83, 1883-1908.

24. HLRO, Commission of Inquiry into Huddersfield Improvement Bill, unpublished minutes.

25. Appendix to the 'First Report of the Commission of Inquiry into the State of Large Towns and Populous Districts' 1844, (572) xvii, 177-8.

26. Case filed in Chancery, 6 June 1862. Applications for Leases 1859- WRRD, Miscellaneous Deeds.

27. Case filed in Chancery, 6 June 1862.

28. WYAS, Wakefield, WRRD, 34/47/29 1891; 42/879/372 19c Ramsden DD/RA. Correspondence Sir John William Ramsden t – June 1885, DD/RA/22/80. WRRD, 16/547/326 1890. WYA: DD/RA/14/1.

29. HLHS, Huddersfield Council Minutes; Committee for the Marsh

30. WYAS, Wakefield, WRRD, 37/8/49/894.

31. WYAS, Kirklees, Thornhill DD/T/315, Thornhill Estate Act 185 papers.

32. WYAS, Kirklees, Ramsden DD/RA/28/2; DD/RA/9/3 correspc John William Ramsden and Mr Habenshon 1862 DD/RA/28/2; D.

33. WYAS, Kirklees, Thornhill DD/T/33. Outlay and Incomes 1858-68

34. WYAS, Wakefield, WRRD, WG. 453/485 1861; 42/8/62 1865; 844/

35. WYAS, Wakefield, WRRD, 834/376/446 1879.

36. WYAS, Wakefield, WRRD, 32/275/148 1887; 13/287/149 1888; 27/822/49 1890; 26/1029/488 1890; 25/426/223 1890; 26/10441/492 1890; 28/653/313 1891; 2/44/208 1897; 2/436/206 1868; 2/439/207 1898.

37. WYAS, Kirklees, Ramsden DD/RE/41, letter from Isabella Ramsden to Lord Fitzwilliam July 1841. DD/RA Box 24 Rough Draft of Report to Ramsden Trustees by George Loch.

38. WYAS, Kirklees, Ramsden, DD/RA Box 28 letter from Sir John William Ramsden to Mr Nelson, 6 November 1859.

39. WYAS, Kirklees, Ramsden DD/RA/21/9. Isaac Hordern's notebook 1846-1911. Miscellaneous Correspondence DD/RA/15-40.

40. WYAS, Kirklees, Ramsden DD/RE/c/94-5, DD/RE/c/87.

41. WYAS, Kirklees, Ramsden DD/RE/c/102.

42. WYAS, Kirklees, Ramsden. DD/RA Box 5 Sir John William Ramsden's Interview and Memorandum Book vol. 7, 1899-1909.

43. WYAS, Kirklees, Ramsden DD/RA/9/1.

44. WYAS, Kirklees, Ramsden DD/RA/c/105.

45. WYAS, Kirklees, Ramsden DD/RA/28/2, DD/RA/9/3, DD/RA/20/10, DD/RA/41/1, DD/RA/37/3.

CHAPTER 19

Parliamentary Politics in Huddersfield, c.1832-53

VIVIENNE W. HEMINGWAY

Huddersfield parliamentary politics in the first two decades after the borough's enfranchisement in 1832 were boisterous, often corrupt, and marked by divisions amongst the various political parties contesting the elections, as well as amongst factions in the majority of the population who could not vote. These interests used several methods of influencing the electorate, yet the main political influence in the borough has always been seen as the Ramsden family.[1] A first glance at the results of the seven elections held in the borough from 1832 to 1852 gives weight to this belief, as the Whig-Liberal candidate favoured by the Ramsdens was elected on each occasion (see Table 1).[2] The question of how much actual influence the Ramsdens had, however, is not easy to assess, nor is it easy to distinguish between what was regarded as "proper" and "undue" influence over tenants. A great deal must have depended on what the tenants themselves thought of as being within normal bounds, and evidence for this is very scarce. Those who opposed the Ramsden candidates also had their own methods of influencing voters, such as putting pressure on shopkeepers, but how far these methods were effective is also open to debate.

One of the reasons why Huddersfield has always been thought of as a nomination borough under the control of the Ramsdens is that, under the second Reform Bill, the boundaries of the borough were limited to the township, in which the Ramsdens owned the majority of the land, rather than the wider parish. The small borough which resulted was given only one MP, in spite of the fact that it was an important manufacturing town and paid more taxes than either Halifax or Bradford, which were to have two. The

Table 1 Voting Statistics, Huddersfield Borough Elections 1832-53.

Date	Whig		Liberal		Tory		Radical		Total
	No.	%	No.	%	No.	%	No.	%	
1832	263	63.4	0	0	0	0	152	36.6	415
1834	234	47.8	0	0	147	30.1	108	22.1	489
1835	241	68.9	0	0	0	0	109	31.1	350
1837	340	54	0	0	290	46	0	0	630
1837	323	51.8	0	0	301	48.2	0	0	624
1847	525	51.8	488	48.2	0	0	0	0	1,013
1852	625	51.4	590	48.6	0	0	0	0	1,215
1853	593	46.8	675	53.2	0	0	0	0	1,268

inhabitants of the town petitioned the House of Commons in February 1832 to extend the limits of the borough to the parish rather than the township, and to allot two MPs instead of one. This petition was forwarded to John Charles Ramsden, eldest son of Sir John, for presentation, which he refused.[3] He stated that he had always believed that if the town was of sufficient importance to be enfranchised, that franchise should be confined to the township, rather than be extended to other areas which were not in sympathy with its interests. He also objected to references to his family in the petition, in which it was stated that, although the inhabitants were sure that Sir John would not abuse his position in the town, it would still leave the borough open to the influence of some future proprietor.[4]

The fact that John Charles Ramsden offered himself as candidate, without being asked, shortly after the Reform Act was passed in June 1832, would also appear to confirm the belief that Huddersfield was a Ramsden borough. As an MP for Yorkshire he was undoubtedly well qualified, but his candidature was bound to be looked on with suspicion by the inhabitants. In the letter announcing his intention to stand for election, he did take care to emphasise that the electors' choice should be motivated by their own 'free will', but, at the same time, he also made several references to the connection between the borough and his family.[5]

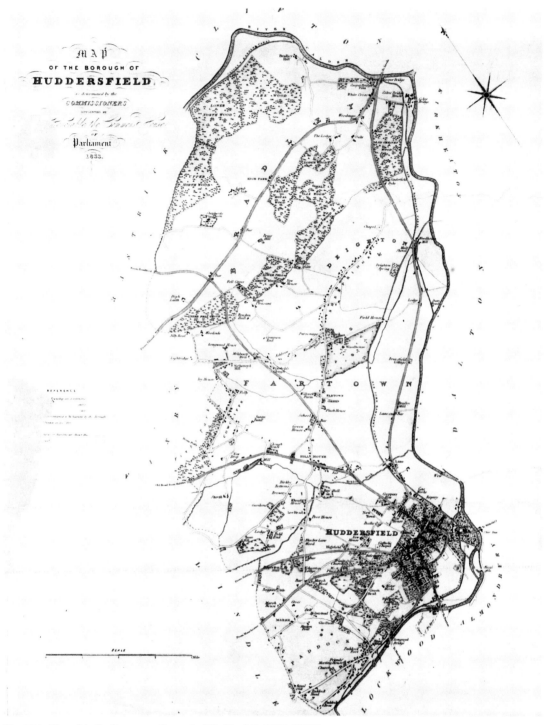

Fig. 19:1 Map of the Parliamentary Borough of Huddersfield, 1833. (KCS)

483

It was probably because of his family connections that John Charles was not well received when he visited Huddersfield on 28 June 1832. His candidacy was also not helped by the fact that, shortly before his arrival, his father had issued a notice to his tenants insisting on the ancient provision, still embodied in clauses in his building leases, that only his corn mills should be used by lessees. This could not be regarded by the inhabitants as anything other than a threat, and, coupled with an election at which his son was a candidate, was not likely to ensure a welcome for John Charles.[6] J.C. Ramsden also made things more difficult for himself. His opposition to Sadler and the Ten Hour Bill was bound to bring out against him the locally popular Richard Oastler and members of the Factory Movement, who were campaigning for a reduction in the hours of labour of children in factories. Although John Charles had stated that he would not interfere with the liberty of conscience of any of the electorate, it appears that he was not averse to trying to use his family's power to try and reduce the influence of a non-elector such as Oastler. He wrote to Oastler's employer, Thomas Thornhill, complaining of Oastler's activities against him, and Thornhill then wrote to Oastler enclosing the letter. It would seem that both Thornhill and Oastler were under the misapprehension that the letter was from Sir John, and so Oastler wrote to Thornhill commenting that:

> Sir John is not correct in saying that 'Oastler opposes **him** in Huddersfield'. That is impossible. It is positively declared by his own party, that **he** has **no** hand in the matter. Even his son says that 'he (Sir John) will punish no one who conscientiously opposes him (Mr Ramsden)', and I am sure that I do, most sincerely and conscientiously.[7]

By this time John Charles Ramsden was seriously beginning to doubt the prospects of his return for Huddersfield, and an *Address* from the Gentry, Clergy, and Electors of the North Riding of Yorkshire, requesting him to allow them to nominate him instead for that Riding, provided him with the excuse he needed to release himself from the unfriendly atmosphere of Huddersfield politics.[8] His place was taken by Captain Lewis Fenton, who does not appear to have received any open endorsement from Sir John, though as his brother, J.C. Fenton, was a Ramsden agent, it is probable that Captain Fenton at least received some indirect Ramsden support. It is impossible to say, however, how much this contributed to his success at the election.[9]

Now then fellow-countrymen,

Behold the *puny* band who have arrayed themselves against you! THE BLACKBURNITES! 234 in number!! and the Sadlerites! 137!!!—After the *iniquitous* Bill had entrusted your rights into the hands of about 1200 Ten Pound Voters—and after the *more iniquitous* clauses had cut them down to 600, instead of that bona fide constituency making up in *patriotic* virtue for their numerical deficiency— what is the result? They have betrayed you into the hands of the Philistines. *They* have a second time set aside the Man of your choice. Yes: and *they* glory in the deed! *They* know your disappointment, but *they* treat it with contempt; and, while *they* affect to call your *patience* stupidity, *they* nick-name *their* own HAUGHTINESS independence. YES, YES, this knot of *exclusives* have indeed sent a *legislator* —what a LUMINARY—to Parliament. *What a sample for the* "COLLECTIVES." *Oh! St. Stephen's, will Lawyers do when Patriots are wanted?* But he is your *mis*-representative; can he be otherwise? Is he not the avowed ENEMY of UNION? The pledged opponent of the *extension* of the *franchise?* Shall all this be suffered with impunity? Oh, no: *they* shall have their own maxims tried upon themselves; "what is sauce for the goose, is sauce for the gander," says the proverb. If these *new* boroughmongers will have the *power* exclusively, let them enjoy *their* TRADE after the same *reforming* fashion. Touch *their* POCKETS, and *their spurious* INDEPENDENCE will lick the dust. WOODITES! look to each other—support one another—by this you will CONQUER. Remember, and never forget, that *labour* is the only earthly handmaid of wealth, power, and *safety*. You, the unrepresented, are the BEES; let the DRONES take care of themselves till *they* learn to whom the hive belongs. By this, you will school them to duty; although, in beings so selfish, it is folly to look for *principle*. Fellow countrymen! *two hundred and thirty-four* cannot rule. The pyramid does not stand on its apex; neither can this *Galtonian* constituency avoid the fate of its prototype. Be united, persevere, and victory will come gloriously crowned with your RIGHTS.

Fig. 19:2 Joshua Hobson's comments on the 1834 election. (KCS)

485

The problem with assessing the amount of Ramsden influence for elections in the 1830s is that there is very little evidence. Following John Charles Ramsden's withdrawal of his candidacy, no references to election matters have been traced in the Ramsden papers until George Loch took over as Steward of the Ramsden Estates in 1844. By this time the Estate was under the control of trustees, as Sir John William Ramsden, John Charles' son, was a minor. It cannot be denied that the Ramsden family were, on the whole, Whigs, and supported Whig-Liberal candidates, but whether this support was active or passive is more difficult to determine. There were, naturally, accusations of the use of Ramsden influence in favour of the winning candidate at all the elections of this period, barring that of 1853. After the 1832 election the Radical candidate, Captain Joseph Wood, stated that Fenton and his supporters had won due to deception, intimidation and influence, a view Joshua Hobson reiterated in his publication of the polling list, entitled *Who does Captain Phantom Represent?*.[10] Similar accusations were also made at the 1834 by-election, held due to the suspicious death (possibly suicide) of Captain Fenton. The *Voice of the West Riding*, which supported Wood in opposition to the Tory candidate, Michael Thomas Sadler, and the Whig-Liberal candidate John Blackburne, claimed that one of Sir John Ramsden's agents had been to see a farmer and told him that he must vote for Blackburne.[11]

Sudden death was a characteristic feature of early Huddersfield politics, and 1837 saw two elections for the borough, one caused by the death of John Blackburne, and the other by the death of William IV. Oastler was the opposing candidate at both. At the first of these elections, Oastler blamed his defeat partly on the influence of Sir John Ramsden, and partly on the presence of the troops who had been called into the town due to fears of disturbances. Oastler was one of the main leaders in Huddersfield of the Anti-Poor Law Movement. The introduction of the 1834 Poor Law Amendment Act into Huddersfield was the great popular issue of 1837, where it provoked outright disobedience, huge public meetings, and riotous assemblies. The essence of the new poor law, directed from London with a view to severe economy, was that those receiving poor relief were much more likely to be incarcerated in large workhouses, rather than being allowed to stay in their own homes.[12]

Oastler's stand against the new law, as against the long hours and child labour of the factories, was rooted in the alliance between paternalist Tory landowners and the popular politics of local workers. It was not surprising that he felt threatened by the influence of the town's leading property owner. Accordingly, he seized every opportunity to neutralise this influence. At the second election Oastler took care to state that Sir John had said:

> that he did not permit the least compulsion to be used to his tenants at Huddersfield, that he felt exceedingly obliged to them for the manner in which they had improved his property; and if anybody had been intimidated in his name it was not in his knowledge nor by his orders.[13]

It is questionable how far the statements of those opposing the Whig-Liberal candidates, and their supporters, can be relied on as evidence that Sir John Ramsden was using his influence to control the results of the elections. As practically all of the borough was owned by the Ramsden family it would be surprising if the defeated parties had not made such statements. It seems likely, however, that they were just the comments of sore losers, rather than having any actual basis of truth behind them. As pointed out above, Oastler himself did not believe that Sir John had instructed his agents to use his influence to manipulate the general election of 1837 in favour of the Whig-Liberal candidate W.R.C. Stansfield. This was perhaps the only election in the 1830s in which Sir John might have thought it necessary to do so if he was at all interested in keeping the borough in Liberal hands. Oastler had lost the 1837 by-election by only fifty votes, and with the Tories and Anti-Poor Law Movement behind him he was certainly not a candidate to be dismissed. If Sir John had been concerned about the direction in which Huddersfield politics was turning, he would naturally have exerted all his influence to increase the majority of the Whig-Liberal candidate. At the 1837 general election, however, Oastler came within twenty-three votes of winning the election. This does suggest that, whatever influences were at work, Sir John's was not one of them. It remains a possibility, however, that during the 1830s his agents, on their own account, were actively canvassing for the Liberal Party and may have used his name to influence voters.

The 1847 and 1852 elections put the question of Ramsden influence into quite another perspective. Here the involvement of the Ramsden agents in local electioneering is not in question, but it is difficult to assess the extent of their activities. At the 1847 election Stansfield stood in opposition to a Liberal candidate, John Cheetham. Cheetham represented those in the town, particularly Nonconformists, who were against state-aided education, and in favour of education being provided by religious voluntary organisations which received no aid from the state. The local Ramsden legal agent, J.C. Fenton, wrote to the steward, George Loch, asking for permission to sign the requisition calling on Stansfield to offer himself for election, stating that he saw no reason why the Ramsden Trustees should not allow a 'proper and cautious' use of their influence.[14] Earl Fitzwilliam, the most prominent of the Trustees, agreed with this view, saying:

> there can be no objection whatever to Mr Fenton signing the requisition to Mr Stansfield; on the contrary, I think it most desirable that he should, and that it should be thoroughly understood that he enjoys the thorough good wishes of the Trustees, though they do not desire to exercise any power, or even influence, over the election.[15]

The Chairman of Stansfield's committee was told that he could advertise the fact that Stansfield had the cordial approval of the Trustees. As the election approached, a decision was taken that the resident agents should visit the direct tenants of the Ramsdens and inform them that the Trustees supported Stansfield and hoped they would vote for him. This was to be the limit of their involvement, but it did not prevent Cheetham's committee complaining to Earl Fitzwilliam that the agents were 'improperly' interfering with the course of the election. This was a question of what was regarded as the 'legitimate' influence of property. The Trustees evidently believed there was nothing wrong in making their choice of candidate known, as long as no threats or intimidation were used.[16] Earl Fitzwilliam was particularly clear on this point, stating:

> the humblest among them has a right to be exempt from any such humiliation, but at the same time it must be made perfectly clear how earnest the Trustees are in their support of Mr Stansfield, and how highly they will appreciate any exertion made in his behalf.[17]

The actual extent of Ramsden involvement in the election is not entirely clear. It is evident that the agents did visit the direct tenants, and it appears that J.C. Fenton made a great deal of effort to persuade Conservatives to vote for Stansfield rather than abstain, though he probably did not do so at the

Fig. 19:3 Alexander Hathorn, Agent for the Ramsden Estate. (KCS)

request of the Trustees.[18] Alexander Hathorn, the Ramsdens' Agent, was accused by Cheetham's committee of visiting tenants who had already pledged their votes to Cheetham, taking with him their employer, after which several of them had announced that they would have to violate their pledges and not vote at all. Earl Fitzwilliam thought these accusations had no foundation in fact, but they do show the amount of influence that could be used to put pressure on electors.[19]

The Ramsden agents were also actively involved in the general election of 1852. Before this, however, discussions had taken place between Stansfield, Loch, Mrs Isabella Ramsden (widow of John Charles Ramsden), and Sir John William Ramsden regarding the future representation of the town. Stansfield wanted to retire on health grounds, and it was hoped that if an election were held after Sir John reached the age of twenty-one, in September of that year, the Ramsden heir would stand as a candidate. There was some idea of proposing him as candidate before he came of age, but it was thought that the inhabitants of Huddersfield would regard the election of an MP who could not vote in Parliament as tantamount to disfranchising the borough.[20]

The Ramsden agents participated more in this election than in the previous one. Even before it was known that Stansfield would be opposed, it seems to have been decided that the resident agents should visit the Ramsden tenants and urge them not to pledge for anyone opposing Stansfield, though this was to be done 'discreetly' and without exercising 'undue' influence. Hathorn, Fenton, and the Ramsden surveyor, Thomas Brook, also attended meetings of Stansfield's committee, and, although it is not clear whether or not they were members of it, they certainly worked for the committee.[21] The opposing candidate, William Willans, after the result of the election had been declared, charged Hathorn in particular with influencing the course of the election, as he had been seen riding beside a cart which contained a Stansfield elector. The *Huddersfield Examiner* also had several comments to make on 'landlordism' and the dependence of the borough on the Ramsden family.[22]

It is apparent that the local Ramsden agents, particularly Hathorn and Brook, were more active in this election than in any other, though it is not clear whether they were working only for Stansfield's committee, or on behalf of the Ramsden Trustees. They were certainly implicated in the illegal practices associated with Stansfield's election campaign. On 24 November 1852 a petition was presented to Parliament alleging that Stansfield and his committee had been guilty of bribery, treating and corruption at the election, and requesting that Stansfield should be unseated and Willans declared elected. A counter-petition was then presented by Stansfield's supporters alleging similar practices by Willans' committee.[23] Both Hathorn and Fenton saw the petition as an attempt to destroy Sir John William's political influence in the borough, Fenton commenting that the opposition was determined

> to overthrow Sir John's interests in Huddersfield as well as that of all the influential part of the inhabitants who are anxious to support him and to admit that property ought to have a **due** influence.[24]

Hathorn was one of those to whom the Speaker of the House of Commons issued a summons, requesting him to appear before a Select Committee which would be held to enquire into the election, taking with

"All are not Men that bear the Human Form."

VIEW EXTRAORDINARY

OF SIR JOHN's

HUDDERSFIELD

MENAGERIE

OF

POLITICAL HOUHYNIMS, OURANG OUTANGS, KAN-GAROOS, LIZARDS, CAMELIONS, CROCADILES, LOCUSTS, AND HYÆNAS:

WITH A VARIETY OF OTHER SECTARIAN ODDITIES OF DISSENT,

CANTWELLS, MAWWORMS, BOOBIES, HUMBUGS, AND HYPOCRITES,

IN THE BROUGHAMIC ORDER OF DEMOCRACY:

"Or Animals one knows not what to call,
Their Generation's so equivocal!"

BY JAY AITCH, "C. & F."

Soon as the potion works, their Human Countenance,
The express resemblance of the Gods, is changed
Into some brutish form of Wolf, or Bear,
Or Ounce, or Tyger, Hog, or Bearded Goat,
All other parts remaining as they were:
And they, so perfect is their misery,
Not once perceive their foul disfigurement;
But boast themselves more comely than before.

MASK OF COMUS.

LEEDS:

PRINTED, FOR THE BENEFIT OF ALL PARTIES, BY J. HOBSON, MARKET STREET, BRIGGATE.

—

1837.

Fig. 19:4 The front cover of a pamphlet written by Jay Aitch (Joshua Hobson) attacking the conduct of the 1837 election. (KCS)

him all papers, books and accounts relating to it. Hathorn commented to Loch that 'luckily' he did not have any documents to produce. He did not say, however, whether he had never had any, or whether he had destroyed, or passed on to someone else, those that he had.[25]

Hathorn did not in the event give evidence at the Select Committee on the Huddersfield Election Petition, held in March 1853. Several witnesses, though, did mention both Hathorn and Brook being involved, albeit indirectly, in the illegal proceedings of Stansfield's Committee. It appears that they had visited four of the witnesses and asked them how they were going to vote. The witnesses were then taken to the George Hotel the night before polling day and given supper, a room for the night, and breakfast, before going to vote for Stansfield. The reason why they were taken to the George was that they lived outside the town, and threats had been made by non-electors who supported Willans that they would kidnap them so that they could not vote.[26] These were not very serious allegations against Hathorn and Brook, and they were not implicated in the general treating that had occurred in the borough, but it does raise the question of whether or not they and the Ramsden Trustees knew what Stansfield's committee were doing. It is hardly likely that Hathorn and Brook did not know what was happening, but it is possible that they worked for Stansfield's committee purely as canvassers and were not involved in any illegal proceedings. It is also possible that the Trustees had not been informed of the activities of Stansfield's committee, and would not have countenanced their agents being involved in any way. The surviving Ramsden correspondence is certainly mute on this point, no mention being made of the agents' activities other than normal canvassing.

It would appear from the evidence of the 1853 Select Committee that Ramsden influence was not the deciding factor in either the 1847 or the 1852 elections, although there is little doubt that the family wished to uphold its political position in the borough. It could be argued that the reason why the Whig-Liberal candidate, Joseph Starkey, lost the 1853 election was that illegal practices had ceased and the Ramsdens found that their influence was not as great as they had supposed. On the other hand, it is also possible that after the Select Committee enquiry they decided they wanted nothing further to do with politics in the borough. Sir John William Ramsden certainly appears to have taken little interest in his estate at Huddersfield, politically or otherwise, and his election as MP for Taunton in April 1853 effectively put an end to any aspirations he might have had to stand for Huddersfield.

Even if Ramsden influence is admitted, though not as a deciding factor in elections, there were also other interests at work to counteract or support it. In the 1830s in particular, both Radical and Tory working class supporters made a great deal of use of the practice of 'friendly' or 'exclusive' dealing. This activity was in many cases by no means friendly, involving threatening and intimidating shopkeepers to force them either to vote for the candidate the working classes supported, or at the very least to make them promise not to vote at all. If retailers did vote for the Whig-Liberal candidate they were faced with the prospect of losing many of their working-class customers. This practice was not confined to Huddersfield borough. The organisation of the Factory Movement, and later the Anti-Poor Law Movement, meant that 'friendly dealing' could be extended to the out-townships where retailers were threatened that if they obtained supplies from traders in Huddersfield who voted for the Whig-Liberal candidate, custom would also be withdrawn from them.

The use of exclusive dealing first appeared at the 1832 election. One meeting in particular, held in support of Captain Wood, objected to the candidature of John Charles Ramsden and the influence of his family, and resolved:

> in order to counteract such unworthy conduct, we, the labouring classes, do here declare that no butcher, barber, publican, shopkeeper, attorney, or medical man, who, by any conduct, shall attempt to return a person in the Ramsden interest, in opposition to Joseph Wood, Esq. a free candidate, shall finger our earnings.[27]

The practice of exclusive dealing does appear to have had some effect on the electors in the retail trade. Nearly 70 per cent of grocers and tea dealers voted for Wood, and 23 per cent of those who chose to remain neutral also had this occupation. These were not enough to offset the votes of Fenton's supporters in other occupations, however.[28] Wood's supporters in 1834 employed the same tactics, which were both criticised and commended in the press. The *Voice of the West Riding* printed several articles and letters in favour of such activities. One letter described exclusive dealing as 'the only just means left to the unenfranchised to work out their political emancipation', and as a counterbalance to the influence of property. The *Halifax Express*, however, condemned the hypocrisy of the Radicals, who spoke of universal rights and liberties, and purity of election, yet attempted to curtail the freedom of the electorate.[29] The shopkeepers were naturally unhappy with the situation. On 2 January 1834 a meeting was held to consider what measures they could take to defend themselves against intimidation. Those present resolved that:

> the present opposition of certain officious individuals, in the Borough of Huddersfield and its neighbourhood, who endeavour by Threatenings and other improper Proceedings, to **intimidate the Electors**, is a violation of conscience, and an arbitrary Attempt to Destroy the Rights of the Burgesses, whose privilege it is TO VOTE AS ENGLISHMEN, according to THE DICTATES OF THEIR OWN JUDGMENT.[30]

The meeting does not appear to have made a great deal of difference to the radical food-retailing vote, however. At the election the Tory and Liberal shopkeeper vote combined could only just equal that of the retailers who voted Radical.[31]

Exclusive dealing does not seem to have been extensively practised at either of the 1837 elections, or if it was, the fact was not openly admitted as it had been at previous elections. This is possibly because Oastler was not in favour of the practice, and did not want to alienate the more respectable Conservatives in the town by sanctioning its use. The Liberals did accuse the Radicals and Conservatives of intimidating retailers, but in fact more grocers and tea dealers voted for the Whig-Liberal candidates at both elections than voted for Oastler. On the other hand, more innkeepers and beersellers voted for Oastler, so it is possible that the non-electors, who were those mainly responsible for carrying out intimidatory practices, had more influence over the drink trade than they had over shopkeepers.[32] As on previous occasions, however, this pressure was not sufficient to determine the course of the election.

By the time of the 1847 and 1852 elections the intimidatory practice of exclusive dealing seems to have died out. This was probably because working-class politics were in disorder after the decline of Chartism, and the more respectable of the labouring classes moved into the mainstream political parties. The practice had not been totally forgotten, however. After the defeat of Willans at the 1852 election a broadsheet was printed entitled 'NON-ELECTORS CAN VOTE ON A SATURDAY NIGHT'. This suggested that non-electors should use their purchasing powers on pay day to buy goods only from those who had voted for Willans, so that when he again stood for Parliament he would be elected.[33]

In addition to the various outside influences that could be brought to bear on electors, there were also the activities of the supporters of the two mainstream parties, the Liberals and Conservatives. There is very little evidence regarding the organisation of political parties in Huddersfield, nor of the way in which they registered voters in the annual revision courts. The Conservatives seem to have been first to establish a rudimentary organisational structure by establishing a news room which opened in March 1833. This was followed three years later by the establishing of an Operative Conservative Society, which by 1838 was reported to have over 200 members. The aim of this Society was to instruct operatives:

> by means of newspapers and other publications, with correct views on political subjects, and to furnish an antidote to those publications which are everywhere intruded upon us; and also to unite with our fellow-townsmen and fellow-subjects in whatever would advance the national welfare, and to resist and oppose whatever would be detrimental to it.[34]

The Society appears to have held meetings twice a month, and organised annual dinners, but much of the work of organising the Conservative electors fell on the parent body, the Huddersfield Conservative Association. This was apparently formed before 1835, though it is only from 1835 onwards that the work of registering Conservative electors in the borough was organised on a more efficient basis.[35]

The Conservatives in Huddersfield do not seem to have actively searched for candidates to stand at elections, however. Sadler and Oastler appear to have been requested to stand by the Short-Time Committee and Anti-Poor Law Movement respectively, and Conservatives then rallied round them. Strangely, at the 1841 general election when the country as a whole was turning towards Conservatism, Huddersfield was one of the few places where a Conservative candidate was not nominated. This was perhaps owing to the fact that with the Tory-Radical alliance of 1837 being split due to Chartism, the Conservatives felt they had little chance of successfully contesting the election.

Even less is known about the activities of the Liberals in organising the Huddersfield constituency. A Liberal Registration Committee was formed in 1835, which was then replaced by a Registration Association in 1837. It is probable that both these organisations were part of a larger Association which looked after Whig-Liberal interests in the town. Further organisation was provided by the Anti-Corn Law League, a branch of which was formed in Huddersfield in 1839. This was a basically Liberal body which campaigned for the abolition of the corn laws, and tried to attract working-class support by holding out the prospect of cheaper bread.[36] As with the Conservatives in Huddersfield, committees to organise the canvassing of electors during elections seem to have been constructed on an *ad hoc* basis. It is not clear how the Huddersfield Whig-Liberal party was organised in the difficult years after 1837, by which time there was a distinct split in the party between those who wanted state-aided education, and those, particularly Nonconformists, who preferred the provision of education by religious voluntary organisations which received no aid from the State.* It is possible that those who supported Stansfield kept hold of the Liberal Registration Association and the main Liberal organisations of the town, whilst those opposed to Stansfield organised themselves around the anti-state church and anti-state education societies.

Up to 1847 none of the mainstream parties appear to have used corrupt practices to influence electors. The split in the Whig-Liberal ranks altered the situation significantly, however, and in the elections of 1847 and 1852 there is proof of substantial corruption. The evidence for this is found in the 1853 Select Committee Enquiry into the 1852 election. The supporters of Willans alleged that Stansfield and his supporters had practised 'gross, notorious, extensive and systematic bribery, treating and corruption', and that the election should therefore be declared in favour of Willans. Willans' supporters also seem to have been guilty of some illegal practices, however, as by the time of the Enquiry an arrangement had been made that Stansfield's supporters agreed to withdraw their petition, if Willans' friends agreed to drop their candidate's claim to the seat.[37]

The Select Committee on the Huddersfield Election Petition sat in March 1853 and heard evidence from over fifty witnesses, mainly innkeepers and beersellers. It emerged that in both 1847 and 1852 members of Stansfield's

*This is explained in more detail in Chapter Twenty-One. EDITOR.

committee had organised an extensive system of treating in many of the inns and beershops in and around Huddersfield. Three witnesses gave evidence that they had provided refreshments at the 1847 election, but had not been paid the whole of their accounts. They had complained about this shortly before the 1852 election and had been given orders to provide breakfasts and refreshments on polling day. They had then added the money they had not received in 1847 to their bill for 1852.[38]

A great deal of the evidence related to the George Hotel, where Stansfield's committee had met. Here it appears that there was practically an 'open house' on polling day, with over 100 breakfasts being provided, and very few people paying for the drinks they consumed. The bills for these refreshments were paid by Frederick Turner, a member of Stansfield's committee, though some innkeepers and beersellers do not appear to have been paid at all.[39] The Select Committee reported its findings to the House of Commons on 15 March. These were that the 1852 election was void due to the 'extravagant' bribery and treating carried on by Stansfield's agents, but that it was not proved that these practices were carried on with Stansfield's knowledge or consent. In conclusion it was stated:

> that the Committee think it right to submit to the consideration of the House, that a system of treating like that which appears to have prevailed for some time in the Borough of Huddersfield must have the effect of exercising an influence over the minds of voters as debasing as direct bribery.[40]

As this system of treating had been in operation for some time, it might be asked why a petition had not been promoted after any previous election. It is possible that the 1852 petition was prompted by the Act of that year for the more effectual enquiry into corrupt practices (15 & 16 Vict. c.57). This provided for on-the-spot Commissions to enquire into corrupt practices at previous elections after a Committee of the House of Commons had reported that such activities had occurred in a certain borough. This would have required a searching investigation into the activities of both parties, however, and it is clear that neither side was free from corruption. Huddersfield was an arena for robust political contest, even by the standards of the day.

On the whole, therefore, there appears to be little evidence that Huddersfield was a nomination borough in the hands of the Ramsden family.

Their agents were involved in rallying support around the candidate they favoured, but such action might be considered within the contemporary bounds of normal political activity. It is evident that during the 1830s a Whig-Liberal candidate was elected because a majority of the population were of that political disposition. This does not, however, rule out the possibility that some electors voted Whig-Liberal because they believed it was in their best interests to do so, rather than from any political conviction. It is worth noting that had Captain Wood not made a last minute decision to stand at the 1834 election, the combined forces of Conservatives and Radicals in support of Sadler would have defeated Blackburne. Of course, some of the Conservative and Radical support was obtained due to intimidation, but the final result of the elections shows how ineffective these practices were in the face of an electorate that was predominantly Whig-Liberal.

For the elections of 1847 and 1852 the deciding factor was not intimidation or the power of property, but the influence of the beer-barrel. The preponderance of Nonconformists in the town with strong views on the subject of voluntary education was evidently sufficient to persuade Stansfield's Committee that, without treating the electors, they had little chance of success. This was particularly the case in 1852 when the opposing candidate, William Willans, was a local man and a leading member of Ramsden Street Congregational Chapel. Stansfield might possibly have won without the aid of corrupt practices, though the result of the 1853 election does not appear to suggest this as the candidate of the Liberals, Lord Goderich, was elected rather than the local candidate, Joseph Starkey. It is probable that the 1853 election was the first in Huddersfield where corrupt practices did not occur, and this election was perhaps the purest in Huddersfield up to the introduction of votes by ballot in 1872.

Vivienne W. Hemingway

Biographical Note

Vivienne Hemingway is currently completing a Ph.D at the University of Huddersfield entitled 'Urban Politics and Popular Protest Movements in the Age of Reform: Huddersfield c.1832-52'. She has held two posts as research assistant at Huddersfield Polytechnic, the first to carry out research for her Ph.D and assist with teaching duties, the second to provide an information technology component on M.A. History courses. She has also carried out research for Barry Sheerman M.P. for a biography of Professor Harold Laski. She is working on a relational database project in the computing service of the University of Newcastle-Upon-Tyne.

NOTES:

1.   N. Gash, *Politics in the Age of Peel* (1953), p.xi & *note*.

2.   Statistics are taken from F.W.S. Craig, *British Parliamentary Election Results 1832-1855* (1977), p.157.

3.   *Halifax Express* 25 Feb. 1832; W(est) Y(orkshire) A(rchive) S(ervice), Kirklees, Tomlinson Collection KC174/115, Printed Notice – 'Moore's Prophecies.'

4.   *Halifax Express*, 3 March 1832, 10 March 1832.

5.   *Halifax Express*, 16 June 1832.

6.   *Halifax Express*, 30 June 1832; [J. Hobson] *Sketch of the Whig Tomfoolery Election* (Huddersfield, 1833), pp.3-4.

7.   *The Fleet Papers*, Vol. 1, No. 7, 13 Feb. 1841; S(heffield) C(ity) A(rchives), Wentworth Woodhouse Muniments G9, J.C. Ramsden to Viscount Milton 4 Aug. 1832.

8.   SCA, Wentworth Woodhouse G9, Requisition to J.C. Ramsden 20 Aug. 1832, Ramsden to Milton 11 Sept. 1832; *Halifax Express*, 25 Aug. 1832.

9.   *Halifax Express*, 22 Sept. 1832; WYAS, Kirklees, Ramsden Papers DD/RA/c/20/26, Sir John to J.C. Ramsden n.d. (*c*.Sept. 1832).

10. P(ublic) R(ecord) O(ffice), Home Office Papers, Counties Correspondence HO52/20, Printed Notice 'Joseph Wood to the Electors and Inhabitants of the Borough of Huddersfield,' 14 Dec. 1832; H(uddersfield) L(ocal) H(istory) L(ibrary), Local Pamphlets Folio 2, 1832 Polling List.

11. *Voice of the West Riding*, 11 Jan. 1834.

12. *Halifax Express*, 13 May 1837.

13. *Halifax Express*, 29 July 1837.

14. WYAS, Kirklees Ramsden DD/RE/c/36, J.C. Fenton to George Loch 26 May 1847.

15. WYAS, Kirklees Ramsden DD/RE/c/36, Earl Fitzwilliam to Loch 29 May 1847.

16. WYAS, Kirklees Ramsden DD/RE/c/36, Fenton to Loch 26 May 1847; DD/RE/c/37, Fenton to Loch 28 June 1847, Alexander Hathorn to Loch 29 June 1847; SCL Wentworth Woodhouse G56/b, Fenton to Fitzwilliam 28 June 1847, Loch to Fitzwilliam 29 June 1847.

17. WYAS, Kirklees Ramsden DD/RE/c/37, Fitzwilliam to Fenton 30 June 1847.

18. WYAS, Kirklees Ramsden DD/RE/c/38, Fenton to Loch 1 July 1847; SCA, Wentworth Woodhouse G56/b, Fenton to Fitzwilliam 2 July 1847.

19. WYAS, Kirklees Ramsden DD/RE/c/38, William Willans to Fitzwilliam 12 July 1847, Fitzwilliam to Willans 16 July 1847, Hathorn to Loch 19 July 1847, Fenton to Loch 19 July 1847.

20. WYAS, Kirklees Ramsden DD/RA/c/60/4, Loch to Isabella Ramsden 24 Jan. 1852, Isabella to Sir John 28 Jan. 1852; Kirklees Ramsden Estate DD/RE/c/92, Isabella to Loch 27 Jan. 1852 & 29 Jan. 1852.

21. WYAS, Kirklees Ramsden DD/RE/c/95, Hathorn to Sir John 25 March 1852, Hathorn to Loch 1 April 1852 & 20 April 1852.

22. *Huddersfield Examiner*, 27 March 1852, 10 July 1852.

23. *Huddersfield Chronicle*, 27 Nov. 1852, 4 Dec. 1852; *Huddersfield Examiner*, 11 Dec. 1852.

24. WYAS, Kirklees Ramsden DD/RE/c/103, Fenton to Loch 6 Dec. 1852, Hathorn to Loch 7 Dec. 1852.

25. WYAS, Kirklees Ramsden DD/RE/c/103, Hathorn to Loch 16 Dec. 1852.

26. *Select Committee on the Huddersfield Election Petition with the Minutes of Proceedings*, P(arliamentary) P(apers) 1852-53, III, Qs 948-1121, 1172-1396, 1397-1524, 1525-1581.

27. *Halifax Express*, 30 June 1832.

28. HLHL, Local Pamphlets Folio 2, 1832 Polling List for Huddersfield Borough; A. White, *History, Gazetteer, and Directory of the West Riding of Yorkshire*, Vol. 1, (Leeds, 1837).

29. *Voice of the West Riding*, 4 Jan. 1834; *Halifax Express*, 2 Jan. 1834.

30. WYAS, Kirklees Tomlinson KC174 'Meeting of Grocers, Drapers, Innkeepers, and other Retail Shopkeepers held at the Ramsden Arms Inn 2 Jan. 1834.'

31. HLHL, Huddersfield Polling List 1834; White, *History and Gazetteer*, Vol. 1, (1837).

32. *Halifax Express*, 13 May 1837; HLHL Polling List 1837 Huddersfield Bye-Election; WYAS, Kirklees Tomlinson KC174 *To the working classes* – partial polling list of 1837 general election.

33. WYAS, Kirklees Tomlinson KC174 *Non-electors can vote on a Saturday night* (1852).

34. *Halifax Guardian*, 12 Jan. 1833, 2 March 1833; W. Paul, *A History of the Origin and Progress of Operative Conservative Societies* (Leeds, 1838).

35. *Halifax Express*, 1 Oct. 1835.

36. *Halifax Express*, 17 Dec. 1835, 27 May 1837.

37. *Huddersfield Chronicle*, 4 Dec. 1852, 26 Feb. 1853.

38. PP 1852-53, III, Qs 2649-1740, 3214-3357, & 3460-3559.

39. PP 1852-53, III, Qs 110-228, 3763-3868, 3878-4066, & 6308-6464.

40. PP 1852-53, III, pp.206-208.

CHAPTER 20

Late Victorian
and Edwardian Politics
in Huddersfield

ROBERT PERKS

Huddersfield's political scene between 1885 and the First World War may seem to be striking for its relative calm and continuity: the Liberal Party triumphed in all but one of the ten parliamentary elections held during that time and remained the largest single party on the Borough Council.[1] In actual fact, however, it was an extremely turbulent three decades, characterised by Liberal splits and the emergence of both radical trade unionism and the Huddersfield Labour Party as a key contender for the working class vote. It was also a time of tremendous social change: of a relative decline in chapel attendances and of demands for far-reaching improvements in living and working conditions in the face of trade competition from abroad which threatened Huddersfield's world lead in high quality fine worsted textiles. By 1914 Huddersfield Liberalism was not the dominating political force it had been in 1885.

Huddersfield was one of the largest single seat parliamentary constituencies in Britain[2] and its boundaries remained unchanged between 1885 and 1914, apart from the addition of Linthwaite in 1888 when Huddersfield became a County Borough, which added a handful of voters for the purposes of local council elections.

Until 1918 relatively few Huddersfield people could actually vote: only 27.8 per cent of the town's total adult population in 1892 and 27.1 per cent in 1910. All women and around 40 per cent of all men were excluded from voting in parliamentary elections.[3] Many were disqualified by the complex workings of the registration system, especially the twelve-month residential

Table 1 Huddersfield Parliamentary Election Results, 1885-1910

Year	Electorate	% Turnout	Result		% Vote
1885	14,991	87.7	E.A. Leatham (L)	6,960	52.9
			J. Crosland (C)	6,194	47.1
1886	14,991	81.6	W. Summers (L)	6,210	50.8
			J. Crosland (C)	6,026	49.1
1892	15,466	90.1	W. Summers (L)	7,098	50.9
			Sir J. Crosland (C)	6,837	49.1
1893 By-Election	15,550	90.7	Sir J. Crosland (C)	7,068	50.1
			J. Woodhead (L)	7,033	49.9
1895	15,832	89.8	Sir J. Woodhouse (L)	6,755	47.5
			Sir J. Crosland (C)	5,868	41.3
			H.R. Smart (ILP)	1,594	11.2
1900	16,770	87.8	Sir J. Woodhouse (L)	7,896	53.6
			E.H. Carlile (C)	6,831	46.4
1906 By-Election	17,568	94.0	Sir J. Woodhouse (L)	6,302	38.2
			T.R. Williams (Lab)	5,813	35.2
			J.F. Fraser (C)	4,391	26.6
1906	17,568	91.2	A.J. Sherwell (L)	5,762	36.0
			T.R. Williams (Lab)	5,422	33.8
			J.F. Fraser (C)	4,844	30.2
1910 (Jan.)	19,021	94.6	A.J. Sherwell (L)	7,158	39.8
			H. Snell (Lab)	5,686	31.6
			H. Smith (C)	5,153	28.6
1910 (Dec.)	19,021	90.5	A.J. Sherwell (L)	6,458	37.5
			J.H. Kaye (C)	5,777	33.5
			H. Snell (Lab)	4,988	29.0

qualification which tended to disenfranchise mobile workers, thereby discriminating unfairly against working-class voters. Levels of local party organisation were crucial as it was the paid party agents who attended voter registration courts to argue about individual claims to be awarded the vote. There are few doubts that the pre-1918 parliamentary electorate in Huddersfield was not conducive to the emergence of a poorly-funded

Table 2 Party Composition of Huddersfield Borough Council,
         1890-1914[1]

Year	Liberal	Conservative	Liberal Unionist	Labour	Independent
1890	38	19	3	–	–
1891	38	19	3	–	–
1892	39	18	2	1	–
1893	38	18	3	1	–
1894	38	18	3	1	–
1895	38	17	4	1	–
1896	37	17	5	1	–
1897	38	16	5	1	–
1898	39	15	5	1	–
1899	38	16	5	1	–
1900	37	19	3	1	–
1901	33	24	2	1	–
1902	33	24	2	1	–
1903	30	27	2	1	–
1904	32	22	2	4	–
1905	32	19	2	6	1
1906	32	17	2	8	1
1907	37	15	1	6	1
1908[2]	37	16	1	5	1
1909[3]	40	14	1	3	1
1910	42	15	–	2	1
1911	34	20	1	4	1
1912[3]	27	25	1	5	1
1913	28	26	1	5	–
1914	30	24	1	5	–

[1] As at 2 November each year.
[2] In 1908 the number of wards was increased to 15 but the total number of Council members remained at 60.
[3] One seat vacant.

political party, like Labour, appealing to working people, the majority of whom did not even possess the vote.

Interestingly, the municipal electorate, which voted on 1 November each year for councillors to Huddersfield Borough Council (one third of a total of sixty retiring each year), was slightly more democratic. In November 1910, for example, 22,269 people were entitled to vote in Huddersfield's local elections compared to 19,021 in the national elections and this included an estimated 4,000 or so women voters.[4] In marked contrast to parliamentary politics, women were entitled to stand for Council, though there was only one such candidate in Huddersfield before 1914, Mrs Julia Glaisyer, president of the Women's Liberal Association, who was twice defeated in South Central ward in 1910.[5]

Women played a distinctly subsidiary role to men in Huddersfield politics and public life before 1914. In July 1910 there were no women councillors, only two women doctors and only two women on an Education Committee of twenty-one.[6] Typically women were confined to welfare provision, deemed to be more suitable; there were twelve women out of forty members of the Board of Guardians, which oversaw local poor law provision. Women joined trade unions, but fewer did so in Huddersfield than in neighbouring Bradford: around half the membership of the Huddersfield branch of the General Union of Textile Workers (GUTW) were women, compared to three-quarters in Bradford. And those who did join never gained prominent positions in the union, despite the GUTW's well-known support for women's suffrage and equal rights.[7] A Huddersfield branch of the National Union of Women's Suffrage Societies (NUWSS) was formed in May 1904 and a branch of the Pankhursts' more militant suffragette Women's Social and Political Union (WSPU) followed in December 1906. However, all the indications are that membership and activity were very low level, and that neither organisation, even at their peak during the 1906 Huddersfield by-election, exercised very much political influence. The only instance of violent suffragette militancy in the town occurred in April 1913 when a plate glass door at Longley Park Golf Club was smashed 'in revenge for Mrs Pankhurst's three years' penal servitude'.[8]

As the Huddersfield constituency stood in 1885 it was roughly diamond in shape, bordered by the constituencies of Colne Valley to the south-west, Elland and Spen Valley to the north, Dewsbury to the east and Holmfirth to the east and south. All were Liberal seats. Huddersfield was a slightly more middle class town than many West Riding towns: in 1901 10 per cent of families had at least one female domestic servant, compared to 8 per cent in Bradford and 7.6 per cent in Halifax.[9] And, if anything, it was more class mixed: the wealthier areas like Marsh, Edgerton, Beaumont Park and Almondbury were less well-defined areas than, say, Headingley in Leeds or

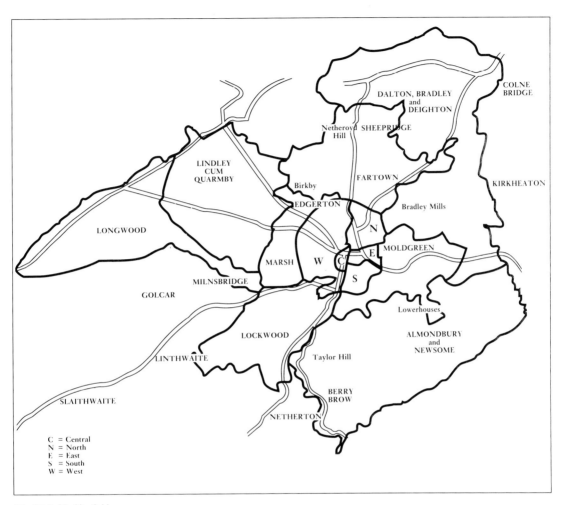

Fig. 20:1 Huddersfield Borough. Municipal Boundaries 1868-1908.

Heaton in Bradford, and were bordered by or amidst poorer working class areas. For voting purposes in local council elections Huddersfield was divided into thirteen wards (fifteen from 1908): between 1885 and 1900 only three solidly elected one party and after 1900 none did, indicating both political change and social mix. Such patterns as did exist over the period reflected a Labour presence in Lindley, Dalton, Moldgreen and North wards; Conservative strength in the East, West and South wards; the remaining six wards were Liberal strongholds.

The influence of family and chapel

By the 1880s the direct political influence of the Ramsden family in Huddersfield, which earlier in the century had been extensive,* had been replaced by a more subtle influence through landowning, which still provided the family with a healthy annual income of an estimated £100,000.[10] The political mantle had passed to a handful of, mainly Liberal, families whose controlling wealth derived from textiles and whose influence was a powerful combination of non-interventionist politics and religious nonconformity. Most prominent were the Hirst, Crowther, Eastwood, Woodhead and Willans families.

Reuben and William Hirst ran the largest cotton spinning mill in the area: they were Baptists and dominated Lockwood Liberal Club. Reuben was Liberal mayor of Huddersfield 1891-93, whilst his brother was a councillor until 1901. Joseph Crowther, a leading Liberal Congregationalist, had interests in seven major textile firms and probably employed more people than any other single manufacturer in the area. Inevitably such influence in the workplace was not irrelevant. It is clear that some employers sought to cultivate paternalistic ties with their workers through mill outings, bonus schemes and ownership of workers' houses. Not all went to the lengths that Titus Salt had done in Saltaire, Shipley, but many made no secret of their wish that employees should vote the same way as their employer.[11]

Joseph Woodhead, pillar of Gladstonian Liberalism in Huddersfield, owned and ran (with his son Ernest) the influential *Huddersfield Examiner*, the town's most potent Liberal mouthpiece with a circulation of over 13,000 in 1885. Although the Huddersfield Liberal Association (HLA) was theoretically democratic, run by a 'caucus' of 'Two Hundred' drawn from the district Liberal clubs, in actual fact local ward feeling was frequently ignored. Individuals like Woodhead, as HLA president between 1885 and 1893, dominated. He was also long-standing president of the Huddersfield Temperance Society and active in the Mechanics' Institution. His wife was prominent in the Women's Liberal Association (established in 1888) and the Women's Temperance Society, whilst Ernest was president of Marsh Liberal club, a key figure in the Junior Liberal Association, and president of the Band of Hope Union.

*A discussion of this influence will be found in Chapter Nineteen. EDITOR.

Fig. 20:2 Joseph Woodhead, MP. (KCS)   Fig. 20:3 Ernest Woodhead. (KCS)

Links between this cabal of leading families were solidified through inter-marriage. Thus the Congregational Liberal Woodheads were connected by marriage to the Congregational Liberal Willans through the daughter of James Edward Willans (who was related to Liberal prime minister Herbert Henry Asquith). The engineering Baptist Liberal Hopkinsons were linked to the Methodist dyers and finishers, the Walkers of Deighton. Such family connections were common and rarely crossed the divide of religion and politics.[12]

Religion and politics went hand in hand: Anglicanism with Conservatism and Nonconformity with Liberalism. The Revd Robert Bruce, minister at Highfield Congregational Chapel in New North Road from 1854 until 1904, was a towering figure in national Congregationalism as chairman of the Congregational Union of England and Wales in 1888. He inaugurated Huddersfield's Free Church Council, was a leading member of the Huddersfield Liberal Association and led the dominating Liberal group on the School Board for twenty-one years. Most significantly, he made Highfield a religious powerhouse of political influence by drawing a congregation which included such Liberal notables as Woodhead, Willans, Wright Mellor, Thomas Denham, Alfred Sykes and Fred Crosland.[13]

Whilst Highfield was certainly the most politically important Nonconformist chapel in the town, by 1885 other less élitist Congregational chapels had gained influence. Ramsden Street attracted such prominent Liberal manufacturers as Charles Henry Jones (Huddersfield's first mayor), William Dawson, Charles Vickerman and William Shaw.[14] Milton Congregational Church opened as a breakaway from Ramsden Street in 1885 and, led by the Revd Stannard won the following of the Hirst and Eastwood families amongst others. Milton was a chapel with a far more populist approach: it organised sports clubs and musical events and was the first in the area to launch a Pleasant Sunday Afternoon.

Huddersfield, like most West Riding towns, was firmly Nonconformist.* In 1893 a lengthy period of chapel building had peaked. Apart from nine Congregational chapels, there were twenty Wesleyan Methodist chapels, ten Free Wesleyan, eight Methodist New Connexion, four Primitive Methodist and seven Baptist, not to mention a host of smaller denominations like the Swedenborgians, Christadelphians and Spiritualists. Taken together, Nonconformist religion in Huddersfield boasted seventy-one chapels and meeting places, compared to twenty-nine Church of England places of worship and two Roman Catholic.[15] In common with most of Britain between 1885 and 1914, however, religious Nonconformity in the town was facing difficulties which combined to reduce chapel attendance relative to population increase.[16] Most important was the 'problem of pleasure': growing urban working class indifference to religion at a time of a rise in popular entertainments (like the music-hall); shorter working hours (Saturday working was being phased out); and the availability of cheap transport (most particularly in Huddersfield, an excellent tramway system).** Church and chapel was marked by a starched middle class respectability that many working people found uncomfortable and often irrelevant to their everyday lives. Although congregations were not deserting in droves, there was a perceptible decline, especially amongst adult attendance. Despite attempts by such organisations as the Pleasant Sunday Afternoon movement, offering more informal 'brief, bright and brotherly' meetings packed with gimmicks like magic lantern shows,[17] the trend was

---

*A discussion of Nonconformity appears in Chapter Six. EDITOR.
**More details will be found in Chapter Sixteen. EDITOR.

Fig. 20:6 Highfield Chapel. (KCS)

Fig. 20:4 Wright Mellor. (KCS)   *Fig. 20:5 Revd Robert Bruce, Pastor of Highfield Chapel. (KCS)*

clear. Between 1851 and 1922 Nonconformist attendance in Huddersfield dropped from 28.8 per cent to 5.5 per cent of the population. With this decline went Liberalism's predominance.[18]

One consistent bright spot on the graph of decline was the temperance movement, a major political and social force in Huddersfield right up to 1914. The Huddersfield Band of Hope, established in 1850 as a means of educating working class children to the evils of drink, formed the nucleus of a Band of Hope Union which had by 1904 a remarkable 12,000 members and eighty individual bands.[19] The Huddersfield Temperance Society, dominated by leading Liberal manufacturers, was an influential pressure group with a regular programme of public meetings in the Market Place declaiming abstinence from alcohol, and a fleet of coffee carts. Apart from supporting a number of temperance hotels, it also ensured that none of the district's Liberal clubs sold drink to members. In fact Liberalism consistently saw drink as the sole cause of poverty, and abstinence as a universal panacea for social ills, a belief epitomised by Liberal manufacturer Samuel Bull: 'if the unemployed drank less it would raise their efficiency and give them employment'.[20] Such attitudes were to be increasingly anachronistic and unacceptable to working people in the face of socialist thinking.

This Liberal synthesis of religious and political influence was thus backed by a clear set of values and beliefs which changed surprisingly little before 1914, notably Irish self-government (Home Rule), free trade, disestablishment of the Church of England and temperance. These were bound up with a strong faith in individual thrift, self-help, self-determination and non-intervention.

The rise of Labour

Before the 1890s it is generally true to say that Huddersfield Liberalism took working class support for granted. Richard Oastler's Tory Radicalism of the 1830s had left no more than a whiff of working class Conservatism by the 1880s. The Huddersfield Working Men's Conservative Association, established in 1867, had declined to virtual insignificance. By 1886 it had dropped 'Working Men's' from its title and moved closer to the wealthy Huddersfield Conservative Association through the influence of Thomas Brooke of Armitage Bridge, whose family dominated Huddersfield

Fig. 20:7 Allen
Gee, JP. (KCS)

Conservatism up to and beyond the First World War. The vast majority of working people in the town who possessed the vote before 1918 did not vote Conservative. Until the 1890s they thronged the seventeen local Liberal clubs which, dominated by local worthies, successfully combined brass bands, crown green bowling, billiards, whist and knife-and-fork suppers with an efficient organisational unit at election times, building partisan feeling and support for key issues. Significantly, it was just such a local network of clubs which was an early priority for the youthful Labour movement in the 1890s and which proved so important to Labour's revival after 1903.

The origins and progress of Huddersfield's labour movement lay as much with trade unionism as socialism. The infamous 1883 Weavers' Strike, the most bitter dispute the area's textile industry was ever to face,[21] had made the Huddersfield and District Power Loom Weavers' and Woollen Operatives' Association the largest and most influential trade union in the town. It led to the creation of the Huddersfield Trades Council in November 1885 and the rise to prominence of Allen Gee, Huddersfield's most important early Labour leader. Gee, born in Lindley in 1852, began work as a weaver but in 1889 became a journalist for the influential Labour paper *Yorkshire Factory*

Times. He went on to become Huddersfield's first Labour councillor and alderman, and first chairman of the Labour Representation Committee (as the Labour Party was then known) in 1900.[22] As first president of the Huddersfield Trades Council Gee led a campaign to increase union membership and co-ordinate the area's diverse and often tiny unions. Like much of the West Riding textile district, Huddersfield had not been marked by its enthusiasm for unionisation, which remained as low as 4.4 per cent of the total working population in 1900 compared to a typical Lancashire figure of 62 per cent.[23] Nevertheless, the late 1880s did see a significant increase, especially amongst textile workers and the unskilled and semi-skilled sector. By 1891 a Huddersfield branch of the Amalgamated Society of Railway Workers had been formed plus a new gasworkers' union, a power loom tuners' association, a brassworkers' union, a cigar makers' union, a painters and decorators' union, and many others.[24] As the *Yorkshire Factory Times* observed: 'even a place like Huddersfield where until the last year or two the spirit of organisation seemed to be dead or dying, is at last awakening to the necessities of the times'.[25]

To some extent this rise in independent working class representation was a result of a growing disillusionment with Liberal political lethargy which had followed the Home Rule crisis. In 1885 the relative political calm which Huddersfield had experienced since Edward Leatham had become MP in 1868 was shattered. Leatham, a Wakefield banker whose brother-in-law was John Bright, refused to accept Liberal Prime Minister Gladstone's conversion to Irish Home Rule and after an acrimonious row he left the Liberal Party to join the breakaway Liberal Unionist Party. The issue divided Huddersfield Liberalism and a number of activists followed Leatham to set up the Huddersfield Liberal Unionist Association.[26]

At first Home Rule attracted considerable local popular support. At the 1886 general election a new pro-Home Rule candidate, William Summers, comfortably beat the Conservative's Joseph Crosland, despite a bitter letter from Leatham calling on Liberal electors 'to give your vote against any one who is ready, like Mr Summers, at the bidding of an imperious autocrat in London, to trample every principle of Liberalism under foot'.[27] However, between 1886 and 1892 political discussion in the town focused on Home Rule to the exclusion of all other issues, as Summers commented: 'With the present condition of things in Ireland it would be idle for us to attempt to discuss any other political question'.[28] It was a Liberal obsession that frustrated Huddersfield's working people at a time when increased foreign competition and American trade tariff protection was threatening local employment. Added to this was the Huddersfield Liberal Party's consistent refusal to allow itself to be represented by working class candidates in local council elections. In November 1890 the party would not endorse Allen Gee as a Liberal candidate for Lindley ward, despite the fact that he was backed by the Trades Council. Although Gee was defeated with ease, standing as a 'Lib-Lab' candidate, it underlined the Liberal Party élite's antagonism to working class representation and demonstrated the need for an independent organisation that could fight effectively for improved wages and conditions for working people.[29] After 1890 Gee was the first of many to abandon Liberalism.

It is notable that Labour's first challenge to Liberalism in Huddersfield had been backed by trade unionism rather than socialism, which came late to the town. It was not until late in 1890 that Huddersfield's first socialist organisation, the Fabian Society, was formed.[30] It had emerged, like many of the town's radical organisations since 1850, from Thornton's Temperance Hotel, nicknamed the 'Centre of Light and Knowledge', which had long been a debating and meeting house for Radicals, Chartists, Secularists, Co-operators and Socialists alike.[31] Early members of the Huddersfield Fabian Society included Ramsden Balmforth (who scored a remarkable victory in 1892 when he was elected to the School Board at the top of the poll,* Joe Dyson, Tom Topping, W.H. Hudson and Jimmy Green, many of whom went on to become prominent Labour leaders. Although much of what they represented differed little from the Liberal Party's more radical spokesmen like Owen Balmforth (Ramsden's brother) and George Thomson,[32] they were united with many local trade unionists on the need for independent working class representation outside the Liberal Party. On 16 September 1891 they came together formally to create 'a distinct and separate Labour Party' known as the Huddersfield Labour Union (HLU), one of the first in Britain.[33] In 1893 it was renamed the Huddersfield Independent Labour Party (ILP) with a new constitution embodying socialist aims, notably: 'to secure the collective ownership of the means of production, distribution and exchange'.[34] The Labour challenge had arrived.

*More details of this are given in Chapter Twenty-One. EDITOR.

The first real test for the new force came in 1893 at a by-election caused by Summers' untimely death, at which the HLA put forward its president, Joseph Woodhead, as candidate. On the face of it he was a good choice; he had been MP for neighbouring Spen Valley and was a solid Gladstonian, but, in contrast to Summers, he opposed the proposal for an eight hour day and was antagonistic towards trade unionism. More advanced Liberal voices in the HLA like Balmforth and Thomson questioned Woodhead's suitability pointing out 'a good deal of feeling amongst the working classes in the constituency against Mr. Woodhead', and a deputation to the HLA from the Trades Council and the Labour Union expressed similar reservations.[35] Labour leader Keir Hardie added his voice to many:

> In Huddersfield not only have the Liberals ignored the Labour Party but they have literally courted destruction by flying in the face of the Labour Party by selecting a candidate who is chiefly known throughout Yorkshire by his hostility to the labour movement: a man who has said . . . that he would rather lose the election than vote for the Eight Hours Bill . . . . That is the man whom the Liberals of Huddersfield have selected to represent Labour in the House of Commons, and those were the men who said they were friends of Labour.[36]

Woodhead's difficulties were compounded when his opponent Joseph Crosland, owner of the *Huddersfield Chronicle*, announced in the closing stages of the campaign that he would support the Miners' Eight Hour Bill if elected. This was enough for the voters to elect a Conservative MP for Huddersfield (the only time this happened between 1868 and 1979, when Geoffrey Dickens was elected).

The shockwaves which the defeat created were far-reaching. For the first time Liberalism began to recognise that it could ill afford to neglect 'bread and butter' policies like working hours, wages and conditions. J.E. Willans reflected this new air of realism on the HLA executive when he noted that: 'The fact is the choice of a candidate for the Borough, that is one who will unite all sections of the Party and thus fight with a good prospect of success, is now a task of unusual difficulty. This is mainly due to the attitude of the Labour Party and the Trades Council. It can hardly be denied that Huddersfield can no longer be considered a safe seat for the Liberal Party'.[37]

Yet such fears were to some extent dispelled by the results of the 1895 General Election when the Liberals recaptured the seat with ease. Labour's candidate, Russell Smart, could muster only 1,594 votes (11.2 per cent of the poll): poor by comparison with Labour's performance elsewhere in West Yorkshire.[38] Labour's challenge had been fatally flawed by an advanced Liberal candidate in Sir James Woodhouse, with a record of support for issues such as the eight hour day; by the continued refusal of the Trades Council to break with Liberalism by advising all trade unionists to vote Labour; and by an immature and impoverished Labour Party organisation battling to keep its seven Labour clubs open. Between 1893 and 1895 the HLA had pursued an aggressive anti-Labour propaganda campaign and overhauled their organisation. After 1895 Labour suffered a downturn; Liberal confidence returned.

Fig. 20:8 Sir Joseph Crosland, Huddersfield's first Conservative MP. (KCS)

Fig. 20:9 Edward Carlile Conservative candidate in the 1900 Election. (KCS)

It was the Boer War that marked the beginning of a change in party fortunes in Huddersfield. The Conservatives, led by a new candidate, Edward Carlile, launched a jingoistic campaign to support the sending of troops to South Africa and capitalise on local Liberal divisions. Though there was never an outright split amongst Huddersfield Liberals, as there was nationally, it is clear that whilst Woodhouse as MP concurred with Liberal leader Campbell-Bannerman in a qualified support for the war, a significant number of local Liberals, clustered around Joseph Woodhead and the *Huddersfield Examiner*, were in outright opposition.[39] A branch of the anti-war South African Conciliation Committee was set up by Woodhead but held no meetings for fear of the sort of violence that had been seen in Birmingham where Lloyd George had spoken against the war and barely escaped a lynch mob.

In the event Huddersfield remained free from violence, but the war brought a wave of patriotic fervour which the Conservatives were able to build on to increase both local party membership and their share of the poll at the 1900 'Khaki' general election. By 1903 the Huddersfield Conservative and Unionist Party (as it was now known) had been able to gain nine seats at successive Council elections, coming within one seat of the Liberals.[40] To some extent the absence of a Labour candidate (due to lack of money and internal disarray) had compensated the Liberals and they picked up votes by offering a limited programme of social reform whilst pointing out that the active prosecution of the war had hit the textile industry, increasing local unemployment.

The revival of Labour

After 1903 local Liberalism quickly revived around its traditional policies. It reunited in opposition to both the controversial 1902 Education Act, which sought to undermine Nonconformist influence by replacing local School Boards with non-elected County Council Education Committees, and Tariff Reform. Tariff Reform struck at the very heart of Free Trade Liberalism by aiming to protect British trade from foreign competition, but it very seriously divided the Conservative Party locally, crucially weakening the party's electoral appeal. From a peak of twenty-seven seats on the Council in 1903 they slumped to fourteen in 1909 and did not recover until 1913.

Conservative performances at parliamentary elections showed a similar decline.

From a low point in 1899, Labour's recovery in Huddersfield began in September 1900 when the Trades Union Congress (TUC) was held in the town, attracting leading labour and socialist speakers and encouraging a mild revival in local trade union membership. Most importantly it led to the creation of the Huddersfield Labour Representation Committee (LRC), based on the national model formed the same year. Though its initial brief was limited to considering 'the question of direct labour representation on **all** local governing bodies',[41] by 1901 the new LRC successfully combined with the Huddersfield ILP and Trades Council to form a committee 'with a view to running a candidate at the next Parliamentary election'.[42]

There were to be another two years of acrimonious debate within the Trades Council, however, before the majority of its membership could be persuaded to select a Labour candidate, during which time the Liberals fought an unsuccessful rearguard action to prevent an ILP takeover of the Trades Council. In the end it was anti-trade union legislation, particularly the infamous Taff Vale decision, and local Liberalism's persistent refusal to use its civic powers to alleviate local unemployment and housing problems, that convinced growing numbers of working people at a mass meeting in 1903 'that the time has now arrived when Huddersfield should be directly represented by Labour in the House of Commons'.[43] The break with the Liberal Party had finally come and in 1904 T. Russell Williams, a mill manager from Keighley, was selected as Labour's candidate.[44]

Underpinning this political shift away from Liberalism was a growing popular interest in socialist ideas and particularly in what could be called ethical or religious socialism. From 1904 Huddersfield was deluged with itinerant socialist speakers, among them Philip Snowden, Victor Grayson, Bruce Glasier, Margaret McMillan and Revd F. R. Swan, all seeking to broaden Labour's appeal beyond 'bread and butter' socialism by offering a 'new Jerusalem': 'a constructive message of social reformation . . . an ideal of human happiness . . . a new politics akin to a religion'.[45] At a time of working class disillusionment with chapel attendance, ethical socialism seemed to offer a real alternative of material advantage within a moral context that was familiar. Important parts of this alternative were the revived local Labour clubs and the Socialist Sunday School (SSS) movement.

Fig. 20:10 Labour Day demonstration, Lockwood 5 May 1907. (KCS)

Socialist Sunday Schools in the Huddersfield area had begun in small way in 1896 as an alternative to Nonconformist Sunday schools. By 1906 the central St. Peter's Street SSS was attracting as many as 400 scholars and two other schools had opened at Paddock and Lockwood.[46] The religious tone of the schools' socialist teachings which epitomised Huddersfield socialism at this time was typified by its aim: 'We desire to be just and loving to all our fellow men and women, to work together as brothers and sisters, to be kind to every living creature and so help to form a New Society with Justice as its foundation and Love its law'.[47]

Though aimed primarily at children, adult members were encouraged through discussion classes on texts by Ruskin, Morris, Blatchford and Marx. A new-found belief in communing with nature and getting back to the land was evident from frequent picnics and excursions, organised not only by the SSSs but also by the Clarion movement and the Cinderella Clubs, to places like Farnley Tyas and Netherton, considered by many Huddersfield children to be truly the countryside.

It is difficult for us to grasp the tremendous popular enthusiasm which characterised the Huddersfield Labour movement throughout this period.

Street corner meetings were held most nights of the week attracting hundreds of people, and 3,000 or more would regularly throng St. George's Square or the Market Place to hear speeches by local and national Labour figures. Most impressive were the annual May Day processions which, in 1907, comprised the Linthwaite Brass Band playing the 'Marseillaise' followed by 200 Clarion cyclists in formation; then came the St. Peter's Street Socialist Sunday School, Paddock SSS and local Labour dignitaries like Alderman Gee and Victor Grayson. They were followed by members of Milnsbridge Socialist Club, Honley Brass Band, Lockwood SSS, Newmill and Holmfirth Labour Parties, Lindley Brass Band, Huddersfield ILP, Moldgreen ILP, Lindley Socialist Institute and Outlane Labour Party. Sporting an array of red banners, rosettes and sashes the procession marshalled at Queen Street South then took a circuitous route around the town arriving in St. George's Square where thousands had gathered to greet them. Three separate platforms for simultaneous speeches were set up at opposite corners of the square and as darkness fell the singing of the 'Red Flag' could be heard several miles away.[48] As Russell Williams remarked: 'Socialism is a religion to our people. They live for it. They would willingly die for it. It is the breath in their nostrils, they talk about scarcely anything else'.[49] Thus was Socialism offering a distinctive working class culture, a new way of life grounded in Christian morality, at a time of disenchantment with a Liberal Party consistently refusing to envisage independent working class representation and offering scant social reform.

Success at the polls came swiftly. At the November 1904 local elections the Labour Party gained three seats out of only four candidates fielded, followed by another at a by-election in North ward, bringing Labour's total number of councillors to five. By 1906 this had grown to a pre-war peak of eight, in which year Labour's share of the poll in Huddersfield local elections reached 40 per cent, easily exceeding the Conservatives' 17.2 per cent and just behind Liberalisms' 42.8 per cent. This new-found electoral success enabled the Huddersfield ILP to raise funds for the parliamentary candidature and for a much needed Labour newspaper to counteract the *Huddersfield Examiner*. From July 1905 the *Huddersfield Worker* was to be a crucial mouthpiece for Labour well into the inter-war period.[50] By the end of 1905 Labour election committees were in place, involving over 500 members in all wards of the constituency and also the first full-time election agent had been appointed.[51]

Writing to Ramsay MacDonald (later to be Labour's first prime minister) on the eve of the 1906 General Election, Russell Williams said: 'We are likely to win Hud. *(sic)* This is no 'bluff': Hudd. is in the reckoning this time. The greatest enthusiasm prevails everywhere I go'.[52] It seemed that Labour's day had come.

The survival of Liberalism

The general election of January 1906 and the by-election which followed in November 1906 (caused by the appointment of sitting MP, Sir James Woodhouse, as a Railway Commissioner) marked the high point of Labour's pre-war fortunes. The party was not to win a higher proportion of the vote until J.H. Hudson actually captured the seat for Labour in 1923, and Labour's municipal representation did not again reach eight until 1937. On both occasions in 1906, Labour came within less than 500 votes of winning the seat from the Liberals, a discrepancy which would undoubtedly have been negated had the franchise not operated against would-be Labour voters. By and large the Huddersfield Liberal Party stuck to its traditional cries of free trade, temperance and Home Rule. Although Arthur Sherwell, their candidate at the by-election, had a record as a social reformer, there is little evidence in Huddersfield of the sort of 'progressive' or 'new' Liberalism apparent in Lancashire at this time.[53] The Huddersfield Liberal Association continued to place its faith in charity and self-help to deal with social problems. The Liberal-dominated Charity Organisation Society, and from 1904 the Guild of Help, both aimed to deal with poverty without recourse to additional legislation. As Ben Riley, Labour councillor for North ward and later MP for Dewsbury reflected: 'How completely out of touch modern local official Liberalism is with the real progressive spirit of the time.... The leading dominant Liberals on the Council are either entirely opposed to enlarging the purpose of their politics or they are far too timid, too nervous, achieving no great aims'.[54]

What *had* been crucial to the Liberal Party's retention of the seat at the by-election was a complete overhaul of its organisation by a new President, William Pick Raynor. The HLA had been alarmed by Labour's showing in January 1906 and in the space of a few months Raynor had forced through a constitutional revision expanding the 'Two Hundred' to a 'Five Hundred', thus allowing an influx of younger Liberal activists; the appointment of Arthur Withy as an organiser 'to carry on our educational propaganda amongst the younger members of the party on Anti-Socialist lines', and a scheme to improve local ward and club organisation.[55] Membership of both the Junior and Women's Liberal Associations increased during 1906 (the latter becoming one of the largest in Britain) and there is no doubt that the reorganisation had done much to offset Labour's propaganda gains since 1903 and undermine Labour's claim to be the only working class party.

The tantalising closeness to victory in November 1906 embittered the Labour Party for some years to come. The period up to the Great War was marked by divisions, dissent and fragmentation within the Labour movement and a decline in popular enthusiasm and electoral success. Harry Snell managed to maintain Labour's vote at the January 1910 general election, but dropped back to third place at the December election of that year in the face of a Conservative revival. The number of Labour councillors had dropped from eight to two by 1910 and Victor Grayson's sensational victory as an independent Labour candidate in the neighbouring Colne Valley by-election in 1907 quickly dissipated into disillusionment as his squabble with the national party became more pronounced and his personal behaviour more outrageous.[56] By 1910 a breakaway Huddersfield Socialist Party had emerged, subsequently to be a branch of the British Socialist Party, which criticised the Parliamentary Labour Party's moderation and lack of socialist commitment. Its evocation of insurrection only speeded the flight of moderate voters from Labour's cause. Industrial syndicalist ideas were also gaining ground; a branch of E.J.B. Allen's Industrialist League was formed in 1909, advocating violent socialist strike action, and had some involvement in the industrial unrest that hit Huddersfield after 1910.[57]

Only on the eve of the First World War is there evidence that Labour was reuniting, by which time Liberalism had re-established credibility amongst working people through their new national welfare policies and their constitutional struggle with the Lords. To an extent school meals, old age pensions and national insurance had stolen Labour's thunder. At a time when a divided local Labour movement lurched leftwards and unprecedented industrial unrest seemed to some to be threatening the social order, voters returned temporarily to the traditional parties. It was to be the social changes of the war and the extension of the vote in 1918 that once again placed Labour in a position to challenge Liberalism. If, by 1914, Huddersfield Liberalism had narrowly avoided defeat, it was a chastened force with significantly less social and political influence than it had had thirty years before.

Robert Perks

Biographical Note

Dr. Robert Perks is Curator of Oral History at the British Library National Sound Archive and Deputy Director of the National Life Story Collection. He took a first-class honours degree in History at Huddersfield Polytechnic, followed by a PhD. which focused on Liberalism and the challenge of Labour in West Yorkshire, 1885-1914. In 1983 he established what is now the North's leading oral history archive, the Bradford Heritage Unit, and is national secretary of the Oral History Society. He co-edits *Oral History* and co-wrote *A Century of Childhood* to coincide with a Channel Four oral history television series about twentieth century childhood.

NOTES

1. *See* Tables 1 and 2.

2. *Public Statutes* 1884-5, (1885) pp.128-214; *Huddersfield Examiner*, 7 March 1891.

3. See census returns. In 1892 61.1 per cent of men could vote, 63.7 per cent in 1900 and 59.8 per cent in 1910. This reflects national trends see N. Blewett, 'The franchise in the United Kingdom, 1885-1918', *Past and Present*, 32 (1965), 27-56.

4. *Huddersfield Examiner*, 22 October 1910.

5. See R.B. Perks, 'The New Liberalism and the challenge of Labour in the West Riding of Yorkshire 1885-1914, with special reference to Huddersfield', (unpub Ph.D. thesis, CNAA/Huddersfield Polytechnic, 1985), from which this article is drawn; also P. Hollis, *Ladies elect: women in English local government 1865-1914 (Oxford, 1987)*.

6. *Huddersfield Examiner*, 9 July 1910: from a speech at the Women's Liberal Federation conference in support of Shackleton's Women's Suffrage Bill.

7. See Joanna Bornat, 'Lost leaders: women, trade unionism and the case of the General Union of Textile Workers, 1875-1914' in *Unequal opportunities: women's employment in England 1800-1918*, edited by Angela V. John (1987).

8. *Huddersfield Examiner*, 21 May 1904, 1 and 22 December 1906; *Labour Leader*, 7 December 1906; H.W. Strong, 'Huddersfield and the Strength of Liberalism', *Independent Review*, February 1907; R.B. Perks, thesis, chapter six; *Huddersfield Examiner*, 12 April 1913.

9. H. Pelling, *Social geography of British elections 1885-1914* (1967), p.301; and census returns. The figure in Harrogate was 35 per cent.

10. See estimates in *Huddersfield Examiner*, 27 April 1895; *The Worker* 21 September 1906.

11. *See* for example Ernest Learoyd's speech to his workers during the 1910 elections: *Huddersfield Examiner*, 15 January 1910, and more generally Patrick Joyce, *Work, society and politics: the culture of the factory in later Victorian England* (1980). On Salt *see* Jack Reynolds' excellent *The great paternalist: Titus Salt and the growth of nineteenth century Bradford* (1983).

12. *See* Clyde Binfield, 'Asquith: the formation of a prime minister', *Journal of the United Reformed Church History Society*, 2, 7 (April 1981).

13. *See* Perks, thesis, pp.84-5 for biographical details of these individuals.

14. Perks, thesis, p.57.

15. Huddersfield Wesleyan Methodist Church, *Tabulated statement as to the provision for religious worship in Huddersfield*, (Huddersfield, 1893); Perks, thesis, p.62.

16. See A.D. Gilbert, *Religion and society in industrial England: church, chapel and social change, 1740-1914* (1976).

17. The story of the PSA is a fascinating one, see: A.H. Byles, *The PSA: what it is and how to start it* (1891); J.W. Tuffley, *Grain from Gallilee: the romance of the Brotherhood Movement* (1935); *Huddersfield Examiner*, 22 October and 30 December 1898, 7 January 1899; Perks, thesis, chapter five.

18. *Religious worship (England and Wales) report*, P(arliamentary) P(apers) 1852-3, LXXXIX, (1); K.S.Inglis, 'Patterns of religious worship in 1851', *Journal of Ecclesiastical History*, XI (1960), 74-87; M. Kinnear, *The British Voter* (New York 1968), p.125.

19. F.W. Dearden, *Huddersfield and District Band of Hope Union: Jubilee memorial 1870-1920 (Huddersfield*, 1920*)*, p.96. See also R. Tayler, *The hope of the race* (1946); L.L. Shiman, 'The Band of Hope movement: respectable recreation for working class children', *Victorian Studies*, 17 (1973-4), 49-74.

20. *Huddersfield Examiner*, 16 December 1893; Anon., *1832-1932: One hundred years of temperance work: souvenir of the centenary celebrations of the Huddersfield Temperance Society* (Huddersfield, 1932); Perks, thesis, pp.291-300.

21. See Ben Turner, *A short History of the General Union of Textile Workers* (Heckmondwike, 1920), pp.28-65; D.F.E. Sykes, *The History of Huddersfield* (Huddersfield, 1911), p.326. For more detail on this *see* Robert Perks, ' ''The Rising Sun of Socialism'': Trade Unionism and the Emergence of the Independent Labour Party in Huddersfield' in *The Rising Sun of Socialism': The Independent Labour Party in the Textile District of the West Riding of Yorkshire between 1890 and 1914* edited by Keith Laybourn and David James (Bradford, 1991).

22. *Dictionary of Labour Biography*, edited by J. Bellamy and J. Saville volume three (1976), pp.81-4.

23. See K. Laybourn, 'The attitudes of Yorkshire trade unions to the economic and social problems of the Great Depression 1873-96', (unpub Ph.D. thesis, Lancaster University 1972), pp.142, 175. See Lady Dilke's speech to the 1900 TUC held in Huddersfield in 1900 in *Huddersfield Chronicle*, 8 September 1900.

24. *Yorkshire Factory Times*, 10 and 17 January 1890; 16 January, 10 April, 29 May, 12, 19 June, 17 July 1891.

25. *Yorkshire Factory Times*, 16 January 1891.

26. *Huddersfield Examiner*, 12 June 1886: the HLUA had three councillors in 1886, rising to five between 1896-1900, and sixty members in March 1887 rising to 170 by 1900. Over the years it gravitated increasingly towards the Huddersfield Conservative Association and was absorbed by it in 1910.

27. *Huddersfield Examiner*, 3 July 1886.

28. *Huddersfield Examiner*, 11 February 1888.

29. *Huddersfield Examiner*, 25 October, 1 and 8 November 1890; *Yorkshire Factory Times*, 31 October 1890.

30. B. Riley, 'A brief account of the rise and growth of the labour and socialist movement in Huddersfield and the Colne Valley' in *The 16th ILP conference handbook*, by B. Riley and E. Whiteley (Huddersfield, 1908).

31. *Huddersfield Examiner*, 30 October 1909; Ben Turner, *About myself* (1930), pp.82-3; E. Royle, *Victorian Infidels: the origins of the British Secularist Movement 1791-1866* (Manchester, 1974), p.227.

32. On Thomson see R.B. Perks, '"Real profit sharing": William Thomson & Sons of Huddersfield, 1886-1925', *Business History*, XXIV (July, 1982).

33. *Yorkshire Factory Times*, 25 September 1891.

34. *Yorkshire Factory Times*, 10 March 1893; B. Riley,(1908); H. Pelling, *The origins of the Labour Party 1880-1900* (Oxford, 1965), p.118.

35. *Huddersfield Examiner*, 14 January 1893.

36. *Huddersfield Chronicle*, 21 January 1893.

37. U(niversity) of H(uddersfield) A(rchives), Liberal Association Minutes: selection committee minutes, 13 October 1893.

38. By comparison Ben Tillett won 23.4 per cent in Bradford West, John Lister 20.5 per cent in Halifax.

39. See R. Price, *An imperial war and the British working class: working class attitudes and reactions to the Boer War 1899-1902* (1972); *The Pro-Boers: the anatomy of an anti-war movement*, edited by S. Koss (Chicago, 1973).

40. *See* Table 2.

41. My emphasis. *Yorkshire Factory Times*, 30 November, 7 and 29 December 1900; *Huddersfield Chronicle*, 24 November 1900.

42. West Yorkshire Archive Service, Kirklees Huddersfield Trades Council Minutes, 27 March and 28 August 1901; E. Wimpenny to J.R. MacDonald, 7 April 1901, Labour Party Correspondence 2/140: *Yorkshire Factory Times*, 6 September 1901.

43. *Yorkshire Factory Times*, 14 August 1903; *Huddersfield Chronicle*, 8 August 1903; J.W. Brierley to J.R. MacDonald, 8 August 1903, Labour Party Correspondence 10/223.

44. *Yorkshire Factory Times*, 12 February 1904; *Labour Leader*, 23 November 1906 for biographical information.

45. F.R. Swan, *Do Socialists Desecrate the Sabbath?* (Huddersfield, nd), p.13. Swan resigned from Marsden Congregational Chapel in 1907 to edit the *Worker* and was secretary of the League of Progressive Thought.

46. *The Worker*, 22 June 1906; UHA, Lockwood Socialist Institute Minutes, 15 July 1906. More generally see F. Reid, 'Socialist Sunday Schools in Britain 1892-1939', *International Review of Social History*, XL (1966), pp.18-47; C. Pearce, 'An interview with Wilfred Whiteley', *Bulletin of the Society for the Study of Labour History*, 1969. Whiteley was superintendent of Lockwood SSS until 1926.

47. *Socialist Sunday Schools: Aims, Objects and Organisation (nd)*.

48. *Huddersfield Examiner*, and *The Worker* 11 May 1907.

49. *Leeds Mercury*, 24 July 1907, also T. R. Williams, *Should the Liberal and Labour Parties Unite?* (Bingley, 1903).

50. Stanley Chadwick's article in *Huddersfield Examiner*, 12 January 1974, and Bob Duncan, *James Leatham 1865-1945: portrait of a socialist pioneer* (Aberdeen, 1978). 80,000 special issues were distributed free in January 1906 and when Leatham joined as editor in 1908 weekly circulation was 6,000.

51. *The Worker*, 19 January 1906; *Huddersfield Chronicle*, 30 December 1905.

52. General correspondence of the Labour Party, 29/466, 8 December 1905.

53. For this debate *see* Perks, thesis, chapter six; K. Laybourn and J. Reynolds, *Liberalism and the Rise of Labour 1890-1918* (Beckenham, 1984); D. Howell, *British Workers and the Independent Labour Party 1888-1906* (Manchester, 1983); D. Tanner, *Political change and the Labour Party 1900-1918* (Cambridge, 1990).

54. *Huddersfield Examiner*, 22 October 1910.

55. UHA, Huddersfield Liberal Association Minutes, sub-committee: 27 February, 23 March and 18 April 1906, executive 1 June 1906.

56. D. Clark, *Colne Valley: Radicalism to Socialism* (1981); and *Victor Grayson* (1985), Reg Groves, *The Strange Case of Victor Grayson* (1975).

57. *The Worker*, 14 August, 2 and 9 October 1909; Perks, thesis, chapter seven for more detail here; Laybourn and Reynolds, *Liberalism and the rise of Labour*, pp.170-3;. also Bob Holton, *British Syndicalism 1900-14* (1976), pp.43-5.

Fig. 21:1 J.A. Brooke.
(UHA)

CHAPTER 21

Politics and Education in Huddersfield in the Late Nineteenth Century

BRIAN MORIARTY

A recurrent theme throughout this chapter is the strength of local Liberalism in Huddersfield in the late nineteenth century. This situation was sustained by the numerical strength and loyalty of Nonconformists in the district. Consequently, the influence of the Liberal party in local bodies elected by the ratepayers was decisive. The links between Liberalism and Nonconformity were matched by those existing between members of the Church of England and the local Conservative party. Religious membership was a primary factor in determining political loyalties. As a consequence, much of the local education debate was on the surface about political attitudes, but the underlying theme was the conflict of religious principles. Educational progress was often conceived and executed in a mood of bitterness and self-satisfaction. Throughout the period, the local educational debate was dominated by the Liberal and Conservative parties. They also enjoyed power. However in the 1890s, a third force – the 'Labour' interest emerged. Its electoral strength was limited, and this meant that its influence on policy remained marginal during the period under review.

The two decades after 1870 were marked by industrial expansion and rapid growth in the local population. According to the census, the numbers living in the borough increased from 70,250 in 1871 to 95,422 in 1891.[1] The population decreased by 366 between 1891 and 1901, and this coincided with a difficult period in textiles, where employment in wool and worsted went down from 15,561 in 1891,[2] to 12,923 in 1901.[3]

The period of prosperity also coincided with an outburst of civic pride. The Huddersfield Gas Company was purchased by the Council in 1871 and the municipal electricity works was opened in 1893. The reservoirs at Deer Hill, Blackmoorfoot and Wessenden Head were opened between 1875 and 1881. The Market Hall began life in 1880, a municipal housing project was undertaken at Turnbridge between 1880 and 1882, the tramway service began in 1883, and Beaumont Park and Greenhead Park were opened in 1883 and 1884 respectively.

The Nonconformists in Huddersfield enjoyed a majority amongst those people who claimed a religious affiliation. From the evidence of the 1851 (religious) census, the Nonconformists claimed 9,347 (61.8 per cent) of the total sittings. The combined total of Church of England and Roman Catholic sittings came to 6,190 or 39.2 per cent of total sittings. The total sittings at 15,789 was 50.11 per cent of the population at large.[4] Local Nonconformists identified closely with the political values and aspirations of Liberalism in the later nineteenth century. This association does a great deal to explain the dominance of the local Liberal party on all important public bodies. The Improvement Commission, which functioned as a modest public health and policing body in Huddersfield, prior to the incorporation of the town as a municipal borough in 1868, appears to have been dominated by people of Liberal persuasion. With reference to its final membership in 1868, fifteen of the nineteen members voted Liberal in the 1868 parliamentary election.[5] The religious affiliations of nine of the fifteen Liberals have been traced: eight were Nonconformists.[6] The first Corporation (1868) was composed of fourteen aldermen and forty-four councillors. It has been possible to trace the religious loyalties of thirty-eight of the fifty-eight members.[7] Twenty-nine of these were Nonconformists, and twenty-eight of that group voted Liberal in 1868.[8] Only one Nonconformist on the first Corporation (where religious membership has been traced) voted Conservative in the 1868 election.

The first School Board of 1871 had thirteen members. The four who belonged to the 'Church' party were members of the Church of England.[9] Six voted Liberal in 1868.[10] One voted Conservative, and Mrs Huth, as a woman, was debarred from voting. The seven Nonconformists represented the Independents, Baptists, Wesleyans, Free Wesleyans, Methodist New Connexion, Primitive Methodists, and Unitarians respectively. Religious background, therefore, played a decisive part in shaping political loyalties on public bodies in Huddersfield at this time, in particular, the voting strength and educational objectives of the School Board.

The political situation in Huddersfield

The Whigs (Liberals after 1853) dominated parliamentary elections in Huddersfield between 1832 and 1914. Conservative candidates were only able to represent the town from 1865 to 1868 and from 1893 to 1895. In both cases, the candidates were members of the Crosland family, who owned the local 'Conservative' paper, the *Huddersfield Chronicle*. The Conservative success of 1865 was followed by an attempt to improve party organisation through the creation of the Huddersfield Working Men's Conservative Association, in October 1866. A permanent secretary was appointed in 1886.[11] The 1893 victory was due to the opposition of working men to the Liberal candidate, Joseph Woodhead, who held hostile views on trade union rights and on proposals to shorten the length of the working day. The Conservatives were never able to dominate the Corporation at this time; no Conservative leader in the town served for long periods. Within the prominent Brooke family, neither Thomas or William Brooke was involved in municipal politics, although their brother, John Arthur, served as an Alderman for a short period at the turn of the century.

The Liberal group was closely identified with Nonconformist interests in the town. It became the practice to hold election meetings in Chapel Sunday Schools. By 1868, the 'Whig' element in the local party was very small: Mellor, the Whig candidate for the Liberal nomination, received nine votes against 250 recorded for Leatham, who went on to contest the seat successfully.[12] The *Huddersfield Examiner*, owned by Joseph Woodhead, was the mouthpiece of local Liberalism, both determining and reflecting party opinion. The Liberal Registration Association was formed at the Queen Hotel on 1 June 1866, to organise support for Liberal candidates.[13] By 1883 it was effectively controlling the selection of undenominational candidates to the School Board.[14] In 1886, it changed its name to Liberal Association. The 1886 Home Rule Bill, which damaged the Liberal party nationally, had no serious repercussions in Huddersfield. The local Member of Parliament was not re-selected, but the Liberals retained the seat. Only four ward party officers and two prominent personalities announced their defection.[15] The crisis was to come later – in 1893 – over the decision of the local Liberal party to field Joseph Woodhead as its parliamentary candidate.

The third, and successful, attempt to form a local Trades Council, in 1885, provided a foundation for the 'Labour' interest in Huddersfield to build on and this was followed by the opening of the Friendly and Trades Club in 1886. In 1890, Allen Gee, a Liberal, and chairman of the Trades Council, put himself forward as a Liberal candidate in the Lindley ward in a local election. The Liberals failed to support Gee, and nominated an opponent, who was successful. This action may have inspired the creation of the Huddersfield Labour Union in September 1891: Allen Gee was a founder member. In 1892, Ramsden Balmforth, an employee at the Co-op, became the first Labour member on the School Board, and topped the poll. Then, in 1893, the antipathy by working men to the Liberal party's parliamentary candidate led to the end of that party's monopoly of power, for the first time since 1868. By 1895 the local Liberals were more willing to listen to the views of working men over the choice of candidate. However, time had moved on: the Labour Union chose to sponsor its own candidate for the coming election. The interests of the Liberal and Labour movements were now on a conflicting course.

The state of education in Huddersfield around 1870

The Corporation, taking advantage of the Education Act of 1870, made arrangements to establish a School Board in Huddersfield.[16] The first elections were held in January 1871. At the last moment, a number of candidates agreed to withdraw, and this saved the ratepayers the expense of a contest.[17] The new School Board conducted a survey of all institutions in the Borough providing schooling for less than ninepence per week.[18] The report indicated that there was a deficiency of places, especially on the south side of the Borough, for example in Dalton and Lockwood, where the population had increased, by 30 per cent and 22 per cent respectively, between 1861 and 1871.[19] On the basis of tests provided by the Education Department in London, the School Board found that schools classed as 'efficient' provided 8,194 places in 1871.[20] By 1881, the Board calculated that 14,240 places would be needed, leaving a shortfall of 6,046. The Board recognised that 894 new places would be available shortly after 1871 and that an additional 1,062 places would be provided by voluntary agencies in new or existing schools. The final deficency figure was, therefore, fixed at 4,110.[21]

The Board now proposed to create thirteen new infant departments and to finance the building of new schools in Dalton, Lindley and Lockwood.[22] The Board's decision to embark on an ambitious programme of school building as soon as funds permitted worried churchmen – the organisers of the majority of voluntary schools. Throughout 1872, there was an acrimonious debate on the potential cost to the ratepayers of School Board policies.

While the School Board concerned itself with the task of providing elementary school facilities to supplement those provided by voluntary (mainly Church) bodies, the organisation of secondary education in Huddersfield was outside the control of public bodies. The town had two proprietary schools – the College and the Collegiate – and two small grammar schools, at Fartown and Almondbury. Several children from the Borough went to the grammar school at Longwood, which was outside the Borough boundary until 1890.

The Collegiate was founded as a Church of England school in 1838 – that is the influence of the Church pervaded the teaching and administration. The

Fig. 21:2 Huddersfield Collegiate School. (KCS)

school was in increasing financial difficulties after 1882, so that its governors asked to join with Huddersfield College in 1885.[23] The Huddersfield College was founded in 1838, in opposition to the Collegiate. The school was supported by the wealthier Nonconformist families in the town, and in the 1860s was over twice the size of the Collegiate. J. G. Fitch, who visited Huddersfield on behalf of the Taunton Commission in 1868, declared that, while the progress of both schools was being impeded by religious jealousy, there was little difference in practice between the religious teaching offered in the two schools.[24]

Almondbury Free Grammar School had thirty-nine scholars in 1868, of whom twenty-seven paid fees. Additional income came from the assets of the Wormall charity and rents from lands in Almondbury and Golcar.[25] The school struggled to pay its way and depended upon generous support from the Brooke family of Armitage Bridge.

Longwood Grammar School had sixty pupils in 1868 with fees fixed at sixpence per week.[26] Like Almondbury it was closely associated with the Church of England. Despite the construction of new buildings between 1879 and 1881, pupil numbers had fallen to forty-five in 1897, due to the attraction of cheaper education in the Technical School, and the opening of the School Board Higher Grade School in 1894.[27]

Fartown Grammar School developed on similar lines to Longwood. It too had close associations with the Church of England, and, between 1881 and 1899, spent much money on improving buildings. Few pupils were to be found in the senior classes: the thirteen to fifteen age range had only thirty-one members. The difficulties facing the school in this period were attributed to the opening of the Higher Grade School.[27]

Liberal Party supporters not only dominated the activities of the School Board, with its obligation to organise and finance the Board's elementary schools; they also were prominent in the running of education, and in particular the Mechanics' Institution. On the evidence of the 1868 poll books, eighteen of the Institution's Committee voted Liberal, three voted Conservative, two remained neutral and the voting choice of the remaining member cannot be traced. Mr and Mrs Huth, both identified as Liberal supporters, at least until 1886, provided the driving force in the Female Educational Institute, which had 146 members in 1868.[29]

Politics and elementary education: local reactions to national policies

The outstanding feature of the 1870 (Forster's) Education Act was the creation of the dual system in English elementary education. Under this system, the Voluntary Schools – run in the main by the Church of England – supported by state grants, fees and private subscriptions, were joined in many districts by the new Board Schools, supported by state grants, fees, and vital revenue from local rates.

Reaction to national legislation in Huddersfield was expressed, predictably, through party groups. The 'Church' interest, united by a determination to preserve and extend the Voluntary system, organised meetings, attended by leading local Conservatives. Correspondingly, the 'Undenominational' interest, whose objective was to enhance the powers and responsibilities of School Boards at the expense of the Voluntary system, held meetings which were dominated by prominent local Liberals.

In 1870 the local Undenominational, or Liberal interest, was far from united in its views on the conduct of elementary education. There was broad agreement on the need to exclude voluntary schools from rate support, to make attendance at school compulsory, to allow voluntary interests 'no period of grace' to build additional schools (the 1870 bill had proposed a period of twelve months), and to insist that the religious teaching given in any school supported by public money should be 'unsectarian' in character. Huddersfield's Liberal Member of Parliament, Leatham, was against enforcement of attendance, and favoured the abolition of all fees as the best means to attract all the children into schools. The 'Church' interest was opposed to compulsory attendance and wanted the school day (in all schools) to commence with a religious service and instruction in the 'great principles of religion'.

The 'Undenominational' interest enjoyed a monopoly of power on Huddersfield School Board throughout its life from 1871 to 1903, and this meant that the case for extending the duties and powers of the local School Board would prevail. The National Education League had been formed to protect Nonconformist interests at a time when the government was proposing to make major changes in elementary education. The first meeting of the Huddersfield branch was held in January 1870 and the platform party was composed entirely of prominent Liberals.[30] The National Education Union was formed to defend voluntary interests, and its first local meeting was dominated by Conservatives and Church of England clergymen.[31] This meeting was followed by a second gathering two weeks later, which was addressed by the Secretary of the National Union.[32]

A meeting of the 'Undenominational' interest, packed with prominent personalities of the local Liberal party, was held in March 1870, to discuss the Education Bill. Motions were carried objecting to plans to allow School Boards to decide on the kind of religious teaching to be given in their schools, to create School Boards only in certain districts rather than throughout the country, and to give School Boards the option of deciding whether or not to enforce attendance. (The meeting wanted universal School Boards, and government legislation making school attendance compulsory). The proposal to allow the Voluntary system a period of twelve months to expand its schools was attacked.[33] The major topic of interest was religious teaching, and the meeting asked the government to ensure that any school receiving support from local rates, or from national funds, should offer instruction free from any sectarian bias. This request constituted a direct attack on the operation of most of the voluntary schools, which were controlled by the Church of England, where the teaching of that Church's practices and beliefs was central to the curriculum. Amendments to the Education Bill in May 1870 were welcomed by the *Examiner* – in particular the decision to elect School Boards by ratepayer vote and the proposal that all religious teaching in Board schools should be 'undenominational' in character.[34] A major objection of local Conservatives was the Bill's proposal to give School Boards power to compel attendance, believing that compulsion would not work before the creation of an adequate school system.[35]

The next major 'political crisis' in the conduct of elementary education came with the Conservative government's appointment of the Cross Commission in 1886. In March 1887, the School Board sent a letter to the Commission asking for changes, including the removal of certain privileges enjoyed by Voluntary schools.[36] For example, it wanted such schools to be audited annually by the Local Government Board, or other suitable authority. There was a desire that the Education Department in London should consult with the local School Board before approving any extension to a Voluntary school. As most training colleges were run by the Church of England, the Board requested that School Boards be permitted to establish Undenominational Colleges similar to those operating in Scotland. Finally, the Board asked for more help for senior classes, declaring that children of school age should not be disqualified from winning a government grant simply because they had already passed the seventh standard. At no time in the letter did the Board use the opportunity to press claims on behalf of all the elementary schools in Huddersfield; its objective was to enhance the position of the Board's own schools.

Mr J.A. Brooke voiced to the Cross Commission the worries felt by the Voluntary schools. Mr Brooke, a dominant figure in local Conservative politics, wanted more government money for Voluntary schools, claimed that Church people found it a great hardship to pay rates for the support of Board Schools, and supported a suggestion that the power to dissolve School Boards should be increased.[37]

From 1886, Conservative governments enjoyed office for twenty years, with the exception of the period from 1892 to 1895. These governments sought to make two changes in the operation of elementary education. First, new funds – from the rates if possible – had to be found to shore up the Voluntary system. Second, the pretensions of the larger School Boards to organise Higher Grade Schools offering a secondary type education had to be inhibited and then curtailed. The changes were to be achieved by making the County and County Borough Councils responsible for both elementary and secondary education under the 1902 act. Consequently, the activities of the Huddersfield School Board in this period tended to be dominated by protests against government education policies. In contrast, the morale of the minority 'Church' party on the local School Board enjoyed an upward surge. The advent of the 'Labour' interest in local School Board elections in 1892 reinforced the trend to greater political organisation of supporters by the respective parties. By 1900, the Trades Council, numerically and financially much stronger in Huddersfield than the Independent Labour Party, was adopting a more aggressive stance on educational matters.

In order that School Boards should speak with a united voice on educational changes, a decision was taken, at a conference in Manchester in March and April 1893, to form an Association of School Boards of England and Wales. The 'Undenominational' majority group on the Huddersfield Board invariably sent two of its members to meetings.[38]

The School Boards in 1900 were attacked on three fronts. First, the grants paid to students for success in a range of 'advanced' subjects were cut.[39]

535

Second, the government proposed that higher grade schools should not take pupils above the age of fifteen.[40] Finally the Cockerton 'Judgement' said that it was unlawful for School Boards to use the rates to support science classes in the Higher Grade Schools.[41]

The decision to cut grants for passes in 'advanced' subjects was attacked by the Chairman of the Huddersfield School Board as 'most hurtful and disastrous to the higher and more progressive education of the children of the working classes . . .'.[42] On the question of the bar to students over fifteen years attending Higher Grade schools, the local School Board in May 1900 voiced its support for the opponents of this proposal.[43] In June 1900, clause six of the Science and Art Directory left the School Board unable to support science classes from its rates: the Borough Council, where the Liberals also enjoyed a majority, came to the rescue by making a grant of £263 12s. 5d. for 1900-1901 from its own rate revenue. The Church Party on the Huddersfield School Board moved a motion that opposed Boards providing any education which was not elementary.[44] Meanwhile, the majority (Liberal) group on the local Board passed a motion condemning the Cockerton judgement.[45]

The Huddersfield Trades Council was the first local body to express its opposition to the 1902 Education Bill, which it described as 'undemocratic, contrary to the spirit of the age, and a violation of the principle of representation with taxation'.[46] The Trades Council wanted the election by the ratepayers of one body solely for educational work. Existing local councils, which were earmarked to do this work, already had a wide range of civic responsibilities. The majority on Huddersfield School Board were critical of the proposal to use rates for the support of Voluntary schools.[47] On two occasions, the leader of the 'Church' group on the School Board moved a resolution welcoming the Education Bill but was not successful.[48]

The Liberal Association and the Huddersfield Free Church Council held a large public meeting on 2 May 1902. A resolution was passed 'calling upon' all the friends of educational progress to unite in resisting and defeating the bill!'[49]

A further meeting, held on 4 October 1902, and sponsored by the Liberal party, the ILP, the Trades Council and the Free Churches, passed a motion asking the government to withdraw the Education Bill or to call a general election on the issue.[50] The struggle to defeat the Government's Education Bill had produced in Huddersfield a remarkable amount of common understanding between the Liberal party and branches of the Labour movement in the borough. With the passing of the 1902 Education Act, the fight for the two principles – that the new authorities for education should have responsibility for education alone and that no local rates should be used to support Voluntary schools – was lost.

The School Board in Huddersfield 1871-1902

Throughout the period from 1871 to 1902, the Denominational (or Church) party were in a minority on Huddersfield School Board. The Undenominational group, assisted by careful organisation of the voters, won all the contested elections. The Denominational party was almost exclusively represented by members of the Church of England, who sought to protect the local Voluntary schools. The Undenominational party tended to be dominated by Nonconformists who were active in local Liberal politics. The control of the two major parties in School Board elections in Huddersfield was not 'formal', in the sense that the Liberal and Conservative Associations did not sit down *en bloc* and choose the candidates to represent their respective interests. However, throughout the period, the political parties took a keen interest in arranging election meetings and in the results which followed. Due to the vested interest the Liberals had in the work of the School Board, the relationship between the Liberal Association and the Undenominational party was closer than that enjoyed by the Denominational (Church) party with local Conservatives. What is certain is that religious views largely determined party loyalty.

The decision to elect a School Board in Huddersfield was taken by the Borough Council in December 1870. Local Conservatives had hoped to delay this decision in order to give the Voluntary schools more time to remedy shortages in provision.[51] Despite the natural Nonconformist majority amongst the electorate, the electoral balance in Huddersfield was sufficiently delicate to inject some drama, and certainly considerable heat, into the contests for School Board places.

The dominant issue at the first, and most subsequent elections, which were held every three years, was the nature of religious teaching to be offered in the Board Schools. The 'Liberal' group wanted the Bible to be read 'without comment', partly because of its fear that, as the great majority of teachers were either Church of England or had been trained at Church of England colleges, much of the religious teaching might reflect the theology of the Established Church.

The *Examiner* accurately predicted how the election contest for the thirteen seats on the School Board would be resolved. It suggested that the 'Liberal' group should nominate six, the 'workers' two, the 'Church' group four, with the remaining seat to be held by a Roman Catholic delegate. The 'Church' group and the Catholic representative would be expected to unite on most issues. The 'Liberal' group clearly anticipated the support of the workers' nominees, as William Marriott was a member of the Liberal Registration Association, and Mrs Huth's husband also belonged to the same body. Marriott and Mrs Huth were returned as 'Liberal' party candidates.

Table 1 provides an analysis of the membership of the first School Board in Huddersfield: three of the 'Liberal' group already had experience in municipal politics and six had associations with the Mechanics' Institution. Only one of the group belonged to the Church of England. All four members of the 'Church' group were Anglicans, but only one had experience of municipal politics.

The 1874 election revealed, perhaps for the first and only time, a serious split within the Nonconformists, who dominated the 'Liberal' group, on a major issue, religious education. The Wesleyans were split, between those who wanted to retain the *status quo* and have the Bible read 'without comment', and those who wanted explanations to be provided. While the 'Church' party might have obtained comfort from this division, it was also worried about the potential power of the School Board to execute an ambitious building programme, and the effect this would have on the numbers of children seeking admission to the Voluntary schools. In the 1874 election, the Conservative party 'placed their rooms at the disposal of the 'Bible candidates'.[52] The platform party at the candidates' adoption meeting was filled by seven prominent local Conservatives.[53] This event, which was held in Queen Street Wesleyan Chapel, was followed soon afterwards by one in the same chapel in support of 'Liberal' or 'Undenominational' candidates.[54] All seven 'Liberal' candidates were returned in 1874 (six had served on the first School Board). The Church party won six seats and the Roman Catholic candidate was squeezed out.[55] Six of the seven 'Liberal' candidates were Nonconformists. One of the six 'Church' candidates was a

Table 1 Members of the Huddersfield School Board, 1871-74

'Party'	Name	Religion	Municipal Politics	Association with Mechanics' Institution 1871
'Liberal'	W Mellor	Independant	Alderman 1868	Annual member
'Liberal'	E Brooke	Weslyan	–	Committee member
'Liberal'	A Crowther	Baptist	Alderman 1868-74	–
'Liberal'	J Dodds	Free Weslyan	–	President
'Liberal'	C Glendinning	Primitive Methodist	Council 1863-83 Alderman 1883-98	Annual member
'Liberal'	W Sykes	Methodist New Connexion	–	–
'Working Men'	Mrs Huth	Unitarian	–	Husband on Committee of Mechanics' Institution
'Working men'	W Marriott	Church of England	Council 1868-74-80	Vice President
'Church'	Rev. W Calvert	Church of England	–	–
'Church'	H Barker	Church of England	Council 1872-75	Annual member
'Church'	J Priestley	Church of England	–	–
'Church'	W Schofield	Church of England	Council 1880-91	–
'R.C.'	Revd S.L. Wells	Roman Catholic	–	

The use of the label 'Working Men' seems to have died out quietly. In the 1874 School Board election; the term 'undenominational interest' was used to cover all the candidates who had stood in 1871 as either 'Liberals' or the nominees of 'Working Men'. This change reflected voting behaviour on the School Board from 1871 to 1874. The two representatives of the 'Working Men' agreed with the 'Liberals' on all issues. The interests expected to work for the promotion of Board Schools therefore had a clean majority with eight of the thirteen seats.

Wesleyan. The Roman Catholic candidate regained a seat on the 1877 School Board, when a contest was not required, and the 'Church' party was reduced to five.[56]

The Conservative newspaper, the *Chronicle*, claimed that the 'Undenominational' or 'Liberal' candidates were chosen at a general committee meeting of the local Liberal party, held in the Guildhall before the 1880 election.[57] The meeting must have been 'unofficial', as no record appears of it in the minutes of the Liberal Association. Liberal influences

Fig. 21:3 Alderman
Owen Balmforth. (KCS)

must have been present in 1880 in the selection process because Mrs Huth – who now wanted the Bible to be read and explained – was not readopted as an official candidate.

The 1883 election involved seventeen candidates fighting for the thirteen seats. All seven of the 'Liberal' group were returned. Mrs Huth, who stood as an Independent, finished bottom of the poll and her poor performance reflected the importance of having the support of the Liberal Association at a School Board election. Her record of devoted service to the School Board was not enough to ensure her success.[58] The Board gained a valuable new member in June 1883, in the person of Owen Balmforth. Balmforth was a Liberal, but as a member of the Co-operative Society and a close friend of leading local trade unionists, his advanced views on education were to act as a spur to progress.

The 1886 election was notable only for the division which occurred within the Church party's ranks. A three-man ginger group sought election as 'economical candidates'. Two of the group were adopted and both were elected.[59] In 1889, both the 'Liberal' and the 'Church' parties found their unity being threatened by minorities seeking representation. Two ratepayers' 'Independent' candidates arrived at the Church meeting; one of these men was a publican. Both were adopted and both were ultimately elected. The *Examiner* claimed that the publican owed his election success to the support he had received from 'beer drinking loafers'.[60] The 'Liberal' group were approached by the Trades Council for support for their candidate, Allen Gee. At a meeting on 4 January 1889, the executive of the Liberal Association failed to support Gee, even though he was a prominent member of the Lindley Liberal Club.[61] The seven strong 'Liberal' group was returned, along with five of the 'Church' party and a Roman Catholic representative.[62]

Between 1871 and 1901, four major issues caused considerable division of opinion between the two parties on Huddersfield School Board; the question of school provision, the form of religious education, the policy towards attendance, and the arrangements for payment of fees. On the issues of fees and religious education, expediency was sacrificed for principle at the expense of the educational interests of the children.

On the issue of school provision, the majority on the School Board faced little opposition to its proposals to place new buildings in outer areas of the borough. As the central area was adequately served by Voluntary schools in

1870, proposals for building there attracted strong opposition. In such cases the Board often abandoned the usual claim that there was a shortage of accommodation and based its case on the need to provide schools which would not have 'sectarian instruction'. Permission was sought, under this pretext, to build a school at Beaumont Street. Permission was eventually granted, but the School Board was not granted an easy-term loan, but had to go to the open market for capital.[63] Attendance at this school in the first week was 462 and this figure seemed to justify the Board's policy.[64] Similar controversy arose over plans to build and extend the Board School at Hillhouse. The Education Department in London sanctioned the construction,[65] but it refused to agree to the extension, three years later, in 1880.[66] Careful presentation of statistics outlining the situation in Paddock, where four-fifths of the population were Nonconformists, won permission for the School Board to open a temporary school in 1881, and in January 1883 the foundation stone for a permanent building was laid.[67]

The decision on the nature of religious teaching to be given in Board Schools was taken in February 1872. Seven members supported the motion to read the Bible without comment. The four members of the 'Church' party wanted suitable explanations. One person abstained. This may have been Mrs Huth, who eventually broke with the majority party on this issue in 1880. The Church party tried to extend the time devoted to religious teaching in February 1875. A moderate motion, to allow the children to read the Scriptures after the teacher, failed in October 1875, by six votes to five.[68] When a majority of the management committee of Almondbury Board School wanted the Bible to be read, and explained, to the senior scholars, the School Board refused to permit it.[69] A request from the Church Institute, a few days before the 1880 election, that headmasters in Board Schools be allowed to give Bible explanations, was also rejected.[70]

The Huddersfield School Board had the power, under the 1870 act, to impose school attendance, and this they decided to do in September 1873. Children between the ages of five and thirteen would have to go to school, although the half-time system applied after the tenth birthday.[71] Initially the 'Church' party argued that this was an invasion of a family's privacy. However, as the annual grant to all schools, from the Education Department in London, partly depended upon the numbers in attendance, the attitude of the 'Church' party to compulsion changed after 1873.

The local School Board decided to base its fee charges (for Board Schools) on the age of the pupils. Fees of pauper children was paid by the Board, until 1 January 1874, when the Board of Guardians assumed responsibility. Rates were, therefore, being used to educate a minority of children in both Board and Voluntary schools, albeit it for only three years. The Liberal group was not happy with this arrangement and it rejected a request in September 1873 from the Church party to pay the fees of poor, as opposed to pauper, children.

The mood of the Liberal group on the local School Board in the years 1870 to 1886 was buoyant – buttressed by the fact that progressive School Boards were for the most part allowed to dictate the pace of change in elementary education. After 1891, the mood of the majority party in Huddersfield changed perceptibly. As the attempts to restore the health of the Voluntary system increased in scope and intent, the Liberals on the Huddersfield School Board began to move on to the defensive.

The 1892 School Board election in Huddersfield was the first held since the decision to abolish fees (under ninepence per week) in elementary schools. Its local significance lies in the fact that it was the first occasion that a member of the ILP won a seat on the Huddersfield School Board. The Liberal party could no longer claim an exclusive right to represent radical interests. The approach of the Liberal party to the 'Labour movement', which initially was patronising, became in time more conciliatory. The Liberal interest had rejected the Trades Council's nominee (Allen Gee) in 1888, but, by 1891, the Liberal Association was advised by its executive to adopt a 'Labour' candidate.[72] The cautious use of the word 'Liberal' to describe Undenominational Board members from 1871 to 1892 can now be dropped. The Liberals and the Trades Council failed to make an agreement over School Board candidates at a meeting, held on 4 January 1892, in the Victoria Hall.[73] In the election, the Liberals reduced their numbers of candidates from seven to six: all were returned. The Church party won five seats and the Roman Catholic candidate was successful. This left the ILP candidate, Ramsden Balmforth, who came top of the poll, holding the balance of power. In practice, he voted with the Liberals on all major issues.[74]

The local Conservative party, having won the by-election of 1893, went into the 1895 Board election with confidence. The Liberal candidates promised to extend 'advanced' teaching in its Board Schools and to support the work of the new Higher Grade School, opened in 1894, for older pupils.[75] The Church party resolved to check School Board extravagance and change the arrangements for the giving of religious education,[76] and the Huddersfield Conservative Association placed its organising secretary in change of the election arrangements for the Church party. While the Liberals won seven seats, the last two candidates just scraped in at the bottom of the poll. The Trades Council provided the Labour representative, while the Roman Catholic candidate lost his seat.[77] The Liberal candidates had been nominated at a meeting of the 'Friends of Unsectarian Education', organised by a sub-committee of the Liberal party.[78]

There was no election contest in 1898. The Liberals had seven seats, the Church party five and the ILP one. In both 1895 and 1898, the Liberals were not prepared to let the ILP hold the balance of power, and went for a straight majority of the thirteen seats. At the final election in 1901, the ILP and the Trades Council jointly sponsored two candidates. The Liberals won seven seats and the Labour group had two for the first time.[79] This increasing strength of the Labour interest was a portent of things to come.

Politics and secondary education in Huddersfield 1870-1902

The evidence for the state of secondary education in Huddersfield around 1870 is derived from the findings of the Taunton Commission, published in 1867 and 1868, and reference has already been made to the schools earlier in the chapter. In this section, the relationship between the two proprietary schools – the College and the Collegiate – will be examined, with an emphasis on the events leading to amalgamation in 1885 and closure in 1893. Then the arguments surrounding the creation of the Higher Grade School and its impact on other institutions will be reviewed. Finally the attempts by Almondbury Grammar School to survive as a viable concern, without sacrificing its position of independence to municipal control, will be discussed.

The existence of two proprietary schools in Huddersfield, the Collegiate and the College representing Church of England and Nonconformist interests respectively, meant that there was wasteful competition for support in the form of capital investments, scholarships and fees. The governing body of the Collegiate included prominent Conservatives, like Joseph Crosland, the borough Member of Parliament from 1892 to 1895. Liberal members dominated the board of the College: the secretary, Revd Dr Bruce, was later chairman of Huddersfield School Board.

It was the "religious" difficulty which presented the biggest obstacle in the negotiations prior to the amalgamation of the College and the Collegiate. The Collegiate governors wanted instruction, during the school day, in the liturgy, catechism and articles of the Church of England, for those who requested it.[80] The College governors objected, and said that such instruction should be given outside school hours. It was ultimately decided to give this teaching at 11.30 a.m. on Saturday mornings![81] The Collegiate proposal, that there should be an equal number of Churchmen and Nonconformists on the new governing body, was rejected by the College, who argued that it should enjoy a majority, as the College was providing the property for the new school, and that it possessed a higher number of scholars in 1885 than the Collegiate.[82] Local Nonconformists regarded Almondbury Grammar school as an Anglican preserve and did not wish to surrender the privileges they enjoyed in running Huddersfield College. However, when the new governing body met on 1 July 1885, it contained twelve members from each of the two participating institutions. Ten of the College's twelve were prominent local Liberals. Five of the Collegiate group, which included two vicars, were active in Conservative circles. The owners of the local

Fig. 21:4 Huddersfield College. (KCS)

newspapers, Joseph Crosland of the *Chronicle* and Joseph Woodhead of the *Examiner*, both sat on the new board.[83] Among the reasons given for the demise of the school in 1893 was the absence of denominational instruction in the curriculum. This argument, which was relayed in the *Chronicle*, was one used by local Conservatives.[84] The College appears to have fallen between two stools; it offered an education too expensive to be acceptable to those artisans in the town who had ambitions for their sons, yet, on the other hand, its facilities and grounds were not up to the standard of the most demanding parents, with financial resources and the will to buy the best in education.[85]

The closure of the Huddersfield College in 1893 provided the buildings for a new Higher Grade School, run by Huddersfield School Board. The Conservative interest fought a campaign against the School Board's decision to use rates to purchase the college building, for £9,000, and to admit students to the new school free of charge.[86] The *Examiner*, in contrast, argued that, with the closure of the College, Huddersfield would find itself with most unsatisfactory provision in the secondary field.[87]

Owen Balmforth, a Liberal member of the Huddersfield School Board, speaking at a Board meeting on 5 June 1893, defended the proposal that negotiations should be opened with the liquidator of the College company for the purchase by the School Board of the College property. He argued that the purchase of an existing building would save the ratepayers the cost of constructing a new building in the future; that new premises were already needed for pupils in standards six, seven and extra seven to relieve congestion in existing schools; that the low level of fees envisaged would attract a great number of working men's children, whose education was only half-completed when they left their desks; that Huddersfield would lose its pre-eminence in the field of education if it failed to act like the fourteen other School Boards who had already established Higher Grade Schools; that it was in Huddersfield's commercial interests to have such a school; that countries like Germany and Scotland, who had schools of this kind, enjoyed education of a superior character; and that a more advanced education was needed to develop the whole range of human faculties. National opinion in 1893, claimed Balmforth, was moving in favour of a system of Higher Grade Education.[88] The Conservative response to Balmforth's proposition was delivered by W.P. Hellawell, a prominent Churchman on the School Board. He doubted whether the Board had a responsibility in this field of education and believed that it would lead to financial burdens for ratepayers. Districts with Higher Grade Schools were often worse off for secondary schools than Huddersfield, he maintained. Hellawell believed that students could go to evening classes to complete their education, and, in view of the trade recession, it was the wrong time to embark on an expensive capital scheme. It was his opinion that the schools at Almondbury, Fartown and Longwood together with the Technical School, would be adversely affected by the plan to charge low or no fees in the Higher Grade School. Hellawell was not sure that the children of working class parents would take the opportunities envisaged. In short, he believed that a large proportion of the scholars at the new school would cater for the middle classes, who could well afford to pay for the education of their children.[89] The issue was resolved in favour of the 'Liberal' majority. The existing secondary provision was deficient in Huddersfield. The new Association of School Boards, formed in 1893, was a source of advice on the problems of starting Higher Grade Schools. 1894 coincided with the election of a Liberal government disposed to encourage such schemes, with a sympathetic minister at the Education Department, A.H. Acland. Under trust deeds, the governing bodies of the grammar schools were dominated by the Church interest. Anglicans perhaps harboured a hidden fear that the Higher Grade School would evolve into a large and successful secondary school, dominated by Nonconformist interests and subsidised by public money.

Almondbury Grammar School enjoyed a precarious existence throughout this period. Liberals regarded the school as an Anglican 'preserve' and used their majority on both the School Board and the Borough Council as a launching pad for negotiations with the Almondbury governors on the question of future public control. In 1881 the governors submitted to the Charity Commissioners a new scheme for running the school. There were to be eight co-opted and seven representative governors. The local School Board was not included, and claimed that, as the local authority responsible for carrying out the provisions of the education acts, it should have the power to nominate a representative governor. Indeed, they wished to nominate three.[90] The Almondbury governors made no concession to this demand from the School Board. These events of 1881 revealed in some degree the tension between rival religious and political interests in the town, and help to explain the stand taken by the College governors in 1885.

ALMONDBURY GRAMMAR SCHOOL. (H.45.)

Fig. 21:5 Almondbury Grammar School. (KCS)

By 1895 the financial position at Almondbury Grammar School had become critical.[92] Bryce, in his report, favoured the transfer of the school to local public control, as this would bring help from the rates and income from the Ramsden charity.[91] By 1897 the Almondbury school had debts of £1,200, despite the receipt of money in 1896 from the West Riding County Council to assist science classes. Mr J.A. Brooke told the Charity Commissioners that a rapid increase in the numbers on the roll was essential. Laboratory facilities urgently needed to be improved, to help the school stand up to competition from the Technical School and the Higher Grade School.[93] The Charity Commissioners produced a fresh scheme for the school in 1898. They proposed that the governing body should have six new representative governors, two from the council and one from the Yorkshire College, together with such other governors as might be appointed for the purposes of the Technical Instruction Act (1889) by the local authority (the Borough Council), charged with the operation of the Act. These proposals for the governing body were endorsed by the Borough Council.[94] As a result, the number of representative governors at Almondbury was increased from seven to eleven, and the number of co-opted governors was reduced from eight to five. The first assistance from the rates came in 1904, with a small grant of £100.[95] The number of Borough Council representatives was increased from three to eight in 1909, but in a governing body of seventeen, these representatives still did not enjoy an absolute majority. The transfer of the school to local authority control was completed in 1922. The saga at Almondbury revealed the determination of the Church interest to avoid any scheme devised for the financial salvation of the school which would involve the acceptance of new forms of control which might threaten the Anglican character of the school.

Politics and technical education in Huddersfield 1870-1902

The subject of technical education is covered in Chapter Twenty-two; its development was marked by the relative absence of the political divisions which were ever present in the elementary and secondary spheres. Consequently a brief treatment of certain issues is appropriate.

The creation of the Technical School in 1883 was the result of co-operation between the Chamber of Commerce and the Committee of the Mechanics' Institution.[96] The Technical Instruction Committee of the Borough Council, created in 1890, reflected the Liberal domination of local politics. There are few indications that it discharged its responsibilities unfairly. The Technical College, successor to the Mechanics' Institution and the Technical School, was brought under the control of the Borough Council for the first time in 1902. The political differences which ensued were not between Liberal and Conservative but between the Trades Council, which was seeking direct representation on the Technical College governing body, and the Liberal majority on that body.

Huddersfield Borough Council had never resorted to the use of the powers, permitted to it under the Technical Instruction Act of 1889, to levy a rate in aid of technical education. The need for more public money for the College was the theme chosen by speakers at the prize day in 1897.[97] When the Borough Council decided to appoint a Technical College Committee to run the College in 1901, the *Chronicle* welcomed this move, saying that the education offered would gain from the exclusion of the School Board from its management.[98] The Trades Council sought representation on the grounds that it had two men with experience on the Huddersfield School Board and that as the official organisation representing the trades in the town, it should have an influence on the kinds of courses offered. The first approach by the Trades Council in 1902 was rejected in March.[99] A second approach in November 1902 was turned down in January 1903.[100] The proposals for the College governing body were made in March 1903. Nineteen of the thirty-seven representatives were to be Councillors, five were to be nominated by existing Technical College governors, but the Trades Council was left out. The fact that the Vicar was included as an *ex-officio* member, while the body officially representing the trades of the town was excluded, seemed a travesty of justice. By way of compensation, Allen Gee, a past president of the Trades Council and a Labour member of the Borough Council, was one of the nineteen nominated Councillors.

The Technical Instruction Committee's task was to distribute annually the financial 'windfall', known as 'whisky money', which emanated from the Local Taxation Act (1890).[101] Huddersfield's share of the County allocation in 1891 was to be £1,956.[102] Monies were distributed on an annual basis. In 1892, the condition restricting the use of money granted to the Huddersfield School Board to evening classes only, was withdrawn.[103] In 1897, Longwood Grammar School asked that it too might use its grant for day classes. Its grant had been cut from £80 to £50 in 1897, at a time when the school wanted to build a suitable science laboratory. Numbers on the roll were falling. The Committee turned down Longwood's request.[104] No evidence is available to explain this decision, but the fact that the Council representatives only formed a small minority on Longwood's governing body[105] may go some way to explaining the attitude. However, the Technical Instruction Committee's meanness on this issue was balanced by a decision to increase Longwood's grant for evening classes from £50 to £95.[106] Longwood made a second application that its grant be used for day classes in 1901, but this was again rejected.[107]

The experience gained by members of the Technical Instruction Committee between 1891 and 1903 was invaluable in the sense that it not only provided them with responsibilities for educational finance, but it also gave them a contact with a variety of institutions over which the Borough

Council, of which they all were members, would one day assume control. However, the Committee found itself powerless to prevent duplication in classes organised by bodies in receipt of grant. The 1899 report of the Science and Art Department in London produced evidence to show that the Higher Grade School, with its policy of low or no fees, was denuding the classes of the Technical College, and placing the future of the College in jeopardy.[108] As long as such institutions were controlled by different bodies, there was little prospect of co-ordination. The 'municipilisation' of the elementary, secondary and technical spheres of education would provide the means to resolve this difficulty.

The state of education in Huddersfield in the early years of the twentieth century

The Borough Council assumed control of elementary education and the Higher Grade School in 1902. This event was not marred by the intense political wrangling which marked the birth of the first School Board in 1871. Despite the change, there was a degree of continuity in organisation. Many members of the old School Board served on the new Borough Education Committee. The elementary schools were administered much as before. Science and Art grants were still obtained for 'advanced' classes, and 'whisky money' was still distributed to technical classes. The major changes were to be in the field of secondary education.

This section will describe first how the Borough Council assumed control of elementary and secondary education in 1903, and technical education also in the same year. Then a brief analysis of the Sadler report in 1904 on secondary and technical education in Huddersfield will be given. Finally a brief survey of local progress in education, especially those changes which were inspired by the Sadler report, is provided.

The arrangements for the Borough Council to take control of the Technical College were completed in the spring of 1903. The transfer was achieved by the Huddersfield Corporation Act (1902) which became law on 22 July 1902, and fixed the date for transfer as any day prior to the 1 November 1903.[109] In March 1903, the General Purposes Committee of the Council appointed a special sub-committee to draw up plans for the assumption of control over elementary education and certain parts of secondary provision in the Borough.[110] Immediately the Trades Council debated the need to be represented on the new Borough Education Committee.[111] On 12 May 1903, the Trades Council sent a three man deputation to a meeting of the General Purposes Committee seeking the right to nominate a member.[112] In the end, the Education Committee was composed of seventeen Councillors (five with School Board experience), and eight co-opted members, including two ladies. Five of the eight had School Board experience. This group of five contained two clergymen, two Liberals and one member of the ILP. All five councillors on the Committee with School Board experience were Liberals. On 23 September 1903 the Trades Council protested at its exclusion.[113] The ILP member of the Education Committee was also a member of the Trades Council. Despite his nomination, the Trades Council continued to protest. The ILP nominee, Riley, never held an office on the Trades Council. As the owner of a printing business he came from a different background to Pickles, the Trades Council candidate, who was a painter. Riley was also known to have ambitions beyond the confines of local politics. The Trades Council may have preferred a more 'parochial' representative.

The Sadler report on Secondary and Technical Education, published in 1904,[114] provided the basis for developments prior to 1918. Sadler believed that Huddersfield's immediate need was for two good secondary schools, but he did not believe that the Higher Grade School should be one of these. Almondbury Grammar School was to be the boys' school, and a new school was needed for the girls. He appeared to have an antipathy to the science-biased curriculum of the Higher Grade School and a preference for classical subjects. Sadler found that there were 708 places in Huddersfield Secondary Schools, or 7.45 places per 1,000 population. This was regarded as poor. For Almondbury to become the boys' public secondary school in the Borough, Sadler said that the representation of the Council on the governing body would have to be drastically increased if the school was to attract a large increase in public funding.[115] Sadler's main reservation against the potential of the Higher Grade School to grow into a proper secondary school was based upon the low staying on rate. Of the 187 pupils enrolled for the four-year science course in 1901, only nine began the final year of study in 1904.[116] Sadler, therefore, felt that the Higher Grade School was not yet ready to become a secondary school, but might do so ten years later, when demand grew. By that time he had envisaged that other schools of the Higher Grade type would have emerged.[117] The main objections to the Sadler report came from the local branch of the National Union of Teachers. Its membership was strong in those elementary schools which sent their best pupils to the Higher Grade School. The NUT objected to the report's support for Almondbury Grammar School, claiming that its curriculum did not meet the needs of local industry and that the school was dominated by a sectarian interest, in the guise of the Established Church.[118]

With regard to the Technical College, Sadler advised the closure of the Day School of Science and suggested that the College should concentrate on offering vocational courses for older students over sixteen years of age,[119] and that the Council devote more resources to the College.[120] The College was run by a Technical College Committee of the Council and Sadler advised that it should be joined with the Education Committee in charge of elementary and secondary education.[121]

How well did Huddersfield respond to the challenges presented in Sadler's report in the years up to 1918? The only scholarships provided by Huddersfield Borough Council at this time were thirty allocated to students at the Higher Grade School who undertook to become pupil teachers.[122] In the Board of Education's list of efficient schools for 1907-08, the two listed for Huddersfield were Almondbury Grammar School and the 'Municipal Secondary School'.[123] It was clear that the Council was not prepared to prevent the Higher Grade School from growing into a proper secondary school. Indeed in 1909, it began to cater for boys only, and a new public high school for girls was opened at Greenhead in that same year, to which the girls from the 'Municipal Secondary School' were transferred. The school at Greenhead was extended in 1917 by the purchase of an adjacent residence 'Longdenholme', the former home of the late Joseph Woodhead. By 1918, the boy's school (the former Higher Grade School) was reported to be overcrowded.[124] Increasing assistance was given by the Council to Almondbury Grammar School after 1904 until its transfer to public control in 1922. The Technical College began a building programme in 1903, costing £35,000.[125] Grants of 'whisky money' continued to be shared amongst local institutions offering technical classes. In 1903-04, the Technical College obtained £1,242 11s. 5d. out of £2,153 17s. 2d. This source of revenue coupled with local rate support insured the future growth of the Technical College. At the end of the war, in 1918, extensions were proposed for the textile, engineering and chemistry departments. Within months, the sum of £32,000 had been raised by subscription alone to help meet the cost of these extensions.[126]

Huddersfield, despite its failings in the secondary and technical spheres of education, possessed a solid base for advance, in the form of an adequate number of elementary schools in all parts of the Borough when the School Board era came to an end in 1903. The managers of the local Voluntary schools had worked hard in an attempt to keep conditions in their schools on a par with those in the Board schools. In 1903 there were seventeen Board schools providing 12,038 places and twenty-two Voluntary schools with 9,496 places. Twenty-one of the Voluntary schools were attached to the Church of England.[127]

In so far as public control led to greater commitment of rates and taxes in support of schools and the Technical College, then political involvement in education was beneficial. To the extent that this was accompanied by bitterness over divisions on issues like religious teaching in elementary schools, then educational progress was impeded. Decisions were, in some cases, guided by moral and party political considerations rather than the educational interests of the children. The monopoly of power enjoyed by the Liberals on Huddersfield School Board led to consistency in aims and in administration. The commitment by this group to expand and improve facilities under its control, may have acted as a spur to those managing the competing Voluntary system. However, there is no doubt that such competition ultimately led to the over-provision of facilities.[128] Indeed, the fact that the Liberals dominated the School Board elections and regarded the Board Schools as 'their schools', coupled with the responsibility that the Church party had for management of Voluntary schools, meant that the latter could rarely field a group of candidates with the quality and experience of its Liberal opponents. The voting on key issues became a formality and the drama associated with boards like Birmingham, where power changed hands, was only rarely present in Huddersfield.

Religious division clearly inhibited progress in local secondary education. Two proprietary schools perished as a result, and Almondbury Grammar School could have suffered the same fate. Municipal control of the Technical College after 1903 clearly brought tremendous benefits.

So, while the Technical College benefited from political control, secondary education in Huddersfield did not flourish because of the religious divisions which existed, and which corresponded closely with political affiliations. On balance, elementary education in the borough gained from the creation of the School Board in 1871 despite the political in-fighting which resulted.

The post-war economic depression deprived the community of the resources need to expand facilities after 1918. Huddersfield would have to wait much longer before it obtained the education system appropriate to the needs of a prosperous industrial and commercial town.

B. D. Moriarty

Biographical Note

Brian Moriarty was educated in Coleraine, Queen's University and Leeds University. He has been on the staff at Colne Valley High since 1966 and is at present Head of Careers. He took a research degree at Leeds University by part-time study. He is interested in economics and environmental matters and helped in construction work at Colne Valley Museum in its early days. His hobbies include transport (rail and air), archaeology, photography, rugby and cricket, sea fishing and walking.

NOTES

1. Huddersfield Local History Library, The Annual Report of the Medical Officer of Health to Huddersfield Corporation (1901), p.9.

2. Census of England and Wales of 1891, P(arliamentary) P(apers) 1893-94 CVI pp.426-431.

3. The 1901 Census for the County of York, Command Paper 1107 (1902) pp.244-245.

4. *Population (Great Britain) Religious Worship (England and Wales)* PP 1852-53 LXXXIX (Summary Table F).

5. Poll Book with a register of candidates' supporters and abstentions for the Huddersfield constituency 1868 (Huddersfield, 1868).

6. This is derived for those members of the Improvement Commission who later served on the Borough Council from O. Balmforth *Jubilee History of Huddersfield Corporation 1868-1918* (Huddersfield, 1918), pp.108-119. (Balmforth's lists give dates of death of all Councillors and these dates have been used to trace obituaries in the local press).

7. Obituaries provide details of religious membership and sometimes of political party.

8. In the Parliamentary Election between Leatham (Liberal) and Sleigh (Conservative).

9. *Huddersfield Examiner*, 28 January 1871. All newspapers consulted were weekly editions.

10. Poll Book 1868.

11. M.G. Clarke 'Development and Purpose in a Local Conservative Association, a study in the Huddersfield Constituencies 1836-1966', p.25 (available on microfilm in Huddersfield Library).

12. Minutes of the Huddersfield Liberal Registration Association, 11 March 1868.

13. Minutes of the Huddersfield Liberal Registration Association, 1 June 1816.

14. Minutes of the General Committee of the Huddersfield Liberal Registration Association, 2 July 1893.

15. Minutes of the General Committee of the Huddersfield Liberal Registration Association, 19 June 1836.

16. School Boards were to be elected by ratepayers and given the task of making good any deficiency in provision in the field of Elementary Education.

17. *Huddersfield Examiner*, 28 January 1871.

18. Report on the Educational Condition of the Borough of Huddersfield, (November 1871).

19. Report on the Educational Condition of the Borough of Huddersfield, (November 1871), p.4.

20. Report on the Educational Condition of the Borough of Huddersfield, (November 1871), p.10.

21. Report on the Educational Condition of the Borough of Huddersfield, (November 1871), p.12.

22. Report on the Educational Condition of the Borough of Huddersfield, (November 1871), pp.13-14.

23. Endowed Charities. *Administrative County of the West Riding of York and the County Boroughs of Halifax and Huddersfield. Vol 3. Western Division*, p.660; and *Report of the Schools Inquiry Commission*, PP.1867-68 XXVIII vol ix, p.653.

24. *Report of the Schools Inquiry Commission*, p.233.

25. *Report of the Schools Inquiry Commission*, Vol XVII, p.20.

26. *Endowed Charities*, p.688.

27. *Endowed Charities*, p.698.

28. *Endowed Charities*, pp.672-673.

29. *Huddersfield Examiner*, 25 January 1868.

30. *Huddersfield Examiner*, 22 January 1870.

31. *Huddersfield Chronicle*, 4 December 1869.

32. *Huddersfield Chronicle*, 18 December 1869.

33. *Huddersfield Examiner*, 12 March 1870.

34. *Huddersfield Examiner*, 28 May 1870.

35. *Huddersfield Chronicle*, 20 July 1870.

36. WYAS, Kirklees: C/E/L6/5 Huddersfield School Board Letter Book, 31 March 1887.

37. Royal Commission inquiring into the workings of the Elementary Education Acts PP 1887 XXX p.149.

38. Huddersfield School Board Eighth Triennial Report 1892-95, p.9.

39. B. Simon, *Education and the Labour Movement*, (1965) p.193.

40. Simon, *Education and the Labour Movement*, pp.194-195.

41. Simon, *Education and the Labour Movement*, pp.195-196.

42. WYAS, Kirklees: KHT22/1/10, Minutes of the Huddersfield School Board, 2 April 1900.

43. WYAS, Kirklees: KHT22/1/10, Minutes of the Huddersfield School Board, 8 May 1900.

44. WYAS, Kirklees: KHT22/1/10, Minutes of the Huddersfield School Board, 3 December 1900.

45. WYAS, Kirklees: KHT22/1/10, Minutes of the Huddersfield School Board, 4 February 1901.

46. WYAS, Kirklees: S/HTC/1/2, Huddersfield Trades Council. Minutes of the General Meeting of 23 April 1902.

47. WYAS, Kirklees, C/E/TH/62, School Board Letter Book, 21 April 1902.

48. WYAS, Kirklees, KHT22/1/11, Minutes of the School Board 1 June 1902; and *Huddersfield Examiner*, 7 March 1903.

49. *Huddersfield Examiner*, 9 May 1902.

50. *Huddersfield Examiner*, 11 October 1902.

51. *Huddersfield Chronicle*, 31 December 1870.

52. *Huddersfield Chronicle*, 17 January 1874.

53. *Huddersfield Chronicle*, 17 January 1874.

54. *Huddersfield Chronicle*, 31 January 1874.

55. *Huddersfield Examiner*, 7 February 1874.

56. *Huddersfield Examiner*, 2 January 1877.

57. *Huddersfield Chronicle*, 17 January 1880.

58. *Huddersfield Examiner*, 2 February 1883.

59. *Huddersfield Examiner*, 23 January 1886.

60. *Huddersfield Examiner*, 3 February 1889.

61. Minutes of the Executive Committee of the Liberal Association, 4 January 1889.

62. *Huddersfield Examiner*, 3 February 1889.

63. Huddersfield School Board. First Triennial Report (1871-74,) pp.19-20.

64. *Huddersfield Examiner*, 10 August 1874.

65. Huddersfield School Board Second Triennial Report (1874-77), pp.22-23.

66. Huddersfield School Board Third Triennial Report (1877-80), pp.12-13.

67. *Huddersfield Examiner*, 20 January 1883.

68. *Huddersfield Chronicle*, 16 October 1875.

69. *Huddersfield Examiner*, 22 November 1875.

70. *Huddersfield Chronicle*, 17 January 1880.

71. *Huddersfield Examiner*, 13 September 1875.

72. Minutes of the Executive Committee of the Liberal Association, 8 December 1891.

73. Minutes of the A.G.M. of the Liberal Association 15 January 1892.

74. *Huddersfield Examiner*, 6 February 1892.

75. *Huddersfield Examiner*, 5 January 1885.

76. *Huddersfield Chronicle*, 5 January 1895.

77. *Huddersfield Examiner*, 2 February 1895.

78. *Huddersfield Chronicle*, 2 February 1895.

79. *Huddersfield Examiner*, 19 January 1901.

80. WYAS, Kirklees: B/HCC/6b-7, Minutes of the Huddersfield College Governors, June 1885.

81. WYAS, Kirklees: B/HCC/6b-7, Minutes of the Huddersfield College Governors, June 1885.

82. WYAS, Kirklees: B/HCC/6b-7, Minutes of the Huddersfield College Governors, June 1885.

83. WYAS, Kirklees: B/HCC/6b-7, Minutes of the Huddersfield College Governors, June 1885.

84. *Huddersfield Chronicle*, 10 June 1893.

85. *Huddersfield Examiner*, 5-12 July 1938.

86. *Huddersfield Chronicle*, 20 January 1894.

87. *Huddersfield Examiner*, 10 June 1893.

88. WYAS, Kirklees: KHT22/1/7, Minutes of Huddersfield School Board, 5 June 1893.

89. WYAS, Kirklees: KHT22/1/7, Minutes of Huddersfield School Board, 5 June 1893.

90. WYAS, Kirklees: C/E/Lb/3. Huddersfield School Board Letter Book, 3 February 1881.

91. *Endowed Charities. Western Division* Vol 3, p.666.

92. *Royal Commission on Secondary Education*, PP 1895, XLV Vol VII for Yorkshire, p.191.

93. G.Hinchcliffe. *History of King James' Grammar School in Almondbury*, (Huddersfield, 1968) p.130.

94. WYAS, Kirklees: KHC8/18, Minutes of the General Purposes Committee of Huddersfield Borough Council, 9 May 1899.

95. Hinchcliffe, *King James' Grammar School.*

96. The Technical School created in 1883, became the Technical College in 1896.

97. *Huddersfield Examiner*, 24 December 1897.

98. *Huddersfield Chronicle*, 23 February 1901.

99. WYAS, Kirklees: S/HTC/1/2, General meeting of the Huddersfield Trades Council, 26 March 1902.

100. WYAS, Kirklees: KHC/8/20, Minutes of the General Purposes Committee of *Huddersfield Borough Council*, 13 January 1903.

101. WYAS, Kirklees: KH/3, Proceedings of the Council of the County Borough of Huddersfield 20 December 1890.

102. WYAS, Kirklees: KHC8/14, Minutes of the Technical Instruction Sub-Committee of Huddersfield County Borough General Purposes Committee, 17 April 1891.

103. WYAS, Kirklees: KHC8/15, Minutes of the Technical Instruction Sub-Committee of Huddersfield County Borough General Purposes Committee, 10 October 1892.

104. WYAS, Kirklees: KHC 8/18, Minutes of the General Purposes Committee of Huddersfield County Borough, 11 October 1897.

105. There was a strong Anglican tradition at Longwood Grammar School.

106. WYAS, Kirklees: KHC 8/18, Minutes of the General Purposes Committee of Huddersfield County Borough, 11 October 1897.

107. WYAS, Kirklees: KHC 8/19, Minutes of the General Purposes Committee of Huddersfield County Borough, 9 July 1901.

108. *Annual Report of the Science and Art Department*, PP 1899, XXXI, Appendix B, p 467.

109. WYAS, Kirklees: KHC 8/20, Minutes of the General Purposes Committee of Huddersfield County Borough, 12 August 1902.

110. WYAS, Kirklees: KHC 8/20, Minutes of the General Purposes Committee of Huddersfield County Borough, 10 March 1903.

111. WYAS, Kirklees: S/HTC/1/3, Minutes of the Executive of the Huddersfield Trades Council, 25 March 1903.

112. WYAS, Kirklees: S/HTC/6/3, Huddersfield Trades Council Eightieth Anniversary Publication 1885-1965, (Huddersfield), pp.38-39.

113. WYAS, Kirklees: S/HTC/1/3, Minutes of Huddersfield Trades Council, 25 September 1903.

114. M.Sadler, *Report on Secondary and Technical Education in Huddersfield*.

115. Sadler, *Report*, p.46.

116. Sadler, *Report*, p.21.

117. Sadler, *Report*, p.57.

118. *Huddersfield Examiner*, 18 February 1905.

119. Sadler, *Report*, p.7.

120. Sadler, *Report*, p.75.

121. Sadler, *Report*, p.101.

122. Education (England and Wales), PP 1906, LXXXII, p.317.

123. Board of Education: list of schools in England recognised as efficient PP 1907-1908, 1908 LXXXIII, p.81.

124. Balmforth, *Jubilee History*, p.41.

125. Balmforth, *Jubilee History*, p.44-45.

126. Balmforth, *Jubilee History*, p.44-45.

127. *Education (England and Wales)* PP 1903, LI, p.722.

128. *Education (England and Wales)* PP 1903, LI, p.722.

CHAPTER 22

From Mechanics' Institution to Polytechnic: further and higher education, 1841-1970

JOHN O'CONNELL

A Huddersfield Scientific and Mechanic Institute was founded in 1825, for 'the supplying at a cheap rate, the different classes of the community, with the advantages of instruction in the various branches of science and the useful arts'.[1] As its first annual report claimed, it 'was ... established under highly favourable auspices', being generously supported by donors and subscribers, led by Sir John Ramsden, landowner of most of Huddersfield, who was its Patron, and endowed with a library of over 700 volumes.[2] But it foundered in its first year – only partly because its bankers failed in the financial crisis of 1826 – and though it lingered on into the 1830s, it changed its character and was re-formed as the Huddersfield Philosophical Society, whose Rules closely resembled its own.[3] It was one of more than twenty such institutes founded in the same year in the Pennine towns of Lancashire and Yorkshire, the first and largest of which were in Manchester and Leeds.[4] They were part of a national movement that followed the foundation – itself taking examples from Edinburgh and Glasgow – of the London Mechanics' Institution, late in 1823, in which the leading figures were Henry Brougham and George Birkbeck. Brougham, a Scottish lawyer and future Whig Lord Chancellor, was already an established champion of 'education for the lower orders'. For him, mechanics' institutes were 'not merely seminaries for teaching mechanics the principles of natural and mechanical sciences, but schools where the working classes generally may learn those branches of knowledge which they cannot master by private reading . . .'.[5] Birkbeck, a Yorkshireman educated in science and medicine in London and Edinburgh – where he and Brougham were college friends –

had given pioneering lectures on science to working men in Glasgow between 1800 and 1804, when he left, to practise medicine in London. These were the foundation of his contemporary and lasting reputation as the 'father' and 'leading mover of the (mechanics' institute) system'.[6] He insisted that mechanics' institutes should be primarily schools of science.[7] This Birkbeckian influence is evident in the stated objectives of the Huddersfield Scientific and Mechanic Institute. As well as the financial disaster, it explains its failure.

From about 1840 it was being complained that mechanics' institutes had failed, on two counts: they did not educate the working classes, and they did not teach science.[8] But already, the narrow view of their being teachers of science to artisans was giving way to a conception of them as general cultural centres. This was the changing climate in which was founded, in May 1841, the Huddersfield Young Men's Mental Improvement Society,[9] and this new climate is the starting point for an explanation of its success. That it was successful, and reputedly, by the end of its first decade, uniquely so among the 600 institutes by then in existence in England,[10] is amply attested. Dr Tylecote quoted contemporaries describing Huddersfield as one of only three 'examples of complete success', where the 'anticipations of their founders' had been 'fully realised', and as 'the only Mechanics' Institute which had any pretensions to meet the needs of the people' and 'the best in England'. 'We know of scarcely another Institute that can compare with it. It reaches the working man and it teaches him.'[11] It did this, not by teaching large numbers of adults eager and able to learn the principles of science, for such numbers did not exist in the Huddersfield district, but by providing elementary education to semi-literate boys and young men.[12] But this function was more generally performed than Huddersfield's reputation for uniqueness suggests. By 1859, elementary classes far outstripped all others in the Yorkshire Union of Mechanics' Institutes, whereas, when the Huddersfield society joined it, in 1843, only 10 per cent of members attended such classes.[13]

The idea of forming the Society originated with five young men employed by Frederic Schwann, a prosperous export merchant who had already provided a library for his employees.[14] They now formed what was intentionally a mutual-improvement society. They first met in the Temperance Hotel, in Cross Church Street, and, with thirty or so others,

Fig. 22:1 Frederic Schwann, first President and benefactor of the Mechanics' Institution. (UHA)

began classes in the British School, Outcote Bank, in reading, writing, arithmetic, grammar, geography, design and French; and a library was begun 'by subscription'. By the time the Committee reported to the first annual soirée, in February 1844, new classes had begun in elocution, vocal music, mathematics and chemistry, and there was a total membership of 410, 'chiefly operatives' enjoying 'the advantages of an elementary education adapted to their occupations in life'. To the then library of 271 volumes, during 1844, and 'in a spirit of liberality above all praise Mr Schwann's workmen merged their Library', to make a total of 773 volumes. General lectures were given, but their number was restricted, so as not to interfere with 'the more necessary branches of elementary instruction'.[15] The 'higher classes' were about to be moved to Nelson's Buildings, New Street (opposite Lockwood's Yard). This first printed Report established the characteristic features of what, in August 1843, had been re-named 'Mechanics' Institution': the primacy of the classes; the importance of the Library; the relative unimportance of lectures; the Committee's concern with the social and recreational development and the moral welfare of members; the availability as teachers of experienced staff from the Huddersfield College and Collegiate proprietary schools; even the holding of meetings in the Philosophical Hall, the largest auditorium in the town.[16]

In 1844, the first paid secretary, Robert Neil, was appointed, but he was a shadowy figure in comparison with his successor, George Searle Phillips, also known by his pen-name, January Searle.[17] Phillips' was, perhaps more than Frederic Schwann's, the most important influence in the formative years of the Institution. Neil set the pattern of regular social events: monthly meetings for talks and recitals; annual local galas, at Fixby pastures and later at Kirklees Hall; day excursions on the new railways; and Easter and Christmas entertainments.[18] Of Phillips, who succeeded him in 1846, it is tempting to ask how far the fame that Huddersfield Mechanics' Institution came to enjoy by the early 1850s is to be explained by its undoubted achievements and how far by Phillips's celebration of them. He immediately set up a probationary class for grading entrants by attainment, and reorganised the classes to establish a regular gradation of instruction;[19] secured revisions of the fees system in an effort to make the institution 'self-supporting'; began a practice of visiting the homes of absent students;[20] and compiled statistics of student achievements and institutional progress. In his

Fig. 22:2 The building of the British and Foreign School Society, in Outcote Bank, occupied by the Young Men's Mental Improvement Society and the Mechanics' Institution from 1841. (KCS)

Fig. 22:3 The site of 'Nelson's Buildings', where classes of the Mechanics' Institution were taught from 1844 to 1850, in the rooms above the sign for Elliot and Hallas. (KCS)

time the curriculum was extended,[21] and the institute was advertised both nationally, in Phillips' own prolific writings, and locally, by his having students hawk round notices of the classes.[22] In 1850 a 'Preliminary Savings Bank' was introduced and run by Charles W. Sikes, of the Huddersfield Banking Company; this was a forerunner of the Post Office Savings Bank. The last notable feature of this Schwann/Phillips era was the purchase of new premises, a former warehouse in Queen Street which was bought, converted and furnished, in 1850, for £1,600.[23] When Phillips left, in 1854, there were 518 students paying fortnightly fees of 7d., and 58 'Presentees', who paid only 1d. a week, because they were sponsored by 'Annual Members', yearly subscribers of £1 1s.0d or more.[24] But Phillips ended his Huddersfield career under a cloud. Student numbers had declined in his later years; he had crossed swords with the President in 1850-51; and the Committee severely reprimanded him for his neglect of his duties in January

Fig. 22:4 The premises in Queen Street occupied by the Mechanics' Institution 1850-61. (KCS)

Fig. 22:5 Frank Curzon, Secretary, Mechanics' Institution, 1854-62. (KCS)

1854.[25] His last full year, 1853, was, as he described it, 'a critical period'. It was so, too, for Frederic Schwann, for it was the year in which he ceased to be President. Strangely, this was not mentioned in an annual report until that of 1856, when a vote of thanks was passed and he was made a life member.[26] He never broke his connection with the Institution: he had kept it solvent till then, and he remained a generous annual subscriber and occasional special donor till his death in April 1882, when a warm tribute was paid to him. His sons followed him as benefactors, and so has his granddaughter.[27] Phillips became agent for the Yorkshire Union, but resigned after less than two years and thereafter played no part in the mechanics' institute movement.

Frank Curzon, his successor, was less flamboyant but no less effective in promoting the interests and reputation of the Institution. Like Phillips, he was to leave to become organising agent and lecturer to the Union, and only retired from that post in his eighty-fourth year, a legendary figure, long and far renowned for the brilliant expository skills he displayed in his 'blackboard lectures'.[28] His reforming zeal is evident in the annual reports for his time, from 1854 to 1862. A prize scheme was introduced, and a donation was made to the prize fund by the Prince Consort. Monthly social meetings became fortnightly, occasional Saturday conferences were arranged between teachers and Committee members, and a system of 'class inspections' by pairs of Committee members was instituted.[29] Curzon found two defects in the class teaching: over-dependence on unpaid teachers, and the use of out-dated books; and complained that, though the Institution was well supported by 'men in authority', it was 'weak where we should look for strength': pupils were educated and rose in the world, but then forgot their Institution.[30] From 1859 he introduced what became standard practice thereafter, tables showing the previous educational achievements of entrants, and their occupational groupings. He represented the Committee as being anxious to preserve the working-class character of the Institution, and a paper he presented to a Bradford meeting of social scientists sought to demonstrate this. A correspondent to the *Huddersfield Chronicle* was to complain that 'not one sixth of the new Committee (for the year 1861) can, strictly speaking, be called working class', and that elections to it were 'a mere farce'; but the seal of approval had been put on the Institution when 'the greatest friend of popular education now living', Lord Brougham, addressed its annual soirée in October 1860.[31]

Fig. 22:6 The Northumberland Street building, occupied by the Mechanics' Institution between 1861 and 1884. (UHA)

As the Phillips, so the Curzon era was marked by a move to new premises, this time the first to be purpose-built, in Northumberland Street. The building, on which 'not a penny has been spent on useless decoration' – and which the complaining letter writer to the *Chronicle* described as 'not only plain but positively ugly' – was paid for entirely by donations, the leading donors, after the proceeds of a Ladies' Bazaar, being the Whig Sir John William Ramsden and then two woollen manufacturers, the Tory family firms of Starkey Brothers, of Longroyd Bridge, and John Brooke and Sons, Armitage Bridge, a striking illustration of how the Mechanics' Institution, then, as always, was supported across the political divide. A list of subscribers to the fund was published with the annual report for 1861: it included the names of dozens of workmen of both the Starkey and the Brooke mills. The Queen Street premises were sold, and the mortgage paid off, and the Institution was free of debt after raising over £4,600 for the new building, its furniture and fittings.[32] The Institution was flourishing, and Curzon's later reports strike an optimistic and confident note: 'at no period has there been so general a recognition of the necessity for the encouragement of sound education among the industrial classes' as in 1860 when there was an increased number of members, perhaps, he coyly suggested, because there were more paid teachers, which a gift of £100 over four years by Frederic Schwann had helped to make possible.[33] 'Prosperity' enveloped the college in 1861, Curzon's last full year. The total paid-up membership was 1,216, and since 1854 the number of weekly classes had risen from 73 to 92, taught by 20 paid and 25 voluntary teachers. There were junior (for boys of 9 to 16) and senior elementary classes, in which mainly the three Rs were taught, and 'special' classes, in history, French, mathematics, drawing, book-keeping and – revived that year – chemistry. Thus, the only recognisable science was chemistry, which, though it had been taught intermittently since 1844, by William Marriott, a manufacturing chemist, and a devoted supporter and future President of the Institution, did not become a sustainable subject until the famous teacher George Jarmain took it over, in 1864. He was to teach it for thirty years.[34] Besides the classes, and lectures, which were never given prominence in teaching, the other principal features of the institute were the Library and the Reading Room. The Library, which benefited from gifts by Sir Robert Peel, son of the former Prime Minister,[35] had between 2,000 and 3,000 volumes in these years, and the Reading Room, which could be subscribed to by non-members of the Institution, was an attraction in the town.

Despite the prosperity, the Institution's educational base was narrow, and it is true to say that 'from educational bankruptcy the mechanics' institutes were rescued by two timely developments – the examination system of the Society of Arts, and the demand for technical and scientific education'.[36] As a direct consequence of the Great Exhibition of 1851, there was created, in 1857, the Department of Science and Art, set up as part of the Education Department of the Privy Council to deal with secondary and technical education. In 1860 it instituted an examination system which was to last for forty years. The Science and Art Department gave approvals for the setting up of 'science schools', many of them in mechanics' institutes, to which it gave grants, on a 'payment by results' basis. The Society of Arts began its examining activities in 1856, and in 1857 held an experimental 'Prize Examination' 'to include Commercial and Trade Schools',[37] choosing the Huddersfield institute as its sole centre outside London. Frank Curzon had warned his students of their disadvantage in competing with people 'from middle class literary societies and private schools', but of the 90 successful candidates at the Huddersfield centre, 32 were from the Institution, and he

Fig. 22:7 George Jarmain: teacher of Chemistry. (UHA)

now enthused about the 'beneficial results', showing 'the importance of accuracy . . . and . . . of clear expression', and about how people who had known nothing of the Huddersfield Institute 'now realise its value'.[38] In 1873 the Society entered the technological field, but handed these subjects over to the newly-established City and Guilds of London Institute (CGLI) in 1880.[39] The first Huddersfield students to be regularly examined were members of George Jarmain's Chemistry classes, who took the Science and Art Department's examinations in 1865. From 1867 candidates were entered from the elementary classes for the examinations of the Yorkshire Board of Education, and the best of them were also candidates for the Society of Arts examinations; and from 1869 students in the drawing classes were examined by the Science and Art Department. By then, too, students in other subjects than Chemistry took its science examinations.[40] The term 'technical education' was first used in the annual report of 1867, when the secretary, Joseph Bate, claimed that the Committee had fostered it 'from almost the commencement of the institution'. Nationally and locally, an important part of the impetus towards its promotion came from the shock to British complacency given by the Paris Exhibition of 1867.* An outcome of this was the setting up of a Parliamentary Committee on Scientific Instruction, before which one witness said: 'I do not know of a single manager of an ironworks in Yorkshire who understands the simple elements of chemistry'.[41] In Huddersfield, the report on the year 1868 spoke of 'reports of practical men who visited the Paris Exhibition' showing that 'the technical education which the operatives on the continent possess may imperil our industrial prosperity'. It boasted of 'the practical direction of the teaching of the Institution', and especially about two developments of that year: the introduction of a class in the chemistry of dyeing, taught by Mr Jarmain, who had been one of 'the practical men who visited the Paris Exhibition';[42] and, in conjunction with the Yorkshire Board of Education, the establishment of science classes for schoolmasters and others in practical geometry and machine drawing. This last development was the first form of teacher training at Huddersfield Mechanics' Institution.

The implementation in Huddersfield of the Elementary Education Act of 1870 was eventually to change the character and identity of the Institution. An immediate consequence was that it added to its sources of income: apart from members' subscriptions, as well as receiving grants from the Science and Art Department, based on examination successes, the institute also received annual allowances from the Education Department, and after 1873 annual examinations of students in elementary classes were conducted by HM Inspectors of Schools. The printed version of the report received at the annual meeting held on 29 January 1876 included an extract from the *Huddersfield Chronicle* commenting on the report itself. The *Chronicle* said that nearly five years after the formation of the Huddersfield School Board, under the 1870 Act, there were both 'elementary schools in superabundance and a Mechanics' Institute preparing to enlarge its classrooms. These two facts . . . seem to bear the relation of cause and effect'; the Institution was 'a great society, quite as worthy as it is able to undertake the higher duties that lie before it'.[43] The annual report for 1879 expressed surprise that 'despite such opportunities to the masses to gain Elementary Education', the attendance at these classes did not fall more, and only in January 1883 did the new Secretary, Austin Keen, remark on 'the decline in the elementary classes' as 'naturally consequent upon the Compulsory Education Act of 1876'.[44] This report shows the extent of change since 1870: it divided the College into the

*David Jenkins comments on the effects of the Paris Exhibition in Chapter Eleven. EDITOR.

Technical School, teaching Cloth Manufacture, with a small, newly-formed Mechanical Engineering class, both examined by the CGLI; the Science School and the School of Art, both examined by the Science and Art Department; 'Higher Grade' classes in French, German, English literature and commercial subjects, examined, where appropriate, by the Society of Arts or the Yorkshire Union; and the elementary classes. This was the institution to which 'just before Whit', 1883, the Committee of the Huddersfield Female Educational Institute – founded in 1846 under the same auspices as the mechanics' institute – 'formally handed over "their work"' and left their Beaumont Street accommodation to join the hitherto all-male institution (except for singing classes) in its new building in Queen Street South.[45]

The Institution's move to a new building and its transformation into a Technical or Trade School were the result of nearly ten years' planning and negotiation. The need for more accommodation to house the expanding science and technological classes was apparent by 1875. In April 1877 a contrived meeting took place between a deputation from the Committee of the Mechanics' Institution and the Council of the Chamber of Commerce, where a move was afoot to convert several local charities to the benefit of a proposed 'Trade School'.[46] The Institution's deputation was led by Alderman John Fligg Brigg, JP, its President, who had been one of the five employees of Frederic Schwann who met in the Temperance Hotel in May 1841, and was now himself a wealthy merchant and a leading citizen. The Council of the Chamber included six men who were or had been Committee members of the institute, two of whom had been President. A report of their meeting was published, addressed to 'subscribers and the public generally', revealing a proposal by the Committee for a 'Trade School', which the Council would consider.[47] The scheme was agreed, the Charity Commissioners approved the conversion of the local charities to this purpose, and an architect, Edward Hughes, was commissioned to design an extension to the Mechanics' Institute. In December 1879 a report of all this, signed by Thomas Brooke, of John Brooke and Sons, Armitage Bridge, who was now President of both the Committee of the Institution and the Council of the Chamber of Commerce – and the driving force behind the scheme – was issued to the public, with an appeal for support.[48] But by June 1880 it was realised that a new building was needed, and Hughes made plans for a new site, on Queen Street South,

Fig. 22:8 Sir Thomas Brooke, Bart., JP, DL. President of the Mechanics' Institution and the Technical School, 1879-86. Older brother of Sir John Arthur Brooke. (KCS)

Fig. 22:9 John F. Brigg, JP, founding member of the Mechanics' Institution in 1841 and continuous supporter till his death in 1899. (KCS)

Fig. 22:10 Sir John William Ramsden. (KCS)

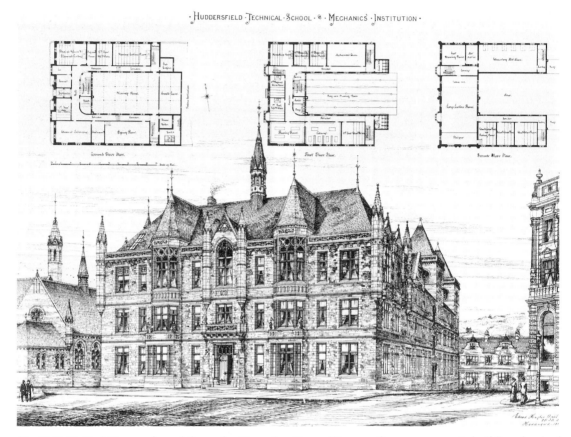

· HUDDERSFIELD · TECHNICAL · SCHOOL · & · MECHANICS · INSTITUTION ·

Fig. 22:11 Huddersfield Technical School and Mechanics' Institution, Queen Street South, opened 7 July 1883. (KCS)

leased from the Ramsden Estate Trustees for 999 years. A building fund of over £15,500 was raised, including £2,000 from the Clothworkers' Company of the City of London, which had, since 1878, subscribed £100 annually to the institute, and awarded two annual scholarships to be taken up at the Yorkshire College, Leeds. A memorial stone was laid by the Master of the Company on 21 October 1881,[49] and the building, and a Fine Art and Industrial Exhibition which was to be visited by 329,639 people in the next six months, were opened on 7 July 1883 by the Duke of Somerset, father-in-law of Sir John William Ramsden. The Mayor of Huddersfield present that day – who was also Vice-President of the Institution – was Alderman John Fligg Brigg, JP.[50] This time, money was spent on decoration: on the facade of the building there were four lions, holding shields which bore the arms of the Clothworkers' Company, the Borough, Sir John William Ramsden, Bart, MP, and the future Sir Thomas Brooke, Bart.

The new institution, now governed by an educational trust, was called the 'Technical School and Mechanics' Institution'.[51] In reality, the mechanics' institute had been absorbed in the technical school. It was a timely transformation. The development by the Huddersfield School Board from the 1880s of evening continuation schools, and its opening of a Higher Grade School in 1894, would largely deprive the Institution of the post-school elementary education in the town, and the more advanced post-elementary work with a scientific or technical bias.[52] But there was powerfully-voiced opinion that the new Technical School should not be a merely technical institute. In 1880, the *Huddersfield Chronicle* had supported the idea of a technical school, but had pleaded for a traditional liberal education to be preserved, and had hoped that attendance at the reading room would not be diminished by the changed status. When he formally inaugurated the new building for classes in March 1885, the Marquis of Ripon – whose father was an early supporter and whose wife had laid the foundation stone of the Northumberland Street building in 1859 – hoped that some or all of literature, classics, history, geography and 'political and social economy' would be taught, and the *Huddersfield Examiner*, reporting this, reminded readers that much of the money subscribed, especially income from the charities, was earmarked for the support of general education.[53] Twenty years later the academic range of what by then had become a municipal college would again be reviewed, in circumstances radically changed by the interaction of national and local pressures.

In that interval technical education made more advances nationally than at any previous time. Technical Instruction Acts of 1889 and 1891 empowered the County and County Borough Councils set up by the Local Government Act, 1888, to establish secondary and technical schools, and to finance them from the rates; and the Local Taxation Act of 1890 enabled these local authorities to subsidise technical education out of the revenues from certain customs and excise duties, which became known as 'whisky money'. There were now, therefore, two authorities locally providing or financing education: School Boards, set up under the 1870 Act to provide elementary education, but in the 1890s often providing 'higher-grade schools' and 'evening continuation schools'; and County and County Borough Councils, authorised to support technical education*. This over-lapping of authority

*Elementary and secondary education and their politics are described in Chapter Twenty-One. EDITOR.

was removed by the 'Cockerton judgments' of 1900-01, declaring expenditure by School Boards on evening continuation and higher grade schools illegal; then, in 1902, the Balfour Education Act abolished School Boards and made the Councils Local Education Authorities (LEAs), empowered to develop 'elementary and other than elementary education', which meant secondary, technical and adult education and teacher training. Already, in 1899, the Board of Education had been established, absorbing the old Education and Science and Art Departments, and the Charity Commission, and creating a single central-government department for education. Within the college, 'the signs of the times', and proof that 'our school is established on a sound basis' were 'the steady decline of the elementary classes and the contemporaneous rise of the higher ones'.[54] The first Principal, Dr G.S. Turpin, was appointed in 1894, but was succeeded in 1896 by Dr S.G. Rawson, like Dr Turpin, a chemist. In that year the School changed its title and became 'The Huddersfield Technical College'. The old mechanics' institute building had been sold in 1887, and a 'Jubilee Extension' fund was opened in 1890 (to celebrate 50 years in 1891), to which the main contributor – of £5,500 – was Sir Joseph Crosland, who was to be Conservative MP for Huddersfield in 1893-95. This fund was allowed to accumulate over nearly ten years before work began to extend the new building to accommodate student numbers that had increased by over 20 per cent, to 1,335, between 1894 and 1900, when the extensions were occupied.[55] But the College had been in financial difficulties from 1888, when the Governors were looking to find new ways 'of bringing the income up to the expenditure'. In March 1890, a deputation to the Town Council had asked for an annual contribution of £600, which would have represented a rate of less than a half-penny in the pound, though the Technical Instruction Act authorised the Council to levy a penny rate to support technical education.[56] But Huddersfield Council chose not to take advantage of the act, and, though, from 1891, the Council did distribute the 'whisky money' received under the Local Taxation Act, the College still had 'need of an increased assured annual income'.[57] Throughout the 1890s it was struggling financially, and negotiations for its transfer to Council control began in June 1899. As the bills for the new extensions came in, it was clear that the burden of 'working and maintaining the College has become almost too great to be borne by a private body'.[58] When the building and equipment were assigned to the Council, under the Huddersfield Corporation Act, 1902, the debt on the current account was £9,000 and on the building account £23,500.[59]

Dr Rawson began the practice of writing annual Principal's reports, and, from 1896 till his valedictory flourish of 1903, he reflected on the College's prospects and problems. He wanted evening students to follow systematic courses, to avoid 'frenzied flitting from one branch of knowledge to another', and the more able to be allowed to attend day classes;[60] he compared support to English technical colleges unfavourably with that given to German Technical High Schools, and pleaded for higher-level work – in Arts subjects and 'Higher Commercial' education as well as in science and technology – to be done in them. For Huddersfield, he hoped the new Authority would allow the College to co-ordinate the work of the evening continuation schools and would 'make regulations to promote a regular flow of the more advanced students to the College'; and he urged the development of the College's pupil-teacher centre into a Day Training College.[61] The Council's new Education Committee, charged with implementing the 1902 Act, was advised on how to fulfil its obligations by a nationally-acknowledged expert, Michael Sadler, then professor of education at Manchester University, and later to be vice-chancellor at Leeds, who received similar commissions from eight other LEAs than Huddersfield.[62] He found advising on the future of the College the most difficult part of his commission. His report, published in 1904, praised 'the pioneers of technical education in Huddersfield' who had started the Technical College in 1884 on so ambitious a scale, but considered the greatest obstacle to their success had been the lack of a good secondary school in Huddersfield in the last twenty years. Had there been one 'there would have been much more practical support for high-grade technical education . . . from the employers of labour than has actually been given'. Having surveyed its thirteen departments, he concluded that the College should concentrate its effort on those where the work stood 'in vital relations to the industries of the Borough. These are the Textile Department, the Art Department, the Dyeing Department (which should be closely associated with the Chemical Department), and the Engineering Department'. Any thought of making 'a University College, with a wide range of academic activities' must be banished. 'The right policy for Huddersfield is to strengthen the (newly-designated) University of Leeds . . .', and, 'like Bradford, to concentrate on developing those technical departments which could help the trade and add to the wealth of the community'. The College's Day School of Science, which had competed, unfavourably, with the Authority's higher grade school (formerly, and again to be, Huddersfield College), should be abolished, as should the Departments of Languages, Commerce and Economics. The Biological Department, which, led by Dr T.W. Woodhead, had an active research record, should merge its work with the University's, Mathematics should be absorbed into Engineering, and Domestic Economy should be assigned to an evening continuation centre. Sadler decided against recommending that the College's Department of Education, by then the only pupil-teacher centre in the town,[63] should become a Day Training College. He stressed the need for co-ordination of the Authority's evening-school work, but did not support Rawson's suggestion that the College should co-ordinate it.[64] Thus, the chemist, Rawson, wanted a liberal curriculum, and Sadler, the classicist, advocated a narrowly-technical college. More of the Rawson than of the Sadler vision would be realised.

In immediate response to the Sadler report the College's secondary day and evening continuation schools were closed, and the Governors sought to develop the Textile Department. The Huddersfield Corporation Act, 1906, empowered the Council to borrow £10,000 to enlarge the Textile and Dyeing Departments, but it turned out that extensions could not be carried out to the existing building. The new Principal from 1904, J.F. Hudson, a mathematician and physicist, still urged, despite the Sadler recommendation, and as Dr Rawson had, the establishment of a municipal teacher-training centre within the College, but equally in vain.[65] In 1905 there was revived talk of university college status, but the College instead became affiliated to Leeds University, which meant that students from Huddersfield's day classes were allowed one-year's remission on university courses.[66] It also successfully applied to become a 'Technical Institution', under the Board of Education's regulations, which required it to give 'organised courses' of advanced, day-time instruction, and a system of College Certificates and Diplomas was introduced, for full-time students on 3-year courses and part-time students on 5-year courses, for which the first awards were made in 1908.[67] There was an attempt to link the Authority's evening schools to the College by a system of scholarships, and 'fixed' or 'group' courses of study were arranged to give evening students a coherent education, as Rawson had advocated.[68] But some Sadler – and Rawson – recommendations were not carried out, as a Board of Education report of 1909 revealed. Though it commended the valuable work done in the College, and the research of some of its staff, it found 'the age and standard of admission are very low for an institution of this character', and 'regretted that the proposed extension of the Textile Department has not been carried out'. It recommended that the Governing Body be re-constituted, to put it more in touch with other educational work in the Borough; that the Principal and the Local Authority's Inspectorate be empowered to devise and enforce a scheme to co-ordinate the evening schools with the College; that the age and standard of admission to the College be raised to fifteen, and the next year to sixteen; that elementary work in commercial subjects be relegated to evening schools; and that students under nineteen should take complete courses, to avoid the 'frenzied flitting' Dr Rawson had condemned.[69] There followed a flurry of activity. A public conference was held in the Town Hall within a month, and 2,000 workers were appealed to in dinner-hour talks at mills;[70] the Governing Body was reconstituted, to give it more LEA representation.[71] The recruitment drive had only a temporary effect, and the College's increased income from Government grants reflected more the rising level of work than increased numbers of students: in 1912-13, when there were 1,764 students, it was £4,000, and total income was £12,878. By then, the admission age had been raised to sixteen, 'except for those who have completed an Evening School course or are qualified by attending Secondary or Higher Elementary School',[72] exemptions which must largely have undermined the rule.

In 1914, with a full-time staff of 42, and 37 part-time staff, the College was teaching students ranging from final honours of London University in Arts and Sciences (principally Chemistry), through its own Diploma and Certificate courses, external examinations of public bodies and professional institutes, and non-examinable classes in languages, literature and history to the first day-release classes for apprentices; and it was a centre for Workers' Educational Association and Oxford Extension classes. It had a public reading room, a library of 9,000 volumes, a museum that provided a service to local schools, whose teachers it helped to train, and an impressive number of scholarship endowments. It had some flourishing College societies, including a Women Students' Association, and had inaugurated Open Days, which it called 'conversaziones'. After a scrutiny by eighteen of HM Inspectors, the report praised its work but stressed its need for more space, especially for the Textile Department.[73]

The 1914-18 War was a stimulus to, rather than a brake upon, the growth of the College: though 200 students had enlisted, the decrease in student hours in the 1914-15 session was less than one per cent.[74] The most important war-time development was the creation, in 1916, of a Coal Tar Colour Chemistry Department, a direct result of the formation of British Dyes Ltd., an antecedent of ICI. Mr Joseph Turner, formerly of Read Holliday, the oldest chemical firm in Huddersfield, and now a director of British Dyes, and later to be Sir Joseph Turner and a College Governor for twenty-four years, promised a substantial contribution to the new department from his company,[75] and Sir John Frecheville Ramsden continued his family's tradition of generous support to the institution with a donation of £3,000 in 1917.[76] This was part of some energetic fund-raising for extensions to benefit the Colour Chemistry, Textile and Engineering departments,[77] and in 1918, there was, it seems, some embarrassment about what to do with nearly £15,000 donated to the support of Colour Chemistry. The Privy Council's approval was sought for the formation of a Research Association under its scheme for Scientific and Industrial Research, and £4,500 was assigned to the endowment of research scholarships, on which the tradition of chemical research in the College was to be based.[78] The building fund was raised because the Board of Education did not contribute to the cost of new building for technical education, and local rate support was limited to 3d. in the pound.[79] When the war ended, it was the long-standing accommodation needs of the Textile and Dyeing departments that took precedence. The generous gifts of textile employers' associations in the Huddersfield district, and the patient acquisition of buildings opposite the College, on Queen Street South, culminated in the approval of a building scheme by the employers and their conveyance of the land and funds to the Corporation, as a gift.[80] The new Textile building, which was opened on 26 October 1920, cost £50,000, and the Corporation contributed £6,000; and the Dyeing Department was also re-housed. But larger hopes that were entertained in the euphoric post-war period, of building a new Technical College and secondary school combined, on a site at Highfields, were never fulfilled.[81]

Teacher training in the College came to an end in 1920, when the pupil-teacher system was abolished, though the Governors tried to persuade the Board of Education to make Huddersfield a centre for training ex-service men as teachers.[82] A new College management scheme was also required under the Education Act of 1918, involving a new composition of the Governing Body, which in 1921 became a Sub-Committee of the Council's Education Committee.[83] Other immediate post-war changes included the transfer of the college museum to Ravensknowle,* after the gift to the Council of his house and grounds by Leigh Tolson, in 1919,[84] and, as numbers expanded in non-vocational adult classes, the creation of a Humanistic Studies department which embraced this work.[85] One hoped-for change did not come about: the Heads of Departments, in their new Board of Studies, persuaded the Authority to approach Leeds University with a suggestion – made for a third time – that Huddersfield become a university college. The University Council met specifically to discuss the proposal, in October 1923, but nothing more came of it.[86] The most constructive development nationally in technical education in the post-war years was the inception of National Certificates and Diplomas, awarded on part-time and full-time courses respectively. They were joint awards of the Board of Education and professional bodies, made at Ordinary and Higher levels. The earliest awards were in Chemistry, Applied Chemistry and Mechanical Engineering; the scheme began in 1921-22, and the first awards were made in 1923.[87] The College's own Diplomas and Certificates continued to be awarded, and to them was added, in March 1923, the College Associateship, which required additional relevant work experience and the submission of a dissertation by diplomates. It was an award sparingly given, and usually to holders of doctorates.[88]

Though the inter-war period was not a creative one for technical education, within the rigid limits set by a national climate of near-stagnation and its being under a Local Authority that did not complete a single new school in the period, Huddersfield Technical College did remarkably well. After falling from a peak of 3,900 in 1923-24, student numbers almost continuously rose from 1924-25 to 1938-39, when the total was 4,379; but there was almost no change in the percentage of full-time students, at about 10, and

*This is described by Stuart Davies in Chapter Twenty-Six. EDITOR.

almost 80 per cent were evening-only students. Mr Hudson's last report, written in late 1937, described the institution as a 'Regional College', a 'University of the people', 'a local centre for advanced study and research in artistic, literary, historical, scientific and technological subjects'. The next year's report, Dr J.W. Whitaker's first, claimed a 'significant movement' towards 'day-time instruction', but it made a plea for more day release of students, and condemned the drawbacks of evening classes in tones reminiscent of Dr Rawson more than thirty years before.[89] The College was now bursting at the seams. It occupied eight separate buildings, and for ten years Principals' reports had sung a litany of complaint about lack of space and over-crowding.[90] The Town Council first approved a proposal to build new Chemical laboratories in 1931, but building, to house the Chemistry, Colour Chemistry, and Dyeing Departments, did not begin till 1936. The foundation stone was laid on 2 July 1937 by Alderman Albert Hirst, Chairman of Governors, and this Chemistry building was completed in 1939, but the hoped-for relief was postponed by the outbreak of war, and the extension was not occupied till 1940.[91] Even then, as was realised from 1937, the outlier buildings were still needed. Academically, the status of the College was raised, and its research reputation established, in these inter-war years. The College had the funds, from its scholarship endowments and grants from the Department of Scientific and Industrial Research, to recruit up to ten full-time post-graduate research students.[92] Annual lists of staff publications were dominated by the research papers produced by Dr H.H. Hodgson, Head of Colour Chemistry, and his colleagues and senior students, but staff across the departments had publications to their credit.[93] Consonant with this academic advance, the College's library services were improved,[94] and student facilities and activities expanded: sporting clubs and a dramatic society prospered, a student magazine, *Mock Turtle*, was launched, and an appointments board was set up to serve full-time students.[95] There were extensive Golden Jubilee celebrations in 1934, and an important regional development involving the College was the formation of the Yorkshire Council for Further Education (YCFE) in 1936-37.[96]

In contrast with 1914-15, the first year of the Second World War saw a drastic fall in student numbers. Thereafter, however, they rose steadily, and the 5,000 in 1944-45 was the highest yet recorded. But the College also contrived to accommodate 300 students from Avery Hill Teacher Training

College, evacuated, with 30 staff, from Eltham, in 1941, who occupied part of the new extension, and who stayed for the duration; classes of soldiers training to be radio mechanics; members of the ATS who were taught commercial subjects; REME fitters, who replaced the radio mechanics in December 1942; and engineering cadets of all the services. As well, girls of Varndean School, Brighton, evacuated to Holme Valley Grammar School, were sent for Botany lessons, and from 10 p.m. to 6.30 a.m. there were crash training schemes for civilians in bench skills.[97] There was little disruption to the staffing of the College: only five men were in the Forces in late 1944, from a total of 75 full-time staff, who were supplemented by 250 part-timers.[98] But, though by the end of the war there were staffing shortages, there was no decline in staff research; and student activities flourished, not least because the Avery Hill students were women.[99] Much thought and discussion were given to post-war developments. The 1943 White Paper on *Educational Reconstruction*, which foreshadowed the Butler Act of 1944, paid only scant attention to further education, but it did acknowledge the contribution the technical colleges made to war-time training needs, and condemn their often poor buildings and the inadequate equipment found in them. Under the Act it became a duty, and not merely a power, of LEAs to provide further education, but, as with the 'continuation school' provision of the 1918 Act, a requirement of compulsory part-time education for school leavers to age eighteen was never implemented. In this connection, one war-time experience brought about in Dr Whitaker a radical conversion. The outbreak of war had caused a postponement of the raising of the school leaving age to fifteen, and he had welcomed two groups of 'junior employees' of fourteen and fifteen, sent on day release. But by the time he resigned, in March 1946, he was convinced this was a 'pernicious' system, and 'against the spirit' of the 1944 Act.[100]

This was one of the items on the first agenda of the new Principal, Dr W.E. Scott, when he took up his post in the following September. Condemning this 'mixing of Junior and Senior students' as bad for both, he was aware that Professor Sadler had done the same more than forty years before, and may well have known that Dr Rawson had done so before that.[101] Other main items were the issues raised in the plethora of post-war educational reports, circulars and memoranda, and the continuous problem of accommodation shortage, made the more acute because student numbers rose precipitately in the post-war years. The educational problems facing the College were those of the whole range of further and higher education, since it had pupils at every level, about 35 per cent of them under eighteen. At the same time as short post-graduate courses were becoming popular, the 'steady increase' in day release had, by 1953, brought to over 2,000 the number attending these courses, 700 more than in 1946-47.[102] But the balance was wrong. Dr Scott complained that the machinery of national and regional councils for Further Education was not working, and that the prestige of university degrees was inhibiting the development of full-time courses for higher technological qualifications, so that universities were expanding, but, at advanced levels, technical colleges were not.[103] Overall numbers kept on rising: in 1945-46 there were over 5,000 students; by 1948-49 well over 6,000; then after a slow-down and even reverse, 7,000 in 1953-54, when another steep upward trend set in. In his first year at the College, Dr Scott had predicted that there would have to be 'a several-storeyed building on the site behind the new extension' (the Chemistry building),[104] but alternatives were explored, and interim solutions sought. Belatedly, a new, pre-fabricated, Domestic Science and Catering building, in Queen Street South, came into use in 1949, but Textiles and other needs remained unmet, and by 1953 'saturation point' had been reached.[105] In 1949 the LEA had formulated a comprehensive building-development plan.[106] It went through many revisions before, in February 1954, it was approved in Council, after a highly-charged debate – because of the housing clearance involved – by 28 votes to 23.[107] Despite these problems, there were major academic initiatives in the immediate post-war years. The nascent 'Huddersfield Technical (Teachers') Training College', which was later to grow on the Holly Bank Campus and in 1974 to merge with the Polytechnic, began its life in the Technical College in June 1947.[108] Within the College, and building on a tradition of providing singing classes through most of its history, and of promotion of the 'Mrs Sunderland' annual competitions from 1889,* the foundations of a Music department were laid in September 1948, by the appointment of a full-time lecturer. The first orchestral concert was given in December 1950, when also was begun what came to be the tradition of the Christmas Festival of Nine Lessons and Carols, and there were concerts to celebrate the College's 110th anniversary, in March 1951, a celebration timed to coincide with the opening of the Festival of Britain.[109]

*More details of the Mrs Sunderland competitions will be found in Chapter Twenty-five. EDITOR.

Another College exhibition was held in March 1956. A few days before it opened, Sir David Eccles, Minister of Education in the Conservative Government, laid before Parliament his long-awaited White Paper, *Technical Education*. Its appearance was timely. In 1954-55 the Ministry had asked the Governors to consider closing some full-time degree and diploma courses, because of small numbers.[110] Nationally, since 1945, though there had been limited expansion of higher technological education, the universities had been the main beneficiaries, and Dr Scott had complained in early 1955 that the role of technical colleges was still not clear.[111] The White Paper was to open an era of rapid expansion, during which priority came to be given to selected technical colleges, and there was established the 'binary system', of spreading higher education generally across the university and the LEA-controlled public sectors. But in the short term there was trouble. The White Paper named Huddersfield as a possible College of Advanced Technology (CAT), to teach exclusively advanced courses; then in 1957 there was the disappointment of Bradford's selection, over Huddersfield, and in July 1958, though 'sandwich' courses in Chemical Technology and Dyeing were approved by the new validating body, the National Council for Technological Awards (NCTA), applications in Mechanical and Electrical Engineering were rejected. Worse was to come. 'Pressure from Regional influences' resulted in the removal of the Dyeing course to Bradford and the cessation of teaching for London external degrees, after sixty years, and despite the Governors' appeal to the Minister. In 1958 the Regional Council (YCFE) recommended that Chemistry and related subjects should no longer be offered at the newly re-named Huddersfield College of Technology,[112] and the National Council did not renew approval of the College's only Dip. Tech. course, in Chemistry, in 1962. Desperately, Governors, Education Committee and Town Council 'combated a suggestion from the Ministry that Regional College status should be withdrawn', and a reprieve was granted.[113] The Principal's advice of April 1956 had been ignored, and he was entitled to castigate the Authority for the slow progress with its building programme and its failure to separate 'the more elementary work'. Hastily, late in 1962, it submitted a scheme for a Branch College.[114]

Ramsden Technical College began life in 1963, taking over 4,000 students, though its separation was made 'in evolutionary manner', and was not wholly completed till 1980.[115] But its existence helped to make openings towards future expansion for the College of Technology. The Robbins Report, published in late 1963,[116] though leaving uncertain the future of Regional Colleges, was expansionary, and its projections of increased student numbers to 1973 were immediately accepted by the Government, as was its suggestion that a Council for National Academic Awards (CNAA), with a much wider subject competence, should replace the NCTA. By 1965 the CNAA had approved honours-degree courses in Chemical Technology and Electrical Engineering at Huddersfield, though a submission in Mechanical Engineering had failed.[117] The 125th anniversary celebrations, in March-April 1966 – which were attended by Frederic Schwann's granddaughter, Mrs Ismena Holland, who marked the occasion by endowing the college with a Founder's Scholarship – were held in a buoyant atmosphere. Two months later, a White Paper named the College as one of twenty-eight on a provisional list of Polytechnics, and Mr Anthony Crosland, the Labour Secretary of State for Education, was to include it on the confirmed list of twenty-nine which he announced to Parliament on 5 April 1967.[118]

In the decade before that the college campus had more than doubled in size. The foundations of the first new buildings – to be the tower blocks – were laid in 1957. There was some accommodation relief in the next session, when the Technical Teachers' College moved out to New North Road, and by September 1959, Catering and Domestic Science occupied its new building and the Textiles and Engineering departments their towers. But these were not net gains: buildings on the west side of Queen Street South had to be demolished[119] and were lost to the College, and such expedients were resorted to as temporarily housing the Music department in the old YWCA building, a former Sunday School and an ex-warehouse, while its block was built.[120] It was clear that a new site was needed for the Ramsden College, which still occupied part of the Old Building. Eventually, one was found, at the old Royal Infirmary, but it was not to be occupied until September 1968.[121] In July 1965 the College was told that the Government had curtailed its building programme, but by September 1966 the Music building was occupied, a start had been made on the Catering annexe and the second instalment of what would become 'Z Block', and a Great Hall/Administration building was planned.[122] The Library and several academic departments moved into Z Block in the autumn of 1968, when also the Catering annexe was occupied, and the Students' Union took up

Fig. 22:12 The Textiles and Engineering Departments were housed in the 'Tower Blocks' in 1959. (UHA)

residence in the old St Joseph's School.[123] The Sports Hall complex came into use in 1969 and the Great Hall building in 1970. By then, the inheritance of the Mechanics' Institution had descended on two distinct colleges, on separate campuses, though not yet wholly separated: Huddersfield Polytechnic, formally designated on 1 June 1970, and Ramsden Technical College, which in July 1971 resumed the name Huddersfield Technical College.

When the 1966 White Paper had named Huddersfield as a proposed Polytechnic, the only degree-level courses it taught were in Chemical Technology and Electrical Engineering. In 1967 an ordinary degree in Chemistry was approved, and preparation was under way of honours-degree submissions to the CNAA in Textile Marketing, Engineering Systems, European Studies in the Humanities Department, and Music, and of an ordinary degree in Catering. Only the first was immediately successful, and its teaching began in 1968. But both Chemistry and Electrical Engineering found difficulty in recruiting students, and a proposal for a degree in Engineering Design was rejected on the grounds of national over-supply.[124]

The academic base was widened when the School of Music gained the CNAA's approval for its honours-degree course and the Humanities Department resumed teaching for London University's external BA degree in 1969.[125]

The College had taken part in another birth, in 1963, than that of Ramsden Technical College. In February, the Chief Education Officer, Harold Gray, had told the Board of Studies of the intention to set up a day training college for teachers. He did this because it was envisaged that staff of the College would be 'responsible for the personal academic education of the . . . students'.[126] The opening of Oastler College of Education in September 1963 fulfilled the hopes of Principals Rawson and Hudson, sixty years before,[127] that there would be a day training college for school teachers in Huddersfield and revived an association with teacher training that the College had had for twenty years, and less systematically for almost a hundred.[128] When the Authority was invited to submit its scheme for a Polytechnic for approval by the Department of Education, it associated both colleges in the proposal. On 17 July 1968 the Secretary of State formally announced that he would be prepared to designate the College of Technology, joined with Oastler College, as a Polytechnic. Staff from both colleges worked with LEA officers to draw up an Instrument and Articles of Government, which the Department accepted in June 1969, and the nucleus of a Polytechnic Governing Body met in October.[129] An interim Polytechnic Academic Board was convened in April 1970, at which Mr K.J. Durrands, who had been appointed Director in November 1969, was present. The Polytechnic was instituted on 1 June 1970, and the official designation ceremony was performed on 23 April 1971 by the new Secretary of State for Education in the Conservative Government, Mrs Margaret Thatcher. There were then 1,540 full-time and about 2,000 part-time students.[130]

Fig. 22:13 The Polytechnic's Central Services Building, opened by H.R.H. the Duchess of Kent in May 1977. (UHA)

John O'Connell

Biographical note

Professor O'Connell was born and went to school in Bury, Lancashire. Following war-time service in the Royal Navy, he graduated in History at Manchester University in 1949. After 14 years as a schoolmaster he joined the staff of the then Huddersfield College of Technology, which became the Polytechnic. He retired in 1989 as Professor and Head of the Department of Humanities. He served on the Schools Council for 15 years, for much of that time as Chairman of its History Committee; and he has been Higher-Education member of the Standing Advisory Committee for History of The Associated Examinining Board (AEB) since 1974. He is author of *Making the Modern World. Britain: Science and Industry* (1970) and of articles on the teaching of history.

NOTES

1. T(olson) M(emorial) M(useum), 'Rules of the Huddersfield Scientific and Mechanic Institute for the Promotion of Useful Knowledge, Established 25 April 1825'.

2. TMM, 'First Annual Report of the Directors of Huddersfield Scientific and Mechanic Institute, as laid before the General Meeting of the Society on Monday, 19 June 1826', p.3; Second Annual Report (1827), p.4.

3. Mabel Tylecote, *The Mechanics' Institutes of Lancashire and Yorkshire before 1851* (1957), p.76, *n.2*; Report of the Huddersfield Female Educational Institute ... (1859), p.8; Rules of the Huddersfield Philosophical Society (MS.) (1843).

4. Tylecote, *The Mechanics' Institutes*, p.57, *n.2*.

5. Quoted in Tylecote, *The Mechanics' Institutes*, p.25.

6. Tylecote, *The Mechanics' Institutes*, p.12, *n.1*. The London Mechanics' Institution is now Birkbeck College, University of London.

7. J.F.C. Harrison, *Learning and Living* 1790-1960 (1961), p.63.

8. The 'failure' of the mechanics' institutes is discussed in Edward Royle: 'Mechanics' Institutes and the Working Classes, 1840-1860', in *The Historical Journal*, XIV, 2 (1971), 305-321; and in Harrison, *Learning*, pp.62-74.

9. Not May 1840, as was printed on later (for instance 1863) issues of the Rules; and not 'Mutual Improvement Society', as reported in the essay by G.S. Phillips on 'Huddersfield Mechanics' Institute' in his collection *Walks around Huddersfield* (1848), p.89, and repeated - presumably following Phillips - by J. Taylor Dyson (an old student) in his *History of Huddersfield* (1932), p.269. D.F.E. Sykes *The History of Huddersfield and its Vicinity* (1898), p.423), who followed the first printed Report, of February 1844, got it right.

10. About a quarter of these were in Yorkshire, and there were more than half a dozen at this time in the Huddersfield district, where more than thirty were founded in all. J.P. Hemming: 'Adult Education in Huddersfield and District, 1851-1884' (unpub. M.Ed. thesis, University of Manchester, 1966), chapter VI; Brian Dingle: 'History of Further Education in Huddersfield and District', (unpub. Dip FE thesis, University of Leeds Institute of Education, 1975), chapter 4.

11. Tylecote, *The Mechanics' Institutes*, p.190.

12. Some students were as young as nine. See TMM, '13th Report to the Committee . . . January 1854', p.9.

13. Figures given in Edward Royle, 'Mechanics' Institutes', p.309.

14. The following account of the early years of the institute is culled from the Minute Book, 1843-8 U(niversity) of H(uddersfield) A(rchives); the printed Annual Reports; the historical accounts given in the Report of January 1853 and the 'Last Report of the Work of the Institute in Northumberland Street, 1884 . . .' (1885); and from Tylecote, *The Mechanics' Institutes*, chapter VI.

15. UHA MI/1/1, 'Report of the Committee of the Huddersfield Mechanics' Institution at their first Annual Soiree, held in the Philosophical Hall, Feb. 13th, 1844, F.Schwann, Esq. President of the Institution in the Chair', p.11; TMM, 'Report on the year 1844 to the Annual Meeting . . . held on January 31st 1845' (no pagination).

16. It belonged to the Philosophical Society, and later became the Theatre Royal. Among the schools' teachers who also taught part-time at the institute from the beginning was G.D. Tomlinson. As a Vice-President, as well as superintendent of the School of Design, in 1856 he was to originate the move to raise money for a new building, and he was President when the building, in Northumberland Street, was occupied in 1861. TMM, 'Report on the Year 1844 . . .'; '16th Report . . . January 1857', p.11; '20th Annual Report . . . January 1861' p.1. *See* p.568.

17. His career and beliefs are discussed in Harrison, *Learning*, pp.137-144, and in J.P. Hemming: 'The Mechanics' Institute Movement in the Textile Districts of Lancashire and Yorkshire in the Second Half of the Nineteenth Century' (unpub. Ph.D. thesis, University of Leeds, 1974), esp.pp.576-578.

18. TMM, 'Report of the Committee . . . January 1847', pp.24-25, for example.

19. TMM, 'Report of the Committee . . . January 1848', p. 3.

20. TMM '10th Report . . . January 1851', p.5; 8th Report . . . , p.6.

21. He tried to retain chemistry, and Latin was introduced in 1852 ('13th Annual Report . . . January 1854', p.10).

22. TMM 8th Annual Report . . . p.6.

23. TMM 10th Annual Report . . . p.5.

24. TMM, '13th Annual Report . . . January 1854.

25. UHA, MI/1/4 Minute Book, 27 January 1851, pp.10-11; 9 January 1854, p.219.

26. TMM, '13th Annual Report . . . January 1854', p.4; TMM '15th Report . . . January 1856', p.17.

27. *See* p 586 for Mrs Ismena Holland.

28. For Curzon, see J.P. Hemming, Ph.D. thesis, pp.578-81; F. Curzon: *Reminiscences of My Life Work* (1904).

29. TMM, '16th Report . . . January 1857', p.8. TMM '18th Report . . . January 1859', p.9.

30. TMM, '14th Report . . . January 1855', p.13; 15th Report . . . pp.14-15.

31. *Huddersfield Chronicle*, 2 February 1861; TMM, '20th Annual Report . . . January 1861', p.6. Dr Hemming (Ph.D. thesis, 'Appendix 1') has calculated that, over the years 1859 to 1882, the percentage of 'factory operatives' in the Huddersfield student body was 32; 'mechanics', so described, constituted 5.5 per cent. The most expanded category over the period was that of 'clerks and book-keepers'.

32. TMM, '21st Annual Report . . . January 1862', p.4; 'List of Subscribers for the Erection of the New Building . . .', 1861. The Queen Street building was demolished in the 1960s; its last occupants were Messrs. Timothy Wood Ltd., ironmongers.

33. TMM, '19th Annual Report . . . January 1860', p.3.; 20th Annual Report . . . p.4.

34. TMM 14th Report . . .; TMM '21st Annual Report . . . , p. 8; Calendar for 1894-95, pp. 2, 89, 96.

35. TMM 16th Report . . . , p.4.

36. Harrison, *Learning*, p.213.

37. Society of Arts Examination Notice, June 1857.

38. TMM '16th and 17th Reports . . . , pp.12; 3-4.

39. Michael Argles, *South Kensington to Robbins* (1964), pp.16-25.

40. Annual Reports on the years 1865-69.

41. Quoted in Argles, *South Kensington*, p.26.

42. His letter to the *Huddersfield Examiner*, 4 January 1868, advocated the establishment of a Central School of Industry in 'some central town in the West Riding, say Leeds . . .'.

43. H(uddersfield) L(ocal) H(istory) L(ibrary), Tomlinson Collection, 35th Annual Report . . . , January 1876; *Huddersfield Chronicle*, 5 February 1876.

44. HLHL, Tomlinson, 39th Annual Report . . . , January 1880, p.7; Report of the Committee . . . January 1883, p.7.

45. HLHL, Tomlinson, Annual Report, 1883 . . . January 1884, p.21.

46. HLHL, Tomlinson, 'Huddersfield Mechanics' Institute: Last Report of the Work of the Institute in Northumberland Street, 1884 . . .' (1885), p.17; *Huddersfield Examiner*, 24 February 1877.

47. The two ex-Presidents were John Dodds and Wright Mellor. HLHL, Tomlinson, 'Trade School for Huddersfield. Report of an Interview . . . on Wednesday, April 11TH, 1877'.

48. HLHL, Tomlinson, 'Scheme for a Technical School for Huddersfield and Report of the Committee of the Huddersfield Technical School and Mechanics' Institute', December 1879.

49. HLHL, Tomlinson, '38th Annual Report . . . , January 1879', p.8. 41st Annual Report . . . , January 1882', p.19.

50. HLHL, Tomlinson, Annual Report, 1883 (1884), p.25; *Huddersfield Examiner*, 7 July 1883 and Supplement; *Huddersfield Chronicle* , 14 July 1883.

51. HLHL, Tomlinson, 'Last Report of the Work of the Institute . . . 1884', (1885), p.11; Calendar for 1896-97, pp.207, 215.

52. This is dealt with exhaustively by Brian D. Moriarty, in 'Politics and Education in Huddersfield in the late Nineteenth Century' (unpub. M Ed thesis, University of Leeds, 1978), especially Chapter 8.

53. *Huddersfield Chronicle*, 7 February 1880; 19th Report . . . , January 1860; *Huddersfield Examiner*, 14 March 1885.

54. H(uddersfield) T(echnical) S(chool) and M(echanics') I(nstitution): Calendar for the session 1885-86, pp.62-3.

55. H(uddersfield) T(echnical) C(ollege): Calendars for . . . 1896-97, p.207; 1890-91, p.132; 1897-98, p.133; 1900-01, p.237; 1901-02, p.215.

56. UHA H.T.S. and M.I.: Calendars for . . . 1888-89, pp.98-9; 1890-91, p.101.

57. UHA H.T.S. Calendar for . . . 1892-93, pp.120, 110.

58. H.T.C. Calendar for . . . 1900-01, p.211.

59. HLHL, Michael E. Sadler, *Report on Secondary and Technical Education in Huddersfield* (1904) p. 70 (Sadler *Report*).

60. UHA H.T.C. Calendar for . . . 1898-99, p.189.

61. UHA H.T.C. Calendars for . . . 1898-99, p.189; 1900-01, pp.239-40; 1902-03, p.273; 1903-04, p.272.

62. *Dictionary of National Biography*, sub nomine.

63. UHA H.T.C Calendar for . . . 1904-05, p.252.

64. Sadler *Report*, pp.70-101; 125-6.

65. H.T.C: Calendar for . . . 1906-07, pp.41, 247-8.

66. H.T.C.: Calendar for . . . 1905-06, pp.234-8; 1906-07, p.247.

67. Sadler *Report*, pp.70-71; H.T.C. Calendars for . . . 1904-05, p.262-4; 1906-07, p.245; 1907-08, pp.250-52.

68. H.T.C. Calendars for . . . 1906-07, p.236; 1908-09, pp.264-5.

69. UHA 'Report on the Technical and Evening Schools in the County Borough of Huddersfield for the period ending 31 July 1909'. Board of Education, 6th August, 1909'.

70. H.T.C. Calendar for . . . 1909-10, pp.268-9.

71. H.T.C. Calendar for . . . 1910-21, pp.vii-x.

72. H.T.C. Calendars for . . . 1912-13, p.276; 1911-12, p.264.

73. H.T.C. Calendar for . . . 1913-14, pp.292-3.

74. H(uddersfield) C(ounty) B(orough) C(ouncil). Council Proceedings: Minutes of the Technical College Governors, 22 February 1916.

75. As above, 2 February 1916.

76. HCBC, Technical College Governors: Textile Sub-Committee, 6 June 1916; Extensions Sub-Committee, 26 June 1917.

77. As above, 26 February 1917.

78. HCBC, Technical College Governors' Minutes, 15 April 1918; Technical College Jubilee Brochure, 1934.

79. HCBC, Technical College Governors' Minutes, 27 February 1919: application to the Local Government Board.

80. HCBC, Technical College Governors' Minutes, 24 September 1918; 17 December 1918, confirmed by Council, 18 December 1918.

81. HCBC, Technical College Governors' Minutes, 28 September 1920; HCBC, Minutes of Proceedings of Education Committee: Technical College Sub-Committee, 21 February 1922; Governors' Minutes, 18 December 1917, 23 July 1918, 27 July 1920.

82. HCBC, Technical College Governors' Minutes, 27 February 1919; Sub-Committees, 2 December 1920, 28 February 1921.

83. HCBC, Technical College Governors' Minutes, 25 November 1919, 24 February 1920, 28 June 1921; Technical College Sub-Committee, 29 November 1921, 4 and 29 May 1922.

84. HCBC, Council Proceedings. General Purposes Committee, 8 May 1919; Governors' Minutes, 24 February 1920.

85. HCBC, Technical College Governors' Minutes, 27 May, 2, 24 June, 9 July, 23 December 1919.

86. HCBC, Council Proceedings: Technical College Sub-Committee, 26 September 1922; Technical and F E Sub-Committee, 18 and 19 December 1922, 14 February, 26 June, 24 July 1923; Departmental Report to the Mayor, 1924.

87. HCBC, Council Proceedings. Technical College Sub-Committee, 20 December 1921, 24 January 1922.

88. HCBC, Technical College and F E Sub-Committee, 27 March 1923. Sixteen Awards had been made by 1934 (H(uddersfield) T(echnical) C(ollege). Principal's Report for 1933-34, p.1).

89. H.T.C., Principal's Reports, 1936-37, p. 8; 1937-38, p.6.

90. Principal's Report, 1927-28, 1928-29, etc.

91. Principal's Report, 1932-33, p.(viii); 1935-36, p.(ix); 1936-37, p.6; 1938-39, p. 9; 1939-40, p. 5.

92. E.g., Principal's Report 1928-29, p.(v)

93. E.g., Principal's Report 1931-32, Appendix II; 1932-33, Appendix II.

94. Cf. Principal's Report 1933-34, p.(v); 1938-39, p.14.

95. Principal's Report 1931-32, p.(viii); 1933-34, p.(vii); 1935-36, p.(ix); 1932-33, p.(viii).

96. HCBC, Council Proceedings: Departmental Report to the Mayor, 1936-37, p.1483.

97. Principal's Report 1939-40 to 1944-45.

98. Principal's Report 1943-44, p.10.

99. Principal's Report 1940-41, p.1; 1944-45, p.6.

100. Principal's Report 1938-39, p.7.; 1944-45, p.2.

101. Principal's Report 1945-46. p. 4.

102. Principal's Report 1952-53, pp.3-4.

103.   Principal's Report 1948-49, p. 4, 1951-52, pp.2-4.

104.   Principal's Report 1945-46, pp.3-4.

105   Principal's Report 1952-53, p.3.

106.   Principal's Report 1949-50, p.2, HCBC, Council Proceedings: Finance Sub-Committee, 20 January 1950, Minute 456.

107.   Principal's Report 1953-54, p. 2., *Huddersfield Daily Examiner*, 4 February 1954.

108   Principal's Report 1946-47, pp. 3-4.

109.   Principal's Report 1950-51, pp.2, 11.

110.   Principal's Report 1954-55, p.2.

111.   Principal's Report 1953-54, p.2.

112.   H(uddersfield) C(ollege) of T(echnology), Principal's Report 1957-58, pp.2-3, 1959-60, p. 4.

113.   HCT, Principal's Report 1961-62, p. 3.

114.   HCT, Principal's Report 1961-62, p.2.

115.   HCT, Principal's Report, 1963-64, pp. 2-3, H.M.Dix, *Twenty Five Years On. A Short History of Huddersfield Technical College (1989), pp.8*, 32, 40.

116.   'Report for the Committee on Higher Education appointed by the Prime Minister' (1963-64).

117.   HCT, Principal's Report 1964-65, p.3.

118.   'A Plan for Polytechnics and Other Colleges', (1966); Parliamentary statement by the Secretary of State for Education, 5 April 1967.

119.   HCT, Principal's Report 1958-59, p.2, 1967-68, pp.9, 19.

120.   Principal's Report 1963-64, p.3, 1965-66, p.13.

121.   Principal's Report 1963-64, p.3, H.M.Dix, *Twenty Five Years On*, pp.13-14.

122.   Principal's Report 1965-66, p.4, 1966-67, p.12.

123.   Principal's Report 1967-68, pp.2, 17-18, 19.

124.   Principal's Report 1966-67, pp.6, 8, 11, 14, 15, 1967-68, pp.7-8, 9-10, 13, 16.

125.   Principal's Report 1968-69, pp.10, 12, 14, 15.

126.   Principal's Report 1962-63, pp.3-4.

127.   H.T.C., Calendar for . . . 1903-04, p.272, 1904-05, pp. 261-62.

128.   H.T.C., Calendar for . . . 1899-1900, p.183, HCBC Technical College Governors' Minutes, 27 February 1919, p.264, 28th Annual Report . . . January 1869.

129.   HTOC, Principal's Report 1966-67, p. 2, HCBC Council Proceedings. Governors of College of Technology and Ramsden Technical College, 22 November 1966 (Minute 296), 18 April 1967 (Minute 553). *Huddersfield Daily Examiner*, 24 October 1967, Principal's Report 1968-69, p.4.

130.   *Huddersfield Daily Examiner*, 23, 24 April 1971.

Fig. 23:1 Lockwood Spa. (KCS)

CHAPTER 23

Health care
in nineteenth-century
Huddersfield

HILARY MARLAND

By the end of the nineteenth century the
inhabitants of Huddersfield had access to a
wide range of health care services.
Although comparing very unfavourably with our expectations of what
medical services should offer, these were impressive enough when set
alongside what had been available at the beginning of the century.
Huddersfield, then 'an insignificant cluster of irregularly built lanes',[1] had no
hospital, and only a handful of surgeons and chemists' shops serviced the
medical needs of its inhabitants. During the course of the century all this
changed. The number of doctors increased rapidly, to over thirty by the end
of the century. Of the medical institutions, the Huddersfield Infirmary was
outstanding; its physical presence was a memorial to Victorian philanthropy,
it made a major contribution to the medical relief of the town's inhabitants,
and it was a symbol of the dynamism and growth in confidence and power of
the local woollen manufacturers, who financed, ran and recommended
patients to the charity. Supplementing the work of the Infirmary were a
variety of smaller charitable enterprises providing nursing and convalescent
care, assistance to the blind, deaf and dumb, support to lying-in mothers, and
home visiting.

Friendly societies were established in large numbers in the Huddersfield
area during the nineteenth century, providing their provident working-class
membership with sickness benefits and medical attendance. In the closing
decades of the century, the municipal authorities began to play a greater role
in health care, with the appointment of John Benson Pritchett as the first
Medical Officer of Health in 1873, and the setting up of an infectious diseases

hospital at Birkby in the same year. For the very poor, the old, the careless and the unlucky, the Poor Law offered a minimum health care service, based on its workhouse sick wards and out-relief. Alongside these institutional and organized forms of medical relief, there existed a rich and diverse self-dosing medical subculture, utilizing family recipes, the chemist's shop, spas and healing wells, and a galaxy of quack doctors and local healers.

This chapter will offer a brief overview of health care in nineteenth-century Huddersfield.[2] In order to narrow down the large area to be covered the account will close around 1870, before the period when the local authority began to provide health services. Rather than simply giving a blow-by-blow account of each medical option, an attempt will be made to explore in what circumstances they were resorted to, what choices people had when they needed medical help, and what paths the population of Huddersfield followed in seeking cures for their ills.

Illness in nineteenth-century Huddersfield

The population of nineteenth-century Huddersfield had ills in abundance. It is the infectious, particularly epidemic, diseases which first catch the attention, diseases which today make their appearance in a mild form or which have been eradicated. Topping the mortality figures was tuberculosis, 'the white plague', the greatest killer disease of the nineteenth century, but measles, scarlet fever, smallpox, whooping cough, influenza, typhus, typhoid and diarrhoea, were also major killers, especially of the young and weak. These ever-present diseases flared up on occasion in epidemic proportions. In 1847, for example, mortality rates in Huddersfield were pushed up by a serious outbreak of typhus; out of 867 deaths, ninety-seven were attributed to typhus, ninety-one to phthisis (pulmonary tuberculosis), thirty-two to scarlatina (scarlet fever), thirty-eight to pneumonia, thirty-one to whooping cough, twenty-five to diarrhoea, nineteen to smallpox, thirteen to bronchitis, and seven to influenza.[3]

Of all the infectious diseases, it is Asiatic cholera which has captured the imagination of contemporaries and historians. Asiatic cholera was a disease new to Europe, which swept through England in four major epidemics during the nineteenth century, in 1831-32, 1849, 1853-54 and 1866. In terms of overall mortality, its influence was not great; rather, its impact was felt at an emotional level. With its high case mortality rate of 40 per cent to 60 per cent, dreadful and speedy progress of a few days or even hours towards death from dehydration, accompanied by violent vomiting and diarrhoea, agonizing cramps, followed by collapse and coldness, when the body took on a vivid blue appearance, cholera was a shocking disease. Like other epidemic diseases, it baffled the medical profession. In Huddersfield the 1849 epidemic was especially severe, resulting in a total of fifty-two deaths.[4] This outbreak was largely confined to areas well known for their environmental problems;[5] Birkby, the workhouse and its environs, and Johnny Moore Hill at Paddock were badly affected. The latter was 'a place notorious for the prevalence of fever and other forms of disease', and out of nineteen dwellings, with a total of 110 inhabitants, twenty cases of cholera and thirty-two cases of diarrhoea were reported.[6]

Chronic complaints were also prevalent amongst the populace of Huddersfield, aches and pains, swellings, itches, skin eruptions, wasting sicknesses, gallstones, bronchitis, rheumatism and gout, aggravated by poor sanitation, urban filth, poverty, poor diets, and damp, dirty and cramped living conditions for some, over-indulgence and too little exercise for others. Occupational diseases, resulting from dust, heat and long hours of labour, were very common, and as frequently unprotected machinery was introduced into local mills, industrial accidents soared, adding to the toll of injuries and deaths in the mines and railway construction. The story of young Joseph Habergam, who in 1833 gave evidence to a parliamentary inquiry into factory conditions, is particularly heart-rending and shocking. Habergam testified to the appalling conditions for young children in local textile mills – long hours, dust, fines and beatings by overlookers, and numerous, often fatal, accidents. For Habergam factory work had resulted in a serious deformity of his limbs. Dr John Kenworthy Walker of the Huddersfield Infirmary and Mr Hey of the Leeds Infirmary, where Habergam had been transferred on the recommendation of Richard Oastler, concluded that Joseph Habergam, then aged seventeen, would be permanently crippled.[7]

Different options were resorted to for different complaints or medical emergencies. Victims of railway, mining or factory accidents would be transported hastily to the Infirmary, where they would remain until ready for discharge or until they died. Infectious diseases, even when life-threatening, would usually be treated at home by a Dispensary doctor, Poor Law surgeon or general practitioner; later in the century sufferers would perhaps be removed to one of the Union workhouses or municipal fever hospitals. But in other cases the path to seeking a cure was more circuitous. The case could be taken, for example, of a labouring man, a textile worker, past middle age but still with a family to support, who was regularly prevented from following his occupation because of recurrent bouts of rheumatism. It is likely that his first step would be to nurse his complaint at home using self-dosing remedies, perhaps applying pig fat, a warm plaster or a liniment of turpentine, rum and neat's-foot oil to the painful areas, or imbibing white mustard, ground-ivy, camomile, woody nightshade, or cream of tartar and gum guaiacum in wine, water or tea. If these failed to bring relief, it is possible that resort would be had to a chemist's shop, a local healer or spa. Both the Lockwood and Slaithwaite spas were reputed to be very beneficial for rheumatic complaints. Or perhaps a visit was paid to Richard Horsfall of Merrydale, the local bonesetter, or to the well-known Whitworth doctors on the other side of the Pennines.[8]

By this time, with the coming of colder weather, and no longer able to work, the friendly society was turned to. After its officials had checked the authenticity of the case, it was agreed that a sickness benefit would be paid, and that the society's doctor would attend. Several months later, the family were in desperate straits; reliant on now reduced friendly society benefits and crippled by debt, the friendly society doctor pronounced the case hopeless. With no employer to protect him, attempts to obtain a ticket of admission for treatment at the Huddersfield Infirmary failed. Besides, chronic cases, in effect lost causes, such as his were not considered 'proper objects' for in-patient treatment. Finally, the aid of the Poor Law Guardians was sought. The family were forced to give up their home and enter the workhouse, the end of the road.

A fictional, rather melodramatic, Dickensian story in the best Victorian traditions. An extreme depiction of what could happen when the poorer classes were overtaken by illness, but not untypical. Historical records alas rarely present us with complete medical and life histories, especially for the poor and illiterate, but elements of each stage in this fictional depiction of the search for a cure are to be found in the Kirklees archives, in the Infirmary records, friendly society papers, Poor Law accounts and diaries. The dabbler in home cures, the chronic invalid appearing year after year in the friendly society accounts under debit, the removal of families blighted by illness to the workhouse.

The medical profession

Servicing the various medical institutions and busy building up their private practices, were a growing number of university educated or apprentice-trained physicians, surgeons and general practitioners.[9] In 1780 Huddersfield was served by only three surgeon-apothecaries, Messrs. Thompson, Tinker and Batty, junior; by 1822 the number of medical practitioners had risen to thirteen, to over twenty by the 1850s, and over thirty by the close of the century. The best-trained and most successful, usually members of the local élite, with high social standing and many local contacts, acquired the sought-after appointments at the Huddersfield Dispensary and Infirmary, were regarded as the town's senior doctors, and often had lucrative consulting practices; men such as Dr Kenworthy Walker, honorary physician to the Huddersfield Dispensary from its establishment in 1814 until 1846, when ill health forced him to resign, George Robinson, in turn honorary surgeon and consulting surgeon from 1814 to 1865, and William Turnbull, honorary physician from 1816 until within a few weeks of his death in 1876, a period of sixty years! Those lower down the social and career scale had to be content with friendly society or Poor Law posts, appointments as factory surgeon or to smaller charitable enterprises, and private practices catering for the less well-to-do.

Until late in the nineteenth century, all doctors were united by their inability to cure many of the illnesses which confronted them, with only a handful of useful medicines and techniques at their disposal, the most outstanding of which was vaccination against smallpox. Only towards the end of the century, with startling advances in the fields of bacteriology and surgery, did medical men obtain a more complete armoury for their fight against sickness. Surgery, justly dreaded, was less widely practised than often believed. Only fifty-five operations took place in the Huddersfield Infirmary in 1875, increasing to four hundred in 1895, usually amputations, cutting for stone,[10] reduction of hernias, eye surgery, and the treatment of a small number of cancers. Until the second half of the century surgery was carried out without anaesthesia, and in the 1870s 'only faint glimmerings of the antiseptic system had reached Huddersfield'.[11] Yet most doctors were also united in their abhorrence of alternatives to their orthodox regimes of bleeding, blistering,[12] cutting, heroic dosing and purging. A few members of the Huddersfield medical profession did dabble with alternative therapies, homoeopathy, phrenology, hydropathy or medical galvanism, but these were exceptions, and throughout the century war was raged against the unorthodox, the quack, the charlatan. But, lacking the ability to cure, the orthodox medical practitioner fought a losing battle against quacks, local healers and self-dosing practices.

Self-dosing

In a great many, perhaps most, cases of illness, relief began at home, without the help of medical men, qualified or unqualified. Self-dosing was practised on a grand scale, a pastime indulged in by all classes, rich and poor, urban and rural, as a cure for sickness and to prevent its appearance. Typically self-dosing was applied to common trivial ailments, aches and pains, coughs and colds, and more persistent conditions, rheumatism, gout, bronchitis and such like. Belief in the need for regular purgings was widespread; 'spring medicine', brimstone and treacle, young greens and castor oil, were used to drive sickness out of the body, to 'clear the system'. The survival of traditional 'folk' remedies in nineteenth-century Huddersfield is evidenced by two recipe books, those of James Woodhead of Netherthong, compiled in 1818, and James Hirst of Huddersfield, put together between 1836 and 1892,[13] both of which contained remedies for a variety of common complaints, using herbs and plant extracts, simple, easily obtainable medicaments, and more curious components, dung of cat, earthworms and dragon's blood! Included amongst James Woodhead's remedies for jaundice, consumption, nervous complaints, blindness, 'obstructions' and 'looseness', was oil of cloves for toothache, a well-known treatment, honeysuckle, sugar and alum for inflamed eyes, and 'powdered dry dew worms' and ale for colic. Alongside remedies for soothing and alleviating, were more drastic solutions for medical emergencies, most notable a recommendation for Widow Welch's Pills 'for young women', a well-known abortifacient, and a remedy of Woodhead's own composition for procuring abortions, made up of iron, aloes and antimony, no doubt powerful enough to produce the desired result.[14]

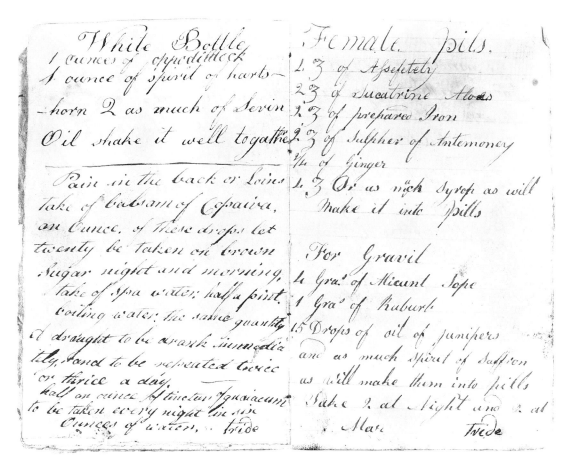

Fig. 23:2 Recipes contained in James Woodhead's book, 1818. (WYAS, K)

By the nineteenth century self-dosing was not limited to the kitchen preparation of simples[15] and herbs collected in the garden and surrounding countryside, but had been supplemented by a wide range of prepared and packaged remedies. Family remedies passed on through the generations could be added to by consulting health manuals, such as John Wesley's *Primitive Physic* and William Buchan's *Domestic Medicine*, newspapers and magazines. Mrs Beeton's *Household Management* and other cookery books contained health maintenance tips, special recipes for invalids, and simple remedies. During the course of the century, chemists and druggists were to become important suppliers of medicaments, the ingredients of family medicine chests (a rather more extensive version of the bathroom medicine cabinet,

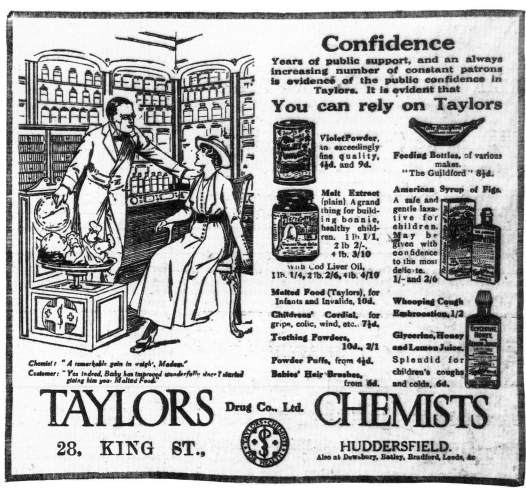

Fig. 23:3 Chemist: "A remarkable gain in weight, Madam" Customer: "Yes indeed. Baby has improved wonderfully since I started giving him your Malted Food". Advertisement for Taylor's Chemists **Huddersfield Examiner**, 2 Feb 1917. (KCS)

including bicarbonate of soda, boracic crystals, senna pods, Indian bark, and perhaps a couple of homoeopathic remedies), family recipes, commercial patented brands, and their own special remedies. In 1810 R. Elliot 'Chemist and Apothecary' of Huddersfield 'strongly recommended to the Public' a selection of his 'valuable medicines, Elliot's Restorative and Healing Tincture, Elliot's Family Cordial, The Ceylonian Powder, and Elliot's Lozenges'. William T. Bygott offered the inhabitants of Huddersfield his own Toothache Elixir, guaranteed to cure toothache in just one minute, while William King advertised King's Glycerine Cough Balsam, a 'valuable remedy' for chest affections.[16]

Medical advice accompanied the sale of medicines, and some chemists also offered the services of dentist, surgeon and man-midwife.[17] The counter-prescribing of chemists and druggists was a source of great grievance on the part of the medical profession, but amongst laymen their services became increasingly popular, as perhaps best demonstrated by the rapid rise in their numbers. In 1790 Huddersfield had only two chemists and druggists, by 1841 eleven, and by 1871 twenty-five,[18] while most surrounding villages had their own chemists' shops or branch establishments. Some gained great repute. George Hall's shop in King Street was 'believed in as a cure-all with a faith greater than ever Gull or Jenner commanded, . . .'.[19] When R.C. Walshaw became successor to George Hall, 'The People's Druggist', towards the end of

Fig. 23:4 Advertisement for Needham Bros., 'Medical Chemists'. Huddersfield Weekly Examiner, *26 July 1884. (KCS)*

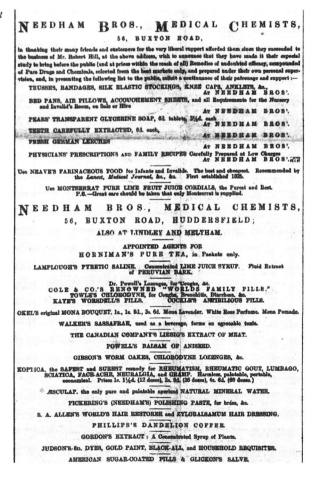

the century, Walshaw promised to give personal attention to the preparing of medicines for small ailments 'for which the late Geo. Hall was so justly noted'.[20]

Yet it was not only the chemist and druggist who supplied the needs of the self-doser. By the nineteenth century newspaper advertisement had become a standard sales technique, particularly for the patent medicine vendor. A glance at any of the newspapers appearing in Huddersfield during the nineteenth century amply illustrates the extent to which medicines were advertised, and the range available, the famed Holloway's Pills, Cordial Balm of Gilead, Dr Locock's Pulmonic Wafers, Frampton's Pill of Health, Dr Taylor's Vegetable Antiscorbutic and Rheumatic Drops, etc., designed to cure all ills to which the flesh is heir, complete with coats of arms and testimonials from satisfied clients. Such preparations were available from a variety of retailers, the newspaper proprietor himself, chemists, stationers, grocers, hairdressers, drapers, and publicans.

In all areas of self-dosing practice, it becomes evident that by the nineteenth century, traditional folk elements were becoming intermingled with commercial practices and scientific (or pseudo-scientific) medical theories. This was no more so than in the case of the water cure, which embraced both traditional and modern features. Several of Huddersfield's local spas were of antique origin, including St. Helen's Well in Honley, whose reputation for curing powers stretched back through the centuries. A number of local wells and springs were revamped during the nineteenth century, transformed with the application of hydropathic theories, into commercial bathing establishments. In 1827 a large spa baths was established by a company of subscribers at Lockwood, on the site of an old sulphur well, where 'the existence of mineral springs had suggested to the speculative mind dreams of an English Baden, or at least of another Harrogate. The river was spanned with a rustic bridge, grounds were laid, and a Bath Hotel opened its doors'.[21] By the 1860s the Lockwood Spa was offering swimming, warm, Buxton, shower, vapour, sulphurous, fumigating and shampooing baths, and in the 1867 season it attracted almost 30,000 bathers.[22]

The spa cure was especially popular amongst the better-off, combining an undemanding cure with genteel entertainments; a round of tea parties, card games and walks in pleasant surroundings. The annual opening of the Slaithwaite Spa each May was a great local occasion, with afternoon tea, a

RULES AND REGULATIONS

FOR THE

PUBLIC BATHS, LOCKWOOD SPA.

OPENED, MAY 1827.

1.—All persons to pay for Bathing, before they are admitted to the Baths.

2.—All Subscribers to the Baths, to pay their Subscriptions on or before the first time of Bathing.

3.—The BUXTON, HOT, and VAPOUR Baths, are kept constantly ready, during the Season, (*from May first, to November first,*) and will be prepared any time afterwards, on two hours notice.

4.—The Baths are always kept in good order.

5.—Separate COLD and HOT Baths are provided for the Ladies.

6.—All persons detected *Spitting* in the Baths, or *using Soap*, to pay ONE SHILLING; and no person will be permitted to make any future use of the Baths, who shall have defiled or improperly used them.

7.—All Visitors looking over the premises, to be charged Threepence each, and Sixpence on Sundays, unless introduced by a Proprietor.

8.—On Sundays the Baths will close to the Subscribers and the Public, at Nine o'clock in the Morning, and open at Five o'clock in the Afternoon, except the applicant produces a Certificate from a Physician or Surgeon.

9.—All persons who bathe or visit the Baths, shall enter their name and residence in a book kept for that purpose.

TERMS FOR BATHING.

NON-SUBSCRIBERS.	s.	d.
SWIMMING BATH		6
PRIVATE COLD AND SHOWER BATHS	1	0
BUXTON BATH 86⁰	1	6
WARM BATH	2	0
VAPOUR BATHS	3	6

ANNUAL SUBSCRIPTION.	£.	s.	d.
FOR ONE PERSON TO THE SWIMMING BATH		10	6
FOR A FAMILY, TO ALL THE COLD BATHS	1	1	0

The Bath-Keepers are not allowed to take any perquisites.

Subscribers of One Guinea, are privileged to have the Warm Baths at half Price.

₄*₄ The Committee have taken into consideration the request of several Trades-people, to reduce the Terms; this has been complied with, which they hope will give general satisfaction.

N. B. PARTIES MAY BE ACCOMMODATED WITH TEA, BY THE BATH-KEEPER, AT ONE SHILLING EACH.

These elegant and commodious Baths, which embrace every comfort and convenience, will open for the season, on the FIRST of MAY next. The Baths are now abundantly supplied with the celebrated SPA WATER, a Steam Engine having been erected to work the pump; and the charges and direction of the whole, will be regulated by a Committee of Shareholders, and managed by an experienced keeper.

The Village of LOCKWOOD is beautifully and delightfully situated, in the valley of the HOLM, about ¾ of a mile distant from the Market-Town of Huddersfield, and lies in a romantic and finely sheltered country, with good roads in every direction. It combines every requisite to comfort, invigorate, and strengthen the weak and sickly. The Spa Water is generally known and highly esteemed for its Medicinal qualities: in particular, it has been found highly beneficial in glandular, rheumatic, gouty, dyspeptic, scorbutic, and all other kinds of cutaneous complaints. The Baths are without doubt, the most complete establishment of the kind, in the West-Riding of Yorkshire; and the private Lodgings in the Village, and in Huddersfield, are excellent and moderate. There are daily Coaches to all parts of the kingdom, from Huddersfield: in short as a summer retreat, LOCKWOOD cannot be surpassed.

If any want of Attention, or Neglect is observed in the Bath-keepers, by the Subscribers, they are requested to report it to the Committee.

Lockwood Baths, April 10th, 1828.——MOORE, PRINTER, HUDDERSFIELD.

Fig. 23:5 Rules and Regulations for the Public Baths, Lockwood Spa, opened May 1827. (WYAS, K)

concert and speeches by Slaithwaite worthies. By the 1850s clients could either pay for individual baths or make an annual subscription of 12s. 6d. for one person for a season or 25s. for a family.[23] True enthusiasts made annual pilgrimages to local spa towns in high season, most usually Harrogate, Buxton or Ilkley. Although it is true that many of their traditional bathing places were taken over for development, the poorer classes were not completely excluded from the new commercial baths. Many visitors were said to be mechanics and factory workers, and at the Slaithwaite Spa a subscription charity was set up for those too poor to pay the admission charges.[24]

The mid-nineteenth century saw the advent of a new brand of self-dosing, medical botany, sometimes known as Coffinism or Thomsonianism, which made a direct appeal to the working man. Medical botany proved popular in northern England, and in Huddersfield, with its assertive and boisterous working class, its appeal was especially strong. For medical botany, with its catch-phrase and promise to make 'every man his own physician', was designed to attract those of the working-class who were educated, politically aware, and radical in their thinking. Medical botany was imported to England from North America by the rather inappropriately-named (or perhaps not!) Dr Isaiah Coffin, who set up botanic societies in a number of northern towns during the 1840s, including Huddersfield. Medical botany emphasized self-dosing; the treatments were simple and herbal based. Handbooks were available to explain dosing and the care of the sick, while the botanic societies offered lectures and the opportunity to exchange information. Although basically a self-dosing system, botanic 'practitioners' also had their role, as suppliers of the necessary herbs and sources of advice. By 1861 six botanic doctors and medicine vendors were listed in the Huddersfield census returns,[25] showing that the shift towards commercialization had also permeated medical botany. It was not only the straightforward remedies, but also the democratic organization of the botanic societies and the emphasis on self-help and self-improvement which attracted the labouring class. Medical botany was likely to involve those who were also active in the Co-operative and Methodist movements, the Mechanics' Institutes or teetotalism. The explicit opposition of the medical botanists to the medical profession also explains the appeal of the movement to a working class disenchanted with regular medical practice, reflected, for example, in popular outbursts against doctors in cholera epidemics and during the 1834 election campaign, when local medics, 'Dead Body-Bill Doctors' had voted in support of Blackburne, the unpopular Whig candidate and supporter of the Anatomy Bill.[26]

Quack doctors and local healers

Although self-dosing was practised by all levels of Huddersfield society, it was the labouring classes and the poor who were depicted as being lured in especially large numbers to the quack, local healer, herbalist and druggist's shop. There is certainly much truth in this assertion, if only for the simple reason that unqualified advice tended to be much cheaper than that offered by the regularly qualified physician and surgeon.[27] As the *Lancet* remarked in 1857:

> Large towns consist almost entirely of operatives who look upon physic as a trade, – and a poor one too, . . . – who rather like some of their own class – who have a strong belief in a natural gift for doctoring, and, above all, believe most fervently in cheap physic, cheap advice, and cheap visits.[28]

Not only was an unqualified healer likely to be of the same class as the client, but he or she would probably be well known in the community. Unqualified healers comprised a broad group, including itinerants, the so-called 'quack doctors' and medicine hawkers, sedentary local healers, midwives, wise women, bonesetters and herbalists, specialists in eye and ear diseases, the treatment of 'bad breasts' and cancers, and dentists, who only late in the century acquired professional trappings. The sole element uniting this group and distinguishing them from 'regular' doctors, was their lack of a formal medical training. We should be wary of making distinctions between qualified and unqualified based on the quality or success of treatment, for qualified doctors had few effective therapies at their disposal until late in the nineteenth century. We should also not brand the unqualified too quickly in a derogatory way, as 'quacks'. Some may have been scoundrels and cheats, some were merely flamboyant and ineffective, but others may well have had a talent for curing, or at least have offered psychological comfort, or a placebo, to the patient.

Fig. 23:6 Richard Horsfall of Merrydale, known popularly as 'Merrydale Dick', a local bonesetter and healer of great repute. (KCS)

Local healers based their practices on recognition, repute and experience, their cures on herbal remedies, folk practices and manual dexterity, often passed down through the generations. Sally Oldfield of Honley was one such healer, a leech gatherer and expert in blood letting.[29] The skills of Sally Dunkirk of Slaithwaite were also well regarded in the Huddersfield area. 'Any bad case of fever, or lunacy, of exceptional emergency, was a call for Sally's services. . . . A most useful woman was she for the times in which she lived.'[30] Trade directory listings reveal a number of local experts; in 1899 seven herbalists were recorded, and a bonesetter, Joseph Oldfield of Berry Brow.[31] Huddersfield was also visited each Tuesday by the 'Batley Bone Setter', M. Spedding, with forty-three years practical experience in treating fractures, dislocations, contracted joints and injured spines.[32]

Early in the century local healers were regularly employed by the overseers of the poor to treat the ailments of those dependent upon the poor rates. Midwives, then lacking a formal training, were often employed in preference to the more expensive surgeon or man-midwife. In March 1788 Dame Haigh was paid 6s. by the Huddersfield overseers for delivering three poor women.[33] The overseers of Mirfield Township employed Molly Holroyd as midwife on a regular basis; for her services she was paid a yearly retainer of six guineas, plus 2s. 6d. per delivery.[34] Bonesetters and other local experts, often women, were regularly called on, and paupers were sent to distant specialists, local spas and even the seaside in the hope of bringing about a cure. In October 1784, for example, the Mirfield overseers paid 2s. 6d. to the 'Boansetter for Bet. Swift', and in April 1795 10s. 6d. 'To Milnes Wife for Cureing (sic) John Child Children'. In April 1807 Widow Jubb was paid one guinea for 'Curing Gladhill', and in July 1818 James Booth was paid one pound for going twice to Buxton to take the waters.[35]

Itinerants were less likely to be employed by the overseers or to have a regular clientele. Travelling from town to town, advertising their progress by means of handbills, they made their appearance on market days to sell medicines, pull teeth, to diagnose and treat a wide range of ailments, to dupe and to entertain. As Sykes reminisced of Slaithwaite in the 1860s:

> in those days quack doctors were very much in evidence. They were very loquacious and talked glibly about the lungs and the kidneys, and the blood and stomach, and all the ills of which the flesh is heir to, and for which they had never-failing remedies and certain cures, with samples available at the moment, and ready to supply a stock of medicines which every family ought to possess.[36]

Many itinerants offered cures for all ills, such as Mrs Drummond, who toured the West Riding during the mid-nineteenth century, together with her assistants and her Famed Herbal Tonic and Aperient Canada Pills, which would cure 'any' disease or debility – stomach complaints, colds, coughs, consumption, jaundice, gout, fever, scrofula, scurvy, rheumatism, piles, cancer, incontinence, smallpox, tumours, ulcers, worms, ague, hysterical fits, wasting, lowness of spirits, pimples, bad breath, and so on *ad infinitum*.[37] Some claimed a whole range of skills, such as the fantastic Anthony Bernasconi Chevalier de la Barre, a frequent visitor to Huddersfield during the 1840s and 1850s, who at various times proclaimed himself dentist, physician, surgeon, aurist, and 'oculist to the King of France'! Others claimed expertise in relieving specific complaints, cancers, blindness, deafness, 'bad legs' or more 'secretive complaints'. The Doctors Henry, who could be consulted twice weekly at 3 Albion Street, Huddersfield in 1839, claimed to be able to 'eradicate every species of Venereal Infection', effecting 'perfect cures' in a week.[38]

Friendly society medical relief

Out of all the working-class organizations to evolve during the nineteenth century, friendly societies, offering insurance against sickness, unemployment and death, proved to be amongst the most enduring, and most capable of attracting support, especially in northern England where they made their greatest impact. By 1803 four friendly societies had been set up in Huddersfield, with a total of 900 members (some 12 per cent of the population of the town). Many of the surrounding villages had their own societies; by 1815 South Crosland had two with 360 members, Saddleworth fourteen and 3,200 members (in both cases 24 per cent of the population).[39] By 1866 Huddersfield was said to have a total of eighty-three friendly societies,[40] including local organizations and the big affiliated friendly societies, namely the Oddfellows, Foresters, Ancients Druids, Shepherds and Free Gardeners.

The assistance given to sick members generally took two forms. Firstly, a weekly benefit was paid to those too sick to follow their usual employment. Once the illness had been confirmed by a society official or approved witness, members would become entitled to a benefit of something in the region of 10s. per week. After several months, or if members were declared permanently incapacitated, the benefit would be reduced. Secondly, a small number of societies provided medical attendance in the person of a club doctor. Medical assistance was usually confined to visiting and medicines, but in the second half of the nineteenth century a few societies paid subscriptions to the Huddersfield Infirmary, thus giving their members access to a wider range of treatments, including surgical operations and nursing care.

Not everyone of course could afford the fees which friendly society membership demanded, something in the region of one shilling a month, often more in the affiliated societies. This largely limited membership to the lower middle class and better paid members of the working class, skilled textile workers, members of the building trades, printers, and small shopkeepers. It was, however, common practice for Poor Law overseers to pay friendly society subscriptions on behalf of paupers or near paupers, thus relieving themselves from the burden of paying out-relief to the sick and from the task of employing medical attendants. High-risk categories were excluded from friendly society membership, which was limited to those aged between around eighteen and forty years old, and, at the time of taking up membership, to those in good health. Relief was frequently restricted to the subscribing member, excluding his wife, children and other dependents, although there were also a number of all-female societies in Huddersfield. Benefit was also denied if it was suspected that the illness of the member in question had been brought about by misconduct or carelessness, frequenting pubs or gaming houses, taking violent exercise or playing football! The Prince Albert Lodge of Ancient Druids in Thurstonland stipulated that no member would receive any benefits for 'hurt or sickness' occasioned by

> drinking, fighting or attending dog fighting cockfighting bullbaiting or mankind fighting with each other, wrestling the veneral (*sic*) disease or attending any demoralizing game or place unless in the capacity of Peace officer . . . or by carrying or firing a Gun except it be in the military service selfe defence or the protection of Property . . . .[41]

Despite all these excluding clauses many Huddersfield people took up membership.

What form of sickness would friendly societies be most often confronted with? It appears that most disbursements were made for long-term and chronic cases, such as rheumatism, bowel disorders, chest complaints and heart disease. Many societies appear to have supported a small number of permanently, almost permanently or seasonally sick members. The same names crop up repeatedly, such as A. Beaumont of Paddock, a member of the Huddersfield Royal Shepherd Sanctuary, who was certified sick in 1837, 1839, 1841, 1842, 1844, and 1846, often for periods of several weeks or months together.[42] At a time when medical science could do little towards relieving chronic illness, friendly societies were valuable institutions. Such cases were normally excluded from the Huddersfield Infirmary, and the payment of a regular benefit went a long way towards keeping a member and his family one step away from the threat of pauperization. But it was the nature of this illness, combined with an aging friendly society membership, resulting in crippling bills for benefits and medical attendance, which proved to be their downfall, and many collapsed towards the end of the century.

The Huddersfield Dispensary and Infirmary

It may seem inappropriate to leave mention of the Dispensary and Infirmary, by far the town's most eminent medical charity, to such a late stage in an account of Huddersfield's health care, but this is intentional. For in so doing, the importance of other systems of medical relief already discussed can perhaps be stressed, the friendly society, the chemist, the local healer and self-dosing, in terms of the numbers making use of them, their cultural and social significance, and their role in treating those not catered for by the Infirmary, the chronic, long-term sick, the incurable.

The Huddersfield General Dispensary began its work in July 1814 in a rented house in Pack Horse Yard, set up ostensibly to commemorate the ending of the Napoleonic Wars. The Wars and their aftermath had resulted in high unemployment, food shortages and acute poverty, and those supporting the Dispensary intended that it should help relieve distress in the town. The nearest hospitals were at Leeds, York and Sheffield, great distances for the sick to travel. Civic pride undoubtedly also played its part. Dispensaries had already been established in Doncaster (1792), Wakefield (1787) and Halifax (1807); the wealthy and influential of Huddersfield were determined not to be left behind in demonstrating their benevolence and civic feelings. The early decades of the nineteenth century were crucial to Huddersfield's development, and the opening of the Dispensary in 1814 fits in closely with the pattern of population growth, civic pride and dynamism, the acquisition of an Improvement Act, the founding of new churches, chapels and schools, the establishment of numerous charitable and cultural societies, and, most important as the source of funding, the enormous expansion of the textile industry.

Just who, then, was responsible for the setting up of the Dispensary? Local doctors played a smaller role than might be imagined, although Dr John Kenworthy Walker was a keen campaigner for its establishment. The

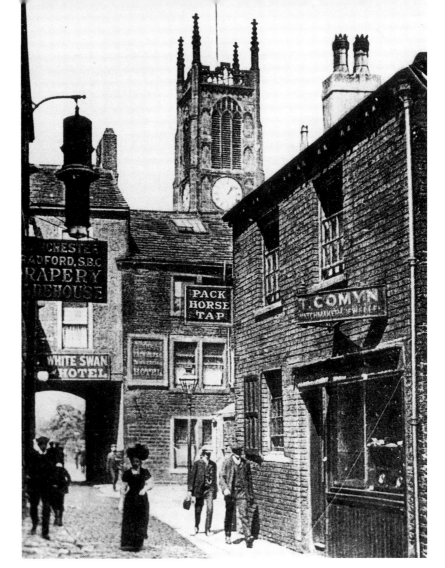

Fig. 23:7 Pack Horse Yard, site of the Huddersfield General Dispensary, established in 1814. (KCS)

charity's founding fathers, officers and committee members were predominantly woollen merchants and manufacturers. The list of those involved reads like a local 'Who's who'; Sir John Ramsden was the charity's first patron, Sir Joseph Radcliffe the first president, and the Firths, Stables, Ridgways, Battyes, Laycocks, Haighs and Brookes were active in financing and management. The Dispensary was funded largely by annual subscriptions of one or two guineas, subscribers obtaining in return the privilege of recommending patients. Donations and benefactions were also important, and lesser sources of income included congregational collections, fines ordered by magistrates, and occasional concerts, bazaars and balls. Local medical men provided their services gratis, attending once or twice a week to examine, prescribe and carry out small surgical operations. A Dispensary post carried great prestige, and no doubt greatly assisted in the building up of a private practice.[43] In addition to the honorary physicians and surgeons, a salaried apothecary or house surgeon was appointed, who did most of the day-to-day work of the charity, functioning as medical attendant, secretary and general manager.

In-patient care was not on offer; patients were either treated at the Dispensary or were visited in their own homes. The charity was to all appearances a resounding success, admitting in the first decade a grand total of 17,579 patients,[44] chiefly victims of epidemic disease. To take just one year, in 1815-16 over 750 of the 1,600 admissions (47 per cent) were infectious disease cases, including 331 cases of smallpox and 246 of scarlatina. Other common admissions were for wasting conditions, respiratory and digestive complaints, eye diseases and rheumatism.[45] Spurred on by the success of the Dispensary, within ten years the committee and medical officers were pressing for the establishment of a purpose-built hospital in Huddersfield, 'for the Reception of a limited Number of In-Patients; more especially for those frequent Accidents arising from the extensive Use of Machinery'.[46] In April 1825 sixteen workmen employed in the erection of the new Independent chapel in Ramsden Street were killed or seriously injured when the platform they were working on collapsed, throwing them to the ground from a height of over fifty feet.[47] Industrial accidents occurred with great regularity, but the horror of the Ramsden Street accident and the numbers involved gave the campaign to establish an infirmary a massive boost. Mr Samuel Clay, a Huddersfield linen draper, entered into the fund-raising effort with particular gusto, raising £3,329 in just one week, a phenomenal amount.[48] Finally, in June 1829 amidst great ceremony the foundation stone of the 'Huddersfield and Upper Agbrigg Infirmary' was laid by Mr John Charles Ramsden, and two years later to the day the building, on the New North Road, opened its doors to the sick of the town.

The scale on which the Infirmary came to operate exceeded all expectations. The grand purpose-built edifice in Grecian Doric style, constructed and fitted out at a final cost of £7,500, required large numbers of medical and nursing staff to cope with the work-load, and cost over £1,500 per annum to run, more than twice the estimate of its founders. Starting out with twenty beds, by 1839 there were thirty-five, and by 1885 eighty-five. In-patient care proved costly, in 1833 calculated at £3 7s. per head compared with a mere 3s. for an out-patient.[49]

Fig. 23:8 Huddersfield Infirmary. (KW)

Admissions rose rapidly, although most patients continued to be seen in the Dispensary, now the out-patients department, or in their own homes, where treatments was offered in a broader range of cases. In 1860-61 some 5,680 out-patients and home-patients received treatment, compared with only 351 in-patients.[50] In some years it appears that around 10 per cent of the population of Huddersfield received some form of treatment by the charity; perhaps only vaccination, tooth drawing or a dose of medicine, or perhaps a more substantial course of treatment.[51] Patients were also admitted from further afield, for example, Brighouse, Holmfirth, Rastrick, Mirfield, and Saddleworth. Even allowing for some statistical acrobatics, and it is clear that figures were presented in their very best light in order to attract support, the Huddersfield Infirmary achieved impressive success rates; in 1870-71 77 per cent of out-patients were 'cured or relieved', the mortality rate was 1.9 per cent.[52] The figures for in-patients, generally more serious cases, fluctuated from year to year, on occasion peaking at 10 per cent, but usually much lower.

Order of the Procession

ON THE

LAYING OF THE FIRST STONE

OF THE

HUDDERSFIELD AND UPPER AGBRIGG

INFIRMARY,

ON MONDAY THE 29th DAY OF JUNE, 1829.

THE Procession will form in the Market-Place, at 11 o'Clock in the Forenoon, and proceed in the following Order, along New-Street, High-Street, Manchester-Street, Upperhead-Row, and Greenside, to the Site; and return along the Halifax Road, Westgate, Kirkgate, Beast-Market, Lowerhead-Row, Castlegate, and King-Street, to the Market-Place.

Constables, and Leeds and Yorkshire Firemen, **Three abreast.**
Music.
The Huddersfield Lodge of Free and Accepted Masons.
MR. OATES, the Architect, with Plans.
Contractors.
High Constable of Upper Agbrigg, and Constable of Huddersfield.

The Vice-President } of the Dinner. }   J. C. RAMSDEN, ESQ. M. P.   { The President { of the Dinner.

Magistrates.
Clergy.
Ministers.
President and Vice-Presidents of the Dispensary.
Treasurer and Secretaries.
Physicians.
Surgeons.
Infirmary and Dispensary Committee.
Subscribers, Inhabitants, and Friends to the Institution, **Four abreast.**
Independent Order of Odd Fellows.
Royal Foresters.
Milton Friendly Society.
And any other Benevolent Society or Club, that may feel disposed to attend.

On arriving at the Ground, the Procession will form as follows, viz. the Clergy, Ministers, and Gentlemen, on the East Side, The Free-Masons on the South, the Independent Order of Odd Fellows, the Royal Foresters, and other Societies on the North Side. The West Side will be reserved for the Ladies.

After the respective Parties have taken their Stations, the Ceremony will commence with singing the following Verses, selected for the occasion.

WHEN, like a stranger on our sphere,
The lowly JESUS wander'd here,
Where'er he went affliction fled,
And sickness rear'd her fainting head.

With bounding steps the halt and lame
To hail their great Deliv'rer came;
The opening ear, the loosen'd tongue,
His precepts heard, his praises sung.

Through paths of loving-kindness led,
Where Jesus triumph'd, we would tread;

To all with willing hands dispense
The crumbs of our benevolence.

Hark! the sweet voice of pity calls
Misfortune to these hallow'd walls;
Here the whole family of woe,
Shall friends, and home, and comfort know.

And Thou, dread Power, whose sov'reign breath
Is health or sickness, life or death;
This destin'd mansion deign to bless;
The cause is thine—O send success.

After which, the VICAR OF HUDDERSFIELD will offer an appropriate Prayer.

THE FIRST STONE WILL THEN BE LAID BY

J. C. RAMSDEN, ESQ. M.P.

After this part of the Ceremony is concluded, the FREE-MASONS will proceed to lay the second Stone with their usual Formalities. After which, will be sung the

NATIONAL ANTHEM.

GOD save great George our King,
Long live our noble King,
  God save the King;
Send him victorious,
Happy and glorious,
Long to reign over us,
  God save the King.

O Lord our God arise,
Scatter his enemies,
  And make them fall;
Confound their politics,
Frustrate their knavish tricks,
On him our hopes we fix;
  God save us all.

Thy choicest gifts in store
On him be pleas'd to pour,
  Long may he reign;
May he defend our laws,
And ever give us cause
To sing with heart and voice
  God save the King.

N. B. Constables will be stationed to prevent the Ground from being occupied by Persons who do not join in the Procession.

MR. BOWER has kindly agreed to form and conduct the Procession.

T. KEMP, PRINTER, NEW STREET, HUDDERSFIELD.

Fig. 23:9 Order of the Procession on the laying of the first stone of the Huddersfield and Upper Agbrigg Infirmary on Monday 29 June, 1829. (WYAS, W)

Abstract of Cash Account from the commencement of the undertaking to June 29, 1832.

RECEIPTS.						PAYMENTS.					

RECEIPTS.

	£.	s.	d.	£	s.	d.
Total donations towards the building, paid up to June 29th, as per printed list	10,114	0	0			
To Interest thereon up to 29th June, 1831	272	5	10			
Transfer from Dispensary Account	73	14	6			
Annual Subscriptions	669	2	0			

DONATIONS, LEGACIES, &c. since June 29, 1831.

	£	s.	d.	£	s.	d.
Miss Hanson's Legacy £500 (Duty £50)	450	0	0			
Thomas Firth, *Toothill*	200	0	0			
Thos. Allen, deceased, per Mrs. B. H. Allen	100	0	0			
Mrs. Middlebrook, (Duty paid by Exors.)	50	0	0			
Balance of Bazaar	49	15	6			
Addition to Subscriptions, (see printed list)	34	17	6			
Frost & Nelson, Donation	31	10	0			
Charles Horsfall, *Liverpool*	20	0	0			
Joseph Schofield, *Rastrick*	15	0	0			
James Spratt, *Hull*	10	10	0			
Joseph Spratt, *London*	10	10	0			
Joshua Riley, do.	10	10	0			
Mrs. C. Rawson, *Halifax*	10	0	0			
Eli Wimpenny, *Holmfirth*	10	0	0			
Philip Bennett, *Wynford*	5	5	0			
John Booth, *Meltham*	5	5	0			
John Jones, *Leeds*	5	0	0			
Joshua Littlewood, *Holmfirth*	5	0	0			
Peace offering in a litigated matter	5	0	0			
John Sutcliffe, *Halifax*	4	5	0			
Edward Parish	4	0	0			
John Dyson, *Honley*	1	1	0			
John Holroyd, *Dalton*	1	1	0			
Friend, per John Newhouse	1	0	0			
W. L. Brook, compensation for assault	1	0	0			
Matthew Hirst	1	0	0			
George Bolland, *Skircoat*	0	10	0			
—— Jarry, *Halifax*	0	10	0			
Isaac Dickinson, *Shelley*	0	10	0	1,043	0	0

CONGREGATIONAL COLLECTIONS.

	£	s.	d.	£	s.	d.
Huddersfield Parish Church	16	14	6			
—— St. Paul's	12	17	6			
—— Trinity	12	4	9	41	16	9
Mirfield Church	10	10	0			
Honley do.	9	11	0			
Woodhouse do.	9	7	6			
Lockwood do.	9	5	0			
Moravians, Mirfield	5	14	2			
Meltham Church	4	10	2			
Longwood do.	3	6	0			
Paddock do.	1	5	0	95	5	7

MISCELLANEOUS.

	£	s.	d.	£	s.	d.
Magistrates, sums paid to them in lieu of Penalties	39	3	5			
Sale of Trusses	3	19	0			
Rev. Mr. Ogilsby for Board of Servant	1	11	6			
Fine, per Mr. Bradbury	1	0	0			
Do. per Mr. Wrigley, *Saddleworth*	0	5	0			
Sale of Engravings	2	5	0			
Mr. Crawshaw, produce of Charity Box	0	10	3			
Mr. John Smith, do.	0	17	0	49	11	2

INTEREST.

	£	s.	d.
From Bankers, on Balance in their hands from June 29th, 1831, to June 29th, 1832	131	12	11
	£12,448	12	0

PAYMENTS.

BUILDING AND FURNISHING.

	£	s.	d.	£	s.	d.
To Joseph Kaye, Mason's Work	3,598	13	1			
— Hepworth and Son, Joiner's do.	1,138	0	0			
— John Newhouse, Plumber's do.	490	10	4			
— T. Clayton, Plasterer's do.	202	10	0			
— J. Crabtree, Slater's do.	153	8	1			
— J. Heaps, Ironmonger's do.	137	9	0			
— J. Lucas, Painter's do.	74	0	0			
— J. Lockwood, Ironmonger	72	15	0			
— J. Oates, Architect	215	15	6			
— J. Nelson, Clerk of the Works	162	0	0			
— Sundries	453	6	3			
— Furnishing	820	2	10	7,518	10	1

HOUSE EXPENDITURE.

	£	s.	d.	£	s.	d.
Drugs and Leeches	247	5	4			
Medical Department, (Trusses, Surgical Instruments, Leather for Plasters, Calico, &c.	20	0	9			
Salaries and Wages	184	10	9			
Flour and Meal	45	19	11½			
Meat	77	11	5½			
Malt and Hops	51	10	1½			
Milk	44	8	7½			
Groceries	35	11	3½			
Eggs	3	11	2			
Coals	35	13	9			
Candles	9	4	3			
Tea and Coffee	13	13	0			
Vegetables	13	12	7			
Petty Expences	4	6	2½			
Printing, Stationery, &c.	52	14	10			
Soap	9	1	7			
Shaving Patients	2	16	0			
Sundries	10	18	9			
Washing and Cleaning	1	11	8			
Wine, Spirits, and Porter	6	13	6			
Water Rent	5	5	0			
	£ 876	0	7			
Deduct for Groceries included in the above Abstract, but not yet paid	18	14	6	857	6	1
Money in Matron's Hands				0	19	6
Dispensary Account				8	8	4
Balance in Banker's Hands, £4000. of which is ordered to be invested on a Mortgage				4,063	8	0
				£12,448	12	0

Fig. 23:10 Abstract of the accounts of the Huddersfield and Upper Agbrigg Infirmary, 1831-32. (WYAS, W)

Although the overall success rate of the charity was good, admissions were limited in a number of ways. Many forms of illness were excluded; 'persons disordered in their senses, subject to epileptic fits, suspected to have the smallpox, measles, itch, or other infectious distemper, having habitual ulcers, syphilis, . . . or those suspected to be in consumption, or in an incurable or dying state', were not to be admitted as in-patients.[53] Admissions were normally regulated by the governors' letters of recommendation and the admissions committee, not by the medical officers, and were strictly controlled according to social criteria. Those too rich or too poor, the middle classes and paupers, were largely excluded (except when the Boards of Guardians subscribed). The charity was basically intended for the 'deserving poor', those who had a role to play in the functioning of the local economy, its purpose 'the speedy return of the workman to his labour, . . .'.[54] While the Infirmary no doubt attracted its fair share of benevolent support, representing altruism and Christian charity, there is little doubt that its overriding purpose was pragmatic, and for the local employer of labour a brilliant solution to the problem of sickness or accidents in his work-force. For a small payment of several guineas a year, he relieved himself from the responsibility of providing medical treatment for his employees, who could be sent with their letter of recommendation to the Infirmary, and from improving the conditions which so frequently were the direct cause of sickness or injury. Accident cases accounted for a high proportion of admissions, many following injury in the workplaces of subscribers. It was not without reason that local manufacturers invested in the 'Joint-Stock bank of Charity'.[55]

Poor Law medical services

The better-off of nineteenth-century Huddersfield had access to a growing corps of professional doctors, as well as to well-tried self-dosing alternatives. The labouring man, meanwhile, had his local healer, chemist's shop, friendly society, or, if lucky enough to obtain a letter of admission, the Infirmary. But what happened to those lacking these possibilities? All too often the very poor had no other resort when taken ill but to turn to the Poor Law. Under this regime they fared badly, although rather better before the imposition of the New Poor Law after 1834, a disaster for northern England and for sick paupers.

Under the Old Poor Law, relief was organized on the basis of local townships, regulated by the overseers of the poor. Medical relief was given on a very small scale (normally accounting for less than 5 per cent of Poor Law expenditure), yet there is evidence to suggest that it was administered in individual cases with some flexibility and generosity, both within and outside of the workhouse. The parish would, in addition to out-relief, pay the medical bills of paupers, or contract doctors would be employed. In 1822 the Mirfield overseers resolved that Messrs Kitson, Parker and Hoyle would take the contract 'in rotation at the sum of Forty Pound pr year'.[56] The most usual cases treated by the Poor Law doctor were broken limbs and other injuries, fevers, children's diseases and chronic ailments of old age. The account books of the overseers list as common items of expenditure, the setting of fractures, bleeding, ointments and salves, pills, charges for doctors visits and for nursing, usually undertaken by poor parish women. Payment for the maintenance of lunatics and childbirth expenses topped the list. As mentioned earlier, overseers employed local healers and made arrangements with friendly societies for medical relief, and a few also paid subscriptions to local dispensaries and infirmaries. The Mirfield overseers even supported a blind boy at the Liverpool School of the Blind, at a cost in 1817 of £12, a vast sum.[57]

Although the total number of people helped was small, considerable sums could be laid out in individual cases, on doctoring and out-relief, and supplements to medical care, food, alcoholic beverages, fuel, nursing attendance, lying-in and funeral expenses. Midwifery expenses would include not only the cost of a surgeon or midwife, but payment of a lump sum to buy clothes and other necessities for the child (a guinea to a married couple, half a guinea to an unmarried mother), grants of extra food, the expenses of churching,[58] and, if the child or mother died, an all too frequent occurrence, funeral expenses. In 1784 the Huddersfield overseers paid 2s. to Dame Tomlinson for delivering Hannah Finsley, 5s. in out-relief, and one week later 1s. 4d. for 'Finsley Child Funeral'. In the same year regular sums were expanded on the Hudson family, almost constant burdens on the poor rate: in May 2s. for a midwife for Nat Hudson's wife Rachel, 9d. for her churching and 3s. 6d. to buy shoes (presumably to present a respectable picture in church) and 7d. for itch salve and brimstone for Nat Hudson, in July 6d. for a Godfrey Bottle [59] for the Hudson baby, in August 5s. to send

Fig. 23:11 William Wilks (1770-1840), honorary surgeon to the Huddersfield Dispensary, and occasional employee of the Poor Law overseers. (WYAS, K)

Nat to the Whitworth doctor, [60] in September 3d. for Rachel to be bled, and so on through the overseers' account book. [61] In 1801 the Mirfield overseers, spent almost £3 on medicines, wine, brandy, and bleeding for a female workhouse inmate, Betty Oates, and in 1817 £9 was paid to Mr William Wilks, surgeon to the Huddersfield Dispensary, 'for attending Mathew Hirst and cutting of (*sic*) his Leg'. [62]

After the passing of the 1834 Poor Law Amendment Act, which reorganized small townships and parishes into large Unions, governed by the Boards of Guardians, the old methods of providing medical relief disappeared. The employment of local healers, the payment of friendly society subscriptions, and instances of individual generosity to the sick were cut at a stroke. The Huddersfield Union, created in 1837 and composed of the parishes of Huddersfield, Almondbury, Kirkburton and Kirkheaton, included thirty-two townships and a population of 100,000, covering a massive 68,640 acres. Any personal contact, such had existed between pauper and overseer under the old Poor Law, was inconceivable. Medical relief became regimented and inflexible.

Most sick paupers continued to be treated in their own homes, perhaps luckily for them, as conditions in the Union workhouses were appalling. The Huddersfield Workhouse was said to be 'wholly unfitted for a residence for the many scores that are continually crowded into it, unless it be that we desire to engender endemic and fatal disease';[63] typhus victims 'lay in overcrowded wards, often for weeks, on bags of straw or shavings crawling with lice, without a change of linen or bed clothes'.[64] In 1857 a special commission reported that the lack of classification in the Huddersfield Workhouse led to 'abandoned women' with diseases of a 'most loathsome character' being mixed up with idiots, young children and lying-in cases.[65] Medical treatment under the new regime was provided by the Poor Law medical officers, often well-qualified and well-meaning men, but badly remunerated and over-worked. Relations between the Guardians and their medical employees were acrimonious, and this led to a rapid turnover of medical officers and a large number of vacancies, and, no doubt as a direct result of this, the occasional appointment of unsuitable and poorly-qualified medical attendants. The pressures on the medical officers meant that treatment was sometimes inadequate, occasionally negligent. In 1858 Mr Roberts, the medical officer for Golcar, refused to attend upon the children of one Rebecca Taylor, and three of her children died of scarlet fever without ever being seen by a medical practitioner. For this Roberts was merely reprimanded by the Guardians.[66]

Parsimony was the most outstanding feature of the New Poor Law; efforts were directed at cost-cutting and keeping the burden of the ratepayer to a minimum. The Guardians refused, despite directives from the Poor Law

Fig. 23:12 Dr William Dean of Slaithwaite, Poor Law surgeon, Friendly Society Medical Officer, police, army and insurance surgeon, and local 'general practitioner' in the mid-nineteenth century. (KCS)

Board in London, to provide better workhouse accommodation (until the opening of the Deanhouse and Crosland Moor Workhouses in 1862 and 1872), to improve medical officers' salaries and conditions, and to treat the very poor, the weak, the old and unfortunate with more humanity. This had a direct effect on how the sick fared. Expenditure provides the best indication of the low priority given to medical relief. As late as 1863 the medical expenses for the Huddersfield Township amounted to only £296; excluding expenses for the maintenance of lunatics this falls to £126, or 1d. per head of the population, and 1.6 per cent of total Poor Law expenditure.[67]

The inhabitants of nineteenth-century Huddersfield were also catered for by various public health services, mental health facilities, and several small-scale charitable enterprises, for example, lying-in charities and missionary societies, which have not been discussed in this chapter. The range of health care options was wider than we might expect. Most people had some choice in determining where, how and by whom they would be treated, although some certainly had more choice than others, medical treatment being dictated more than anything by the ability to pay. This would determine whether a family would employ a physician or a much cheaper surgeon-apothecary, whether a man-midwife or midwife would attend at the birth of a child, whether a friendly society subscription could be afforded, or whether a more costly patented and pre-packaged medicine would be chosen in preference to a simple herbal remedy.

The nineteenth century saw the development in Huddersfield of two channels through which the wealthy classes provided medical relief to the poor – the voluntary Huddersfield Dispensary and Infirmary and the rate-supported Poor Law medical service. These differed from the other forms of medical options which have been considered, in that they were created and controlled by a group, made up chiefly of local manufacturers, for the assistance of another group, of rather groups, the Infirmary for the 'deserving poor', the labouring man who had fallen on hard times, the Poor Law for the destitute. Yet the nineteenth-century expansion of institutional services did not force out or diminish the role of friendly societies, self-dosing or fringe practices. Rather they survived and thrived, bolstered by the possibilities of commercialism. In 1844 it was calculated that 5,905 persons were treated annually by the medical officers of the Dispensary and Infirmary, a substantial slice of the population, but the vast majority would have received only out-patient care. The Poor Law, however, was helping only 1,600 individuals out of the entire Huddersfield Union, 1.47 per cent of the population.[68] Given the high profile of sickness in the lives of Huddersfield's inhabitants, other medical options were necessary to make up the short-fall. Yet the friendly society, the local healer, the quack, the chemist and self-doser were not just significant because they filled a gap; they treated cases shunned by the institutional services, and, more importantly, they represented an independent and vibrant medical culture outside the Infirmary and Poor Law.

Hilary Marland

Biographical Note

Dr Hilary Marland obtained a PhD from the University of Warwick in 1984 with her thesis on medical practice in nineteenth-century Yorkshire, published as *Medicine and society in Wakefield and Huddersfield 1780-1870* (Cambridge University Press, 1987). She is author of *The Doncaster Dispensary 1792-1867. Sickness, Charity and Society* (Doncaster Library Service Occasional Papers, 1989), and, together with Valerie Fildes and Lara Marks, editor of *Women and Children First: International maternal and infant welfare, 1870-1945* (Routledge, 1992). She has also published on the nineteenth-century medical profession, chemists and druggists, and Dutch midwives. Now employed as Research Officer at the Institute for Medical History, Erasmus University Rotterdam, Dr Marland's research interests include the history of preventive medicine in the Netherlands, women medical practitioners, and the history of Dutch midwives 1700-1945. She is currently editing a volume on early modern midwives, *The Art of Midwifery: early modern midwives in Europe*, for the Routledge Wellcome Series on the History of Medicine.

NOTES

1. 'Supplement' to the *Morning Chronicle*, 18 Jan. 1850 in J.T. Ward, *The Factory System* (Newton Abbot, 1970), p.162.

2. Little detail can be given here of each form of medical provision, but for a deeper analysis and full bibliographical references, see Hilary Marland, *Medicine and society in Wakefield and Huddersfield 1780-1870* (Cambridge, 1987).

3. Other causes of death were not given. W(est) Y(orkshire) A(rchive) S(ervice), Kirklees KHT9/1. The Minutes of Proceedings on a Preliminary Inquiry on the Huddersfield Improvement Bill, held February 1848, Evidence of Mr Joshua Hobson, p.8.

4. C. Creighton, *A History of Epidemics in Britain* (2nd ed., 1965, first pub. Cambridge, 1894), vol. II, p.844.

5. The subject of public health will not be covered here, but see Marland, *Medicine and society*, chapt. 2.

6. J. Taylor, MD, 'On the Mode of Origin and Propagation of the Epidemic Cholera, In Huddersfield and the Neighbourhood, in the Autumn of 1849', *Medical Times*, 23 (1851), 256-59, 340-44, 399-402, esp.p.341.

7. D.F.E. Sykes, *Huddersfield and Its Vicinity* (Huddersfield, 1898), pp.307-13.

8. The Taylor family of Whitworth, Lancashire, famed throughout the north of England for their bonesetting and surgical skills, during the eighteenth and nineteenth centuries. See J.L. West, *The Taylors of Lancashire. Bonesetters and Doctors 1750-1890* (Worsley, 1977).

9. See chapts. 7 and 8 of Marland, *Medicine and society*, for the numbers, training, practices and appointments, professional activities, social standing and civic involvement of the Huddersfield medical profession.

10. The operation to remove bladderstones, now known as lithotomy, since the seventeenth century part of the surgeon's repertoire, and one of the first surgical procedures to be carried out on a regular basis.

11. WYAS, Wakefield C500/5/18. 'A Review of the Surgery of the Huddersfield Infirmary for the Last 23 Years. A paper read before the Huddersfield Medical Society, on Dec. 9th, 1896', by John Irving, Honorary Surgeon to the Infirmary, pp.6, 4.

12. Bleeding or blood-letting, using lancets or leeches, was a common therapeutic technique for a whole range of ailments, including fevers, headaches, eye diseases and abdominal conditions. Blood-letting, together with vomiting, purging and sweating, was linked to the belief that sickness marked the build-up in the body of noxious substances; these substances had to be expelled by one or more of these techniques to restore the patient to health. The application of blisters was based on the principle of counter-irritation, that by setting up an inflammatory reaction, the disorder would be decoyed to a safer place. Many self-dosers also made use of these techniques.

13. WYAS, Kirklees KC190/1. J. Woodhead, Netherthong, recipe book, 1818; WYAS, Kirklees Diary: James Hirst, Notable Things of various Subjects, 1836-c.1892.

14. WYAS, Kirklees KC190/1. J. Woodhead, recipe book.

15. A single herb, in effect medicine in its most 'simple' form.

16. *Wakefield Star*, 2 Feb. 1810; *Huddersfield Examiner*, 1 Jan. 1870; *Huddersfield Weekly Examiner*, 26 July 1890.

17. See Hilary Marland, 'The medical activities of mid-nineteenth-century chemists and druggists, with special reference to Wakefield and Huddersfield', *Medical History*, 31 (1987), 415-39.

18. Marland, *Medical History*, 31, p.425.

19. G.W. Tomlinson, *History of Huddersfield (Home Words)*, 1885-1887 (Huddersfield, 1887), p.30.

20. County Borough of Huddersfield. *Official Handbook of Her Majesty's Diamond Jubilee Celebration, June 22nd, 1897* (Huddersfield, 1897), p.198.

21. Sykes, *Huddersfield and Its Vicinity*, pp.404-405.

22. C.P. Hobkirk, *Huddersfield: Its History and Natural History* (2nd ed., London and Huddersfield, 1868), p.10.

23. *Huddersfield Examiner*, 1 May 1852.

24. A.B Granville, *Spas of England. 1: the North* (1841, reprinted Bath, 1971), pp.406-407.

25. Census enumerators' books, Huddersfield Township, 1861.

26. H(uddersfield) L(ocal) H(istory) L(ibrary). A Copy of the Poll. Borough of Huddersfield, 1834.

27. By mid-century a general practitioner generally charged between 5s. and 10s. per visit, a consultant upwards of three guineas. There was enormous variation in the charges of unqualified healers, but it was likely to be in the range of a few shillings, in exceptional cases £1, for an entire treatment. Many operated on a 'no-cure, no pay' basis.

28. 'Quackery in the Manufacturing Districts', *Lancet*, II (1857), 326.

29. M.A. Jagger, *The History of Honley* (Honley, 1914), pp.100-101.

30. J. Sykes, *Slawit in the 'Sixties* (Huddersfield and London, n.d.), pp.127-28.

31. *Halifax and Huddersfield Trade Directory 1899*.

32. *Official Handbook*, p.176.

33. WYAS, Kirklees P/HU. Huddersfield Town Book, 1784-93.

34. WYAS, Kirklees P/M. Township of Mirfield, Overseers Accounts, 1772-1803.

35. WYAS, Kirklees P/M. Overseers Accounts, 1772-1803, 1805-26.

36. Sykes, *Slawit in the 'Sixties*, p.129.

37. *West Riding Herald*, 6 April 1836.

38. *Leeds Mercury*, 1 June 1839.

39. *Abstract of Returns relative to the Expense and Maintenance of the Poor*, P(arliamentary) P(apers) 1803-1804, XIII, 175; 1818, XIX, 82.

40. W. White *Directory of Leeds, Bradford, Huddersfield, Halifax, Wakefield, Dewsbury* (Sheffield, 1866), p.292.

41. WYAS, Kirklees S/TD 5. Prince Albert Lodge of the Ancient Order of Druids, Thurstonland, Sick Rules, 1856-63, pp.5-6.

42. WYAS, Kirklees S/SR14/2, 3/2. Royal Shepherd Sanctuary, No. 99, Huddersfield, Treasurer's Book, 1832-1870, Notices of illness of members.

43. See Hilary Marland, 'Lay and medical conceptions of medical charity during the nineteenth century. The case of the Huddersfield General Dispensary and Infirmary', in *Medicine and Charity before the Welfare State* edited by Jonathan Barry and Colin Jones (London and New York, 1991), pp.149-71.

44. WYAS, Wakefield C500/1/33-44. Annual Report, Huddersfield General Dispensary, 1823-24.

45. WYAS, Wakefield C500/1/33-44. Annual Report, Huddersfield General Dispensory 1815-16.

46. WYAS, Wakefield C500/1/33-44. Annual Report, Huddersfield General Dispensory 1822-23.

47. *Leeds Mercury*, 30 April and 7 May 1825.

48. *Leeds Mercury*, 28 May 1825.

49. WYAS, Wakefield C500/1/33-44. Annual Report Huddersfield Infirmary, 1832-33.

50. WYAS, Wakefield C500/1/33-44. Annual Report Huddersfield Infirmary 1860-61.

51. For details of admissions and rates of cure, see Marland, *Medicine and society*, esp.pp.101-108.

52. WYAS, Wakefield C500/1/33-44. Annual Report Huddersfield Infirmary, 1870-71.

53. HLHL. Rules and Regulations of the Huddersfield and Upper Agbrigg Infirmary, 1834, p.17.

54. WYAS, Wakefield C500/1/33-44. Annual Report Huddersfield Infirmary, 1862-63.

55. WYAS, Wakefield C500/1/33-44. Annual Report Huddersfield Infirmary 1838-39.

56. WYAS, Kirklees P/M. Township of Mirfield Vestry Minute Book, 1758-1834, Meeting of 2 May 1822.

57. WYAS, Kirklees P/M. Township of Mirfield, Overseers Accounts, 1805-26.

58. A service of thanksgiving and cleansing performed usually one month after childbirth.

59. An infant calmative, with a large opium content.

60. See note 8.

61. WYAS, Kirklees P/HU. Huddersfield Town Book, 1784-93.

62. WYAS, Kirklees P/M. Township of Mirfield, Overseers Accounts, 1772-1803, 1805-26.

63. *Leeds Mercury*, 5 Feb. 1848.

64. Public Record Office MH12/15070. Newspaper cuttings enclosed in Huddersfield Correspondence, May to June 1848.

65. WYAS, Kirklees P/HU/m. Minute Book of the Huddersfield Boards of Guardians, vol. 9, 8 May 1857.

66. WYAS, Kirklees P/HU/m. Minute Book of the Huddersfield Board of Guardians, vol. 9, 7 May 1858.

67. WYAS, Kirklees P/HU/cfo. A Statement of the Accounts of the Huddersfield Union, 1861-73. The Huddersfield Township in Account with the Huddersfield Union, for the Year ended March 25th, 1863.

68. *Report from the Select Committee on Medical Poor Relief. Third Report*, PP 1844, IX, 531, Evidence of H.W. Rumsey, App., Schedules 1, 2 and 3.

Changing the Pattern: Everyday Life 1800-1900

JENNIFER STEAD

Everyday life in Britain over the past forty years has, in its essentials, changed very little, but in 1880 people looking back forty years, especially in industrial areas, had good reason to be shocked by the enormous changes, economic and social, which had transformed their lives. The writers of numerous local histories and recollections published in the late nineteenth century described the tough living conditions they endured up to mid-century, when at last trade began to improve, wages rose and food prices lowered. They saw the effects of mains water, drainage and improved hygiene and also the cumulative effects of railways, gas lighting, Factory and Education Acts, efficient law and order provision, co-operative and temperance movements, chapels, mechanics' institutes, clubs and societies, all of which helped to curb the rebellious spirit and to wipe out the old, rough way of life, including many traditional customs and pastimes. These "improving" influences may be divided into those imposed from above by officialdom, and those which sprang from within the ranks of the working class, such as self-help groups, some inspired by a religious and morally improving spirit, others by a humanist one. In this account of change in the Huddersfield district as exhibited in some of the small details of everyday life, the first half of the nineteenth century will be referred to as the early period and the second half as the later period.

Rough Behaviour

'Savage actions and coarse language . . . have given place to more moral conduct and intellectual knowledge', wrote Mrs Jagger of the Huddersfield district in 1914. Other hill and mountain regions had also been 'savage' and 'coarse', but Huddersfield and its moorland hamlets and villages to the south and west seem to have been especially so, having been always isolated from main routes of communication and civilising influences, and never having felt subject to authority. John Wesley's remarks[1] about the extraordinary wildness of Huddersfield people are well known, as are John Pawson's in 1765 describing them as 'heathens, ignorant and wicked to a degree'. In 1825 a new doctor in Bradford wrote that Bradford people were 'little removed above the brute creation', they thought nothing of killing each other, even so 'I have been told they are worse at Halifax and Huddersfield but I think it scarce possible'. Even richer clothiers were crude and rough because they retained the vulgar manners of their low origins.

In 1805 a vigilante group had to be set up in Honley to combat drunkenness and disorder.[2] Hall Bower Sunday School and day school was built in 1814 in an attempt to tame the 'wild, rough youths of the neighbourhood'.[3] In the *Leeds Mercury* of 11 January 1845, a correspondent making a plea for a mechanics' institute at Honley described the working classes there as more than ordinarily debauched; the drunk and disorderly did a great deal of damage at night, and 'vice and immorality prevail to a great degree'.

Strangers to a village would be likely to have stones and sods thrown at them. New residents were attacked and harassed until they won acceptance by showing courage – a submissive attitude brought only scorn. For a youth to go courting a girl in another village, even another part of his own village, was foolhardy and dangerous; he might be assaulted and forced to pay 'pitcher' money, that is dropping coins into his assailants' pitcher for their ale, and if he refused he was met with great violence. In 1875 two Almondbury youths were fined £4 for pitchering a Huddersfield youth who had come courting to Almondbury, and at Smithy Place, Honley, another man was pitchered by being thrown into a sumphole, where he almost suffocated.[4]

There were running battles between villages; at the bull-baitings, held in Thirstin, Honley, up to the 1820s, local gangs regularly fought with those from Skelmanthorpe and Crosland, and Honley people were attacked by the inhabitants of Almondbury on their way to and from, and even in, Almondbury church, while Melthamers were attacked on their way to

Honley. Skelmanthorpe was 'a village in which it was said that a whole man did not exist at that time, having lost fingers, ears, noses. . . , owing to their love of personal warfare'.[5] The men were notorious for their 'lug-biting' and 'shin-poising'. On May Day at Slaithwaite lads from rival villages, such as Golcar and Marsden, would fight each other, stripped to the waist, until unrecognisable. 'The wonder is they did not kill each other, so brutal were the methods adopted.'[6] No wake or feast was thought to be complete unless the men had been involved in personal combat. There is a story that at Longwood Thump 'a father addresses his stalwart son, "Jack, has te foughten?" Jack replies, "Noow, father," and the affectionate parent rejoins, "Kum then, get thee foughten, and let's gwoa whom" '.[7]

Ignorance and superstition

In the early period a great many working people were illiterate and innumerate, largely because from early childhood they would be involved in cloth production, coal-mining or other work, or because their parents were too poor to pay the schoolmaster's fee. Many did not go to Sunday school. The ignorant had to develop *aides-mémoires:* the manager who was at Woodsome Hall about 1815 could not count his sheep so had to memorise all their faces;[8] women had to calculate when to expect their babies by putting a cinder on the mantelpiece as each month passed. The extreme ignorance of many people in the eighteenth century meant they were still susceptible to belief in charms, well-worship, boggarts, fairies and witches, superstitions which persisted strongly until 1800 and beyond. Ordinary mishaps were attributed to the intervention of witches; for example one weaver in 1790 suffered a bad misfortune when a joint of 'hung beef' fell off the beam and broke his warp; he fetched a charm to stop it happening again – this was a bottle of his 'watters' placed in the chimney – and 'as they wasted it would side away t'witch'.[9]

It is easy to dismiss these superstitions as 'quaint' without making the mental effort of entering the ignorant person's mind. Pitch darkness out of doors held dangers both real and imaginary, while in the near-darkness indoors, flickering flames created disturbing moving shadows. Accidents happened, people and animals fell ill and died from no apparent cause. In these circumstances it would seem reasonable to blame an unknown power, and prudent to carry a charm or a piece of 'wiggin' (ash-twig).

Weddings, christenings and funerals

Celebrations such as weddings, childbirth and funerals were attended by much drinking, mirth and matchmaking or 'leetings on'; indeed, funerals could prove to be more rumbustious than weddings. In the early period a birth at Saddleworth was celebrated by 'wetting the baby's head' or 'yed-weshing', which involved much tapping of beer barrels, singing, telling of ghost stories and men and women pairing off in the dark.[10] In Almondbury parish, at weddings it was common for bride and groom to creep separately to and from church by different routes, in their weaving and working aprons, to escape the rough and indecent pranks which were sure be be played.[11] By the end of the century the funeral 'drinking' and 'yed-weshing' had been replaced by a sedate ham tea and a christening tea, and the uproarious wedding 'do' by a formally seated wedding breakfast.

Feasts

In the early period the local feast or wake was the most important time of the year, when family members and ex-residents returned home, relationships were reinforced and new friendships and matches made. These annual feasts[12] included Almondbury Rushbearing, Honley Feast, Saddleworth Wakes, Kirkheaton (Yetton) Rant, Kirkburton 'Trinity Burton', Meltham Bartleby, Slaithwaite 'San Jimis' (St. James) and Longwood Thump. Vast crowds attended and walls were pulled down to accommodate them. The attractions included a circus, menagerie, strolling players, waxworks, mountebanks, games and rides, sports and races, conjurors and scalding-hot porridge eating competitions. Even those who were living at subsistence level in the early period contrived to enjoy the special fare: currant puddings, followed by veal and fruit pies, then roast beef and pickled red cabbage and home-brewed beer; drunkenness was tolerated. In c.1860 the old sports and races, sideshows and theatre in Honley were replaced by travelling fairs, then in 1869 the Feast fields were enclosed. The Feast decayed as education and railways advanced; the crowds, instead of descending on the village, increasingly took seaside excursion trains.[13]

On Honley Feast Sunday from 1825 onwards crowds of Methodists, before going to Honley, would converge on Salem Love Feast at Berry Brow, led by local preachers such as the charismatic 'Little Abe' Lockwood. Both

JUNE 16.06
TEMPERANCE FETE BERRY BROW

Fig. 24:1 Self help played an enormous part in improving lives: Temperance Societies effected a significant reduction in drunkenness. In this Temperance procession at Berry Brow in 1906, several neighbouring villages are represented, the Taylor Hill group being in the middle of the photograph. (Private collection)

the love feast and the temperance movement provided drama in the shape of confessions, conversions, and wringing of the emotions, and had a considerable civilising influence. Temperance was a vitally important self-help movement, for the Beerhouse Act of 1830 had allowed any household to brew and sell beer, and it was calculated only three years later that one in eight of all heads of households in Huddersfield was a drunkard.[14] Most recreations were centred around the public house and most men went there.

Holidays

In the first three decades of the nineteenth century many people's working day was twelve to fourteen hours long, they worked till 2 p.m. or 4 p.m. on Saturdays and were allowed only two half-day holidays in the whole year – the afternoons of Good Friday and Christmas Day.[15] As the century progressed, Factory Acts shortened working hours, and weight of public demand lengthened the local Feast to four days. Eventually, also through public demand, whole days were secured at Christmas, and at Easter and Whitsuntide, when railways offered cheap trips.[16]

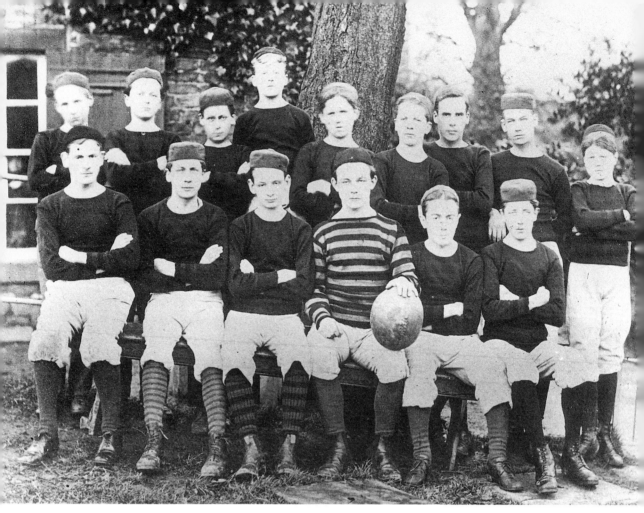

Fig. 24:2 Almondbury Grammar School rugby team in 1878. The brutally rough, unregulated game of football as played for at least 600 years on open field and heath by an unlimited number of players was standardised in 1863 and 1871 by the Football Association and the Rugby Football Union respectively. These set up proper rules, which encouraged the attitude of fair play. At the same time, the rough game of 'lakin' at bad' [bat] was transformed when players adopted the Marylebone Cricket Club rules, which resulted in the encouragement of gentlemanly behaviour. (KCS)

Christmas began to be celebrated nationally in a recognisably 'modern' way from the 1850s, but the Huddersfield district clung to old habits. Here 25 December had not been important, real Christmas was celebrated on Twelfth Night, 6 January, with wassail and Twelfth cake. Even in the 1870s when most people would go a-wassailing (carrying a wessel bob, or evergreen garland) on the 'new' style wassail night, 31 December, people at Holmfirth would still only wassail after dark on 6 January. In earlier years on old Christmas Day, following ancient tradition, there were football games between rival villages across three miles or so of fields and rough country, for example, between Honley and Meltham. Even when nowhere near the ball, men kicked each other ferociously and walls were demolished. The last such game between Almondbury and Farnley Tyas was in 1819.[17] Local writers have left us no clues as to the reasons for its discontinuance; protests of property owners may have played the largest part.

Popular anarchy and public censure

Many societies have traditionally sanctioned periodic role reversal, male/female, master/servant, and allowed limited periods of anarchy, but licensed anarchy was severely reduced in England in the nineteenth century. Old Mischief Night, 30 April, was one of the festivals when mayhem reigned: farm animals were released, swill and weeting (urine) tubs were overturned, windows and doors whitewashed, snecks tied to imprison people indoors, gates and every removable thing stolen and property destroyed. The old and unmarried bore the brunt. The innocent were sometimes blamed; feuds were created which could last a lifetime and revenge could be wreaked with impunity. It continued to the late nineteenth century; Easther wrote in the 1870s that 'a great deal of damage was done formerly . . . Policeman X is now the spoiler of this sport'.[18] Other writers mention that gas-lit streets, mechanics' institutes and evening classes were all factors in its demise.

One way of getting back at a bullying policeman was to pillory him with a 'stang-riding', (such a case happened about 1870)[19] but this 'punishment' was usually reserved for those who were considered to have broken the accepted code of relations between the sexes: adulterers, wife-beaters, husband-beaters or couples courting or marrying with too large an age gap. An effigy of the culprit(s) mounted on a pole (stang) or ladder was paraded by a noisy crowd making 'rough music' by beating pots and pans and chanting a nominy, such as,

> with a ran-ran-ran, an old tin-can,
>
> A women has been paying (thrashing) a man,

and then the effigy was burnt. It was thought that if the stang-riding be performed in three townships it was quite legal and the police could not interfere,[20] but in fact stang-riding was ignored or condoned by the authorities as it was a form of censure for unacceptable behaviour. Documented examples are to be found in Crosland (1786),[21] Honley (1857),[22] Silkstone (1860),[23] Cowcliffe (1874)[24] Lockwood (1876),[25] and also in the 1870s one at Lindley (involving a crowd of 400 people)[26] and several at West Vale;[27] many more went unrecorded.

A less dramatic form of village censure was carried out at night; weeting tubs would be emptied over the culprit's steps, or white lines drawn between the doors of offending couples. Up to 1750, 25 per cent of all brides

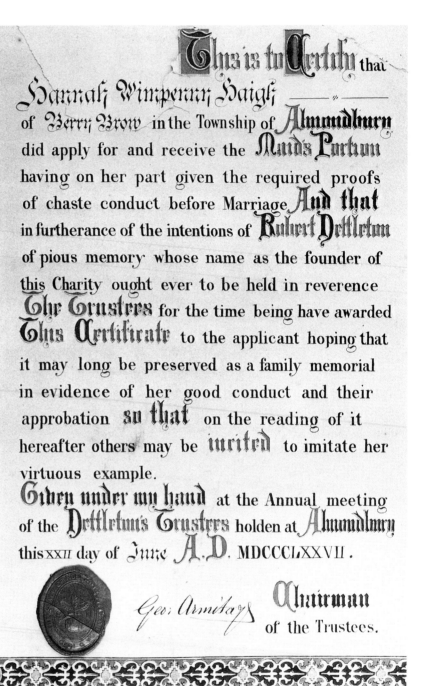

Fig. 24:3 This certificate of chasity plus a small gratuity were awarded to Hannah Haigh in 1877. Part of Robert Nettleton's Charity, 'The Maid's Portion', was shared out between applicants: these were newly-wed women who had not produced a child within forty weeks after marriage. For example at the Trustees meeting at The Woolpack 27 June 1860 when fourteen women attended to present their certificates of marriage and birth of first child, the amount each received was 15/–. Such rewards of virtue were part of an overall effort to reduce the high rates of illegitimacy. (Private collection)

were pregnant, between 1800 and 1850 this rose to 38 per cent.[28] Little shame attached to this, as a promise of marriage was regarded as binding. In an effort to improve matters in the parish of Almondbury, part of the Nettleton Charity, the Maid's Portion, was devoted to rewarding those brides who had been married for nine months without producing a baby. This was but one of the influences which helped to bring about a significant reduction in illegitimate births by the end of the century.

Leisure

Some leisure activities changed radically. In the cottage industry there had been no clear division between labour and leisure; workers had flexible time and could 'lake' (play) if they felt like it, then 'wake' at night, that is work by candlelight to compensate.[29] The weaver was always quick to leave his loom for a bear-baiting, or more often, a bull-baiting, as held, for instance, at Bull Ring Longwood, Quarmby Clough and Moles Head Hill, Golcar.[30] Mastiffs or bulldogs were kept for the purpose.[31] The last bull-baiting on Almondbury Common was at the 1824 Rushbearing; 'the public voice' and legislation put a stop to it.[32] Betting was an addiction, and the weaver would also skip work for a dog-battle or a cock-fight. These sports were never stamped out, because they could be conducted in secret, although regular fines were levied, for example at Paddock, Honley and Meltham in 1856. Other cruelties continued: young animals and birds were tortured or 'spanghewed', while 'rabbit worrying, boring out birds' eyes to make them sing better, and eating live rats for a show (are) . . . still lingering among us'.[33]

Following hounds, foot-racing, whippet-racing, pigeon-flying and knurr and spell were acceptable leisure activities.[34] 'Lakin at bad' (bat) , a primitive form of cricket,[35] and the fierce unregulated football played, even in the dark, in any rough meadow after the mill 'loosed' by up to fifty men, each playing for himself, were gradually turned into regulated games, played on Saturdays by skilled teams.[36] The Football Association drew up rules in 1863, which induced principles of fair play; by the 1870s cricket was inspiring gentlemanly behaviour. Dangerous games continued to be suppressed by police, for example in the 1870s the police issued edicts against 'pig', a boys' game played with a long piece of wood pointed at both ends.[37]

Evening merry-meetings in cottages were called 'laikin-neets' (playing nights) and these survived to the 1890s. At the decorous, tea-drinking kind, recitations, songs and games were enjoyed, some of these being survivals of medieval courtship games. The other sort of laikin-neet was attended by 't'pubby lot' who drank ale, played cards, clog-danced, and gambled on everything. 'Rough? Some o't'roughest games you ever saw'.[38] A very interesting game called Ringing Adam Bells, survived at these laikin-neets into the 1880s (and more innocently as a child's and party game it survived much longer) . It was played by adults only, in firelight, once the door had been locked and the blinds drawn. The women, seated in a circle on the floor, facing a circle of men, sang these lines:

> Ringing t'owd Adam Bells
> Kitlins in t'clough
> Who can see my bare arse

at which the women rolled over backwards and the men finished the verse,

> Me, fair enough.

The game was once played openly at weddings in indecent and uproarious fashion, but at a Newsome wedding in 1844 only women took part; it is clear that by this date men were beginning to be discouraged from joining in when it was played at a public function, on account of a new sense of decency.[39]

Music

Music was an improving influence and played a large part in people's lives.[40] From the eighteenth century there were bands, orchestras, choirs and handbell ringers. In the early period people would walk long distances to practices after working all day, for example from Penistone to Honley and back in the dark.[41] Local rhymes and songs reinforced local identities.[42] Huddersfield was renowned for the singing of very long songs, especially hunting songs.[43] By about 1840 there were at least three public houses in Huddersfield town designated as 'singing halls', the forerunners of music-hall; these were the Argyle in Manchester Road (later the Greyhound), the Cambridge Hall and the Navigation Hotel, Aspley.[44] There was 'music in every corner . . . beautiful voices can be heard side by side with the rattle of the loom'. Massive outdoor local sings drew crowds from surrounding towns.[45] Huddersfield Choral Society was founded at the Plough Inn in 1836. Other 'improving' leisure activities involved clubs and societies, and many places such as Slaithwaite, Farnley Tyas and Honley had a book club or lending library offering serious literature and philosophy, though these libraries were feared by some members of the middle class because it was thought that they engendered seditious thoughts.[46]

Homes and sanitation

Weavers' cottages in the early period were devoid of comfort. Furniture was simple, for there was little room left when weaving, spinning, winding and (the abominably stinking and messy) warping and lecking were performed at home. People were born, slept and died in the loomgate or jennygate. Beds were sometimes placed on tops of looms or across stair steps, or were fastened to the wall by day, and called 'shut-up', or 'turn-up' beds.[47] In the period between 1800 and 1830 in a weaver's cottage of only two rooms there would probably have been two looms, a spinning wheel, a winding wheel, a turn-up bed, a chaff or straw mattress, a delft rack, a table, two or three simple chairs or buffets, an ark, a cradle, a bread reel for drying oatcake, a bakestone, an iron set pot, and a stone sink which sometimes had drainage to the outside. The chamber would be open to the stone slates, walls would be whitewashed, or coloured ochre or blue.[48]

By the 1850s, however, millworkers were aspiring to better things. James Mellor of Crosland Moor, who earned £1 for a sixty-one-hour week at a Huddersfield mill in 1851, was able to buy 'a good second-hand piano' for his little boy.[49] By the 1880s most working class homes had gas light, running water and drainage, and a great many had a carpet or rugs, horsehair-padded chairs, a mahogany sideboard and soft furnishings.

In the early period, cottages were lit by dim rushlights which lasted only one hour, candles, which were expensive and used sparingly, whale-oil lamps or firelight. 'Cannel-coil' (candle-coal), carbonised roots dug from fissures in the moors, provided free, clear lighting (and heat).[50]

Sanitation was primitive; even in the 1840s there was no proper drainage, and slop water thrown out by cottagers collected in stinking slimy open sewers called 'sower-oils' or 't'sink'.[51] Communal privies in folds or yards were described as 'vile'. At the edge of the stone flags inside these privies was a drop to the ashpit and at 'more or less inconvenient distances' from this edge were two or three poles stretching from side wall to side wall, used as 'pearks' or perches for both poultry and humans alike, and with no privacy whatsoever. Nor was the introduction of a long 'seat' with holes of various sizes much improvement.[52] At the end of the nineteenth century, even after the introduction of better earth closets and water closets, old habits died hard. In the hills of the Colne Valley in the 1890s at least one farmer's family was still using 't'back o't'booise' (cow stall); the women when outside would lift their skirts and urinate where they stood,[53] both of which habits had once been preferable to using a communal yard privy.

Water supplies in the early period were unreliable especially in summer; the fountain at Newsome, for instance, would dry to a trickle and hundreds of pitchers would be lined up waiting to be filled.[54] Although houses in Huddersfield were supplied with tap water in the 1840s, outlying districts did not receive a supply until the 1880s, for example Honley in 1881.[55] Piped water cut off yet another communal activity, however, since meeting, queueing and gossiping at the well and fetching water for neighbours had formed no small part of village life, reinforcing its public nature. Personal cleanliness improved, though, as the burdens of washday lessened, and especially so after the heavy soap taxes were removed in 1853;[56] nevertheless, some old people in the 1870s continued to wash themselves in urine.[57] The death rate fell gradually, but as late as 1886 the Newsome vicar was still burying twice as many children as elderly people. He attributed the 'improvement' he had seen in the previous ten to fifteen years 'to the greater wisdom of the parents in clothing the arms of their children, as well as the chest'. Epidemics and consumption carried off most.[58] At this date the percentage of people over the age of sixty had not yet risen back to the level it stood at in 1720; this was to take another thirty years.[59]

Housework

As late as 1856 half the woollen industry was still carried on in cottages by out-workers.[60] Even in the 1880s hand-loom weavers were needed at Skelmanthorpe for weaving short runs of fancy waistcoatings. Women were fully employed in clothmaking, but they also managed to rear infants, cook, brew, clean, churn, milk, wash, and sew. A Slaithwaite woman said 'I had to rock and weave at the same time by fastening the cradle band to the sley board of my loom, working all day, and had to do the home work, baking and washing, at nights'.[61] In hand-loom weavers' cottages, cleaning started when weaving stopped, at 4 p.m. on Saturdays, when the 'fruzzins' (hairs off wool) and sand would be swept up, the floor scoured and perhaps a 'list' or 'yeld' (heald) rug put down[62] (made from the spare cloth or thrum of a woven piece which was the weaver's perk, until the practice was stopped in the 1870s).[63] Sunday was looked forward to as the only quiet day, when clog-irons would not be grinding on sanded stone floors. After the flagged floors were scrubbed with urine and hot water to remove the grease,[64] scouring stone was rubbed on, either ochre 'ruddle', or 'pottery-mould' or 'idle-back' which could be white or blue. White idle-back was used on the hearthstone. Patterns could be made with two colours, for example a continous circular one was originally intended to keep away evil influences.[65]

In the early period, clothes which had been washed were smoothed in the big box mangle at the manglehouse in each village. Mangles were costly and villagers would club together to buy one, sometimes along with a gophering iron, to set up some poor widow so that she could earn a few shillings.[66] The manglehouse was a regular 'callin-oil' or gossip-shop; in Berry Brow the manglehouse was in Waingate, and at Lockwood it was at the Green.[67] Men would often help to turn the heavy wheel. Other expensive equipment such as loom gears and brewing vessels were constantly lent and borrowed, as were daily necessities such as yeast, weeting and fire.

Dress and personal appearance

Up to about 1850 men and master shared the same speech, and the master's manner of dress was little better than his workman's, even though he was much better off. In the 1830s even the Sunday wear of nine-tenths of the people had been ill-fitting fustian and clogs, the women wearing a shawl pinned over their heads in chapel in lieu of bonnets, except in one enterprising congregation where each Sunday a different woman wore the communal bonnet.[68] On weekdays the men often went unshaved. Many people were undersized through poor nutrition, often with faces disfigured by smallpox and missing teeth.[69] Men and women took snuff, or smoked long clay pipes, the women 'holding the pipe between the teeth like a sweet morsel'.[70] Men's clogs had thick iron plates on the sides as well as iron 'skellets' on the soles, very useful for 'poising' (kicking) shins. Cleaned clogs or clean working trousers were regarded by the males with scorn and invited a roughing up. By 1880, however, Board Schools and severe schoolmasters such as John Mellor at Slaithwaite had effected a total reversal, since cleaned clogs were now the rule. By this date only colliers wore the old heavy clogs, and on a Sunday most men wore boots.[71] Men now wore broadcloth and tweed, while women sported a variety of materials made up by the local dressmaker into a semblance of the current fashion.

Diet

Until the 1860s diet was extremely simple, based mainly on oatmeal. However, in the eighteenth century, before large scale enclosures, weavers had enjoyed a better diet, a broth or stew being the usual weekday dinner. But in the 1760s, food prices started to rise, and by the 1780s the clothing districts were in distress. For the next seventy years there were long periods when families had to subsist on porridge three times a day, eked out with oatcake, potatoes, a little bacon and blue milk (skimmed), and with what greenstuff they could get, usually nettles and 'fat hen' (chenopodium album).[72] There was mint tea to drink; tea, white bread and meat were saved for Sundays only. The porridge 'dip' was milk, buttermilk, skimmed or blue milk, whey, beer, saim (lard) or treacle. Porridge in the early period was eaten straight out of a communal bowl or pan with the eaters standing round the table.[73] Variations could be made by adding onions or nettles and bacon fat. 'Wattergruel' was thin porridge, and starving weavers subsisted on this, especially in the 'dreadful barley time' of the 1790s, 'the great panic' of 1826 and the 'hungry forties'. Drinks, which in the early period had been traditional northern ones of beer, water, milk, buttermilk, skim milk, whey and herbal drinks, gave way after mid-century to beer and tea. The universal oatcake, eaten by masters as well as men, gave way to wheat bread. The salted 'hung beef' which clothiers had once relied on to last through the winter was gradually abandoned as fresh meat became more affordable. Likewise farmers in the Scammonden Valley no longer had to buy barrels of salt herrings to last the winter.[74] The sharing and charitable giving of offal at pig-killing time also died out as the opportunities for keeping pigs diminished; so ended another form of communal feasting, along with the 'payscalding' or pea feast, the quilting feast, and the 'harvest home' which was discouraged because it was too rowdy, and replaced with the church harvest festival.[75]

Cast-iron ovens

The introduction of the cast-iron oven caused a significant change in food habits. Up to about 1820 there was perhaps only one oven in each neighbourhood, as at Newsome where the oven belonged to Dame Eastwood, who sold bread to her neighbours. After the Napoleonic wars foundries which were no longer making cannon began to produce cast-iron ranges with fireside ovens, cheap enough for even the working class to buy in the 1820s and by 1850 most working class houses had one. Until the repeal of the Corn Laws in 1846, however, only a modicum of baking can have been done. But then gradually began what Peter Brears has described as 'a golden age of home baking'.[76] Compressed yeast, cheaper sugar, jam and dried fruit

Fig. 24:4 Most people had no oven until the 1820s; from this time, cast iron ranges with ovens and water boilers began to alter domestic life radically. They made possible a new level of hygiene and comfort and, after the repeal of the Corn Laws in 1846, facilitated 'a golden age of baking' (Peter Brears). The cast iron range was yet another 'improvement' which served as a means of standardising people's lives. (Drawing by Nick Stead).

appeared in the 1840s and reliable baking powder in 1850. Women whose cooking had been done only on the open fire, bakestone or griddle, now found their repertoire enormously increased; besides meat and vegetables they were able to bake pies, tarts, bread, cakes, biscuits and puddings, and hospitality became lavish at all times, not just during wakes week or Christmas. These mass-produced cast-iron ovens could stand as a metaphor for nineteenth-century industrialisation and improvement: the ordinary man now enjoying the new freedoms of, and at the same time in the thrall of, the uniformly cast boxes of efficiency and standardisation, decently black and gleaming, standing at the very heart of family life. The old independent habits and free behaviour were being forced into a regulated mould which in turn created new opportunities.

At the end of the period, after decades of improvements, Huddersfield people were indeed less savage and coarse. Even the 'terrible roughness of their speech' was modified, with the barbaric-sounding gutturals in their dialect softening to consonants: for instance peh became peff (cough), druhhen became drukken and druffen (drunken), sloughen became slokken and sluffen (satiate); words like Haigh, Keighley, tough, trough, laugh, enough, changed similarly. But the dialect, even though it was still 'drated' (drawled), had lost little of its 'raciness, copiousness and vigour' and its speakers had not lost all of their old character, they were still 'not exactly what would be termed a polite people'.[77] It remained true that even 'if we are slow of speech, we are swift to wrath, and quick to resent an injury'. Some continued to 'act in their own defence without the help of law'.[78] Many were still hostile to visitors[79] and cold to 'comers-in', to inquisitive people or to those offering sympathy: 'We are silently determined not to be trifled with ... we are apt to hide our feelings either beneath rude speech or silence'.[80] Fierce scrubbing and cleaning was still often a substitute for soft feelings.[81] Even women kissing the bride at a wedding were scorned, 'Sitha, sitha, they're kussin' one another, the maungy things'.[82] There were few soft words. Proposals of marriage were still abrupt on the lines of 'Thee and me'll get wed', even in the late nineteenth century.[83] It was still considered unmanly to raise one's hat to a superior.

D.F.E. Sykes's *History of Huddersfield* ends with a typical high Victorian eulogy to the staggering improvements made throughout the nineteenth century, 'the story of the rise and progress of this district is an almost unbroken record of victory joined to victory'. As an example of the improvement in crime rates, he cites the number of prosecutions in 1869, which was 598 out of a population of 70,000, whereas in 1896 the number had dropped to only 252, in a population of 105,000. Also 'the sports of the people have changed, and changed for the better. The theatre and music-hall have supplanted the prize ring and the cockpit. Football and cricket are the games of rich and poor alike'.[84] The only regrets of Sykes and the other local writers were the increasing pollution of air and rivers, the people's increasing self-indulgence and love of comfort (for example they would no longer walk ten miles to a music practice or a preaching), the reading of trash instead of good literature, but above all the loss of simplicity, genuineness and individuality. 'There is less of that sturdy independence now, and less originality. We are all woven by one pattern now.'[85] Sykes's words might be applied with even more truth today.

Jennifer Stead

Biographical Note

Jennifer Stead holds an M.A. in Fine Art and formerly lectured in art history at Bradford College of Art. She now writes on local and social history, specialising in food history. She was a co-founder and is a co-editor of *Old West Riding* magazine. Publications include *Food and Cooking in 18th Century Britain (English Heritage, 1985)*, and contributions to *Food and Society Series*, editor C. Anne Wilson, (Edinburgh University Press): *Banquetting Stuffe: The Fare and Social Background of the Tudor and Stuart Banquet* (1990); *Traditional Food East and West of the Pennines* (1991); *Waste Not Want Not: Food Preservation from Early Times to the Present Day* (1991); *Food for the Community* (1993).

NOTES:

1. John Wesley's words may be found in Chapter Nine by John A. Hargreaves.

2. *The Journal of Dr John Simpson of Bradford, 1825* (Bradford, 1981), pp.11, 19, 28, 30, 74. Mary A. Jagger, *The History of Honley* (Huddersfield, 1914), pp.93, 34, 4.

3. Revd Stuart W. Roebuck, *Chapel Folk, the Story of the First 175 years, Hall Bower Sunday School* (1989), p.14.

4. Revd Alfred Easther, *A Glossary of the Dialect of Almondbury and Huddersfield* (1883), p.102.

5. Jagger, *Honley*, pp.122, 188, 79; Mary A. Jagger, 'Some account of the Parish Church of St. Mary's, Honley', *Yorkshire Notes and Queries*, II (1890), pp.200, 234; Revd Joseph Hughes, *The History of the Township of Meltham* (Huddersfield, 1866), p.13.

6. John Sugden, *Slaithwaite Notes of the Past and Present* third edition, enlarged (Manchester and London, 1905), pp.7, 182; John Sykes, *Slawit in the 'Sixties: Reminiscences of the Moral, Social and Industrial Life of Slaithwaite and District In and About the Year 1860* (Huddersfield and London, 1926), pp.68, 112.

7. Easther, *Glossary*, p.49.

8. Easther, *Glossary*, p.137.

9. Easther, *Glossary*, pp.148-149; Jagger, *Honley*, pp.118-120; Ammon Wrigley, *Saddleworth Superstitions*, (Oldham, 1909), pp.20-30; Sugden, *Slaithwaite Notes*, pp.24, 25; Sykes, *Slawit*, p.9.

10. Joseph Bradbury, *Saddleworth Sketches*, (Oldham, 1871), p.176.

11. Jagger, *Honley*, p.136.

12. *See also* Chapter Four by E.J. Law.

13. Jagger, *Honley*, p.123; Sykes, *Slawit*, pp.63-69; Sugden, *Slaithwaite Notes*, pp.150, 186.

14. Janet Burhouse, 'Increase of drunkenness in Huddersfield', *Old West Riding* 5 no 2 (Winter 1985), p.34.

15. 'Local Notes and Queries', *Leeds Mercury Weekly Supplement*, 22 December 1888.

16. *Leeds Mercury Weekly Supplement*, 16 August 1890.

17. Easther, *Glossary*, pp.xvii, 142, 145, xix.

18. Jagger, *Honley*, pp.42, 128; Easther, *Glossary*, p.87; Wrigley, *Saddleworth Superstitions*, p.41.

19. Walter E. Haigh, *A New Glossary of the Dialect of the Huddersfield District* (Oxford, London, 1928), p.118.

20. Jagger, *Honley*, p.136; Easther, *Glossary*, p.129; Wrigley, *Saddleworth Superstitions*, p. 33; Bradbury, *Saddleworth Sketches*, p.179.

21. Almondbury Parish Registers, marriages 1786.

22. Easther, *Glossary*, p.129.

23. Revd Joseph F. Prince, *The History and Topography of the Parish of Silkstone* (Penistone, 1922), p.92.

24. *Parkin's Family Almanack* (Chronological history of Huddersfield and neighbourhood compiled by Allan Parkin) (1874), part 33, p.2.

25. Brian Clarke, *The History of Lockwood and North Crosland* (Lockwood, 1980), p.41.

26. West Yorkshire Archive Service; Wakefield. Huddersfield Borough Police Occurrence Book, 25 August 1873.

27. J.H. Priestley, 'The Illustrated Diary of Mr W.H. Stott', *Transactions of the Halifax Antiquarian Society* (1955), p.88.

28. Leonore Davidoff, 'The Family in Britain', in *Cambridge Social History of Britain, 1750-1950*, edited by F.M.L. Thompson, vol 2, (1990), p.91.

29. Easther, *Glossary*, p.144; Sykes, *Slawit*, p.159.

30. D.F.E. Sykes, *The History of Huddersfield and its Vicinity* (Huddersfield, 1898), pp.257-58; Wrigley, *Saddleworth Superstitions*, p.45.

31. Jagger, *Honley*, pp.149, 302.

32. Easther, *Glossary*, p.xv.

33. Easther, *Glossary*, pp.125, xvi; Sugden, *Slaithwaite Notes*, p.61.

34. Jagger, *Honley*, pp.155-56; Sugden, *Slaithwaite Notes*, p. 61.

35. Easther, *Glossary*, p.7.

36. Sykes, *Slawit*, p.159; Mary A. Jagger, *The Early Reminiscences of Mrs Jagger* (Honley, 1934), p.21.

37. Easther, *Glossary*, pp.7, 101.

38. Jennifer Stead, 'A Note on Laikin-neets', *Old West Riding* 1 no. 1 (Spring 1981), p.23.

39. Jennifer Stead, 'Ringing Adam Bells, a Yorkshire game discovered', *Old West Riding* 1 no. 1 (Spring 1981), p.5; 1 no. 2 (Autumn 1981) pp.34-36.

40. A detailed account of music in Huddersfield occurs in Chapter Twenty-five by David Russell.

41. Y(orkshire) A(rchaeological) S(ociety), MS 1156, letter 23 June 1848; Jagger, *Honley*, p.140.

42. 'An Invitation to Queen Victoria to Visit the Village of Holme, 1847,' *Old West Riding* 1 no. 1 Spring 1981), pp.37-38.

43. *From Village to Town: A Series of Random Reminiscences of Batley During the Last 30 Years* (Batley, 1882), p.69.

44. *The Huddersfield Examiner* 28 April 1921.

45. Jagger, *Honley*, p.142; Jagger, *YN & Q,* 237.

46. Jagger, *Reminiscences*, p.8; Sugden, *Slaithwaite Notes*, p.128.

47. Revd Thomas Lewthwaite, *Home Words, Newsome Parish Magazine*, (Huddersfield, December 1884); Sugden, *Slaithwaite Notes*, p. 212.

48. Peter Brears, *Traditional Food in Yorkshire* (Edinburgh, 1987), pp.6, 7, 197-202; *From Village to Town*, pp.73-75.

49.   YAS, MS 1156, letter 22 October 1851.

50.   Easther, *Glossary*, p.76; Corney Crake, 'The Humble Homes of Sixty Years Ago', *Huddersfield Cuttings*, p.86 Huddersfield Local History Library; Hughes, *Meltham*, p.2.

51.   D.F.E. Sykes, *The Life of James Henry Firth: Temperance Worker* (Huddersfield 1897), pp.29-30; Jagger, *Honley*, p.61; Corney Crake, *Huddersfield Cuttings*, p. 87; Lewthwaite, *Home Words*, (March 1886); D.L. Clarkson, 'An Outbreak of Cholera at Paddock in 1859', *Old West Riding* 7 no. 1 (Spring 1987), p.27; Alfred Taylor, *The History of Wilshaw*, second edition, (1961), p.13.

52.   Corney Crake, *Huddersfield Cuttings*, p.87.

53.   Oral communication, Scapegoat Hill, 1981.

54.   Lewthwaite, *Home Words* (September 1886).

55.   Jagger, *Honley*, p.169.

56.   Jagger, *Reminiscences*, p.19.

57.   Easther, *Glossary*, p.146; Jennifer Stead, 'The Uses of Urine', *Old West Riding* 1 no. 2 (Autumn 1981), p.13.

58.   Lewthwaite, *Home Words* (April-June 1886).

59.   Peter Laslett, 'The Welfare State: As old as English History', lecture, Yorkshire Archaeological Society, 25 March 1981.

60.   D. Elliston Allen, *British Tastes* (1968), p.159.

61.   Sugden, *Slaithwaite Notes*, p.92.

62.   Corney Crake, *Huddersfield Cuttings*, p.86.

63.   Easther, *Glossary*, p.139.

64.   Corney Crake, *Huddersfield Cuttings*, p.86.

65.   Jagger, *Honley*, p.100; Peter Brears, *North Country Folk Art* (Edinburgh, 1989), p.138.

66.   *Leeds Mercury Weekly Supplement*, 13 November 1886.

67.   Clarke, *Lockwood*, p.132.

68.   Jagger, *Honley*, pp.114-15; Jagger, *Reminiscences*, p.15; Easther, *Glossary*, p.80.

69.   Jagger, *Reminiscences*, p.17; YAS, MS 1156, letter 10 November 1847, letter 22 October 1851.

70.   Sugden, *Slaithwaite Notes*, p.73.

71.   *Leeds Mercury Weekly Supplement*, 22 June 1889.

72.   Easther, *Glossary*, p.44.

73.   Bradbury, *Saddleworth Sketches*, p.185.

74.   Peter Brears, *Traditional Food*, p.116.

75. Wrigley, *Saddleworth Superstitions*, p.40; Easther, *Glossary*, pp.98, 106; Brears, *Traditional Food*, p.3; 'Rural Life around Huddersfield', *Huddersfield Cuttings (Huddersfield Examiner*, 21 August 1937), p.33.

76. Brears, *Traditional Food*, pp. 50-53, 86.

77. Easther, *Glossary*, pp.x, 89.

78. Jagger, *Honley*, pp.91-93.

79. Easther, *Glossary*, p.89; W.A. Hirst, 'Yorkshire Reminiscences', *Huddersfield Cuttings* p.141 (*Huddersfield Examiner*, 31 May 1931).

80. Jagger, *Honley*, p.93.

81. Sugden, *Slaithwaite Notes*, p.76.

82. Easther, *Glossary*, p.84.

83. Oral communication.

84. Sykes, *Huddersfield and its Vicinity*, pp.433, 437, 438.

85. Sykes, *Huddersfield and its Vicinity*, p.267.

CHAPTER 25

Music in Huddersfield, c.1820-1914

DAVE RUSSELL

T he West Riding textile district was much vaunted as a musical centre in the nineteenth century and the Huddersfield area was undoubtedly one of the most musical places within this most musical of regions. Indeed, in terms of the number of performing musical organisations per head of population, Huddersfield and its environs formed one of the most intensely musical communities in Victorian England. A music journalist claimed in 1908 that:

> The casual visitor to Huddersfield would hardly imagine that he was amongst some of the greatest music lovers in the country. There is no festival here, no Hallé orchestra, and no Richter or Henry Wood. But, in an unpretentious way, the people of Huddersfield give probably more time to music than do those of any town of a similar size in England.[1]

Before exploring the patterns of this vigorous local musical life it is necessary to clarify the scope, both musical and geographical, of this study. The town of Huddersfield, while a major musical centre in its own right, stood at the centre of a far wider area, much noted for the richness of its musical culture. Considerable elements of the town's musical activity, and some of its reputation, depended upon the skills and enthusiasm of those in neighbouring communities. Therefore, while every attempt has been made to place Huddersfield at the core of this chapter, historical accuracy demands regular excursions a little further afield and particularly into the Colne and Holme valleys.

The problem of geography, however, is insignificant in comparison with the difficulties of focus presented by the sheer volume and variety of local musical life. Focusing simply on what might be termed amateur musical societies — choral societies, brass bands, orchestras and so forth — the town of Huddersfield alone produced at least thirty such bodies between 1820 and 1914, while the Holme and Colne valleys together produced approximately another sixty.[2] Local churches and chapels played a major role in the provision of music and the training of musicians. Concert life too, was varied, ranging as it did from the philanthropic concerts, such as those organised by local notables in 1852, aimed at elevating the 'common people' through the 'sacred art' of music, to the rather more fashionable events connected to the 1881 festival which accompanied the opening of the town hall.[3]

At the same time, Huddersfield supported a music-hall-cum-singing-room industry from the mid-nineteenth century, a number of public houses providing music and entertainment in their 'saloons' and 'concert rooms' from at least the 1840s. From the late nineteenth century, the town was served by a number of larger halls, ranging from the relatively simple Rowley's Empire, run in the 1880s and 1890s by J.W. 'Over' Rowley, (so nicknamed because of the somersault that accompanied one of his songs) a leading national music-hall performer in the late nineteenth century, to the two rather more sumptuous variety palaces, the Hippodrome and the Palace, opened in 1905 and 1909 respectively.[4] A local music service industry also flourished in a number of guises, stimulated above all by the strength of domestic music-making. A directory published in 1899, recorded fourteen 'music and musical instrument dealers' within a few miles of the town centre, by late twentieth century standards an impressive number to serve 95,000 people.[5]

This rich musical life promoted many interesting individual institutions and careers worthy of study. Clearly, it is utterly impossible to do justice to such varied activity and a relatively specific core has to be found. It is the amateur musical culture of bands, choirs and orchestras that has been selected for detailed treatment here. Some elements of this history are already reasonably well-known, through, for example, R.A. Edwards's detailed study of the Huddersfield Choral Society, *And the Glory*. Nevertheless, a general account of this element of musical life is valuable, for it sheds much useful light on the relationship between music and society, as well as illustrating the central role that leisure activity held in the lives of many Victorians and Edwardians. This chapter focuses on the factors underpinning the origins of amateur musical life in the eighteenth and early nineteenth centuries, then investigates the major forms of musical organisation in turn, before considering the importance of music to the local community. Throughout, the emphasis is on the *social* rather more than the musical history of these bodies.

Contemporary observers put forward a variety of, often rather fanciful, theories to explain the highly developed local musical traditions, especially choral singing. They emphasised such elements as the hilliness of the local terrain, which supposedly developed lung-power for singers, and on the vowel sounds peculiar to the local dialects, which were regarded by some as an aid to clear articulation.[6] It is more fruitful, however, to search for explanation in the social and economic realities of local life. Mono-causal explanation of nineteenth century musical aptitude and interest is not possible; rather, an inter-relationship of several factors operating in the later eighteenth and early nineteenth centuries generated a climate propitious to musical endeavour. Of undoubted significance was the influence of religion and especially Methodism, a powerful local presence, as is shown elsewhere in this volume. The great stress placed by Methodists on music (sometimes in ways antagonistic to the desires of John Wesley) is well known.[7] Certainly, it would be wrong to assume, as sometimes has been done, that Methodists absolutely dominated local musical life. In his *And the Glory* Edwards is correct to stand out against the rather simplified popular perceptions of eighteenth and nineteenth century musical development which would have us see, for example, the early Huddersfield choral singers as, in his words, 'untutored, non-conformist millworkers'; he notes the presence of many Anglicans in their number. Similarly, in the mid-nineteenth century, the Roman Catholic St. Patrick's church became one of the most celebrated musical centres in the town.[8] However, although musical enthusiasm was not confined to Nonconformists, and Methodists in particular, their great importance lay both in their general encouragement of music, and in the fact that they drove others, especially in the Church of England, to place equal emphasis upon the musical elements of worship, or risk losing a sizable section of their congregation. As one worried commentator noted, albeit with a little of the exaggeration he disclaimed: 'it is not rashness to assert that for one who has been drawn away from the established church by preaching, ten have been induced by music'.[9]

A second key influence was the role of individual members of the local élite in encouraging and supporting music amongst the working classes. Although this has sometimes been exaggerated, both by contemporaries and more recent commentators, as though no popular creative activity could possibly take place without élite intervention, there is no denying the significant level of assistance given to musical ventures amongst the less affluent element of the local population by some individuals. To give an example from a later period, the Brook family of Meltham Mills, enthusiastic philanthropists on a number of fronts, gave important financial help to Meltham Mills Brass Band, supplying £390 between 1872 and 1883 by doubling the prize money gained at one contest per year at which the band won first prize.[10] Motives for such generosity comprised a mixture, varying in proportion from individual to individual, of genuine desire for the spread of musical education and the belief, so common in the period, that music was a particularly potent vehicle for the inculcation of morality and political quiescence. A celebration of northern choral singing written in the 1830s claimed that: 'sentiments are awakened which make them love their families and their homes; their wages are not squandered in intemperance; and they become happier as well as better'.[11]

The development of musical life was further assisted, at least in the late eighteenth and early nineteenth centuries, by the relatively flexible work patterns of many workers, especially in the textile trade, who still maintained sufficient control over their working environment to allow for the development of work routines which incorporated time for rehearsal, concerts and so forth. Finally, the intense local community pride so typical of Huddersfield, and of the textile district as a whole, led to both a search for excellence and a determination to match the efforts of 'rival' towns. This continued throughout the period to 1914 and beyond, well exemplified by Huddersfield's decision to launch a music 'festival' in 1856 in honour of local favourite, Mrs Sunderland, who had been 'snubbed' by the organisers of the Bradford music festival.[12] The relationship between music and local pride and patriotism will be considered in some detail at the end of the this chapter.

By the late eighteenth century a dense network of clubs and groupings had emerged in the Huddersfield area. Nearly all were anonymous, for there was little need for nomenclature in a society where opportunity for public performance, and thus the need for publicity, was limited. Little hard evidence is available relating to the social base of these organisations, but it seems reasonable to suggest, on the basis of evidence from neighbouring towns, that they were composed for the most part of domestic outworkers, artisans and tradesmen, groups which would be characterised later in the century as the upper working and the lower middle classes, with perhaps a leaven from rather higher in the social scale. Most clubs included both singers and instrumentalists, their repertoire drawn largely from the current stock of glees, hymns, oratorio, especially *Messiah*, and, in some cases, operatic overtures.[13]

In the late nineteenth century, a number of writers recorded important reminiscences of this musical culture. Interviewed in 1889 for the *Magazine of Music*, octogenarian William Blackburn recalled the leading local clubs:

> The most important of these were at Almondbury, Mirfield, Deighton, Kirkheaton and Dewsbury, between which societies there was a regular interchange of courtesies, members of each club or band frequently walking distances of from two to eight miles after work hours.[14]

Writing in John Spencer Curwen's *Music at the Queen's Accession* in 1897, Fred Brook of Shelley recalled how 'working people would sometimes meet at a given house and sing glees, hymns and songs, accompanied by fiddle, flute, piccolo and bass'. Another contributor, recording conversations with his grandfather, concentrated on the hardwork and self-sacrifice required, expensive printed music being hand copied and bound in brown paper, 'and most carefully guarded and used as long as the paper would hang together. . . . It was no uncommon thing for a person to sit up all night copying'.[15] There is undoubtedly a little rosy nostalgia here, aimed at a late Victorian public removed from the necessity of copying, or 'pricking' out as it was known locally, by the development of a cheap printed music industry, but it is hard not to be impressed by the undoubted level of commitment. Many, probably most, of these players and singers also performed together in a variety of religious and quasi-religious settings, in choirs, in the church and chapel bands that were so important before the spread of the organ from the early and mid-nineteenth century, and at the 'sitting-ups', the Sunday school anniversaries which were such noted annual musical occasions. Here, singers and players from all denominations would come together to perform. This tradition was kept alive through the 'sings', the community singing for charity, that became a marked feature of local musical life in the late nineteenth century (and which continued until the late twentieth century in some local areas).[16]

It is from this configuration that many of the formally organised musical societies began to emerge in the 1820s and 1830s. Various segments of these local clubs began to coalesce into such bodies as the Huddersfield Philharmonic, founded around 1820, the Huddersfield Glee Club (1827), the Huddersfield Friendly Musical Society (1832) and, of course, the Huddersfield Choral Society (1836).[17] Paucity of records from this period makes it hard to pin down the exact motives which led to the foundation of a more formal type of organisation, but a number of possibilities present themselves. Perhaps the most likely explanation stems from the response of musicians to the rapid social and economic changes of the early nineteenth century. The period saw greatly increased opportunity for public performance. An expanding urban population, the desire of the middle classes for respectable, improving recreation, the increase in the number of individuals and institutions – millowners, temperance bodies, Sunday schools and so forth – all looking for musical events to dignify or jollify their outings and meetings, all helped increase the demand for public music-making. If musicians were to benefit from this and extract the maximum opportunity to perform, it was clearly sensible to abandon anonymity and develop clear, public forms of organisation, so that 'customers' knew exactly who and what they were dealing with.

Conversely, while the process of formalisation is to an extent explicable in terms of reaction to the 'positive' aspects of urbanisation and industrialisation, for some musicians, especially less affluent ones in trades directly affected by technological change and new working habits, it might have been a response to rather more negative elements. There is not space here to discuss the impact of industrialisation and urbanisation on the working class, and it has to be remembered that the experience of different occupational groups varied quite strikingly. Nevertheless, many local textile workers will have experienced some of the wage-cutting, longer hours and dislocation of working practices that were such a feature of the period from 1815 to 1850. It may well be, therefore, that for some formal organisation, with its rules, fines and regular patterns of rehearsal and performance, were all mechanisms for maintaining contact, discipline and finance during difficult times.[18]

The choral society was, for the most part, the most common outcome of this process of formalisation and the choral tradition was to form a crucial component of local nineteenth-century musical culture. Initially, choral societies tended to be fairly small, rather club-like bodies, but they took on an ever higher public profile as the century progressed, tailoring their efforts to various types of public performance. From 1820, 'in or about the year' that the first formal body, the Huddersfield Philharmonic was founded, until the outbreak of the First World War, at least fifteen choral societies had been founded merely within a three-mile radius of the town centre, and this number is almost certainly an underestimate. If the radius is extended to five miles to take in the Colne and Holme valleys to the south, villages such as Kirkheaton to the east and more substantial neighbouring towns such as Elland and Brighouse to the north, the number rises to approximately fifty. Obviously the membership of many of these choirs overlapped to an extent, and doubtless some choirs were fairly short-lived, but the number is striking. There were broadly three types of choral groups in nineteenth century Britain. The first might be termed oratorio choirs, those skilful enough – and, given Victorian taste, large enough – to tackle the major works in this musical field. Most early Huddersfield choral societies performed, sometimes in full but more often in selection, such central works as *Messiah*, *The Creation*, and *Elijah*, and throughout the period, most choirs worked quite happily on certain areas of the oratorio repertory. The Huddersfield Choral Society, however, was undoubtedly the leading local choir of this type, certainly by about 1860, performing the fullest range of works during the period under study. There is not space to develop a study of its repertoire here, but it clearly reflected the major trends in choral performance in this country. There is some evidence that the choir would have liked to have been a little more 'experimental', but were unwilling to risk financial loss by offering the public more than a minimum of new works. Secretary John Eagleton noted in 1896 that 'unfortunately the public stayed away in such large numbers when a new work was performed that the society lost an enormous amount of money'.[19]

The second grouping might best be referred to as cantata choirs. Mixed voice choirs usually of between sixty and one hundred voices, their typical concert would combine one of the many cantatas of the period – Gaul's

Holy City (1882), Sterndale Bennett's *May Queen* (1858) and Sullivan's *Golden Legend* (1886) were particular favourites – with vocal and/or instrumental selections. Third, although often overlapping with the cantata choirs, came the mixed and male voice competitive choirs which grew in number from the late nineteenth century, stimulated by the growth of the choral contest from the 1880s and 1890s. These choirs specialised in glees and partsongs, including those of Bantock and Elgar, both of whose vocal music was an important part of what many musicologists refer to as the 'English musical renaissance' of the late Victorian and Edwardian period. Probably the most successful competitive choir in the area, until its abandonment of the contesting arena due to rising costs in 1905, was the Huddersfield Glee and Madrigal Society. Originally founded in 1875 by Ben Stocks, choirmaster of the Brunswick Street Methodist New Connexion Chapel, merely to compete at a single event in Manchester, it remained together to become a nationally regarded choir.[20] Many of its members were, like Stocks, also members of the Choral Society and leading figures in various church and chapel choirs, a further reminder of the intensity that so many of these singers brought to their chosen social activity. Although not strictly a 'choral society', it is also worth noting here that the amateur operatic society became an increasingly common feature of musical life from around the turn of the century. Many of these bodies appear to have originated in church and chapel institutes and similar social centres, illustrative of the relative loosening of High Victorian morality by this stage.

While serving as a central element of local musical life, the choral society was at the same time arguably an important force for social integration. First of all, it brought together a broad spectrum of social classes, ranging from the skilled working class to the upper ranks of the middle class. (The poor were largely excluded from this, as so many areas of organised leisure activity, by lack of money and lack of access to the sponsoring institutions). In the mid-1890s, for example, the Huddersfield Choral Society drew almost equally from the skilled working, the lower middle and upper middle classes.[21] Admittedly, the Huddersfield Choral, with over 300 members at this time, was big enough to allow for the avoidance of social mixing with any other group that people felt 'undesirable', and it is also likely that the smaller choirs, in which proximity with one's fellow members was more difficult to avoid, attracted far fewer members from the local élite. Nevertheless, the fact that in 1895, Almondbury weaver Sam Shaw could stand alongside solicitor E.J. Woodhead amongst the Choral Society basses, serves as a valuable corrective to more simplistic notions of class-division within Victorian and Edwardian leisure.

At the same time, choral music also brought together individuals from a variety of religious backgrounds. Certainly, some choirs maintained a fairly clear denominational identity. Golcar Baptist Choir, a much respected late Victorian mixed-voiced choir under the baton of Richard Stead, provides an obvious example. However, the bigger choirs were often essentially amalgams of the best local church and chapel choristers, thus allowing for a type of rank and file ecumenicalism, not always encouraged by religious leaders.

Choral singing also became an increasingly important social outlet for women as the century progressed. The early societies were undoubtedly male dominated, although important soloists like Mrs Sunderland were enormously fêted. In 1837, only eight of the Huddersfield Choral Society's fifty-four members were women; by 1895, they represented a clear majority, comprising 187 of the 330 members.[22] It is not easy to disentangle the musical from the social forces underpinning this important change. Certainly from the 1840s, composers, led by Mendelssohn, showed an increased preference for the contralto over the male alto and this obviously benefited women. However, it is equally the case that the influx of women singers illustrates, especially amongst the middle classes, an increased desire for access to respectable public forms of recreation.

Whether or not their passage into the choirs represents a form of social emancipation for women, however, is debatable. Of crucial importance here is the fact that from early in the twentieth century, there is plentiful evidence that middle class males were less inclined to show an active interest in 'serious music' either as performer or spectator. For example, drawing from evidence in adjacent towns, the Huddersfield sources being too thin, in 1895, approximately 40 per cent of the male members of the Leeds Philharmonic Choral Society were drawn from employers and the professional and managerial classes. By 1909, this figure had fallen to about 25 per cent. Similarly, in nearby Bradford, there is clear evidence that middle class males formed a decreasing element of the audience at the local subscription concerts.[23] It would be surprising if similar trends were not experienced locally. It is perhaps the case that while women's arrival in the choral society initially represented a significant breaching of a male space, this was far less the case by about 1906. Women by this stage were predominating in a leisure pursuit that was losing favour with the key status-setting group, the middle class male. At the very least, though, a growing number of women, especially from the middle classes, were able to enjoy an 'acceptable' form of public recreation and thus expand their leisure-time horizons.

The other principal feature of amateur musical life was, of course, the brass band. The very first formally organised, named wind bands began to appear in the Huddersfield area, as they did in many other parts of Britain, around 1820. (Before the 1840s and early 1850s most bands played a combination of brass and reed instruments, so the term 'brass band' is technically inappropriate for this early period and is used here for convenience only). While many early bandsmen grew up in the informal club-based musical culture already described, the linkage between this activity and banding is less clear-cut than that with choral music. There were certainly other routes into banding. In particular, it is probable that some local bandsmen received initial training in the militia and volunteer bands that were established during the wars with France between 1793 and 1815.[24]

Inevitably, given the great pride in individual bands that so typifies the band movement, much effort has been dedicated to discovering the identity of the "first" band. In the final analysis it is a fairly hopeless quest. First, many bands existed anonymously, as a loosely organised village or town band, from late in the eighteenth century and this really nullifies the search. At the same time, the scarcity of records makes the recording of band activity much before the 1850s a very hazardous pastime. The safest statement in the Huddersfield context is that the area saw a number of bands emerging in the second and third decades of the century. A reed band is believed to have existed in Slaithwaite by 1819, Holme Band dates from 1820, again initially a reed band which changed to brass in 1837, while Kirkburton Old was founded in 1821.[25] Over the period between 1820 and 1914 some thirty-five bands came into existence within five miles of the town centre. Once again, scarcity of records makes exact delineation of the overall growth of banding difficult, but there appears to have been two broad periods of growth. The first was in the 1840s and 1850s when a combination of slightly improved standards of living for some, the development of a related family of brass instruments and the beginnings of a network of contesting, made banding a serious leisure-time proposition. The second period came in the 1880s and 1890s encouraged by, amongst other factors, a further rise in living standards, increased free time for certain industrial groups and skilful marketing by the brass band service industries. Although bands often attracted supporters from the middle classes, the playing membership throughout the period was drawn almost exclusively from the ranks of the skilled and semi-skilled working class; they also remained resolutely male organisations until the 1940s and 1950s.

The *town* of Huddersfield was never to produce a brass band of real distinction. The 'Huddersfield' bands which featured so successfully in national competition – Linthwaite, Holme and above all, Meltham Mills, under John Gladney winners of a Belle Vue championship hat-trick in the three years from 1876 to 1878, were in fact drawn from the industrial villages in the surrounding area.[26] In general, the top-flight brass bands were very much the product of such places, benefiting from the local ties of community and the shared workplace experience of many members, crucial when arranging rehearsal and performance schedules. One of the most striking

Fig. 25:1 Meltham Mills Brass Band.
(D. Rawlinson)

features of the band movement has always been the role of the family as an agent of musical socialisation and education, and family links were especially important in the smaller village bands. At one stage in the history of Holme Band, for example, when bad trade led to Joseph Clough and his five sons leaving the band, his younger brother rescued it by joining along with his six sons. At the same time, at least until the improvement in transport opportunities in the late nineteenth century, the workers in such communities had far fewer alternatives in terms of commercially provided leisure. Theatre, circus and the public house singing room must have acted as something of a counterbalance to the development of banding within the town of Huddersfield itself.

All this is not to suggest that there were no town bands. Huddersfield Band, playing Wegel's overture to *The Swiss Family*, appeared at the prestigious Hull contest of 1856, an event attracting 14,000 people, although little is known of this band's subsequent history.[27] Most of the town's bands appear to have been founded in the later nineteenth century. Their number included the Huddersfield Borough, Catholic, Fire Brigade, Friendly and Trades and Princess Street Mission Bands. Interestingly, as these names suggest, most of them were connected with some form of voluntary society, a common starting point for bands in the urban setting, providing the focus and organisation otherwise denied. The Huddersfield Military Band, founded in 1892, also featured strongly in local musical life in the late nineteenth and early twentieth centuries. They gained their title not from any connection with the army or volunteer force but because they adopted a combination of reed and brass instruments normally associated with army bands. They were possibly the best of the Huddersfield town bands, good enough to play at the Greenhead Park band concerts on a number of occasions. The popularity of these concerts from the 1890s onwards, and the quality of the bands that performed there, illustrates well that while top-flight bands may not have flourished in the town, there was nevertheless a clear appetite for their music.[28]

The brass band was in certain senses the most important public musical institution in the area throughout this period. It fulfilled numerous functions, playing at the head of all manner of processions, providing background music at feasts and flower shows, acting as a dance band, performing at concerts as well as in many, although not all cases, taking part

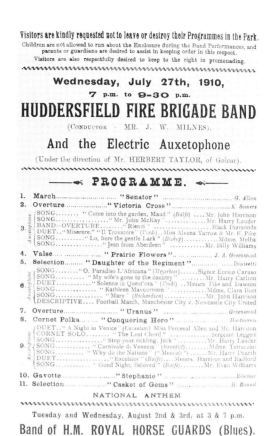

Wednesday, July 27th, 1910,

7 p.m. to 9-30 p.m.

HUDDERSFIELD FIRE BRIGADE BAND

(Conductor - MR. J. W. MILNES).

And the Electric Auxetophone

(Under the direction of Mr. HERBERT TAYLOR, of Golcar).

⟶ PROGRAMME. ⟵

1. March.............................. "Senator" .... G. Allan
2. Overture ...."Victoria Cross".......................... K. Somers
3. *(Auxetophone)*
   - SONG........ "Come into the garden, Maud" (Balfe) ....Mr. John Harrison
   - SONG...................."Mr. John McKay" ....Mr. Harry Lauder
   - BAND—OVERTURE........ "Rienzi" ....Black Diamonds
   - DUET.."Miserere." "Il Trovatore" (Verdi) ..Miss Alvena Yarrow & Mr. E. Pike
   - SONG........."Lo, here the gentle Lark" (Bishop)..........Mdme. Melba
   - SONG................"Jean from Aberdeen " ....Mr. Billy Williams
4. Valse..... .... "Prairie Flowers"... .... J. A. Greenwood
5. Selection......... "Daughter of the Regiment"............. .....Donizetti
6. *(Auxetophone)*
   - SONG........"O, Paradiso L'Africana" (Meyerbeer)......Signor Enrico Caruso
   - SONG........."My wife's gone to the country " ....Mr. Harry Carlton
   - DUET............"Solenne in Quest'ora" (Verdi) ..Messrs Pike and Dawson
   - SONG............ "Kathleen Mavourneen" ....Mdme. Clara Butt
   - SONG.............. "Mary" (Richardson) ....Mr. John Harrison
   - DESCRIPTIVE.... Football Match, Manchester City v. Newcastle City United
7. Overture...................... "Uranus" ....Greenwood
8. Cornet Polka........ "Conquering Hero" ....Hartmann
9. *(Auxetophone)*
   - DUET.."A Night in Venice" (Lucantini) Miss Perceval Allen and Mr. Harrison
   - CORNET SOLO........ "The Lost Chord" ....Sergeant Leggett
   - SONG................"Stop your tickling, Jock "..........Mr. Harry Lauder
   - SONG............ " Carnivale di Venezia " (Benedict)........Mdme. Tetrazzini
   - SONG.......... " Why do the Nations " (" Messiah ")......Mr. Harry Dearth
   - DUET............." Excelsior " (Balfe)....Messrs. Harrison and Radford
   - SONG........... ' Good Night, Beloved " (Balfe)........Mr. Evan Williams
10. Gavotte......... ...."Stephanie " ....Rimmer
11. Selection...... ...."Casket of Gems " ....H. Round

NATIONAL ANTHEM

Tuesday and Wednesday, August 2nd & 3rd, at 3 & 7 p.m.

Band of H.M. ROYAL HORSE GUARDS (Blues).

Fig. 25:2 Greenhead Park concert programme, 1910. (KCS)

in contests. As a result of this wide range of engagements their repertoire was broad indeed, encompassing, to name only some major forms, polkas, contemporary musical comedy, hymns and operatic selections. They played an important part in the musical education of the area, often providing audiences with their first experience, albeit often in truncated and heavily rearranged form, of many pieces both 'serious' and 'light', to use two rather unsatisfactory terms. Linthwaite Band's popularisation of Wagner in the late 1870s, via the 'Bayreuth' selection arranged by their conductor, ex power-loom weaver Edwin Swift, provides a notable example of the former.[29]

The brass band was the best known instrumental ensemble to flourish in the local community, but it was not, as is often assumed, the only one. Huddersfield, and its environs, was also an important centre for handbell ringing. This activity was initially associated with the church, but the ringing of secular pieces by teams of ten to twelve performers seems to have become a fairly established musical pursuit for working men, at least in the industrial districts of Yorkshire and Lancashire, from the mid-nineteenth century.[30] Little is yet known of the early ringing in the Huddersfield area, but in the late nineteenth and early twentieth century a surge of interest in the activity saw the establishment of at least fourteen teams in a six-mile radius of the town. Huddersfield and district emerged as one of the major centres of ringing in Yorkshire and thus in the country as a whole, a Huddersfield and district team winning the annual Belle Vue ringing championship every year between 1898 and 1912.[31] Much contemporary evidence implies that the majority of players were drawn from the working classes, although some undoubtedly were small businessmen and tradesmen; Thomas Cartwright, for example, described on his death in 1914 as 'one of the finest ringers in the district', ran a small painting and decorating business.[32] Like brass bands, they played a wide-ranging variety of music, although French and Italian opera seemed particularly favoured in the contest arena.

Crosland Moor United, founded in 1890, was probably the finest English handbell team of the later Victorian and Edwardian period. Under the conductorship of Albert Townend, a local violinist and music teacher, they recorded a hat trick of wins at the Belle Vue competition between 1901 and 1903, and then, having stood down for a year in accordance with competition regulations, repeated this achievement in the years 1905 to 1907.[33] In August

Fig. 25:3 Crosland Moor "United" hand bell ringers. (KCS)

1911 they set off on a lengthy tour of Australia and New Zealand, a remarkable travel opportunity for this period. The Edwardian period saw a number of musical tours to the colonies, partially designed to forge a sense of imperial unity between colonists and 'Motherland'; this tour appears to have been essentially commercial in aim, although in certain towns the presence of significant numbers of Huddersfield émigrés allowed for some very specific displays of local pride within the context of Empire. This was well illustrated when, billed as the Huddersfield Bell Ringers, Crosland Moor played their opening concert in Dunedin, with the event advertised by a poster in the claret and gold of Huddersfield Northern Union Rugby Club, with a rugby ball at the centre. Significantly, Crosland Moor were not the only local ringers deemed good enough for international exposure; Almondbury undertook two tours of Canada and the United States in the early years of the twentieth century.[34]

The region also supported a number of amateur orchestras. There had been a significant local tradition of orchestral playing in the late eighteenth and early nineteenth century but until about the 1860s, local orchestras tended to be adjuncts of choral societies, rather than freestanding bodies. The Huddersfield Choral Society admittedly made a point of allowing its orchestral members a certain autonomy; in 1856 the committee agreed that every rehearsal should open with an instrumental piece and that the May and August meetings would be dedicated purely to orchestral performance.[35] From the later nineteenth century, possibly because these type of arrangements were becoming less frequent, and especially from the 1880s, the number of amateur orchestras began to grow quite rapidly. Probably the first 'free-standing' orchestra in Huddersfield was the Huddersfield Philharmonic, founded c.1862 by Unitarian minister J.G. Thomas as the Fitzwilliam Street Philharmonic Society. (It took on its new name in 1871).[36] Even this body seems to have drawn quite heavily on members of the Choral Society orchestra. Over the period to the end of the century, at least four other orchestras came into existence within a five-mile radius of the town centre, with several others in a further five-mile belt.

It is harder to pin down the class base of the orchestras than of the brass bands and choral societies, and indeed, it may well have varied from orchestra to orchestra. It is probable that the majority were from the lower middle class and 'upwards', music being perceived as an eminently suitable 'rational' recreation for this group. Nevertheless, working men were also drawn into the orchestral world, encouraged to some degree by the spread of school violin lessons from about the turn of the century. Under schemes set up and partially financed by instrument manufacturers, schools allowed children to buy their instruments by hire-purchase. However, it was not always possible for them to find or afford tuition on leaving, and many instrumentalists settled instead for the brass band movement.[37] Unlike banding and handbell ringing, orchestral playing did provide opportunities for women performers, although these were limited. In 1888, Harriet Thomas, leader of the Huddersfield Philharmonic and daughter of its founder, was the orchestra's only woman player; by 1912 the Slaithwaite Philharmonic could boast four women performers, but they represented only a very small proportion of the total membership.[38]

The orchestral repertoire varied according to the institution, but concert performances usually included a Haydn symphony, an overture, or possibly two, from early to middle nineteenth century Italian or French opera, a waltz or other lighter piece, combined with an instrumental solo and very often some vocal works performed by a guest singer. At the very end of the period, opportunities arose for contesting, and here Slaithwaite Philharmonic, under Arthur Armitage, was extremely successful, winning first prizes in the orchestral sections at the Midland Music Festival in 1912 and 1913, the Blackpool Festival in the same years, and the Morecambe Festival in 1913. Although it has to be said that for these events this amateur orchestra was toughened by the addition of a number of professional players, there can be no doubt that contesting of this type pushed the best orchestras into a more demanding repertoire. Slaithwaite, comfortably the best of the local orchestras by this time, had to come to terms with, amongst other pieces, Wagner's *Meistersingers* overture, Mozart's G minor Symphony and Schubert's *Unfinished* Symphony.[39]

There may appear to be a certain 'whiggishness' about some of the preceding narrative, a rather 'onward and upward' tone, depicting the amateur musicians of Huddersfield and district moving from a rather primitive type of musical culture to an ever more sophisticated one. This implied notion of 'progress' is a dangerous one if pushed too far. In a certain sense, a trajectory of progress can be plotted; by 1914 institutions and individuals could very often perform to a technical level beyond that of their predecessors, while at the same time purveying a far broader repertoire. However, general concepts of progress are misleading if they lead to the assumption that certain forms of music and music-making are inherently 'better' than others. There were undoubted losses involved for the rank and file players over the period, especially in regard to control of the repertoire. In its early period, for example, if the practice of the Huddersfield Choral Society was in any way typical, members could choose which pieces they wanted to sing, and could make critical remarks afterwards. This was occasionally abused; Luke Liversedge was threatened with expulsion from the Huddersfield Choral in 1864 unless a full apology followed his 'insults' to the conductor, R.S. Burton.[40]

By the later years of the century, although many choirs maintained a broad democracy via elections of key committees and sometimes conductors, members were likely to have the choice of music dictated to them by their conductor or music committee, and opportunity for discussion and criticism amongst the rank and file was far more limited. This was, of course, partly a function of the increasing control by professional musicians over choral

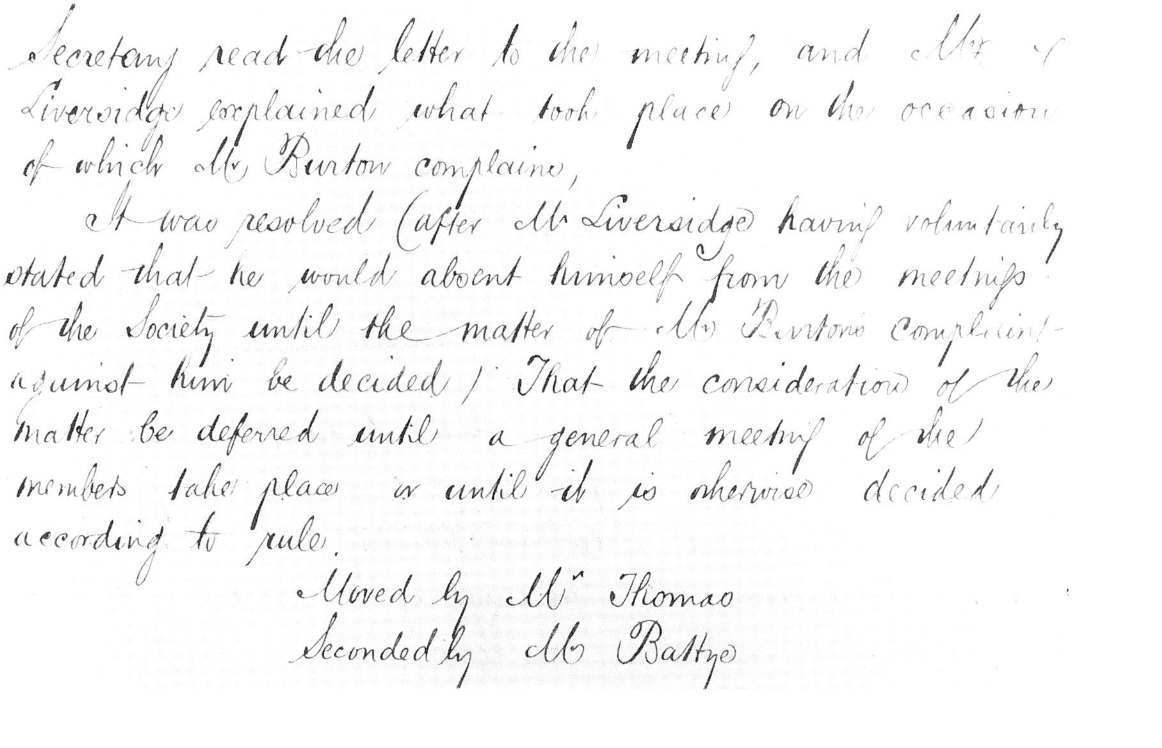

Fig. 25:4 Huddersfield Choral Society Minutes, 8 December 1864. (WYAS, K)

Secretary read the letter to the meeting, and Mr Liversidge explained what took place on the occasion of which Mr Burton complains,

It was resolved (after Mr Liversidge having voluntarily stated that he would absent himself from the meetings of the Society until the matter of Mr Burton's complaint against him be decided) That the consideration of the matter be deferred until a general meeting of the members take place or until it is otherwise decided according to rule.

Moved by Mr Thomas
Seconded by Mr Battye

Fig. 25:5 Sir Henry Coward. (KCS)

music, particularly in high status organisations like the Choral Society. It is inconceivable that as eminent a choral trainer as Henry Coward, who was appointed as conductor in 1901, would have tolerated open and free discussion of his methods. Similarly, in the brass band field, some control was lost as a result of the progressive abandonment from the later decades of the nineteenth century of the 'own choice' test piece (pieces selected by the bands themselves) in favour of test pieces imposed by contest organisers. This policy probably helped raise standards by forcing bands to master a wider variety of pieces, but not all bandsmen would have been in total agreement with it.[41]

On a more general level, it is also important to appreciate that from the early years of the twentieth century, there were signs that musical organisations of most types (amateur operatic societies appear to have been an exception) were occupying a less central position within local society. Choral societies were particularly troubled, experiencing both a fall in public support and in recruitment of male singers. Even brass band commentators expressed some concern over the recruitment of younger players. 'Can anyone account for the apathy of the younger generation against becoming bandsmen?', lamented the Yorkshire correspondent of the *British Bandsman* in 1910, referring specifically to the Huddersfield district.[42] Certainly, the problems experienced by bands before 1914 were minimal compared with those which awaited in subsequent decades and it should also be acknowledged that correspondents of this type were prone to complain and pass judgment, often on the flimsiest of evidence. Nevertheless, the *Bandsman* contributor was not alone in expressing these worries. The growth of alternative leisure pursuits, especially sport and the cinema, were cited, probably with some justification, by all types of musical organisation as a root cause of their problems. For the choral society specifically, the beginnings of a decline in levels of church membership coupled with the development of a popular recreational taste, placing slightly less emphasis on the 'respectable' and the 'improving', caused a further set of problems. The first signs of the stemming of the flow of recruits to their main nurseries, the church and chapel choirs, and the fact that significant sections of the population wanted rather different musical fare, began the long but definite process which saw the choral society increasingly cut adrift from the mainstream of popular culture.

In many ways, however, this bleaker view moves the focus beyond 1914. There can be no denying that the popular musical society played a key role in local society throughout the nineteenth and early twentieth centuries and helped shape the experience and attitudes of both performers and audience. For the members of the local musical community, apart from the artistic 'remuneration', there were also numerous social and economic benefits. At the most basic but crucially important level, there existed the pleasures of companionship with those sharing similar aims and interests, often combined with the opportunity for travel. The diary of Maggie Woodhead, a teenage member of Slaithwaite Philharmonic, recording a long but rich day in Birmingham for the Midland Music Festival, captures this splendidly:[43]

May 18 1912. A Great Day. Birmingham Music Festival. Left Slawit at 8.16 . . . . From Birmingham station went to Queen's College to practise. Had to wait until 1.30 until all the students had gone. We girls and Sam got shown into a room at the top where there was lovely view. Had a game of tippit . . . . Then had a look round Birmingham – tried to find a china shop – but couldn't. Went to the Cathedral. Some most lovely Burne Jones windows . . . . Then went to the Imperial Institution to get ready for playing. We played last, Birmingham 2nd, Nelson 1st. We got 1st-97; Nelson 2nd-87; Birmingham last-78? We were excited and rushed off to send our telegrams. Only half an hour for tea, had to play at the Town Hall at 6.30. Left my 8/6d where we had played. Was lucky and found it again. During the concert remembered I had left my cloak at Lyons where we had tea. Found that too. Went to the pictures with Mr Clay, Mr Mayall and Sam and the other girls . . . . Then went to the Empire which was not at all bad . . . . Got to Slaithwaite at 4.30 – a glorious morning.

Fig. 25:6 A.W. Kaye.
(KCS)

That extract indeed encapsulates much of the essence of involvement in amateur musical life. There was, too, opportunity for part-time paid musical work and, for the favoured few, a route into a full-time professional musical career of varying lengths and types. (The best known career, that of Mrs Sunderland, will be looked at shortly). By 1874, for example, it was claimed that thirty-four Huddersfield singers had gone on to become cathedral choristers, while William Todd and Joel Hirst, both members of the Choral and the Glee and Madrigal, toured the United States and Canada with the Sam Hague Minstrels in the early 1880s. A number of brass bandsmen gained places in orchestras or, like Joe Jessop, a cornet player with Huddersfield Temperance Band when aged only seven, joined touring concert parties. Jessop's specialism in the 1890s was a solo in which he played cornet and piano at the same time.[44] Admittedly, pay and conditions for professional musicians, especially those at the lower end of the business, were often poor, and thus not all of these examples demonstrate upward social or economic mobility. At the very least, however, there may well have been an enhanced job satisfaction for many.

At the same time, local musical culture could carry important meanings for the people of Huddersfield and district. In particular, it became an major vehicle for displays of civic pride. The idea of civic pride is a troublesome one, for it does tend to assume a unified community bound together by a consensus of interests, and in this context, it would be very bold to claim that musical activity had either the capacity to dampen all social tensions or to appeal to all classes and interest groups. Nevertheless, sufficiently large numbers from across the social spectrum took enough interest in local musical life to suggest that it could act as an effective agent for the construction of community focus and identity.

An intense interest was taken by local people in the careers of their local celebrities of all types, but musicians ranked particularly highly in this respect. Undoubtedly the most marked example is provided by public response to the career of Mrs Sunderland, the so-called 'Yorkshire Queen of Song'. Interestingly, given the great esteem she was held in by the people of Huddersfield, she was actually born in nearby Brighouse, in 1819. The daughter of a gardener, she began public performance in 1834, becoming a founder member of the Huddersfield Choral Society in 1836, enjoying a successful career as a soloist, which ended in 1864 with a farewell concert in

Huddersfield Town Hall. The audience was so large that many had to stand outside and hear the concert through the window. A leading British oratorio soprano, she earned her soubriquet 'Queen of song' as the result of a Royal Command performance in 1858. After her retirement she was honoured locally in a number of ways, most notably via the establishment of the Mrs Sunderland Music Festival in 1889. Whether she represented a focus of pride for all social classes is unclear, but it is perhaps significant that Ben Turner recalled in his autobiography, that tickets for her concerts (and, indeed, for those of other 'notables') were raffled in the mill where his father worked.[45]

If we can accept even some of the often rather overblown testimony of the local press, the smaller towns and villages in the area showed a similar affection for those who 'bring honour to our good town'. In 1911, the *Huddersfield Daily Examiner* spoke of a concert at Marsden as 'an occasion for the recognition of native genius, for Sam Dyson, who is principal baritone at Canterbury Cathedral, and Miss Maud Sykes, who has this year made an appearance at the Queen's Hall, are Marsden people'.[46] In the same year, the *Colne Valley Almanac*, commenting on a concert by violinist and ex-Slaithwaite cotton-spinner Tom Clay (the same Mr Clay who went to the pictures in Birmingham with Maggie Woodhead and her friends) noted that 'Slaithwaite is today proud of having produced such a musical genius from the ranks of the working class'.

Local pride was probably at its most intense when the town was represented by an institution rather than an individual. In 1887, a male voice and a mixed voice choir, both largely, although not exclusively, based on the Glee and Madrigal Society, attended the choral contest at the Welsh National Eistedfodd, held that year at the Royal Albert Hall in London, as part of an attempt by Welsh cultural leaders to 'uplift Wales in the eyes of its London critics'.[47] In the week before the contests, the *Examiner* gave extended coverage to the event, carrying a very detailed technical piece on the test pieces and claiming 'extraordinary interest' in the town. On the days of the contest three-quarter page articles were printed. In both contests, the Huddersfield choirs shared first place with Welsh choirs, unleashing a great wave of local patriotism. The *Examiner* printed favourable reviews culled from the national press, as well as a list of names of all 246 singers taking part.[48] The reception accorded to the choir on arrival at the railway station was remarkable, 'great crowds' assembling, president Allen Haigh and conductor Johnny North, once an errand boy at Woods music shop, having to appear at a window in the George Hotel, at which point the crowd sung 'For he's a jolly good fellow', while a cornet player began 'See the conquering hero comes'. This was a style of homecoming identical to that given to successful sports teams.[49]

It is important to avoid over-romantic interpretations of these events. Some of those present at the station in 1887 will simply have been attracted by the presence of a crowd in the first place. Further, one wonders just how much interest there would have been if the choir had been unsuccessful. Nevertheless, displays of this sort say much about the depth of popular musicality in the area and its marriage to an intense local pride. From the late nineteenth century, music has been one of the major vehicles through which the people of Huddersfield, or at least sizable sections of the population, have been able to impose their town on the national consciousness. There was genuine local delight in 1887, for example, that Huddersfield had been England's representative in the vanquishing of the Welsh. Although the *Examiner* was generally sympathetic to the Welsh singers, it quoted with approval, the words of the *St. James's Gazette*:

> Mr Richard's (Henry Richard MP) speech was calculated to give his countrymen an excellent opinion of themselves. They might not play cricket or football, but they could sing and play the harp like angels. And then, to have to share first prize with Huddersfield.

Subsequent *Examiner* editorials developed the idea of Yorkshire superiority through criticism – albeit later challenged by a 'Melthamer' now resident in Wales – of the Welsh choirs' supposedly poor sightsinging ability.[50]

The later success of the Huddersfield Choral, under Sir Malcolm Sargent from 1932, did much to cement the notion of the town as a centre of musical excellence, both locally and on the 'mental map' of British people in general. Indeed, this continues to the present day, the Huddersfield Choral Society becoming a kind of cultural icon for Yorkshire patriots.[51] All this is a forceful reminder that it is through popular leisure that communities develop key elements of both their own self-image and that of others. Huddersfield Town Football Club, especially in the inter-war period, arguably served a similar function. What people do in their 'time off' is a much more important historical issue than is sometimes appreciated. The singers and musicians of Victorian and Edwardian Huddersfield, of course, would have needed little reminding of that.

Dave Russell

Biographical Note

After teaching in schools in Bradford and Leeds for six years, in 1985 Dr. Russell took up his current post as Senior Lecturer in the Department of Historical and Critical Studies at University of Central Lancashire. He has published a number of articles on the history of English popular leisure and popular culture and is the author of *Popular Music in England, 1840-1914. A Social History* (Manchester, 1987).

NOTES:

1. *Musical Home Journal,* 10 March 1908.

2. Exact measurement would only be made possible by a massively time consuming trawl of local newspaper sources and even this would not record all of the early societies. The figures here are very much 'best guesses'.

3. *Leeds Intelligencer,* 13 March 1852; R.A. Edwards, *And the Glory* (Leeds, 1985), p.61.

4. G.J. Mellor, *Northern Music Hall* (Newcastle, 1971), pp.17, 91-2, 187.

5. *Halifax and Huddersfield Trade Directory,* 1899.

6. W.L. Wilmshurst and S.H. Crowther, *The Huddersfield Choral Society* (Huddersfield, 1961), p.6; E.C. Bairstow, 'Music in Yorkshire', *Music and Letters,* October, 1920, p.343.

7. See particularly, E. Routley, *The Musical Wesleys* (1968).

8. Edwards, *Glory,* p.x; Anon, *Incidents in the Life of a Veteran Organist with Recollections of Local Musical Celebrities* (Huddersfield, 1874), p.5.

9. Quoted in J.S. Curwen, *Studies in Worship Music* (1881), p.31.

10. *Brass Band Annual,* (1896), pp.19-23.

11. *The Harmonicon,* quoted in *Mainzer's Musical Times,* 15 Nov. 1842.

12. Edwards, *Glory,* p.41. Not to be confused with the permanent festival held from 1889.

13. For a more detailed survey. D. Russell, *Popular Music in England. A Social History* (Manchester, 1987), pp.147-156.

14. 'The Huddersfield Choral Society, part 1', *Magazine of Music,* (June, 1889).

15. J.S. Curwen, *Music at the Queen's Accession* (1897), pp.24-25, 29-30.

16. See A. Smith, *An Improbable Century. The Life and Times of the Slaithwaite Philharmonic Orchestra 1891-1990* (Golcar, 1990), pp.157-58 for some interesting comments on the recent history of the sings.

17. Edwards, *Glory,* p.1.

18. Russell, *Popular Music,* pp.158-161. This emphasis on the late eighteenth and early nineteenth centuries should not obscure the existence of a local popular musical tradition *before* 1750. Unfortunately, sources are extremely scanty and this important aspect of musical life must remain shadowy for the present.

19. W(est) Y(orkshire) A(rchive) S(ervice), Kirklees, KC200 Huddersfield Choral Society, minute book, 15th April 1896.

20. Anon, *The Huddersfield Glee and Madrigal Society; a Jubilee Record,* (Huddersfield, 1926) p.5.

21. This information was extracted from the chorus membership lists, now with WYAS, Kirklees in conjunction with local trade directories. For full details, D. Russell, 'The Popular Musical Societies of the Yorkshire Textile District 1850-1914' (unpub. D.Phil thesis, Univ. of York, 1980), pp.66-86 and appendix 2.

22. Russell, *Popular Music*, pp.210-211.

23. D. Russell, 'Provincial concerts in England, 1865-1914: a case-study of Bradford', *Journal of the Royal Musical Association*, 114 (1989) 50-51.

24. T. Herbert, 'Nineteenth-Century bands: The making of a movement'. *The Brass Band Movement in the 19th and 20th Centuries* edited by T. Herbert (Milton Keynes, 1991), pp.7-56. A. Taylor, *Brass Bands* (St Albans, 1979), pp.7-21 is also useful on what he terms the 'pre-history' of bands.

25. Anon, *Slaithwaite Band: Golden Jubilee Year, 1925-1975*, souvenir programme, p.5; *Brass Band Annual* (1899), p.32; *British Bandsman*, December 1891.

26. Taylor, *Bands*, pp.259-274 for full contest results for Belle Vue (1853-1914) and Crystal Palace (1900-1914).

27. *Brass Band Annual* (1899), p.32; *Leeds Intelligencer*, 5 July 1856.

28. The Greenhead programmes are held in the Huddersfield Local History Library and are a useful source for the study of the band repertoire at this time.

29. See Russell, *Popular Music*, pp.187-194

30. P. Bedford, *An Introduction to English Handbell Ringing* (Chelmsford, 1974) is a good introduction.

31. *Huddersfield Daily Examiner*, 20 September 1912.

32. *Huddersfield Chronicle*, 21 March 1914.

33. *Huddersfield Daily Examiner*, 20 September 1912. Townend conducted from 1898 to 1912. *Colne Valley Guardian*, 24 August 1912.

34. *Huddersfield Daily Examiner*, 21 November 1911. Townend sent a series of letters to the *Examiner* which were published over the course of the tour. Apart from the musical comments they contain a number of interesting remarks on colonial life and travelling conditions. See, for example, 4 October 1911, 1 November 1911, 30 May 1912. For Almondbury, *Huddersfield Daily Examiner*, 20 September 1912.

35. WYAS, Kirklees, Huddersfield Choral Society minutes, 16 December 1856.

36. For a history of the orchestra, *see* S. Crowther, *A Hundred Years of Making Music* (Huddersfield, 1974). The Choral Society orchestra was strong at this time with about 35 members.

37. Russell, *Popular Music*, p.47.

38. Evidence gained from the marvellous photo of the Slaithwaite orchestra in Smith, *Improbable*, pp.64-5.

39. Smith, *Improbable*, pp.52-79.

40. WYAS, Kirklees, Huddersfield Choral Society minutes, 8 December 1864. Presumably he did apologise for the two are recorded as falling out again, 15 January 1867. Burton was a notoriously difficult character who clashed at some time with most choirs under his

guidance. Even allowing for personality clashes, however, tensions were all the more likely to occur at this time, a transition period between the older club atmosphere and one typified by the more 'professional' approach demanded by Burton, the first conductor from outside of the town and a man with a reputation to defend. Russell, *Popular Music*, p.213, for Burton.

41. Taylor, *Brass*, pp.76-8.

42. *British Bandsman*, 30 April 1910.

43. A. Smith, *Improbable*, pp.45-46.

44. Anon, *Recollections*, p.33-4; WYAS Kirklees *Pastime*, n.d. cutting in Huddersfield Glee and Madrigal collection, *Cornet*, August 1894.

45. *Old Yorkshire*, edited by W. Smith, series 2, vol. 2, (1890), pp.235-38. B. Turner, *About Myself*, (1930), p.24. Turner claims that he accompanied his father to at least one of Mrs Sunderland's concerts, but given that he was only months old when she retired, this seems to be a case of the unreliability of autobiography.

46. *Huddersfield Daily Examiner*, 3 October 1911. See also *Colne Valley Guardian*, 6 October 1911.

47. H.T. Edwards, 'Victorian Wales seeks re-instatement', *Planet*, 52, August-September, 1985, pp.13-24.

48. *Huddersfield Daily Examiner*, 3 August, 10 August 1887.

49. *Huddersfield Daily Examiner*, 13 August 1887.

50. *Huddersfield Daily Examiner*, 12, 17, 19 August 1887.

51. See, for example, Roy Hattersley, *Goodbye to Yorkshire* (1976), pp.115-21.

Fig. 26:1 Dr. T.W.
Woodhead. (KCS)

CHAPTER 26

The making of a municipal museum: Huddersfield and the naturalists

STUART DAVIES

O ne of the most common characteristics of Victorian towns is that, with the growth of prosperity and the acquisition of all the basic amenities necessary in an urban environment for health, safety and good government, municipal cultural institutions were eventually established. Huddersfield was not really an exception; its townspeople simply took longer than some to persuade the corporation to support their cultural aspirations. This chapter examines the history of the museum movement in the town from the middle of the nineteenth century until the opening of the Tolson Memorial Museum in 1922.[1]

In many northern towns the municipal museum was founded on an earlier one created by a philosophical society.[2] The Huddersfield Philosophical Society had been formed in the 1830s as a successor to the Huddersfield Scientific and Mechanic Institute founded in 1825. Its rules stated that the objectives of the society included 'the formation and maintenance of a Library, Reading Room and Museum'. There is, however, no evidence that the museum project ever got off the ground and the Philosophical Society itself faded away, although it did have its own Philosophical Hall, later the Theatre Royal.[3] The making of a municipal museum in Huddersfield followed a different route.

One consequence of industrialisation was that working men welcomed every opportunity to escape from the mill and town. In the early nineteenth century, therefore, arose a passionate following for 'collecting nature'. This usually entailed shooting, picking or seizing specimens to be added to the collector's personal cabinet of curiosities. But these men also gathered together in 'societies', often based in a public house, where they would meet regularly and even house some of their specimens in what came to be known as 'inn-parlour museums'. These public houses were also the focal point for trading in specimens or the place where collectors met with one of a number of 'birdstuffers' to be found in the district. From these public house encounters emerged larger societies, more formally organised and more scholarly in their intentions. The remainder of this chapter traces how, from these modest beginnings, Huddersfield managed to establish its own municipal museum, into which many of the specimens collected by the Victorian 'bird-men' and others eventually found their way.[4]

The Huddersfield Literary and Scientific Society, founded in 1857, seems to have lost little time in establishing a small museum at its rented premises in South Street.[5] Some of the earliest donations included an 'American snake captured alive at the Huddersfield Railway Station, in June 1857' and a locust captured at the Huddersfield Infirmary in June 1858.[6] At the Society's 'Conversazione' on 28 March 1860 a large number of natural science exhibits was on display, on loan from various society members.[7] By March 1861 at least one cabinet had been glazed ready for specimens and it seems likely that the museum was formally established during 1861.[8] The Society's annual report for 1861-62 reported that:

> The formation of a museum has occupied a prominent share of the attention of the Committee during the past year. It is greatly to be regretted that in a town like Huddersfield, so much dependent upon the cultivation of science for its prosperity, so little public feeling should be manifested on this subject, and that we should be so much behind other towns in the West-Riding in the possession of a good local Museum.

The purchase of glass cases to display specimens was dependent on financial donations and, as a result, zoology and botany collections were almost unrepresented in the museum. The Committee had, therefore, created a new class of membership in the hope of raising the subscription income so as 'to be able to devote small sums annually in furtherance of this most desirable object'.[9]

In its early years the museum attracted a number of donated specimens from local naturalists and, in 1861-62, a series of fossils from 'the Members of the Huddersfield Museum Field Club'.[10] But funding continued to be a problem. In 1864 the Committee lamented the lack of funds but expressed the hope of soon establishing a museum 'worthy of the society, and of the wealthy neighbourhood in which it exists'. A year later the Society reported that the 'Museum has steadily increased in size and importance' and the Committee considered 'that the time is fast approaching when an appeal must be made to the public, in order to enable the society to enter upon or build such a suite of rooms as would at once accommodate the various operations of the Society and prove an ornament and credit to the town. The necessary funds for its maintenance could be guaranteed'.[11]

During the following year, through want of funds and accommodation, little was added to the museum. The Society decided to take action. It called a meeting with the Huddersfield Naturalists' Society and the Huddersfield Archaeological and Topographical Association (the forerunner of the Yorkshire Archaeological Society) and proposed that the three should set out to raise sufficient funds to erect a building ('to be called the Athenaeum') to be shared by them all and to pay the salary of a curator. The Naturalists' Society declined to be involved but the other two were joined by the Huddersfield Athletic Club and pressed on. It came to nothing, and once again the Society bemoaned the lack of 'public spirit' and support for education, literature, the arts and sciences from the inhabitants of Huddersfield.[12]

By 1870 the Society was seriously worried about its future. Fewer and fewer young people seemed interested in the lectures they offered, the conversaziones made a loss and both the museum and library stagnated for want of space and funds. Nevertheless, it still had nearly 200 members and in 1871 took the decision to purchase the Mission House in South Street. 'The Building comprises a Lecture Hall and Geological Museum on the ground floor, and upstairs a suite of rooms, which it is proposed to convert into a General Museum for Botany, Zoology, Chemistry and the principal manufactures of the district'.[13] The Society seems to have revived in the 1870s and with it the museum. As was common with similar societies, it was the practice to appoint honorary curators for various parts of the collections. Thus for most of the 1870s, C. P. Hobkirk was curator of Botany, Joseph Tindall curator of geology, William Nettleton curator of zoology and H. G. Brierley curator of microscopy.

In 1881 the Society acquired 295 cases of British birds, the collection of Alfred Beaumont of Honley, part of which had been exhibited at the Society's conversazione in 1860. It was purchased for £200 'by a gentleman in the town, with the view of the collection forming the nucleus for a Town's Museum. It is intended that the purchase money shall be raised by public subscription. Your Committee having been requested to house the collection until such a museum is established, having consented to do so, and your Committee feel certain of the support of the members in assisting the promoters of a scheme for obtaining a museum in Huddersfield. . . . It is the intention of your Committee to exhibit the collection to the public at a small charge. . .'. The 'gentleman' was probably Major Graham, agent for the Ramsden Estate, and he clearly hoped not to have to bear the whole cost of the purchase.[14]

The acquisition of the Beaumont collection was the last recorded noteworthy act of the Literary and Scientific Society's museum. In January 1884 the newly established Huddersfield Technical School and Mechanics' Institution* received a deputation from the Literary and Scientific Society. The society offered to hand over the museum into the care of the Technical School in return for the use of a room at the School for their fortnightly meetings. Major Graham, as part owner of the former Beaumont collection of birds, was apparently happy with this proposal, provided that the collection was accessible to the public for a nominal fee. The Committee of the Technical School agreed in May 1884 and began preparations to temporarily house the museum in a large shed at the rear of their new Queen Street South premises, (opened in 1883), previously used for part of the Huddersfield Fine Art and Industrial Exhibition, with which the building opened in 1883. The collections were eventually moved there in February 1885. Meanwhile, the Huddersfield Literary and Scientific Society itself had been absorbed into the Technical School.[15]

In April 1885 the Technical School agreed that they needed to extend one wing of their building in order to house classrooms, a physical science lecture room and the museum. Unfortunately they were unable to finance this work, which was going to cost nearly £10,000. They did manage to purchase Graham's birds from his widow, but little else was done to further the cause

*This was the successor of the Huddersfield Mechanics' Institution, whose story is told in Chapter Twenty-Two. EDITOR.

*Fig. 26:2 Technical
College with the extension
of 1900. (KCS).*

of the museum. In May 1887 various societies from the town sent a
deputation to demand that the Technical School took action, but discussions
dragged on throughout the 1890s. Some collections were offered during this
time, including Samuel Learoyd's mineral collection (first displayed in the
new Corporation Art Gallery in 1898), 'South African weapons' and cotton
samples from Messrs Horrockses, Miller & Co. of Preston. But it was not
until 1900 that the extension was finally built and the museum opened.[16] By
this time a curator had been appointed. He was Seth Lister Mosley, a man
already well experienced in natural history and museums.

Seth Lister Mosley was in many ways the most extraordinary of the
Huddersfield naturalists.[17] He was born at Lepton in 1848, the son of James
Reid Mosley, a joiner and handloom weaver, who took up taxidermy in the
late 1840s to become, according to his son, 'the most famous birdstuffer this
district has produced'. This fame did however have a cost; shortly before

685

James' death (mercifully perhaps) in 1881, 'his extremeties were paralysed by the arsenic he used in curing skins'. Seth Lister's fascination with nature grew from his father's work and particularly the field excursions to collect specimens.

The family moved from Lepton to Fenay Bridge (where Seth was seriously ill and not expected to live) and then to a newly-built house on Almondbury Bank in 1853. The setting could not have been better for a young boy interested in nature. Because of his poor health his total formal schooling, on his own admission, 'did not amount to six months'.[18] Instead, he spent a lot of his time drawing and painting birds and butterflies. He began painting on glass, selling the products to his father's customers, 'the bird men who came on Sundays'. Towards the end of the 1850s he even formed a "society" with four other boys. They met and created a "museum" in the pigsty where Seth kept rabbits. Two of his companions became collectors: James Brier of birds and Joseph Whitwam of land and freshwater shells, his collection eventually ending up in Tolson Museum. Mosley himself was encouraged to collect by Alfred Beaumont, for whom his father was doing a great deal of stuffing at that time.

In 1863 Mosley briefly attended drawing classes at the Mechanics' Institution in Northumberland Street, before being apprenticed as a painter and decorator to the firm of Carter and Stuttard. In 1869 he married Sarah Taylor and they moved to another house on Almondbury Bank, on 'Lodge Row'. The following year he suffered a serious attack of typhoid fever. While recuperating, he produced more and more paintings of butterflies, and started offering them for exhibition. He was so encouraged by the response that he spent as much time as possible developing this skill. He earned money through house painting, but still found it necessary to join the Huddersfield Naturalists' Society because he could no longer afford to buy books. He later became their Secretary for many years. In the 1871 Census he was entered as 'Painter and Naturalist', no doubt his own description.

Mosley also developed his museum interests. Following his early endeavours in the pigsty, he used to shoot small birds, stuff them, and mount them in cases in the parlour. His father's customers admired them and began purchasing them. After his illness at Lodge Row, he fitted up a room with cased birds and 'opened the door and invited people to come and see . . . and made no charge'. While a parlour full of cased birds opened on this rather *ad hoc* basis barely meets modern expectations of a museum, nevertheless the educational spirit behind Mosley's museum was a laudable one and is the foundation for his later claims to have had over fifty years experience 'in museums'.

During the 1870s he remained at Lodge Row, and continued to paint and exhibit. By 1877 he decided, following a successful exhibition in London, to devote his whole life to natural history. To support himself and his family, he began producing limited-edition hand painted works, which sold well. He went all over the country painting specimens in taxidermists' and private collections, and at the museums in South Kensington, Norwich, Liverpool, Newcastle, Edinburgh, York and 'many other places'. In 1879 he joined with John E. Robson of Hartlepool to produce a penny weekly called *The Young Naturalist*, though he withdrew from the venture after two years. Nothing is known about his "museum" at Lodge Row. It was probably as much a commercial venture as an educational one, specimens being collected, stuffed, exhibited and then sold to other collectors as need arose. In 1880 he built a small house at the top of Dungeon Wood near Crosland Moor. While it was being built Mr. H. F. Beaumont gave nearby land for the creation of Beaumont Park. Mosley apparently immediately fitted up a museum room in his new house, for an advertising handbill for 'Mosley's Museum' survives from 1880-81. He also opened 'temperance refreshment rooms' at the same address. However, when the park was opened in 1883 he renamed it the 'Beaumont Park Museum' and then the 'Educational and Economic Museum'. Mosley tells us that 'it soon became well known and we had plenty of visitors'. The museum grew and he erected a second building. On the first floor there was a single room measuring 15 feet by 30 feet, heated around with hot water. This was the museum room.

The Educational and Economic Museum is much more recognisable as a public museum. Mosley's circular advertising the museum gave a clear idea of its purpose. The museum was open daily, refreshments and accommodation were available, but prospective visitors were warned that 'it is not a place of amusement, but an Educational Institution'. It had been established 'for the propagation and diffusion of a knowledge of natural history and its economic application'. Subscribers (paying not less than one guinea a year) were supplied with educational cases 'which if placed in Schools, will help in the work of the Museum', while Associates (paying 2s.6d. per year) 'have access

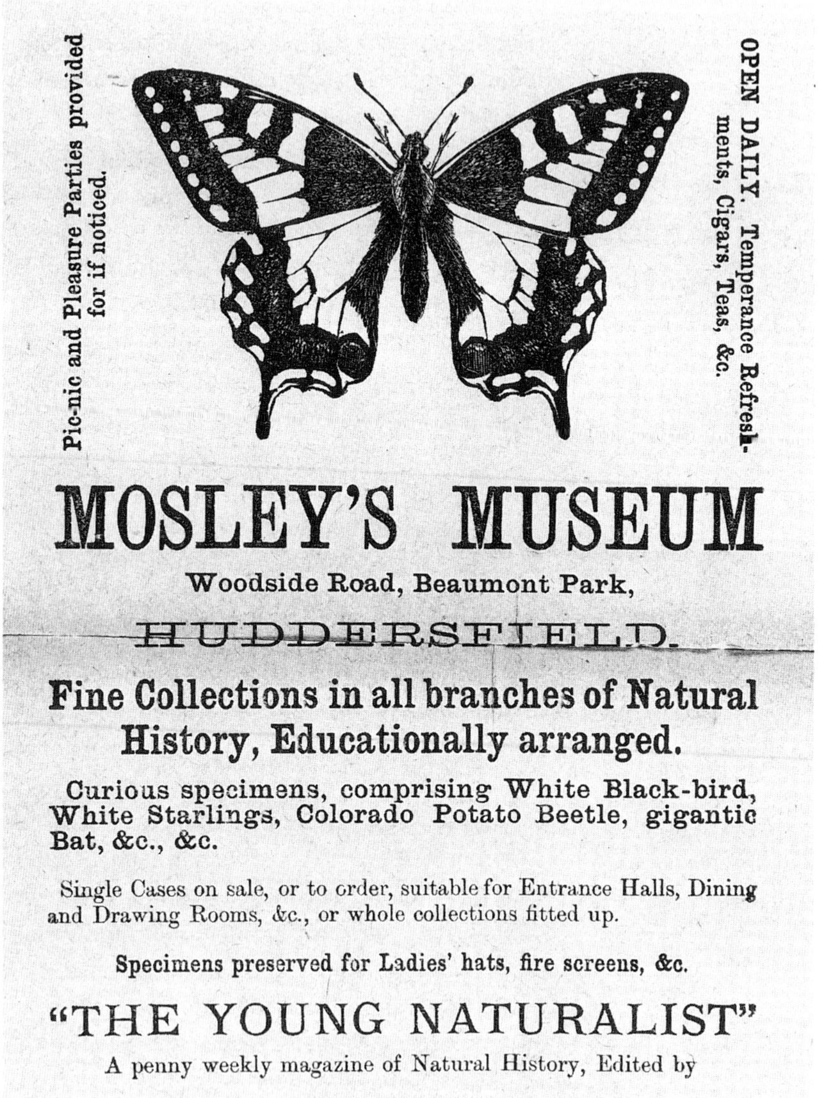

Fig. 26:3 Poster advertising S.L. Mosley's museum at Beaumont Park. (KCS)

to the Museum, and may attend all Lectures, Meetings or Excursions'. So access was limited to those who could afford to pay.

Mosley claims that it was here that he 'instituted the exhibiting of fresh wild flowers in a museum, now so largely imitated in other towns'. More important was his promotion of the 'economic' value of museums. From about the time he moved to Beaumont Park, Mosley had developed an association with Miss E. A. Ormerod, the economic entomology adviser to the British Board of Agriculture. He recognised the importance of studying insects, which had an economic impact on crops (whether beneficial or harmful), and the need to research and publicise these effects. He consequently produced display cabinets on this subject for many places, including the Bethnal Green Museum in London.

When Thomas Greenwood, the most celebrated authority on museums in Victorian England, visited the museum in 1888 he was told by Mosley that it had been 'established to promote a love of nature and decrease of intemperance; every assistance will be given to students, who are permitted to see the private collections any Wednesday evening during the winter, or on Sunday mornings during the summer. The public collections consist of a rich collection of British birds, educational collections of insects, as supplied to the Royal Gardens, Kew, Museums and Schools, collections of insects injurious to farm and garden plants, with methods of prevention'. Greenwood observed that Mosley had struggled to keep his museum going while the people of Huddersfield had twice refused to establish a public library and museum in the town. He hoped they might have a change of heart 'and accept as a nucleus of their work this little Museum which has been offered to the town'.[19]

While at Beaumont Park a change appeared in Mosley's view of the role of the 'naturalist' in society. 'During this time leading thoughts about Nature took a different turn, the old mania for collecting waned, and there seemed a desire for a new way of approaching the objects around us. My change of attitude towards religion had brought me to a different state of mind, and I was quite prepared to be less sympathetic with wholesale slaughter. . .'. His commitment to God did indeed come to play an increasingly important part of his life as he got older and his conscience was clearly troubled by the years of 'shooting and stuffing' so familiar to him in his younger days and commonplace in his father's time. He wrote in the preface to his book about

Huddersfield birds (published in 1915): 'I regret that the book is a record of murder and plunder from beginning to end'. Remembering how he had been responsible for sending over 70 cases of birds to elementary schools, he considered that this had been a mistake. 'We ought not to encourage children to take pleasure in looking at dead creatures, and so long as they are accessible in a public museum when required for reference, good pictures answer all practical purposes both for educational uses and private study'.[20]

By 1899 Mosley was openly confessing his difficulties in keeping all his many interests going. In May of that year he wrote that 'this month has been one of heavy work, ever since the commencement of the year the mental strain has several times threatened a breakdown. I am afraid I have made a machine almost too large for me to work'.[21] Even apart from the workload of making up and regularly dispatching cases of specimens to subscribers, his other museum duties would be quite enough for most men. But the museum was only one of his many interests. He was a prolific writer, not only contributing to the publications of many societies but also, since 1894, editing, publishing and mostly writing each month, *The Naturalists Journal*. Furthermore he ran natural history classes, gave sources of lectures each year and was also a lay preacher. He worked tirelessly in the cause of temperance and closely linked the study of nature with the knowing of God.

However, the Educational and Economic Museum was nearing the end of its days. In 1896 Mosley had accepted an invitation to become the curator of the museum of the Technical College, as the Technical School had become in that year. This was, he wrote 'not owing to my ability for I am only untrained, non-schooled working-man, but no less a lover of nature because I have learned to trust God'.[22] Mosley had already had a long association with the Technical College collections. In 1877 Charles Hobkirk had asked him to help sort out the Literary and Scientific Society's insect collection and in 1885 Mosley appears to have organised the move of the Society's collections to the Technical College.[23] He was, therefore, a natural choice for the post, particularly since the new extension now looked as if it was actually going to happen and an experienced curator would be needed to prepare and display the collections.

In 1900, having apparently received an assurance from the governors of the Technical College that their new museum should be open to the public, Mosley closed his own museum and transferred all the best specimens to the

Fig. 26:4 The Museum Room in Huddersfield Technical College. (UHA)

college. 'Mr S. L. Mosley's Museum at Beaumont Park is now closed as a public institution. There or elsewhere it has been open to the public, either free or at a nominal charge, for 30 years. The formation of a town museum in Huddersfield, and the appointment of Mr Mosley as curator, renders its existence no longer a necessity. It will be continued, however, as a Laboratory of Christian Natural History. Many specimens not needed in this capacity have been removed to the new museum at the Technical College Mr Mosley will now cease to "deal" in natural history specimens'.[24]

The opening of the new museum immediately attracted the deposits of existing collections. The Huddersfield Naturalists' Society originated in 1848 but was not formally established until 1850. It subsequently amalgamated with the Huddersfield Photographic Society (founded 1888) to form the Huddersfield Naturalist and Photographic Society in 1893. Although the society accumulated specimens, held occasional exhibitions and had at least some members in common with the Literary and Scientific Society (Alfred Beaumont, for example, was its President in 1864), it never established a museum, although that had been one of its aspirations from at least the 1870s.

Unfortunately there had never been sufficient space or money to set up their own museum and repeated petitions to the Town Council, in 1883, 1887 and 1893 for example, were unsuccessful. Finally, in 1901, it decided that its specimens should be labelled and deposited in the Technical College Museum. Other collections and their library also went to the same place, where the society's members could enjoy much improved study opportunities.[25]

The new museum also received, in August 1901, the collection of stamps, "curios" and pictures bequeathed to the town by Robert Holliday of Ravensknowle Hall. This, it was thought at the time, would open the way for the "municipalisation" of the Technical College museum in order to meet Holliday's hope that his collection would form the nucleus of a town museum.[26] This, technically, did indeed happen, when the Technical College was assigned to the Council under the Huddersfield Corporation Act in 1902. However, the museum remained where it was, in the absence of more suitable premises elsewhere, and the general public had only limited access to it.

Mosley, who continued as its curator, found this most unsatisfactory. In 1913 he complained that it was still essentially a private teaching museum for the benefit of the college rather than the people of Huddersfield generally. 'Although the museum has since become town property, and the public are admitted on two half days each week, it has never been a public museum, and up to the present the corporation has no museum policy, it having come to them as a part of the college, to be of service to the teaching staff, and its interest and usefulness in that line having grown from the beginning, it is now made use of by nearly every department in the college, as well as by the elementary schools both in the borough and district. There is a loan collection and a daily intercourse between the museum and the day schools, and for the last nine years a teachers' class has been held, either in the museum or out of doors, weekly. Classes from schools outside the borough are often brought to the museum'.[27] The museum was therefore carrying out a useful educational function, but it was not a fully operational public museum.

Mosley, as one might expect, had decided views about what a museum should be. He believed that a museum should have two distinct (but not necessarily separate) sections, one for students, the other for the public.

Fig. 26:5 Seth Lister
Mosley. (KCS)

'The students' portion should be kept in closed cabinets away from the light, as nearly all specimens deteriorate by exposure and spoil for scientific purposes. There should be certain times set apart for students (including art students) when the public are not admitted, and a reference library should be attached containing works on every department of nature, and plenty of accommodation for taking notes'. The public portion of a museum, he suggested, was often spoilt by there being too many specimens, leaving the visitor bewildered and without any definite impressions. Labels should contain more information than just the name of the object and 'the English name should be shown in all practicable cases'. He advocated the use of pictures rather than specimens, partly because they caused far less destruction of life and spoilation of the countryside, but also because of the shortcomings of specimens themselves. 'As I visit different museums and see cases which were done twenty or twenty-five years ago, the specimens faded and unrecognisable, one cannot but think that it would have been much better to have kept the specimens in dark drawers for reference by students, and replaced by permanent paintings for the public. Faded specimens are not only useless but are positively misleading by misrepresenting what they actually are'.

Mosley supported the idea of 'qualified demonstrators' giving daily talks to visiting parties. He had long done this with casual visitors to his own museums. Finally, he advocated that a museum should be more than just local. 'While a museum should fully represent the products of its own district – natural, commercial and historical – it is unduly cramped if confined entirely within these limits, as no locality can furnish illustrations of all the main types of animal or plant life. . .'.[28]

While the museum remained at the Technical College it was unlikely that Mosley would have the chance to put his views into full operation. The problem of finding suitable accommodation remained until after the First World War. The opportunity to create an adequate municipal museum came in 1919, when Legh Tolson, a cotton manufacturer, local historian and heraldry enthusiast, gifted to the town his house at Ravensknowle for a museum in memory of his two nephews, who had been killed in the war. Ravensknowle Hall had been built between 1859 and 1862 by John Beaumont, a fancy waistcoat manufacturer. The grounds were to become a public park, thus creating an excellent setting for the museum.

Fig. 26:6 Tolson Memorial Museum. (KCS)

But it was not Mosley who determined the development of the museum. That opportunity fell to Dr Thomas William Woodhead, the head of the biology department at the Technical College. Woodhead was a natural scientist with a doctorate gained in 1906 at Zurich for a thesis on the ecology of Huddersfield woodlands, and an honorary MSc from Leeds, in 1915, in recognition of his wide-ranging scientific work. Woodhead achieved an international reputation for his pioneering work in plant ecology, although he is now largely forgotten, unknown outside Huddersfield.

Legh Tolson offered his house at Ravensknowle to the Council, provided that it be converted to a museum for demonstrating 'the influence of all conditions existing in the neighbourhood upon the plant, animal and human life of the town and district'. Tolson himself invited Woodhead to prepare a brief scheme for the development of a local museum, and this was delivered as a speech at the Town Hall on 8 August 1919. His *Scheme for the Development of a Local Museum* was subsequently printed, adopted by the Council in December, and Woodhead was appointed Director of the new museum. Woodhead's *Scheme* became the blueprint for the museum's foundation, purpose and development.

A Museum should be an educational institution, and should provide practical illustrations of the main factors in the environment of the community. The objects should be so arranged as to show the influence of these factors on the organic life of the neighbourhood, and these in turn on the evolution of man's activities and social development.

Although realising that 'for a complete understanding of local conditions a wide outlook is involved', Woodhead grasped the essential importance of local studies both as an educational tool and as an effective piece of collection management.

In founding a Local Museum it is important to remember that space and funds are limited. It is, therefore, useless to attempt the accumulation of universal objects. It is only in a National Museum and with national resources that this can be done with any approach to success.

A provincial museum should be essentially local, and the advantages of such a policy are:

(1) It prevents the accumulation of miscellaneous objects which, being too miscellaneous to be of educational value, are little more than curiosities.

(2) It will serve to concentrate study on local objects and aims, which are of greater value to the community, and ultimately of greater value to the State.

(3) A Local Museum should serve to cultivate local patriotism of the most desirable kind, and develop concentrated study rather than discursive and superficial interest. Its educational value will thus be greatly enhanced.

In creating the displays Woodhead aimed to put before the public an account of the total environment of the Huddersfield district, working systematically through from geology to botany and thence to animals and finally people. The activities of the latter necessarily occupied only a small part of the museum and were rather superficially treated. The strength of the Tolson Memorial Museum, when opened in 1922, was its geology and natural history displays.

There were a number of key elements in Woodhead's museum. The first was its meticulous and logical organisation: it was didactic in the extreme, reflecting part of its purpose, which was to instruct students of natural sciences. Secondly, the labelling was very detailed and very technical, again being targeted at Woodhead's Technical College students. Thirdly, the displays needed to be seen in conjunction with a series of handbooks published by the museum to support them. Fourthly, the museum was intended to become the focal point for local studies. Woodhead promoted it vigorously in the local press and elsewhere, and encouraged societies and groups to hold their meetings there, an aim greatly facilitated by the addition of two lecture rooms in 1936. Finally, the museum ran a school loans service from the start and encouraged formal school loans. A room was available for class work and a large number of loan cases (with accompanying notes) was available for borrowing by schools.

While doing all this Woodhead still managed to develop the collections through gift, fieldwork and, occasionally, purchase, as in 1927 when the Porritt collection of insects was acquired for £4,000, raised entirely by voluntary subscription. The following year the Miers Report described the Tolson Museum as 'the best example of a really local museum ... a remarkable example of one man possessed by a dominating idea'. Woodhead died in 1940, distinguished as an ecologist and a member of that 'band of highly individualistic seekers after knowledge' for which the Pennines were famous.[29]

Much of the detailed specimen preparation (and perhaps display) was the work of Seth Lister Mosley. After Woodhead's appointment as 'Director' of the museum, Mosley was offered the post of Curator in 1920, although not until after a measure of negotiation about the terms and conditions of his appointment. Mosley was, it would seem, a little aggrieved by the situation. He made a statement to the Borough Council's Sub-Committee in March 1920 outlining his qualifications:

> I was born in a museum, and have been connected with museums ever since. Seen all the principal museums in this country and done work for most of them.
>
> I have been working for a museum for Huddersfield since I was 16, and the existence of this present museum is due to my efforts. From 50,000 to 75,000 specimens in this Museum belong to me. They were brought down here and the Beaumont Park Museum was closed on the supposition that I should be able to carry on here the work I had established there, but I have been unable to do so.

He went on to say he was willing to continue at the new museum provided that he had an Assistant, that his duties would be to superintend museum work and 'continue local investigations on my own lines' and that the appointment be for life. He also offered to hand over his own collections for £200.

A handwritten note about the appointment (probably by Woodhead) casts a different light on Mosley's case. The writer declares that Mosley's scientific knowledge 'is very patchy and incomplete on Natural History subjects' and that control by the Committee will be essential 'to prevent blunders'. Mosley had apparently wanted to spend a great deal of his time publishing leaflets but 'however interesting this might be as a matter for the newspaper[30] we cannot sanction the issue of such inaccurate and misleading stuff. . . . What the Committee need first is a *Museum* not leaflets . . . . The most valuable work Mosley could do would be to get specimens suitably mounted and ready for display when the whole building becomes available. In this work he needs assistance. His son Charles would be a very useful man. . .'. And so Seth Lister Mosley was appointed Curator (on £150 per annum) and Charles Mosley as Assistant Curator (on £200 per annum). Mosley's collections were acquired although 'the majority are not local . . . have no special scientific value . . . the local ones are poor specimens chiefly and so mounted as to greatly reduce their value and usefulness'.[31]

In June and July 1920 the cases were removed from the Technical College to Ravensknowle. Legh Tolson (who was retiring to the Lake District) did not move out until August, which meant a delay in carrying out structural alterations. The curator set about re-casing the bird collection and setting up a 'bird room'. Several volunteers, including eminent scholars, came in to help advise on other areas of the collections.[32]

Seth Lister Mosley stayed at the Museum long enough to set up a new Bird Room in the extension of 1925. He then retired, on a Council pension, eventually dying in 1929. Charles succeeded him as Curator and remained at the museum until 1933. This brought to a close an association between the Mosleys and museums in Huddersfield stretching back for nearly eighty years. The opening of the 'Bird Room' may also be seen as the culmination of nearly a century of collecting of specimens by the naturalists of Huddersfield, finally recognised in the town's own museum. Mosley and the other 'working men naturalists' are never likely to be academically respected. They

Fig. 26:7 The bird room at Tolson Memorial Museum. (KCS)

were too practical for that. They were also too passionate in their quest for new discoveries, self-improvement and the sharing of what they found with others. Their achievement lies not in tedious perfection but in the vision of sharing their enthusiasm with ordinary people. This is the purpose of a public museum and Tolson is their monument.

Stuart Davies

Biographical Note

A graduate in History from Westfield College (University of London) and the London School of Economics, Dr Davies worked in Gloucester and Birmingham before his appointment with Kirklees. He is the author of *By the Gains of Industry: Birmingham Museum and Art Gallery 1885-1985, Treasures for the People: The story of museums and galleries in Yorkshire and Humberside* (with Peter Brears) and numerous articles on museum management and local history.

NOTES and REFERENCES

1. I am pleased to acknowledge the help given by John Rumsby, Janet Kenyon and Hilary Haigh in the development of this article.

2. P. Brears and S. Davies, *Treasures for the People* (Leeds, 1989), pp.16-30.

3. T(olson) M(emorial) M(useum), 'Rules of the Huddersfield Scientific and Mechanic Institute for the Promotion of useful knowledge' (1825); Annual Reports, 1826, 1827; Huddersfield Local Studies Library, 'Rules of the Huddersfield Philosophical Society', (1850); O. Balmforth, *Huddersfield Past and Present* (Huddersfield, 1894), p.29.

4. C. Mosley, 'Inn-Parlour Museums', *Museums Journal* xxvii, (1928) 280-1; S. L. Mosley newspaper clippings (Tolson Museum).

5. C. P. Hobkirk & F. Curzon, *A Short Description of the town, its public buildings, Manufacturers and Antiquities* (Huddersfield, 1883), p.4.

6. H(uddersfield) L(iterary) and S(cientific) S(ociety) Annual Report 7 March 1859. No complete set of the Society's reports appears to have survived. Both Kirklees Libraries (Huddersfield Local History) and the University of Huddersfield Archives hold various items. The references here are to copies held at Tolson Memorial Musuem.

7. TMM, HLSS Conversazione catalogue 28 March 1860. Nearly all of eighty cased 'British Birds' lent by Mr Alfred Beaumont of Honley were subsequently purchased on the Society's behalf in 1881 (for £200) and exhibited at the Huddersfield Fine Art and Industrial Exhibition in 1883.

8. TMM, HLSS Annual Report 4 March 1861.

9. TMM, HLSS Annual Report 10 March 1862, p.5.

10. TMM, HLSS Annual Report 10 March 1862, p.9.

11. TMM, HLSS Annual Report 18 March 1864; HLSS Annual Report 17 March 1865.

12. TMM, HLSS Annual Report 19 March 1866; HLSS annual report 11 March 1867. H. H. Charlesworth and M. A. Ellis *The History of a Society 1850-1968* (Huddersfield, 1968), pp.12-13.

13. TMM, HLSS Annual Report 8 April 1872.

14. TMM, HLSS Annual Report 17 March 1881; *The Naturalist*, vol. vii (1881-2) pp.36-7.

15. U(niversity) of H(uddersfield) A(rchives), *Technical School and Mechanics' Institute Council Minutes* 14 January 1884; 8 May 1884; 30 June 1884; 3 November 1884; Letters Out, 23 February 1885.

16. UHA, Technical School Committee Minutes, 28 April 1885; 23 May 1887; Letters Out, 6 July 1885; 5 November 1895; 28 September 1896.

17. The biographical information on Seth Lister Mosley is largely drawn from two sources; his own autobiography (up to 1912) was published in *Nature Study* vol. xx (1912-13) and some further papers are to be found in the Tolson Museum.

18. S. L. Mosley, 'Reminiscences', *Naturalists Journal*, vii, no. 78 (Dec, 1898), 184.

19. T. Greenwood, *Museums and Galleries*, (1888), p.152.

20. Mosley (1912-13), p.25; S.L. Mosley, *An Account of the Birds of the Huddersfield District* (Huddersfield, 1915).

21. *The Naturalists Journal*, viii, no. 83 (May 1899).

22. *The Naturalists Journal*, v, (1896).

23. UHA, HLSS Minute Book, 14 August 1877; 11 September 1877; Technical School Letters Out 23 February 1885.

24. *The Naturalists Journal*, ix, (Sept 1900), p.143.

25. Charlesworth and Ellis, pp.25-6; G. T. Porritt, *Our Society, and its Work* (Huddersfield, 1898); Annual Reports and Monthly Circulars of the Huddersfield Naturalists' Society (Huddersfield Local Studies Library).

26. *Huddersfield Daily Examiner*, 4 October 1901.

27. Mosley (1912-13), p.29.

28. Mosley (1912-13), pp.29-30, 33.

29. T. W. Woodhead, *Scheme for the Development of a Local Museum* (Huddersfield, 1919); S. Caunce, 'Dr. Woodhead and the Tolson Memorial Museum', typescript, Tolson Museum (1983); J. Sheail, 'T. W. Woodhead and the Study of Vegetation and Man in the Huddersfield District', *The Naturalist*, 987, (1988), pp.125-39.

30. Mosley had been writing a weekly column for the Huddersfield Examiner since 1914.

31. TMM historial files.

32. TMM Draft First Annual Report by Charles Mosley (1921).

Index